NORTHUMBRIA'S
GOLDEN AGE

This book is dedicated to
the memory of
Jim Lang

NORTHUMBRIA'S GOLDEN AGE

EDITED BY

JANE HAWKES & SUSAN MILLS

SUTTON PUBLISHING

First published in the United Kingdom in 1999 by
Sutton Publishing Limited · Phoenix Mill
Thrupp · Stroud · Gloucestershire · GL5 2BU

British Library Cataloguing in Publication Data
A catalogue record for this book is available from the British Library.

ISBN 0-7509-1685-0

Title page illustration: 7th-century gold plaque, Bamburgh, Northumberland. (Drawing: Yvonne Beadnell)

 ALAN SUTTON™ and SUTTON™ are the trade marks of Sutton Publishing Limited

Typeset in 11/14 pt Sabon.
Typesetting and origination by
Sutton Publishing Limited.
Printed in Great Britain by
Butler & Tanner, Frome, Somerset.

CONTENTS

CONTENTS

LIST OF PLATES AND ILLUSTRATIONS

Plates (between pages 212 and 213)

Illustrations

CONTRIBUTORS

Gerald Bonner Durham
George Hardin Brown Department of English, Stanford University, California
Craig Cessford Cambridge
Rosemary Cramp Department of Archaeology, University of Durham
Robin Daniels Tees Archaeology, Hartlepool, Cleveland
Carol A. Farr London
Edwin & Joyce Gifford Southampton
Christopher Grocock Surrey College, Guildford
Richard Hall York Archaeological Trust
Jane Hawkes Department of Archaeology, University College, Cork
Isabel Henderson Nigg, Scotland
Nicholas Higham Centre for Medieval Studies, University of Manchester
Arthur Holder Church Divinity School of the Pacific, Berkeley, California
Catherine E. Karkov Department of Art, Miami University, Ohio
James Lang[†] Centre for Medieval Studies, University of York
Kevin Leahy Museum and Art Gallery, Scunthorpe, North Lincolnshire
Sam Lucy Department of Archaeology, University of Durham
Thomas W. Mackay Orem, Utah
Douglas Mac Lean Austin, Texas
Perette Michelli Art Department, St Olaf College, Minnesota
Susan Mills Bede's World, Jarrow
Catherine Mortimer Ancient Monuments Laboratory, London
Nancy Netzer Department of Fine Art, Boston College
Carol Neuman de Vegvar Department of Fine Arts, Ohio Wesleyan University
Éamonn Ó Carragáin Department of English, University College, Cork
Elisabeth Okasha Department of English, University College, Cork
Fred Orton Department of Fine Art, University of Leeds
David Parsons Department of Adult Education, The University of Leicester
Erica Paterson York Archaeological Trust
Dominic Powlesland Malton, North Yorkshire
Julian D. Richards Department of Archaeology, University of York
Mark Stansbury Department of History, Boston College
Christopher D. Verey London

Leslie Webster Department of Medieval and Later Antiquities, British Museum, London
Niamh Whitfield London
Susan Youngs Department of Medieval and Later Antiquities, British Museum, London

† deceased

ARCHAEOLOGY AND HISTORY

CHAPTER 1

THE NORTHUMBRIAN IDENTITY

Rosemary Cramp

For now dawns the Golden Age of the English Church wherein learning and the arts prospered to such an extent that during the sixty-six years between the arrival of Theodore (669) and the death of Bede (735) the remote province of England . . . achieved a position that without exaggeration may be described as supreme in western civilization.

(Kendrick 1938, 119)

This period was for Kendrick an Anglo-Saxon renaissance 'in the direct pedigree of the great classical tradition', although he recognized the co-existence and achievements of the 'barbaric' native art of the indigenous Celtic and Anglo-Saxon peoples. The achievement of Northumbria in this Golden Age now seems to be accepted as combining in a unique manner the native and classical traditions.

It is also generally accepted that when it was politically successful, between the early 7th and mid-8th century, the foundations of its achievements were firmly laid so that even with the economic and political decline of the kingdom in the next century the influence of its scholars and craftsmen was still felt outside its borders. Moreover, there was something distinctive in the style of its art which could be termed 'Northumbrian'. These are assumptions to be further considered.

Bede, whose works provide the fullest account of the dominant Anglo-Saxon personalities of the 6th to 8th centuries, as well as the origin legends of the Anglian peoples, and the definitive statement concerning the early use of the name of the kingdom, fittingly epitomizes the Northumbrian achievement (Houwen & MacDonald 1996).

Nevertheless, his account of early Anglo-Saxon England has not been without criticism. If his origin myths are now seen as too simplistic (Scull 1995, 71–2), it may also be questioned whether we are still too influenced by his, and other early textual descriptions of political and ethnic divisions. It is easy to create cultural divisions among the Anglo-Saxon kingdoms where they did not exist. One may ask whether the perceived differences are largely the result of differential survival of evidence. Why should Northumbria's identity differ from that of western Wessex for example? Textual sources suggest Anglo-Saxon ascendancy was established over a British population after a long and bitter struggle in both areas; both areas bordered on independent native kingdoms, and the Irish influence, even presence, is as well attested in Wessex (eg at Glastonbury and Malmesbury) as it is in Northumbria.

Does the distinctiveness of the two areas derive from ethnic differences: Angles being different from Saxons, the south-western Britons different from those of the north, or is it a question of population balance: fewer Anglo-Saxons in Northumbria with Irish and Pictish kingdoms on its borders? The fact that the constituent parts of Deira and Bernicia retained their topographic Celtic names and the '*Humbrenses*' or '*Northhumbrenses*' took a locational name rather than some form of tribal name, such as the North Angles, can be contrasted with the overarching name 'West Saxon' which came to prevail in the south-west. It may also be significant that not only did the British rulers of the sub-Roman kingdoms identify themselves by the collective term, 'The Men of the North', but the Anglian peoples continued to use a topographical term even after the Scandinavian settlement.

Was there something deeply influential in the terrain, which created differences in its inhabitants from prehistoric times onwards (Fox 1959)? Was it the nature of the Roman legacy of *Britannia Inferior* and *Britannia Superior*, or a question of post-Roman contacts and communications which gave different identities to the two areas? Some of these points are discussed below, but one may simply note here that western Wessex was oriented towards the continent across the narrow English Channel, with the Bristol Channel providing access to the western seas and Northumbria fronted two seaboards. The trading connections of each coast, for the early period at least, seem to have been distinct, but the western ports were subjected to massive silting in the post-Roman period and only the Humber estuary on the east provided a major sea port for long-distance trade. The question of how post-Roman communications shaped Northumbria's identity certainly needs further exploration.

Although there seem to be universal differences in temperament and lifestyle between mountain and lowland dwellers, it is perhaps because highland zones provide inaccessible refuges that the terrain shaped post-Roman Northumbria:

> . . . however Romanized the Celtic establishment of lowland Britain may
> have become, the survival of a Celtic aristocracy such as the house of

Gododdin or of Urien of Rheged even in isolated pockets in the highland zone could have been sufficient to ensure a full regeneration of Celtic life as soon as the military and economic conditions which supported the veneer of Roman civilization had been removed (Smyth 1984, 4).

The nature of Roman settlement in the north and south of Britain was significantly different, and the subsequent effect in acculturation of the indigenous population has been much debated (Millett 1990; Cleary 1989; Higham 1992). The south had a network of small and large towns; York was the only major urban centre in the north, and fittingly survived as the only Northumbrian minting centre. The close-packed networks of Roman estates with many elegant houses in the south compare with the simpler dwellings, thinly spread through Yorkshire and as far north as Durham. These villas and many smaller roadside settlements, in what became Deira, differ from the forts, *vici* and individual farms of the military zone which became Bernicia, and this is paralleled in differences in the later Anglo-Saxon settlement (see Lucy, below). Despite evidence for post-Roman reoccupation of some of the wall forts (Dark & Dark 1996), the *vici* of the forts along and north of the Wall did not provide the same focus for future settlements as the lower lying or riverine forts, or more cogently the villa estates. There is no evidence from Northumbria to parallel Pearce's (1982) account of the West Saxon minster churches and their estates which seemingly coincide with the distribution of Roman villas, although comparable charter evidence does not exist for the north. Nevertheless, it can be demonstrated archaeologically (eg at Yeavering and Heslerton) that there is often coincidence between, if not continuity from, pre- and post-Anglo-Saxon cult centres in the north as well as the south.

It is generally agreed that change in Roman Britain towards an indigenous life-style began in the 4th century, proceeding with a change from literate to oral culture (Richter 1994, 14–16), from large industries to small-scale production controlled by regional potentates, and from stone to timber architecture. In the 4th and 5th centuries the Men of the North formed their power bases and for a time successfully contained the Picts, until they were bypassed by sea in 367. It is possible that, as elsewhere on the continent, local military commanders took over a screen of east coast defences and their surrounding regions, with control points on major roads and river mouths (Hope-Taylor 1977, 276–309; Casey 1994).

The theory that in the 6th century the role of coastal defence was then handed over to Anglo-Saxon mercenaries – perhaps Octha and Ebissa as mentioned in the *Historia Brittonum* (Morris 1980, 29, 76, 77) – and from there sprang the Bernician dynasty, cannot be proved or disproved, but archaeological evidence does not contradict it. It is also now generally accepted that after the initial settlements of the Anglo-Saxons in Lindsey, the east coast and inland in eastern Yorkshire, there was a lull before swift expansion in the 6th century, the period when the Angles become clearly visible in cemeteries and settlements elsewhere in Northumbria (see Lucy and Powlesland, below), although it seems major expansion inland occurred earlier in Deira than Bernicia. Nevertheless, victories may have been swiftly followed by colonization of newly acquired territories, as described by Bede (Colgrave & Mynors 1969, 116–17, I.34). Hope-Taylor's model for Yeavering and its development is vitiated only by the fact he saw it as so specifically Bernician. There seems no doubt, however, that to understand the process of assimilation of peoples and replacement of power structures in Northumbria only very extensive excavation of sites can provide answers.

I will take as one example of these processes, Catterick, a site for which there is documentary evidence, Roman, native and Anglo-Saxon, and which has been intermittently excavated over the last fifty years (Alcock 1983, 14–17). It is located alongside a major river, and dominates strategic routes west and north. The Roman name for the Roman town and fortress, *Cataractonium*, appears in a variety of sources from Ptolemy onwards with various spellings. Whether we accept Rivet and Smith's (1979, 302–4) interpretation of its name as derived from British, meaning 'place of the battle ramparts'; or Jackson's (1969, 83) as derived from the obscure Latin, *cataracta*, meaning 'rapids', either would be topographically appropriate. On the east of the site, hidden by the present army camp, is a long spur of land called Castle Hills, enclosed by rapidly flowing waters. Vestigial earthworks indicate a pre-Roman or sub-Roman British camp, a strong point which could have been taken over by the Angles.

In the post-Roman record there are references in the *Gododdin* poem to a place called *Catraeth* where a confederation of British princes led by the king of the Gododdin met the combined Anglian forces of Deira and Bernicia and suffered a terrible slaughter (Jarman 1988, *passim*). This was about the time of Urien of Rheged's death, c 590–600, and the two events may be linked. In the Taliesin poems addressed to Urien he is described as Lord of Catraeth, and in his latter years, or immediately after his death, the Anglian leaders could have moved decisively to capture such a strategic point. But post-Roman archaeological evidence is not so precisely datable that it can point to such sudden events.

Roman structures on the site reveal extensive rebuilding after 400 and a timber building was occupied into the 5th century, but a sunken hut, previously dated by pottery to the 5th century, is now redated to the 6th century, and so Anglo-Saxon occupation as opposed to burials is not evidenced until about the time of the postulated battle of *Catraeth* (Wilson et al. 1996). Nevertheless, there could have been an Anglian presence in the area before that time – even mercenaries serving British leaders.

Recent excavations under Catterick racecourse have revealed a Roman amphitheatre, about 140 m in diameter, built over a very large late Neolithic/early Bronze Age burial cairn; as at Yeavering an earlier prehistoric focus seems to have been intermittently revived. Later an Anglian cemetery was placed alongside the amphitheatre, and these burials, like the many others found in the abandoned buildings of the Roman fort, seem to date to c 450–550. It is a pity that such evidence cannot tell us if Urien ruled over a mixed ethnic group or whether the Angles only flooded in after his death, but by the reign of Edwin, Catterick was an important royal vill where Paulinus preached and baptized in the River Swale. Later, in the 8th century (in 762 and 792), two royal marriages took place at Catterick according to the *Historia Regnum*, and in 769 it was burnt by the tyrant Eanred (Arnold 1885, 42, 44, 54). Perhaps at that stage the focus of the settlement was changed, and the area over the old Roman *vicus* and fort, which had been so extensively used as a burial ground, was abandoned for a new Christian focus in what is the present village. Catterick, however, remained an important estate, and was one of the largest in Richmondshire at the Domesday survey.

The newly discovered grave goods include a small penannular brooch of the native British type also found in other Northumbrian cemeteries (Sherlock & Welch 1992a; Hirst 1985). There is no doubt that in the competitive world of North Britain, when Briton, Angle, Pict and Scot fought each other in differing alliances, dress fastenings and jewellery could proclaim different identities and the modest little ring brooches of the Britons in the hands of other immigrants like the Dál Riata Scots assume the scale and elaboration of an Anglian square-headed brooch.

Both the Angles on the east coast of Britain and the Dál Riata Scots from Ireland on the west began their land takings c 500, and as incomers to the island both may have encountered similar problems. Certainly there is ample evidence for contact at the leadership level with the Bernician Angles. The Deiran royal family seems initially to have had friendly contact with the Britons of the west, if the story of Edwin's stay with Cadfan of Gwynedd is to be credited, and despite his later wars with the Britons he may have learnt something of Roman traditions from them as well as from his East Anglian and Kentish contacts. His reign saw the conversion of parts of Northumbria to Christianity after his marriage to a Kentish princess, and he seems to have forged conscious links to Roman traditions, such as his use of standards in his progress, his provision of public order and public amenities, and his baptism at York (Colgrave & Mynors 1969, 192–3, II.16). (This attachment to Roman traditions does seem to be a trait which distinguishes Deira from the rest of Northumbria.) Edwin's Bernician successors looked north and west for their alliances: Oswald, Oswiu and their brothers and retinue were in exile among the Dál Riata Scots, and were linked with Irish, British and Pictish lineages through marriage.

The amalgamation of Germanic and Celtic traditions clearly took place first in the secular courts; in cultural terms this is manifested in prestigious items of metalwork. In Ireland and Dál Riata the kings seemingly exercised controls over the craftsmen and their products, and as Nieke has fully considered, the brooches and pins produced in royal centres conveyed prestige and perhaps signified allegiance as well as identity (Nieke & Duncan 1988; Nieke 1993, 128–9). There are significant differences between the penannular and related round brooches of the Celts but once the distinctive and highly decorated form had been developed it was remarkably long-lived among the Irish and the Picts. In contrast, the expression of the Anglian identity in brooches and other dress fastenings is not long-lasting and during the 7th century the prestigious fashions of Kent come to prevail.

It is interesting that in the Dunadd excavations not only were moulds found for casting bird-headed ring brooches but also a single cabochon garnet in an elaborate gold setting. Such bird-headed brooches are seen as Celtic copies of a Germanic motif (Campbell & Lane 1993, 54–7), but perhaps one should also remark that such brooches are not common outside Northumbria among the Anglo-Saxons, and their discovery in large cemeteries such as Sewerby, as well as the most westerly of the Northumbrian graves at Occaney Beck and the two Roman sites of Chesterholm and Chesters along the Wall (Miket 1978, 178) could well indicate a perceived common identity.

Among the Anglo-Saxons, although the story of the cruel control of Weland by Nithhad may hint at the subjection of smiths to kings, no fine metalworking production sites of this period have been found in Northumbria, save for the tantalizing fragments of crucibles at Yeavering (Tinniswood & Harding 1991, 103–5). The Anglo-Saxon acceptance of Christianity may have been a factor in proclaiming a common identity by their dress fastenings, although one might imagine that close links with Iona could have inhibited this development in Northumbria in the 7th century.

The Ionan monks' arrival at Lindisfarne in 635, and the new contacts and patronage they established, are often seen as introducing Hiberno-Saxon art traditions and the Golden Age. This is clearly demonstrated in manuscripts where fragmented and ambiguous patterns, in which bird, beast and human merge, give way to a clear differentiation of motifs: spiralform patterns and geometric interlace, together with a geometric layout holding the motifs together. This differentiation was a contribution from Celtic art, but all the Insular tribes were involved in artistic experimentation and assimilation. Acceptance by Irish artists of animal ornament, both Germanic and Romano-British, began in the secular world, but the understanding and acceptance by the Northumbrians of human and realistic figural sculpture and such Mediterranean motifs as late classical vine-scroll was the result of wider ecclesiastical contacts in the late 7th century.

It is unfortunate that, save for the Cuthbert relics, we have no surviving fine metalwork from Lindisfarne, and for that reason the moulds from its satellite Hartlepool are all the more important since they show the same type of ribbon animal ornament, and the same type of evangelist symbol as in the *Lindisfarne Gospels* (Cramp & Daniels 1987). This, although a slender clue, suggests that in the monastic colonies different affiliations, religious as well as lay, were emphasized through pattern as well as form.

The most significant metal ornament from Lindisfarne is the Cuthbert pectoral cross, described by Bruce-Mitford (1974b, 295) as:

> Celtic in fundamental form, southern in fashion and in the goldsmith's craft-traditions it exemplifies, yet with a strong local complexion, [it] seems to be like St Cuthbert himself and the famous monastery he adorned, essentially Hiberno-Saxon.

The wearing of gold and garnet jewellery was adopted by many rulers of the north-west Germanic kingdoms in emulation of east Christian fashion and, as already mentioned, reflects Kentish fashion. If the famous Cumberland sword pommel and Dalmeney pyramid, as well as the Boldon strap dispenser, Uncleby brooch and Dunadd cabochon are any indication, then garnet settings were an established part of the repertoire of the secular Northumbrian goldsmiths before Cuthbert's death. Although the pectoral cross design reflects the geometry of the *Lindisfarne Gospels* (Coatsworth 1989), it is difficult to accept that its fundamental form is Celtic. This has been reasonably compared with continental altar crosses, but from the plethora of cross shapes available to artists there do seem to have been local preferences, and possibly significant groupings, and some may be linked to the influence of one outstanding piece, not necessarily now surviving.

In trying to recreate the past one is repeatedly tantalized by the feeling that lurking just out of view are images which must have been potent and influential to the contemporary viewer. We can still see their vestiges in the shadows they cast, but can only guess at their substance. If one could but see certain outstanding objects, now lost, much might be explained. Publicly accessible objects (the gold embroidered overtunic sent by the Pope to Edwin, Paulinus's great gold altar cross, Oswald's banner, the icons brought by Benedict Biscop to Wearmouth-Jarrow), not to mention the more private objects available to an elite group (the gospels in letters of gold on purple vellum commissioned by Wilfrid, the illustrated history of the world with which Ceolfrith bought land from Aldfrith), may all have been influential.

Yet new discoveries continue to be made, and Cuthbert's cross is not as isolated as when last discussed. The tiny fragment of a cross of similar shape found at Dunbar (Holdsworth 1993, 40–2, fig 9) supports the idea that this narrow splayed-arm type was especially favoured in Bernicia just as a more widely splayed-arm type was cultivated further south at sites such as Hartlepool and Whitby (Cramp 1993, 67–8).

Other centres such as Hexham and Jarrow have stone crosses which obviously mirrored prestigious metalwork, possibly altar crosses, but the cross shapes are different again. Interestingly the shape which Collingwood (1927, 94–8) called 'lorgnette' or 'spine-and-boss', which Bailey more recently has called 'cruciform head-pattern' (Bailey & Cramp 1988, 33–5), is long-lived in the North Riding and western Cumbria. This is the shape of a cross with expanded arms incised on the Ripon 'Adhyse' cross (Collingwood 1927, 94, fig 117). Collingwood noted the motif's resemblance to an appliqué in form. More recently Kelly (1992, 75–6) has identified some Irish stone crosses which reflect wooden matrices with metal appliqués, and has also contrasted the Irish shape of the 'tall Latin cross' with the Anglo-Saxon form of the 'equal-armed cross elevated on a pillar' (Kelly, D 1993, 221). The Ripon cross, like those from Whitby which I have compared elsewhere with wooden prototypes (Cramp 1993, 69), is of this 'Irish' form. In the complex history of Ripon (see Hall, below) there were Insular influences. The inspiration for the lorgnette group may have been some prestigious artefact from Ripon, which, having made its early mark, continued to inspire a school of sculptors, casting a long shadow into the monastery's possessions in the British west.

It is sculpture, often located where it was originally placed, that can demonstrate unambiguously what was visible and influential in Northumbria, and how varied and inventive the craftsmen's achievements were. The different background inspiration for these monuments is apparent in their forms: the wooden cross introduced to Bernicia from Dalriada; the stele and processional or altar crosses from Gaul and Italy; the Roman funerary and triumphal monuments in Britain and on the continent.

Northumbrian sculptors appear to have a particular understanding of late classical proportions in figure sculpture and of the nature of stone as its own medium. The deep 'Roman' carving is partly a period trait but is particularly apparent on those individual and apparently influential monuments which I have called 'originals' (Cramp 1992, 63).

Iconographic analysis of the more complex monuments has over recent years unveiled how contemporaries could have derived from these icons a depth of spiritual and scriptural understanding (Ó Carragáin 1986, and below), but such monuments are also a conspicuous testimony to the united power of the church and secular rulers. Not for nothing are the finest examples on the borders of kingdoms, on well-trodden routes: Ruthwell near a major crossing of the Solway, Bewcastle on the Maiden Way, Abercorn and Aberlady on the Firth of Forth. Even when the elaborate monuments appear in ecclesiastical establishments they were clearly meant to be seen, either on the edge of the enclosures, as at Jarrow or Tynemouth, or in the church. Many of these crosses are also literate monuments.

The Irish between the 4th and 6th centuries developed not only their own individual style of writing but effective methods of learning Latin as a written language (Ó Cróinín 1995, 204). From the Ionan mission in the 7th century, and the visits to study in Ireland which Bede records, the Northumbrians benefited from these skills and enthusiastically took them forward. They developed parallel Latin and vernacular written cultures, and used their native runes for epigraphic display (eg the Ruthwell cross). It is possible this public display of literacy was encouraged by Roman inscriptions still visible in the landscape as well as by contemporary epitaphs which travellers to Rome recorded. Northumbria is indeed distinguished among the Anglo-Saxon kingdoms by its early monumental stone inscriptions. If one considers Okasha's distribution map of all pre-Conquest inscriptions on stone (1971, 140) the quantity is apparent, and if only the pre-10th-century inscriptions, then the concentration in Northumbria is even more striking.

A monument from one site will suffice to illustrate the distinctively Northumbrian characteristics in sculpture. Dewsbury is the centre of a huge parish today, and by oral tradition has been associated with Paulinus. It is in a frontier area between Northumbria and Mercia, and was possibly a royal foundation. Although nothing survives from the 7th century, the number and quality of the extant 8th- to 10th-century monuments indicate the importance of the mother church (Collingwood 1915, 162–71).

Inscriptions on the Dewsbury monuments, both memorial (Collingwood 1915, 166*k*) and descriptive (op. cit. 162*a*, 164*f*) suggests a literate community, a suggestion supported by the kneeling figure of a monk at the feet of an angel which illustrates the link seen by early Christian writers between the monastic and angelic life (Cramp 1995a, 131). Other fragments have strong doctrinal and liturgical resonances: on the Virgin and Child shaft two 'Eucharistic' miracles – the turning of water into wine and the multiplication of loaves and fishes – are divided by explanatory inscriptions in display capitals (Fig 1.1). Likewise Christ is depicted seated and surrounded by standing figures who could be apostles and saints, with one figure (Collingwood 1915, 162*b*) whose cap indicates, as at nearby Crofton (op. cit. 161*a*), that he is a bishop, possibly Paulinus. Stylistically the figures are close to Crofton, but this must have been a remarkable monument, perhaps standing within the church as a devotional focus, of the same fashionable 'Carolingian' type as Reculver or Masham.

The solemn figure of Christ in glory and judgement (Fig 1.2), sometimes accompanied by the twelve apostles, is one of the commonest images in Northumbrian sculpture. In an earlier period the standing Judge is found on the Cuthbert coffin lid, at Bewcastle, Ruthwell and possibly Hoddom, and seated accompanied by saints and angels at Easby, Hoddom and Halton. Christianity brought hope to the Anglo-Saxons: of a protective Creator who harmonized the natural world so that birds and beasts no longer struggled, against themselves and humanity, but happily found their place and sustenance on the true vine. (This image of the inhabited vine-scroll is more fully developed in Northumbrian sculpture than elsewhere in western Europe; even in neighbouring territories, in Ireland or Pictland, it appears as only fragmentary or sketchy, not a developed theme.)

When Cædmon found his voice to utter the first Northumbrian hymn it was to praise the might and protective power of the Creator (Colgrave & Mynors 1969, 414–17, IV.24), and Bede's articulate *thegn* saw Christianity as providing

Fig 1.1. Dewsbury, part of a shaft showing the miracles of turning the water into wine and the multiplication of the loaves and fishes. (Copyright: R. Cramp)

Fig 1.2. Dewsbury, part of a columnar shaft showing Christ in Majesty. (Copyright: R. Cramp)

certainty for the future – no longer a short passage of life from darkness into darkness (Colgrave & Mynors 1969, 182–5, II.13). Nevertheless, there was (as Bede said in his own vernacular 'death song'), an inevitable journey for every person, and after that the anxious knowledge of individual judgement (Smith 1933, 15–17, 42–3). Of course Christians elsewhere understood this also, but it was left to the Northumbrians uniquely to articulate the joy and the grave responsibility of created being.

I think we can accept that Northumbria in its Golden Age did have a distinctive identity. This identity was partly shaped by its geography – its highlands which allowed refuge in times of stress, and its seaboards, in particular the open way to the British west and to Ireland – but also by Roman territorial development and the early takeover by unruly native tribes who called themselves the Men of the North. The fact that a new Irish kingdom established itself at the same time as the Britons, Angles and possibly Picts were all struggling for territory and identity was crucially important. There were undoubtedly distinctions in the vernacular dialects, north and south, which everyone used as their first or second language, but the evidence is too scanty to consider here.

Northumbrian art, particularly the Christian art of the 7th to 8th centuries, embodied certain distinctive characteristics but it would be too simplistic to say that Bernicia looked to the Celtic north and west and Deira to the south – that is true in some places and at some times. In the remarkable achievements of the Northumbrian craftsmen, there are various competing centres which contribute to the creative energy of the whole. Neuman de Vegvar (1987, 275–7) in her account of the 'Northumbrian Renaissance' identified three modes of acculturation: assimilative, emulative and synthesizing, rightly stressing that one must look to the conditioning factors which produced such modes. In the distinctive articulation of word and image which emerged from the Northumbrian artistic crucible, the introduction of exotic foreign artefacts such as those imported by Benedict Biscop, Ceolfrith and Wilfrid must have been very influential.

The Franks Casket has been seen by many as summarizing the influences reflected in the Golden Age of Northumbria and its synthesis of the oral and literate heritage of several cultures confidently recast in one style. Kendrick (1938, 122) doubted whether the carver 'had any intention of expressing an intelligible sequence of events', but more recent scholars have seen subtle (antithetical) links within and between the scenes as well as a possible multiplicity of meaning (Lang, below). A good example, not unrelated to my discussion of the sculpture, is the theme of Judgement, expressed in the judgement of Christ juxtaposed with the judgement of the Jews and the Roman sack of Jerusalem, as well as the punning use of *dom* as 'judgement' or 'glory'.

The casket parades literacy, but its images come from an oral culture. The distinctive gifts of the Magi, for instance, include contemporary visualizations of gold overflowing from a goblet, incense smoking in a censer, and myrrh as a branch; the craftsman must have been told that myrrh was an aromatic shrub. This recalls Gregory of Tours' famous story of how the wife of Bishop Nametius of Clermont decorated the church she had built with coloured frescoes. She held a book from which she read stories of past events, telling the workman what she wanted painted on the walls (Dalton 1926, II, 59). The visualization of the Weland legend perhaps came easily to the craftsman, but when he depicted the Adoration of the Magi, although he may have had some image of the three figures and the Virgin and Child, he transformed the anonymous gifts usually featured in this scene to something that linked word and image in a way he could understand. For me that type of creative interpretation is an important part of the identity and confidence of the Golden Age of Northumbria.

CHAPTER 2

CHANGING BURIAL RITES IN NORTHUMBRIA AD 500–750

Sam Lucy

This chapter includes a Gazetteer of the Anglo-Saxon Cemeteries of Northumbria, 5th–8th Centuries.

INTRODUCTION

The early Anglo-Saxon pre-Christian burials of Bernicia (for present purposes taken to be northern England east of the Pennines, between the Tees and the Tweed), have given rise to much debate in recent years. In this chapter these debates will first be reviewed, and the particular issues for which these burials have been used as evidence will be considered. The evidence itself will then be examined, using a chronological approach and taking into account recent excavations and summaries of the material.[1] After comparing this evidence with that of Northumbria south of the Tees, this chapter will conclude by arguing that the mortuary evidence can be seen to suggest a range of more interesting and appropriate questions than those which have been asked in the past.

RECENT DEBATES

Ideas about the Anglo-Saxon pre-Christian burials of Bernicia can be seen to have changed as more information on them has been collated and made public. Miket (1980), drawing on recent excavations, antiquarian accounts and unpublished work (Keeney 1935) produced a supplement to the gazetteer included in Meaney (1964) which can be seen to have brought about a new generation of enquiry into these remains. Prior to this, opinion on these burials can be typified by Faull (1977, 10) who considered their most striking feature to be their undistinguished nature, with the singular exception of the Castle Eden burial with its 6th-century claw beaker.

Alcock disagreed with this view, arguing that 'Bernician graves may be few, but they are frequently rich' (1981, 168). In this chapter he argued that these remains

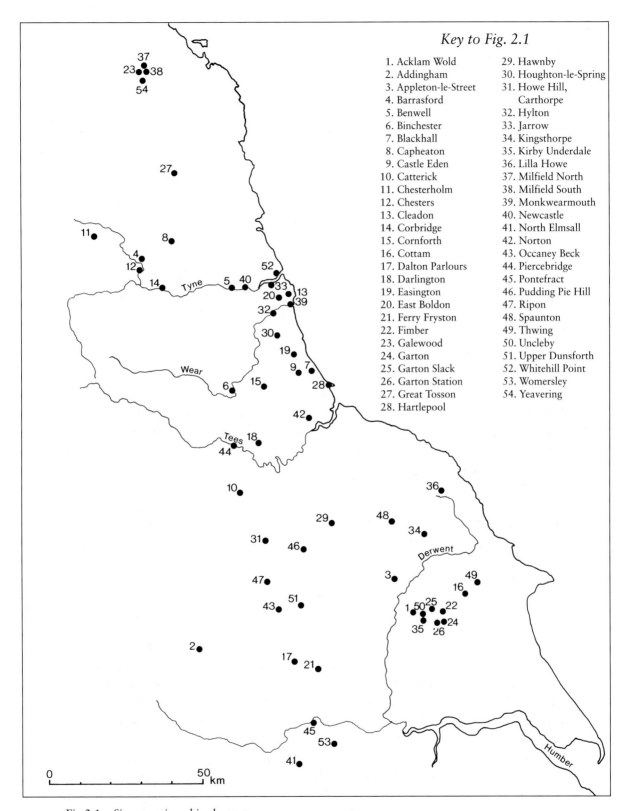

Key to Fig. 2.1

1. Acklam Wold
2. Addingham
3. Appleton-le-Street
4. Barrasford
5. Benwell
6. Binchester
7. Blackhall
8. Capheaton
9. Castle Eden
10. Catterick
11. Chesterholm
12. Chesters
13. Cleadon
14. Corbridge
15. Cornforth
16. Cottam
17. Dalton Parlours
18. Darlington
19. Easington
20. East Boldon
21. Ferry Fryston
22. Fimber
23. Galewood
24. Garton
25. Garton Slack
26. Garton Station
27. Great Tosson
28. Hartlepool

29. Hawnby
30. Houghton-le-Spring
31. Howe Hill, Carthorpe
32. Hylton
33. Jarrow
34. Kingsthorpe
35. Kirby Underdale
36. Lilla Howe
37. Milfield North
38. Milfield South
39. Monkwearmouth
40. Newcastle
41. North Elmsall
42. Norton
43. Occaney Beck
44. Piercebridge
45. Pontefract
46. Pudding Pie Hill
47. Ripon
48. Spaunton
49. Thwing
50. Uncleby
51. Upper Dunsforth
52. Whitehill Point
53. Womersley
54. Yeavering

Fig 2.1. Sites mentioned in the text.

could be ranked in three distinct grades: graves with weapons would fall into those with swords, those with spears, and those with just knives or buckles. While acknowledging that the ranking of burials with jewellery is a more subjective process, he nonetheless went on to produce a gazetteer of burials in Bernicia, where each site was allocated according to these grades of *alpha*, *beta* or *gamma* (the grade of the site being calculated on the basis of the overall status of the individual burials contained within it). The high ratio of *alpha* to *beta* sites was then used to infer a different social structure from Anglo-Saxon society south of the Humber, and Alcock concluded that 'a very few Anglian *thegns*, supported by a small number of retainers, took over the territory and organization of the British Votadini as a going concern' (1981, 179).

Cramp in turn contradicted this, pointing out that later 6th- and 7th-century furnished burials tended to contain richer goods than earlier graves, and therefore arguing that:

> . . . the distribution of furnished graves in Northumbria probably reflects the date at which there was effective Anglian control within an area rather than the status of the Angles *vis à vis* the native population (1983, 269).

She concluded that 'all in all it is very difficult to speculate with any precision on the numbers and status of the invading English as well as of surviving Britons in the north' (1983, 270–1).

Sherlock and Welch, however, with the knowledge of the 'community'-type cemeteries excavated at Norton and Easington in the 1980s and early 1990s, stated in contrast that:

> . . . it can now be argued with some justification that the Tyne-Tees region was probably settled by many small Anglian farming communities of the Norton type in the 6th century. This would seem more convincing than a series of, so far unidentified, British settlements, which presumably had been subjected to overlordship by a small, well-armed, Anglian elite (1992a, 104).

More recently, Higham (1993, 75) has stated categorically that 'there can be little doubt that Bernicia contained no more than a tiny minority of immigrant stock'. The nature of the supposed incoming Anglo-Saxon population is therefore an issue which has generated much debate.

Other aspects of burial practice in the north have also been discussed. Cramp (1983, 268) noted an interesting coincidence of furnished Anglo-Saxon burials with Roman forts in the area, which was thought perhaps to signify a tradition adopted from the native British population. Others have also suggested partial adoption of indigenous rites. Miket (1980, 300) suggested that this may be where the antecedents of the regional pattern of burial in stone cists lay. Similarly, Sherlock and Welch (1992a, 27, 103, following Faull 1979) argued that the high proportion of crouched burials in the Norton cemetery could be seen as evidence for the strong influence of native traditions, perhaps for intermarriage of the Anglian settlers with their native British neighbours. Cramp (1983, 270) had, however, already pointed out that crouched burial is a rite found elsewhere in England during the Anglo-Saxon period and which continues into the later medieval period. She also suggested (Cramp 1988, 74) that the Anglo-Saxons had adopted all aspects of the 'native' burial rite, thus rendering themselves archaeologically invisible, and possibly accounting for the small numbers of furnished burials which are found.

A third area of debate surrounds the issue of where the boundary between Deira and Bernicia lay. Cramp (1988, 74) wondered whether the whole of the Tees valley should be considered to fall within the sphere of Deiran influence, something which Sherlock and Welch considered unlikely 'in view of the general similarity of the cruciform and small-long brooches recovered from sites between the Tyne and the Tees valley' (1992a, 6).

There are thus three main areas of debate surrounding Bernician pre-Christian burials: the status of the incoming Anglo-Saxons – whether this was elite take-over or peasant migration; their relationship with the indigenous population and the influence of native burial traditions; and the location of the boundary between the neighbouring kingdoms of Bernicia and Deira.

THE SIGNIFICANCE OF BURIAL PRACTICE

In recent years there have been major theoretical advances in understanding the significance of burial practice. In the 1980s it became widely believed that the material culture patterning seen in burials does not constitute a mirror image of social organization (Barrett 1990, 181; Hodder 1982, 14; Morris 1987, 38); a person buried with weapons, for example, need not have been a warrior in life, a point more recently supported by Härke's (1992) comparisons of artefactual and skeletal data which has emphasized the symbolic role that such grave goods can play. Aspects of social theory have also been drawn upon by those studying burial practice, leading to the belief that death and burial are essential parts of human existence, and that burial practices are actively created by those affected by death (Barrett 1990; Thomas 1991). Mourners are thus seen as the active participants in burial practices (Barrett 1990, 182). In contrast to previous analyses of Anglo-Saxon burials, where it was almost as if the corpse buried itself with its favourite belongings, the role of the mourners comes to the fore. It is they who must decide what goods to bury with the corpse and how to arrange them; how deep and wide a grave to dig; and where the grave should be positioned in the landscape (Lucy 1998, 24).

If burial is viewed in this light, then the mourners create the burial rite; they create the artefactual and spatial patterning which we, as archaeologists, study. This highlights the importance of studying cemeteries within a chronological framework. If burial practice is viewed as an active creation it must be subject to change, and those changes over time are presumably meaningful to the burying community. Similarly, funerary rites should also be studied from a local perspective, as any spatial patterns seen on distribution maps are, first and foremost, the creation of individual and neighbouring communities choosing to adopt similar ways of burying their dead.

Along with such archaeological critique there has also been much historical work on the subject of ethnicity. Historians have demonstrated that ethnic names, when they appear in documentary sources, need to be examined in context in order to understand what those names mean. Although, traditionally, names such as Angles and Saxons have been taken to mean racial groupings, consisting of people linked by blood-ties and common language and culture, recent work has shown the concept of early medieval ethnicity to be something far more fluid and ambiguous. It is now viewed by many as being intimately involved with relations of power, politics and loyalty (Amory 1993, 2–3; Geary 1983, 16; Hedeager 1993, 123), with ethnic identity only being judged important enough to mention in certain situations (Geary 1983). Early medieval peoples should be viewed more as temporary groupings, brought about by specific circumstances, than as permanent biological entities (James 1989, 47).

Some archaeologists have already identified the difficulties involved in distinguishing named ethnic groups of the English through analysis of grave goods (Austin 1990; Cramp 1988, 73; Lucy 1998). The historical critique outlined above emphasizes the flaws inherent in approaches which attempt to reconstruct ethnic groupings in this way. For what then, do Anglo-Saxon cemeteries provide evidence? It can be argued that examining the archaeological evidence from a chronological and regional perspective can shed some interesting light on previous debates.

THE BURIALS OF THE NORTH

The 6th-century evidence north of the Tyne is extremely sparse, and in many respects odd (Fig 2.2). Aside from the chance finds in the Roman forts on the Tyne at Benwell, Chesterholm and Corbridge, there remain only three sites with possible remains of this period: the inhumation at Galewood, with two, probably annular, brooches, a pottery vessel and a large bead, with two nearby spearheads, which is dated to the later 6th or earlier 7th century; the confused report of an Anglo-Saxon buckle as possibly coming from one of four Bronze Age cists at Great Tosson; and the possibly 6th-century burials within the ring-ditch associated with the 'ritual complex' at Yeavering, just two of which were furnished, with iron knives.

Following recent excavations and publications, there is now quite extensive evidence for burials between the Tyne and the Tees. Aside from the burial in the Roman fort at Binchester and the chance find of a cruciform brooch at Piercebridge, there is also evidence for 'community'-type cemeteries at Darlington, Easington and Norton, sites which exhibit considerable differences in

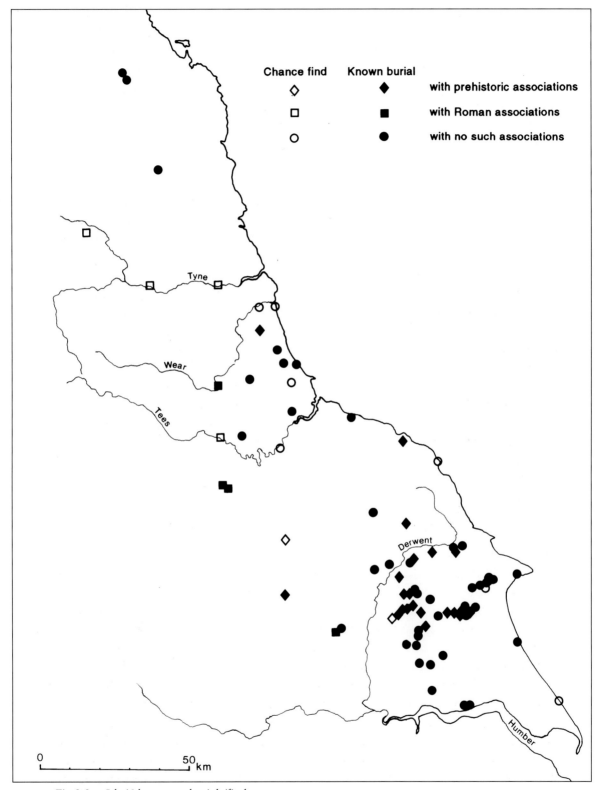

Fig 2.2. 5th-/6th-century burials/finds.

orientation and positioning. Burials at Norton are mainly oriented N–S, those at Darlington W–E, and those at Easington both W–E and NE–SW. Approximately half of the burials at Norton are crouched, while those at Easington are found in a variety of positions. There are also the cist burials at Blackhall, Castle Eden, Cornforth and Houghton-le-Spring, as well as chance finds of brooches, possibly suggesting burials, at Cleadon, Hylton and Whitehill Point. With the exception of Houghton-le-Spring, none of these is known to be associated with a prehistoric earthwork, such as a round barrow, a great contrast with cemeteries in Northumbria south of the Tees where this is a common feature (Lucy 1998).

The area between the Derwent and the Tees seems to be where these different traditions intermingle, with the cist graves at Appleton-le-Street and Spaunton, the burials in the Roman fort at Catterick, and the burials in prehistoric barrows at Upper Dunsforth, Kingsthorpe and Pudding Pie Hill. This is emphasized by the lack of cemeteries with Roman associations from East Yorkshire, east and south of the Derwent.

In the 6th-century burials of Northumbria, therefore, we seem to have various different features, such as barrow burial, cist burial, inhumation in Roman forts and cremation (rarely found north of the Tees), which all have very different spatial distributions (see Fig 2.2). All, however, are associated with items of material culture commonly linked with the 'Anglian' area of England, such as cruciform, square-headed and annular brooches and certain styles of decoration on metalwork and pottery.

Graves from the 7th century are identified by their association with distinctive items of material culture, such as hanging bowls, bronze workboxes, seaxes, gold and garnet jewellery, silver and gold pendants, and by the use of Salin Style II zoomorphic decoration (Geake 1997).

It is only in the 7th century that the practice of furnished inhumation in the area north of the Tyne becomes truly visible (Fig 2.3). Again, there are chance finds in Roman forts along the Tyne, with the square-headed brooch found at Benwell, and the Style II decorated annular brooch from Chesters. There are also, however, two sites associated with barrows, at Barrasford and Capheaton, and one with a henge monument, at Milfield North.

In contrast with this picture, the area between the Tyne and the Tees is virtually blank for this period, with only the 'rock tomb' burial at East Boldon, with its gold and garnet buckle.

Between the Tees and the Derwent there are two, possibly three, sites associated with prehistoric barrows: those at Hawnby and Lilla Howe, and possibly also that at Howe Hill, Carthorpe, where such an association is suggested by the name of the site. There is a single cist grave at Occaney Beck with two Style II decorated annular brooches, and three other sites where the precise location of the grave is not recorded.

It is only in the 7th century that burials in West Yorkshire are found, with just the single inhumation in the Roman villa at Dalton Parlours, the male skeleton

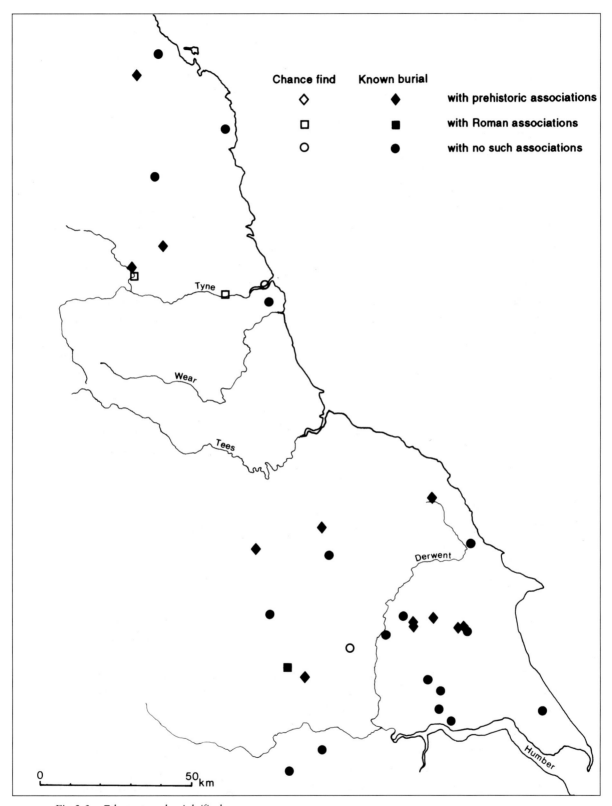

Fig 2.3.   7th-century burials/finds.

with a spearhead and an interlace belt at North Elmsall, the burial with a gold and garnet pendant at Womersley, and a possible weapon burial at Ferry Fryston.

In East Yorkshire the tradition of burial associated with prehistoric round barrows continues in the 7th century, with the cemeteries or burials at Acklam Wold, Fimber, Uncleby and Kirby Underdale. However, this rite also expands to include other forms of prehistoric earthwork, with the cemetery based on a linear earthwork at Garton, and also the extremely unusual cemetery at Garton Station, based around an Iron Age square barrow cemetery. A curiously high proportion of these cemeteries has predominantly crouched burial, which has been argued elsewhere to represent a new innovation in this area, rather than a continuation of native rites (Lucy forthcoming). No 7th-century cist burials or cemeteries with Roman associations were found in this area, however.

In the 7th century, therefore, the tradition of interment in Roman sites seems to have been declining, while that of barrow burial has spread outside East Yorkshire, and the tradition within East Yorkshire has expanded to include cemeteries based around other kinds of prehistoric earthwork. The tradition of cist burial also seems to be in decline, with just two recorded examples, both lying between the Tyne and the Derwent.

8th-century burials fall roughly into two types (Fig 2.4). There are those associated with known monastic or ecclesiastical foundations, such as those around Ripon, Addingham, Pontefract, Hartlepool, Jarrow, Wearmouth, Newcastle and the postulated church at Yeavering (although some of the burials at Hartlepool, Wearmouth and Jarrow may be slightly earlier, Cramp, pers comm). These are typically unfurnished burials, usually oriented W–E, but with the occasional E–W burial. These are usually dated by radiocarbon testing, and only the site at Newcastle is recorded as being in association with Roman features, in this instance, the interior of the fort.

The other type of cemetery is perhaps best thought of as a variant on the 'Final Phase' type (Geake 1992). These too are predominantly unfurnished, but burials are occasionally interred with a knife, a buckle, coins or other such small items. These are also generally extended and supine burials, oriented W–E, but they are distinct in that they are usually associated with a prehistoric earthwork. Such sites include the cemetery at Milfield South, associated with a henge monument; at Cottam, associated with the Bronze Age barrow Kemp Howe; the burials associated with linear earthworks in the eastern half of the Garton cemetery, and also that at Garton Slack (where coin evidence dated a burial to the 8th century); and finally, the site at Thwing, where the cemetery was located at the centre of a Bronze Age earthwork. It is notable that, with the exception of Milfield, all these 8th-century cemeteries with prehistoric associations are found in East Yorkshire. They may, of course, be Christian, and associated with unlocated churches or mortuary chapels, but it is still of note that they are linked to these prehistoric features in the landscape. This can easily be seen as a continuation of the rite from the 7th century.

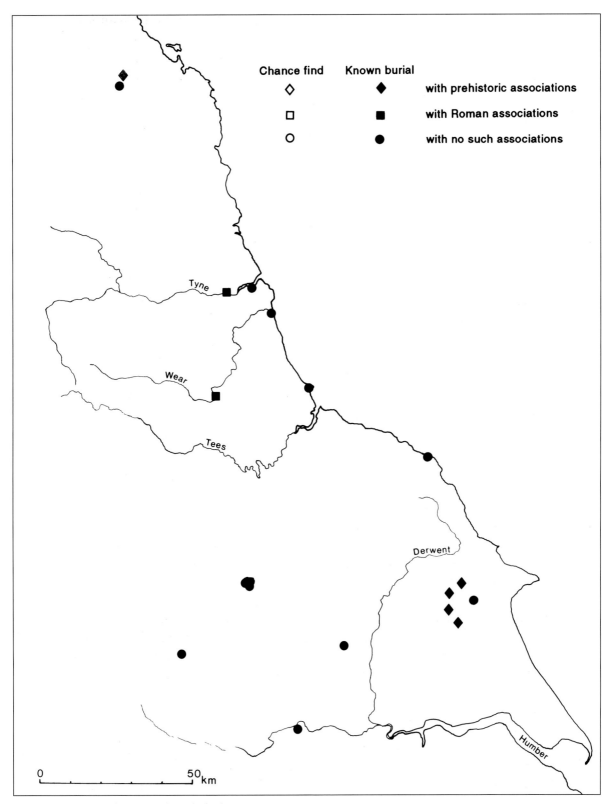

Fig 2.4.   8th-century burials/finds.

ASKING NEW QUESTIONS

It can be argued that the mortuary evidence outlined above cannot be of assistance in the debates that have so far surrounded this period, but that it can raise different questions. The issue of how burial evidence might be interpreted needs deeper and more careful thought, both in the light of the many variations in practice which have been outlined above, and in view of the theoretical reconsideration currently being given to early medieval burial practice (Lucy 1998 and forthcoming). Given that there are overlapping distributions of these different practices such as cist burial, cremation, barrow burial and crouched burial, can burial evidence really be used to reconstruct a political boundary, such as that between the later documented kingdoms of Deira and Bernicia? Even if, in the 6th and 7th centuries, this boundary was viewed in geographical terms, rather than as a boundary between the members of different political groupings, why should we expect it to be reflected in the way in which a few people buried their dead? Given all these variations on a theme, perhaps burial practice should be interpreted on a more localized level, as differences between and similarities with neighbouring communities, rather than as an expression of some abstract political allegiance (cf Lucy 1998, where it was argued that burial rites provide one of the media through which social groups can define both themselves and others).

Similarly, the suggestion of continuity from native burial practice or the adoption of 'British' rites can be questioned. As Miket (1980, 299) pointed out, we have yet to identify the 'native' burial rite of the 5th to 7th centuries in this area. As the only burials which are known, and are capable of being dated, are those with an Anglo-Saxon colouring, perhaps we should regard this rite as the only one used which is now archaeologically recoverable. Access to 'Anglo-Saxon' goods was presumably not limited to certain sectors of the population. The determining factor would have been whether or not people wished to bury their friends and relations with such goods, something which presumably was not determined by genetic origins.

Likewise, the debate over the status of the Anglo-Saxon population can be undermined. The only possible evidence for elite burial which is known from Northumbria are the burials at Yeavering, a documented royal centre, which are also among the plainest burials known from this area. What does this say about the signalling of status through burial ritual? It could be argued that those already in positions of power had no need to emphasize their status in society through the destruction of wealth as grave goods. Perhaps furnished burial was a tactic employed by those 'on the way up', whatever their origins.

Instead, it can be argued that by asking different questions of the burial data, more interesting lines of enquiry can be pursued, which are more in keeping with the actual contexts in which burials take place. Such questions might include: what localized identities are being emphasized by the different features of 6th- and 7th-century burial practices? Did the practice of cist burial mean something different to those doing the burying than secondary burial in a barrow? Did it mean the same to bury in a round barrow as in a linear earthwork? Did the location of cemeteries in the landscape imply different things to the wider community?

What was the significance of burying the dead in Roman forts, and why did this decline in the 7th century? Perhaps this represents a reaction against the tide of Roman Christianity sweeping the country. Or perhaps, with the conversion, were Roman places now seen to be the property of the Roman church, and thus unsuitable places for non-Christian furnished burial?

What was the relationship of burial practice with Christianity? It has been argued in other areas that 'Final Phase' cemeteries are a sort of last-ditch statement against conversion, a kind of defiant paganism (Carver 1989, 155; Geake 1992, 90–1). Perhaps in 7th-century Northumbria the continuation of association of burial with prehistoric earthworks performed a similar function to the raising of barrow mounds over burials at Sutton Hoo.

CONCLUSION

Theoretical reconsideration of the significance and meaning of burial practices can help shed new light on old debates surrounding the material, and can suggest new questions which can be asked of it. It is extremely difficult to use archaeology to identify ethnic groupings in the past, especially in the realm of burial archaeology (Austin 1990; Hedeager 1993; Lucy 1998), because the decision to bury a person and include grave goods with them is a deliberate one which can only be made by the mourners (Barrett 1990, 182; Thomas 1991). Viewing burial practice as something which is the creation of the mourners, who are able to choose how to bury a person and what to bury with them, forces us to see burial, not as something which can reflect ethnic or political groupings, but as an active creation of a local society at a particular time. When similarities in aspects of burial practice are found over long periods of time, or over large areas, this needs explaining in dynamic terms, as the result of an accumulation of individual decisions and actions. Viewing the 5th to 7th centuries in terms of people, rather than abstract ideas of 'Britons' and 'Anglo-Saxons', has the potential to offer exciting new insights into the period.

In short, archaeologists have for too long been using this burial evidence in the wrong debates. Burials cannot be used to reconstruct political history. They are only evidence for the ways in which people buried their dead, and for the light this throws on the ways they lived.

ACKNOWLEDGEMENTS

I am extremely grateful to Professor Rosemary Cramp for reading and commenting on a draft of this chapter, to Niall Hammond for providing information from the County Durham SMR, and to Yvonne Beadnell for producing the illustrations.

NOTE

1. This evidence is available in the form of a gazetteer accompanying this chapter, listing a summary of all Anglo-Saxon cemeteries and related finds of the 5th–8th centuries, with full references, from the pre-1974 counties of Yorkshire, Durham and Northumberland. This gazetteer draws heavily on those compiled by Meaney (1964), Eagles (1979), Faull (1979), Miket (1980), Alcock (1981), Geake (1997) and Lucy (1998). References to all sites are given in the appropriate gazetteer entry, rather than in the text. Sites mentioned in the text are shown in Fig 2.1.

GAZETTEER OF THE ANGLO-SAXON CEMETERIES OF NORTHUMBRIA 5TH–8TH CENTURIES

I. 5th- to 6th-century Burials

East Yorkshire
Birdsall (SE824629)
1868 – in Mortimer Barrow 108 Aldro Group, a clean well-burnt deposit of unurned calcined bone with a bronze ferrule, two bronze pieces with inset glass or crystal, and further bronze implements.
Refs: Mortimer 1905, 56–7, figs 107–8 (who cites Sherwin MS vol).

Bishop Wilton (SE78055648)
1876 – in Mortimer Barrow 199, 'Kity Hill', many pieces of the iron umbo of an Anglo-Saxon shield and flat pieces of iron also belonging to shield were found W of the centre near the surface.
Refs: Eagles 1979, 423; Mortimer 1905, 149.

Bishop Wilton (SE81235635)
1866 – in Mortimer Barrow 69, Beacon Hill, near the centre, 6 in deep, were found an Anglian skull and parts of arm bone, with an iron spearhead and portions of two blades of iron shears. The barrow was partly destroyed during construction of the beacon in 1588.
Refs: Brown 1915, 805; Eagles 1979, 423; Meaney 1964, 288–9.

Boynton (TA125674)
1951 – an Anglian burial with a shield boss and an iron spear, discovered by a local farmer. Further burials *in situ* were not recorded.
Refs: Eagles 1979, 424; Meaney 1964, 282; OS Records.

Bridlington (TA20556911)
1959 – Thirty-eight graves were excavated by Rahtz, after seven inhumations had been discovered during farmhouse construction in 1958.
1974 – ten further burials were excavated by Hirst in advance of building works. A maximum of fifty-nine individuals were recorded, of variable orientation, with mainly 6th-century goods.
Refs: Hirst 1985; *Medieval Archaeol* 4 (1960), 137.

Driffield (TA01995749)
1893 – several skeletons were found while levelling two small fields adjoining King's Mill Road. Some early Frankish pottery and twelve skeletons were recorded. These were men, women and children, with heads to various points, some of whom were crouched. The site was situated on a slight rise, with a possible Bronze Age inhumation in the middle, suggesting a barrow.
Refs: Eagles 1979, 427; Faull 1979, 309; Meaney 1964, 286–7; Mortimer 1905, 294–5; Smith 1912b, 86–7; Swanton & Myres 1967, 49, fig 3.1; *Trans Hull Scientific & Field Naturalists Club* 4 (1918), 314.

Driffield (TA02975748)
1876 – during excavation of a railway siding at Driffield Cake Mill several interments were found, some accompanied by bits of iron and fragments of Anglo-Saxon pottery. There were also traces of at least one cremation.
Refs: Eagles 1979, 428; Meaney 1964, 287; Mortimer 1905, 293; Smith 1912b, 86; *Trans Hull Scientific & Field Naturalists Club* 4 (1918), 314.

Driffield (TA025579)
1924 – reference was made to 'Anglian skeletons and finds'.
Refs: Loughlin & Miller 1979, 90; OS Records.

Driffield (TA02355830)
1858 – when removing part of Moot Hill, Anglo-Saxon remains including a sword were found.
Refs: Eagles 1979, 427; Meaney 1964, 287; Mortimer 1905, 294; Smith 1912b, 86; *Trans Hull Scientific & Field Naturalists Club* 4 (1918), 314.

Driffield (TA028576)
1935 – a skeleton and a fragmentary Anglo-Saxon pot were found near Routh Hall.
Refs: Eagles 1979, 428; RCHM Records.

Driffield (TA042578)
1845 – ten to fifteen skeletons were found when half a barrow was levelled.
1847 – Thurnam levelled the rest of the mound, finding eight more burials.
1871 – Mortimer reopened the mound, finding eleven Anglo-Saxon inhumations and one cremation. The finds comprised annular and cruciform brooches, bead strings, knives, buckles, and a single shield and spear.
Refs: Akerman 1855, 13–19; *Archaeol J* 8 (1851), 97; Eagles 1979, 427–8; Elgee & Elgee 1933, 183–4; *J British Archaeol Assoc* 2 (1847), 54–6; Meaney 1964, 285; Mortimer 1905, 286–95; Smith 1912b, 84–6; *Trans Hull Scientific & Field Naturalists Club* 4 (1918), 314.

Etton (SE952428–954428 or 958428–962428)
Pre-1866 – in a field adjoining the new railway line between Market Weighton and Beverley, seventy skeletons were found contracted, but there was no sign of a barrow. Greenwell excavated there for one day, and thought them Anglo-Saxon; Meaney considered this doubtful.
Refs: Eagles 1979, 430; *Gentleman's Magazine* 1 (1866), 494; Greenwell's notebook in Dept of Medieval and Later Antiquities, BM; Meaney 1964, 288.

Ganton (SE991781)
Pre-1974 – an Anglian cemetery was found near Windale Beck Farm.
Refs: OS Record SE97NE45; Purdy 1974, 208.

Ganton (TA003762)
Pre-1877 – Greenwell found a secondary Anglo-Saxon burial in Barrow 29, with only a single tooth remaining, accompanied by woollen fabric, three cruciform brooches, a buckle, a necklace and food vessels.
Refs: Eagles 1979, 432; Greenwell & Rolleston 1877, 178; Meaney 1964, 288; Smith 1912b, 93.

Haltemprice (TA021265)
1952 – Anglo-Saxon beads and pottery were found when a drain was cut at Tranby, Hessle, probably indicating at least two burials.
Refs: Eagles 1979, 435; Hull Museum Records; Meaney 1964, 291.

Haltemprice (TA033264)
Pre-1907 – an Anglo-Saxon cist was found under the tower of Hessle church.
Refs: Elgee & Elgee 1933, 181; *Hull Museum Publications* 46 (1907), 64; 117 (1919), 319; Meaney 1964, 291; *Trans East Riding Archaeol Soc* 14 (1907), 64; *Trans Hull Scientific & Field Naturalists Club* 4 (1918), 319.

Hayton (SE82484698)
Pre-1979 – potsherds, an iron knife and human remains were found in a gravel pit at Burnby Gates.
Refs: Eagles 1979, 436; RCHM Records.

Heslerton (SE918767)
1977–86 – excavations were carried out by J.S. Dent, then by D. Powlesland of an extensive Anglo-Saxon cemetery. In total, 184 inhumations and 10 cremations were excavated (with more remaining under the A64 which bisects the site), in association with prehistoric earthworks. The finds comprised jewellery, metalwork and pottery from the mid-5th to the 7th century. There was also a 'ritual' horse burial.
Refs: Powlesland et al. 1986; Powlesland 1989; in press.

Hornsea (TA207484)
1913 – while levelling a slight ridge, bones and beads were found. Sheppard excavated and found twelve skeletons, most flexed or crouched on one side, with heads to various points. Half had brooches or other ornaments.
Refs: Brown 1915, 803–4; Eagles 1979, 437; Faull 1979, 98; Meaney 1964, 291; Sheppard 1918.

Huggate (SE858559)
Pre-1984 – an Anglo-Saxon burial urn was found in a chalk bank at Cross-dykes.
Refs: Dent 1984, 33.

Kilham (TA07926598)
Pre-1824 – in a chalk pit approximately two miles N of Kilham, several urns and other relics were found in the first quarter of the 19th century.
1824 – in a sandpit at Kilham where excavations had previously 'been successful', a skeleton was found with a buckle, brooches, wrist clasps and beads. York Museum also has from this site a 5th-century square-headed brooch, a radiate brooch with geometric decoration, a developed cruciform brooch of the 6th century, five pairs of wrist clasps, three pairs of flat annular brooches and two odd ones, a bronze ring, strap ends, two buckles and weapons including spearheads and a shield boss.
Refs: Brown 1915, 806–8; Eagles 1979, 211; Elgee & Elgee 1933, 180–1; Meaney 1964, 292; Mortimer 1905, 344 (in part quoting from *Scarborough Repository* of 1824); Smith 1912b, 87–8.

Kilham (TA057646)
Pre-1979 – a child burial with two annular brooches and a bronze pin was excavated by the Grantham brothers.
Refs: Eagles 1979, 438.

Kirby Grindalythe (SE88046690)
c 1798 – no record of Sykes's opening of the Howe.
1890 – Mortimer re-excavated Howe Hill, Duggleby, which began as a round barrow and ended as the base for a post-mill, finding evidence for at least two Anglo-Saxon inhumations, plus many

animal bones including ox, goat/sheep, dog/fox, red deer and horse, and an iron knife, bits of iron and many potsherds.
Refs: Eagles 1979, 439; Meaney 1964, 291–2; Mortimer 1905, 23–6.

Kirby Underdale (SE82465826)
1867 – secondary in Mortimer Barrow 102 was found a crouched skeleton with a knife.
Refs: Eagles 1979, 209; Mortimer 1905, 123.

Kirby Underdale (SE827585)
1877 – in Mortimer Barrow 200, three cattle buried in the plague of 1866–7 had destroyed at least one burial accompanied by a thin bronze cup and the iron spike of an Anglo-Saxon spear.
Refs: Eagles 1979, 439; Meaney 1964, 296; Mortimer 1905, 120.

Kirkburn (TA017567)
1851 – Lord Londesborough opened a Bronze Age barrow, examining the central Bronze Age cist, and ten other skeletons, of whom Mortimer thought three to five were British, and the rest Anglo-Saxon.
1870, 1872 – Mortimer reinvestigated the site, and found twenty-seven more Anglo-Saxon inhumations, most heads being oriented to the centre of the barrow. Finds included annular and cruciform brooches, beads, purse rings, knives, buckles, spears and three shields.
1887 – workmen discovered thirteen more burials with similar goods.
Refs: *Archaeologia* 34 (1852), 251–6; Elgee & Elgee 1933, 183; Mortimer 1905, 271–83; Smith 1912b, 82–4; *Trans Hull Scientific & Field Naturalists Club* 4 (1918), 313–14.

Kirkburn (TA002562)
1870 – part of a large bronze cruciform brooch was found on a mound, Mortimer Barrow 137, possibly representing a ploughed out secondary burial.
Refs: Eagles 1979, 440; Meaney 1964, 292–3; Mortimer 1905, 262.

Kirkburn (SE98665752)
1868 – four secondary burials were found in the barrow ditch of Mortimer Barrow 112, being crouched with heads to various points. One was buried with a knife.
1872 – Mortimer found a further burial, which was contracted and associated with animal bones.
Refs: Eagles 1979, 440; Meaney 1964, 290 (giving incorrect location as SE950610); Mortimer 1905, 245–6; Smith 1912b, 80–1.

Kirkburn (SE97175757)
1872 – in Mortimer Barrow 146 an Anglo-Saxon burial was found, almost fully extended, with head to S, and an iron piece.
Refs: Mortimer 1905, 235; OS Records.

Langton (SE80326837)
Pre-1877 – when a barrow, 50 yd NW of a great entrenchment running N–S across the racecourse, was levelled there were found many fragments of Anglo-Saxon pottery and remains of probably cremated interments just below the surface.
Refs: Eagles 1979, 440; Greenwell & Rolleston 1877, 136; Meaney 1964, 293 (giving location as SE815686); Smith 1912b, 100.

Londesborough (SE87154625)
1870–95 – many inhumations were discovered during chalk-quarrying, with glass and amber beads, bronze brooches, bronze and iron buckles, iron knives and food vessels.

1880 – two skeletons were found, about 2 ft down. One was extended with the head to NW, two bronze brooches, a bronze bracelet, a bead, a buckle, some iron 'blades or arrowheads' and a possible key. Later, another was found contracted on the right side, with the head to WNW, a knife, annular brooches, and other ornaments.

1884 – among finds given to Cambridge Museum were the head of a small-long brooch, two Roman coins, a strap end and a bead.

1895 – a visit by the East Riding Archaeological Society excavated a burial with head to E, laid on its back/left side and crouched, with a food vessel, a bronze square-headed brooch and two bronze clasps. Also given to York Museum were two annular brooches and glass and amber beads.

Pre-1940 – other items probably from this site in Hull Museum include four cruciform brooches, two of which were very large and elaborate, a pair of girdle-hangers, six flat annulars, a large deer horn annular, wrist clasps and a long necklace.

Refs: Brown 1915, 804; Cramp & Miket 1982, 6–8, fig 5; Eagles 1979, 441; Meaney 1964, 294; Mortimer 1905, 353; Smith 1912b, 77–8; Swanton 1964; *Trans Hull Scientific & Field Naturalists Club* 4 (1918), 314–15.

Market Weighton (SE8741)

1906 – a prone female burial was found in a rock-cut grave, with an amber and glass necklace, a pair of massive developed cruciform brooches, a single cruciform brooch, a possible belt plate, two pairs of wrist clasps, a horn ring, a pair of girdle-hangers and food vessels. Also found was a male grave with probably 7th-century goods.

Refs: *Antiquary* 42 (1906), 333–8; *Hull Museum Publications* 33 (1906), 10–18; 117 (1919), 319; Meaney 1964, 295; Smith 1912b, 74–5; *Trans East Riding Archaeol Soc* 14 (1907), 77; 16 (1909), 67; *Trans Hull Scientific and Field Naturalists Club* 4 (1918), 319.

Nafferton (TA060587)

1850–55 – Mr Longbottom, while digging in a sandpit, found frequent interments associated with relics including iron spears, knives, bronze fibulae and pottery. There may possibly be another cemetery, as the 'brickyard between the church and the Pottery' was said to be where many urns and other Anglo-Saxon relics were discovered by Longbottom (Eagles gives the location as TA05235890).

Refs: Bowman 1855, 28–9; Eagles 1979, 442; Elgee & Elgee 1933, 180; Meaney 1964, 295; Mortimer 1905, 343–4; Smith 1912b, 87.

North Cave (SE905321)

Pre-1891 – some skeletons were found at the Everthorpe cutting of the Hull and Barnsley Railway, with 'Roman helmets', probably Anglo-Saxon shield bosses.

Refs: Eagles 1979, 443; Smith 1891, 278.

Nunburnholme (SE86404887)

1851 – three skeletons were found in a chalk pit, in a crouched position, with heads to E. Associated goods included silver earrings, silver finger rings, three brooches, two wrist clasps, toilet implements, an urn, iron objects, a bronze buckle and a bead necklace.

Refs: Bowman 1855, 62–3; Eagles 1979, 444; Faull 1979, 96; *Gentleman's Magazine* (NS), 40 (1853), 269–70; Morris 1907, 15; Phillips 1853, 231.

Rillington (SE850741)

1954 – a skull and arms were exposed during excavation of a trench across the pavement on the S side of Westgate. The skeleton was lying E–W with calcite-gritted ware sherds at the E end.

Ref: OSSI 03465.00020.

Rudston (TA097677)
Pre-1912 – a pair of 5th-century cruciform brooches were found.
Refs: Brown 1915, 806–7; Meaney 1964, 297; Smith 1912b, 89.

Rudston (TA11326721)
Pre-1960 – an inhumation burial and knife were found by the Grantham brothers.
1960 – a biconical urn and iron spear ferrule were found with the remains of an inhumation burial.
Refs: Eagles 1979, 445; Faull 1979, 307 (citing J. Bartlett HM letter 9/12/60 to A.L. Savill).

Rudston (TA11216746)
1830 – urns, swords and spears, probably Anglo-Saxon, were found when fishponds were enlarged at Thorpe Hall.
Refs: Eagles 1979, 445; Sheahan & Whellan 1856, 489.

Sancton (SE903402)
1873 – urns were marked on the OS map as found in a chalk pit to the NE of the village.
Pre-1875 – Rolleston illustrated a talk with eight urns and associated goods including clasps, beads, cruciform and annular brooches.
Pre-1882 – Foster recorded a site a mile N of the village – an area 150 x 50 yd was reported as filled with urns.
1891 – Richardson of South Cave excavated an urn.
1891–4 – Hall dug further urns, but located them in a different place. Fragmentary urns had been disturbed by ploughing or later burials. Some had been protected by flat stones. Usually no implements or ornaments were found associated.
1892 – Hall found an urn 7.5 in high. Three others were found in the same year.
1894 – Hall found a large urn with ridged bosses, bones and a knife.
Pre-1909 – Sheppard described and illustrated nineteen urns belonging to Wilson from Sancton. Eleven contained goods, including brooches, beads, clasps, toilet implements and combs.
1953 – Taylor found broken pottery near the chalk pit.
1954 – Sutton of Hull Museum put down some trial trenches and found six urns and numerous fragments. Among the cremated bones were miniature knives, shears, tweezers and beads.
1955 – excavations continued to the N; twenty-eight pottery positions were located, some with two or more urns. Associated goods included combs, fused bronze and glass.
1956 – more excavations to N and E located sixty-three pottery positions, over 50 yd². The remains of glass vessels as well as normal objects were found.
1957 – eighty pottery positions were found, although only eight urns were complete. They appear to have been scattered over the site with no regular system of spacing. About 200 were found, either plain cooking pots or food vessels, or ornamented cremation urns. They had sometimes been deliberately holed before burial.
Refs: *Archaeologia* 45 (1880), 409–10; *Archaeol Aeliana* 4 ser, 25 (1947), 38; Brown 1915, 803; Eagles 1979, 446; Elgee & Elgee 1933, 179–80; *Hull Museum Publications* 66 (1909), 67; Meaney 1964, 298–9; Smith 1882, 12–13; Smith 1912b, 75–6; *Trans East Riding Archaeol Soc* 4 (1897), 115–20; 14 (1907), 63; 16 (1909), 50–66, 70; *Trans Hull Scientific & Field Naturalists Club* 4 (1918), 318–19.

Sledmere (SE90766131– 91046144)
c 1850? – a contemporary of Mortimer's grandfather remembered the discovery of inhumation burials, one with a sword, 300 yd N of Fimber Station.
Refs: Eagles 1979, 448; Mortimer 1905, 192–3.

Tibthorpe (SE941561)
1850 – several inhumations were found when excavating a well to the N side of Angas Farm.
Refs: *Proc Yorkshire Geological & Polytechnic Society* 11 (1890), 452.

Warter (SE870505)
Pre-1979 – a gravedigger at Warter Priory found an iron spearhead with a split socket beneath later burials.
Refs: Eagles 1979, 451.

Warter (SE899531)
1851 – a secondary inhumation burial with a sword and pot was found in a round barrow at Blanch.
Refs: Eagles 1979, 451; Mortimer 1905, 322.

Welton (SE975268)
Pre-1907 – a bead and small penannular brooch were found with a skeleton at Melton Hill.
Refs: *Hull Museum Publications* 46 (1907), 64; 117 (1919), 319; Meaney 1964, 295; Smith 1912b, 74; *Trans East Riding Archaeol Soc* 14 (1907), 64; *Trans Hull Scientific & Field Naturalists Club* 4 (1918), 319.

Wharram (SE83606272)
1868 – Mortimer found two inhumations in the upcast of a ditch which cut a Bronze Age round barrow. The burials were extended, with heads to SW and no goods.
Refs: Eagles 1979, 422; Meaney 1964, 303; Mortimer 1905, 50–2.

Wharram (SE858642)
Pre-1935 – a Saxon interment was found near Wharram Percy House.
Refs: Clark 1935, 39; Eagles 1979, 453.

Wharram (SE865635)
Pre-1859 – during construction of the Burdale Tunnel on the Malton and Driffield Railway, a well-preserved skull was found with other remains and iron weapons, including a Saxon sword.
Refs: Bateman 1861, 237; Eagles 1979, 453; Faull 1979, 318; Whellan 1859, 209.

Willerby (TA02287930)
1937 – during construction of a petrol station, human bones were found on an upper hill-slope. Sheppard investigated, and described four well-furnished grave groups.
1939 – Gwatkin excavated, and recovered at least five more graves, two with crouched burials. He also found five flat annular brooches, an iron knife and a large fragment of an urn.
1936–52 – the site was excavated on various occasions, producing around eighty grave groups, most of which disappeared during the Second World War. The site was used possibly from the 5th to the 8th centuries.
Refs: Eagles 1979, 453; Faull 1979, 98; Meaney 1964, 301–2; Sheppard 1938.

Withernsea (TA34102815)
1908 – fragmentary pots (probably cinerary urns) were found when digging a well on the W side of Bannister Street.
Refs: Eagles 1979, 454; Miles & Richardson 1911, 7; *Trans East Riding Archaeol Soc* 14 (1907), 74.

North Yorkshire
Appleton-le-Street (SE733714)
Pre-1859 – an Anglo-Saxon cist grave was found on Hepton Hill, containing gold earrings, an amber necklace, a small food vessel and a comb.
Refs: Eagles 1979, 415; Elgee & Elgee 1933, 181; Meaney 1964, 282; Whellan 1859, 210.

Barnby (NZ830130)
Pre-1930 – an unburnt Anglo-Saxon burial with the remains of an iron spearhead was found at the base of a probably prehistoric monolith.
Refs: Elgee 1930, 106; Meaney 1964, 282.

Broughton (SE771728)
Pre-1798 – a number of cremation urns were found, probably Anglo-Saxon.
Refs: *Antiquity* 2 (1928), 74–5; Brown 1915, 391; Eagles 1979, 415; Elgee & Elgee 1933, 179, 245; Hinderwell 1811, 19; Meaney 1964, 282–3; Phillips 1853, pl 33; Smith 1912b, 100.

Catterick (SE225988)
Pre-1849 – two square-headed brooches of the 6th century were found on a Roman site.
Pre-1957 – four more brooches of early Anglo-Saxon date were found.
1958/9 – excavations by Hildyard found evidence for four or five adult burials and one or two infants, accompanied by 'Saxon knives'.
Refs: *Archaeol J* 4 (1849), 216; Hildyard 1953; 1957, 224 n 5; Meaney 1964, 284–5; Sherlock & Welch 1992a, 6; Smith 1912b, 100; Wilson et al. 1996, 4, 47–9.

Catterick (SE239973–244974)
1939 – approximately five skeletons were found in a Roman building – one with a large cruciform brooch; one with two buckles; two others and a single skull with erratic orientation.
1959 – rescue excavations by Wilmott produced six spearheads, a great square-headed brooch, an iron 'dagger' and a shield boss. The burials may have been in cists.
1964/6 – a female burial with 6th-century grave goods was discovered at RAF Catterick, possibly associated with those found in 1939.
1981/2 – eight further Anglian burials were found cut into Roman buildings. There were other features which may also have been graves.
Refs: Alcock 1987, 252–3; Cardwell 1988; Cramp 1970b, 206 n 6; Hildyard 1953; *J Roman Stud* 30 (1940), 166; Meaney 1964, 284–5; Pocock 1970; Wilson 1982; Wilson et al. 1996, 29–45; *Yorkshire Archaeol J* 35 (1940), 98.

Catterick (SE231986)
1995 – excavations at Catterick race-course produced evidence for forty-four burials associated with brooches, beads and weapons of the mid-5th to mid-6th century.
Refs: *Medieval Archaeol* 40 (1996), 291; Wilson et al. 1996, n 17, n 162.

Catterick (SE232976)
1970s – two cist burials containing children were found cutting through a layer containing 6th-century pottery.
Ref: Wilson et al. 1996, 45–7.

Heworth (SE610519)
1878, 1880 – remains of cremation urns were found, reconstructed to form at least forty-two examples; one containing bronze tweezers, others with fused glass, probably dating to the 5th or 6th century.
Refs: *Ann Rep of Council of Yorkshire Phil Soc* (1878), 8–9; *Archaeol Aeliana* 4 ser, 25 (1947), 39–40; Brown 1915, 802–3; Elgee & Elgee 1933, 179; Smith 1912b, 103; *York Museum Handbook* (1891), 216.

Kingthorpe (SE834857)
1853 – a disturbed Anglo-Saxon secondary burial was excavated near the apex of a barrow,

consisting of some bones, a bronze cruciform brooch, a boar's tusk and a vessel rim.
Refs: Bateman 1861, 235; Meaney 1964, 292.

Maltby (NZ46001320)
1990 – metal detector finds including a blue bead string, a pair of small-long brooches and a
cruciform brooch, dating to the late 5th/early 6th century, possibly representing a single
inhumation.
Refs: Sherlock & Welch 1992a, 6; 1992b.

Pudding Pie Hill (SE436810)
Pre-1891 – a large shield boss, shield handle and spearhead were found in a barrow.
Refs: Elgee & Elgee 1933, 183; Meaney 1964, 296; Sherlock & Welch 1992a, 6; Smith 1912b, 96;
York Museum Handbook (1891), 210.

Robin Hood's Bay (NZ948052)
1912 – in Pickering Museum were goods including an urn and two jars, beads, tweezers, two
square-headed brooches and annular brooches.
Refs: Elgee & Elgee 1933, 180; Meaney 1964, 296; Smith 1912b, 93.

Hob Hill, Saltburn (NZ651205)
1909–10 – inhumations, cremations and possible half-cremations were found intermingled. Goods
found with cremations included pots, buckles, beads and tweezers. The inhumations were richer in
artefacts including spears, knives, beads, brooches and pottery. All are suggestive of a 6th-century
date. Graves 17–40 were possibly deposited in two parallel lines running N–S. One burial had
traces of a coffin.
Refs: Brown 1915, 808; Elgee & Elgee 1933, 180; Gallagher 1987; Hornsby 1912; Meaney 1964,
297; Sherlock & Welch 1992a, 6; Smith 1912b, 93–6.

Spaunton (SE724899)
Pre-1933 – a cist burial of a male with a small pot and beads was excavated.
Refs: Elgee & Elgee 1933, 181; Meaney 1964, 301.

Thornaby (NZ450162)
1987/8 – a chance find of an Anglo-Saxon spearhead of Swanton type C1 dating to the mid-
5th–mid-6th century.
Refs: Sherlock 1988; Sherlock & Welch 1992a, 6.

Upper Dunsforth (SE426633)
c 1785 – human bones and cremation urns in a barrow indicate a mixed rite cemetery.
Refs: *Gentleman's Magazine* 57 (1787), 564–5; Hargrove 1789, 256–7; Meaney 1964, 287.

Yarm (NZ421117)
Pre-1958 – an isolated cremation burial and a class F copper alloy penannular brooch were found.
1976 – a class F penannular brooch was found S of Yarm.
1977 – a similar brooch was found within a few yards of the previous year's find.
Refs: Brown 1977; Meaney 1964, 303; Myres 1977, fig 332.150.

York, The Mount (SE593511)
1859–60, 1950–6 – finds of whole and fragmentary cremation urns, representing an extensive
Anglo-Saxon cremation cemetery NW of the main Roman road.

Refs: *Archaeologia* 42 (1869), 433; *Archaeol Aeliana* 4 ser, 25 (1947), 40–1; Brown 1915, 802; Elgee & Elgee 1933, 179; Meaney 1964, 303; *Medieval Archaeol* 1 (1957), 149; Smith 1912b, 104; *York Museum Handbook* (1891), 216; *Yorkshire Archaeol J* 39 (1958), 429–35.

County Durham

Binchester (NZ210313)

1978 – in the *praetorium* of the Roman fort were found the remains of a woman of 20–30 years, oriented N–S with no coffin, crouched on the back, with a bronze S-brooch with birds' head terminals, glass and amber beads, an antler disc, antler ring and bronze fragments, probably dating to the 6th century.
Refs: Briscoe 1968; Coggins 1979, 236, fig 17.1; Miket 1980, 297; Sherlock & Welch 1992a, 4.

Blackhall (NZ471388)

c 1900 – 8 km to the SE of Easington a burial of a child with a single bead in a cist was found.
Refs: Durham SMR no 526; Hamerow & Pickin 1995, 35; N. Hammond (pers comm).

Castle Eden (N427385)

1775 – an inhumation with a blue glass claw beaker inverted over the mouth was found with head to E in a stone cairn.
Refs: Alcock 1981, 173; Austin 1987, 57–60; *British Museum Quarterly* 15 (1941–50), 73; Brown 1915, 484, 810, pl 124; Evison 1982, 60–1, pl 7a; Harden 1956, 139, fig 25b.1; Hodges 1905, 215; Meaney 1964, 83; Miket 1980, 292.

Cleadon (NZ43875601)

1983 – a chance find of a bronze small-long brooch dating to the later 5th/6th century.
Refs: Miket 1984; Sherlock & Welch 1992a, 3.

Cornforth (NZ313329)

1822 – eight or nine skeletons were found in cists, two with iron spearheads. The bones of a horse and probably a dog were found in one. Orientation was not E–W.
Refs: Alcock 1981, 173; Fordyce 1857, 400; MacKenzie & Ross 1834, 321; Meaney 1964, 83; Miket 1980, 292; Surtees 1823, 397.

Darlington (NZ28621507)

1876 – six skeletons of men, women and a child were found with heads to W. Each had a small pot at the head. Also a number of bronze brooches, some gilded, were found. These included two great square-headed brooches, two small-long brooches, two circular brooches and two cruciform brooches, along with pins, bronze tweezers, a necklace, at least three spearheads, two shield bosses and two swords, of the late 6th century.
Refs: Alcock 1981, 174; Brown 1915, 810, pl 31.4; *Darlington and Stockton Times*, 22 Mar 1905; 20 Oct 1962; Hodges 1905, 211; Miket 1980, 293; Miket & Pocock 1976; *NE Independent*, 1 Feb 1879; *Proc Soc Antiq Newcastle* 3 ser, 3 (1907), 34, 36; Sherlock & Welch 1992a, 2–3; Wooler 1913, 38.

Easington (NZ417427)

1991–2 – eight or nine burials were found, four oriented E–W and two NE–SW. Four contained jewellery and one had weapons. Two were extended, one was flexed, one was crouched and one was prone. The goods were mainly 6th century, although one buckle was possibly 7th century.
Refs: Hamerow & Pickin 1995; Pickin 1991; 1993; Sherlock & Welch 1992a, 5.

Houghton-le-Spring (NZ353492)
Pre-1914 – an inhumation burial was found, unfurnished in a cist grave, with head to W, secondary in a barrow.
Refs: *Archaeol Aeliana* 3 ser, 11 (1914), 123–30; Miket 1980, 300.

Hylton (NZ343567)
1981 – a chance find of a bronze small-long brooch of the later 5th/6th century.
Refs: Miket 1982; Sherlock & Welch 1992a, 3.

Norton-on-Tees (NZ44882256)
1980s – 120 inhumations, all but 3 of which were oriented N–S. Approximately half were crouched.
Refs: *Medieval Archaeol* 28 (1984), 173–5; Sherlock & Welch 1992a.

Piercebridge (NZ214156)
1989 – chance find by divers of a C2 cruciform brooch on the river bed, close to the bridge.
Refs: N. Hammond (pers comm); Selkirk 1989; Sherlock & Welch 1992a, 5.

Northumberland
Benwell (NZ215648)
1935 – a chance find of a 6th-century cruciform brooch.
Refs: Brewis 1936; Cramp & Miket 1982, 8, fig 6.6, pl 1.6; Jobey & Maxwell 1957; Miket 1980, 290–2; Sherlock & Welch 1992a, 3.

Chesterholm (NY771804)
Pre-1975 – a chance find of a 6th/7th-century bronze annular brooch.
Refs: Henig 1975, 13, fig 5; Miket 1978, 178, fig 4.2; 1980, 293.

Corbridge
1984 – two small-long brooches were found by metal detecting S of Corbridge (or possibly Newton Kyme)
Refs: Miket 1985.

Corbridge (NY982648)
1907 – a pair of late 5th-century bronze cruciform brooches with some small beads were found in the Roman fort, probably representing an inhumation.
1908 – a small Anglo-Saxon urn was found near a stone cist. A scabbard mount was also found in the fort.
Refs: Alcock 1981, 174; *Archaeol Aeliana* 3 ser, 5 (1909), 342, 406–8, fig 25; 3 ser, 6 (1910), 272; *Proc Soc Antiq* 33 (1911), 215; Sherlock & Welch 1992a, 3.

Galewood (NT912324)
c 1852 – a body was found with two probably annular brooches, a pottery vessel and a large bead. Two iron spearheads were also found several feet off.
Refs: Alcock 1981, 174; Keeney 1936; Maclauchlan 1867, 26, n 8; Meaney 1964, 193; Miket 1980, 294.

Great Tosson (NU028005)
1858 – four Bronze Age limestone cists were discovered, one of which was reported as having an Anglo-Saxon bronze buckle, but this is more likely to have come from one of the graves excavated at the same place, which were extended, with heads to W.

Refs: Alcock 1981, 174; Davis & Thurnam 1865, 54–7; Greenwell & Rolleston 1877, 432; Meaney 1964, 198–9; Miket 1980, 294; *Proc Soc Antiq Scotl* 4 (1863), 58–63.

Yeavering (NT925305)
1953–7 – some 'British' burials were excavated, one of which contained possibly Anglo-Saxon goods.
Refs: Hope-Taylor 1977, 108–16, 244–50; Meaney 1964, 199; *Medieval Archaeol* 1 (1957), 148–9; 24 (1980), 265–70; Miket 1980, 296; Sherlock & Welch 1992a, 3.

II. 7th-century Burials

East Yorkshire

Acklam (SE792611)
Pre-1866 – skeletons were found from time to time 500 yd SW of Greet's Chalk Pit.
1860 – a labourer found one or more bodies with a few amber and glass beads and a circular gold pendant with filigree plaitwork and garnet bosses.
'A few years later' – the same labourer found another body with pieces of iron, a knife, a sword, an iron ferrule, part of a sharpening iron and the remains of a buckle and plate.
1878 – Mortimer found six adult burials, four crouched, two extended, of which four graves contained iron knives and other iron objects.
1980 – a pattern-welded sword was found with an inhumation burial and a plain pot on Acklam Wold.
Refs: Brown 1915, 805; Eagles 1979, 421; Elgee & Elgee 1933, 182; Meaney 1964, 282; Mortimer 1905, 94–5; Smith 1912b, 92–3.

Burton Pidsea (TA252311)
1818 – two skeletons were found 5–6 ft below the surface, which crumbled when exposed. No coffins were seen. Goods included blue glass and gold earrings and a gold ring.
Refs: Eagles 1979, 426; Meaney 1964, 283; OS Records; Poulson 1841, 44.

Elloughton (SE941278)
1940 – an Anglo-Saxon inhumation cemetery was found during house construction on top of a hill. Skeletons were found 1–1.5 ft deep in the gravel. Men and women were found, and also a child which seems to have been deposited in a sack. Burials were in shallow pits, placed anyhow; some were face down, and one was headless. Goods included annular brooches, beads, buckles and iron tools.
Refs: Eagles 1979, 429; Meaney 1964, 287–8; Sheppard 1940, 161–4.

Fimber (SE894606)
1863 – at least six bodies were found 80 yd SE of Fimber church, crouched with fragments of iron and pottery. These were mostly small people, women and children.
c 1870 – two bodies were found close to S side of church, one with a late penannular brooch. The barrow on which the church was built seemed to have been used for Anglo-Saxon burial.
1884 – an Anglo-Saxon spear was found while cleaning out the mere just below the church.
Refs: Eagles 1979, 431; Faull 1979, 319; Meaney 1964, 288; Mortimer 1905, 190, 192; Smith 1912b, 79.

Garton (SE980577)
1985–6 – an Anglo-Saxon inhumation cemetery was excavated, comprising forty-three individuals in thirty-five graves, within an Iron Age square barrow cemetery. Burials were accompanied by annular brooches, beads, dress pins, knives, buckles, spears and swords.
Refs: British Museum Records; Stead 1991, 17–24.

SAM LUCY

Garton (SE988577)
1870 – twenty-six graves were excavated in a Bronze Age mound and linear earthwork, and were quite richly furnished, with goods including a workbox, food vessels, annular brooches, a jet and gold pendant, a circular gold pendant, bone combs, iron knives, buckles and bridle bits; 46 ft E a group of thirty, probably 8th-century, graves were also excavated.
Refs: Elgee & Elgee 1933, 182; Geake 1997, 158; Meaney 1964, 289; Morris 1983, 55; Mortimer 1905, 247–57; Smith 1912b, 79–80; *Trans Hull Scientific & Field Naturalists Club* 4 (1918), 312–13.

Kirby Underdale (SE82195941)
1868 – an inhumation cemetery centred on a Bronze Age barrow was excavated by Greenwell, who located seventy-six individuals in seventy-two graves. Goods included annular brooches, bead strings, pendants, knives, swords and workboxes.
Refs: Brown 1915, 805–6; Eagles 1979, 439; Elgee & Elgee 1933, 184; Greenwell & Rolleston 1877, 135–6; Meaney 1964, 302–3; Mortimer 1905, 118; Smith 1912a; 1912b, 89–92; *Trans Hull Scientific & Field Naturalists Club* 4 (1918), 311.

Kirby Underdale (SE823582)
1862 – a chalk pit in Pudsey Plantation encroached on a barrow, exposing two extended burials with heads to W.
1870 – the centre of the barrow was explored revealing a disturbed skeleton and fragments of Anglo-Saxon pottery.
1871 – further chalk quarrying exposed an adult skeleton, extended, with head to the NW.
1876 – Mortimer explored the rest of the mound (Barrow 4) and found one burial extended, with the head to SSE, and another crouched on the right side, with the head to WSW, accompanied by an annular brooch, beads, a bronze workbox, and possibly the remains of a chatelaine, suggesting a 7th-century date.
Refs: Brown 1915, 805; Eagles 1979, 439 (giving location as SE82215935); Meaney 1964, 295–6; Mortimer 1905, 114; Smith 1912b, 92.

Kirkburn (TA000563)
1936 – at the NW corner of the aerodrome was found an extended skeleton with a fragment of an iron ring under the head. Other objects found in the dump included a sword, six knives, three hones, a buckle, a ring, a key, two annular brooches, a gold tab set with garnets and some beads, suggesting at least twelve graves.
Refs: Eagles 1979, 440; Meaney 1964, 293; OS Records; *Yorkshire Archaeol J* 34 (1939) 44–7.

Market Weighton (SE8741)
1906 – a male grave with a knife, part of a scramasax, a small spear and an iron buckle was found. A female with 6th-century goods was found in an adjoining grave.
Refs: *Antiquary* 42 (1906), 333–8; Meaney 1964, 295; *Hull Museum Publications* 33 (1906), 10–18; 117 (1919), 319; Smith 1912b, 74–5; *Trans East Riding Archaeol Soc* 14 (1907), 77; 16 (1909), 67; *Trans Hull Scientific & Field Naturalists Club* 4 (1918), 319.

Newbald (SE909368)
Pre-1901 – a skeleton was found with the body doubled over. Later, a child's skeleton was found with a hole in the skull and 'other remains of a more or less significant character were subsequently found'.
1901 – another skeleton was found extended on the back, with pottery. Above this was another skeleton, also extended, with a knife, a scramasax, a steel and small iron points.
1901–2 – Sheppard excavated three skeletons close together. The first was on its side, with the legs

partly drawn up, accompanied by a bronze annular brooch, beads, a knife and keys. The other positions are unknown. Sheppard speaks of 'numerous skeletons buried in shallow graves in the sand. These were carefully and gradually examined, so as not to make too great inroads on the farmer's crops'.
Refs: *The Antiquary* 38 (1902), 106–7; Eagles 1979, 443; *Hull Museum Publications* 3 (1901), 10–12; 11 (1902), 1–8; 46 (1907), 63; 117 (1919), 317; Meaney 1964, 295; *Trans East Riding Archaeol Soc* 14 (1907), 63; *Trans Hull Scientific & Field Naturalists Club* 4 (1918), 317.

North Cave (SE900310)
1958 – a number of skeletons were excavated in a field. Finds in Hull Museum include a blue glass pendant with a silver mount and beads found with a female skeleton, and a bronze wire finger ring and iron knife found with a male.
Refs: J. Bartlett HM letter 9/12/1960 to A.L. Savill; Eagles 1979, 443; Meaney 1964, 288.

Rillington (SE85677442)
1980 – an Anglian burial with two cruciform brooches was discovered during the excavation of an Iron Age crop-mark site. From the same excavation came a bronze strap end. A local man brought some earlier finds along to the excavation, including brooches matching the 1980 finds, and dating to the late 6th/early 7th century.
Refs: *Yorkshire Archaeol J* 53 (1981), 139; 55 (1983), 1–9.

Seamer (TA028841)
c 1845 – quarrymen found a number of skeletons which they buried in Seamer churchyard. It was not remembered if any ornaments were present.
1857 – workmen found several gold ornaments and other articles. Lord Londesborough and T. Wright investigated, sifting the excavated earth and finding an urn, a gold and garnet pendant, two gold rings, a silver ring, two gold pins, two gold pendants, three triangular gold and garnet tabs, a large silver annular brooch, beads, a jet ring, a pierced coin and some broken pottery. Trenching the ground above, they found a crouched skeleton with a bronze girdle ring, a small knife and fragments of bone and iron.
1871 – in Hull Museum two large ?keys on an iron ring were labelled M. Seamer 1871.
Refs: Brown 1915, 809; Eagles 1979, 418; Elgee & Elgee 1933, 182; Gomme 1886, 192–3; *J British Archaeol Assoc* 19 (1865), 329–32; Meaney 1964, 300; *Report of the Scarborough Philosophical & Archaeological Society* 26 (1857), 16–17; Smith 1912b, 100.

Stamford Bridge (SE734554)
1937 – during excavation of a gravel pit, human bones were found with a white metal serpent bracelet. Around the same time, a toilet set was found in the spoil. A Roman burial had previously been found in the same place, but these goods suggest an Anglo-Saxon burial.
Refs: Clark 1943, 339; Eagles 1979, 449; Meaney 1964, 283.

North Yorkshire
Carthorpe (SE309838)
1865 – at Howe Hill, four W–E burials and more bones were found. One had four small monochrome beads; one had a small bronze buckle, a small plain strap end and knife; another had a buckle and knife; the last was unfurnished. One was extended and two were crouched on the right side.
Refs: Elgee & Elgee 1933, 186; Meaney 1964, 283–4; *Proc Soc Antiq* 8 (1880), 409; Sheppard 1979, catalogue 1 type 6; *Yorkshire Archaeol J* 1 (1870), 175–81.

Hambleton Moor (SE552807)
Pre-1912 – from a woman's grave came a plain annular brooch, a small buckle, a silver pin and part of a workbox with chain.
Refs: Meaney 1964, 290; Smith 1912b, 96.

Hawnby (SE526893)
Pre-1865 – barrows excavated at Sunny Bank produced a woman with a leather girdle with gold and garnet decoration, gold and silver hairpins, four silver and one bronze annular brooch, blue glass beads, a hanging bowl and knife. Only two or three of the other eight barrows produced remains: one flexed burial, oriented W–E, with no goods; another extended on the right side, oriented N–S, with a bronze workbox, an annular brooch and a small knife.
Refs: Brenan 1991, 55, 68; Brown 1915, 809; Elgee & Elgee 1933, 184–5; Geake 1997, 189–90; *Proc Geol Soc W Riding Yorks* 4 (1865), 497–9; Sheppard 1979, catalogue 1 type 1/2; Smith 1912b, 96; Youngs 1989, 48.

Lilla Howe (SE889987)
Pre-1871 – a secondary burial in a barrow was found with four silver ornamented strap ends, two roundels of gold filigree work, plain gold rings and a gold brooch with white stone.
Refs: Elgee & Elgee 1933, 185–6; Meaney 1964, 293–4; *Trans Hist Soc Lancs & Cheshire* (NS) 11 (1871), 200.

Occaney Beck (SE352621)
1949 – an E–W oriented burial was found in a grave lined with limestone slabs. It was thought to be a male aged 25–35 years with two bronze Style II annular brooches.
Refs: *Archaeological Newsletter* 2 (1949), 51; Meaney 1964, 295; *Yorkshire Archaeol J* 37 (1951), 440–1.

York, Castle Yard (SE604514)
1829 – a bronze hanging bowl and two pots were found, probably representing inhumations.
Refs: Brown 1915, 809; Elgee & Elgee 1933, 185; Meaney 1964, 303; *Reliquary* (NS) 12 (1906), 60–4; Smith 1912b, 104.

West Yorkshire
Dalton Parlours (SE402445)
1977 – a single inhumation was found overlying a Roman villa, semi-flexed on the left side with a small annular brooch.
Refs: Dickinson 1990; Faull 1981, 180; *Medieval Archaeol* 22 (1978), 150.

Ferry Fryston (SE473425)
1811, 1863, 1962 – in Greenwell Barrow 71 were found at least four secondary inhumations, one of which was said to be 'in armour' perhaps implying a weapon burial. All were extended, with heads to W.
Refs: Faull 1981, 180; Greenwell & Rolleston 1877, 371–2; Pacitto 1971.

North Elmsall (SE417127)
1962/3 – a male skeleton with a spearhead and a gilt bronze interlace belt was found.
Refs: Faull 1981, 180; *Medieval Archaeol* 8 (1964), 238, pl XIX, E.

Womersley (SE5319)
1860 – a skeleton was found with a gold filigree and garnet pendant.
Refs: *Archaeologia* 96 (1955), 163; Brown 1915, 809; Campbell 1982, 42; *J British Archaeol Assoc* 16 (1860), 289; Meaney 1964, 303; Smith 1912b, 98.

County Durham

East Boldon (NZ3661)

1800–1840 – an inhumation burial was found in a rock tomb with a gold and garnet brooch/buckle.

Refs: Åberg 1926, 128, 216 no 93; Alcock 1981, 172; *Archaeol Aeliana* 1 ser, 4 (1855), 19; Brown 1915, 349, 810, pl lxxi, 5; Cramp & Miket 1982, 9–10, fig 6.11, pl 1.11; Hodges 1905, 213; Meaney 1964, 83; Miket 1980, 294; Sherlock & Welch 1992a, 4.

Whitehill Point (NZ367674)

1892 – a great square-headed brooch was dredged from the Tyne dating to the early 7th century.

Refs: Åberg 1926, 56, 194, tab 1 group v no 238; *Archaeol Aeliana* 3 ser, 5 (1909), 408; Brown 1915, 269 pl XLV no 6; Cramp & Miket 1982, 9, fig 6.10, pl 1.10; Leeds 1949, 81, 86, pl 137; Leeds & Pocock 1971, 32–3; Miket 1980, 296; *Proc Soc Antiq Newcastle* 2 ser, 5 (1891–2), 236, 239.

Northumberland

Barrasford (NY919736)

Pre-1875 – an inhumation burial was found secondary in a barrow with a silver ornamented shield boss, a two-edged sword and knife.

Refs: Alcock 1981, 172; *Archaeol Aeliana* 2 ser, 7 (1876), 14–15; Collingwood-Bruce 1880, 67–8, pl XXII; Dodds 1897, 311; Meaney 1964, 198; Miket 1980, 290; Sherlock & Welch 1992a, 3.

Benwell (NZ215648)

1957 – a square-headed brooch was found near a glass vessel – possibly suggesting an inhumation dating to the 7th century.

Refs: Alcock 1981, 172; *Archaeol Aeliana* 4 ser, 13 (1936), 117–21; 4 ser, 35 (1957), 282–3; Cramp & Miket 1982, 8, fig 6.7, pl 1.7; Jobey & Maxwell 1957; Leeds & Pocock 1971, 32–6; Meaney 1964, 198; Miket 1980, 290.

Capheaton (NZ017796)

Pre-1813 – a mound was excavated, finding a 'great many cartloads of human bones and skulls' – finds included a hanging bowl, a finger ring and some copper pieces.

Refs: Alcock 1981, 173; *Archaeol Aeliana* 1 ser, 1 (1822), 3, 32; 2 ser, 4 (1860), 251; Brenan 1991, 55, 68; Cowen 1931; Cramp 1967, 11 no 13; Cramp & Miket 1982, 10, fig 7.12, pl 2.12; Geake 1997, 172; Hodgson 1827, 229 n; Meaney 1964, 198; Miket 1980, 290; *Proc Soc Antiq London* 22 (1907–9), 74–5; *Proc Soc Antiq Newcastle* 4 ser, 4 (1930), 255–8; 4 ser, 5 (1931), 12, 287; Sherlock & Welch 1992a, 3.

Chesters (NY912704)

19th century – a chance find of a bronze annular brooch with Style II decoration.

Refs: *Archaeol Aeliana* 5 ser, 6 (1978), 177, fig 1.1; Miket 1980, 293.

Hepple (NT983025)

Pre-1877 – several Anglo-Saxon burials were found in a quarry with goods including an ear scoop, a workbox chain, tweezers, an earring and a barrel-shaped bead.

Refs: Alcock 1981, 174; *Archaeol Aeliana* 5 ser, 2 (1974), 275–80; Cramp & Miket 1982, 4–5, fig 3.2; Greenwell & Rolleston 1877, 432; Meaney 1964, 199; Miket 1980, 295; Sherlock & Welch 1992a, 3.

Howick Heugh (NU236168)

1928–30 – quarrying produced at least fifteen burials, variously oriented, mostly crouched, with a few iron knives, some spearheads and some Anglian beads.

Refs: Alcock 1981, 174; *Archaeol Aeliana* 4 ser, 16 (1939), 120–8; Cramp & Miket 1982, 5–6, fig 4.2; Keeney 1939; Meaney 1964, 199; Miket 1980, 295; Sherlock & Welch 1992a, 3.

Lowick (NU005410)

1841, 1860 – a small seax in the British Museum is marked from Lowick. Three burials excavated with heads to E are not necessarily connected.
Refs: Miket 1980, 297–8; Sherlock & Welch 1992a, 3.

Milfield N (NT934348)

1975 – five graves were discovered during the excavation of a henge monument. They were oriented roughly W–E; one had two knives, one had a knife and buckle, one had a knife, an annular brooch and a chatelaine, one had a knife, buckle, girdle ornament, two annular brooches and a pin.
Refs: Harding 1978; *Medieval Archaeol* 20 (1976), 168; Miket 1980, 295; Scull & Harding 1990; Sherlock & Welch 1992a, 3.

III. 8th-century and Later Burials

East Yorkshire

Cottam (SE96166628)

1878 – in Mortimer Barrow 209, Kemp Howe, were found six adult interments from the SE side of the mound in narrow graves, with the knees slightly flexed, all heads to the NW and no goods.
1969 – Brewster re-excavated the barrow, finding a further seven burials in coffins without grave goods, suggesting a Christian/late cemetery. C14 dates centring between 725 and 745 have been obtained.
Refs: Brewster 1969, 241; Department of Environment 1968, 13; Eagles 1979, 427; Faull 1979, 303; Meaney 1964, 292; Mortimer 1905, 336–7.

Garton (SE988577)

1870 – 46 ft E of the 7th-century graves, thirty graves on a different orientation were excavated. Of these, only one was furnished, with a box.
Refs: Elgee & Elgee 1933, 182; Geake 1997, 158; Meaney 1964, 289; Morris 1983, 55; Mortimer 1905, 247–57; Smith 1912b, 79–80; *Trans Hull Scientific & Field Naturalists Club* 4 (1918), 312–13.

Kilham (TA047645)

Pre-1979 – at least six burials were found in coffins in a water-main trench.
Refs: Eagles 1979, 438; Faull 1979, 306.

Sledmere (SE95666181)

c 1800 – at Garton Slack ten or twelve skeletons were found by workmen.
1860 – a skeleton was found on each side of the road by workmen.
1866 – Mortimer records forty-two graves in the earthwork known as the Double Dyke, all W–E, supine, with twenty-eight extended, one contracted and nine crouched. Only some fragments of Anglo-Saxon pottery, and one or two knives, a spearhead, arrowhead and bone comb were found.
1959 – 300 ft to the E, seven W–E burials were found, one with an iron knife, one with 8th-century coins.
Refs: *British Numis Jnl* 30 (1960–1), 6–53; Geake 1997, 158; Grierson & Blackburn 1986, tab 13; Meaney 1964, 289–90; Mortimer 1905, 264–70; Smith 1912b, 82; *Trans Hull Scientific & Field Naturalists Club* 4 (1918), 313.

Thwing (TA0370)
1970s/80s – an Anglo-Saxon settlement was excavated within a Bronze Age ringwork, with an Anglo-Saxon cemetery at its centre, containing at least 132 individuals. This was probably a Christian cemetery, associated with a mortuary chapel. Amber and glass beads and a knife were found in one grave (C14 dated to 789–992); other C14 dates centre on the 7th and 8th century.
Refs: Geake 1997, 159 (citing Terry Manby pers comm).

North Yorkshire
Lamel Hill (SE614509)
1847-8 – a Civil War battery was built on the site of a cemetery by scraping up earth containing burials to form a mound, and this was excavated by Thurnham.
1983 – part of the undisturbed flat cemetery was excavated, locating thirty-eight graves in three groups. Most were W–E oriented, although two or three were E–W oriented. Most were unfurnished, but one had a knife and a small iron buckle.
Refs: *Archaeol J* 6 (1849), 27–39, 123–36; Elgee & Elgee 1933, 186–7; Geake 1997, 190; *Interim* 9.3 (1983), 11–13; Meaney 1964, 293; *Medieval Archaeol* 28 (1984), 249; Sheppard 1979, catalogue 1 type 5.

Ripon – Ailcy Hill (SE31737114)
1986-7 – 37 graves were excavated on a natural mound 200 m E of Ripon Cathedral, and remains of least 140 further individuals were also found. There appeared to be three generations of burials; one of the earliest was buried with a double-tongued buckle and a knife (C14 dated to 563–661). Most of the burials were oriented W–E, supine, extended and uncoffined. All the sexable remains were male, but some infant and juvenile remains were found in the disarticulated bone.
Refs: Geake 1997, 189; Hall & Whyman 1996, 65–124; *Interim* 11.4 (1986–7), 29–37; 12.3 (1987), 15–22; *Medieval Archaeol* 31 (1987), 169; 32 (1988), 290.

Ripon – Deanery Gardens (SE315712)
1977 – three W–E oriented burials were found 80 m N of Ripon Cathedral. There was no direct dating evidence, though these may be outliers of Ladykirk. A gold and garnet plaque was recovered from a demolition layer within the site.
Refs: Geake 1997, 189 (citing York Archaeological Trust archives); Hall & Whyman 1996, 130–6.

Ripon – Ladykirk (SE316712)
1955 – thirty-six graves were excavated on the W side of St Marygate, Ripon, 120 m N of the Cathedral, roughly W–E oriented. Four had combs of the 9th to 11th centuries. A late 8th-century sculpture fragment was found with another.
Refs: Geake 1997, 190; Hall & Whyman 1996, 124–30; Morris 1983, 61.
Whitby (NZ903113)
Pre-1943 – there are suggestions of the excavation of an 8th-century cemetery associated with the abbey.
Refs: *Archaeologia* 89 (1943), 27–88; Cramp 1976a, 223–9, 455–7; Rahtz 1976a, 459–62.

West Yorkshire
Addingham (SE08464972)
1991 – fifty-seven W–E oriented graves were excavated to the W of the present churchyard, with C14 dates of the 8th, 9th and 10th centuries.
Refs: Adams 1996; Geake 1997, 191.

Pontefract (SE46152613)

1885 – human remains were found with a possible iron ladle.

1985–6 – two different phases of burial were found predating the church, the earlier phase with a C14 date of 600–780 and one burial with a pair of tweezers.

Refs: Adams 1996; *Curr Archaeol* 9 (1987), 340–4; Faull 1981, 180; Geake 1997, 191; *Medieval Archaeol* 30 (1986), 178–80; 31 (1987), 172; Sheppard 1902.

County Durham

Binchester (NZ210313)

Pre-1983 – Cramp refers to more than forty-four unpublished inhumations from the fort excavated by John Rainbird and R. Jones, with C14 dates centring on the 8th and 9th centuries.

Refs: Cramp 1983, 268.

Hartlepool (NZ530335)

19th century – a number of N–S oriented burials were excavated at Cross Close, laid in rows, with inscribed stones (some of which may be 7th century).

1972, 1976 – sixty-eight further burials were found, unfurnished and oriented W–E in rows, with C14 dates of the 7th–9th centuries.

Refs: *Antiquaries Journal* 2 (1922), 141–3; *Archaeol Aeliana* 4 ser, 34 (1956), 196–212; *Archaeologia* 26 (1882), 479–82; Daniels 1992; Geake 1997, 148; *Gentleman's Magazine* 102 (1833), 218–20; Hodges 1905, 212–13; *J British Archaeol Assoc* 1 (1846), 185–96; Meaney 1964, 84.

Jarrow (NZ339652)

1963–7, 1969–71, 1990 – some of the burials excavated may predate the monastic cemetery, as some were found on a different orientation, and three were accompanied by beads (possibly indicating an earlier date). There were also 109 burials of the conversion period.

Refs: Cramp 1969, 45; 1976a, 236; Geake 1997, 184–5; *Medieval Archaeol* 16 (1972), 150; 35 (1991), 194.

Monkwearmouth (NZ403577)

1959–67, 1969, 1971 – a heavily disturbed cemetery was excavated, with generally W–E orientation and supine, extended burial. Single coins were found in three graves (one Roman, two Anglo-Saxon), along with a boar's tusk, and some gold thread (possibly suggesting an earlier date for these burials). There were also instances of prone burial, and burial on the right side. The monastic cemetery seems to have lain to the E and the lay cemetery to the W.

Refs: Cramp 1969, 31–4; 1976a, 231; Geake 1997, 1; *Medieval Archaeol* 9 (1965), 171; 16 (1972), 150.

Northumberland

Milfield S (NT939335)

1977–8 – twenty-four graves were excavated of a probable total of forty-five within the henge monument. There were skeletal remains in three, and grave goods in one: two or three knives, a perforated spatulate tool, a lace tag and buckle. All were oriented W–E.

Refs: Geake 1997, 172; *Medieval Archaeol* 22 (1978), 149; Miket 1980, 296; Scull & Harding 1990.

Newcastle (NZ250639)

1970s/80s – 660 W–E oriented graves from the early 8th century onwards were excavated, some of the early burials being uncoffined, and some having pillow-stones.

Refs: P. Graves, pers comm; *Medieval Archaeol* 23 (1979), 246; 26 (1982), 211; 27 (1983), 206; 30 (1986), 170; 35 (1991), 194–5; 37 (1993), 285–6.

Yeavering (NT925305)
1953–7 – various areas of unfurnished, W–E oriented burials were excavated, some associated with a possible church.
Refs: Geake 1997, 172–3; Hope-Taylor 1977, 67–78, 244–67; Meaney 1964, 199; *Medieval Archaeol* 1 (1957), 148–9; 24 (1980), 265–70; Miket 1980, 296.

CHAPTER 3

ANGLO-SAXON SETTLEMENTS OF THE GOLDEN AGE

Julian D. Richards

It is frequently suggested that one of the strengths of archaeology is that it is able to complement history based on documentary sources and dominated by the deeds of kings and archbishops. Archaeology, it is argued, is about the everyday lives of everyday folk. Unfortunately, one searches hard for the everyday villages and farms to place alongside the rich manuscript and sculptural evidence of 7th- and 8th-century Northumbria. Certainly there are a number of key sites, but these are royal palaces such as Yeavering (Hope-Taylor 1977), Milfield (Gates & O'Brien 1988) and Sprouston (St Joseph 1982), or monasteries such as Whitby (Peers & Radford 1943), Wearmouth-Jarrow (Cramp 1969; 1976a), Hartlepool (Daniels 1988), and Whithorn (Hill 1988). Since the 1980s rescue archaeology has begun to improve this imbalance. In 1985 the first Northumbrian trading settlement, or *wic*, was found during the excavations at 46–54 Fishergate in York (Kemp 1996). It is not known how far Anglian *Eoforwic* extended, although Hall (1994, 42) estimates that by the Viking Age York had c 15,000 inhabitants. Nevertheless, it is unlikely that more than 5% of the population of Northumbria lived within *Eoforwic* and the restricted nature of its food supply, as shown by the animal bones from the site (O'Connor 1991, 277–83; 1994), indicates that there was only limited contact with the hinterland.

Of that hinterland we know very little as there have been relatively few excavations of typical rural sites. At Heslerton (North Yorkshire) an extensive settlement has been excavated, including both sunken and post-built halls (Powlesland, see below); the discovery of Northumbrian *stycas* suggests that parts of the site at least were still occupied in the 8th century. Excavations at Thwing have revealed a number of Anglo-Saxon buildings, including post-built structures and a sunken-featured building containing a large oven. Occupation debris, including *sceattas* and *stycas*, indicates activity from the 8th century onwards

(Manby forthcoming). At Wharram Percy investigations of the desertion of the medieval village have revealed that it had Middle Saxon origins although we have little information about settlement organization at this date (Hurst 1984; Milne & Richards 1992; Stamper & Croft forthcoming). Further north an upland site has been examined at Simy Folds (Coggins et al. 1983) although the difficulties of dating the stone buildings and associated field systems emphasize the problems of mapping upland settlement patterns. In summary, in terms of saying anything about where the mass of the people lived, the Golden Age of Northumbria is still a Dark Age.

Ironically, we know as much about Middle Saxon settlement patterns from so-called treasure hunters as we do from archaeology. In the 1980s Anglo-Saxonists defined a new category of Middle Saxon site which they christened 'productive' or 'prolific'. The sites were unusual in that they had not been found by traditional methods of air photography, field-walking, geophysics or excavation. In fact they were invariably discovered by metal detector enthusiasts and characterized by large numbers of Middle and Late Saxon coins and other artefacts. Such find spots were rarely examined archaeologically and came to be regarded as a rather special category of site of unknown function but unusual status. Productive sites have now been reported from much of eastern England, including Yorkshire, Lincolnshire and East Anglia, although their known distribution is limited to those areas where archaeologists have been prepared to collaborate with 'treasure hunters'. In Northumbria there are more known productive sites than there are excavated settlements but our knowledge of them is limited. It has been suggested that they may be periodic markets (Newman forthcoming), but this is largely on the fairly negative grounds of the lack of settlement evidence recovered from excavations at Barham in East Anglia (Wade 1984). It has become important to discover more and to try to fit these sites into a settlement hierarchy for Northumbria. Here I shall describe the interim results of a research project on one such productive site, in the area of Cottam on the Yorkshire Wolds, and I shall speculate how the development of Cottam might be modelled within Middle Saxon settlement evolution.

The site to be considered is that at Burrow House Farm, Cottam, some 20 km from the east coast, and 10 km north-west of the modern market town of Driffield. The existence of an Anglo-Saxon settlement at Cottam came to light as a result of the discovery, over many years, of large numbers of Anglo-Saxon artefacts. From 1987 to 1989 some 200 man-hours of searching by metal detector users yielded over sixty pieces of 8th- and 9th-century date. The find spots have been systematically recorded and the objects published (Haldenby 1990; 1992; 1994). Several of the metal items are quite corroded, having suffered from agricultural disturbance, whereas much appears to have only been ploughed up in recent years and is still in a good state of preservation. To date, the detected finds include some forty simple pins, as well as disc-headed and racket-headed forms, over thirty 9th-century strap ends, eight finger rings, two disc brooches and a caterpillar brooch, a gilt mount, three buckles, a fragment of rolled gold sheeting, over thirty 9th-century *stycas*, and some twenty Roman coins. There is also evidence of domestic activity, including ten lead spindle whorls, and over forty iron knife blades. There are also a few Anglo-Scandinavian finds, including a Jellinge-style brooch and two so-called Norse bells. The metal detector enthusiasts did not make any systematic attempt to recover the non-metal artefacts, although they acknowledge that substantial quantities of both pottery and bone were observable in the plough soil.

The mapping of crop-marks from aerial photographs of the surrounding area reveals a landscape dissected by ancient trackways and partitioned by extensive field systems. Many of these form so-called 'ladder patterns' comprising series of rectilinear fields or paddocks defined by ditches and often fronting onto a trackway, with occasional settlement enclosures. Elsewhere in the Wolds this landscape has generally been assumed to be Iron Age and Romano-British. This is true in some cases, such as south of Wharram-le-Street, where the Roman road south of Malton cuts obliquely across the field systems and trackways. However, the Cottam project has allowed the definition of different categories of enclosure and the dating of some of them to the early medieval period.

The Anglo-Saxon finds from Cottam are largely coincident with a sub-rectangular crop-mark enclosure (henceforth described as Cottam B), immediately to the west of Burrow House Farm (Fig 3.3). Despite exhaustive metal detecting across the rest of the area, Anglo-Saxon artefacts have not been found further away from the enclosure, suggesting that it is contemporary with the finds. Unusually, the enclosure does not appear to be linked with an associated field system but rather it appears to sit astride a trackway which skirts the dry valley and then runs south-east to a more typical ladder-pattern enclosure (known as Cottam A) which was confirmed as a Romano-British farmstead by excavation in 1996, and then continues south to the earthworks of the deserted medieval village of Cottam (Fig 3.1).

The correspondence of the Anglo-Saxon finds with the sub-rectangular enclosure leads to the conclusion that the enclosure is itself of Anglo-Saxon date. This has been confirmed by two trenches which revealed post-hole buildings and settlement debris of the 8th and early 9th centuries (Richards 1994, and in prep). The excavation yielded chalk thatch weights, a ceramic lamp and other finds indicative of permanent structures rather than a temporary market. Although there was little pottery which could be confidently placed in the 8th or 9th centuries this seems to be a common feature of contemporary sites in the region; there was plentiful bone debris from butchery of farm animals, and indications of non-ferrous metalworking in the locality. To the east of one of the buildings was a circular pit, c 1.5 m in diameter, towards the middle of which was an adult female skull, radiocarbon dated to 664–775 at the 68% confidence limits. The upper fill of the pit contained a Wessex silver penny of Æthelberht, dated 858–62, an Anglo-Saxon dress tag, and two decorated comb fragments.

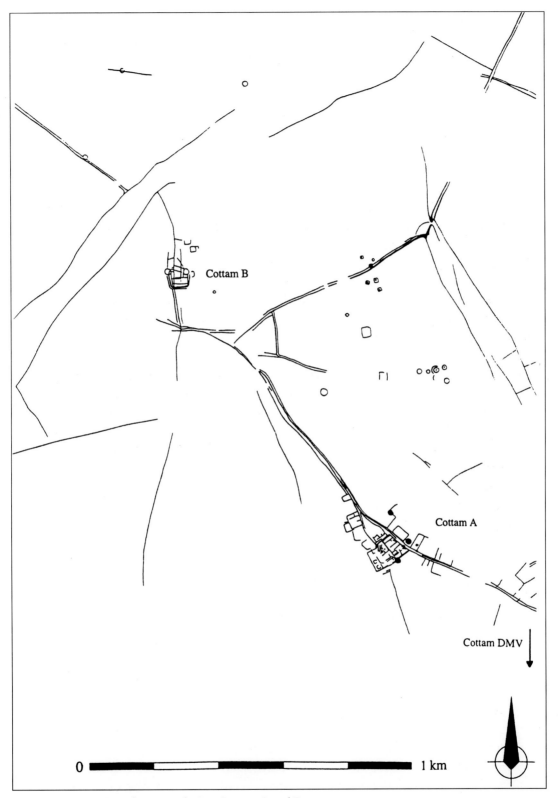

Fig 3.1. Location of crop-mark sites Cottam A and B.

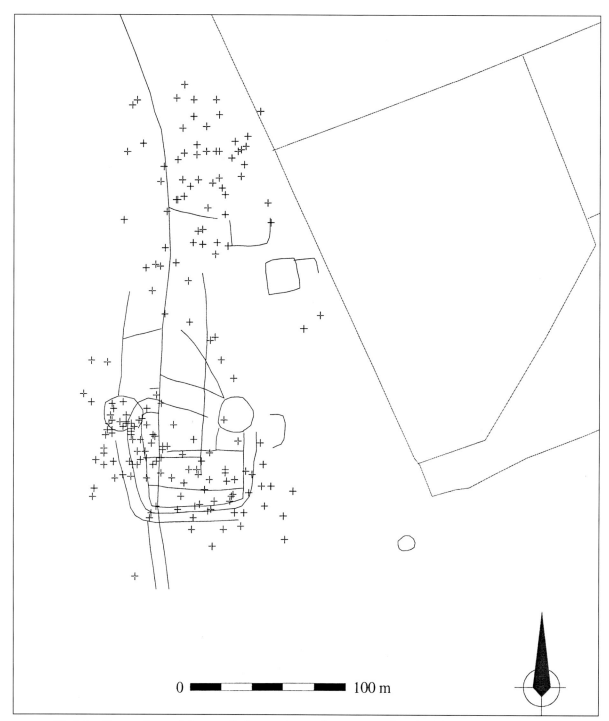

Fig 3.2.   Cottam B: metal detector finds superimposed on crop-marks. (ARC/INFO 7.0; J.D. Richards 1997; finds database: T. Austin, C. Buckley and J. Kenny)

The contents of the pit were sieved and yielded skeletons of frogs and water voles which must have stumbled into it while it lay open. By this stage, therefore, it is proposed that this area of the site had been abandoned.

In one area, to the north of this Anglo-Saxon enclosure, the distribution of metal detected finds spreads beyond the crop-marks (Fig 3.2). However, a magnetometer survey in this area has revealed a series of further sub-rectangular enclosures laid out on either side of a trackway. Excavations revealed that the features in this area were generally very shallow, with some ditches only surviving to a depth of less than 0.1 m, insufficient to affect crop growth, although the trackway itself was entered through a massive ditched and banked gateway. Excavation has confirmed what was already suspected from field-walking and the surface distribution of datable objects, that after a localized settlement shift a Viking-Age farm had been constructed to the north of the abandoned Middle Saxon settlement. Occupation here appears to have been relatively grand but short-lived, perhaps spanning some fifty years or a single generation only, from the late 9th to early 10th centuries. At that point it is proposed that the settlement shifted again, probably to the site of the medieval village at Cowlam or Cottam.

In summary, the excavations at Cottam have revealed a shifting and evolving early medieval settlement pattern. It is difficult to escape the conclusion that the sub-rectangular enclosures at Cottam B represent Anglo-Saxon and then Anglo-Scandinavian farmsteads, while the more traditional ladder-pattern farmstead at Cottam A is confirmed as Late Iron Age and Romano-British. This work may therefore allow a reassessment of the typology of crop-mark enclosures and a re-examination of the large number of undated enclosures known from the Yorkshire Wolds (Fig 3.3). It is anticipated that far more may turn out to be of early medieval rather than of Iron Age or Romano-British date.

Secondly, the productive site at Cottam B was shown, on excavation, to have the structural features, including pits and post-hole buildings, and material debris that one would expect of a normal settlement site. There was little to suggest that this was a periodic market or trading community. The site had been created as a result of deep ploughing which had disturbed the Anglo-Saxon cultural layers. This ploughing had removed the upper levels of the crop-mark features and distributed the debris into the plough zone. Nevertheless, the question remains as to whether this debris is richer and more plentiful than one would expect of a 'typical' Middle Saxon settlement.

In order to resolve this it may be useful to compare the finds from Cottam with those from other excavated Northumbrian sites. If the productive sites are somehow special or of particularly high status then they should yield more metalwork than other settlements.

The settlement at Wharram Percy, some 12 km further west, appears to share many features with Cottam. The deserted medieval village made famous by Beresford and Hurst's excavations has also been shown to overlie a Romano-

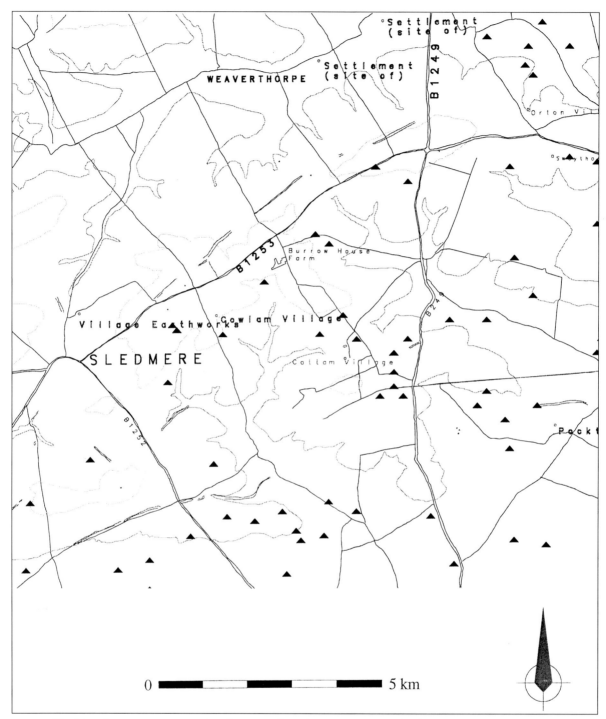

Fig 3.3. Cottam environs: undated crop-mark enclosures. (Topography from OS 1:50,000 map.
Crown copyright reserved. ARC/INFO 7.0; J.D. Richards 1997; digitised by H. Fenwick)

British ladder settlement pattern, although the origins of the medieval village again lie in the Middle Saxon period (Beresford & Hurst 1990). Excavation has revealed Middle Saxon activity throughout much of the area of the medieval village (Milne & Richards 1992, fig 44). During the Middle Saxon period we also have evidence for the first post-Roman laying out of boundaries and enclosure of the landscape at Wharram Percy. The late Roman field systems had by now undergone considerable silting but surviving hollows were sometimes used as convenient sites in which to erect sunken-featured buildings (Milne & Richards 1992). Two Middle Saxon boundaries were recovered from the South Manor excavations; both were E–W ditches, the second apparently replacing the first. The later ditch was contemporary with a smithy; the earlier was sealed and cut by smithing activity. This redefinition of the boundary 1 m to the north indicates that there was relatively little pressure on land at this stage and that the Middle Saxon occupants of the South Manor site were thereby able to extend their holding (Stamper & Croft forthcoming).

How far is the Wharram metalwork assemblage comparable with that from Cottam? At first sight, the absolute numbers of a few diagnostic categories of finds appear to be much lower (Table 3.1). Thus, from the South Manor at Wharram Percy there is only one 8th-century coin, one strap end, and eleven copper alloy pins, whereas metal detector finds from Cottam B include four 8th-century coins, thirty-four strap ends, and sixty-three copper alloy pins. However, this has to be understood in the context that the metal detector users had intensively worked an area of c 30,000 m^2, and that the site is now considered to be 'worked-out', with modern agricultural practices having brought most of the metalwork into the plough soil.

At Wharram, by contrast, only a fraction of the settlement area estimated at c 6% has been dug and the rest is undisturbed by modern ploughing or metal detecting (Beresford & Hurst 1990, 131). The South Manor site comprises an excavated area of c 900 m^2 but, as has been noted above, Middle Saxon finds are widely distributed across the village. If, rather than take the absolute number of finds, we base comparison on the relative density of these indicators we find that Wharram Percy is also a 'productive site' with the figures for the average density of finds per 100 m^2 similar to those for Cottam (Table 3.2).

In comparison with the possible monastic sites at Flixborough and the known Middle Saxon monastery at Whitby, however, both Cottam and Wharram fare rather poorly, having significantly lower densities of most of the chosen artefact types. Flixborough is clearly unusual, with high proportions of 8th- and 9th-century coins, five times the density of strap ends and at least ten times the number of dress pins. Whitby also has much greater densities of metalwork than Cottam or Wharram but, with the exception of 9th-century coins which simply reflect Whitby's survival beyond Flixborough, it has lower densities than the Humber site (Peers & Radford 1943). Hartlepool, on the other hand, has densities which are comparable with Cottam, apart from the lack of 9th-century coins which is explained by its abandonment in the later 8th century (Daniels 1988, 175).

The artefact densities for Cottam are lower than for the excavations at Fishergate (Rogers 1993). The density of coins at Fishergate is comparable to that of Flixborough, although the proportions of strap ends and dress pins are lower, being comparable with the figures from Whitby, although still ten times higher than at Cottam.

In conclusion, Cottam can be seen to have an artefact fingerprint similar to that of Wharram Percy. It may therefore be instructive to examine the nature of the Middle Saxon society and economy seen at the South Manor at Wharram Percy.

In terms of diet it appears that the inhabitants of Wharram were largely dependent upon their own resources. The pattern of animal husbandry is basically characterized as a self-sufficient economy. Sheep were the most numerous animal, but cattle probably formed the most important element of the diet, while pig contributed little. The South Manor cattle had a multi-purpose role, for dairying, traction and meat. Killing and unspecialized butchery was carried out on site; there was no evidence for any selection of joints, in comparison with contemporary deposits from York Minster and Fishergate (O'Connor 1991). There were also few imported species; oysters from the Yorkshire coast or Humber estuary were about the most exotic element of the Middle Saxon diet (Stamper & Croft forthcoming).

The animal products also seem to have supported a small domestic textile industry. The finds include loom weights for use with a warp-weighted loom, spindle whorls of clay, stone and antler, bone pin-beaters, and glass linen smoothers. There is also a large amount of bone and antler combs and pins, presumably made locally from shed antlers gathered in woodland. The range of iron objects indicates the working of wood, textiles and leather, as well as agricultural activity (Stamper & Croft forthcoming).

In the cereal crops too there are few surprises at Wharram Percy. The principal crops were wheat, barley and oats, with small traces of rye. Peas were an important crop; the cultivation of flax was also likely. Some items must have been brought from further afield. Fruits and nuts of the woodland margins were used to supplement the diet; as the environmental evidence for the pre-Conquest period suggests an area of mixed arable farming and grazing land, with very few trees (Hurst 1984, 87), these may have been fetched from some distance, together with the antlers needed for comb manufacture. Rushes, hay and heather must have been brought to the site from heathland; the nearest source is the North Yorkshire Moors, some 15–25 km away. In contrast to contemporary urban sites, however, there is very little evidence of luxury cultivated and imported fruits, herbs and spices. The dietary evidence, therefore, suggests quite a low level of subsistence; as at Cottam there appears to have been little trickle-down from the thriving *wic* site in York (Stamper & Croft forthcoming). As other evidence suggests that the inhabitants of Middle Saxon Wharram should have been able to afford such goods we may conclude that they were simply unable or unwilling to obtain them.

The evolution of the settlements at Wharram Percy and Cottam can also be seen to fit into the same model. Both areas were extensively farmed during the Roman period from ladder-settlement farmsteads. Towards the end of the Roman period these farms fell into disuse. There is little evidence of activity in the early Anglo-Saxon period; field systems were abandoned and the landscape may have become more open, although the system of trackways was preserved, and at Cottam the trackway was still important enough in the 8th century for settlement to develop along it. This settlement was replaced by a grander farmstead at the point of Scandinavian first contact, although the new farm was only short-lived and was soon itself given up in favour of a site which it has been suggested developed into one of the local Domesday manors.

In 1984 John Hurst suggested that the most likely date at which Wharram Percy became a nucleated planned village was during Scandinavian reorganization in the 10th century (1984, 86); this likelihood is reiterated in Beresford and Hurst (1990, 84). From field-walking in the Wharram area it is also clear that the pattern of Middle Saxon pottery finds supports the idea of scattered settlement at this stage, while Late Saxon pottery is only found at the nucleated village sites (Hurst 1984, 82; Hayfield 1988). Although the case remains unproved, there is a deal of circumstantial evidence which still supports both a 10th-century laying out and an Anglo-Scandinavian context for it. The late 9th and 10th centuries were a time of tenurial change, due to the Viking settlement. A number of former large, often ecclesiastical, estates were being fragmented and passing into private ownership (Richards 1991, 30–1). In Yorkshire the *Anglo-Saxon Chronicle* informs us that in 876 'Healfdene shared out the lands of the Northumbrians, and they [the Scandinavians] proceeded to plough and to support themselves'. The Yorkshire Wolds are one of the main areas where we believe that Scandinavian landlords took control of former large estates. In the erstwhile East Riding of Yorkshire 48% of place-names are Scandinavian-influenced.

It is proposed, therefore, that at both Cottam and Wharram Percy the Scandinavian settlement disrupted existing settlement patterns and led to the nucleation of villages. As the Golden Age of Northumbria came to an end the medieval and modern settlement pattern was thus defined. Of the Northumbrian settlement pattern very little survived. Instead of a pattern of dispersed Middle Saxon farmsteads, Scandinavian lords now held power through nucleated villages. The Middle Saxon landscape was lost. However, by pooling the information that productive sites can provide and putting it alongside that derived from excavations, we are able nevertheless to describe in some detail an Anglo-Saxon settlement hierarchy for the kingdom of Northumbria.

	8th-century coins	Copper alloy strap ends	Copper alloy dress pins
Cottam B	4	34	63
Wharram Percy: South Manor	1	1	11
Flixborough	29	22	445
Hartlepool	2	1	4
Whitby	17	14	114
Fishergate, York	18	5	74

Table 3.1: Total numbers of selected categories of finds from Middle Saxon sites in Northumbria.

	Approximate area investigated (m^2)	8th-century coins	Copper alloy strap ends	Copper alloy dress pins
Cottam B	30,000	0.01	0.11	0.21
Wharram Percy: South Manor	900	0.11	0.11	1.22
Flixborough	4,000	0.73	0.55	11.13
Hartlepool	1,500	0.13	0.07	0.27
Whitby	5,000	0.34	0.28	2.28
Fishergate, York	2,500	0.72	0.2	2.96

Table 3.2: Average density of finds per 100 m^2.

CHAPTER 4

The Anglo-Saxon Settlement at West Heslerton, North Yorkshire

Dominic Powlesland

The excavation of the Early Anglo-Saxon settlement at West Heslerton, North Yorkshire, undertaken on a seasonal basis between 1986 and 1995, has produced evidence that indicates that we have underrated the complexity and sophistication of settlement development in the Early Anglo-Saxon period. This excavation formed the latest stage of nearly twenty years of fieldwork funded by English Heritage and their predecessor organizations as parts of the Heslerton Parish Project (Powlesland, Haughton & Hanson 1986). The excavation of an associated cemetery, completed in 1987, had already offered new insights into the Early Anglo-Saxon or Anglian population and material culture, particularly from a large body of mineral-replaced textile remains (Powlesland & Haughton forthcoming). Situated on the southern margin of Northumbria on the southern side of the Vale of Pickering at the foot of the Yorkshire Wolds, West Heslerton is perhaps most important because of the very extensive areas examined. If not totally excavated, the whole area of the settlement was observed and 50% or more of most features excavated (Fig 4.1).

Prior to the completion of work on the site during 1995 it appeared that there was little that was exceptional about the nature of the settlement at West Heslerton and that the site may have followed what might be proposed as a standard sequence of development from a Late Roman farmstead to a Late Saxon settlement. New evidence recovered in 1995 has cast some doubt on this view, with the Late Roman activity at the site relating to some sort of ritual use associated with a spring rather than to domestic settlement. There is good reason to see this ritual component at the site continuing as an element of the Early Anglo-Saxon landscape, and it appears that this aspect provided the impetus for

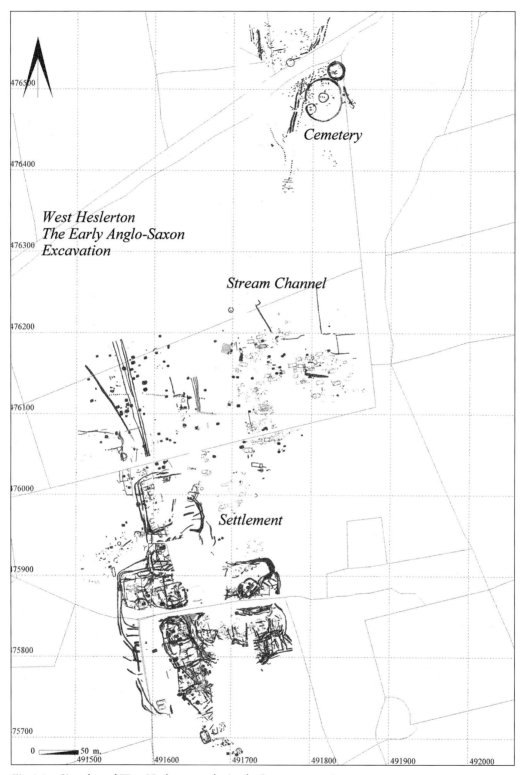

Fig 4.1.   Site plan of West Heslerton early Anglo-Saxon excavation.

settlement at this location during the Early Anglo-Saxon period. It is perhaps most remarkable that there was no indication of the ritual nature of the settlement core in areas examined prior to the final season. The new evidence offers the possibility for a somewhat unique context for the Early and Middle Saxon settlement and makes it even more important to establish to what degree, this, the most extensively excavated site of its kind in England, can provide testable models of settlement morphology and evolution during the formative years of the English nation.

Excavation of the Anglo-Saxon domestic deposits is now complete and although many questions relating to the Roman to Saxon transition remain unanswered, the comprehensive excavation of the Anglo-Saxon features reveals a remarkable settlement of unparalleled size and complexity. The quality, scale and uniformity of the evidence recovered will enable us to both ask and answer fundamental questions relating to most aspects of the development of an Early Anglo-Saxon settlement in a way that has not been possible before.

The theory put forward prior to the last season's work, that the settlement relocation, which is a feature of the Early Anglo-Saxon landscape, may have had its roots in a major reorganization of land-holding structure in the closing decades of the Roman period, gains less weight from the new evidence if its ritual nature is confirmed. The excavation, one of the largest ever undertaken in Britain, has produced a wealth of new evidence, the importance of which is both intrinsic to the material itself and also a consequence of the uniform and detailed spatial record generated in the field. The excavation has been the setting for one of the most extensive applications of computers in the field and has produced perhaps the most significant spatially referenced data-set for any site of this period. The excavation has formed the proving ground for a number of innovative approaches to data collection, recording and management which have an importance extending beyond the regional or temporal boundaries of the site in its local setting.

The settlement covered a far larger area than was originally anticipated, Early Anglo-Saxon features being widely distributed over an area of more than 13 hectares (32 acres). The layout of the settlement includes a remarkable degree of spatial variation with distinctive areas for housing, craft/industry and agricultural processing and indications of a deliberate separation between secular and ritual space. With the post-excavation analysis in its infancy it is not yet possible to precisely phase much of the activity. However, the overall assemblage indicates that occupation continued at the site from the late 4th century until the 9th century. To what degree continuity can be demonstrated from Roman to Saxon remains to be seen; nevertheless, the view established during excavation indicates that some continuity occurred even if this relates mostly to the use of space. Much of the northern half of the settlement was without any internal divisions or property boundaries. The occupation and associated activity in the southern half of the settlement contrasts with that to the north in that an extensive network of ditched and fenced enclosures spans the complete period of occupation at the site. At the southern limit of the domestic occupation a series of large post-hole structures and substantial fence slots appear to define the boundary between the secular space and the apparently ritual space which dominated the Late Roman landscape contained within a dry valley running due south from an active spring to the foot of the north-facing scarp of the Yorkshire Wolds.

It was not possible to fully examine the Roman evidence; however, enough was examined to give some indication of the layout and nature of the Roman activity. A series of sub-rectangular enclosures around the spring-head, one containing a small round-house, was established during the late 4th century. To the south of these enclosures a large structure constructed on rammed stone rafts appears to have blocked off the entrance to a dry valley which, beyond this building, had been terraced by the deliberate dumping of large quantities of material. A number of structures were cut into the sides of the valley overlooking the terraces; these included a complex of bread ovens, a large unusual and finely built structure, with flattened apses at each end cut back into the valley side and apparently deliberately removed to re-establish the valley profile, a large well and fragments of other structures again cut back into the side of the valley. The bread ovens and extensive spreads of oyster and mussel shells associated with the structure built across the valley might be interpreted as the sort of food bars we find at pilgrimage sites today. Basic pottery kilns produced exceptionally crude Romano-British ceramics and may have produced some of the pottery which appears to span the transition from the Roman to Saxon periods.

Whatever the nature of the Roman activity it clearly provided the setting for the establishment of the Anglian settlement. What is most remarkable is that during the Early Saxon phase the site was established on a huge scale covering most of the total utilized area of the settlement. Early material and structural techniques are found throughout the site; only during the Middle Saxon phase does the settlement contract to cover little more than the Roman core of the site. The picture that emerges is not one of a cluster of small farmsteads gradually being replaced in such a way as to move the settlement across the landscape as we find in the interpretation for instance of the settlement at Mucking, Essex (Hamerow 1993). It appears that from the outset the settlement was well organized with areas set aside for particular functions (Fig 4.2). This factor and the very high degree of architectural uniformity at this and all other sites of the period points to a far more sophisticated society than has traditionally been accepted. At the centre of the settlement a stream ran due north from the spring and bisected the northern half of the site. The initial settlement appeared to have been established with four distinctive zones. To the north-east lay an extensive area of housing consisting mostly of rectangular post-hole buildings and a relatively small number of associated *grubenhäuser*. To the north-west an area containing no post-hole structures but a large number of *grubenhäuser*, metalworking furnaces, a malt-kiln and very extensive butchery deposits appears to have formed a craft and industry zone. To the west of the stream channel a triple-ditched enclosure adjacent to the stream may have been used for crop processing and stock management. Only around the spring and to the south does the simplicity of the division between the areas in the northern part of the site give way to a much more complex multi-function zone with extensive enclosure complexes and the complete range of structural and other activity. If, as the evidence seems to indicate, the division of the site into different zones in its earliest Anglo-Saxon phase is confirmed during the analysis, then this may be interpreted almost as an attempt to establish some sort of urban centre. It implies a high degree of social organization; to what degree we see this as a product of a highly stratified society may be determined from the structural remains which are highly uniform and, with the exception of a single large structure, situated transversely across the dry valley, and appear to be all of much the same scale, standard and construction.

An important aspect confirmed by the excavation is the high degree of structural uniformity in Early Anglo-Saxon buildings, something already identified in the comparison between the post-hole buildings occurring at sites as far apart as Thirlings, Northumberland and Cowdery's Down, Hampshire (O'Brien & Miket 1991; Millett 1983). The excavation has included the examination of over 220 structures including 130 *grubenhäuser* and at least 90 post-hole structures; all are interpreted as having had raised floors, providing a dry air space beneath. The function of a number of the *grubenhäuser* as grain storage buildings can now be demonstrated from the environmental evidence. In other cases they appear to have formed general purpose storage buildings associated with small-scale craft and industrial processes, and animal processing. There is no clear evidence that these structures served as housing or as weaving sheds as has been suggested in the past, although debris from weaving activity is plentiful in their fills. Ultimately, following the decay or removal of the structures themselves, the pit providing a dry air space beneath the floor boards was exposed and filled with rubbish. The data from these features offers immense research potential. The problems of dating and sequencing sites of this class will require extensive multivariate analysis of the *grubenhäuser* fills which include material indicating the survival of this structural type until the desertion of the site in the 9th century. An analysis of the post-hole structures from this site and other published examples indicates that, in contrast to the view most recently expressed by Marshall and Marshall, these buildings are most likely to have utilized tie-beam construction and could in the larger cases have incorporated an upper storey (Marshall & Marshall 1994; Clemence 1993).

The extensive complex of overlain enclosure ditches which dominated the southern part of the settlement provides a complete stratigraphic sequence covering the life of the site and make it possible to try and identify individual 'properties' while providing a complete contrast to the open-plan nature of most

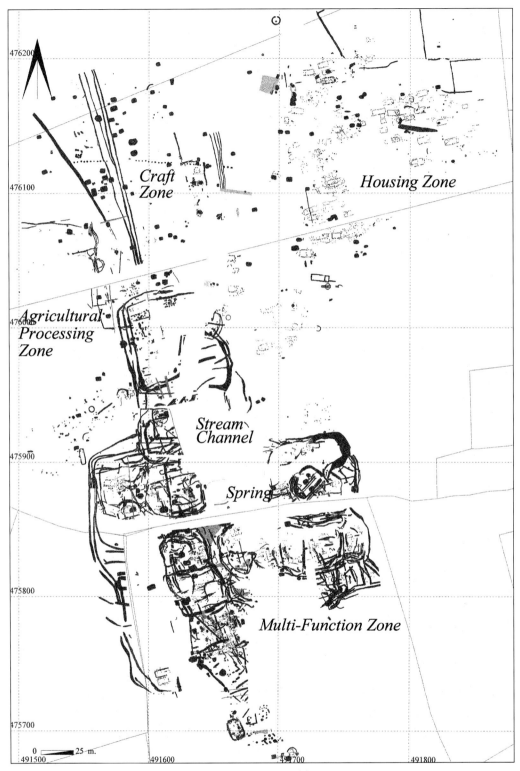

Fig 4.2.   Anglo-Saxon settlement plan showing structured layout.

of the site to the north. Clearly, the initial layout of enclosures can be attributed to the Roman occupation and use of the site associated with the activities in the valley behind, but when the settlement was finally deserted many of the early enclosures were still in use although each had been redefined a multitude of times. An extensive programme of phosphate data collection and analysis undertaken during the 1995 excavation season coupled with soil micromorphological analysis may assist us in determining the degree to which these enclosures served as stock compounds.

The site has produced one of the largest and best documented environmental data-sets from a site of this period, with one of the largest and most complete faunal assemblages, the analysis of which will have considerable bearing upon the comparative analysis of the large Roman and medieval assemblages from urban centres. The initial examination of the plant macrofossil evidence indicates that a wide range of species are present, including crops as well as fruits and berries; the majority of the crops appear to have been grown on the broad flat margins of the Vale of Pickering to the north of the site. The examination of the charcoal has revealed a surprising variety of species. Although oak and hazel dominate the assemblage, there is extensive evidence of fruit woods, perhaps indicating the maintenance of orchards. Soil micromorphology has shown an increase in agricultural activity at the foot of the Wolds during the Roman period and demonstrated the use of some of the enclosures for stock, perhaps including wintering of animals within the immediate vicinity of the settlement core to the south. The presence of a possible mill in one area was indicated by clear signs of water-course management, the distribution of quern fragments, and a series of features identified through geophysical survey; this feature was not examined on account of limited time and resources to undertake what would have been a highly complicated piece of excavation.

The site has produced a large artefact assemblage of considerable significance. For example, long-distance high-volume trade is reflected in the significant quantities of Niedermendig lava quern-stone fragments and hone stones. High status items such as glass vessels, while not common in the assemblage, show a distribution increasing towards the southern end of the site and appear to be Early Saxon rather than of an earlier date. The wealth of artefacts and ecofacts and the high quality of the record provide an opportunity for the examination of disposal practices, fragmentation, preservation and site formation processes to a degree not possible from smaller scale excavations.

Discrete areas show remarkable functional differences such that the region to the east of the stream channel was utilized almost exclusively for housing and that to the west for storage, craft and industry and agricultural processing. Only at the southern end of the site, where the character is fundamentally different on account of the extensive network of enclosure ditches and fence lines initially established in the Roman period, is there any clear evidence of mixed function. The principal Anglo-Saxon occupation phase extends beyond that of the associated cemetery covering the Anglian or Early to Middle Saxon periods ending at c 850.

The structural evidence for the Anglo-Saxon period as a whole is remarkable; all the recognized types of Early and Middle Saxon post-hole structures are represented. The *grubenhäuser*, however, are all of the twin-post construction type with a single post at each end, although a number show evidence of additional posts representing repair or replacement.

The nature of the evidence from this and other similar sites is such that interpretation is fraught with difficulties; the use of supported timber floors in all structures has deprived us of the sort of *in situ* floor deposits that we anticipate in both earlier and later contexts. The *grubenhäuser*, which contain a large percentage of the material evidence, require careful interpretation if we are to put to rest the past arguments about the role of these structures. While it is clear that very little at most of what these features contain relates to any primary activity associated with the structures, the rubbish deposits with which they were ultimately filled seem not even to be primary deposits and may represent secondary or tertiary disposal of material gathered elsewhere on the site. The very incomplete nature of the ceramics discarded in the *grubenhäuser* fills may indicate that these features were rarely used for primary rubbish disposal, in which case we may see night-soiling as a primary mode of disposal and what we are left with is just a small fraction of the discarded material. While the structural technique used in these buildings was uniform there is a wide variation in scale and this is probably matched by function. It seems increasingly likely that grain storage was a primary function in some cases, the cavity floor created by digging a pit beneath the floor securing a dry environment for the preservation of seed corn. Others may have served a more general purpose associated with other activities such as butchery, textile production and metalworking. Much weight has been put on the survival of loom weights in these features; however, they have tended to be seen in isolation rather than within the broader assemblage which always included a large quantity of faunal material and other debris. The unfired loom weights manufactured using clays available within 50 m of the settlement would, once dried, be brittle, non-durable and difficult to rework; it would have been easier to make new ones as required. Short-term storage of these objects was probably facilitated using a stick or pole and so we need to be careful not to overemphasize their occasional discovery in lines in the base of these features. That textile production was an important activity at this and other Early Anglo-Saxon sites is clear; however, the extent and the degree to which this generated any large surplus is difficult to determine. The evidence does not indicate large-scale production, rather a continuation of a textile tradition identified on sites in the region from the Iron Age onwards.

During the Middle Saxon period from c 650–850, the settlement area contracted to cover little more than the Late Roman core of the site. It is difficult without detailed analysis of the assemblages to determine the level of population during this late phase. Only three Middle Saxon post-in-trench structures and part of a fourth were located in the areas examined, and the difficulty of distinguishing between some of the ceramics without more detailed analysis make the level of activity unclear. The lack of any artefacts in the fill of the Anglo-Saxon well (constructed during or soon after 724) may indicate that occupation died out earlier than is implied by the coin series; however, this seems unlikely. There was certainly intense activity during this period in the southern part of the site and it is likely that a number of structures, both *grubenhäuser* and post-built structures, may be related to this phase in the final analysis. Two of the *grubenhäuser* examined in 1995 were certainly filled in during the Middle Saxon period, one containing a *sceat,* the second imported glazed pottery. The extensive deposits of ash and burnt/decayed daub examined in 1995 may help in the identification of a broader range of late features. At a relatively late stage in the project the recovery of a pit group incorporating large amounts of pottery in association with two *stycas* allowed us to identify at least one class of pottery as certainly Middle Saxon. This had previously been thought to be Bronze Age in date. One aspect of the ceramic assemblage as a whole which may support a view that the site was not of particularly high status is the rarity of obviously imported material.

The very small number of extensively excavated Early Anglo-Saxon settlements compared to the very large body of funerary evidence and the tremendous difficulty in dating material in the immediate post-Roman and Early Anglo-Saxon periods makes the whole process of excavation and analysis of sites of this type particularly challenging. The biased nature of the available evidence relating to Early Anglo-Saxon England, a function of random discovery and historical inference, has in the past given us little opportunity to take a broad view. Much like looking through a stained-glass window, only isolated fragments of the picture let light through; we have, for instance, never been able to apply or test the social models proposed for the cemeteries on settlement sites. The sudden and dramatic emergence of fully-formed and all-encompassing Anglo-Saxon material culture, which has in part fuelled the arguments about invasion or migration, and the difficulties in identifying native or continental individuals within the cemeteries have in the past contributed to the concept of the 'Dark Ages'.

The public perceptions of the 'civilized' Roman and the 'pagan' Saxon are completely outdated, but in many ways we have been without the raw materials to combat these views. One of the greatest privileges in the excavation of West Heslerton has been the ability to see the whole site and therefore make sampling decisions on the basis of a known quantity of evidence. The combined evidence from the cemetery and the settlement form an important analytical resource, allowing us to pursue many different threads of evidence and concepts using a complete body of evidence, a body of evidence which is of course massively depleted as a result of disposal practices, deformation processes and modern plough damage, and yet more comprehensive than any we have seen before.

Regardless of the view we take with reference to the Late and sub-Roman activity at the site, the emergence of a large and clearly zoned settlement during the Early Anglo-Saxon period indicates a well-organized society. The uniformity of the structural remains might indicate a highly egalitarian society rather than one dominated by a small social elite; this view is also given some support from the examination of the grave assemblages which do not appear to indicate massive differences in the availability of disposable wealth. The zoning that is so obvious at West Heslerton is concerned both with the human use of space in addition to other areas of functionality such as crop or animal processing. This points to a more cohesive population than might be accepted if we view the settlement as a shifting group of loosely related farmsteads as in the traditional model. The widespread use of almost identical structural forms and the trade both in luxury items as well as the more mundane imply that this level of cohesion is not of purely local importance and provides an ideal and stable setting for the emergence of the Anglo-Saxon kingdoms.

The grand scale of the earliest Anglo-Saxon phase at West Heslerton may be indicative of great ambition among the leaders of the population, establishing a new settlement, forcing a break with the past but also perhaps offering a better future than was possible within the ladder settlements which follow the wet margins of the Vale of Pickering, where increasing ground water levels would have made life more difficult than it had been earlier during the Iron Age and early Roman period. There is no evidence of coercion either within the cemetery or from the settlement and the apparently uniform adoption of early Anglo-Saxon material culture indicates cooperation rather than an aggressive dominant elite using the native population as slaves. Whatever the social and political mechanisms that combined to bring native and Angle together into this emergent new culture, by 600 the Vale of Pickering, as in most other areas of south and eastern England, was dotted with Anglo-Saxon settlements.

The apparent contraction of the settlement to about two-thirds of its original size during the Middle Saxon period may reflect the need for greater security. The enclosure network which dominates the southern part of the settlement is generally insubstantial and provided stock management functions rather than anything we may see as defensive. There is some indication that fenced enclosures were established within the larger ditched enclosures but it is not yet clear whether these minor features can be shown to have acted as property boundaries. We still have a lot of analytical work to do to isolate the Middle Saxon from the earlier material within the overall assemblage since it appears that many of the early ceramic fabrics continue in use into the Middle Saxon period. Some new ceramic types are introduced in addition to new types of metalwork which are clearly Middle Saxon in date; other changes are indicated both in the faunal and plant macrofossil evidence indicating changes in agricultural practices and diet.

The Anglo-Saxon coin series indicates that occupation of the site ended by the middle of the 9th century. We assume that at this point the modern settlement at

West Heslerton is first established in a location situated above and around the present church, a much more enclosed and secure setting than the relatively open one of the early Anglo-Saxon settlement. It is tempting to invoke the Viking raids as the reason for this shift. Extensive burnt and ashy deposits filling the final phase features of the settlement might be used to argue that the settlement had been burnt down. This material was all *ex situ*, however, there is no evidence that any structures burnt *in situ* and thus this burnt material may well be derived simply from cleaning up debris rather than from a more dramatic event.

Clearly the data recovered from West Heslerton will allow us to reappraise much that has been said about early Anglo-Saxon settlements, their development economy and environment. Once the analytical programme is complete and the results fully published we may finally be able to define testable models of settlement morphology and development which should help in identifying and evaluating other sites.

CHAPTER 5

(RE)CONSTRUCTING NORTHUMBRIAN TIMBER BUILDINGS: THE BEDE'S WORLD EXPERIENCE

Susan Mills

The museum and project now known as Bede's World, which is devoted to illuminating the life and times of the Venerable Bede, could be said to have begun with the excavation from 1963–78 of the site of St Paul's monastery, Jarrow, where he appears to have spent most of his life. The results of this work revealed what is still the most complete plan of the main buildings of a monastery of the 7th–8th centuries in Europe to have been excavated (Cramp 1994). Such was the interest in this that a museum was opened in 1974 in a nearby late Georgian building, Jarrow Hall, where it was hoped that the story of Bede, the monastery and its place in the culture of early medieval Northumbria could be told. A new exhibition was opened in the hall in 1979, following the end of the excavation, and the museum became known as the Bede Monastery Museum.

Over the years the museum developed and by the mid-1980s was planning an expansion that would involve the construction of a larger museum building. The advent of Tyne and Wear Development Corporation in 1988, with its remit to regenerate the Tyne river frontages from Newcastle to the river mouth resulted in the development programme taking on a different character. It was then possible to plan a capital programme that included a superb new museum building adjacent to Jarrow Hall, where there would be new exhibitions about the life and times of Bede, including new displays of the museum's collections, largely comprising the excavated assemblage – a chance for the first time to do justice to the story of Bede. Another opportunity presented itself, however: to the north of

Jarrow Hall was a large area of former industrial land, derelict since the demolition in 1985 of twenty oil storage tanks, some of which had been constructed audaciously close to the hall. From an initial suggestion to create an urban farm on this 15 acre wasteland eventually emerged the idea of planning and developing an agricultural landscape which would demonstrate elements of farming and secular life in Bede's time, as a counterbalance to the monastic story to be told in the indoor museum.

The farm was given the name *Gyrwe*, the English version of Ingyruum the name used by Bede in the *Ecclesiastical History* to describe the place where Benedict Biscop was given land by King Ecgfrith to found the second part of 'the monastery of St Peter and St Paul which is at Wearmouth and Jarrow' (Colgrave & Mynors 1969, 566–7, V.24). The name has been interpreted most satisfactorily as 'the place of the marsh-dwellers', an extremely apt description of the landscape adjacent to the monastery which, until earlier this century, was bounded on the south side by salt marsh and the little River Don, and on the east by a large inter-tidal mud flat known, at least since the late 18th century, as Jarrow Slake.[1] The farm was planned not necessarily to represent what this particular area of land would have looked like in Bede's time, when it would undoubtedly have been part of the monastic estate of Wearmouth-Jarrow, but to illustrate elements of an agricultural landscape – with wood and grassland, fields systems, animals, crops, activities and buildings – with which Bede and his contemporaries would have been familiar.

The development of the farm has been a salutary experience not without its trials, tribulations, near disasters – including having to deal with the difficulties of poor tree growth, to the extent that it will probably be some time in the middle of the twenty-first century before the woodland is as we had envisaged it – but also some triumphs, in spite of recalcitrant rare breeds of sheep, pigs, fowl and cattle. That is the subject of another paper (Fowler 1997, Fowler & Mills forthcoming): this paper will focus on the part of the farm development that arguably has remained particularly true to the tenets of the original plan, that of working only according to the principles used in the time of Bede.

The decision to construct timber buildings developed from the same fundamental aim of showing secular life in Bede's time. It was considered important to provide a contrast with the very exotic (to Northumbria) continental environment of the early medieval monastery, with its stone-built, plastered walls, richly decorated with stone carvings, paintings on wooden boards, and coloured glass windows; the norm for most people in the secular world appears to have been timber buildings of a wide range of sizes, shapes and designs, though generally conforming to a specific 'two-square' module (Hope-Taylor 1977, 125–8, 136–9, 213; James et al. 1984), probably also elaborately decorated in a style appropriate to the timber tradition. The buildings were to be chosen from the admittedly relatively few settlement sites that had been excavated in the area formerly comprising the kingdom of Northumbria at its apogee, that is, the land between the Firth of Forth to the north and the Humber estuary to the south. Only the tools and techniques known to have been used at the time would be employed to build them; this would obviously have a considerable impact on the construction timescale.

In keeping with the intention of founding the work on sound academic principles, a workshop was held at Bede's World in May 1993 to discuss the experiment. Archaeologists involved in the excavation of early medieval settlement sites, and someone with experience of timber building reconstruction elsewhere, participated.[2] The discussion ranged over a number of issues: types of wall construction; flooring; roof framework and roofing materials; internal surface treatments; decoration; furniture and fittings. Buildings were then selected to demonstrate variety of scale, construction technique and type. They were chosen initially from just three sites: the royal residence of Yeavering, north-west of Wooler in north Northumberland (Hope-Taylor 1977); the single phase settlement of Thirlings, a few kilometres to the north-east of Yeavering (O'Brien & Miket 1991), and the largely unexplored site of New Bewick, in the same area, which had provided the only excavated example of a *grubenhaus* in Bernicia, the northern province of Northumbria (Gates & O'Brien 1988, 5–8).

It was intended that at some time in the future one of the halls from Yeavering, probably Phase IIIC Building A4, 'the largest and most massively impressive of all the great halls on the site' and associated by Hope-Taylor (1977, 58–62, 129–41) with the reign of King Edwin, would be constructed. At 26.5 m × 12.8 m, this would be the largest building (re)construction of any period in Britain. It was felt, however, that it was important to begin the experiment with a smaller structure so that the construction techniques could be learned and perfected. Another compelling reason for this arose from the need to create at an early date a striking vertical element in the farm landscape – a smaller building would obviously be completed more rapidly. After considerable discussion, Building A from the Thirlings site (O'Brien & Miket 1991, 61–4, 84–5) was chosen.

The discussion focused on the detailed 'design' features of this building and on the types of timber to be used. There was also some debate about *grubenhäuser*, perhaps destined to be the second type of building constructed, the nature and purpose of their pits and whether or not floors were suspended over them. The debate over this issue became quite heated, some people considering that all had suspended floors, while others thought that some probably did and others did not.

No particular site layout was established for the buildings, though the 'basin' at the north end of the farm was their designated location: later their positions were drafted on a plan and three others were selected from Thirlings and Yeavering. Since then, and partly resulting from our experience of construction so far, the plan has been modified and we now intend to construct buildings from a wider range of sites, including the early medieval monastic site at Hartlepool, Co Durham (Daniels 1988) the monastic site of Whithorn in south-west Scotland

(Hill 1997) and the large planned settlement of West Heslerton in North Yorkshire (Powlesland 1989; 1997 and above).

The detailed planning for the construction of *Gyrwe* Building 1 then began.[3] Thirlings A was a large building, c 12 m × 6 m, which may well have been the main hall in the settlement, perhaps where everyone gathered for feasts and meetings. The building had a foundation trench c 0.80 m deep, in which stains of the post and panel positions had survived and from which it was possible to suggest the type of wall construction. The ground plan was used to prepare working drawings for the construction. The diameters of the timbers (0.30 m) were based on those of the stains in the foundation trench. The height of the long walls was assumed to have been about 2 m. Other calculations were made by working out what was most likely from the ground plan; there are only so many permutations for a superstructure based on this and decisions have to be made; the most important one is, of course, to ensure that the building stands up and can withstand the most severe weather conditions. The others – the type of roofing material, the finish of the walling between the main structural posts, carving if any – are more qualitative than quantitive and, although mapped out at an early stage, were not determined finally until work was already well under way.

Before the work began a constructor had to be found to carry it out. We were fortunate that a man with experience of traditional boat-building, where adzes (arguably one of the early medieval carpenter's most important tools) were still used, was interested in working on the project. In due course a joiner came to the museum and was trained by our constructor. At the end of his training we began to employ him as an assistant constructor. Since work on the hall began in April 1994 there have usually been only two men preparing the timbers, although they have trained two volunteers who are now extremely proficient. Many people have of course been involved in the construction – digging foundation trenches, helping to raise the gable uprights and the ridge poles, thatch the building, make, daub and limewash the wattle panels, but the timber preparation is what takes time and it is only too evident now that the Anglo-Saxons must have worked in larger teams.

The foundation trench was actually excavated by hand, as we intended to adhere rigidly to the principle of replicating all original techniques. Unlike the original builders at Thirlings, however, who were digging trenches in light sands and gravels, our volunteers were hacking their way through heavy, clayey, reclaimed soil, containing a variety of foreign bodies – bricks, pipes, even twisted wire cable. The trench was backfilled as soon as the posts were in place and the wall plates fitted and now no one can tell how it was excavated; in the face of time and financial constraints, there are limits to verisimilitude – ultimately it is what remains visible that counts.

The posts were placed exactly as in the original trenches; the plan indicates how, in spite of being based on the two-square module, the building was irregular, with unevenly spaced posts, two opposing doorways of different widths and one end narrower than the other, necessitating the use of a two-piece ridge pole and resulting in a roof which slopes down considerably at one end.

It has taken c 30 tons of green, fifty- to sixty-year-old oak of the correct diameter from a local estate for the main structural timbers; substantial quantities of willow, hazel and birch for the wattle panelling (though the advantage is that small and otherwise waste pieces unsuitable for fencing can be utilised for this); c 25 tons of local boulder clay, straw and water for the daub; slaked lime, water, brickdust (for colouring) and boiled linseed oil (waterproofing) for the limewash. For the roof, seventy ash poles from Suffolk were interwoven with hazel rods from Cumbria; 1,800 bundles of reed from Tayside were used for thatch; in the *Ecclesiastical History* Bede mentions a church on Lindisfarne being built 'after the Irish method, not of stone but of hewn oak, thatching it with reeds' (Colgrave & Mynors 1969, 294–5, III.25). A total of 125 bundles of sedge from Cambridgeshire were used for the ridge (Plate 1).

Wherever possible local supplies of timber were sourced, but the project has revealed that in the North East of England there are no longer areas of hazel, willow and ash coppice capable of providing large quantities of timber; there are now a number of projects in the region to establish new deciduous woodlands and this situation may improve in future years.

The panelling on the hall was woven but not daubed until the roof had been thatched; a professional thatcher was employed to do this, but he also trained a member of the museum staff to thatch. While this was being done, the constructors began the New Bewick *grubenhaus*. The original building had a pit 4.7 m × 3.9 m and 0.5 m deep (Gates & O'Brien, 1988, 5–8). These dimensions and the presence of posts placed centrally on the short end were replicated. The poor quality soil necessitated the use of a wattled revetment in the pit. The roof was constructed with a ridge pole and rafters of ash interwoven with hazel, on to which heather thatch was applied. Heather was probably a popular roofing material in moorland areas, where it can occasionally be found on buildings today; it has proved to be an excellent, waterproof material. The roof sits on the ground around the pit. The gable walls were constructed of horizontal oak planking with half-lapped joints, the planks pegged on to a triangular frame. The door was made of vertical planks and fitted, in the absence of any surviving evidence, with a sliding lock mechanism. Sockets in the frame were lubricated with beeswax, enabling the pivots of this heavy door to move with ease.

This *grubenhaus* was left with a sunken floor; a flight of wooden steps, fitted with handrails to satisfy modern regulations for visitors, was constructed. The structure is, to use a phrase beloved of estate agents, 'deceptively spacious' and has accommodated, albeit very briefly, more than twenty adults during a site tour! It seems likely that such buildings were used, as has been noted elsewhere (Rahtz 1976a, 70–81; Powlesland 1997, 104–7 and above), for a variety of purposes, including the ubiquitous weaving shed (Hamerow 1993, 17–19; Hamerow forthcoming;[4] Smith et al. 1995, 106, 115) and perhaps even as more than adequate sleeping accommodation (Plate 2).

The sunken floor remains somewhat damp, however; indeed, it really never dried out completely and now, protected by the substantial walls and an extremely sound roof, the dampness is maintained rather than eliminated. A certain level of dampness was apparently something of an advantage for weaving linen (Hamerow 1993, 17–19; Hamerow forthcoming), but for other uses a damp floor can surely not have been a particularly desirable situation. To keep the dampness under control we have cut drainage channels around the *grubenhaus* at ground level, as well as a channel below ground from a corner of the pit. Most of the *grubenhäuser* excavated so far have been on light, well-drained soils on sites identified by air photography and, where the original ground surfaces have survived, there appear to be no traces of drainage channels. Were these sunken buildings never built on heavy clay soils like ours or, if they were, was drainage incorporated in the design?

The construction of the hall has also raised a number of questions. The labour involved has already been mentioned; it has taken about three years with a very small team working to complete it; during that time, of course, these men were acquiring the skills of timber construction to create buildings the originals of which were the products of several centuries-worth of experience.

Daubing the walls proved an illuminating experience. Various proportions of clay, straw and water were tried and recorded. Even with the best mixture there was substantial shrinkage and cracking which fluctuated according to the weather conditions (the daubing was begun at the end of March 1997 and completed in May); the solution was to allow it to dry out then fill cracks and gaps repeatedly until the shrinkage ceased. Different limewash recipes were also tried. The linseed oil added to provide a waterproofing element caused the limewash to slide off the previous coat; a small amount of boiled linseed oil in the mixture seemed to work best. Even so, on an extremely wet day in June, with rain lashing against the north gable wall, the limewash and the daub began to soften, bubble and disintegrate. It is likely that the maintenance of the limewashed daub in a sound condition was an annual task on these buildings.

Finally, when the foundation trenches were excavated at the doorways to insert the door sills, it was found that the posts were already beginning to rot after only three and a half years in the ground. Had the soil been light and well drained, or solid, anaerobic clay, this might not have happened. Only the sapwood, however, was affected, which raises the possibility that the Anglo-Saxons had enough large diameter timber and labour at their disposal to enable them to use only the heartwood, thus ensuring (except in case of fire) the longevity of their buildings.

The hall is now partly furnished and is used by living history groups and by the museum's education service for exploring Anglo-Saxon life and skills, as well as providing a source of information for students and, indeed, all our visitors. The *grubenhaus* will soon be fitted out as a weaving shed with a warp-weighted loom. Other questions and perhaps problems will no doubt be raised as we use these buildings and construct others.

ACKNOWLEDGEMENTS

I am grateful to everyone who took part in the original workshop, particularly Rosemary Cramp, Peter Fowler and Colm O'Brien for their continued involvement and support, and Richard Darrah, for preparing the working drawings and training our constructors: William Tegetmeier, who thatched both buildings and trained Mark Connelly, the farm manager, to thatch; Ulfric, for making the door hinges; Colin Brooke, Kevin McCulla, Malcolm Nicholson and David Temple for their assistance with some of the construction work. Members of Dunholm and the Northumbrians living history groups help to bring the buildings to life. It is to Michael Hayes and Mark Stewart, the constructors, their voluntary helpers Sydney Perry and George Richardson, and Mark Connelly, however, that I and the Bede's World project owe most gratitude, since without their ever-increasing skill and expertise the timber building programme would not have achieved its already considerable measure of success.

NOTES

1. I am grateful to Victor Watts of the University of Durham for this interpretation.
2. Those taking part in the workshop were as follows: Heather Clements, Rosemary Cramp, Peter Fowler, Peter Hill, Richard Darrah, Helena Hamerow, James Llyal, Martin Millett, Susan Mills, Dominic Powlesland, Andrew Nicholson and Colm O'Brien. Robin Daniels was unable to attend but has since maintained close contact with the project, and in fact made the choice of the Hartlepool building along with the author.
3. Meetings took place between Colm O'Brien, Richard Darrah and the author. Following this, Richard Darrah, who has extensive experience of working with timber using only traditional techniques, initially at West Stow and latterly on a range of projects, then prepared the working drawings from which the published plans were drawn by Yvonne Beadnell.
4. I am grateful to Helena Hamerow for making available to me a chapter of her book in advance of publication.

CHAPTER 6

THE ART OF ANGLO-SAXON SHIPBUILDING

Edwin & Joyce Gifford

Clinker (or lap strake) boat construction appears to have been developed along the shores of the southern Baltic during the 3rd and 4th centuries by the Germanic people, whom Bede later called Anglo-Saxons. In this method of building, the planks overlap and are fastened to each other with iron rivets which, when compared with earlier sewn seams, greatly improve the stiffness and water-tightness of the hull. The form of the hull is created by the shipwright who varies the width and curvature of individual planks as they are cut and fitted. The frames are shaped to fit after the planking is finished, thus completing a monolithic three-dimensional structure of great strength (Fig 6.1).

With their art of clinker construction the Anglo-Saxons were able to build much lighter, stronger ships than before. A good example of this technique is the 23 m Nydam ship of the 4th century (Akerlund 1963) now in the Schleswig-Holstein Museum (Fig 6.2). One can assume that clinker-built boats were used for the migrations into Britain and that the Saxons had probably adopted the Mediterranean square-sail which they would have seen in use by the Romans, by 473 when Sidonius Apollinarius was describing the Saxons as '. . . ready to unfurl their sails for the voyage home from the Continent' (Haywood 1991, 71). The Karlby stone (Fig 6.3), which has been dated to about the 7th century, appears to illustrate a square-sail on a hull of Saxon profile.

The finest example of all Anglo-Saxon ships is the 27 x 4.5 m Sutton Hoo royal longship buried in East Anglia in the early 7th century and found in 1939. The beautiful shape of the hull preserved in the sand (Fig 6.4) clearly shows that the ship was designed to sail fast:

(i) The mid-ship section has a markedly flat bottom with round bilges, which is good for carrying sail and for speed, and is not a shape commonly associated with a galley or barge.

Fig 6.1. Planking of *Ottor* complete and riveted before framing. (Photograph: E.W.H. Gifford)

(ii) The waterline shape has a fine entry and run indicating an underwater form which will generate resistance to leeway when travelling at speed.

(iii) The plan-form is leaf-shaped in a manner generally associated with sailing vessels, as distinct from the near parallel sides of a rowing galley, such as the Nydam ship, which are designed to give maximum output from the oarsmen with the minimum resistance from the hull.

(iv) The closely spaced gunwhale to gunwhale frames provide adequate strength to resist the small sailing forces of the single square-sail rig.

(v) There are additional frames in the stern to strengthen the hull against the heavy rudder loads of sailing, whereas a rowing galley needs only a light steering oar and no special framing.

Fig 6.2.   The 23 m Nydam oak ship, early 4th century. (Photograph: E.W.H. Gifford)

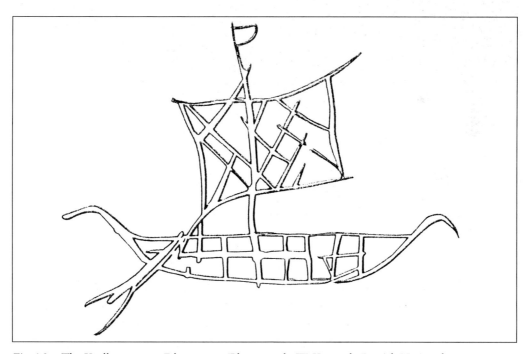

Fig 6.3.   The Karlby stone, c 7th century. (Photograph: W. Kanasch, Danish National Museum)

Fig 6.4.   The Sutton Hoo ship burial, early 7th century. (Photograph: C.W. Phillips)

(vi) The stem and stern posts have a larger projection beyond the planking than is needed for strength, but which is helpful in resisting leeway when sailing.

(vii) Fastening spikes for the oar-tholes were found only in the fore and aft parts of the Sutton Hoo ship with none in the mid-ship area, a distribution typical of the type of rowing and sailing vessel shown in the Bayeux tapestry and commented on by Bruce-Mitford (1975, 420).

Many of these features are among those listed by Goodburn (1986, 41) as characteristic of an Anglo-Saxon clinker boat-building tradition.

Striking evidence of Anglo-Saxon sailing is given by Hunebec's description of Willibald's voyage from Hamwic in 721 (Talbot 1954, 157):

. . . they embarked on a ship. When the Captain of the swift-sailing ship had taken their fares, they sailed, with the west wind blowing and a high sea running, amidst the shouting of sailors and the creaking of oars. When they had braved the dangers at sea and the perils of the mountainous waves, a

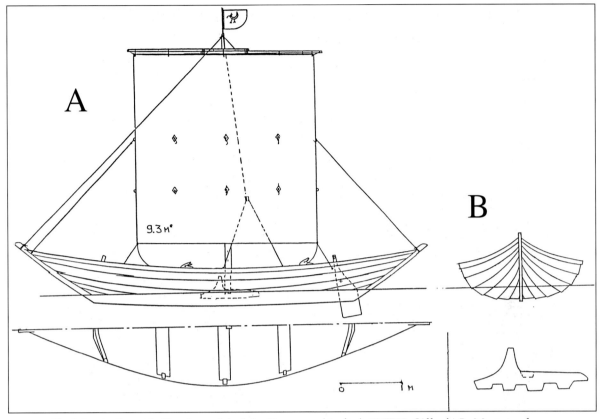

Fig 6.5. A. *Ottor*, half-scale model of the Graveney ship find. (E.W.H. Gifford.) B. Mast step from Kingshithe, Kent. (E.W.H. Gifford after Goodburn 1986)

swift course brought them with full sails and following wind safely to dry land. At once they gave thanks and disembarked, and, pitching their tents on the banks of the river Seine, they encamped near the city which is called Rouen, where there is a market.

A 10th-century trading vessel of about the same beam, but half the length of the Sutton Hoo ship, was found in 1970 at Graveney, Kent. Excellent details and drawing of the find and a proposed reconstruction are published (Fenwick 1978). Recently, many boat fragments of this period have been found along the Thames and recorded by the Museum of London (Goodburn 1994, 40). This archaeological evidence alone is not enough for predictions to be made of the speed and seaworthiness of these ships, so the authors decided to build and sail half-scale models, starting with the Graveney ship as its small size entailed less effort in building and crewing. Model testing at reduced scale is a well-established technique in naval architecture (Gifford & Gifford 1995, 121). Much would also be learnt about the art of Anglo-Saxon boat-building.

BUILDING AND TRIALS OF THE GRAVENEY SHIP MODEL, *OTTOR* (FIG 6.5A)

As the model was intended primarily for sailing trials, as well as for gaining experience in Anglo-Saxon boat-building techniques, it was essential that the hull should be geometrically similar and this was achieved by halving all the critical dimensions, giving a vessel of 6.7 x 2 m. For economy, some materials different from the original were used where this would not compromise the project. Sawn Scots pine, 12 mm thick, was used instead of the cleft oak of the original, ballast being added to compensate for the difference in weight. Internal frames were made from laminated pine instead of grown oak, as such changes would have no effect on the shape of the hull and would provide adequate strength.

The Graveney ship when found had a keel-plank which was notably smooth and unworn. Three 25 mm diameter holes, appropriately placed for keel trenail fastenings suggest that a badly worn false keel was removed at some time towards the end of the ship's sailing life and the trenail holes plugged.

In neither ship was a mast step found, but such a relatively small piece of wood might have been removed on abandonment of the Graveney ship or in preparation for the burial at Sutton Hoo. After the completion of our boat-building project, the Museum of London made the remarkable discovery of an early 11th-century mast step at Kingshithe, Kent (Fig 6.5B), which could have been fitted over frames with the spacing of those of the Graveney ship. Such a useful timber might well have been removed from an abandoned ship for reuse elsewhere.

The hull was built right way up, planking first and frames fitted last. When building the original ship the required shapes of the planks would have been either in the mind of the shipwright or stored in some physical record, such as templates. In our case, the shapes were obtained by making a quarter-scale model with moulds derived from McKee's drawing (Fenwick 1978, fig 10.1.1) and scaling these up to give half-size templates for the planks of *Ottor*.

As there is no direct evidence of the type of sails used on Anglo-Saxon ships, we looked back to Roman evidence and forward to early Viking usage. A simple square-sail has been fitted, without lifts or braces, with the mast supported by the mid-ship frame. No rudder was found at Graveney so the design used is similar to that reconstructed by Goodburn (1993, 56) from the finds from the Thames embankment.

As this project has been a continuous learning process, not only of the characteristics of *Ottor* but of all aspects of building, rigging and sailing of small, square-rigged open vessels, this experience has been set down chronologically.

The first trips were made in Southampton Water during 1988 in very light winds with a total crew of four. *Ottor* proved easy to row with two oarsmen, surprisingly responsive to light airs when sailing and steered well, although needing occasional help from a lee-bow oar when tacking. Leeway was about 30°, which prevented windward progress, except when helped by the oar. Later tests

Fig 6.6. *Ottor* sailing in Southampton Water on a broad reach at 4 knots. The angle of the wake shows the small amount of leeway. (Photograph: J. Bird)

in moderate winds with crews of six persons showed a decrease in leeway to about 20°, which enabled some windward progress to be made. The false keel of 40 mm projection was then fitted. This reduced the leeway by about half and greatly improved the weatherly qualities. With a crew of only three persons in Force 4–5 and one reef, the boat could work about 70° to windward in smooth water with a speed of 2 knots through the water. With the wind abeam and on the quarter, speeds of 5 knots were recorded by an accompanying boat, corresponding to 7 knots in the full-size vessel. In a later trip with a similar wind and weight of crew, but with steep and confused seas, it was not possible to maintain a windward position, but the boat remained stable and dry and sailed well with the wind free. *Ottor* steers well, being extraordinarily light on the helm and gives a great feeling of 'looking after the crew' (Fig 6.6). At no time has the crew member charged with the responsibility of dropping the sail in an emergency been called upon to do so.

During early trials the sail was set without bow-lines, but as confidence grew these were fitted and caused us no difficulty. They flatten the otherwise inward curling luff which controls the angle of incidence of the sail to the wind, such that *Ottor* can now sail at about 70° to the wind in moderate seas, when properly ballasted. The trials showed, without question, that the hull form is well suited to sailing. Tacking is remarkably simple and quick, the boat responds readily to the rudder and, once the luff is aback, the boat spins round quickly, no doubt assisted by the rockered keel, and is ready to sail on the other board just as soon as the tacks and sheets can be hauled. With the present keel and rudder, *Ottor* can make 1 knot directly to windward. In favourable wind conditions, speeds of up to 7 knots when running and reaching could be expected with the full-size ship.

A comparison of the hull shapes of the Graveney and Sutton Hoo ships reveals a close similarity, despite the time difference of 300 years. The sections at the forefoot are also nearly identical (Gifford & Gifford 1996, 12). The main difference is between a slender longship and a shorter trader. This comparison encouraged the authors to build a half-scale model of the Sutton Hoo ship.

BUILDING AND TRIALS OF THE HALF-SCALE MODEL OF THE SUTTON HOO SHIP, *SÆ WYLFING* (PLATE 3; FIG 6.7)

The building methods were the same as for *Ottor*, but seasoned pine was used for the planking except for the two top strakes which were of oak. The rig was the same type as in *Ottor*. The rudder was based on that of the Nydam pine boat (Rieck 1993, 3). *Sæ Wylfing* was launched on Southampton Water in May 1993. Since then twenty-two outings have been made, giving about 100 hours of actual sailing and rowing.

These extracts from the log of *Sæ Wylfing* indicate the breadth of experience gained in her:

19.8.93 Solent and Southampton Water
Returning from Cowes after Classic Boats Parade of Sail. Crew of seven. Moderate SW . . . turned NE and ran at a good speed to Calshot Spit. Shook out last reef and the escort boat with GPS measured 5.3 knots over the ground, against a strong ebb. Tidal information indicated 1 knot, so speed through water at least 6.3 knots. Reefed again before turning round Calshot, heading for Fawley (WSW). Measured 4.5 knots close-hauled – no tidal stream in bay.

5.6.94 Solent and Southampton Water
Crew of six plus 70 kilos of water ballast. Wind NW, 16 knots . . . hoisted double-reefed sail . . . passed over Calshot Spit ridge, sounding with the rudder. Shook out one reef and made for Stone Point – wind backed west so headed for Cowes. Tacked towards Calshot shore and made very good speed head-reaching in excess of 7 knots (estimated) with very little leeway. Everybody very pleased. Landed near beach café, the fore-foot slid over the shingle and four men hauled the boat almost out of the water. Later, although the tide had left her quite dry, launching down the beach was very easy. Wind had freshened, so double-reefed and sailed close-hauled up Southampton

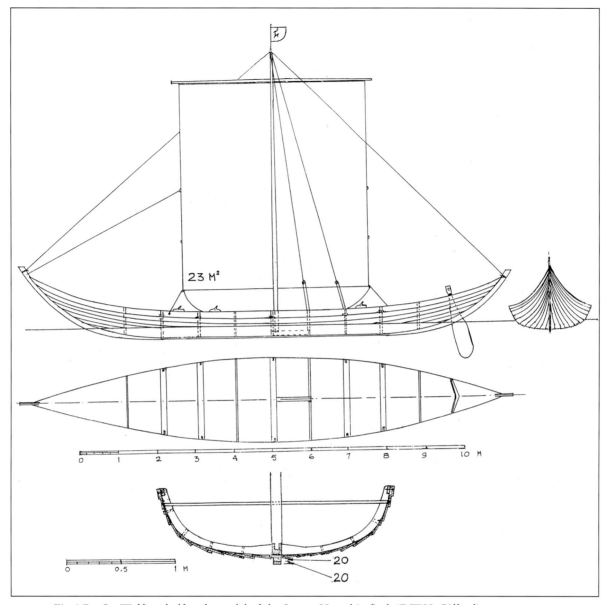

Fig 6.7. *Sæ Wylfing*, half-scale model of the Sutton Hoo ship find. (E.W.H. Gifford)

Water, passing close to Calshot Castle. Continued on towards Fawley, boat making no progress to windward although travelling fast. Wind increasing, so tacked with help of lee bow oar and headed back to Calshot, but still no gain to windward. Decided to lower mast, first time afloat and row. Continuous washes and choppy seas, but reasonable progress made upwind. Wind gusting to 22 knots. This trip confirmed good sailing ability – fast and weatherly with single reef. Double-reefed sail (half full sail area) made the boat very stable and safe in a fresh breeze, but could not make to windward.

11.6.94 River Deben below Woodbridge
At the invitation of the Sutton Hoo Society. Crew of eight and a favourable wind. Crew all sitting on bottom boards. Made very good speed to Sluice Cottage, Ramsholt, getting ahead of the Hoppitt's boat, which was known to be doing 6.5 knots [Plate 3].

18.6.94 River Blackwater at the Maldon Festival of Traditional Sail
Crew of eight. Wind NW Force 4. Rowed clear of Maldon slipway, hoisted full sail on the ebbing tide. Sailed straight down the main channel around Northey Island past Heybridge Basin, passing other craft going to the start of the Barge Race and being passed by none. Barges were anchored or sailing to and fro near the starting line between Osea Island and the mainland where the channel becomes wider. Sailed at high speed between the barges, certainly in excess of 7 knots, trying to keep out of the main channel and with the crew sitting in the weather bilge for long stretches. Marconi Sailing Club anemometer reading top of Force 4 (16 knots). (Comment of barge skipper while looking at *Sæ Wylfing* in Maldon next day: 'Yew 'ad a good little blow around yesterday, and don't she point well?' This seemed an excellent summary.)

20.7.94 Île Tatihou, Baie de la Seine, at ISBSA Conference
Crew of nine. Light east wind. Rowed and sailed round the island before making several trips with eminent archaeologists aboard; on one occasion with 15 people. Sailed and rowed well in light breeze despite nautical and linguistic confusions! (Following discussions on the keel, it was agreed that the experimental additional projection of 50 mm for two-thirds the length was inappropriate, and on returning to Southampton it was changed to an additional 20 mm over the full length, giving a total of 40 mm as deduced from the Nydam pine boat.)

16.8.94 River Itchen and Southampton Water
Crew of eight. Wind SW, 15 to 20 knots. Left hard of Itchen Sailing Activity Centre, Southampton, and rowed to Dock Head against flood tide and wind, one nautical mile. Hoisted sail with one reef and close-reached down the line of heavy moorings in Southampton Water. GPS gave 4.8 to 6 knots. Leeway, measured with hand-bearing compass, from 10 to 15°. Gybed round After Barn buoy off Netley and returned close-reaching to Dock Head. Wind gusting to 22 knots. GPS gave maximum of 7 knots.

9.9.95 Cadland House Beach, Solent, at the Cerdic Conference
Crew of ten, with weapons. Fresh SW wind, one reef. Gave second demonstration at 13.30 just after high water. Backed off beach with stern pair of oars and turned with starboard pair. Rowed clear and hoisted sail on starboard tack towards Isle of Wight. Wore round comfortably in fresh

Fig 6.8. *Sæ Wylfing* making an assault on Cadland Beach, Solent. Note the raiding party ashore dry shod, and the bow-hand braced to hold the boat straight against beam wind. (Photograph: P. Williams)

breeze (the Meteorological Office recorded 27 knot gusts in this area at this time) and returned at high speed to the shore. Just before landing, the crew moved aft except for one man at the bow who leapt ashore with a stern rope to hold the boat against the wind. The bow slid clear of the water up the shingle beach and ten members of Colchester Historical Enactment Society leapt ashore dry shod, the whole operation taking less than one minute [Fig 6.8]. Subsequently, eight men pulled the boat, on greased skids, up the steep beach completely clear of the water.

From the beginning, *Sæ Wylfing* has given the crew confidence in her seaworthiness and expectation of good performance. She looks, feels and sails like a thoroughbred but handles like a large, docile family dinghy, being stable, easy to steer and predictable. At no time has there been any likelihood of a capsize, and water has been taken over the gunwale on only one occasion when the main sheet was eased too slowly in a squall. The steep, breaking washes of fast motor yachts were an occasional hazard but caused no problems. With increased skill and the strengthened rig, confidence has increased until full sail can now be carried at the top of Force 4 (16 knots), or even above.

DATE	PLACE	WIND SPEED KNOTS	SAILING MODE	SAIL AREA[5]	MODEL SPEED KNOTS	LEEWAY DEGREES	KEEL PROJECTION
1. 19.8.93	Solent	12	Run	Full	5[2]	0	20 mm over full length
2. 19.8.93	Solent	16[3]	Close-hauled	One Reef	4.5[2]	20	Ditto
3. 2.9.93	Southampton Water	8	Close-hauled	Full	3.5[1]	10–30[4]	Ditto
4. 5.6.94	Southampton Water	18[3]	Fore Reach	One Reef	7 plus	10	Additional 50 mm over middle two-thirds keel
5. 11.6.94	River Deben	16 plus	Fore Reach	Full	7[1]	10	Ditto
6. 18.6.94	Maldon	16[3]	Fore Reach	Full	7 plus	10	Ditto
7. 16.8.94	Southampton Water	15–20[3]	Fore Reach	One Reef	6[2]	10–15[4]	40 mm total over full length
8. 16.8.94	Southampton Water	22[3]	Fore Reach	One Reef	7[2]	10–15[4]	Ditto

Notes:
1. Speed measured by calibrated electronic log on board or on boat alongside.
2. Speed measured by GPS on board or on boat alongside.
3. Hand-held anemometer, checked against land station.
4. Leeway measured by hand-held bearing compass.
5. Sail area – full sail 23 m², with one reef 17 m².

Table 6.1: *Sæ Wylfing*'s sailing performance.

The results above show that the model reached speeds of 7 knots in 16–18 knot winds with full sail of 23 m². This would be equivalent to 10 knots in the full-size ship in the same wind speed with a sail area of 180 m². Although the ship could carry this area, it is likely that for convenience of the size of spars a smaller sail of say 150 m² would have been used. This would give the same 10 knot ship speed in a stronger wind of 20 knots (Gifford & Gifford 1996, 20). The choice of sail area would depend on the purpose of the ship, the generally prevailing wind speeds and the nerve and skill of her crew.

The windward performance varied considerably, depending on sea state and reefing. In smooth water with waves less than about 300 mm and with full sail, the model could generally make good 1 knot (1.5 knots full-size ship speed) directly to windward when sailed upright, which proved more effective than when heeled. Performance fell off when reefing was needed so that with two reefs in a short sea of about 600 mm, it was only just possible to keep station. But at no time in the weather conditions tested was *Sæ Wylfing* driven to leeward by the wind. The increase in keel projection from 20 mm to 40 mm reduced leeway from 20° to 12° which is helpful if progress to windward is required, but not essential otherwise.

As it may be assumed that the Anglo-Saxons would have awaited a favourable wind and tide, it might seem that undue emphasis has been given to windward ability in these trials. This is partly because *Sæ Wylfing* had an escort boat on only two occasions and so her extraordinary performance with the wind free could only be enjoyed for a short while without the need for a long sail or row home, and partly because modern sailors always ask 'how does she go to windward?'

The two beach landings have indicated both the possible speed of attack and that, if the ship were caught on a lee shore in a strong wind, she could be run up a beach and hauled clear. Beaching would be possible even in a high surf as the markedly upswept stern would give protection against swamping and indeed, would help to drive the ship further up.

CONCLUSION

Our experience in sailing *Sæ Wylfing* has been a revelation. The performance of Rædwald's ship, built and maintained to a high standard, would have been truly remarkable. It was able to reach and run, in winds of Force 4 and above, at speeds of 10 knots and more over an arc of 200° and to average 7 knots when on passage with favourable winds. Ships such as this, each with a maximum capacity of 100 people, would have provided a superlative means of transport, hitherto unsuspected, with possible journey times of:

Rendlesham, Suffolk, to Canterbury	:	½ day
Canterbury to France	:	½ day
Rendlesham to York	:	1½ days
Rendlesham to the River Idle, Lincoln, via the River Witham	:	1 day
York to Canterbury	:	2 days

The 0.6 m draft would have allowed confident sailing in shallow coastal waters and, with the bold sheer, to beach-land even in high surf.

This combination of high speed, shallow draft, easily raised side-rudder and surf beach-landing capability would have made her a safe ship for the waters of the east coast of England and the southern North Sea. Whenever possible, her crew would have awaited a favourable wind as, in 690, did Ecgberht (Colgrave & Mynors 1969, 478–9, V.9) and as indeed have all sailing ship captains until the 19th century. Open boats would not generally be sailed during the winter in these northern waters.

As Blair (1976, 94) observed, 'given a measure of good luck and the good sense to choose the right season of the year, the sea voyage may well have been not only safer but also quicker'. It is notable that practically all early Anglo-Saxon settlements are on, or near, coasts or navigable rivers, indicating that water transport was of prime importance. One can image Rædwald voyaging speedily over the shallows of the Thames estuary to visit Æthelred and Augustine at Canterbury (Colgrave & Mynors 1969, 190–1, II.15) and using his ships, when assisting Edwin to gain the Northumbrian throne, to reach the River Idle in time to defeat Æthelfrith 'allowing him no time to summon and assemble his whole army' (op. cit. 1969, 180–1, II.2). Did Paulinus use such a vessel when he took Queen Æthelburh 'by ship to Kent' after Edwin's death in 633 (op. cit. 1969, 204–5, II.20)? To what extent did Anglo-Saxon ships facilitate the rapid spread of Christianity? They must have been important in gift-giving and maintaining order through an extensive realm.

The beautiful hull buried at Sutton Hoo reveals that problems of shape, strength and fitness for purpose had been fully resolved by the end of the 6th century. This was a high point in the Anglo-Saxon art of clinker construction. In the following 800 years clinker ships would be built for a variety of purposes and some would be beamier, deeper and heavier, but it is unlikely that the skills exhibited in Rædwald's long ship were ever surpassed.

GLOSSARY OF TERMS

Abeam: From the side.

Beat: Sail to windward on a series of courses or boards.

Bilge: Lowest internal part of a hull or transition between bottom and side of hull. Weather bilge is on windward side.

Close-hauled: Sailing as close to the wind as possible, with sheet and tack hauled in tight fore and aft.

GPS: Global Positioning System. Instrument for navigating from observation of satellites.

Gunwhale: The upper strake (plank) of side of vessel, usually the strongest.

Knot: One nautical mile per hour, approximately equivalent to 1.1 land miles per hour.

Leeway: Sideways deflection by the wind of vessel from course steered.

Quarter: Portion of vessel on either side of stern.

Reaching or *Broad reaching*: Sailing with wind abeam. Head-reaching is with wind ahead of the beam, but not close-hauled.

Reef: Reduce sail area by rolling up a part and securing it, or the part so rolled up, one reef, double-reef.

Sheer: Upper edge of hull or curvature of that edge.

Sheet: Rope controlling aft corner of square-sail.

Spars: Generic term for mast and yard.

Tack: Rope controlling fore corner of square-sail. Turn towards wind between boards when beating, difficult with square-rig.

Wear: Turn downwind between boards when beating, simple in a square-rigged vessel. See tack.

Yard: Spar across top of square-sail.

CHAPTER 7

THE MIDDLE SAXON SITE AT FLIXBOROUGH, NORTH LINCOLNSHIRE

Kevin Leahy

Imust begin with two admissions; firstly this is not, and cannot pretend to be, an authoritative account of the Flixborough site. Post-excavation work is underway on this complex site and a full analysis of the finds may well present a different picture from that suggested here. Secondly, despite the best efforts of the Northumbrian kings, Lindsey, and thus Flixborough, lay outside the kingdom of Northumbria. However, as the site lies only 8 km to the south of the eponymous Humber estuary, it is hoped that this geographical slip will be overlooked.

The village of Flixborough lies in North Lincolnshire just to the north of Scunthorpe. Prior to the excavation it was chiefly known as the site of the 1974 chemical works explosion in which twenty-eight men died. There were other large industrial plants in the area: immediately to the east was Lysaght's massive Normanby Park steelworks, the slag heaps of which came perilously close to the edge of the archaeological site. Lysaght's works closed in 1981 and its site is being reclaimed as an industrial estate. The Anglo-Saxon site itself lay around a large sand dune banked up against the side of the Liassic escarpment, about 1.4 km east of the River Trent (Plate 4).

Archaeological interest in the site started in 1933 when Derreck Riley and Jim Walshaw found a large amount of animal bone, some 'Roman' pottery and two clay loom weights (Dudley 1949, 175; Riley, diary entry for Saturday, 23 September 1933). Later, on 6 January 1934, test pits were dug at the base and on the top of the dune. These produced more pottery, bones and a fragment of a spindle whorl. More recent finds include an Anglo-Saxon coin, a pottery spindle whorl and a gilded copper alloy disc of 8th-century date. Interest in the site was rekindled in 1988 when planning permission was sought for a sandpit. The application was passed to the Humberside Archaeological Unit where the potential importance of the site was recognized; it lies immediately adjacent to the abandoned church of All Saints, North (or Little) Conesby (a deserted village), and traces of the village might be expected. While it was likely that there would be archaeological remains in the field, there was insufficient evidence to contest a planning application. Luckily the operator of the sandpit, George Jewitt, was interested in archaeology and did all he could to help. With his cooperation it was agreed to maintain a watch on the site when sand extraction started.

Work began with the removal of the topsoil by a bulldozer while Irene MacGrath (with her metal detector) and I conducted a 'watching brief'. I was only there for conscience's sake; the chances of seeing anything in the tracks of the machine seemed remote, even if there was anything there. Irene picked up a coin, an Anglo-Saxon *sceat*, which cheered us up a bit. On the second day things started to happen; Irene found an early Anglo-Saxon great square-headed brooch and, more importantly, some iron hinges and fittings from a coffin. In the days that followed we excavated eleven oriented burials, some of which had been interred in wooden coffins. These were fitted with hinges and hasps suggesting they may have served as chests during the lifetimes of the occupants, *memento mori*. The human remains had almost totally dissolved away, leaving only fragments of bone and teeth.

Field-walking to the north of the sand dune produced, as Riley and Walshaw had found, a scatter of occupation debris. The pottery was Anglo-Saxon and, on checking the 1933 pottery finds at Scunthorpe Museum, we found that they too were Anglo-Saxon and included the spout from a large Ipswich ware pitcher. A geophysical survey was carried out to the north of the dune and, when this failed to give any useful results, a trial excavation was organized. This revealed the edge of a large ditch which contained Anglo-Saxon material. Ben Whitwell of the Humberside Archaeological Unit then drafted a project design which English Heritage accepted, agreeing to sponsor a ten-week excavation. The work on the site was carried out by the Humberside Archaeological Unit (now the Humber Archaeological Partnership) between 1989 and 1991. The small team was directed on site by Dave Tomlinson with Ben Whitwell and myself as co-directors.

A week before the excavation started crop-marks appeared in the ripening cereal grown on the field and, with the aid of a local pilot, they were photographed from the air. From the aircraft a thin green line could be seen surrounding the sand dune. This was odd; if the dune was a natural feature why should anyone dig a ditch around it? We could also see the shape of the old churchyard marked by a relict hedge line and some large green patches to the north of the dune near the position of the test pit. This would be the excavation site.

The plough soil was removed from a large area revealing, as a black band across the yellow sand, the ditch observed from the air. Although the crop-mark showed the ditch curving south to encircle the dune it proved impossible to trace its western side by excavation. As with other remains on this side of the site, it was probably truncated by erosion and ploughing. Again there was a striking amount of archaeological debris. It became clear that very few of the finds could not be dated to the Middle Saxon period. There would be few problems of re-deposited material from earlier periods or intrusive later material; the economy of the Middle Saxon period was laid bare. Unfortunately though, there was no sign of any buildings.

It was around this time that we started to get interested in the top of the sand dune, hitherto thought to be a purely natural feature as there was no sign of archaeological debris in the earth dug out by the rabbits that infested it. However, archaeological material seemed to be coming from the side of a test pit dug into the edge of the dune. Another test pit revealed a limestone gravel surface about 1.5 m below the surface of the dune. A black occupation layer then appeared in the face of the advancing sandpit to the south and all became clear. The site had been buried by a deep layer of wind-blown sand, preserving it like an Anglo-Saxon Pompeii. It was here that we found our first buildings.

All the buildings shared the same NE–SW alignment and were found on top or to the north of the dune. The area to the south was not excavated, but finds from the sandpit's power-sieve suggested that the settlement did not extend over that area. There were, however, other graves in addition to the eleven already excavated. This was demonstrated by the experience of an unfortunate house-holder who received, along with her load of building sand, a free skeleton. The buildings were relatively large timber structures represented by stains in the sand marking the post-holes and trenches in which their wall posts had been placed. These were sometimes difficult to find. Early in the excavation, in an area thought to be finished, we found, some days later, the outline of a building actually standing above the level of the surrounding sand. The wind had eroded sand from the surface of the site but the fill of the wall trenches retained moisture and was more resistant. At intervals along the excavated trench stone slabs were found on which the building's wall posts had rested. The excavation team developed considerable skill in finding the faint traces of structures which had sometimes been rebuilt on a number of occasions (Plate 5). Other structures were uncovered; many of the halls contained hearths and were connected by paths and areas of limestone rubble. These are important as they provide stratigraphic links across the site which will help resolve the relationships between buildings. Some areas of the site underwent changes in function; a building in the north-east corner was demolished to make way for a series of ovens which, in turn, were built over.

A feature of the Flixborough site was extensive layers of dumped occupation debris which overlay some buildings and were cut through by others. These layers were eventually covered by a deposit of dark soil containing material derived from the final period of Anglo-Saxon activity on the site. This, in turn, was engulfed by a deep layer of sterile wind-blown sand sealing the deposits and protecting them from later disturbance. There was some evidence for later activity. During the high medieval period an oven and pit were dug into the dune and a large E–W ditch cut across the northern part of the site. The site remained otherwise undisturbed until excavated.

In the absence of any direct documentary evidence the chronology of the Flixborough site must be based on the finds although, in many cases, the stratigraphy at Flixborough will be used to date the finds. The quantity, quality and degree of preservation of the finds at Flixborough are remarkable and constant sieving and metal detecting during the excavation gave a very high rate of recovery.

The most datable objects are the coins and Flixborough has, with sixty-eight recorded finds, produced more Anglo-Saxon coins than any other site in Lindsey (Blackburn 1993, 86). Coins were not issued by the independent kings of Lindsey and finds include East Anglian, Northumbrian, West Saxon and Frisian issues. Frisian *sceattas* are relatively common finds in Lindsey and their presence need not be seen as significant. During the period of the site's occupation, Lindsey was a province of Mercia, having been lost to Northumbria, following a long struggle, in 679. Despite this, Northumbrian coins are the most common, suggesting that Flixborough was involved in the Northumbrian economic sphere for at least part of its existence.

The coin sequence at Flixborough begins with a series D *sceat* dating to around 700–715 and terminates with Lunette-type pennies of Alfred struck around 874–5. There is an unstratified late 10th-century penny of Edward the Martyr but, in the absence of any other 10th-century finds, this may be seen as a casual loss with the main period of occupation on the site terminating in the late 9th century. Some caution is needed when using coin dates to construct a chronology for the Flixborough site. The pattern of coins on the site strongly reflects the general pattern of coin use in Lindsey (Blackburn 1993, 83). Anglo-Saxon coins earlier than the series D *sceattas* are very rare in Lindsey and there is a general lack of early 10th-century coinage.

The pottery found at Flixborough will form an important part of the final report. Most is of the shell-tempered Maxey-type ware which was the characteristic Middle Saxon fabric in the region. There is also a substantial quantity of East Anglian Ipswich-type ware. Both Maxey and Ipswich wares are well-known Middle Anglo-Saxon pottery types but the sequence of finds from Flixborough may help to further define their development and dating. The earliest phases at Flixborough are associated with Early Anglo-Saxon wares which pre-date the introduction of Maxey ware. Although the date of the transition is open to doubt, their presence suggests that occupation started in the late 7th century. The ceramic evidence also has a bearing on the end of activity on the site and supports the dates suggested by the coins. The later phases of the site contain some Torksey ware and Lincoln kiln-type wares, fabrics which seem to have come into use in the third quarter of the 9th century.

There is a little imported continental pottery at Flixborough but this does not occur in large enough quantities to suggest that the site was a *wic* and involved in overseas trade. In view of Flixborough's location close to a major waterway this is surprising. There is some imported glass, but the most common imported material is fragments of Mayen lava quern-stone from the Eiffel mountains in Germany.

The metalwork found at Flixborough (Plate 6) was remarkable for its quality, quantity and range (Webster & Backhouse 1991, no 69a–w; Whitwell 1991, 244–7). This material, particularly the stratified finds, will do much to refine the chronology of object types and decorative styles during the Middle Saxon period. There are four pieces of Early Anglo-Saxon metalwork, but as these objects are 6th-century types they pre-date the start of occupation in the late 7th century. Some of the copper alloy pins may be 7th century, but they could be later. There is a striking absence of 10th-century Anglo-Saxon and Viking metalwork although this material is common in Lindsey. In general the copper alloy objects found at Flixborough support the date ranges provided by the coins and pottery.

The evidence for on-site manufacture of non-ferrous objects at Flixborough is limited. Although there are a few mould fragments, an initial examination of the copper alloy objects suggests that few were unfinished and in the process of manufacture. The large number of metal objects found must have been made elsewhere. Lead objects such as weights, whorls and possible window came were found, but the amount of lead waste was particularly striking. This consisted mainly of droplets of lead melt but off-cuts were also found. Lead waste occurs on other rich Middle Saxon sites and is a feature of the 'productive sites' (see below). Its source and function are not understood.

In contrast to the human remains found to the south of the dune the bones from the main areas were exceptionally well preserved, and around 5,000 kg of animal, bird and fish bone were retrieved. This has great potential as it can all be dated to the Middle Saxon period. Large numbers of bone objects were found but there is, so far, no evidence to suggest that bone was being worked on the site. In the absence of any water-logged deposits no wood or leather objects were preserved. Although no textiles survived, Flixborough produced a remarkable amount of material relating to all aspects of cloth manufacture. Clay loom weight fragments were very common and must represent some hundreds of weights. The site also produced carding-comb teeth, spindle whorls, bone pin beaters and needles in unparalleled numbers, suggesting the production of cloth on an industrial scale.

In view of the site's location on the edge of Scunthorpe, now an important steel-making centre, the presence of large numbers of well-preserved iron objects and smithing off-cuts may be significant. Direct evidence of iron-working is provided by the presence of slag. It would, however, be unwise to place too much emphasis on Flixborough as an iron-working centre; while slag was common, it did not occur in the vast quantities found on smelting sites. Smelting was certainly being carried out in the Flixborough area, but it was not taking place on site.

Iron objects were both common and well preserved. The most significant find was the hoard discovered in the sandpit after the excavation had concluded. This was contained in two lead vats and consisted of axes, adzes, draw-knives, spoon bits and a slashing bill (Leahy 1995), all the tools that a joiner would need to make a building, or a boat. In addition to the 303 knives and 34 pairs of shears, a wide range of iron fittings were found. If these objects had not been found in dated contexts they would not have been dated to the Middle Saxon period. There was little agricultural equipment, but a large iron plough-share was found in a small pit together with a fine, 2 m long, cauldron chain. Two lunette-bladed knives may provide evidence of leather-working or dressing.

The single most important discovery was the evidence for literacy (Plate 7). This included a lead plaque listing seven Old English personal names and a silver ring bearing the first eleven letters of the Latin alphabet (Webster & Backhouse 1991, no 69b). These objects do not, in themselves, prove the literacy of anyone other than those who made them, or at least originated the inscriptions. The presence of twenty-seven styli, however, must demonstrate the existence of a large number of literates among the community.

An important consideration is the nature and function of the Flixborough site. What activities could have given rise to this vast array of finds? While it is premature to attempt to define this complex site, others have not been reticent in describing it as an 'Anglo-Saxon nunnery' and it is perhaps worth reviewing the evidence here.

Before looking at the evidence, however, some caveats must be expressed. Firstly, it may be a mistake to consider Flixborough as only having one function during the 200 years of its occupation. The copper alloy metalwork appears to suggest a change in the site's nature or status between the 8th and 9th centuries, with earlier material appearing more plentiful and of better quality. Some areas underwent changes in function, with buildings being replaced by ovens, and one structure containing both burials and a series of well-used hearths again suggests a change in status. Secondly, we cannot assume that the area excavated was typical of the entire site; the main part may have lain on the top of the escarpment and, lacking the massive dump layers, have been devoid of finds.

While much has been made of the richness of the Flixborough site these riches are, in the main, quantitative rather than qualitative. Most of the finds, including the decorated objects, can be paralleled on other sites in the region. Middle Saxon Lindsey (and, to a lesser extent, Deira) appears to have been surprisingly rich and the material found need not be seen as the sole prerogative of an aristocracy. What impresses at Flixborough is the sheer quantity of finds, with 68 coins and a startling 917 recorded non-ferrous finds. It must be emphasized, however, that other sites, while not as rich as Flixborough, have produced large amounts of Middle Saxon metalwork. The site most comparable to Flixborough is the Anglo-Saxon monastery at Whitby, where excavations during the interwar years produced 150 coins and 140 Anglo-Saxon non-ferrous objects (Pirie, pers comm;

Peers & Radford 1943, 27–88). It would, however, be wrong to assume that Flixborough was monastic on the basis of parallels with Whitby. Other attested monastic sites have been excavated and have yielded only modest numbers of finds, as at Jarrow (Cramp 1976b, 249–60) and Hartlepool (Jackson 1988, 182, fig 33). Even at Whitby the high number of finds may relate not to the religious community but to commercial activity around the monastery gate.

The other parallels for the Flixborough finds are presented by the so-called 'productive site phenomenon'. This was first recognized by numismatists who, while recording metal detector finds, realized that some sites were producing surprisingly large numbers of Middle Saxon coins. Productive sites are known in Lincolnshire, but the most fully investigated examples are in East Yorkshire (Leahy forthcoming a). The largest collection of finds is from South Newbald, East Yorkshire (*ibid*) where 126 coins and 114 objects were found. On the basis of an historical and topographical study it was suggested that the site may have been a market nucleated around a possible minster. The nature of the finds from Newbald stands in sharp contrast to the wide range of domestic finds from Flixborough. Newbald produced large numbers of coins and dress fittings but no pottery, animal bone, loom weights or other evidence for human occupation.

Metal detecting at the productive site at Cottam, East Yorkshire, has also retrieved large numbers of coins and finds, although here the assemblage looks more balanced, having also produced domestic and agricultural equipment (Haldenby 1990, 51–63; 1992, 25–39; 1994, 51–6). The metal detecting has been followed by a series of excavations carried out by the Department of Archaeology of the University of York; this is producing settlement evidence (Nenk et al. 1994, 228–9).

Excavations on the site of the massive prehistoric ring-work at Thwing, East Yorkshire, produced evidence for Middle Saxon buildings and a cemetery containing 132 oriented burials, 23% of which were in iron-fitted wooden coffins of the type found at Flixborough (Manby 1986, 1–8; 1988, 15–18). The evidence suggests that the site was some sort of administrative centre, but the excavations produced only sixteen coins and thirty-seven objects (Leahy forthcoming b), although an aristocratic element in the population would seem likely.

Some types of object are of particular importance in the interpretation of sites and the discovery at Flixborough of twenty-seven styli and other evidence for literacy is significant. Styli are uncommon finds and only one of the many other sites from which I have recorded metal detector finds is producing styli. There are six from Whitby (Peers & Radford 1943, 64–5, fig 15) and two from Jarrow (Webster & Backhouse 1991, no 105d). During the Middle Saxon period the ability to write was uncommon outside the clergy and the discovery of this number of styli suggests that the site was a monastery, or at least had a strong clerical presence. The absence of carved stones or grave markers at Flixborough may be significant (Cramp 1993, 64–73). These occur on Anglo-Saxon monastic sites (Whitby, Jarrow, Hartlepool) and the discovery of them at Flixborough would have supported such an interpretation. However, their absence need not preclude the site being a monastery and there are Middle Saxon burials, some of which came from the possible church. The other potentially monastic feature is the great, and long-lived, ditch which may have encircled the dune. This could have been a monastic *vallum*.

The presence of a church and churchyard immediately adjacent to the site may be significant. We are fortunate that a 1778 estate survey by John Snape (North Lincolnshire Museums, Sheffield Papers A/9/2) has, as a marginal illustration, a carefully executed view of the now demolished church. This shows it to have been a simple two-cell structure of probable Norman origin. There was more than one church at Conesby with references, in 1455, to the manorial chapels of St John the Baptist and Holy Cross (Owen 1975, 18). The dedication of the church adjacent to the site of All Saints may point to the existence of a third church, but this could simply be a post-Reformation renaming of one of the chapels. That Conesby should have three places of worship is significant; a number of the Anglo-Saxon monasteries in Lincolnshire consist, not of one site, but of a series of dispersed foci each with its oratory (Stocker 1993, 101–22). The two churches at Conesby may be a relic of this or, more probably, a Saxo-Norman refounding as occurred elsewhere (Whitby, Crowland, Bardney). The 1455 references to the chapels show that they were (or were supposed to be) served by the parson of West Halton (Owen 1971, 134; 1975, 18). This link with West Halton is interesting. By tradition St Æthelthryth founded a monastery at West Halton during her flight from her husband, Ecgfrith of Northumbria, in the late years of the 7th century. West Halton parish church is dedicated to her and there is Anglo-Saxon material from the village. Although the two sites are 7.5 km apart, West Halton and Flixborough are linked in other ways: until rationalization of boundaries in the 19th century there was an outlier of West Halton within the parish of Flixborough. We may be looking at another dispersed monastery.

What I have tried to do here is to give an account not of the Flixborough site but of its discovery and the excavation itself. I have described how things appeared at the time of their discovery and on first reflection. Some of these interpretations will be modified in the light of further research but I believe that they, and the story of the excavation itself, are worth recording. In our (rightly) objective accounts of excavations we sometimes lose sight of ourselves and the excitement of discovery. Archaeology, and particularly Anglo-Saxon archaeology, is exciting, and we should pass on the story of our adventure so that others can share our experiences. It was this sense of enthusiasm and excitement that Jim Lang never lost, and was so successful in communicating to others.

ACKNOWLEDGEMENTS

I would like to offer my thanks to the manager of the Flixborough Project, Dr Chris Loveluck, for his helpful comments on an earlier draft of this chapter. While his assistance is acknowledged, the views expressed here are my own and may not be shared by him.

CHAPTER 8

Dynasty and Cult: the Utility of Christian Mission to Northumbrian Kings Between 642 and 654

Nicholas Higham

An Irish mission was established within Bernicia at the invitation and under the protection of King Oswald of the Bernicians in the mid-630s (Colgrave & Mynors 1969, 219, III.3; Mayr-Harting 1991, 98). Thereafter, until Bernician royal patronage was revoked by his brother, Oswiu, in 664, the patronage of immigrant clergy and the growing ranks of their Northumbrian acolytes was to be a central feature of royal policy. Leading clerics had several functions, serving to legitimize, sustain and enhance kingly power *vis-à-vis* rivals both at home and abroad. The clergy had their own objectives, of course, and on occasion conflicting views on some areas of royal policy, but, despite the mission-centric version of history offered by Bede, power lay primarily with the royal house. The presence of Irish clergy in Northumbria depended on their utility to successive kings and was a consequence of royal, not clerical, initiatives.

It would be a mistake to imagine that all the Northumbrian kings who variously patronized the Ionan church had identical objectives. Rather, each pursued a variant of the core policy of patronage to his own specific advantage. The foundation of monasteries provides perhaps the clearest evidence of the distinctiveness of royal initiatives, as each king sought to strengthen his own regime. By 663, Oswald's foundation on Holy Island (Lindisfarne) was competing for status and authority with his son Œthelwald's Lastingham, his brother Oswiu's Whitby (among others), his sister-in-law's foundation at Gilling and his nephew's at Ripon, each of which was established by the grant of royal estates in pursuit of specific purposes. By such grants, kings sought to provide themselves with high-status sepulchres under the protection of a permanent cult centre, but far more might be intended: Gilling was founded to resolve the peculiar difficulty of a murder perpetrated within the royal kin (Colgrave & Mynors 1969, 257, 293, III.14, 24); Whitby was so generously founded and ably led by a succession of royal abbesses that it became the principal school in Northumbria in the late 7th century, overshadowing Holy Island (Blair 1985). It was no coincidence that it was also the setting chosen by the king for the best-known synod of the Northumbrian church, under his presidency and called into existence largely to do his will (Cubitt 1995, 289).

Church and kingship were, therefore, highly interdependent. As further illustration this chapter will focus on just two issues: the first is the interaction of dynastic politics and religious patronage within the struggle between Oswiu and Oswine between 643 and 651; the second is the political utility to Oswiu of the mission to the East Saxons, c 653.

OSWIU AND OSWINE

Oswald has received considerable attention from the academic community in recent years (Stancliffe & Cambridge 1995), although there has been comparatively little interest in the consequences of his sudden death in battle in 642. The religious policies of his full brother, Oswiu, have received much less attention – excepting his role at the synod of Whitby, of course – despite his far longer reign (642–70). One suspects the baleful influence of Bede may have been responsible for this comparative neglect. Although the venerable monk considered his kingship the apogee of English imperium in his *Historia Ecclesiastica* (II.5), he had a far poorer opinion of Oswiu than Oswald, whom he variously described as *vir Deo dilectus* and *sanctissimus ac uictoriosissimus rex* (Colgrave & Mynors 1969, 214, 232, III.1, 7), even despite Oswiu's triumph over the pagan Mercians in 655 and his responsibility for uniting the Northumbrian and Canterbury churches at Whitby in 664. Bede's treatment is masterly but circumspect. Although his criticism of Oswiu is implied, it is so heavy his audience can have had little doubt as to the inferences they were expected to draw.

The kingdom ruled by Oswiu at the start of his reign, which was suffering penetrating Mercian raids, was much reduced from that which Oswald had enjoyed. His brother's death at the hands of the pagan Midlanders arguably discouraged him from testing the damaged efficacy of the god of Iona in battle against the Mercians, and it was thirteen years before Oswiu took the field to oppose Penda. When he eventually did so, it was only *in extremis* and his chances seem to have been discounted in advance by those in a position to judge – such as his nephew Œthelwald (Colgrave & Mynors 1969, 290, III.24). His reign was long tainted by his brother's defeat, therefore, and by a lack of confidence in improvement under the protection of Aidan's rituals and cult practices. Furthermore, it may be that he was not Oswald's intended heir once Œthelwald was born, and may have been in exile in Ireland during his brother's reign (Ireland 1991, 77–8). Yet Oswiu seems to have had considerable political flair. His development of a novel royal cult around his brother reveals the fertility of his imagination and a determination to turn Oswald's death to his own advantage. At the same time, his marriage to Princess Eanflœd – Edwin's daughter via the Kentish Æthelburh and then in Kent – had some potential to bring him the friendship of the only other English court which was securely Christian at this date.

Oswiu's relationship with Lindisfarne was, however, far from simple. Bede referred to his 'partnership' with Oswine, who ruled Deira between c 643 and 651 and was also a patron of Holy Island but, uniquely, not a member of the Bernician dynasty. It is the four-cornered relationship between Bede as narrator, Bishop Aidan and Kings Oswiu and Oswine which offers insights into the relationship between power and religious policy during these years (Higham 1997, 226–31).

Oswine's history is exclusively told by Bede in Chapter 14 of Book III in the *Historia Ecclesiastica* (Stenton 1971, 83; Yorke 1990, 78, 80; Higham 1995, 167–8) – supposing references in the *Anglo-Saxon Chronicle* to be entirely derivative (Swanton 1996, 27–8). This chapter comes immediately after a group which characterizes Oswald and Aidan as saints. It starts with notice of Oswiu's succession, aged about thirty, to rule for twenty-eight troubled years – troubled that is by Mercian attacks and those of his own son and nephew. Bede then notes Paulinus's death and replacement at Rochester in 644, presumably because that fitted his chronology at this point, but he turns thereafter to Oswine, whom he describes variously as Oswiu's 'consort in royal dignity', 'a man of great piety and religion', 'tall and handsome, pleasant of speech, courteous in manner, and bountiful', 'modest', 'humble' and 'beloved by all'.

This is exceptional treatment and worthy of comment, particularly given Oswine's parentage – his father was, after all, the infamous apostate Osric. His idealized characterization at this point in the narrative naturally inclines his audience to see Oswine, not Oswiu, as the moral successor of the saintly Oswald, and this must have been Bede's intention. By contrast, Oswiu was depicted as cruel, malicious, a troublemaker and the ultimate cause of Oswine's foul murder. His characterization was, therefore, comparatively evil, in contrast to the virtues of Oswald and Oswine, and his entire reign tainted at the outset by the comparison. Yet it was Oswiu, not Oswine, who was Bernician (like Bede); Oswiu not Oswine who killed the terrible pagan king Penda; Oswiu who was named as the very apogee of English kingship; and Oswiu who united English Christianity at Whitby. Oswine, by contrast, achieved nothing whatever of note.

Bede's treatment of these two kings diverges significantly from his normal prejudices, therefore, to the extent that it requires some explanation. Certainly, sanctity had been attributed to Oswine by the 730s and that may have influenced Bede, but there seems more to his perspective than that. The crux of the matter seems to lie in relations between both kings and Aidan.

Oswiu's succession in 642 was presumably accommodated by Aidan, his brother's cult leader and a senior figure in the Bernician regime, albeit one who was entirely dependent on royal patronage for his own episcopal status. Aidan perhaps preferred a baptized, adult heir to the child Œthelwald at this time of crisis and he may have played a significant role in legitimizing Oswiu's accession. Even if Oswiu's treatment of Oswald's physical remains in 642–3 was an embarrassment to the Irish clergy, as Thacker (1995) has quite properly suggested, the inception of a royal cult of Oswald is unlikely to have seriously offended them.

Oswiu's marriage to Eanflæd, c 643, had, however, considerable potential to sow dissension between Aidan and his royal patron. Oswiu was the grandson of King Ælle of the Deirans via his mother. Eanflæd was the granddaughter of the same Ælle through her father, making husband and wife first cousins and thus well within the prohibited degrees of consanguinity for Christian marriage. Oswiu was following the normal pattern of taking a bride once he had secured the throne, irrespective of previous relationships and his paternity of various children. There is no evidence that the contract alarmed Eanflæd's protector, Eorcenberht, sufficiently to oppose the match, even despite his enforcement of Christianity (Colgrave & Mynors 1969, 236, III.8). Nor is Eanflæd known to have objected to a marriage which returned her to a position of influence within her father's erstwhile territories. The marriage arguably offered important political benefits to all involved and sealed a new amity between two Christian kings and two dynasties which now put behind them the tensions which had characterized relations between their predecessors.

However, their complacency is unlikely to have been shared by Aidan, a bishop from that same Irish stable whence Columbanus had fulminated against the marital affairs of the Merovingian kings a generation earlier. What is more, Oswiu's pre-existing children by two different women of high status may well have encouraged Aidan to consider his marriage to Eanflæd bigamous. If so, the bishop was well placed to know the facts. Bede's reticence means that we are not, but his doubts concerning Aldfrith's relationship with Ecgfrith (Colgrave & Mynors 1969, 430, IV.26) certainly leaves room for speculation.

From Oswiu's perspective, the advantages of his marriage were considerable: it linked the two leading Christian, English courts; Eanflæd was Edwin's sole surviving descendant, so the marriage reinforced his own claim as Ælle's descendant and Oswald's heir to the throne of the Deiri; lastly, the marriage distinguished Oswiu's regime from that of his brother, who had linked himself with Wessex rather than the Deiran-Kentish family.

Despite Oswiu's machinations, however, Oswine obtained Deira, and there can be little question as to which of the two candidates the Deirans themselves preferred. Oswine's religious background was cosmopolitan. He was perhaps baptized in his youth under Edwin, but his father reinstated and legitimized non-Christian rituals in 633. When Osric was killed, Oswine fled to the non-Christian West Saxons, enemies of Edwin, while Edwin's descendants went to their kin in Christian Kent and then on to Francia. The West Saxons then themselves experimented with Christian cult during the 630s. Consequently Oswine returned north with a breadth of religious experience which can only have encouraged him to adopt an opportunistic attitude to religious affiliation when he became king. In some respects his political stance was closer to Oswald's than was Oswiu's: his West Saxon sojourn duplicated contacts made there by Oswald; in contrast, Oswiu allied himself with his brother's erstwhile rivals – that branch of the Deiran royal house which descended from Edwin and his Kentish marriage.

In many respects, Oswine's more obvious course would have been to refound the York diocese and so provide himself with an independent religious authority against Oswiu and Aidan, and reinforce his claim to the kingship by posing as the great Edwin's ideological heir to augment his descent from Osric (Kirby 1991, 92). He did not, however, perhaps because Oswiu's marriage to Eanflæd had already committed Canterbury and its king, and a Romanist bishop for York could only come from Canterbury. Oswine was left, therefore, to compete with Oswiu for influence with, and the support of Aidan. It is typical of these convoluted struggles that it was probably the very same act on Oswiu's part which cut Oswine off from the Roman church that threw the Irish bishop into the arms of his rival.

Oswine apparently enjoyed the full support of Aidan, who was represented by Bede as the king's close associate, confidant and loving friend. In this respect, Oswine clearly won the competition between the two kings for the amity of the bishop. What is more, Aidan mattered. He had religious authority across every community which had recognized Oswald as king: one king; one bishop (Angenendt 1986, 773–5). Post-642 and Deiran rejection of the Bernician dynasty, two kings from rival lineages and with competing affinities, representing houses which had recently ruled over both peoples, shared a bishop whose territorial diocese had been forged in the very different circumstances of Oswald's reign. Neither king, neither regime, neither people, can have felt comfortable with this situation or expected it to continue long. Nor, surely, did Aidan, who apparently displayed his own preference by his familiarity with Oswine – although open opposition to Oswiu is unrecorded.

Put simply, following Oswiu's marriage, Aidan seemingly withdrew support from the brother of his earlier patron, Oswald, and backed his cousin. By so doing, he legitimized Oswine's ambitions to be king of both the Deirans and Bernicians and placed at his disposal the potent support of the Ionan god. This circumstance arguably accounts for Bede's remarkable characterization of Oswine as the perfect Christian king and he was thereafter remembered within the northern church as the saintly patron of Aidan. Their joint ambitions necessarily had a political dimension, which was to oust Oswiu, and Bede remarked on Oswine's recruitment of warriors from numerous peoples (Campbell 1986, 133). They were thwarted by Oswiu's sudden recourse in 651 to war, then the murder of his enemy despite their close kinship. That Aidan died only twelve days later (Colgrave & Mynors 1969, 260, III.14) may not be entirely coincidental if his attitude towards Oswiu was as hostile as is here suggested.

What emerges from this conflict is the importance of mission within the political and dynastic issues of the day. A king such as Oswiu and a bishop such as Aidan had very different perceptions of Christianity and the behavioural demands which that might make on the individual. Oswiu was apparently ambushed by what must to him have been inexplicable hostility to his marriage from his own bishop. The king's resolution of the problem was typical of the man, but the eight years of competition emphasizes the centrality of both clerisy and cult to the rule of the north even as early as 642 – as a major source of legitimacy, authority, and mediation with the divine. It was only with both Oswine and Aidan dead that Oswiu was able to establish a new Irish bishop and pursue a more aggressive policy towards his neighbours – which once again is most easily identified via missionary activity (Angenendt 1986, 775–6).

THE BERNICIAN MISSION TO THE EAST SAXONS

The formation of a dynastic alliance cemented by marriage between Penda's son Peada and Oswiu enabled the Northumbrian ruler to extend his influence into Middle Anglia and dispatch Irish and English clergy there (Colgrave & Mynors 1969, 278, III.21). Peada's baptism by Finan deep inside Bernicia at the instigation of the Bernician prince Alhfrith (already his brother-in-law) implies that Oswiu was the senior partner in this relationship. The clergy thereafter dispatched to Peada's court were necessarily to be the Northumbrian king's eyes and ears on the eastern fringes of Mercia since they reported back to Finan on Holy Island and were subject to his authority.

Beyond Middle Anglia lay the East Saxons, and Bede describes how Oswiu's *amicus*, Sigeberht, was king there and another frequent visitor to Northumbria (Colgrave & Mynors 1969, 280, III.22). At Oswiu's urging, Sigeberht too, with his own *amici*, accepted baptism at Wall at Finan's hands. Again, the relationship was presumably unequal and once again clergy were dispatched, although on this occasion a bishop was somewhat tardily appointed to head the mission.

The creation of a new diocese under Oswiu's patronage has perhaps not received the attention it deserves, given that this was the first occasion on which the monumental unity of the territorial diocese dependent on the Bernician kingship had been fractured. Hitherto, the see of Holy Island had extended as far as the influence of its royal patrons, and so had been a highly changeable entity which shrank inwards in times of adversity but extended into Middle Anglia in 653. Cedd's consecration as bishop to the East Saxons reflects a change of policy which occurred not when the mission was first dispatched but only once it had reported back to Northumbria.

That report arguably included reference to the current crisis within the church of Canterbury. Archbishop Honorius was presumably adult when he arrived in England (by 601), so was at least in his seventies by 650. His appointment of Englishmen as bishops to Rochester (644) and successively to the East Angles in c 647 and 652 underlines his isolation as the last survivor of the Italian mission. Honorius's death in September 653 was followed by an eighteen-month vacancy before Deusdedit, a West Saxon, was enthroned as archbishop of Canterbury on 26 March 655 (Colgrave & Mynors 1969, 276–8, III.20).

Cedd was, therefore, consecrated by Finan as bishop to the East Saxons at a time when Italian leadership of the Kentish church was either moribund or entirely at an end and no clear way forward had yet been established. Bede emphasizes the canonical legitimacy of his consecration by three bishops, and this arguably contrasts with the uncanonical appointments of Ithamar to Rochester and Bertgisl to the East Angles at this date. The sudden appearance of a properly consecrated Bernician bishop on the north side of the Thames looks like an opportunistic move by the Ionan-Bernician church and its royal patrons to encroach on the Romanist dioceses of the south-east, which were either vacant or held by English appointees whose consecration was, at best, questionable.

This interpretation becomes clearer when the ecclesiastical organization of the new see is examined. Bede portrayed Cedd as active across the whole East Saxon kingdom, establishing churches in various places and ordaining priests to assist him. However, he focused his mission on *Ythancaestir* (*Othona*: Bradwell-on-Sea) and Tilbury: 'In those places, having collected a throng of Christ's servants, he taught them to observe a rule of regular life, to the extent that these ignorant folk were able to receive it' (Colgrave & Mynors 1969, 285, III.22). 'Christ's servants' were necessarily local men and new converts who were to become monks in two new focal foundations.

Cedd was accustomed to an ecclesiastical system which centred on monastic houses – primarily, but not exclusively, Iona and Holy Island – and naturally set about duplicating this pattern in his own new see. The contrast has frequently been drawn between the Irish-type, coastal or riverine, marginal sites of these churches and Mellitus's earlier reuse of Roman London (eg Mayr-Harting 1991, 100–1). The comparison is, however, less than adequate on its own as an explanation of the sites chosen: firstly, *Othona* was a Roman masonry fort of Saxon Shore type which had closer similarities to London than Holy Island, as had the church Cedd supposedly commissioned for the site (Stenton 1971, 111, 121); secondly, neither is likely to have been an island, and there were such available; thirdly, it is strange that Cedd should have developed two focal sites for the diocese of a single people when all precedents imply that one would have sufficed. It is not an adequate response to simply ignore Tilbury as most modern writers have done (excepting Campbell 1986, 99, whose interest lay in the nomenclature).

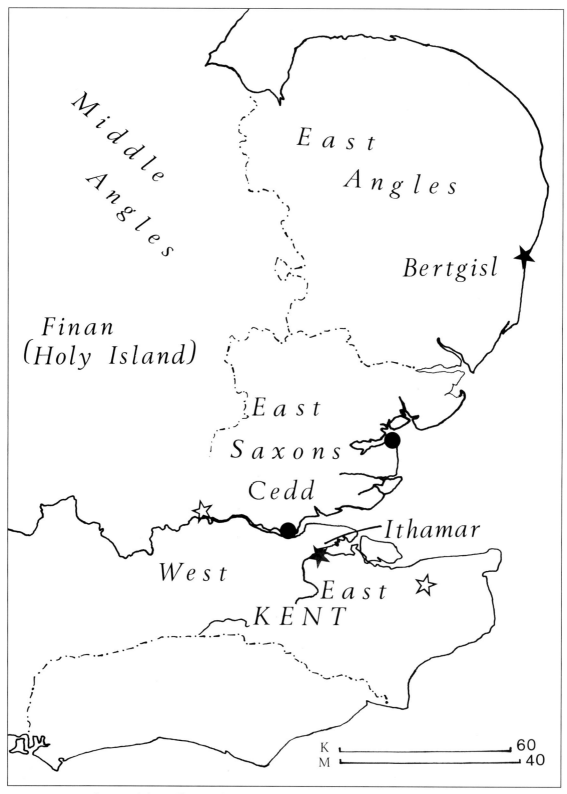

Fig 8.1. Bishops and dioceses in south-east England in 654. Circles represent Holy Island's authority, stars that of Canterbury. Vacant sees are represented by the symbol in outline only. Some pre-1974 shire boundaries have been added for guidance purposes only.

Cedd's foundations may, therefore, indicate that factors other than the particular value-system of the Ionan church were in play. To place the locations chosen in context, it is noticeable that Æthelberht of Kent had earlier established bishops for the West Kentings and East Saxons on the very edges of their respective territories, at sites which offered significant advantages to a king whose influence was based on East Kent (Fig 8.1). A similar phenomenon occurred later in Northumbria, with the establishment of a diocesan centre for the Picts at Abercorn in Bernicia, a short boat trip from Pictland. It seems likely that Cedd's foundations were subject to comparable considerations, acting as both necessarily did as foci of external influence in a client kingship.

Firstly, the location of Bradwell-on-Sea: when Oswiu had dealings with Kent early in his reign, his ambassador, the priest Utta, travelled overland but brought Eanflæd back by sea (Colgrave & Mynors 1969, 260, III.15). A decade or so earlier, Æthelburh and Paulinus had retired to Kent from Deira by boat (Colgrave & Mynors 1969, 204, II.20). Given the difficulty of maintaining contact between Northumbria and Essex in the early 650s across a Mercian-dominated hinterland, it seems likely that Cedd and his colleagues normally travelled by sea. In that case, the Roman fort and fleet base at Bradwell-on-Sea offered an apposite focus for a Northumbria-centric cult at the very bridgehead of Oswiu's influence. Thence, with local royal support, his clergy could effectively marginalize rival cult centres and refocus cult and ritual on themselves. *Othona* therefore resembles Æthelberht's earlier redevelopment of London and the locality of both should be interpreted in a broadly colonial role, as part of the wider strategy of *imperium*-wielding or seeking kings.

Secondly Tilbury: this is a rather different proposition, yet similar logic may have lain behind its foundation. On the edge of the Thames at a place whose name already implied some defensible properties, its most striking feature is its close proximity by boat to West Kent. If Oswiu and Cedd were seeking to refocus the Rochester diocese on a new Ionan-Bernician foundation, then Tilbury seems a good choice: like Rochester, it lay just the width of a river-crossing from West Kent but inside territory secured by royal protection; like Rochester, it offered access to Watling Street, the principal arterial road across northern Kent; like Rochester, it offered access by droveways and river valleys to the west Kentish hinterland (Everitt 1986 *passim*); lastly, it was about as close to Rochester as circumstances and the geography of the East Saxon kingdom would permit (Fig 8.1).

There can be no certainty, of course, but Cedd's foundation of a focal site at Tilbury at precisely the time when Canterbury was in crisis lends itself to interpretation as a Bernician attempt to replace the Romanist church of Kent, much as Holy Island had earlier replaced York. Given that Ithamar was the sole bishop then active in Kent, Cedd's instructions may even have been to effect what amounts to a reverse takeover of the entire southern archdiocese, from an initial foothold in its least successful province – that of the long bishopless and pagan East Saxons. Behind Cedd, one must again see the interests of Oswiu, whose agent he undoubtedly was (Higham 1997, 235–7). From the perspective of the Bernician king, the dispatch of clergy and then, once detailed information came back to him, of a bishop to the East Saxons arguably reflects colonial and imperial pretensions and the desire to expand his own influence deep into the heartland of the Roman church in England.

CONCLUSION

These two case studies illustrate the interconnection of dynastic and religious policy in Northumbria even as early as 642–54. Aidan's involvement in Oswiu's conflict with Oswine underlines the importance of episcopal support to one or other side in a struggle between rival dynasts. His attitude was arguably determined by a breach of one of numerous behavioural changes which Christianity demanded of its adherents, but his preference for Oswine was a critical factor in the race for control of Northumbria. Cedd's subsequent career as bishop to the East Saxons illustrates the potential of the Ionan-Bernician church as a vehicle for the acquisition and consolidation of Bernician influence over distant kingships and kingdoms. Christianity was, *ab initio*, integral to the wider political aspirations of kings, who generally supported mission as an instrument of their own outreach.

CHAPTER 9

The Anglo-Saxon Monastery at Hartlepool, England

Robin Daniels

INTRODUCTION

This chapter summarizes for the first time the range of archaeological information available for the Anglo-Saxon monastery at Hartlepool and puts forward a suggestion for the location of the focus of the monastery. Hartlepool (NZ 529 337) is one of the most extensively explored of the Northumbrian monasteries of the 7th to 8th centuries and excavations have revealed evidence of buildings, boundaries and cemeteries, as well as artefacts of international significance. Five major sites have been investigated (Fig 9.1): the Cross Close cemetery which yielded the name stones in the 19th century, Lumley Street excavated by Durham University and Hartlepool Archaeological and Historical Society in 1968, Church Walk excavated in 1972 and 1976 by Durham University and Cleveland County Archaeology Section respectively and Church Close excavated in 1984, again by Cleveland County Archaeology Section (now Tees Archaeology). Additional investigations have yielded further information which add to the picture but do not make a significant contribution.

In the 640s a monastery was established at 'Heruteu' by Heiu; this was given into Hild's hands by Aidan and she then set about reorganizing the community under Aidan's guidance. In 655 King Oswiu of Northumbria gave his daughter, Ælfflæd, into Hild's care at 'Heruteu' following his success at the battle of Winwæd. In 657 land at 'Streanæshalch' (Whitby) was given to Hild for her to found a monastery and she moved there, retaining control of the monastery at 'Heruteu'. Once Hild moved to Whitby ecclesiastical and royal attention moved with her and 'Heruteu' disappears from the record (Colgrave & Mynors 1969, 293, 407–9, III.24, IV.23).

Hartlepool had been traditionally associated with the monastery at 'Heruteu' and this identification was confirmed by the find of the inscribed stones at Cross Close in the 19th century, and the accumulation of evidence since.

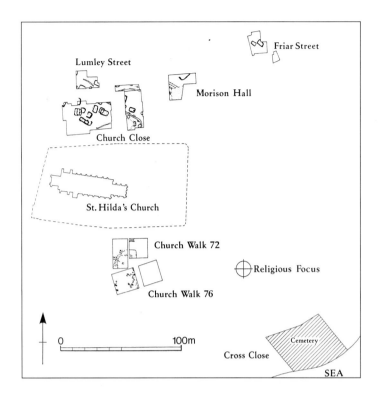

Fig 9.1. The archaeological evidence for the Anglo-Saxon monastery at Hartlepool.

LUMLEY STREET 1968 AND CHURCH CLOSE 1984

These two sites lie in close proximity to each other; Lumley Street has been examined by Cramp (1976a) and Church Close published in the *Archaeological Journal* (Daniels 1988; 1990). Both of these sites recovered the ground plans of small timber buildings (Fig 9.2) with an initial period of post-in-trench and post-hole construction followed by the insertion of stone footings. The transition to stone-footed timber buildings is particularly significant as this type of construction was also encountered at Whitby (Rahtz 1976b, 461) and in both cases the transition seems to date to the mid-8th century. At Church Close this date is provided by coinage associated with occupation material within one of the stone-footed structures.

The size of the buildings is of particular note in that they are much smaller than the 'hall' type buildings associated with secular sites of this period and could only have been used by one or at most two individuals. This has social implications which suggest that a monastic context is the only possible reason for such a quantity of buildings of this size. These buildings have been interpreted as monastic cells provided for individual study and worship, perhaps the manifestation of the structures at Coldingham described by Bede (Colgrave & Mynors 1969, 425, IV.25).

Three different types of boundary features were present at Church Close and Lumley Street: a substantial palisade-type boundary; a lighter subdividing fence

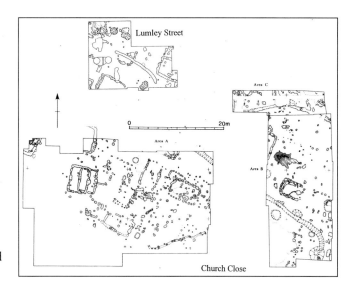

Fig 9.2. The earthfast timber buildings from Church Close and Lumley Street.

line; and a clear space containing no features. The palisade ran NW–SE across the site and represents a substantial enclosure boundary of two phases; the first comprised a sequence of substantial post pits which would have been linked by fencing and the second consisted of a palisade trench which terminated at the southern edge of the Church Close site, indicating an entrance to an enclosure at this point. The size of this boundary structure suggests that it served to compartmentalize a part of the monastic precinct; presumably visual and physical access to this enclosure was strictly controlled.

The enclosure defined by the palisade was subdivided by a light fence line which was aligned NE–SW and was probably joined to the palisade, although this was not seen. The fence line again had an opening at its east end and terminated in a slight return at its west end. The majority of the buildings were set inside the area defined by these two features. The SW boundary to the group of buildings, comprising an empty space, is of particular interest. It is not an accident of archaeological recovery; in contrast to all the adjacent areas there were no features at all cut into the bedrock, and this would seem to suggest the use of space as a delineator and may indicate that this enclosure had some kind of focus towards the south-west.

None of the artefacts recovered from Lumley Street and Church Close is of a high quality and none is particularly indicative of the sex of the occupants of the site; however, the recovery of metalworking material from the fill of the palisade trench at Church Close and an ingot mould from Lumley Street (Cramp pers comm) was significant. Examination of the material revealed that non-ferrous metals including silver were being worked, as was enamel; this suggests high quality metalwork and is confirmed by the moulds. There were three decorated moulds of which the most important was a complete mould depicting a calf, the symbol of

107

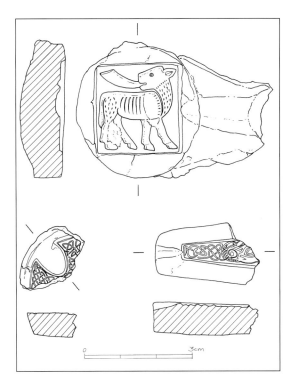

Fig 9.3. The clay moulds from Church Close. Scale 2:1.

St Luke with a back-turned head and trumpet (Fig 9.3). This 'trumpeting' symbol is also seen in the *Lindisfarne Gospels* and indicates that a full knowledge of the contemporary imagery of Christianity was present at Hartlepool, as were craftsmen of sufficient skill to execute exquisite pieces. Radiocarbon dating from the earlier phases at Church Close provided a date of 658–687 (Daniels 1990, 407).

CHURCH WALK 1972 AND 1976 (FIG 9.4)

These sites were excavated by J. Hinchcliffe for Durham University and M.M. Brown for Cleveland County Archaeology Section. Neither has been published, although a draft report for Church Walk 1972 has been prepared and I have produced a working draft report of the 1976 excavations.

The two excavations revealed different parts of the same cemetery with the additional recovery of a building in the northern part of the 1972 excavation. A clear boundary was seen to the cemetery along its north and part of its eastern edges; the type of boundary defining this edge is, however, unclear and a hedge line had been suggested. Within, the cemetery space was used as the major divider between clearly distinct groups of burials and in this the cemetery echoes the use of space at Church Close.

The cemetery contained male, female and infant burials oriented NW–SE and laid out in rows; the orientation is similar to that of the Church Close buildings

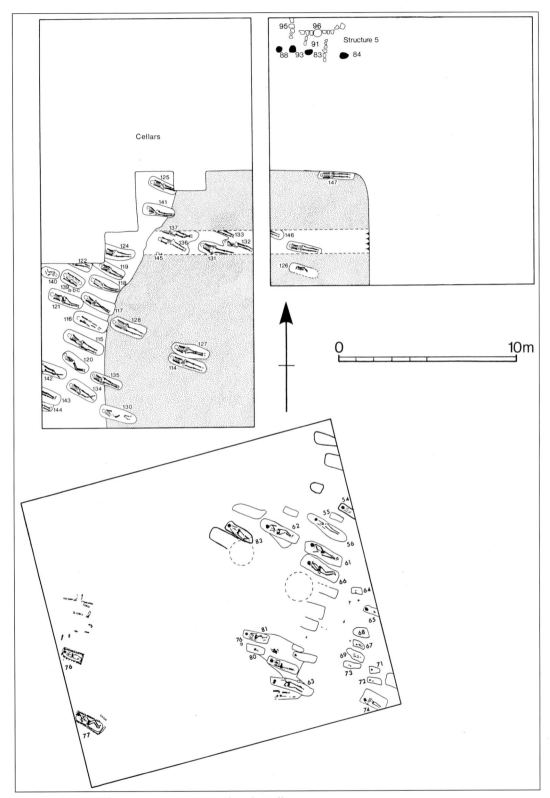

Fig 9.4.   The 7th-century cemetery at Church Walk.

but very different from that of the present church. The total number of burials excavated was c 77 but the full extent of the cemetery is unknown and even within the excavation areas a considerable number were not excavated. This would indicate at least 106 burials being contained within the cemetery and the figure may be considerably in excess of this. Five radiocarbon dates have been obtained for the site and once calibrated and combined these yield a combined date range of 678–782 (Jordan pers comm), which places the cemetery firmly within the datespan of the monastery.

It is possible to discern five distinct groups within the cemetery: group A consists of three rows of adult burials in the north-eastern part of the site; group B comprises a concentration of infant burials in the south-east corner of the cemetery; group C, a concentration of burials focused on a primary interment in a coffin with iron fittings; and group D represents a number of graves (see below) with pebble edgings around the top (comprising at least one adult and one infant burial). Group E may be a later extension of group A containing at least six distinct rows of adult burials.

There is insufficient space within this chapter to explore the full significance of these groupings, but the cemetery certainly demonstrates horizontal groupings probably of social and religious as well as chronological significance. It is suggested that this cemetery represents a lay population which had close links to the monastery, and the cemetery is certainly viewed as a component of the monastic organization.

CROSS CLOSE CEMETERY

This cemetery was first discovered in 1833 by workmen building houses and all subsequent finds from it have been in the context of construction work rather than archaeological excavation. It is from this cemetery that the Hartlepool inscribed stones originate. No similar finds have been made from Church Walk and this must lead to the conclusion that this was the most important cemetery of the monastery and that the names of the stones relate to the monks and nuns of the monastery. I do not intend to describe the finds of this cemetery any further, as Okasha has already done so (see below; cf Cramp 1984, 97–101, 153). I would, however, like to make two points about the site.

The first concerns its N–S orientation and the reported presence of objects in at least one of the graves. As Okasha points out, this may well indicate a pre-Christian date for this cemetery, but if this is so there must have been a considerable imperative at work to result in the new Christian community respecting the same alignment and using the same cemetery. Such an imperative may have been rooted in the status of Hartlepool as a royal estate and conjures up the possibility that it functioned as a relatively important royal centre in the first half of the 7th century.

The second point about this cemetery is that there is a hierarchy within the cemetery ranging from the highest status burials with inscribed stones and pillow-stones, to burials with only pillow-stones, and lastly unaccompanied burials. There is also an impression from the descriptions that the inscribed stone/pillow-stone burials occupy the northern edge of the cemetery; did this place them in closer proximity to the religious focus of the site?

ADDITIONAL SITES

While none of the other sites have revealed significant remains from the monastery, they do add to the picture and the table below sets out the type of remains encountered in all the Hartlepool sites which have revealed information about the Anglo-Saxon monastery. I would draw particular attention to the find from Baptist Street.

In 1995 a small-scale excavation was mounted here in one of the few opportunities to carry out archaeological excavation in the vicinity of the Cross Close cemetery. No burials were recovered, indicating that the Cross Close cemetery did not extend this far north; however, a fine gilded silver alloy disc-headed pin depicting confronting animals was recovered. The pin adds to the number of high quality objects found in this immediate area.

EXCAVATIONS	FINDS	BUILDINGS	BOUNDARIES	CEMETERIES
Cross Close	*			*
Lumley Street 1968	*	*	*	
Church Walk 1972		*	*	*
Church Walk 1976			*	*
Church Close 1984	*	*	*	
Morison Hall 1987			*	
Friar Street 1987		*		
Baptist Street 1995	*			

Table 9.1: Investigations in Hartlepool yielding evidence of the Anglo-Saxon monastery.

DISCUSSION: THE LOCATION OF THE MONASTIC FOCUS

The monastery at Hartlepool contained both monks and nuns and it may therefore be incorrect to speak of a single focus, though Bede's references to Whitby, organized by Hild in the same way as Hartlepool, give no indication of more than one focal area for the monastery. The question stands as to where this could have been at Hartlepool.

It was generally supposed that the present church of St Hilda, built at the end of the 12th century, occupied the position of any earlier churches at Hartlepool. There are, however, two arguments against this. The first is the complete absence of any 7th- or 8th-century stonework from the present church or its vicinity. There is nothing built into the fabric, nothing loose, and certainly nothing *in situ* in the existing fabric. This is in marked contrast to the administrative centres of the monastic estates of Hartlepool, all three of which (Billingham, Hart and Greatham), have extant or surviving evidence, however fragmentary, of early stone churches. It would seem unlikely that stone churches were commissioned at these locations and not at the monastery itself. The total absence of remains must therefore be a result of their total demolition and location elsewhere than the vicinity of the present church.

A range of archaeological evidence, somewhat circumstantial but nonetheless convincing, has now accumulated to suggest an alternative location for the monastic focus. The most compelling of these pieces of evidence is the location of the Cross Close cemetery. If this is accepted as the earliest and most important cemetery, containing the professed of the monastery and their inscribed stones, then it is inconceivable that this should be removed a great distance from the church(es). It would seem very strange if the lay (?) cemetery at Church Walk was situated closer to the religious focus of the site than the cemetery of the monks and nuns.

The Church Walk cemetery may also offer a clue as to the location of the religious focus. The positioning of the infant burials at the Church Walk cemetery, in its south-east corner, would echo a theme seen elsewhere in cemeteries of this period, where infant burials were sited as close as possible to the church. The two cemeteries could therefore be seen to provide pointers to a religious focus which lay to the immediate north of Cross Close and to the east or south-east of the Church Walk cemetery.

Such a location is reinforced by even more circumstantial evidence of artefact distributions. The finds from Church Close and Lumley Street comprise everyday objects supplemented by evidence of high quality metalworking and artistic skills. The high quality objects were not, however, being used in this area. The part of the monastery which has produced high quality artefacts is the Cross Close area, with the inscribed stones and latterly the fine gilded silver alloy disc-headed pin found to the immediate north of the Cross Close site. These objects define this area as being that of the 'consumption' of high quality artefacts, as one might expect at the centre of the establishment.

The end of the Anglo-Saxon monastery at Hartlepool does not seem to have come violently; none of the sites excavated shows any sign of a Viking onslaught and we must perhaps view the end as a process of decay as the interlinked system of Northumbrian monasteries fell apart in the political troubles of the late 8th and 9th centuries. We can only hope that it will be possible to carry out further archaeological work in Hartlepool to test some of the hypotheses set out above.

ACKNOWLEDGEMENTS

I would like to thank Dr Okasha for allowing me to see the text of her chapter before publication, Peter Hart-Allison of Tees Archaeology for the illustrations, and Pip Daniels for reading and commenting on the text.

CHAPTER 10

THE INSCRIBED STONES FROM HARTLEPOOL

Elisabeth Okasha

INTRODUCTION

Between July 1833 and April 1985 a considerable number of skeletons and at least ten inscribed stones were found at Hartlepool (Cramp 1984, 97–101, 153, pls 84.429–85.449, 154.800). Most were unearthed during building work, although the stone most recently found was discovered during excavation. Similar inscribed stones have been found at Whitby, Lindisfarne and other places in the north of England and these bear a resemblance to some inscribed stones from Scotland and Ireland. The Hartlepool stones are generally accepted to be of 8th-century date and the cemetery to belong to the Anglo-Saxon monastery which was founded in the 7th century. Traditionally it has been assumed that the monastery was destroyed by the Vikings in the 9th century. However, the monastic buildings, located and excavated in the 1980s, showed no signs of deliberate destruction and, as Daniels suggested, it may be that the monastery simply declined (Daniels 1988, 202).

Since 1833 many people, myself included, have written a great deal about these inscribed stones, in particular about the language, script and likely date of their texts. Rather less has been written on the find-reports of the stones although they were discussed by Haigh (1846), Brown (1919) and Scott (1956). A fresh and critical reading of these reports can help to answer three questions: firstly, where was this cemetery located? Secondly, what was the orientation of the burials in the cemetery? Thirdly, what was the function of the inscribed stones in the cemetery?[1]

DISCOVERY AND SUBSEQUENT HISTORY OF THE STONES

Hartlepool 0, along with stones 1, 2, 3, 4 and 5, was found in July 1833 in a field called 'Cross Close' adjoining Hartlepool Moor. In 1858 Haigh recorded the stone as lost (Haigh 1858, 18) but in 1875 he said that it, along with the others, was still in existence (Haigh 1875, 366). This 1875 article, however, is inaccurate even by Haigh's standards and, in view of his earlier statement, it is likely that he was in error here. The stone has never reappeared but fortunately rubbings of it are preserved in the library of the Society of Antiquaries in London. The rubbings were done by or at the instigation of a local man, Sir Cuthbert Sharp, and drawings from them were made to accompany Gage's article (Gage 1836). These drawings are also kept in the Society of Antiquaries' library. In 1956 Scott remarked in a rather caustic footnote that no one who had written about this stone had ever actually seen it (Scott 1956, 211–2 n 48). Strictly speaking, this is true, but the rubbings still exist and can be examined without difficulty.

Hartlepool 1 was also found in July 1833 and Haigh said that it was still in existence in 1875. However, in the light of his account of stone 0, this cannot be taken as certain. Hartlepool 1 was recorded as lost in 1901 (Chadwick 1901, 83) but by 1921 it was in Ipswich Museum at which date it was assigned a re-accession number: 1921–56.9. The museum's register entry is undated but is in the handwriting of Guy Maynard who was curator from 1920 to 1953. It states that the stone had been donated by a Mrs Bulmer and that it was returned to Hartlepool under the following circumstances:

A young domestic servant from Hartlepool was on holiday in Suffolk and came to Ipswich where she saw the Hildred stone in the Museum. She subsequently told her employer – a nonconformist minister who informed the municipal council with the result that a request to the Ipswich Council for the return of the stone was made. The approval of the representatives of the finder who had settled in Ipswich was obtained and the Ipswich council authorized the transfer.

This transfer was in or before 1928 (— 1928, 524).

In 1956, however, a different version of this story was published by Scott, whose information was taken from the papers of his late grandfather, Mr C.I. Smyth, who may perhaps have been the clergyman in question (Scott 1956, 210 n 1). According to Scott, the builder who found the stone had given it to a timber merchant whose daughter, a Mrs Ensor, had presented it to Ipswich Museum where it was seen by a former clergyman of Hartlepool (Scott 1956, 196). By 1956 the stone was in St Hilda's Church, Hartlepool, where it remains.

Hartlepool 2 and Hartlepool 4 were also found in July 1833 and were acquired by Sir Cuthbert Sharp who exhibited them at the Society of Antiquaries in London in 1835. In July 1845 he presented the stones to the Society of Antiquaries of Newcastle upon Tyne and they are kept in the Museum of Antiquities in Newcastle.

Hartlepool 3 and Hartlepool 5 were also found in July 1833 and, along with stone 7, passed into the hands of the Revd William Greenwell of

Durham. This is likely to have been before 1858 since Haigh said that some of the stones from Hartlepool were then owned by Greenwell (Haigh 1858, 17). Items from Greenwell's antiquarian collection were subsequently acquired by A.W. Franks and in March 1880 he presented the Hartlepool stones to the British Museum where he was Keeper of British and Medieval Antiquities and Ethnography. The stones have remained in the British Museum since then.

Hartlepool 6 was found in October 1838 by workmen digging a cellar in South Terrace, Hartlepool, close to where the earlier finds had been made. The *Gateshead Observer* of 20 October 1838 noted that:

> The men have been offered a sovereign by one gentleman, and by the Greek Professor of Durham University, Mr. Jenkyns, two guineas for the stone; but we trust that the possession of the relic will be reserved for the Antiquarian Society of Newcastle.

However, whether through the offices of Professor Jenkyns or otherwise, the stone went to Durham Cathedral Library where it remains. It was first recorded there in 1894 (Hodges 1894, 6–7), but it may well have been there by 1858 since in that year Haigh mentioned 'the museum at Durham' as one of the places where Hartlepool stones were kept (Haigh 1858, 17).

Hartlepool 7 was found in September 1843 by workmen cutting a drain in South Terrace. Greenwell acquired it and in March 1880 it, along with stones 3 and 5, was presented by Franks to the British Museum where it remains.

Hartlepool 8 was found in October 1843 near to where stone 7 had been found, also during the digging of a drain. Haigh acquired this stone, perhaps as a result of his appeal in 1858 (see below) and in July 1859 he presented it to the British Museum where it remains. In 1844 it was stated that two out of stones 6, 7 and 8 'have been deposited in the college at Durham. One of the latter stones is in the possession of the clergyman's son' (— 1844, 188). If the first part of this statement refers to stones 6 and 7, it is not inconsistent with the history of these stones as outlined above. The second part is less easy to understand since no clergyman had previously been mentioned in the article and his identity, and that of his son, remains obscure.

Between 1843 and 1985 there is no record of the discovery of any further inscribed stones from Hartlepool. Other discoveries, however, were made. In October 1921 workmen found the remains of a skeleton on the promenade in front of South Crescent. In November 1921 this area was reopened and examined and parts of five other skeletons were found but no inscribed stones (Jones 1922, 141–3). Scott notes that in 1932 another skeleton was dug up by workmen, again without any stones being observed, but it is unclear exactly where this discovery was made. Stones with markings were found during construction of a bathing pool but, despite instructions to the contrary, these were destroyed (Scott 1956,

197, 210 n 11). Between 1972 and 1976 excavations were undertaken at Church Walk, near St Hilda's Church. An extensive early cemetery was found but neither plain nor inscribed stones.

Hartlepool 9 was discovered in April 1985 in a medieval cesspit during excavation of Church Close. It is now owned by Hartlepool Museums Service.

These ten stones, nine existing and one preserved only through rubbings, are all that now remain though others were apparently found. In the *Durham Advertiser* of 26 July 1833 it was stated on page 2 that:

> . . . from the circumstance of these stones having been much scattered and got into different hands, the opportunity of comparing them together has been lost to the public.

In 1858 Haigh said that of the stones discovered in 1833, both inscribed and uninscribed, 'the most were dispersed immediately after their discovery'. However, one was apparently 'purchased on the spot, by a commercial gentleman' and another was 'conveyed to York' (Haigh 1858, 17). Haigh expressed the hope that the then owners of the stones would communicate rubbings or tracings of them to the Society of Antiquaries of Newcastle, or to the publisher of his book. It is possible that it was as a result of this appeal that Haigh acquired stone 8 since there is no mention of his owning it until he presented it to the British Museum in 1859. Apart from this, there is no record that any of the owners of the stones paid attention to Haigh's helpful suggestion. He added an amusing anecdote:

> The ready sale which these stones commanded, on their discovery, encouraged one of the labourers employed, to fabricate a stone similar to No. 5, which he afte[r]wards *discovered* in a railway cutting, at Sandy, in Bedfordshire, and sold to a lady, who presented it to the Bedford museum (Haigh 1858, 18).

This stone seems to have vanished without trace.

FIND-REPORTS OF THE 1833 FINDS

Five reports appeared within the two years following the finding of stones 0–5 in 1833. The first was in the *Durham Advertiser* of 12 July 1833. Here it was reported on page 3 that 'Within the last few days, a great number of human skulls and other remains of mortality' had been discovered by workmen who were digging for the foundations of a house 'in a field adjoining Hartlepool Moor'. It was reported that no skeleton was complete but no mention was made of the orientation of the bodies. The article continued:

The heads of the deceased seemed to have been all placed, when interred, either on or against a square or oblong flagstone, ornamented with some device, and apparently bearing an inscription in Saxon or other characters.

The second report was in the same newspaper, on 26 July 1833, page 2, and contains further details. We learn that the location of the finds was 'on the southern part of the promontory of Hartlepool' and that the skeletons 'were all found lying from north to south'. In addition the inscribed stones were described as 'monumental or head-stones'. A third report on page 3 of the same newspaper appeared on 2 August 1833 accompanying illustrations of stones 1 and 2. The date of the original find was there given as 6 July but no further details were added.

Newspaper reports today are not renowned for the minute accuracy of their information and it is hard to believe that the situation was much different in 1833. Nevertheless, there would have to be firm evidence for us to totally disregard these reports which record the find spot as a field beside Hartlepool Moor, on the southern promontory, and say that the skeletons, although not complete, were lying N–S. This much seems clear. As regards the location of the stones with respect to the bodies, the position is more ambiguous. The second report described the inscribed stones as 'monumental or head-stones' and I take the term 'head-stones' to mean 'stones standing at the head of the body'. The first report, however, stated that the skulls seemed to be 'on or against' an inscribed stone. Does this mean that some skulls were *on* and some were *against* an inscribed stone? Or does it mean that the finders were uncertain whether the skulls had been placed on or against the inscribed stones? This ambiguity is unfortunate, not least because people subsequently reading these reports understood them to have stated unequivocally that some inscribed stones were found beneath skulls.

The fourth report to appear was an anonymous article (initialled 'X.Y.') published in the *Gentleman's Magazine* (X.Y. 1833, 218–20). It states that the author knew of the earlier reports; nevertheless, a considerable amount of additional information is given. We learn that the finds were made about 135 yds south-east of the churchyard, in a field called 'Cross Close' and that the house whose foundations were being dug belonged to a Mr John Bulmer, presumably a relative of the Mrs Bulmer who presented stone 1 to Ipswich Museum. The skeletons were found about 3.5 ft below ground level and were 'lying in a position nearly north and south'. We are told that the 'bones were carefully removed under the superintendance [*sic*] of Mr. Bulmer and Mr. Ecles, and deposited in the church-yard'. The inference is that some of this additional information came from these two gentlemen who, if not eyewitnesses to the actual finding of the stones, were at least on the spot fairly soon afterwards.

The report continued:

A large number of the skulls were resting on small flat plain stones, varying from four to five inches square, and under a few were discovered stones bearing inscriptions, and marked with the cross.

If this were certainly information from Mr Bulmer and Mr Ecles, or other eyewitnesses, it would be very valuable evidence and would help elucidate the ambiguous earlier report. It may, or may not, be an eye-witness account. We would feel more confident about its authenticity if we knew who 'X.Y.' was (for example was he a local man, or did he travel to Hartlepool to talk to people?); if we knew who Mr Ecles was; if we were actually told the source of the additional information; and if we were certain that 'X.Y.''s article was altogether independent in its information of the *Durham Advertiser* reports.

The final report to appear soon after the finding of the stones was a letter dated 7 May 1835 from John Gage to Sir Henry Ellis, secretary of the Society of Antiquaries of London (Gage 1836). Gage remarked that he had tried to see more of these stones but had not been successful. He did not state whether or not he had visited Hartlepool but there is no evidence in his letter to suggest that he had. He gave his sources as the *Gentleman's Magazine* article and subsequent correspondence with Sir Cuthbert Sharp and the Revd William Knight of Hartlepool.

Gage states, on the authority of the *Gentleman's Magazine*, that the stones were found in the field called 'Cross Close', that the skeletons were lying on the inscribed stones and that the bodies were lying in a N–S direction. He gives as the authority for his additional information 'the testimony of Mr. Jackson, a respectable surgeon, who was present at the time the skeletons were found, and who assisted in removing them', this testimony having reached Gage from the Revd William Knight. Clearly they were having quite a party in the field at Hartlepool in early July 1833. With so many people around, it does not seem surprising that some of the stones disappeared but it does make more difficult the evaluation of what is, and what is not, reliable eyewitness evidence.

According to Gage, according to Jackson, the skeletons had been 'placed in order, close to each other' and 'the heads lay upon the stones, as upon pillows'. He continued:

These flat stones . . . are said to measure generally from four to five inches square, though some are larger; some have inscriptions cut upon them, and crosses, in relief, varying in form (Gage 1836, 480).

This picture of a neatly excavated cemetery, with all the bodies lying tidily in rows, each with their own pillow-stone, sounds a little idealized. It is perhaps to be seen as a polished report for the polite audience of the Society of Antiquaries in Burlington House. Certainly, it seems somewhat removed from the original newspaper reports. Nevertheless, although we must approach Gage's evidence cautiously, it cannot be dismissed. He gives us his authority as that of a man present when the bones were removed.

FIND-REPORTS OF THE 1838 FINDS

Four reports appeared in the year following the 1838 finds but only the first gives actual information, the rest all being dependent on it. This appeared in the weekly *Gateshead Observer* dated 20 October 1838. It was reported that workmen digging a cellar in South Terrace had found during the previous week 'several human bones, each skeleton having a flat stone beneath the head'. Subsequently, on the Monday of the week of issue, the men found stone 6 but it is not stated where it was found relative to the skeletons. The bodies were said to have lain 'in two lengths only, north and south' and the stones to have been about 1.5 ft from the surface. The report included an illustration of stone 6 and invited interpretation of its text.

In the next issue, on 27 October, an unnamed person described as 'a gentleman of great antiquarian research and of sound judgment' offered a reasonable interpretation of the text. Meanwhile, there appeared an anonymous account of the stone in the November issue of the *Gentleman's Magazine* (— 1838, 536). This stated that the information and illustration were from the *Gateshead Observer* and some of it is indeed taken verbatim. An interpretation of the text was also given. Finally, a paragraph appeared in the *Gateshead Observer* of 10 November 1838.

The first report of the 1838 finds confirms the location of the cemetery and the orientation of the skeletons. It also states that the skulls were lying on plain stones. It is possible that the workmen who found the skeletons, or the writer of the article, or both, were aware of the 1833 discoveries and so were on the look-out for stones beneath the heads of the skeletons. No indication is given, however, as to the location of the inscribed stone in relation to the skeletons, whether it was under or beside a skull. This suggests that the account may be a trustworthy one, offering description rather than interpretation of what was found.

FIND-REPORTS OF THE 1843 FINDS

Two reports appeared following the 1843 finds, the first being a brief mention in the *Gentleman's Magazine*. The stones were said to have 'lately been found in cutting a drain near the remains of the monastery at Hartlepool' (— 1843, 637). There is no mention of skeletons and no further details are given. The second report appeared anonymously in the *Gentleman's Magazine* for February 1844 accompanied by illustrations of stones 7 and 8 (— 1844, 187–8). The author cited earlier accounts before reporting that stone 7 was found in September 1843 by workmen 'cutting a drain near the South Terrace. . . . Close to the edge of the cliff'. The men thought that there were two graves about 4 ft beneath the ground but the skeletons were apparently incomplete since they found 'several bones, and at the spot where they supposed the head had rested' they found the inscribed stone. Some modern finds were also made. There is thus no evidence as to the orientation of the skeletons nor the relationship of the stone and the skeleton.

Stone 8 was found in October 1843 when a drain was being dug 'not far from the last'. The stone was found on top of a skeleton whose skull was 'resting on a small square stone'. Nearby was another skeleton 'taken up very perfect'. It was lying E–W and in this case also the skull was lying on a small square stone but 'neither of these pillow-stones had any inscription'. Two further skeletons were found lying on top of each other. This may imply that the bodies had been disturbed; no information was given as to their orientation or whether their heads lay on pillow-stones.

It seems clear from these reports that some bodies were interred with the heads resting on small plain pillow-stones and that at least one body was found lying E–W.

FIND-REPORTS OF THE 1921 FINDS

In October 1921 another skeleton was discovered in the same area. The report of this find appeared in the *Northern Daily Mail* of 14 October 1921. Workmen were digging 'in connection with the building of the new South Cliff Promenade', in front of South Terrace, when they came upon 'the remains of a skeleton'. After an account of the 19th-century finds the report continued: 'The skeleton now found was lying north and south, as was expected, but there was no stone under the head'. This firm statement would seem to be good evidence were it not that the report continued 'little of the skull remains except the teeth, which are wonderfully preserved'. If the skeleton was only 'remains' and the skull only teeth, we may legitimately enquire whether it was certain which way the body had been laid and where any pillow-stone might have been placed.

In November 1921 the site was reopened and an account given by the Revd Bertram Jones of Hartlepool (Jones 1922). This account confirmed that only the lower part of the body had been found earlier and that it had been lying N–S. The top part of the skeleton had fallen into the main town sewer located nearby. Excavation was then made 2 ft further west and two more sets of bones were discovered. Both bodies were lying N–S but the top parts had disappeared, presumably into the sewer. No stones were discovered. Further excavation 1 ft east of the original discovery was then undertaken. One thigh bone and a complete skeleton were found. The skeleton was lying N–S and underneath the skull was 'a flat stone . . . wedged in between other smaller stones'; these stones were all plain. Jones added that the 'soil surrounding the skull was minutely examined . . . but no sign or trace of any cut stone was found' (Jones 1922, 142).

The report continued:

A number of responsible witnesses who saw the stone [that is, the stone beneath the skull] in position are all firmly convinced that this resting-place of stone had been made for the head, and that the stone did not come there by chance, there being no similar stones found during the whole excavation (Jones 1922, 142–3).

One of these 'responsible witnesses' was a Mr Smyth who is referred to in a letter from S.F. Sainty to Baldwin Brown dated 26 November 1921. Unfortunately this letter has now disappeared but I saw it in the British Museum in 1964–5 and took careful notes from it. Sainty wrote that on reopening the site:

. . . other skeletons appeared, all in line with the previous one recently discovered. Only one had the skull remaining. . . . The one skull remaining of the skeletons exposed was resting upon an irregular shaped stone (local magnesian lime-stone) which was superimposed upon a similarly irregularly shaped piece. I took rubbings of the edges of these, and enclose tracing of same.

There was no sign of the tracing with the letter (Barty 1967, 270–1). Sainty's letter continued:

I fear nothing has been done in the ordered way one would have desired, but everything was unfavourable to this, and I was not able to get over myself until yesterday, the excavation being done on Thursday. The site is in a populous district where (as Mr Smyth remarked – and he was there all day in a heavy pall of fog) one was subject to the captious wit of a crowd imbued with prurient curiosity. The only gratification seems the confirmation of the site.

Sainty's concluding remark seems too pessimistic. Not only was the site of the cemetery confirmed but its known width was extended and the bodies were again found to be oriented N–S. If, as seems likely, one skull was found on a pillow-stone, this seems to have been rather different from the small square stones previously found beneath skulls. It may be that a slightly different burial practice was observed here.

FIND-REPORTS OF THE 1932 FINDS

In 1932 a skeleton was discovered while a gas pipe was being re-laid. This information was given to Scott by Mr H. Wilson, an employee of the Hartlepools Gas and Water Company. According to Scott, the skeleton was lying N–S 'but no stone was found on this occasion' (Scott 1956, 197). Scott notes that other discoveries may have taken place around this time:

A workman engaged in making the adjacent bathing-pool told Mr. H.R. Carter, verger of St. Hilda's, that stones with markings were then found, but, despite instructions, 'went into the concrete-mixings' (Scott 1956, 210 n 11).

These stones may or may not have been associated with the cemetery. Moreover, it is unclear whether Scott is referring to the bathing pool in the sea at the bottom of Baptist Street or to the paddling pool by the pier which was opened in July 1923.

FIND-REPORTS OF THE 1972 AND 1976 FINDS

In 1972 and 1976 excavations were conducted in the area adjacent to Church Walk, near St Hilda's Church by, respectively, John Hinchcliffe and Marilyn Brown.[2] A fairly extensive cemetery was found which has been dated by radio-carbon analysis to 678–782, suggesting that it was contemporary with the monastic buildings excavated in 1984–5. Daniels estimates that this cemetery contained at least 100 and perhaps as many as 130 individuals, of which more than one-third were infants. The bodies were laid NW–SE in rows. No grave goods were found but one burial appeared to have been in a coffin and some graves were pebble-edged. No inscribed stones were found, nor were any plain stones found under the skulls.

FIND-REPORTS OF THE 1985 FINDS

Stone 9 was discovered near the church, in Church Close. Excavations here established that this was the site of the early Anglo-Saxon monastery. The stone was found in a secondary context, a medieval cesspit (Daniels 1987, 274). Its finding does not therefore cast any light on the location or organization of either cemetery.

CONCLUSIONS

At the beginning of the chapter, three questions were posed. The first was, where was the cemetery containing the inscribed stones located? This can now be answered with some certainty.

The 19th-century finds were made in and around the field 'Cross Close' during the construction of houses in Henry Street and South Terrace, now South Crescent (Fig 10.1). No finds were noted when George Street or the streets further east were being constructed, nor in those west of Baptist Street (Daniels pers comm). (On the map, Baptist Street is the unnamed street immediately west of Henry Street.) In 1921 further finds were made in front of South Crescent, during the construction of South Cliff Promenade. Excavations some 25 m to the rear of South Crescent in 1985 and 1995 revealed no further traces of the cemetery (Daniels pers comm). The stones found during construction of the bathing or paddling pool must be disregarded since it is not clear where exactly they came from nor whether they were associated with the cemetery. The outer boundaries of the cemetery thus seem to have been Baptist Street to the west,

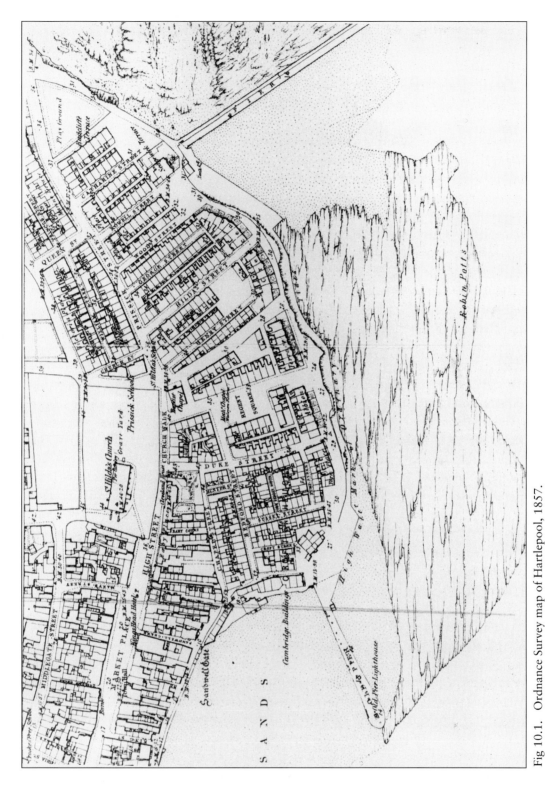

Fig 10.1.   Ordnance Survey map of Hartlepool, 1857.

George Street to the east, the back of South Crescent to the north and the sea cliff to the south.

The second question concerned the orientation of the burials in the cemetery; this too can now be answered. Around twenty-five burials are recorded: about thirteen separate ones and two groups described as containing several skeletons. All the burials seem to have been of adults and the bodies were buried in rows. Many of the bodies were oriented N–S; the orientation of a few was unclear and only one skeleton was found lying E–W. A comparison of the two cemeteries, both of which date from the 7th–8th centuries, would reward investigation.

The third question asked was: what was the function of the inscribed stones in the cemetery? The 1833 find-reports allow at least three interpretations of the evidence. The first is that all, or nearly all, of the bodies were buried with the head resting on a stone, some being small and plain, others larger and inscribed. The second is that all, or nearly all, of the bodies were buried with the head resting on a stone, some being small and plain, others larger and inscribed, but in addition some bodies, presumably those without an inscribed stone in the grave, were buried with an inscribed head-stone above the grave. The third is that all, or nearly all, of the bodies were buried with the head resting on a plain stone, but in addition, some were given a head-stone above the grave, in the centuries since interment, the head-stones fell into the graves so that by 1833 it was not possible to distinguish where they had been placed originally.

The 1838 reports suggest that all the skeletons discovered then had the skulls resting on plain stones. The 1843 reports suggest that some skeletons had the skulls resting on plain stones but that other skeletons were disturbed. Neither set of reports provides clear evidence as to where the inscribed stones were found. The 1921 reports note that the only complete skeleton found had the skull lying on a small plain stone but a stone that may have been of a different shape from those found previously. No inscribed stone was found on this occasion. The one skeleton found in 1932 had no stone of any sort found with it.

Unfortunately, the existing material evidence does not help us to choose between the three possibilities. No small plain stone found in use as a 'pillow' has been preserved. Of the eight surviving inscribed stones, some are considerably more weathered than others. Stone 6, for example, is hardly weathered at all while stone 5 is badly deteriorated. A stone standing for some time above a grave might become more weathered than one that had always been interred. Alternatively, could one accept Brown's idea (1919, 205) that the stones were placed recumbent rather than erect as head-stones? In this case, some might have been quickly covered with soil, thus preserving them, while others remained on the surface and became weathered. The problem with both these sets of arguments is that the stones are not all geologically identical, so like is not being compared with like. The atmospheric and soil conditions presumably weathered some sorts of stone more, and more quickly, than others.

Some, again for example Brown (1919, 206), argued that a stone inscribed 'pray for so-and-so' must have been addressing a human audience; he goes on to say that this does not, however, imply that they were originally located above ground. It seems to me that, were the stones addressing a human audience, they must certainly have been visible above ground. However, I have suggested elsewhere that such inscribed texts could also have been addressing a divine audience, God and the saints, and in this case it would not matter where the stone was placed (Okasha 1995, 71).

So which of the three interpretations is likely to be correct? Certainty is clearly impossible, but my preference is for the third: that the bodies were buried with most but not all of the heads resting on a small plain stone. Some of the bodies were distinguished by being given an inscribed stone above the grave. I do not think that there is sufficient evidence to be sure whether these were recumbent or free-standing. With the passing of time, these inscribed stones fell into the graves. On their discovery it then appeared as if they had been actually buried with the bodies.

ACKNOWLEDGEMENTS

The map is reproduced by kind permission of Alan Godfrey Maps of Newcastle. Dr Steven Plunkett, Keeper of Archaeology, Ipswich Borough Council Museum, kindly supplied me with a copy of the register entry relating to Hartlepool 1 and gave me permission to quote from it. I am most grateful to Robin Daniels for his help and for putting at my disposal his unpublished work on the Hartlepool excavations. Needless to say, he is not responsible for conclusions that I have drawn from his work.

NOTES

1. The stones are published in Okasha 1971 and Okasha 1992. They are numbered here as in these publications, the numbering being based on that of Haigh 1846.
2. I am most grateful to Robin Daniels for providing me with information about these excavations.

CHAPTER 11

WHITBY, JARROW AND THE COMMEMORATION OF DEATH IN NORTHUMBRIA

Catherine E. Karkov

Very little is known for certain about the monastery of Whitby and its first abbess, Hild. It is unclear whether the site identified by Bede and his contemporaries as *Streanæshalch* is the site now called Whitby, although no satisfactory alternatives have been suggested. It is clear from the documentary sources that the monastery was an educational centre and the burial place of royalty, although the material evidence for these functions is ambiguous. Similarly, while Bede describes the abbey's first abbess, Hild, as a wise, important and saintly woman, aside from denouncing Wilfrid to the Pope and dying, there is no record of anything she said or did. Most intriguingly, neither Hild's full name (and thus her full identity), nor the location of her grave and the manner of her burial have been preserved. The absence of Hild from the historical record has been a point of fascination for scholars interested in the histories of Bede, the poet Cædmon, and Anglo-Saxon monastic women (eg Fell 1981; Blair 1985; Hollis 1992; Lees & Overing 1994), but equally important is the absence of her corpse, memory, and commemoration from Whitby itself, not least because, ironically, this may say much about the active presence of other women in the Northumbrian church.

Quite a lot of evidence for the dead and their commemoration actually survives from Anglo-Saxon Whitby in the form of memorial sculpture and in the documentary record, particularly the *Life of Gregory*, originally written by a nun or monk of Whitby, probably between 704 and 714, but now surviving only in a 9th-century copy (*St Gall, Codex 567*). There is also a significant corpus of memorial monuments and written texts recording who the 'special dead' were and how they were commemorated at the monasteries of Wearmouth-Jarrow and

Lindisfarne, and a comparison of the evidence from these sites may have significance not only for our understanding of Whitby, but also of the relationship between these centres and the Northumbrian court during the 7th and 8th centuries.

All three monasteries enjoyed royal patronage. Lindisfarne was founded at the invitation of Oswald in 635; Whitby was founded in 657, possibly on one of the twelve grants of ten hides of land given to the church in 665 by Oswald's brother and successor, Oswiu (Colgrave & Mynors 1969, 292–3, III.24). Oswiu's son, Ecgfrith, donated fifty hides of land for the foundation of Wearmouth in 673, and a further forty hides for the foundation of Jarrow in 681/2. Only two of these kings seem to have been actively commemorated within the monasteries they helped to found. Oswald's head was buried at Lindisfarne and eventually placed in the coffin of St Cuthbert, and Lindisfarne became a part of the royal saint's cult, although it could not compete with Bamburgh which housed Oswald's incorrupt hand and arm. (As the arm was preserved through the blessing of Aidan, however, it too could be considered a Lindisfarne relic.) The rest of Oswald's bones were translated by his niece Osthryth to Bardney in Mercia.

Bede tells us that Oswiu was buried in the church of St Peter at Whitby, along with his wife, daughter, and 'many other nobles' (Colgrave & Mynors 1969, 293, III.24). Perhaps Ecgfrith was among them, for there is no special commemoration of him at Wearmouth-Jarrow. His name appears on the dedication stone at Jarrow, but this says only that the church of St Paul was dedicated in his reign, and does not assign him an active role in the foundation. Peter Brown (1996, 212) has, however, pointed out that:

> Like Sutton Hoo . . . [Wearmouth-Jarrow] spoke of the power of a ruler who could afford to cast so much wealth, beyond recall, into an institution closely connected with the remembrance of the dead.

One could also argue that despite Wearmouth-Jarrow's efforts to maintain its independence from local authority, the textual record produced by Bede has proved the most enduring form of commemoration for the Northumbrian court as a whole.

Virtually all our information on the religious founders also comes from Bede. Aidan died leaning against the buttress of his church on a royal estate near Bamburgh in 651. He was buried in the cemetery of the brothers at Lindisfarne and translated in the late 650s to the right (south) side of the altar in the newly built church of St Peter (Colgrave 1940, 273, *V Pros* 33). Aidan was commemorated not only by his tomb, but also by the relics taken to Ireland by Colman after the Synod of Whitby; by the miraculous preservation through two fires of the wooden buttress against which he had been leaning when he died; the cures worked by splinters from the buttress; the later (Romanesque) church built on the site; and by Bede's own words, which he explicitly states were a form of commemoration:

I have described in a straightforward manner those things which were done by him, praising such of his qualities as are worthy of praise and preserving their memory for the benefit of my readers (Colgrave & Mynors 1969, 264–7, III.17).

Aidan's cult was later eclipsed by that of Cuthbert who died in 687. Cuthbert's body was dressed in bishop's robes, wrapped in a cloth given to him by Abbess Verca, and placed in a stone sarcophagus, donated by Abbot Cudda, on the right side of the altar in the church of St Peter, Lindisfarne – presumably near to the body of Aidan, although neither Bede, nor Cuthbert's anonymous biographer state this. Cuthbert, as a number of scholars have noted (Campbell 1989, 11; Stancliffe 1989, 22; Thacker 1989, 113), usurped Aidan's position as founding father, or head of the Lindisfarne episcopal dynasty. Cuthbert's superior position is emphasized by his first translation in 698 to a more visible location within the church, the incorrupt state of his body which visibly seemed to hover between life and death, and the fact that it was his body and not Aidan's that attracted subsequent burials. Bishop Eadberht (d 698) was buried beneath Cuthbert in his original sarcophagus (Colgrave & Mynors 1969, 444–5, IV.30). Bede's account of this event in both the *Ecclesiastical History* and the prose *Life of Cuthbert* makes the relationship between the bishops explicit:

His body was placed in the sepulchre of the blessed Father Cuthbert and they put over it the coffin in which they had laid the incorrupt limbs of the father (Colgrave & Mynors 1969, 445, IV.30).

Eadberht's successor, Eadfrith, was buried near Cuthbert in 721 (Colgrave 1940, 311), as was the anchorite Œthelwold in 699 (Colgrave & Mynors 1969, 456–7, V.1). Cuthbert was further commemorated by a series of miracle-working relics (his shoes, chasuble, fragments from his oratory on Farne, pieces of his hair), by the *Lindisfarne Gospels*, written at least in part for him, and by three *Lives* in addition to sections in the *Ecclesiastical History*.

In both the textual and material record Cuthbert became the father of a family of saintly bishops, but Bede was also unwilling to let Aidan be forgotten. In the anonymous *Life* Aidan appears only in Cuthbert's vision of his death, so that within the narrative Cuthbert creates, or at least guarantees, Aidan's status as a saint. Bede's prose *Life* includes the vision, but adds that it was this event that caused Cuthbert to enter the monastic life: while Cuthbert is responsible for Aidan's saintly status, Aidan is responsible for Cuthbert's status as a monk and future saint; both men are reborn into a new life. Aidan reappears in the prose *Life* when Cuthbert enters Lindisfarne, Bede writing that Aidan was the first bishop of Lindisfarne and responsible for establishing the monastic and episcopal order that Cuthbert was now inheriting (Colgrave 1940, 208–9, V *Pros* 16).

The process by which Cuthbert's body replaces Aidan's as the focus of cult at Lindisfarne, and the fact that Bede manages to keep Aidan's memory alive (Stancliffe 1989, 22), may have considerable significance for our understanding of Hild's death and commemoration, or lack thereof, at Whitby. Hild, like Aidan, may have been relegated to obscurity by attempts to establish a new focus of cult.[1]

The surviving sources of information on Hild are exclusively textual, and here there is a problem because Hild's full name has nowhere been preserved. Hild is an abbreviated form or nickname, always appearing in Anglo-Saxon England as an element in a compound name such as Hildegyth or Hildeburh (Fell 1981, 78). Bede records that Hild's parents were Hereric and Breguswith, and that her sister was named Hereswith, a name which joins the first and last syllables of her parents' names. Hereswith's name thus unites and commemorates the identity of her parents as well as signifying her own lineage. Hild's abbreviated name, on the other hand, sets her apart from her own family.[2]

Bede is the only source of information on Hild's death, which was a good death, similar to those of Æthelthryth of Ely, Cædmon and Cuthbert. She was tried with a long and debilitating illness lasting seven years, during which time 'she never ceased to give thanks to her Maker and to instruct the flock committed to her charge both in public and in private', and she died urging her nuns to 'preserve the gospel peace among themselves and towards all others' (Colgrave & Mynors 1969, 413, IV.23). Æthelthryth died exulting in the pain from the tumour in her neck and the lesson in vanity that it provided (Colgrave & Mynors 1969, 395, IV.19). Cædmon ignored all signs of his illness and died assuring his monastic brothers of his charity towards them, and being assured in return of their charity towards him (Colgrave & Mynors 1969, 420–1, IV.24). Cuthbert, also racked by illness, died commanding his companions to maintain peace and charity, to study, and to have nothing to do with those who celebrated Easter at the wrong time (Colgrave 1940, 284–5, V Pros 39). One major difference between these deaths is that Bede gives us the words of Æthelthryth, Cædmon and Cuthbert, but not of Hild; we hear their voices, while Hild remains silent. Bede also neglects to say where or how Hild was buried, in contrast with Cuthbert, Æthelthryth, Aidan, Benedict Biscop, Ceolfrith and their successors at Wearmouth-Jarrow. Moreover, as in the anonymous *Life*'s version of Aidan's death, proof of Hild's sanctity is guaranteed only by the visions of others. A good death alone is not sufficient proof of sanctity; Cædmon, for example, never achieves sainthood despite his exemplary death.

There is a similar absence in Bede's first account of the foundation of Whitby (Colgrave & Mynors 1969, 290–1, III.24). The subject of the chapter is actually Oswiu, but Bede digresses to say that, in thanks for his victory over Penda of Mercia in 655, Oswiu pledged his infant daughter Ælfflæd to perpetual virginity, and that she entered the monastery at Hartlepool of which Hild was then abbess. Two years later she moved with Hild to Whitby:

. . . the king's daughter was first a pupil and then she became a teacher, of life under the Rule; then about the age of sixty, the blessed virgin [Ælfflæd] departed to be united with the heavenly bridegroom. She is buried in this monastery together with her father Oswiu, her mother Eanflæd, her grandfather Edwin, and many other nobles, all in the church of the holy apostle Peter (Colgrave & Mynors 1969, 293, III.24).

Neither Hild nor the whereabouts of her grave are mentioned and Bede returns immediately to the story of Oswiu. Bede's second account of Hild's move to Whitby (Colgrave & Mynors 1969, 408–9, IV.23) also distances her from the monastery's foundation, stating that she either founded, or set it in order, and that the task was appointed or imposed upon her. As Cuthbert eclipsed Aidan at Lindisfarne, so Ælfflæd and her family seem to have supplanted Hild at Whitby, and just as Bede emphasizes the saintliness of Aidan despite Cuthbert's superior status, so he provides information on Hild's praiseworthy qualities in spite of Ælfflæd's dominant presence. Bede cannot be held responsible for silencing Hild, or reducing her to the role of spiritual mother, although overall his treatment of women is, as many have noted, problematic (Hollis 1992, 128–9, 205–7; Lees & Overing 1994, *passim*). His discussion of Whitby is superficial in comparison to that of other monasteries – Lindisfarne, Ely, Barking, and Coldingham, for example. Moreover, he seems to silence Hild in favour of the patriarchal voices of Cædmon and himself, while his summary narrative of the 'central' events in Whitby's history – its foundation, the Cædmon story, the Synod of 664, and Hild's death – remove Hild physically from her own history. We neither hear her voice nor see her actions. However, Bede seems to have genuinely admired in Hild some of the same qualities he saw in Cuthbert and Aidan: humility, learning, devotion, charity, prudence, and the fact that she taught by personal example. If we learn nothing of her words, actions, or cult, it may be because she had already been relegated to obscurity by the time of Bede.

Hild died in 680 and was succeeded by the co-abbesses Eanflæd, whose date of death is unknown, but was probably c 704, and Ælfflæd, who died c 714. On the subject of Ælfflæd, Bede has much to say. In the *Ecclesiastical History* he seems to have nothing but praise for her, his words often echoing those applied to Hild. He commends her royal status, virginity, and wisdom, and grants her the 'weighty epithets' of *magistra* and *doctrix* (Thacker 1992, 143). But then the *Ecclesiastical History* depicts the Northumbrians as a chosen people and is dedicated to a Northumbrian king. Bede's portrait of Ælfflæd in his prose *Life of Cuthbert*, written for the monks of Lindisfarne, is markedly different. He still praises her; she is a 'venerable handmaiden of Christ', a virgin, a good mother to the nuns in her charge, and a woman who 'increased the nobility of a royal pedigree by the much more potent nobility of highest virtue' (Colgrave 1940, 231, V Pros 23), but his description of her actions portrays her as proud, foolish, over-emotional, worldly and far too concerned, perhaps, with matters outside the church. When incurably ill, rather than ignore the pain, or embrace it as evidence of her unworthiness and a sign that she is about to enter the eternal life of heaven – as do virtually all Bede's dying abbots, abbesses, bishops, saints, and cowherd/poets – she prays to Cuthbert for a cure, which she is granted. He sends her his girdle. The resulting miraculous cure is a testimony to his saintliness, but also to Ælfflæd's weakness (Colgrave 1940, 232–3, V Pros 23). The episode is not recorded in the anonymous Life of Cuthbert.

Immediately after her cure Ælfflæd meets Cuthbert on Coquet Island. Her concern appears to have been primarily with her secular family and the royal succession. She asked Cuthbert first to prophesy how much longer her brother Ecgfrith would live, and who would succeed him at his death. Bede tells us that she fell at Cuthbert's feet and begged him for an answer, burst into tears when she received one, then with feminine audacity (audacia feminea) began to ask about the succession (Colgrave 1940, 234–7, V Pros 24). Only after ascertaining that her half-brother Aldfrith would succeed did she ask Cuthbert whether or not he would accept the bishopric that her brother intended to offer him (Colgrave 1940, 102–5, 234–7, V Anon III.6, V Pros 24). The differences between the account of this incident in the anonymous Life and in Bede are well rehearsed (Hollis 1992, 109, 207); suffice it to say that while Ælfflæd's questions are no less persistent in the former (Colgrave 1940, 102–5, V Anon III.6), the description of her 'humbly' and politely kneeling at the saint's feet contains none of the emotional pleading, drama, and feminine audacity of Bede's version. Eddius Stephanus, in his Life of Wilfrid, implies that after Ecgfrith's death she continued to be privy to royal decisions during Aldfrith's reign. She and Abbess Æthelburh were the primary witnesses to Aldfrith's dying words, and it was Ælfflæd who made them public at the 706 council of Nidd, where she related that Aldfrith expected his son Osred to succeed him and desired peace with Wilfrid (Colgrave 1927, 130–3, lx). While she may have been acting according to Aldfrith's wishes, it is Ælfflæd's words that authorize both the succession and Wilfrid's reinstatement.

Bede's most critical portrait of Ælfflæd comes in the prose Life (Colgrave 1940, 261–5, V Pros 34), where Ælfflæd detains Cuthbert, who has come to Osingadun to dedicate one of her churches, at a 'carnal banquet' (carnalibus epulis). When Cuthbert drops his knife and turns his mind to spiritual matters Ælfflæd asks him why he has stopped eating, and receives the curt but, Bede assures us, humorous reply 'Can I eat all day?' The next day, when Ælfflæd learns that Cuthbert's vision of the death of a member of her community has proved true, she bursts into the dedication ceremony with 'woman-like astonishment [stupore femineo] as if she were announcing something new and doubtful'. In contrast, her behaviour in the anonymous Life is humble, reverent, and full of awe for the power of Cuthbert (Colgrave 1940, 126–9, V Anon IV.10).

Bede's description of Ælfflæd is no doubt exaggerated for the worse. To him, her political interests and 'extramural' activities would have been anathema, compared with those of Hild, whose concerns appear to have been focused exclusively on the church. Nevertheless, Bede's portrait of Ælfflæd may indeed be accurate in its reflection of a religious woman who maintained an active interest in the politics of both her church and nation, as well as the lives, status and memory of her family.

Support for Bede's portrait of Ælfflæd is provided by the *Life of Gregory*, the only major text known to have been produced at Whitby. Internal evidence in the *Life* indicates it was written after Eanflæd's death and while Ælfflæd was still abbess. The priest Trimma who is sent to search for Edwin's bones is described as living in 'a monastery of the South English, in the days of their king Æthelred, while Eanflæd was still living in the monastic life', and Whitby is 'the well-known monastery of Ælfflæd' (Colgrave 1968, 18, 103). This means that the *Life* was written c 704–14, at least fifteen years before Bede completed the *Ecclesiastical History* (c 731).

The *Life of Gregory* is unusual in that it is written in very poor Latin, and uses the first person, singular and plural, to a much greater extent than the roughly contemporary *Lives* written by Bede, Eddius Stephanus, and Cuthbert's anonymous hagiographer. Although its primary subject is Gregory, the author devotes as much space to Northumbria, the court, and the translation of Edwin, as he or she does to Gregory and Rome. Northumbria replaces Kent as the goal of the first Roman mission, and the roles of Æthelberht of Kent and Augustine in bringing Christianity to England are downplayed in favour of Ælle of Northumbria and Gregory himself. There are repeated plays on the Trinitarian significance of the names Ælle and Edwin (Eadwine). The author tells us that:

> Though it is the name of a king, *alle* also signifies the Father, *lu* the Son, and *ia* the Holy Spirit. . . . Edwin's name, consisting of three syllables, truly signifies the mystery of the Holy Trinity which He taught, inviting all to come to Him and be baptized in the name of the Father, the Son, and the Holy Spirit (Colgrave 1968, 97, 13–14).

There are also repeated attempts to establish Northumbria's, and particularly Whitby's, direct links back to Rome and Gregory by such devices as redirecting the first mission, or linking names in groups of three to form a spiritual genealogy that runs from Gregory and Ælle to Ælfflæd. Christianity, for example, descends from Æthelberht to Ælle to Edwin (Colgrave 1968, 95, xii).

Chapters 18 and 19 are devoted to the translation of Edwin's relics from Hatfield Chase to Whitby, and contain the only passages that deal directly with the monastery itself. Trimma, who eventually finds Edwin's bones, is instructed by a heavenly visitor to take them to 'the well-known monastery of Ælfflæd, a most religious woman and the daughter of queen Eanflæd, who was herself . . . the daughter of Edwin' (Colgrave 1968, 103, 18). The bones are then buried 'in the church of St Peter, the chief of the Apostles, together with other of our kings, on the south side of the altar which is dedicated in the name of the blessed Apostle Peter and east of the altar dedicated to Gregory' (Colgrave 1968, 105, 19). Nowhere is Hild mentioned, which is surprising in a text so devoted to the spiritual and biological origins of Northumbria. It is important to note that Hild is also excluded, as far as we can tell, from the Lindisfarne *Liber Vitae*, which does record the names of Ælfflæd and Eanflæd.[3]

The fact that Hild and Ælfflæd were adversaries when it came to the issue of Wilfrid may have been reason enough for the lack of commemoration of Hild. Hild wrote letters denouncing Wilfrid to the Pope, while Ælfflæd gave him her active support and was crucial to his reinstatement. However, there may have been more to it than that. The *Life of Gregory*, along with Bede's account of Ælfflæd and her family, is often taken as evidence that Ælfflæd's intention was to establish Whitby as a royal cult centre or, more specifically, a monument to the Deiran dynasty. This would certainly accord with her interest in her royal family, but then why no mention of Hild? Or naming of those unnamed kings among whom Edwin was buried? At Whitby Ælfflæd seems to have been more interested in creating a monument to herself and her immediate forebears, *possibly* with an emphasis on the female relatives and descendants of Edwin. In the *Life* it is only Ælfflæd, Eanflæd and Edwin whose names are connected with the monastery. It might be possible, however, to supplement the documentary record by turning to the material evidence.

Higgitt (1995, 231, fig 4) has suggested that a cross head from the abbey (Whitby IV) inscribed in Latin lettering +AHHAE+ may commemorate Edwin's sister Acha. He has also suggested that a fragmentary cross shaft from Hackness, a daughter house of Whitby, inscribed in Latin letters 'Oedilburga blessed forever' (OEDILBVRGA BEATA [AD S]EMPER) and, probably, 'religious abbess Oedilburga pray for . . .' (OEDILBVRGA ORATE) may commemorate, or possibly have enshrined Ælfflæd's grandmother, Edwin's queen, Æthelburh, who became abbess of Lyminge after Edwin's death (Lang 1991, 135–41, pls 454–66). The stone, Hackness 1, includes runic inscriptions, and is dated to the late 7th to 9th century. (Hawkes, pers comm, dates it closer to the 9th century on stylistic grounds, but this does not exclude its commemorating Æthelburh.) If these identifications are correct, Whitby and its daughter house(s) had a dynasty of hallowed queens and abbesses to rival those of the bishops of Lindisfarne, or the abbots of Wearmouth-Jarrow, although the Whitby dead formed a biological rather than a purely, or largely, spiritual family.

As elsewhere in the medieval world, early Anglo-Saxon England seems to have had a tradition of women maintaining family-based cults. It was the unfortunate Osthryth, Ælfflæd's sister, who first discovered and translated the bones of Oswald (Colgrave & Mynors 1969, 246–7, III.11), while Ælfflæd's creation of a monument to Edwin and his female relatives can be related to contemporary events at Ely where Abbess Seaxburh began the transformation of the monastery into a shrine to herself, her sisters (the daughters of King Anna of East Anglia), and her female descendants. The shrine eventually included the bodies of the three sisters Æthelthryth, Seaxburh and Withburga, Seaxburh's daughter Eormenilda, and possibly Eormenilda's daughter Werburh (Ridyard 1988, 50). Ælfflæd's actions might also be compared with those of the later Anglo-Saxon and continental women responsible for the preservation of Oswald's cult (Ó Rian-Raedel 1995).

Whether the monuments from Whitby and Hackness commemorated Edwin's wife and sister or not, the focus of Whitby's memorial monuments, like the sections dealing with England in the *Life of Gregory*, was on names. The Whitby sculptures are unusual in the Northumbrian corpus in consisting primarily of simple standing stone crosses inscribed with individual names, like the AHHAE cross, and plain crosses on which names may have been painted. Some are clearly skeuomorphs of wooden crosses, and Cramp has suggested that these might be intended to commemorate Oswald's wooden cross (Cramp 1993, 69, fig 7.4; Thacker 1995, 106). Oswald's familial ties to Whitby would certainly make this an appropriate form of commemoration.[4] If, as Cramp (1993, 70) and Bailey (1996a, 51–2) have suggested, Whitby pioneered the development of the standing stone cross, these highly unusual monuments might themselves have commemorated the role of Oswald and the Northumbrian royal family in bringing Christianity to the north, a role also glorified in the *Life of Gregory*, although admittedly the *Life* does not mention Oswald. Further, the early use of the cross as a commemorative monument at Whitby might have implications for our understanding of the Bewcastle cross (Bailey & Cramp 1988, pls 90–117), which is roughly contemporary with the Whitby sculptures. Bewcastle is an aristocratic, commemorative monument, a sculptural *liber vitae* (Ó Carragáin 1987b; Karkov 1997), inscribed with the names Kyneburg[5] and (probably) Alhfrith. It possibly commemorates Ælfflæd's half-brother, who attended the Synod of Whitby, and his wife. In any case, it certainly has more in common with the large visible commemorative monuments of Whitby than it does with the small, far less visible (if not invisible) name stones of Lindisfarne and Hartlepool (see Okasha above).

Ultimately, the commemoration and manipulation of the dead that took place at Whitby, Lindisfarne, and Wearmouth-Jarrow has far more to tell us about the living than it does about the dead. As Geary has pointed out:

the right to speak the past also implied control over that which gives access to the past – the 'relics' by which the past continued to live into the present. How these tangible or written relics of the past were preserved, who preserved them, and who could therefore make them to disappear were fundamental aspects of power and authority (Geary 1994, 7).

The disappearance of Hild and the appropriation of her founding position by Ælfflæd, Eanflæd and Edwin are a testament to Ælfflæd's power and authority within Northumbria, which Thacker has stated may have been rivalled only by that of Wilfrid (Thacker 1995, 110). In her power to create a monastic history, to preserve the memory of the dead, or to make them disappear, she may also have rivalled Bede himself.

NOTES

1. Aidan and Hild are also linked by the fact that he was her spiritual father. He summoned her back to Northumbria from the East Anglian court, instructed and advised her and, presumably, helped to establish her first in her little cell on the banks of the Wear, and subsequently at Hartlepool.

2. Hild's story is characterized by continual separation from her family: her father is already dead when she is born; she is exiled to the court of her nephew in East Anglia, from which her sister has already departed for Chelles; and her attempts to be reunited with her sister in the convent at Chelles (a sort of false *peregrenatio*) are abandoned when Aidan summons her back to Northumbria.

3. Cross (1979) argued for the existence of a lost *Life of Hild* based on evidence from the much later *Old English Martyrology*. His argument, however, was based exclusively on minor differences between the accounts of Hild's life in Bede's *Ecclesiastical History* and the *Martyrology*. Moreover, he did not suggest when, between 680 and the 10th century, the lost *Life* might have been written.

4. Many of the Whitby crosses, however, are similar in form to the cross carved on the base of Cuthbert's wooden coffin. Given the particularly close relationship between Ælfflæd and Cuthbert, a relationship between the monuments from the two sites should not be ruled out (see Bailey 1996a, 51).

5. Kyneburg's name appears on the north face of the cross, a location that may reflect the traditional association of women with the north side of churches or monuments (see Gilchrist 1994, 133–5).

CHAPTER 12

WILLIBRORD'S 'FRISIAN' MISSION AND THE EARLY CHURCHES IN UTRECHT

David Parsons

INTRODUCTION

Northumbrians had been interested in the Low Countries as a possible mission field since the initial foray of Wilfrid in the late 670s. That interest culminated nearly two decades later with the arrival in the Netherlands of Willibrord and his subsequent consecration as (arch)bishop of the Frisians in 695 (Levison 1946, 45–69; Parsons 1996, 30–1). In a career lasting almost fifty years his building activities amounted to very little, if we are to believe the contemporary and later medieval sources. Bede records laconically that he 'built a number of churches . . . and established several monasteries', but does not reveal how many or where they were located (Appendix I (a)). Alcuin's *Life* claims that 'he traversed every part of the country', where he ordered churches to be built on estates donated by his converts, and gives the impression that there were many such properties (Appendix I (c)). Alcuin fails to define the 'country', however, but it is unlikely to have been the whole of Frisia, and there is evidence to suggest that Willibrord's activities were largely restricted to the area south and west of the Rhine–Maas delta, Bede's *citerior Fresia* (Colgrave & Mynors 1969, 480, V.10). A recent review of the known early church foundations in the Low Countries reveals a noticeable clustering in present-day Belgium and the more southerly parts of the Netherlands (Parsons 1996, 37–43, fig 5).[1] This observation is reinforced by the addition of further instances of churches for which there is only documentary evidence (Appendix II). A revised map of church sites is given here as Fig 12.1. The same conclusion is reached by the compilers of the map of Merovingian church buildings displayed at the exhibition 'Die Franken' (Päffgen & Ristow 1996, Abb 321). This distribution strongly suggests

136

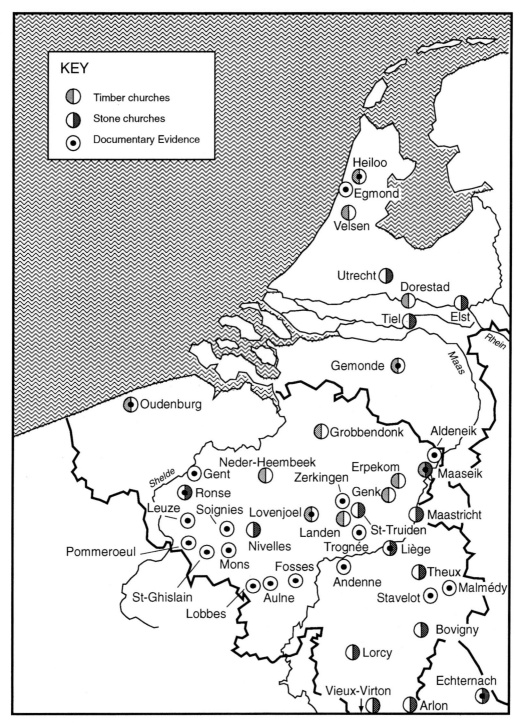

Fig 12.1. The Low Countries, showing evidence for churches up to the mid-/late 8th century. (After: Parsons 1996, Fig 5, with additions and amendments)

that Willibrord's activity was limited to that part of Frisia which was under Frankish control throughout most of his missionary life, but with outposts in North Holland. The failure to have any significant impact on the northern parts of Frisia is borne out by the need for Boniface to attempt a missionary campaign there in the 750s. This apparent relationship between missionary activity and political and military colonialism is a well-recognized phenomenon (Päffgen & Ristow 1996, 408–10; Dierkens 1996, 465). Seen in this light the position of Willibrord's diocesan centre at Utrecht takes on added significance, not only as the symbolic centre of his episcopal authority but as an ecclesiastical 'frontier post' on the very edge of Frankish territory. It is no coincidence that Willibrord was established in his see by Pippin, Mayor of the Merovingian palace, himself.

THE EARLIEST CHURCHES OF UTRECHT: THE EVIDENCE OF THE NARRATIVE SOURCES

The Content of the Documents

The documentary evidence is complex and requires careful interpretation. The only strictly contemporary account, Bede's *Ecclesiastical History*, is terse, saying simply that 'the reverend bishop built a church' in Utrecht (Appendix I (a)). A dozen years after Willibrord's death, his younger colleague Boniface, in a letter to the newly installed pope, gave a much more circumstantial account (Appendix I (b)). Evidently there were two churches which had been built by Willibrord, one dedicated to St Saviour, in which his see appears to have been located, the other dedicated to St Martin, built on the 'ruins of a certain little church destroyed by the heathen'. Later Utrecht tradition, represented by a 13th-century inscribed panel formerly in the cathedral, claimed that this earlier church had been founded in the reign of Dagobert and was originally dedicated to St Thomas (Appendix I (e)). This tradition was repeated in the 14th century by Jan Beke whose writing has been brought into prominence recently (Broer & De Bruijn 1994; 1995). He wrote two chronicles, one in Latin and the other in the vernacular; the wording of the two is not identical.

Both versions of Beke's *Chronicle* agree with the panel in the cathedral in ascribing a St Thomas dedication to the early church destroyed by the pagan Frisians (Appendix I (f)). On the site of this ruined church Willibrord built a collegiate church which was to house his *cathedra*, but the dedication of the new church is not mentioned. Beke goes on to say that Boniface later founded another collegiate church known as the Old Minster close to the ancient chapel of St Saviour; however, he admits a degree of uncertainty here, reporting a contemporary opinion that this church had been built by Willibrord for eighty prebendaries, forty of whom he later transferred to St Martin's. Beke also provides the main reference to a further church dedicated to Holy Cross, though there had been an earlier brief allusion to a church with the joint invocation of Holy Cross and St Mary in Theofrid's *Life of St Willibrord* (Appendix I (d)), a text based on Alcuin's *Life*, Bede, other saints' lives and the Echternach charters (Talbot 1954, 2). According to Beke, Holy Cross was built by Willibrord close to the ruins of the earlier church of St Thomas, and housed the baptismal font.

Discussion of the Narrative Sources

The 13th- and 14th-century documents are potentially of great interest, but have not to my knowledge been referred to previously in any English-language publication. *Prima facie* their credibility is not great, on account of their late date, but the inscribed panel formerly in Utrecht Cathedral is entirely consistent with the relevant part of Boniface's mid-8th-century letter, except in one particular: it claims that the ruined church restored by Willibrord was originally dedicated to St Thomas. This seems an unusual invocation for the cathedral clergy to have invented in the 13th century, and it presumably reflects an earlier tradition, though it does not appear to have been mentioned in any previous document.

Beke's chronicles, on the other hand, are clearly riddled with misconceptions or with deliberate distortions introduced to accommodate the changed circumstances of the later Middle Ages. Nevertheless, he demonstrably relies on earlier, superficially more dependable, material, for example the letter of Boniface to Pope Stephen, as Broer and De Bruijn have shown (1995, 33).

Extract from St Boniface's letter of 752–3	Jan Beke, *Chronographia*
... *fana et dilubra destruxit et aecclesias construxit et sedem episcopalem*	... *fana et dilubra destruxit et ecclesias construxit et sedem episcopalem in honore sancti Martini*
et aecclesiam in honore sancti Salvatoris constituens in loco et castello, quod dicitur Traiectum	*et basilicam in honore sancte Crucis in loco et castello, quod dicitur Traiectum*

The extent to which Beke's text is derivative is plain. Equally clear are the adjustments made to Boniface's text, which are signalled above (my emphases). The change in the dedication of the episcopal see to St Martin reflects the fact that St Martin's had in fact been the cathedral for some centuries by the time Beke was writing, despite the implication of Boniface's text that the original cathedral was St Saviour's. At the same time, Boniface's account should not necessarily be taken at face value, since he was engaged in a dispute with the bishop of Cologne over control of the Frisian see, and sought to influence the Pope in his favour. In some quarters an extremely negative view is taken of Boniface's reliability, and he is accused of systematic falsification. This view is represented by Van Welie 1996, who argues that there is no evidence of a *sedes episcopalis* in Utrecht after 719 until donations by Pippin III in favour of St Martin's, 751×3. Nevertheless, Van Welie shows that St Saviour's was the principal church in the early period and that the tradition of baptism attached to it at a later date (1996, 60). It is safe to assume that Boniface would know what the facts were, even though it might suit his purpose to put a gloss on them. His letter referred to Willibrord's lifetime, for the greater part of which St Saviour's was the only major, and thus *de facto* episcopal church; its seniority was recognized in the title Old Minster, which is attested from the early 12th century (Stöver 1996, 78 n 2), by which time St Martin's had become the cathedral.

The second change introduced by Beke into Boniface's text is the reference to Holy Cross in place of St Saviour. Elsewhere he says that Willibrord established a baptismal font in Holy Cross (Appendix I (f)). Since the rite of baptism was initially the responsibility of the bishop, and since St Saviour's was apparently the original episcopal church in Utrecht, there is every reason to accept a connection between the two churches, so that Beke's amendment may not be so drastic as it appears. He also records the building of the Old Minster close to the 'ancient chapel of St Saviour', and Broer and De Bruijn see this as a case of the transfer of the dedication to the new church, while the ancient chapel was given an alternative, though related, invocation (Broer & De Bruijn 1995, 49–53). Holy Cross may always have been or may have continued as a structurally independent baptistery to St Saviour's in the classical manner.

How these various churches relate to the later topography of the city depends on the identification and location of the early, probably 7th-century, church, to which the late medieval sources attribute a St Thomas dedication. Boniface states that Willibrord rebuilt this church and reconsecrated it in the name of St Martin, which presumably reflects his close links with the Frankish court, where Martin had the status of patron saint. Since that is also the dedication of the later cathedral, the most obvious location for the early church is in the northern part of the Roman fort, where parts of the Gothic cathedral still stand. However, this does not seem to be the position indicated on a 17th-century map, which purports to show Utrecht as it was in 690 (Fig 12.2). This somewhat speculative document places the church of St Thomas apparently outside and to the north of the walled area. Further, the later medieval descriptions use the Latin *prope* or the Dutch *bi* (near) to express the location of the church in relation to the *castrum/casteel* (Appendix I (e) & (f)), rather than *infra/in/binnen*, which would be expected if its position had been inside the walls, though Beke's chronicle is not consistent in this respect. Broer and De Bruijn explain, however, that in the later Middle Ages the 'castle' was synonymous with the bishop's palace to the south of the axis of the Roman fort (1995, 21); the church of St Thomas/St Martin, lying to the north of

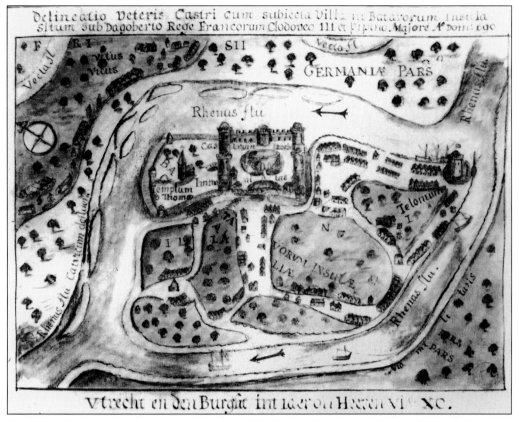

Fig 12.2.   Utrecht: map showing city as of AD 690. (Source: Broer & De Bruijn 1995, Afb 2)

the axial line, counted as 'outside'. It is in any case unlikely that the earliest church would have been anywhere but inside the Roman walled area or that it would subsequently have become a candidate for cathedral status if it were not so, and it seems reasonable to accept that St Thomas's was situated in the northern half of the fort. Near to the ruins of St Thomas's, Beke tells us, Willibrord built the Holy Cross chapel; its successor stood immediately to the south of the destroyed cathedral nave (Fig 12.3, no 1) until 1829, when it was demolished.

THE EARLIEST CHURCHES OF UTRECHT: THE ARCHAEOLOGICAL EVIDENCE

The Chapel of Holy Cross

Excavations on the Domplein in 1929 exposed the remains of Holy Cross, which were dated to the 10th century (Van Giffen et al. 1938). Further investigations in the 1930s added details to the plan of the chapel, which

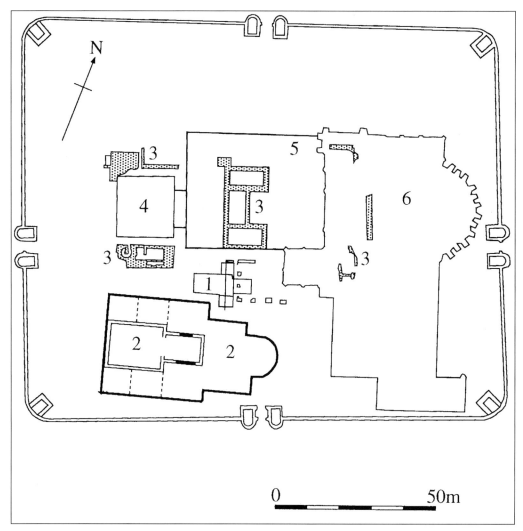

Fig 12.3. Utrecht: ecclesiastical buildings in the fort interior. 1: Holy Cross with the NW corner of the *principia*; 2: extent of St Saviour's (outline) with proposed early church; 3: excavated evidence for pre-Romanesque forerunner of cathedral; 4: cathedral tower (still existing); 5: extent of demolished cathedral nave; 6: outline of surviving Gothic cathedral. (After: De Groot 1994, Afb1, and Stöver 1996, Fig 3)

consisted of a nave, a narrower chancel, and two transeptal side chambers aligned with the east wall of the nave (Fig 12.4). In 1993 the opportunity arose to reinvestigate part of the structure, whose renewed exposure unleashed a flood of interpretation and counter-interpretation. In the following year contributions to the debate – archaeological, historical and topographical – were published in a special double issue of the *Bulletin* of the Koninklijke Nederlandse Oudheidkudige Bond (De Groot 1994, Rijntjes 1994, Broer & De Bruijn 1994, Stöver 1994).[2]

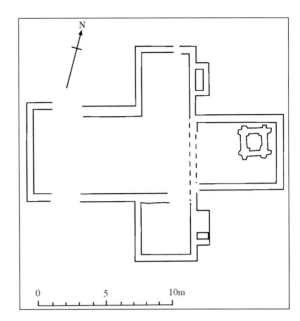

Fig 12.4.   Utrecht: plan of Holy Cross chapel. (After: Stöver 1994, Afb 5)

One of the objectives of the 1993 investigation was to test Van Giffen's somewhat subjective dating. To this end charcoal from the construction mortar was sampled for radiocarbon testing. The resulting determinations appear to confirm the likelihood of a date in the 10th century: there is a 95% probability that the date falls between 876 and 1008 (De Groot 1994, 140, 193). A review of the 1929 excavation material suggested an earlier – possibly 8th-century – date, however (De Groot 1994, 136, 193), and a systematic attempt was undertaken to reconstruct the successive ground levels in the area of the Domplein. The top of the chapel foundations lay 3.7 m above NAP (Dutch Ordnance Datum), noticeably lower than the general 10th-century level which was around +4.5 m. Between the two were decorated stone sarcophagi dated on art-historical grounds to the 8th and 9th centuries at +4.1 m and +4.4 m respectively (De Groot 1994, 144, 193). Despite the radiocarbon evidence, therefore, a date in the early 8th century is proposed.

The chapel was built immediately over the destruction levels of the Roman *principia* and incorporated Roman building materials. Unless it can be shown that the *principia* survived into the 10th century, this also implies an early date for the chapel. At the time when it was built the general lines of the *principia* were clearly still visible, since Holy Cross was oriented in relation to it and precisely located across its north-western corner so as to incorporate the well of its atrium in the chancel of the new building. It is tempting to see some ritual purpose in this deliberate arrangement, and Jan Beke's reference in the 14th century to a baptistery in Holy Cross may be significant here. What is unconvincing in De Groot's chapter is his suggestion that Holy Cross was the church built (or rebuilt) by Willibrord in honour of St Martin (1994, 147, 193–4). There is no suggestion in the excavated evidence of the chapel itself of an earlier church and a later rebuild phase, though it must be admitted that the destruction referred to in the documents may have been partial and confined to the above-ground fabric. Willibrord's 'rebuilding' may have amounted to no more than a superficial patching up and reroofing that left no trace in the below-ground archaeology. On the other hand, De Groot has drawn attention to a phase between the Roman *principia* and the Holy Cross chapel, consisting of secondary walls constructed between the column bases of the atrium. The north and south foundations of the chancel of Holy Cross cut the west wall of this atrium reconstruction. De Groot hints that the rebuilt atrium might have been the 'predecessor' of Holy Cross (1994, 145, 146, 193). If this was the Frankish church destroyed by the Frisians, then it is not easy to accept that Holy Cross, which just cuts its west end, could be the Willibrordian reconstruction described in the documents.

A further, non-archaeological, objection to the interpretation of Holy Cross as Willibrord's St Martin's concerns the later history of the buildings in the fort. A transfer of a St Martin dedication from this chapel to the later cathedral is unlikely, since as Broer and De Bruijn (1994) point out, there was never any connection between the cathedral and Holy Cross, which was always linked to St Saviour's.

Reverting to the interpretation of the archaeological data, Rijntjes claims that Holy Cross *was* a two-period building (1994, 152–6; 1996, 49–50), which could make credible the progression from an early Frankish church to St Martin's. He draws attention to the differences in foundation details and quality of masonry between the south transeptal annex and the remainder of the building and concludes that the annex was built as a free-standing cult building (possibly a *cella memoriae*, though with its implication of burial this is unlikely inside a Roman enclosure at an early date) and that the nave, chancel and north annex were added to it at a later stage. His 1996 article includes a reference to 'Pl.IID', which is supposed to show the junction between the south annex and the nave and to reveal their chronological relationship; there is no such plate, and the reference should presumably be to Pl.IIIA, which is, to say the least, inconclusive. However, Rijntjes's 1994 interpretation held that the south annex was the original *ecclesiola*, and the remainder of the building Willibrord's church of St Martin, and therefore of early 8th-century date. His more recent discussion of the completed ('Phase 2') church, despite citing parallels universally earlier than c 750, concludes that the building should be dated to the second half of the 8th or the first quarter of the 9th century, on the grounds that the 'external reflection of the internal altar-arrangement is a Carolingian rather than a Merovingian architectural feature' (Rijntjes 1996, 54). The matter hinges on comparisons of plan form, and they in their turn depend on the integrity of the Holy Cross plan. Despite his two-phase interpretation, Rijntjes argues that 'the church . . . must have been planned as a whole', which is the best argument against the development of the building from an isolated *cella*. The unified symmetrical plan, the orientation and the exact placing of the church to enclose the Roman well are hardly likely to have arisen in the piecemeal building development proposed by Rijntjes. He may be right in seeing a chronological progression within the fabric, but if so his two phases must be stages within a single campaign of construction. The finished building clearly has many parallels: the Old Minster at Winchester and many other Anglo-Saxon examples have been cited, along with an equally impressive array of continental comparanda. Whether the affinities of Holy Cross are Anglo-Saxon or Frankish must be argued elsewhere.

Pending the full publication and discussion of the 1993 excavation, it seems best to avoid over-elaborate interpretations. Broer and De Bruijn (1995), for example, propose a development sequence for the area as a whole involving the use of part of the *principia* as the first church. While this is far from improbable and parallels could easily be found for it, there is no direct archaeological evidence for such a phase, though De Groot 1994 hints at the rebuilt atrium as a possible predecessor of Holy Cross (see above). Holy Cross must be taken at face value, together with the admittedly late evidence of Beke's *Chronicle*, as representing a foundation of Willibrord with baptismal facilities, and possibly therefore the forerunner of St Saviour's.

The Church of St Saviour (Old Minster)

The medieval church of St Saviour was demolished in 1587 and its foundations were dug out. In the 19th century its western half was covered by the buildings that still survive. Much of the eastern half of the church is known from excavation, which has also revealed two parallel wall foundations, possibly of 8th-century date, in the central part of the transept. An archive of drawings, including plans, has survived, and a combination of information from these sources and the results of excavations has made possible the reconstruction of the ground plan of the church prior to its demolition (Stöver 1994, Afb 10; 1996, Fig 2). On the basis of the unusual proportions of this plan and the early foundations excavated in the centre of the transept Stöver has further proposed a reconstruction plan of a putative earlier church, which he ascribes to the time of Willibrord (Stöver 1996, Fig 3). This church consisted of an aisleless nave, 18 m long and 12 m wide, with a narrower chancel, some 12.5 m long and 9 m wide (see Fig 12.5). As an extension to this hypothesis one might suggest that the areas of the side aisles flanking the short medieval nave and the chapels added outside them could represent early transeptal annexes. These have been added to the plan as a *ballon d'essai*, and it should be stressed that they form no part of Stöver's reconstruction. However, with these hypothetical additions the plan looks very familiar, and many of the dimensions are approximately one and a half times the length of their Holy Cross counterparts. The length of the chancel as

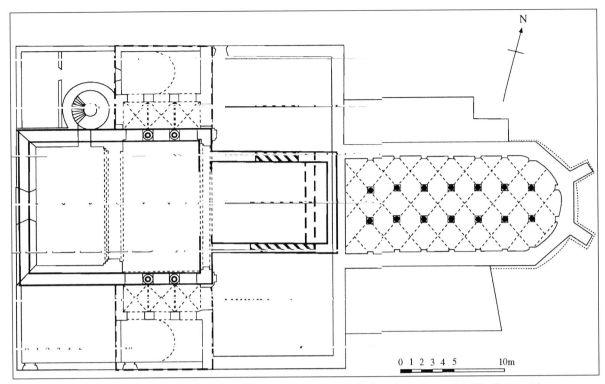

Fig 12.5.   Utrecht: St Saviour. Reconstructed extent of church demolished in 1587 (fine line) with proposed early church (heavy line) based on excavated walls (hatched/shaded) and the proportions of the later building; broken heavy line = hypothetical transeptal adjuncts and termination to chancel. (After: Stöver 1996, Figs 2 & 3)

proposed by Stöver is rather too great, but a reduction to 10 m, which corresponds with the end of the southern excavated foundation, brings the chancel into the right relationship with that of Holy Cross. In view of the relationship between the two churches, as expounded by Broer and De Bruijn 1994, this series of correspondences takes on some potential significance.

CONCLUSION

What the three or four early churches of Utrecht (depending on whether the *ecclesiola* and St Thomas's were one and the same) have in common is their location within the walls of the former Roman fort. The site of Holy Cross is known and that of St Saviour can be assumed on the basis of the archaeological evidence for the Romanesque church. The site of the *ecclesiola* and/or St Thomas's, assuming that the objection to the interpretations of Holy Cross as the *ecclesiola* is accepted, is not known, but it is likely to have been in the area of the later cathedral of St Martin, where only 10th/11th-century evidence has so far been revealed by excavation. The relative status of these churches has given rise to much controversy, especially in terms of identifying which of them acted as Willibrord's cathedral, and the recent re-excavation of Holy Cross has added fuel to the debate. What has received little attention is the significant placing of Holy Cross in relation to the *principia* of the fort and the placing of its chancel over the Roman well, which is suggestive in view of the late tradition that this church incorporated a baptistery. In discussing this, Parsons (1996, 36–7) referred to some early churches built in or over major public buildings in Roman towns or *principiae* of Roman military enclosures. These are generally not the cathedrals of the respective towns, though at a later date York is an exception. For example, St Nicholas in Leicester is potentially an early church, but there are good arguments in favour of St Mary de Castro as the site of the Anglo-Saxon cathedral, and it is noticeable that this church is located not in the town centre but close to the southern defences. Similarly, Lincoln Cathedral developed not on the site of St Paul in the Bail in the forum courtyard, but on the edge of the upper town, eventually growing out across the Roman circuit wall. There are many other instances of the peripheral siting of cathedrals, the prime example being St John Lateran in Rome. It could thus be argued that St Saviour's in Utrecht must have been Willibrord's cathedral because of its 'classic' position in the south-west corner of the fort. The restricted area inside the defences robs the argument of much of its force, however: if the early Frankish church, whether dedicated to St Thomas or not, occupied a fairly central position under the present cathedral, there were few options available to Willibrord for the siting of a second church, which regardless of status would necessarily have to be built towards the edge of the enclosed area.

The debate about whether St Saviour's or St Martin's was the 'original' cathedral is somewhat sterile, and perhaps even anachronistic. There is a growing literature on the concept of 'families of churches', which appears to have been common in the early medieval period, especially in cathedral towns (Metz is a much cited example, see Van Welie 1996, 59–60, and the literature cited at 67 n 31). It is perhaps best to regard the Utrecht churches as such an episcopal group, with the various churches and their functions complementing each other. Such a close relationship is implied by the late tradition that Willibrord provided St Saviour's with eighty prebendaries, but transferred forty of them to St Martin's. Boniface may have been right to locate his *sedes* in St Saviour's, though Beke recorded the setting up of the *cathedra* in the successor church to St Thomas's, equated with St Martin's on the evidence of the 13th-century panel in the cathedral. Beke also refers to a baptistery in Holy Cross, which may therefore have had a special function within the episcopal group, though the earliest direct references to a font associate it with St Saviour's (Van Welie 1996, 60, 67 n 33). The early churches and their functions appear to be so interconnected as to justify Bede's vagueness in attributing the see generally to the 'castle' of Utrecht, rather than to a particular church (*locum cathedrae episcopalis in castello . . . quod . . . Traiectum vocatur*: Appendix I(a)).

NOTES

1. In connection with the discussion of individual church sites in Parsons 1996 it may be noted that Willibrord's monastery and church at Echternach are now the subject of an excellent paper summarizing the results of unpublished recent excavations (Krier 1996).

2. These Dutch language articles were accompanied by helpful English summaries (pp. 193–5), which were nevertheless too brief to allow Anglophone readers to follow the detail of the arguments. The recent publication of the British Archaeological Association's Utrecht Conference Transactions, however, includes English-language contributions from some of the scholars working on the interpretation of the material (Rijntjes 1996, Van Welie 1996, Stöver 1996), though unfortunately neither a report on the Holy Cross excavations nor the unconventional and somewhat controversial views of Broer and De Bruijn have found a place in the volume, so that they are still available only in Dutch. With a substantial part of the debate now easily accessible to English readers, however, the time seems ripe to attempt a review of the archaeological evidence.

APPENDIX I: DOCUMENTARY EVIDENCE

(a) Bede, *Ecclesiastical History*, V.11 (731)

Pippin gave him [Willibrord] a place for his episcopal see in his famous fortress, which . . . is called *Traiectum* (Utrecht). The reverend bishop built a church here. . . . He also built a number of churches throughout those districts and established several monasteries (Colgrave & Mynors 1969, 486–7).

(b) Letter from Boniface to Pope Stephen II (752/3)

Willibrord . . . built churches, establishing an episcopal see with a church in honour of the holy Saviour in a fortified place called Utrecht. . . . But now the Bishop of Cologne . . . declares that it [Willibrord's see] belongs to him on account of the ruins of a certain little church destroyed by the heathen. This Willibrord discovered razed to the ground within the fortress of Utrecht, rebuilt it from the foundations with his own labour, and consecrated it in honour of St Martin . . . the ruined church was given by Dagobert, formerly King of the Franks, to the diocese of Cologne . . . (Talbot 1954, 146, no 47; Rau 1988, no 109).

(c) Alcuin, *Life of St Willibrord* (c 790 [Levison 1946, 54])

[Willibrord's mission] set out for the Castle of Utrecht . . . where some years afterwards . . . Willibrord placed the seat of his bishopric (Talbot 1954, 7). He traversed every part of the country . . . he ordered churches to be built [on properties donated by converts] (Talbot 1954, 11).

(d) Theofrid, *Life of St Willibrord* (late 11th century)

Not far from the bank of the river Rhine he built a chapel and dedicated it in honour of the Cross of Salvation and of Mary ever Virgin, Mother of God (*Acta Sanctorum*, November III, 414–500, here 465; author's translation).

(e) 'Domtafel' (late 13th century)

At the time of Dagobert king of the Franks . . . there was established near the castle at Utrecht (*prope castrum Trajectum*) a church of St Thomas, which the wild Frisian people destroyed. But later . . . Clement [Willibrord] rebuilt it in honour of St Martin (Broer & De Bruijn 1995, 74; present author's translation).

(f) Jan Beke, *Chronicle* (14th century)

In (*infra/binnen*) the precinct [of Utrecht] an early church was built in honour of St Thomas . . . but . . . the Frisians . . . destroyed the ancient church (Ch 4/IV; Broer & De Bruijn 1995, 75). Near the ruin of the primitive church of St Thomas (*prope ruinam/vaste bi sunte Thomas kerke, die . . . vervallen lach*) [Willibrord] built a chapel in honour of Holy Cross, in which he consecrated a baptistery (Ch 9/IX; Broer & De Bruijn 1995, 75). [Willibrord, having been consecrated bishop] built a collegiate church of canons on the site of St Thomas's basilica (*in fundo basilice sancti Thome/optie selve stede daer sunte Thomas kerke hadde ghestaen*) near the castle at Utrecht (*prope castrum Traiectense/bi den casteel Utrecht*); in this church he ordered his *cathedra* to be set up (Ch 10/X; Broer & De Bruijn 1995, 76). In the town of Utrecht Boniface founded a collegiate church of canons next to and touching the ancient chapel of Saint Saviour . . . commonly known as Old Minster. While the principal church of Utrecht has been renovated at some time, the original (timber) structure of this church has survived unrestored to this day. Some say, however, that this same church was originally built by Clement [Willibrord] for eighty prebendaries, forty of whom he himself transferred to the church of St Martin (Ch 15B/XVI; Broer & De Bruijn 1995, 76; present author's translation).

APPENDIX II: SUPPLEMENTARY LIST OF CHURCHES IN THE LOW COUNTRIES

An attempt at a comprehensive listing of churches in existence at the time of St Willibrord's mission or founded by him and his associates in the course of their missionary activity (that is, up to the mid-/late 8th century) has recently been published (Parsons 1996, 35–43, fig 5). That list did not include a systematic search of the primary literature, which has since been carried out with the aid of the extracts published by Knögel-Anrich 1992 for the Merovingian period and by von Schlosser 1892 for the Carolingian period. No attempt has been made to extend the literature searches of these authors or to consult unpublished manuscripts. Von Schlosser 1892 contains no entries referring to sites in the Low Countries in the second half of the 8th century, and all the references in this supplementary list have been taken from Knögel-Anrich 1992, whose entry numbers are given in each case.

Aldeneik (no 635); *Andenne* (nos 510, 511, 618); *Aulne* (no 652); *Egmond* (nos 458–9); *Emberen* (no 392); *Fosses-la-Ville* (no 595); *Gent* (nos 173, 471–2, 508); *Leuze* (no 471); *Lobbes* (nos 166–7, 652–3, 749–51); *Malmédy* (nos 165, 713); *Mons* (nos 628, 770); *Pommerœul* (no 680); *Saint-Ghislain* (no 627); *Soignies* (no 657); *Stavelot (Stablo)* (nos 165, 713); *Trognée* (no 390); *Zerkingen* (no 391).

This adds a further seventeen sites to the twenty-nine of the original list (Parsons 1996, 41), all but one of them in Belgium. Almost all of them are ascribed to Gallo-Roman or Frankish founders, of whom the most famous was Amandus, and where dates are stated or implied by the sources they precede Willibrord's arrival on the continent. They therefore provide no evidence for the activities of the Anglo-Saxon missionaries in the Low Countries. The sole exception is Egmond, where a wooden chapel was built by Adalbert, a Northumbrian disciple of Willibrord. This foundation is further evidence for Anglo-Saxon missionary activity beyond the Rhine/Maas delta, adding to the small cluster of foundations in the province of North Holland. As predicted in the discussion of the original list, the sites for which there is documentary evidence alone emphasize the bias in the distribution of early churches and confirm the expectations of the previous discussion (Parsons 1996, 41). It should be noted, however, that Knögel-Anrich did not make use of local charter material and that reference to this may modify the revised distribution pattern shown in Fig 12.1.

CHAPTER 13

RELATIONS BETWEEN THE BRITONS OF SOUTHERN SCOTLAND AND ANGLO-SAXON NORTHUMBRIA

Craig Cessford

INTRODUCTION

The 'Golden Age' of Northumbria, like all golden ages, exists largely in the eye of the beholder and with the advantage of hindsight. One particular problem is that the perceived brilliance of golden ages can obscure neighbouring groups. Among the many cultures that interacted with Northumbria were the British kingdoms of southern Scotland. The relationship between these groups is usually viewed from the perspective of Northumbrian documentary sources, principally Bede. Possible alternative sources for examining this relationship include British documentary sources, British objects recovered from Anglo-Saxon contexts and vice versa, and British sites subsequently occupied by Anglo-Saxons.

The largest of the patchwork of British kingdoms occupying southern Scotland during the 5th to 7th centuries were Strathclyde in the north-west centred on Dumbarton, Gododdin in the north-east based around Edinburgh, and Rheged in the south-west centred upon Carlisle. There was also a number of smaller states, such as Aeron in Ayrshire (Fig 13.1). The sources that survive are too scanty and unreliable to define exact boundaries for these kingdoms or construct conventional narrative accounts of their histories. The Britons have not attracted the same amount of attention as their neighbours; there are various reasons for this but it is largely due to their failure to leave behind major documentary sources such as Bede's, a corpus of art like Pictish sculpture, or to form the basis of a medieval kingdom as the Scots did. The Britons have also never quite

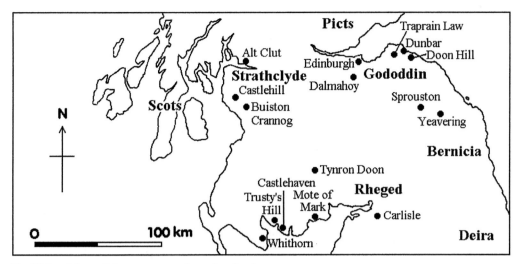

Fig 13.1. 5th- to 7th-century southern Scotland.

escaped the shadow cast by Bede's dislike of them due to differences concerning the Easter and tonsure questions.

The most typical British settlement sites are small- to medium-sized hillforts and crannogs. Burial was by extended inhumation in stone-lined cists without grave goods, often in large cemeteries, and with the dead occasionally commemorated by Latin inscriptions on rough standing stones. Most of their extant tools were iron and there is evidence for items made of wood, leather, bone and stone. They possessed glass beads and vessels, and had access to redware bowls and amphorae imported from the Mediterranean and tableware from France. A range of items of personal adornment such as brooches and pins were made of copper alloy and there are also items made of silver and gold, as well as a range of clay moulds and other objects related to metalworking.

BRITISH DOCUMENTARY SOURCES

The British documentary sources which survive have been relatively neglected compared with Anglo-Saxon sources which have dominated interpretations of the period. There are two major reasons for this: many of the British sources were originally oral and were not written down until several centuries later which creates serious problems concerning their reliability (Dumville 1977b, 178–9). In addition, most of the British sources were not attempts to write historical accounts and do not lend themselves particularly well to this purpose. Instead they are literary products such as the poetry attributed to Taliesin (Williams 1968) or Aneirin (Jackson 1969; Jarman 1988) and the Welsh Triads (Bromwich 1961) which do, nevertheless, provide a considerable amount of valuable information.

Many Anglo-Saxon sources, particularly Bede's *Historia ecclesiastica gentis Anglorum* (Colgrave & Mynors 1969), view the Anglo-Saxons, and Northumbria in particular, as the successors of the Old Testament Jews, a latter-day chosen people with a manifest destiny to rule the world, or at least northern Britain. Not surprisingly the British sources disagree, at best simply portraying Northumbria as one kingdom among many; more usual and less complimentary is the presentation of the Northumbrians as illegitimate upstarts. References to Anglo-Saxons and Northumbria are considerably less frequent than is often assumed and when they occur they are often later interpolations. Taking the Gododdin poem as an example, one of the commonest terms, *lloegrwys*, generally translated as 'men of England', need not refer to England at all and other terms thought to relate to Northumbria could have other meanings (Cessford 1995). The few unambiguous references to Angles and Saxons occur in contexts linking them to individuals from Wales and are probably later interpolations. Many British sources only survive because they were transmitted to Wales and eventually written down there. This led to later Welsh relations with England being anachronistically imposed upon the sources and this has been reinforced by the biases of later Celtic scholarship. Another example of a similar phenomenon is the *obsesio Etin* (siege of Edinburgh) in 638, recorded in two sets of Irish annals (Mac Airt & Mac Niocaill 1983, 120–1). This event has attracted considerable scholarly attention (Jackson 1959, 36–8; Kirby 1974) and often features in general accounts of the period as a Northumbrian victory heralding the downfall of the kingdom of Gododdin (Higham 1993, 99; Ritchie & Ritchie 1991, 148). The annals state neither who was involved in the siege nor give its outcome. Alternative possible scenarios include a purely British struggle or a Pictish attack; even if Northumbria was involved it need not have been victorious. The interpretation of the siege of Edinburgh as a Northumbrian victory is an unproven hypothesis symptomatic of a desire to create a grand tale of Northumbrian expansion.

When Anglo-Saxon and British sources relating to the same events survive they often provide substantially different viewpoints. The death of Æthelfrith of Northumbria in 616 and his successor Edwin's baptism in 627 are described by Bede with no reference to British involvement (Colgrave & Mynors 1969, 174–83, 186–9, II.12, 14), in contrast with the British sources where there is a strong British involvement with the Briton Ysgafnell killing Æthelfrith (Cessford 1994a) and Edwin being baptized under the auspices of Rhun of Rheged in 626 (Morris 1980, 38, 46, 79, 86; Smyth 1984, 22–3). There is no obvious reason to dismiss the British sources and it is likely that Bede simply failed to mention any British involvement because it did not accord with his general narrative purposes. Both British and Anglo-Saxon sources stress violent military aspects of relations between the two groups, primarily because of the biases of their authors and the nature of the sources, such as heroic poetry, which glorify martial prowess. There is some evidence for more peaceful interaction such as dynastic intermarriage, for example between Oswiu of Bernicia and Rhiainfellt of Rheged in the 630s (Morris 1980, 36, 77). Such events were probably more common than the few surviving references suggest (Cessford forthcoming a).

British documentary sources are in no sense superior to Anglo-Saxon sources but do provide an alternative viewpoint. Both are biased but by comparing them it is possible to identify some of the biases and arrive at a more balanced understanding of the period. It is crucial when doing this to return to the original sources to discover exactly what they themselves tell us as opposed to later interpolations or scholarly translations and interpretations.

BRITISH METALWORKING

There is evidence that the Britons of southern Scotland produced items of wood, leather, bone, iron and stone but the best evidence is for a flourishing tradition of ornamental metalworking using copper alloy and, to a lesser extent, silver and gold. Objects were produced using two-piece clay moulds which were broken to remove the finished item and then discarded. These have been recovered in large quantities at the Mote of Mark where there is evidence for the production of a range of penannular brooches, pins, buckles, studs and rivets (Curle 1914, 141–52, 157–60; Laing 1973b, 100, 123, 125; 1975, 102–8; 1993, nos 18, 48, 52, 137–8, 140–2, 148–57, 192–4, 198–205; Longley 1982, 133; Swindells & Laing 1980). Other metalworking-related finds from the site include crucibles, heating trays, nozzles for a bellows, slag and ore, and some evidence for the use of gold and silver. Similar evidence on a lesser scale has been found at Alt Clut (Alcock & Alcock 1990, 108–9, 113–14), Buiston crannog, where the Britons had a profitable sideline forging early Anglo-Saxon gold *tremisses* (Bruce-Mitford 1975, 676; Munro 1882, 230–2), Dalmahoy (Stevenson 1949, 196) and Whithorn (Hill 1997, 397–404). It has recently been recognized (Snape 1992) that late 4th- and early 5th-century type D7 penannular brooches were produced around Hadrian's Wall, indicating that native traditions may have had a much deeper and earlier influence on Northumbrian metalworking than is usually assumed feasible. British metalsmiths were familiar with a wide range of techniques and, while most of the items they produced were of competent rather than high quality, there is no reason why they could not have manufactured artefacts as technologically and artistically advanced as anywhere else in these islands.

A number of large, double-linked silver chains with terminal rings are known from Scotland (Cessford 1994b; Douglas & Alexander 1881; Edwards 1939; Henderson 1979; Laing 1993, nos 221–2; Smith 1874; Stevenson 1956) and their distribution strongly suggests that they were produced in the kingdom of Gododdin (Fig 13.2; Alcock 1983, 14; Cessford 1994b, 23–4). They are of a high standard of workmanship and analysis of their metal content shows that they were produced using late Roman silver (Stevenson 1956) such as that deposited

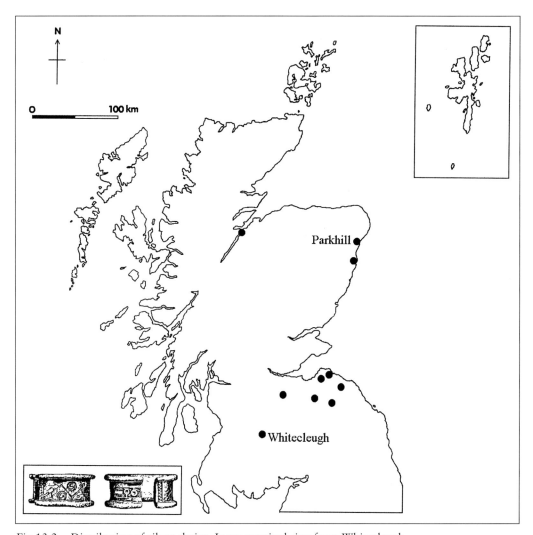

Fig 13.2.   Distribution of silver chains. Inset: terminal ring from Whitecleugh.

in the early 5th-century hoard at Traprain Law in the same kingdom (Curle 1923). These chains have a silver content of between 76.5% and 92.7% and weigh over 1.5 kg (Douglas & Alexander 1881, 69–70; Ralston & Inglis 1984, 55); they consumed the largest quantities of precious metal of any items produced in Britain and Ireland during this period and indicate a wealthy kingdom with access to raw materials and craftsmen. Terminal rings attached to the chains from Parkhill and Whitecleugh have incised symbols inlaid with red enamel similar to those on Pictish sculpture (Henderson 1979; Laing 1993, nos 221–2). This has sometimes been taken as evidence that the chains were produced by Pictish craftsmen but this is contradicted by the evidence of their distribution, and the various suggestions of how they were produced in northern Scotland but deposited further south are unconvincing (Henderson 1979, 22; Ritchie &

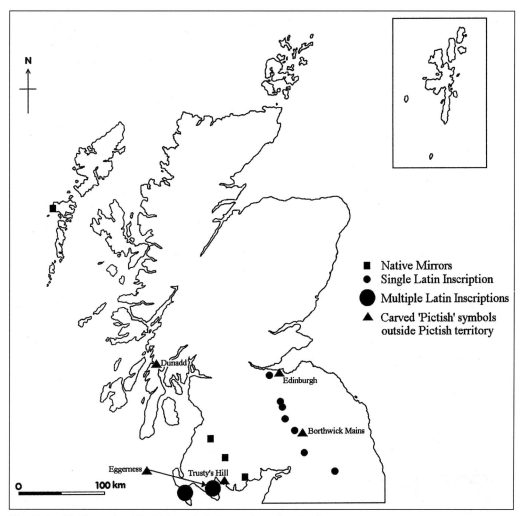

Fig 13.3. Evidence for 'Pictish' symbols in southern Scotland.

Ritchie 1991, 173). One possible solution is that the so-called 'Pictish' symbols are not specifically Pictish but were used by a wider range of groups, including the Britons of southern Scotland.

The current distribution of such symbols is based almost entirely upon examples carved on stone, but these symbols were probably derived from earlier proto- or ur-symbols which were mainly executed on perishable materials that do not survive (Alcock 1996; Laing & Laing 1993, 106–7; Cessford forthcoming c). The distribution of 'Pictish' symbols only delineates the area where such symbols made the transition to the medium of stone (Fig 13.3). 'Pictish' symbols on stone are probably names on grave markers (Samson 1992; Close-Brooks 1984); in southern Scotland at this time Latin inscriptions fulfilled a similar function, removing the need to carve 'Pictish' symbols (Thomas 1992). This hypothesis is supported by several strands of evidence. Some 'Pictish' symbols are based upon artefacts such as native Celtic mirrors, the 'mirror' symbol finding its best archaeological parallels in south-west Scotland at Balmaclellan, Carlingwark and Lochlee (Cessford forthcoming b). The symbols on a rock outcrop at Trusty's Hill have often been linked to Pictish raiders, but it is possible that only two of them were carved by Picts and that two others were carved by Britons familiar with such symbols (Cessford 1994c). Carvings of deer and horses on rock outcrops at Eggerness have affinities with 'Pictish' art and some may pre-date the 'Pictish' symbols (Morris & Hoek 1987, 35–8). Doubt has been expressed concerning the date of a fish symbol from Borthwick Mains but it is possible that it was carved by a native Briton and relates to contemporary fishing rights on the river Teviot (Cessford 1993). This evidence suggests that the label 'Pictish' is slightly inaccurate, that the use of such symbols was more widespread throughout Scotland, and that they are only 'Pictish' because the Britons did not utilize them on grave markers. This has profound implications for the study of Picto-Northumbrian artistic interaction.

GERMANIC OBJECTS FROM BRITISH CONTEXTS

A range of Germanic objects is known from British settlements, the most common type of material being fragments of glass vessels which have been recovered in large quantities from the Mote of Mark (Curle 1914, 152–6; Laing 1973b, 123; 1975, 100; Longley 1982, 133), and Whithorn (Hill 1997, 297–315), and in lesser amounts from Alt Clut (Alcock & Alcock 1990, 108, 113–15), Buiston crannog (Munro 1882, 232–3) and Castlehill (Smith 1919, 127). Alcock (1963, 52–3) suggested these fragments were imported as cullet for use in metalworking, but recent work has shown that they arrived in the form of complete vessels (Campbell 1989; forthcoming). Such vessels are mentioned in the Gododdin poem (Jarman 1988, lines 625, 776, 883) and Adomnán's *Life of Columba* (Anderson 1991, 142–3, ii.33). Glass fragments are relatively uncommon finds on Anglo-Saxon settlements and occur more frequently and in greater quantities on British sites. It is unlikely that the Britons acquired their glass vessels from Northumbria, and more probable that they were obtained from the continent via Irish Sea trade routes and may be linked to a trade in wine.

Other Germanic material includes bucket mounts from the Mote of Mark and a cup mount from Buiston crannog which occur as scrap but originally arrived as complete items (Laing 1973b, 125; Graham-Campbell 1991, 221–3). Another find is an iron spearhead from Castlehill belonging to Swanton's type F1 (Smith 1919, 129; Swanton 1974, 40). Only a limited variety of Germanic objects have been recovered from British settlements compared to the possible range of items the Britons could conceivably have obtained. The Britons seem to have been interested only in gaining access to a few Germanic items, most notably glass vessels, which were the result of long-distance trade that did not involve

Northumbria and were probably obtained in conjunction with imported wine. Their popularity may well be due to them being associated by the Britons with the consumption of wine.

BRITISH OBJECTS FROM ANGLO-SAXON CONTEXTS

A number of Anglo-Saxon settlements and burials in Northumbria have produced items made by British craftsmen. The most distinctive are of metalwork, notably hanging bowls and penannular brooches (Fig 13.4). Hanging bowls have been recovered from the monastic site of Whitby and burials at Capheaton, Garton Slack, Hawnby, and Castle Yard, York (Brenan 1991, nos 13, 15, 29, 33, 68), but unfortunately all are from poorly understood old discoveries or disturbed contexts. There is considerable debate concerning where they were produced but it is unlikely that it was in southern Scotland. Only a single bowl has been recovered from a British settlement, a recent discovery from Buiston crannog (Crone 1991, 295), and there is no mould evidence to indicate their production. Hanging bowls were probably produced in northern Scotland where they are more common, with finds from Aberdour, the Brough of Birsay, Castle Tioram, Clatchard Craig, Tummel Bridge and a mould from Craig Phadrig (Brenan 1991, nos 14, 58, 4.1, 4.3, 4.7–4.9).

Penannular brooches are known from a number of burials in Northumbria, at Driffield, Londesborough, Norton and Catterick (Dickinson 1982; White 1988,

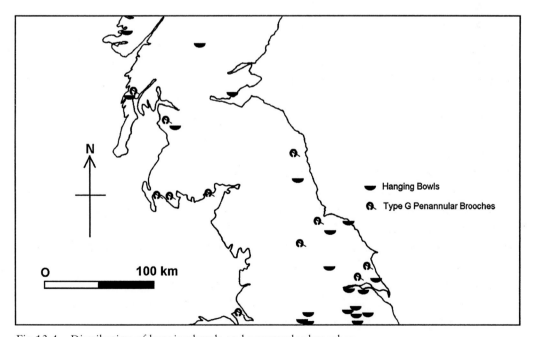

Fig 13.4. Distribution of hanging bowls and penannular brooches.

6–26; Moloney 1996, 130–1). Much attention has been paid to such discoveries but penannular brooches formed only a small part of much larger assemblages dominated by Germanic brooch types. Two such were recovered from female burials at Norton, Cleveland, where a small but elaborate G2 related penannular was found in grave 40 along with a considerable assemblage of other items including pairs of annular brooches, wrist clasps and silver bracelets (Sherlock & Welch 1992a, 40–1, 149, 167). This brooch is stylistically similar to a mould from the Mote of Mark (Curle 1914, 144) and brooches from Castlehill (Smith 1919, 128–9) and western Scotland (Dickinson 1982), so it may have been imported from southern Scotland. The woman in grave 40 was obviously of some importance, but the penannular brooch is outweighed by Germanic elements in the assemblage so she was presumably Anglo-Saxon. The presence of the penannular brooch is linked to the ability to obtain exotic artefacts rather than ethnic identity. A larger plain type G1.7 penannular was recovered from grave 65, a poorer burial otherwise containing only a knife. Given the lack of identifiable Germanic elements, this woman may well have been a Briton. Stylistically, the best parallels for the brooch come from western England in Cornwall, Somerset and Merseyside (Dickinson 1982, 49). The best parallels for the G1.5 and 1.8 brooches from Driffield, Londesborough and Wooler also come from western England (op. cit. 48–50). Hanging bowls and penannular brooches are no more common in Northumbria than in other Anglo-Saxon kingdoms. Most were probably not produced in southern Scotland and it is notable that no silver chains, the most distinctive type of metalwork from southern Scotland, have been recovered from Northumbria.

Whetstones made of greywacké, a stone occurring in south-west Scotland and north-west England, have been found on British settlements in southern Scotland such as Tynron Doon (Williams 1971, 115), Anglo-Saxon settlements such as Heybridge (Drury & Wickenden 1982, 29) and in Anglo-Saxon burials at Harrold, Uncelby and Fonaby. Decorated examples are known from Hough-on-the-Hill and Sutton Hoo (Bruce-Mitford 1978, 311–93; Eagles & Evison 1970, 42–3; Evison 1975, 78–9) which are paralleled by an example from Lochar Moss (Laing 1973a, 46). Their distribution suggests an east coast trade network, possibly involving Northumbria. It has recently been suggested that the find from Lochar Moss was not a whetstone, that the Sutton Hoo whetstone belongs to a Germanic tradition and that the stone may have been obtained from Northumbria rather than a British kingdom (Ryan 1992, 86 and 90). Ryan proposes no alternative function for the Lochar Moss find and its most plausible function remains a whetstone. While the carving on the Sutton Hoo whetstone may well be Germanic, it is unlikely that Northumbria had expanded far enough westwards at a sufficiently early date to provide the raw material for its manufacture.

The range of British objects found on Anglo-Saxon sites in Northumbria is quite restricted and the volume of material involved is not particularly large.

Most of the evidence points to long-distance contacts between Northumbria, northern Scotland and western England rather than direct links between Northumbria and southern Scotland.

ETHNIC TRANSITION SITES

During the 7th century Northumbrian expansion led to its gaining control of much of southern Scotland at the expense of Rheged, Gododdin and, to a lesser extent, Strathclyde. At a number of sites such as Doon Hill, Dunbar, the Mote of Mark and Sprouston it has been suggested that incoming Anglo-Saxons took over existing British settlements. The idea of such transition sites often relies heavily upon place-name evidence (Alcock 1988, 3–9). A number of Anglo-Saxon settlements mentioned by Northumbrian authors have names containing Celtic elements. It is assumed that such settlements must have been previously occupied by Britons from whom the incoming Anglo-Saxons learned the site's existing name. This ignores the possibility that such names may have related to unoccupied sites, such as prehistoric or Roman settlements, which were still distinctive elements in the landscape and would have possessed British names regardless of whether or not they were occupied.

Archaeologically, the identification of such an ethnic transition is more difficult than is often suggested. Structurally the main type of building identified in southern Scotland is the large timber hall used by both Britons and Anglo-Saxons. At a number of sites, the classic examples being Yeavering and Doon Hill (Hope-Taylor 1977; 1980), it has been suggested that British halls were succeeded by Anglo-Saxon halls. The ethnic labelling of such structures is problematical (Dixon 1982), a point graphically illustrated by the fact that a supposed early medieval hall at Balbridie turned out to be Neolithic (Fairweather & Ralston 1993). Such halls are a hybrid of Romano-British and Germanic elements (James et al. 1984) and Hope-Taylor's ethnic labelling is based principally upon historical frameworks which are profoundly insecure and open to alternative interpretations (Scull 1991). The other type of structure is the *grubenhaus* which has been excavated at Dunbar (Holdsworth 1993, 34–6) and identified from aerial photography at Sprouston (Smith 1991, 274–6). *Grubenhäuser* are distinctively Germanic structures with no British parallels and are good evidence for a Germanic presence. The *grubenhaus* from Dunbar is dated to the second half of the 6th century and may pre-date the Northumbrian conquest of the area (Holdsworth 1993, 46). It is possible that the presence of *grubenhäuser* need not indicate ethnic transition, where Anglo-Saxons replace Britons, but could represent the integration of both groups at a single site. This contradicts the generally accepted view of Brito-Northumbrian relations but accords well with the evidence for intermarriage mentioned previously.

Artefacts provide another form of archaeological evidence for ethnic transition but they too are problematical. As already discussed, Germanic artefacts, particularly glass vessels, occur on British settlements, so the presence of such objects cannot be taken as evidence of an Anglo-Saxon presence. More mundane artefact types, such as the pottery and loom weights found at Dunbar (op. cit. 35–6) and Yetholm (Laing 1973a, 46), may provide better evidence for the presence of Anglo-Saxons, but as with *grubenhäuser* they cannot distinguish between ethnic transition and integration.

It is plausible that Northumbrians took over and occupied existing British settlements but the criteria used for identifying such sites need to be more stringent than those often applied previously. It is necessary to demonstrate periods of British and Anglo-Saxon occupation, to prove that the evidence indicates ethnic transition rather than coexistence, and to show that there was no significant intervening gap. This is impossible using historical frameworks, place-name or aerial photography evidence and is problematical even with excavation. The ethnic labelling of particular types of structure or artefacts is difficult and the meaning of the presence or absence of particular 'ethnic' elements at a settlement is a matter of interpretation open to a variety of explanations.

CONCLUSION

The British kingdoms of southern Scotland were among Northumbria's closest neighbours and Brito-Northumbrian relations were crucial to the 'Golden Age' of Northumbria. The study of these kingdoms has been relatively neglected and British documentary and archaeological evidence is often ignored in favour of Anglo-Saxon sources. British documentary sources can provide a valuable alternative viewpoint on the period and, while in no sense superior to Anglo-Saxon documents, they are equally valid and can help expose the biases of the Northumbrian sources. Northumbria did not exist in a cultural vacuum but took over areas with flourishing cultural and artistic traditions. Much of the evidence for Brito-Germanic relations suggests that the most influential contacts were not directly between geographical neighbours but took place over longer distances between southern Scotland and the continent and between Northumbria and western England or Ireland. The British and Northumbrian kingdoms existed on fundamentally similar cultural levels, despite differences of emphasis and detail, and their relations should be viewed as between near equals.

ACKNOWLEDGEMENTS

Thanks are due to everyone who aided me with this chapter, especially Anja Wolle and in particular all those who were so helpful at the Golden Age of Northumbria conference.

MATERIAL CULTURE

CHAPTER 14

THE DUPPLIN CROSS: A PRELIMINARY CONSIDERATION OF ITS ART-HISTORICAL CONTEXT

Isabel Henderson

On July 6th [1891], went to Forteviot, accompanied by Mr A. Hutcheson. We first inspected the Dupplin Cross. It is protected by a wooden railing, and there is a notice-board close by requesting that the cross may not be injured by anyone. This is the only thing of the kind I saw throughout the whole of Scotland

(Allen 1892, 254).

The astonishingly complete, free-standing Dupplin cross stands on rising ground, within the Dupplin estate, north of the River Earn as it flows into the Tay estuary (Figs 14.1 and 14.2). Opposite is Forteviot, site of a Pictish and later Scottish (Dál Riata) royal centre (Airlie 1994, 34–6). To the south, just as the Earn enters the estuary, lay another possibly more ancient Pictish royal site, Abernethy (Anderson 1980, 92–6), while approximately three miles to the east is the fort of Clatchard Craig, which at the time of its Pictish occupation was producing fine metalwork (Close-Brooks 1986).

The Alcocks' (1992) report on the excavations of the Forteviot site included a well-illustrated discussion of the sculpture there and of the Dupplin cross. Subsequent to this, the panel at the top of the shaft on the western face has been

Fig 14.1. Dupplin cross, Perthshire, east face. (By permission of the Trustees for the National Museums of Scotland)

Fig 14.2. Dupplin cross, Perthshire, west face. (By permission of the Trustees for the National Museums of Scotland)

found to contain a seven-line inscription in Roman letters, and the base of the cross to have an ogham inscription (Forsyth 1995).

The complete state of the cross, one of a handful of undamaged free-standing crosses of the pre-Romanesque period to survive in Scotland, is its most precious attribute aesthetically and art-historically. That it also has a clear topographical association with a documented royal centre that has been archaeologically attested is remarkable. But that it should have a vernacular inscription, in a vernacular script as well as 'the longest Roman alphabet inscription from early medieval Scotland' (op. cit. 240), one which moreover contains the name of a historically identifiable person, places it, unarguably, in the small class of pre-eminent early medieval monuments in Britain.

Even the most perceptive assessment of the cross (Curle & Henry 1943) relied on Romilly Allen's on-site description and diagrammatic drawings of all four faces (Allen & Anderson 1903, III, 319–21, fig 334A–D). The drawings, on two facing pages, have impact, and are still useful, but blanks were left where Allen could not make out the designs and they are inaccurate in detail. They cannot convey the bold architectural form of the cross and the subtleties of its style, both decorative and representational. The lack of published photographs of the cross and its comparative inaccessibility combined to conceal its quality and significance, a situation changed by the Alcocks' powerful response to the monument.

Art historians have always associated the Dupplin cross with Forteviot, and the rise of the Dál Riata leader Cináed mac Alpín, who in the mid-9th century permanently established the Scots in the east, and who died at Forteviot around 858 (Anderson 1980, 250). To support a mid-/late 9th-century date for the cross Stevenson pointed to its 'imported' features: the form of the cross, the grape-less vine ornament, and the confronted 'Anglian' beasts. He ascribed the figurative style to 'local' taste, pointing to the 'very poor David'. The moustaches and close-set composition of the soldiers he regarded as comparable to features in early 10th-century Irish crosses, and conjectured that Scots rather than Picts were represented. Stevenson also saw in Dupplin's decorative repertoire symptoms characteristic of late 9th- and 10th-century taste: the key patterns, repetitive C-scrolls, and two-ply interlace. He admitted, however, that it is 'not that these motifs are now introduced but that they now become very fashionable' (Stevenson 1955, 126).

The reading of the Latin inscription forces a reconsideration of the chronological and cultural significance of these traits. Not all of it, as yet, is legible, but by great good fortune the prevailing weather has spared its first two lines, so that after painstaking scrutiny, it can be read as *Custantin*, or *Custentin*, *filius Fircus*, a name identifiable with Constantine son of Fergus who reigned over the Picts for thirty-one years, until his death in 820, and simultaneously over Dál Riata for the last ten years of his reign (Forsyth 1995, 242). The nature of relationships between kings of the Picts and Scots at this period remains unclear but there seems no doubt that on whatever terms, Constantine was the first leader to hold both kingships (Anderson 1982, 109–10). The natural conclusion is that the Dupplin cross dates to the reign of Constantine or to shortly after his death, that is, to the first quarter of the 9th century. The chances are, therefore, that the decorative repertoire of the Dupplin cross was a cause rather than an effect of fashion.

In general, the cross has been associated with the Scots rather than the Picts because it does not display Pictish symbols and is a free-standing cross rather than a cross slab. It has also been associated with Northumbrian sculpture because the cross head was treated as decoratively distinct from the shaft, was ringless, had double-curve arms, and on its east face was decorated with vine-scroll surrounding a central boss. These assumptions need to be re-examined, along with some aspects of its iconography.

The cross, set on a broad base, is monolithic but unremarkable in scale. Its height from the bottom of the shaft is 2.6 m, approximately the same as that of the Iona school cross at Kildalton on Islay. The Dupplin shaft is somewhat thicker than Kildalton's but in this it approximates to the slab fragment at Dunkeld, Perthshire, apparently a once-massive monument with ambitious iconography (RCAHMS 1994, 89, 96), and the shaft of the cross at Mugdrum, Fife (Fig 14.3), south of the Firth of Tay about two miles east of Abernethy and a mile west of Clatchard Craig. Mugdrum (Allen & Anderson 1903, III, 367) was a much larger cross than Dupplin and when complete would have compared with St Martin's Cross on Iona. At St Andrews the shaft of a cross (no 19) stands at 2.5 m (Hay Fleming 1931, 23). These remnants of very large monuments in Fife and Tayside indicate that in terms of endeavour Dupplin is unique only in its completeness.

While it is true that free-standing crosses are not nearly so numerous as slabs in the Pictish area it has been demonstrated that there are developments within the symbol-bearing cross slabs which show full knowledge of the free-standing cross (Henderson 1978). A free-standing cross stands between enthroned figures on the cross slab at Dunfallandy in Perthshire; three Pictish symbols are carved above the scene (Allen & Anderson 1903, III, fig 305B). The designs of crosses on symbol-bearing cross slabs such as Fowlis Wester, Perthshire (3.1 m high) and Cossans, Angus (2.2 m high) make it obvious that free-standing crosses with rings and bases were well known to the Picts (op. cit. III, figs 306A, 230A).

Although, as yet, no trace of a symbol-bearing free-standing cross has been found, there are symbol-less slabs, clearly related to mainstream Pictish sculpture, such as the 'Daniel Stone' at Meigle (op. cit. III, fig 311). The choice of a free-standing cross by the Dupplin patron obviously has significance, but the erection of such a monument was well within the technical capacity of Pictish sculptors and indeed from their point of view was already within their repertoire. Basically, the presence of the symbols is an indicator of a function relating to the symbols and is not a *sine qua non* of Pictish sculpture, just as the ring, base and capstone have been shown to be optional for Irish sculpture and not a rigidly defining nationalistic formula (Kelly, D 1993, 221).

The double-curved arm may, as Cramp (1984, 9, pl 195.1099) has suggested, have had its origin in Lindisfarne, but by the early 9th century, the time of the erection of the Dupplin cross, this type of cross is integral to the Insular repertoire. It appears in Irish metalwork on the 8th-century Lough Kinale, Co Longford, book-shrine (Kelly, E P 1993), in the slab art of Hoddom, Dumfriesshire (Craig 1991) and of Gilling West, North Yorkshire (Lang & Morris 1978, 128–9, pl 20), in the design of the Insular-inspired Rupertus cross dated to the second half of the 8th century (Webster & Backhouse 1991, no 133), on the 8th-century Rothbury cross (Hawkes 1996b) and on St John's Cross, Iona,

Fig 14.3.   Mugdrum cross, Fife, reverse. Riders with hounds chasing stags. (Photograph: T.E. Gray)

Fig 14.4. Kirriemuir no 17, Angus. Cross slab fragment. (Photograph: T.E. Gray; by permission of The Meffan Institute, Forfar [Angus Council Cultural Services])

although this last example ended up with a ring encircling its double-curved cross head (RCAHMS 1982, 197–204). The Picts were aware of cross designs with true rings and quadrilobate rings (their difference has been overemphasized) from the outset of the slab series. A fragment of a slab decorated with a ringed double-curved cross has recently come to light at the sculptural centre of Kirriemuir, Angus (Fig 14.4). The inspiration for the Dupplin patron must surely have been Iona. Whatever the origin of the double-curved arm on Iona, after its appearance there one need not look further afield for the source of its use at Dupplin.

The aspect of the Dupplin cross head which gives it a special lightness and elegance is the treatment of the moulding of the double curve (Fig 14.1). At the top of each curve, at the cusp, the sections of the moulding interlock to form a double scroll which is neatly emphasized by a second internal moulding. The idea of scrolled cusps may originate in two-dimensional cross designs with spiral attachments on the terminals. In three dimensions the Dupplin moulding recalls a feature of brooch design. For example, the inner edges of the terminals on the front of the Hunterston brooch end in a small tight spiral (Youngs 1989, no 69, plate on 75; see Whitfield below). Also comparable is the treatment of the Crieff mounts where the marginal curves meet the base line of the design in roundels of spirals, giving them an 'architectural' form (Spearman 1993); the Dupplin cross employs a strongly defined outline to the same effect. Crieff, the provenance, but not certainly the origin of the mounts, lies approximately twelve miles up the River Earn from Forteviot. An even closer metalwork parallel is the decorative contouring of the recently found plaque from Asby Winderwath Common, Cumbria (see Youngs below). Scrolled cusps, to my knowledge, are unparalleled in sculpture, suggesting that for this aesthetically pleasing device the sculptor was copying directly from a metalwork model.

Viewed from the side the scrolling creates cylinders within the angles of the cross arms comparable to a feature on some of the Irish high crosses, as on the east face of the cross head of the Tower cross at Kells, Co Meath (Henry 1967, pl 75). The scrolled ends to the straight-sided terminals of the cross of the Scriptures at Clonmacnoise provides only a loose parallel (op. cit. pl 90). The most direct design analogy between Dupplin and the Irish crosses is the extended length of the top arm. Simply as a matter of proportion this could be an Ionan feature but at Dupplin a clear decorative distinction is made between the extension and the rest of the arm. Even more significantly the top of the cross appears to be tegulated. Such skeuomorphic tiled terminations for upper arms are a distinctly Irish trait.

The spread of vine-scroll over the eastern face of the Dupplin cross head (Fig 14.1) has always been regarded as the clearest indication of conscious emulation of Northumbrian sculpture. The scroll is composed of two stems, arranged as a medallion scroll enclosing the central boss. The plants emerge sturdily from brick-like plinths, rather than the chalice or earth-pile more usual in Insular art. The closest parallel is on a fragment from Hulne Priory, Northumberland, dated to the first half of the 9th century, where a spiral plant-scroll grows out of a stepped base (Cramp 1984, 193, pl 188.1035). The Dupplin stems divide so as to provide a shoot, which itself divides to fill the cross arms with two coiled tendrils. The main stems proceed upwards around the boss to fill the lower section of the top arm with a pair of coiled tendrils set one above the other. The growth in the bottom and side arms has leaves, those in the bottom arm taking the form of a central pointed leaf with basal lobed leaves.

The diagonal movement of the stems from the outer corners, with linked leafy shoots within the first crossing, is readily relatable to the design on the Hexham 'Acca' cross, the ultimate source of carved medallion vine-scrolls (op. cit. 174–6, pl 168.898–9). The Dupplin leaf type is found on a cross arm from Cumbria (Carlisle no 2), part of a cross head that presumably had vine-scroll on all four arms. Cramp argues that this finely carved piece, possibly derived from metalwork, dates to the 8th century. She notes the close parallel in the plant in the upper field of the initial B of *Britannia*, the opening of Chapter I in the 8th-century *St Petersburg Bede* (fol 3v; Bailey & Cramp 1988, 85–6, ill 204). This plant type has long been related to forms in the *Book of Kells* (Dublin, Trinity College MS 58; Schapiro 1958).

Other examples of Northumbrian cross heads with double-curved arms, central bosses and vine-scroll are found at Masham, and Lastingham (no 3). The latter has an arm span of 1.5 m and its total height has been estimated at over 6 m. This imposing monument dated by Lang (1991, 168–9, ill 587) to the late 8th to early 9th century, contemporary with the Dupplin cross, will have been influential. The way in which the foliage is arranged round the boss and its spiral-scroll tendrils is certainly comparable to the design on Dupplin. Lang associates Lastingham with the vine-scroll on the arm of the Masham cross (Collingwood 1927, fig 133).

The dating of these Northumbrian sculptural parallels adds weight to the view that the Dupplin cross was erected during or shortly after Constantine's reign. Any general assessment of the period motif of vine-scroll on cross heads (Cramp 1978, 9) will, however, now have to take into account this dated regional example.

The choice of the vine-scroll motif itself, and the specific type (berryless medallion scroll, with pointed/lobed leaves) can be accounted for within the context of the diverse plant-scrolls, inhabited and uninhabited, found in Pictish sculpture, some of it on symbol-bearing cross slabs (Henderson 1983, 243–68). All the types there are themselves reflected in Northumbrian sculpture, so Dupplin is not peculiarly 'non-Pictish' in respect of this relationship to Northumbria.

On the other hand if, as suggested earlier, the motivation for choosing a double-curved arm type came from Iona then the serpent bosses that dominate the cross heads there might also have been expected as the Dupplin patron's choice of motif for his cross head. Vine-scroll is used in frames on Pictish slabs at Tarbat and Hilton of Cadboll in Easter Ross. Easter Ross sculpture also uses serpent bosses, most notably at Nigg, so vine-scroll does not preclude their use. Vine-scroll decorates the edges of Pictish slabs which are probably later than both the Easter Ross sculpture and the Dupplin cross – for example, the 'Drosten Stone' at St Vigean's, Angus, and 'Sueno's Stone' near Forres, Moray. It is also used on at least one side of the Mugdrum cross. It seems that as the 9th century progressed, vine-scroll was favoured for prestigious monuments in eastern Scotland, superseding serpent-boss ornament – a shift from the resurrection symbolism of the serpent (Henderson, I 1987; Mac Lean 1993) to the more scripturally specific eucharistic resonances of the vine (Matthew 26.26–9; John 15.1).

While the Picts were familiar with the vine-scroll motif as such, it would be perverse not to associate the placement of this symbolic motif on the cross head with knowledge of Northumbrian monuments such as Lastingham. Vine-scroll is not used in this position on Pictish crosses or in the surviving Iona school sculpture, although on the east face of the Kildalton cross (RCAHMS 1984, 211) two confronted peacocks peck at a bunch of grapes; the peacocks' legendary immortality gaining further nourishment from the wine of the Eucharist. The same imagery appears in the portrait of Christ on fol 32v of the *Book of Kells* (Henderson, G 1987, pl 224). Some of the more complex vine-scrolls in *Kells* are paralleled in Easter Ross sculpture and, as we have seen, foliage in *Kells* shares with Pictish and Northumbrian sculpture the use of pointed/lobed leaves. Dupplin's Northumbrian 'importation' in respect of vine-scroll is therefore of a very limited nature.

The Dupplin cross like many Northumbrian and Irish monuments has panels of carving on the sides of the shaft and arms, and the ends of the transom arms. These display the variety of treatment typical of a prestigious monument and they deserve detailed study. Here it must suffice to say that side decoration is a feature of the taller, later, Pictish cross slabs (Henderson 1978). It is, for example, a notable feature of the symbol-bearing cross slab at Rosemarkie (Allen & Anderson 1903, III, 67) and the slab fragment with characteristically Pictish animal ornament at Forteviot (Alcock & Alcock 1992, 223, ill 4). The decoration of the sides of slabs is symptomatic of the influence of free-standing cross design generally. There is no need to suppose that the weight of the panelled side decoration of Dupplin represents a fresh response to Northumbrian or Irish sculptural conventions.

The decorative repertoire on the western face of the cross head is typically Pictish (Fig 14.2): the boss marking the crossing is decorated with a key pattern; the arms combine animal-headed interlace and spirals. The boss is surrounded by interlacing so irregular as to have defeated Romilly Allen; he seems also to have missed pairs of confronting animal heads within the inner curve of the arms. The interlace is adjacent to spiral ornament, possibly running into it, as one would expect at this period. Triple spirals connected by C-curves (Allen & Anderson 1903, II, 389, no 1054) is a mainstay of the later Pictish or Picto-Scottish repertoire. In a raised form, and with quadruple spirals (op. cit. II, no 1055), it is used to cover the cross on the symbol-bearing cross slab at Shandwick, Easter Ross (op. cit. III, fig 66B), and on two symbol-bearing slabs at St Vigean's (op. cit. III, figs 250B, 253). Animal-headed interlace disposed around a circular element was in the Pictish repertoire as early as the carving of the Glamis Manse symbol-bearing cross slab (op. cit. III, fig 234A). Of great interest is the use of almost identical animal-headed interlace on the unpublished slab fragment with a double-curved arm ringed cross at Kirriemuir (Fig 14.4). Here, the panel at the crossing is square. This fragment portrays a cross head comparable to that of the ringed St John's Cross of Iona, but decoratively shares this aspect of Dupplin's ornament, so combining the two designs and the decorative repertoire.

At this period, the ribbon bodies of the Dupplin 'animals' could be expected to have run onto the central boss. However, one of the most surprising things about the cross is the severity of the designs of the central bosses. Both have a deep, ribbed border enclosing a gently domed field. The front boss appears to be worn smooth but that on the west face contains traces of either a step pattern or angular interlace. A domed deep-bordered boss was found quite recently at Norham in Northumberland (Bailey & Cramp 1988, ill 675) but the proportions of the Dupplin boss type look more like the skeuomorphic studs in deep metalwork settings such as those on the arms of the Lough Kinale book-shrine (Kelly, E P 1993, fig 20.1). The domed field with its step pattern translates into the metal inlays within cast glass studs used in such settings (Youngs 1989, no 209). Heavily ribbed settings are a design feature of the Bologna shrine which has rectangular settings comparable to the raised bosses on the cross head of the Aberlemno roadside symbol-bearing slab (Henderson, I 1993, fig 26.4a, c). Boss ornament showed great diversity in Pictish and later Picto-Scottish sculpture. The versatility of the suite of bosses on the Nigg cross slab is well known (Ritchie 1989, 35), but more immediately relevant to our understanding of the choice made by the Dupplin carvers is the spiral-covered boss at the centre of the ringed cross on a slab at Crieff (Fig 14.5). Here the central boss is covered with spirals that run off its surface to turn into foliage filling all four arms. Crieff is yet another example of how the repertoires of the free-standing cross and the cross slab develop side by side.

Decoratively and formally the Dupplin cross head is treated as quite separate from the shaft. This distinction is a characteristic of Northumbrian cross design (Kelly, D 1993). On the Iona school crosses, the bottom arm of the cross head follows the line of the shaft, creating a Latin cross, not a Greek cross set on a pedestal shaft. There is, however, a decorative distinction on some of the crosses. For example, all four arms of the eastern face of St Martin's Cross have large bosses, and both sides of the Kildalton cross have a scheme of decoration responsive to the cross head. On Pictish cross slabs there is both a decorative and formal distinction in the representation of the cross head (Henderson, I 1993). It is seen on very early slabs like Eassie, Angus, and later slabs like those at Dunfallandy and Meigle (op. cit. fig 26.2). So again, the Northumbrian influence in this respect had long been absorbed by the time of the erection of the Dupplin cross.

On the eastern face, the shaft contains three panels separated by narrower bands of geometric pattern. Immediately below the lower arm at the top of the shaft, in the position corresponding to the inscription on the western face, the image of a single rider fills the whole panel. If this rider is a representation of Constantine, king of the Picts, later King of the Picts and Scots, then the only roughly contemporary comparison is the seemingly secular standing figure, with a falcon on his wrist, carved at the bottom of the Bewcastle cross. The Northumbrian figure is set within an honorific arch, below an inscription which is too weathered to read as a whole, but which is apparently commemorative (Kitzinger 1993, 10–13; Bailey & Cramp 1988, 65). The Repton rider, fully discussed by the Biddles (1985) is a closer parallel in form, but only a fragment of this originally tall cross has survived so we can only conjecture whether there would have been an accompanying inscription. Whether or not the Repton rider portrays the warrior-king Æthelbald of Mercia (d 757), there can be little doubt that he represented a member of the aristocracy.

Representation of riders is pervasive in Pictish sculpture. Often the leader is shown alone or on a larger scale. Well-known examples are on Meigle nos 2 and 5, Hilton of Cadboll, Dunfallandy, Elgin and Woodwray (Allen & Anderson 1903, III, figs 311B, 314B, 59, 137A, 258B). On three slabs, Edderton, Fordoun and Rossie, the rider is carved on a panel within the cross (op. cit. III, figs 82, 217B, 322B). At Fowlis Wester, on a tall slab with the transom of the cross projecting from its edges, a rider tops the reverse (op. cit. III, fig 306B). All these slabs are symbol-bearing, and on some the symbols are in direct proximity to the rider which, if not certainly equivalent to an inscription, are identifiers of some sort. A section of an ogham inscription on a fragment from Abernethy, described by Allen as carved on 'a horizontal raised band' below horses' legs may provide an example of a rider or riders with an inscription (op. cit. III, fig 323). Many more examples of rider imagery could be cited. It is clear that the very portrayal

Fig 14.5.   Crieff, Perthshire.
Cross slab, obverse.
(Photograph: T.E. Gray; by
permission of the Trustees for the
National Museums of Scotland)

of a single rider on the Dupplin shaft represents, indisputably, a thoroughly Pictish cultural convention (Henderson, I 1994b, 48–53).

The rider's bodyguard of four foot-soldiers fills the panel below him. Shield-bearing foot-soldiers accompanying a rider are depicted on a panel at Dull in Perthshire (Allen & Anderson 1903, III, fig 329) and are shown in ceremonial dress, accompanying a leader, on foot, on the symbol-bearing slab from Birsay (Ritchie 1989, 52).

What is unusual about the shaft imagery is the change in figurative style, even though the preferred Pictish profile viewpoint is maintained. The static position of the Dupplin horse, with all four hoofs on the ground, and the tight reining-in of the horse's head has been interpreted by the Alcocks as a deliberate move away from the fleeting, more narrative portrayal of Pictish riders to an iconic image of permanence and authority (Alcock & Alcock 1992, 240). The same stance is found on a cross slab fragment, Dunkeld no 2, where riders are accompanied by four foot-soldiers and three prostrate figures representing the fallen enemy (RCAHMS 1994, fig B) and at Mugdrum (Fig 14.3) and Forteviot no 4 (Allen & Anderson 1903, III, fig 338).

Even more remarkable is the proportionately large head of the rider. This convention is used deliberately for affective reasons in Insular Evangelists' portraits (Kitzinger 1993, 12). Where the pose is frontal, as in the case of the Evangelists, the greater head size is less disconcerting for it obviously insists on direct communication with the viewer. Profile enlargement is seen at its most extreme on the Germanic gold bracteates based on Roman imperial medallions, where only the head of the rider is placed on the horse's back (Webster & Brown 1997, pl 57). Confirming this conscious use of a more expressive approach to style is the linear elongation and close-packed nature of the guarding wall of foot-soldiers at Dupplin. Even the lunging hounds within the bottom panel of the shaft, paralleled at Mugdrum, adopt a dynamic style appropriate to the subject matter.

The moustaches of the single rider and the two more senior looking soldiers on the south side of the shaft have often been noted and declared to be 'Irish'. In a recent study of the Northumbrian Rothbury cross Hawkes (1996b, 30) has addressed the question of the use of moustaches as a feature of its head types. She suggests that moustaches were a useful means of identifying different grades of people. This view clearly fits their use on Dupplin (Alcock & Alcock 1992, 240). The Picts seem to have been aware of this convention; the two patrician figures on the St Andrews Sarcophagus have facial hair while the more humble foot-hunter is clean-shaven (Ritchie 1989, 40).

The most unusual feature of the Dupplin head type is the block-like nose and frontal eye. On the soldiers this profile suggests helmets with nasals but the profile of the harpist in a panel on the north side makes it clear that a stylized facial type is represented (Alcock & Alcock 1992, ill 13; Fig 14.6). The starkness of this formula for a profile face occurs in the *Book of Kells*, but the closest

Fig 14.7. Moone cross, Co Kildare, north side detail. Meeting of St Paul and St Anthony. (By permission of the Department of Arts, Culture and the Gaeltacht, Ireland)

Fig 14.6. Dupplin cross, Perthshire, north side detail. David harping.

analogy is on the cross at Moone, Co Kildare (McNab 1988, fig 3; Fig 14.7). Here, the formulaic frontal style is paralleled on the cross slab fragment at Dunkeld where the respective sets of Apostles are drawn in playing-card mode. The many stylistic and iconographical connections between Pictish sculpture and all the sculpture at Moone deserve further study (de Paor & de Paor 1958, 150; Macquarrie 1992, 122; Henderson 1997, 20). It is noteworthy that the foundation at Moone has, traditionally, a Columban association (Herbert 1988, 282 n 378). What must be emphasized is that *pace* Stevenson the figurative style of the Dupplin cross does not represent a decline from Pictish naturalism to regional barbarism but rather shows a sophisticated awareness that style in itself can be a bearer of meaning. Interestingly, however, the influence of Pictish slab layout is still apparent on the Dupplin cross, and to some extent on the slab fragment at Dunkeld (RCAHMS 1994, 96, fig B) where, respectively, the parade of soldiers and the cavalcade spill into the edge space. The narrative benefits of the roomy, traditional cross slab do not transfer satisfactorily to the shaft format.

The panel beneath the inscription on the west side of the shaft consists of a central roundel of interlace surrounded by four pairs of birds, two at each corner, with beaks and legs interlocked (Fig 14.2). The interlace is cruciform, and identical roundels of this admittedly comparatively simple pattern are found at the bottom of two columns of the canon table on fol 5 of the *Book of Kells* (Henderson, G 1987, pl 202). There are bird motifs on this page also, and of course birds abound in Insular art, inhabiting vines, enmeshed with each other or in processions. The Dupplin panel could simply be an ornamental space-filler separating the inscription from the biblical iconography below. Harbison (1986, 49–85, 79) has compared the Dupplin birds with the triquetra of birds placed under the cross arms on the Cardonagh cross, Co Donegal, and more specifically with the pairs of confronted birds with interlocked beaks within the pediment-like top of the east face of the slab in the churchyard at Fahan Mura, also in Donegal. Henry has stressed the potentially Columban associations of this sculpture through the nearby Columban monastery of Derry (Henry 1965, 127–8).

These plump and sharp-beaked birds might reasonably be thought to represent doves. The exegesis on the dove available to Insular commentators has recently been fully explored in connection with this imagery in the *Book of Kells* (O'Reilly 1994, 347–53). For this purpose one may simply note Adomnán's words in the second preface to the *Life of Columba* where he informs the reader that divine providence had given the saint the name Columba, meaning 'dove'. He then develops the theme:

> For it is shown by the Gospels that the Holy Spirit descended upon the only begotten Son of the everlasting Father in the form of that little bird. For this reason, in the Scriptures the dove is generally taken allegorically to represent the Holy Spirit. Likewise the Saviour himself in the Gospel told the disciples that they should have the simplicity of the dove in a pure heart. For the dove is indeed a simple and innocent bird, and it was fitting that a simple and innocent man should have this for his name, who through his dove-like life offered in himself a dwelling for the Holy Spirit (Sharpe 1995, 104).

Adomnán is thinking of Christ's words to his disciples in Matthew 10.16: 'Behold I send you out as sheep in the midst of wolves, be ye therefore wise as serpents, and simple as doves'. The Dupplin doves surrounding the symbol of the cross could be a visualization of the second half of the verse, rather than of the first ('as wise as serpents'), familiarly alluded to in the roundels of serpents found in the *Book of Kells* and on Pictish, Ionan and Irish sculpture – a dove 'boss' (albeit in shallow relief) rather than a serpentine one.

David protecting the sheep is shown in the bottom panel. David, accompanied by his dog, confronts the lions in virtually identical pose as on the symbol-less cross slab from Aldbar, now in Brechin Cathedral (Allen & Anderson 1903, III, fig 259B). Fitted into the remaining space a larger figure, wielding a stick, holds firmly with his left hand the tail of a quadruped that paces forward in the Pictish naturalistic fashion. Presumably this is David killing the bear. The role of David as a type both of Christ the Saviour and as a model for kingship has been much discussed (Bullough 1975; Webster & Brown 1997, 226–30) but given the emphasis on the native leader, both visually on the east face and textually in the inscription on the west, it is worth remembering that it was David's prowess against both lion and bear that convinced Saul that he could defeat Goliath (1 Samuel 17.31–7). The portrayal of David's encounters with wild animals is therefore redolent not only of Christ's Salvation, but serves also as a reminder of the qualities necessary for a warrior who can save his people. At Aldbar, David wears a belted tunic, and in other Pictish sculpture he wears rather grand attire (Henderson 1994a, 80–1). In both motifs on the Dupplin shaft David appears to be naked. The unencumbered figures resemble the imagery of David on the ends of the transom arms of the Kells Tower cross, where, on the south side, David's knee presses down on the lion's back in Mithraic pose (Harbison 1992, II, fig 352). On the north side, the bear (op. cit. II, fig 357) jumps up at David, who in a gesture reminiscent of the Dupplin version, grasps the back of its neck while raising his club to strike it. Harbison considers the 'bear' to be more lion-like, but a fierce predator is all that is required, not a naturalistic rendering, and other writers have accepted the images as a pair depicting the confrontations with both lion and bear (op. cit. I, 216).

On the top arm of the east face of the Kells Tower cross David is shown enthroned, playing what Harbison believes to be the only example of a triangular harp in Irish sculpture (op. cit. I, 214). In Pictish sculpture David's harp is invariably triangular, so there is no doubt that the impressive instrument which the enthroned David plays on the north side of the Dupplin cross is conceived within the Pictish tradition (Fig 14.6). On the other hand, an enthroned David harping conforms to Irish and Northumbrian iconographical practice. The Dupplin image is a remarkably naturalistic representation of a harp being played; the player's fingers are clearly depicted plucking the strings. The effective depiction of hands functioning is a distinctive trait of Pictish sculpture. However, as mentioned earlier, there is nothing Pictish about the harpist's profile. He has the block-like nose which became part of the repertoire of Picto-Scottish sculpture, to appear unambiguously on, for example, the symbol-less slab from Benvie, Angus, now in the Dundee Museum (Allen & Anderson 1903, III, fig 260B). This small slab, about 1 m high, depicts two armed riders in a style clearly derived from the Dupplin cross.

The aims of this chapter have been to show that the Northumbrian associations of the cross, though present, have been overstated. The break with the Pictish sculptural tradition has also been exaggerated. The choices made by the Dupplin patron for the monument show his familiarity with Insular sculpture in general, but retain a high proportion of specifically Pictish traits drawn from the evolving art of the symbol-bearing cross slabs. A fundamental and enduring feature of the Pictish monumental tradition was the use of rider imagery to portray the secular elite. To the extent that Dupplin complies with this convention it cannot be described as a fundamentally post-Pictish monument, a description queried by Wormald (1996, 135). Of more cultural significance than the Northumbrian traits are the stylistic and iconographical innovations related to sites and sculpture with Columban associations.

What was the motivation behind the erection of the monument? To 20th-century eyes the single rider set above his protecting wall of shields has more impact than the vine-covered cross head. For the 9th-century viewer, however, vine-scroll would not have been mere decoration. The protection of a strong leader was necessary for survival in this world but as Bailey (1996a, 52) points out, for 'the medieval Christian the vine-scroll was always potentially a symbol of Christ and his Church – and of them as sources of sustenance and protection'. The imagery of the cross has to be looked at in the context of Psalm 32 (*Douai Bible*): 'Give praise to the Lord on the harp' (verse 2); 'the king is not saved by a great army' (verse 16); 'vain is the horse for safety' (verse 17); and 'the Lord . . . is our helper and protector' (verse 20).

On the east face of the Dupplin cross the necessary equilibrium between church and state, cross head and cross shaft, is carefully observed. On the west face images of David, a type of both Christ and the ideal ruler, maintain the same balance. If the results of recent research are sustained Constantine himself was both a warrior-king who brought stability to the peoples he controlled, and a warrior for Christ (Clancy 1996). Until now the association of Constantine with Dunkeld, the cult centre of Columba, depended on a late note attached to the Gaelicized version of the Pictish king list (Anderson 1980, 194). If, as has been argued by Clancy, a portion of Columban relics came to Pictland shortly before Constantine's death then his early association with Dunkeld is strengthened. It is possible therefore that by the 820s Columba was already returning centre stage to eastern Scotland and that this was due to Constantine's personal devotion to the saint – a devotion apparent on his monument.

Osbald, briefly king of Northumbria, possibly with blood on his hands, was exiled in Pictland for a short period during Constantine's reign. In 798 Alcuin wrote an admonitory letter to him suggesting that one way of obtaining God's grace for himself would be 'to exhort the race among whom you are exiled concerning its salvation'. While it may seem far-fetched to see the dissemination of the notion of the vine-clad cross head as part of Osbald's soul-saving effort, no doubt, as at other periods, the presence of a Northumbrian royal exile will have had cultural effects (Higgitt 1982, 318; Brown 1972, 235–43). Northumbrian knowledge of Constantine's piety will certainly have been increased and the testimony of Osbald, who became an abbot and was buried at York, may have played a part in securing the inclusion of Constantine's name in the *Liber Vitae* of Lindisfarne, or possibly, Jarrow (Webster & Backhouse 1991, no 97).

Viewing the cross as a link with Columban Dunkeld supports Spearman's conjecture (1993, 136) that the carved arch from Forteviot may have been part of the palace chapel located there, dedicated to Columba, and able periodically to provide protection for the Dunkeld reliquaries. The principal figure on the arch presents a fine example of the moustached, block-nosed, frontal-eyed facial type (Alcock & Alcock 1992, 225, ill 6). He holds a massive sword or staff over his knees, and with his attendants protects both his flock and a draped pedestal or altar, on which stands a cross, now defaced. However interpreted, the figure is basically a Defender of the Faith represented by the altar, cross and, possibly, the *Agnus Dei*.

The arch ended up in the Water of May, below Holy Hill at the west end of Forteviot. Other fine sculptures at Forteviot, including a free-standing cross with a ringed cross head, were broken up. We must be grateful that by a miracle or quirk of fate or, more mundanely, as a result of the protection of the wooden railing, the Dupplin cross survived, unimpaired except by wind and weather. Art-historically it affords the key to much of the sculpture of the 9th and 10th century in Scotland, bridging as it does the rider monuments of the Pictish tradition and the eventually more clerically oriented sculpture of the later medieval period. It now has a firm date bracket and a firm association with a royal patron. Its potentiality for Insular sculpture in general, in these respects, has yet to be exploited.

Note: since this paper was written the Dupplin cross has been removed from the Dupplin estate and is currently on display at the Museum of Scotland in Edinburgh.

ACKNOWLEDGEMENTS

For references and other help I am indebted to Norman Atkinson, Tom Gray, Peter Harbison, James Lang and Michael Spearman.

CHAPTER 15

NORTHUMBRIAN VINE-
SCROLL ORNAMENT
AND THE *BOOK OF
KELLS*

Douglas Mac Lean

Schapiro (1980) derived the foliate decoration of the *Book of Kells* from Northumbria, although Meyvaert (1989) proposed a Coptic source, while recent scholarship emphasizes the Eucharistic dimension of the motif. Any relationship between Northumbrian vine-scrolls and those in the *Book of Kells* may be explored in two ways. Isabel Henderson's (1987) approach to the manuscript's snake ornament provides the methodology best suited to deciphering any meaning intended by the illuminators in their placement of its foliage, while corresponding forms may indicate links between the manuscript's scriptorium and specific Anglo-Saxon ateliers or their sources.

PLACEMENT AND MEANING

Henry (1974, 209) distinguished two types of foliate ornament in *Kells*: either 'light, feathery sprays practically incorporated in the text' or fully developed vine-scrolls, although the latter may be further subdivided into inhabited and uninhabited variants. Examples of foliate sprays are found in the numerical columns of three of the canon tables; those on folios 1v and 3v are somewhat vestigial (op. cit. pls 2, 6).

Sprays are occasionally set in chalices, as in the *capitula* of John (fol 25v) at the beginning of the Passion (op. cit. pl 18). Meehan (1994a, 46) lists additional examples on folios 21r–22r, 48v, 106v, 257r, 276v and 326r. That on folio 276v follows Luke 22.40, set in the Garden of Gethsemane on the Mount of Olives: 'And when he was come to the place, he said to them: Pray, lest ye enter into temptation', a passage suggestive of the vine-scroll ornament of both the *Kells*

Fig 15.1. *Book of Kells* (*Dublin, Trinity College Library, MS 58*), fol 276v. (The Board of Trinity College, Dublin)

Fig 15.2. *Book of Kells*, fol 309r.

Temptation and 'Arrest' miniatures. An eagle turns toward a cluster of three berries on a spray on folio 276v (Fig 15.1), as do the birds on the Jedburgh shrine (Fig 15.3), a product of the same Jarrow milieu that produced the Ruthwell and Bewcastle crosses (Cramp 1984, 16). The eagle and chalice comprise a 'turn-in-the-path' connecting the end of their line of text with the line below, while the chalice's upper spray points to the word *calicem* in the second line of the facing folio, 277r, Luke 22.42: 'Father, if Thou wilt, remove this chalice from me' (McGurk 1990, 139, for textual variants).

One spray in the *Book of Kells* becomes a proper vine, on folio 309r (Fig 15.2) following John 6.40 '. . . every one who seeth the Son and believeth in Him, may have life everlasting, and I will raise him up in the last day' (op. cit. 146). The vine's trefoils are tinted green or yellow, while the vine itself is red, its alternately oriented tendrils enclosing rosettes of red dots. Such an uninhabited vine-scroll pattern is common to the Hexham school, exemplified by the analogous Hexham 3D (Fig 15.4), datable between the mid-8th century and the first quarter of the 9th (Cramp 1984, 15, 177), contemporary with the generally accepted parameters for the *Book of Kells*. Even the manuscript's simple foliate sprays allude to both principal types of early Northumbrian sculpted vine-scrolls: the inhabited ones derived from Jarrow and the uninhabited developed at Hexham.

Uninhabited vines recur throughout the manuscript. The upper and lower right corner protrusions of the Virgin and Child miniature's border (fol 7v) enclose vases housing vines with bluntly pointed leaves. Vines fill the second and last registers within the frame of the facing folio 8r, the *Nativitas XPI incipit* of Matthew's *capitula* (Meehan 1994a, 59, figs 7–8). One blue and one yellow vine zigzag from a chalice against the right edge of the second register, forming a trellis of lozenges framing vine tendrils with yellow, mostly trefoil rounded leaves, with trefoils of rounded blue leaves in the triangular interspaces. A more austere Bernician relative covers one face of the Abercorn, West Lothian, cross shaft (Cramp 1984, Pl. 266, 1435). Henderson (1983, 254, figs 104a, 106b) relates the *Kells* lozenge trellis to the single zigzag vine stem in the left border of the Pictish Hilton of Cadboll slab and the Jarrow usage of diagonal stems within vine-scroll roundels, seen, for example, in the lower four at Jedburgh (Fig 15.3). Green and blue vines grow from a central chalice in the last enframed register of the *Kells Nativitas* page, with trefoil and quatrefoil rounded leaves. The vine to the left of the chalice includes grape clusters and terminates in an elongated central pointed leaf, between two rounded leaves or buds.

Related forms adorn the vines curling from two vases mounted in the lower frame of the arch in the 'Arrest' miniature (fol 114r). The pots and vines are blue, as are the vases and the central undulating vine stems in the lowest rectangles of the columns supporting the arch, where the interlaced tendrils also sprout rounded and pointed leaves (Henry 1974, pl 45). Nordenfalk (1977, 276) thought that the vines framing the phrase *in montem Oliveti* recalled the description in the *De Locis Sanctis* by Adomnán, who depended upon the travelling Frankish bishop Arculf, according to whom, 'it is rare to find any other trees on Mount Olivet except vines and olives' (Meehan 1958, 64–5). But the miniature's vines transcend topography. Insular exegesis successively layers the *locus sanctus* with Christ's Passion, Ascension and final return (Farr 1994, 445–8). The potted vines seem to grow from the heads of the two figures flanking Christ, whom Farr (1994, 445–6) identifies with John's two witnesses in Apocalypse 11.3–13, 'the two olive trees, and the two candlesticks, that stand before the Lord of the earth', echoing the prophet Zechariah's (4.2–14) vision of the temple's golden menorah between two olive trees, 'the two sons of oil who [also] stand before the Lord of the whole earth'. O'Reilly (1993, 111) relates the chrismal implications to Bede's commentary on Christ's Ascension from the Mount of Olives (*CCSL* 121, 9, *Exp Act Ap* I.12), commonly seen as a place of unction.

Fig 15.3.   Jedburgh shrine. (Copyright Department of Archaeology, University of Durham. Photograph: T. Middlemass)

Fig 15.4. Hexham 3D cross-shaft. (Copyright Department of Archaeology, University of Durham. Photograph: T. Middlemass)

Fig 15.5. Hexham 3A cross-shaft. (Copyright Department of Archaeology, University of Durham. Photograph: T. Middlemass)

The trefoil rounded leaves terminating the *fuits* on the first page of the Lucan Genealogy of Christ (fol 200r) become occasional sprays on the second and fourth pages (fols 200v, 201v), but disappear from the third page (fol 201r), where a merman grasps the *fuit* opposite the name *Iona*, the Hebrew equivalent of Latin Columba, or 'dove', an equation known to Columbanus and Adomnán of Iona, as Meyvaert (1989, 6–9, fig 1) has shown. The point may be emphasized by the replacement of the preceding genealogy pages' foliage with birds, perhaps a general reference to doves (Meehan 1994a, 64), whose broader exegetical implications O'Reilly (1994, 345–54, 376–7, pls 37–40) has discussed.

Foliage reappears on the last page of the Lucan Genealogy (fol 202r), terminating in 'the blond figure of Christ himself' (Meehan 1994a, 60) standing behind a double frame enclosing interlaced peacocks on the left and interlaced vines set in a blue chalice on the right (Fig 15.6). The leaves are virtually all rounded and the vine coils enclose a grape cluster on the left. The complexity of the vines' interlace is comparable to the equally uninhabited and contemporary Hexham 3A (Fig 15.5), although the *Kells* vines are somewhat less controlled.

The *verso* of the same folio, the Temptation miniature (fol 202v; Henry 1974, pl 68), has an angel in each upper corner, attending vines in differing vessels, a

Fig 15.6. *Book of Kells*, fol 202r. (The Board of Trinity College, Dublin)

vase on the left and a chalice on the right. Rounded leaf trefoils predominate on the left, while the right-hand vine includes two grape clusters and two triplets of pointed central leaves between rounded buds. Patristic and Insular exegesis helps identify the angels with the two cherubim set above the ark in both the Tabernacle and the Temple, while the miniature's body of Christ becomes the new Temple or church (Farr 1991, 133–5; 1994, 439–40; O'Reilly 1994, 359–61, 370, 375–82). The vine-scrolls, possibly overlooked in this context, prompt one to go further: the right-hand angel's chalice and grapes combine Christ's body with his blood, visually paraphrasing the *Stowe Missal's* Old Irish treatise on the mass, which equates the chalice and the church (Warner 1915, 40). The 'figure waiting behind the vine-scroll at the end of the list of the church's spiritual ancestors on fol 202r' (Fig 15.6) affirms the sacerdotal aspect, foreshadowing 'the high priestly figure standing among the new chosen people in the corresponding position' in the following Temptation miniature, in a recasting of the priesthood of Aaron (O'Reilly 1994, 365, 383–8).

One member of that priesthood, Zacharias, descended from Aaron through Abia, while his wife Elizabeth was 'of the daughters of Aaron' (Luke 1.5). The decoration of Zacharias name in the *incipit* of the Lucan *capitula* (fol 19v) underscores 'the eucharistic sacrifice of the new high priest' (O'Reilly 1994, 358), with its inhabited vine-scroll sprung from a chalice, where the letters A, C and A, but not the H, have feline bodies and the first A shelters a bird (Meehan 1994a, fig 69). The leaves are all rounded and bird and animals alike eat the grapes, as do those on the west face of the Ruthwell cross (Cramp 1984, Pl. 254 1427).

Three of the *Kells* canon tables also have inhabited vine-scrolls. Birds of the Lindisfarne type, identified by Meehan (1994a, 57, fig 3) as 'peacocks', inhabit the vines grown from a central inverted chalice in the arch on folio 2r. The leaves are mostly rounded, with a few pointed examples. Foliate sprays appear underneath the second and third numerical columns (Alexander 1990, 306). Vines with rounded leaves grow from a vase, framed by peacocks' feet, above the centre of the arch of the canon table on folio 3r, a Eucharistic reference to Christ's blood, when combined with the image of Christ's body atop the facing canon table, folio 2v (Ó Carragáin 1994b, 426–9, pls 2–3). On folio 4r vases house vine sprays alongside the Matthew and John symbols above the outer numerical columns (Meehan 1994a, 59), while the vine-scrolls in the two central architectural columns comprise roundels enframing sets of rounded leaves, inhabited by occasional birds (Henry 1974, pl 7).

The peacocks standing in vines in the chalices flanking the enthroned Christ (fol 32v) link the Eucharist to the Resurrection. All the leaves are rounded, but only the vine on the left has grapes. Both vines entwine the feet of the peacocks, established as symbols of immortality in early Christian art and patristic texts (op. cit. 209, pl 26; Henderson, G 1987, 159; Meehan, 1994a, 57).

The *Tunc dicit* of Matthew 26.31 (fol 114v), following the 'Arrest' miniature on the *recto*, becomes an inhabited vine-scroll with two grape bunches, mostly pointed leaves and the tongues of the animal-head terminals of the T and D participating in the ornament (Henry 1974, pl 46; Alexander 1990, 310–11). Liturgical links to Holy Thursday (Farr 1994, 440–3) tie the decoration to the Last Supper and the institution of the Eucharist.

Inhabited vines appear in the frames of two of the four-symbol pages in the *Book of Kells* (Meehan 1994a, 60, figs 5, 38). Diagonal blue vases in the upper right and lower left corners of folio 27v, preceding Matthew, anchor vines with paired birds. Two small panels set in each long side of folio 129v, preceding Mark, have central vases placed against the right edges, flanked by pairs of confronted birds, their beaks meeting above the outwardly coiling vines.

Three of the major initial pages have inhabited vine ornament. An inverted chalice, at the top of the bottom right corner bracket of the *chi-rho* page (fol 34r), sprouts a vine-scroll inhabited by paired birds (op. cit. 1994a, 60, fig 73). The bottom disc of the *Quoniam* page's Q (fol 188r) encloses a cruciform arrangement of vines with rounded trefoil leaves, densely inhabited by four pairs of birds and four quadrupeds, all gobbling grapes, with four knotted snakes attacking four vine roundels (but cf Henry 1974, 209–10, fig 65, pl 115). The animals' bodies of the letters RIN of John's *In Principio* (fol 292r) inhabit a vine potted in a chalice on the right. I cannot find the peacocks Meehan (1994a, 60, fig 72) claims for this composition but support his suggestion that its scribe or artist may also be credited with folios 8r (*Nativitas*) and 19v (*Zachariae*), both notable for their vine-scrolls (Meehan 1994b, 194).

Another inhabited vine-scroll, issuing from central chalices on all four sides, fills the border of the *Una autem* page (fol 285r) introducing the Lucan account of the Resurrection (Henry 1974, pl 89). Pairs of elongated quadrupeds are confronted over each chalice. Werner's (1994, 465, 472) identification of the Eucharistic symbolism, 'necessarily referring to the sacrifice of Christ', is undoubtedly correct, but may be expanded.

Ó Carragáin (1986, 383–9; 1988b, 4–6, 20 n 2; 1994b, 422–33) has focused attention on Northumbrian and Irish liturgical use of the Old Latin Canticle of Habbakuk 3.2, 'In the midst of two animals you will be recognized'. Noting the common comparison of the phrase to Christ crucified between two thieves, Jerome drew parallels between it and God speaking to Israel between the two cherubim over the Ark of the Covenant, God revealed between the Old and New Testaments and God the Father made known in the Trinity between the Son and the Holy Spirit (*CCSL* 76A, 620–1, *In Abac* II.iii.2). Bede further saw the phrase as a metaphor for Christ recognized at the Transfiguration between Moses and Elijah (*CCSL* 119B, 383–4, *In Cant Abac* 60–79). Ó Carragáin (1986, 384–8; 1994b, 423–4) additionally applies the canticle to the Christ over the Beasts panels of the Ruthwell and Bewcastle crosses, as well as the figures flanking Christ in the *Kells* 'Arrest' miniature (where the 'inhabitants' are vined, rather than the vines inhabited). The comparably habitual pairing of creatures inhabiting *Kells* vine-scroll compositions recalls Christ's statement at the Last Supper (John 15.5), 'I am the vine; you the branches' (cf O'Reilly 1993, 110–11).

Foliate ornament in the *Book of Kells* shows a particular affinity for Luke: in Zacharias name in the Lucan *capitula* incipit, the *Quoniam* page, the Lucan Genealogy of Christ, the Temptation miniature in Luke's gospel, and the texts beginning Luke's accounts of Christ's Arrest and the Resurrection. Such reiteration supports O'Reilly's exposition of the iconographical theme of priestly sacrifice in Luke's gospel in the *Book of Kells*.

Isabel Henderson (1987, 60–4) perceptively notes that snake ornament and vine-scrolls, as new motifs to the *Kells* artists, 'would have been used more consciously than the old repertoire of spiral, interlace and fret'. But they are used in somewhat different ways. As Henderson has shown, snakes appear on all four gospel initial pages and the *chi-rho* monogram, while vine-scrolls are restricted to three of those five pages. Five of the *Kells* canon tables utilize foliate decoration, but only one (fol 5v) uses snakes to form two of its grid lines (Meehan 1994a, 53; Henderson, G 1987, fig 203). Snakes decorate a single four-symbols page (fol 27v), while two have vine-scrolls in their decoration. The 'Arrest' and Temptation miniatures feature snakes, but vine-scrolls appear on all three full-page illuminations, including the Virgin and Child miniature. Snake imagery 'is used consistently to highlight the text of the Passion' in the *Book of Kells* (Henderson, I 1987, 64), underscoring the miracle of the Resurrection. In contrast, foliate ornament embellishes textual references to the priest Zacharias and Christ's genealogy, birth, the Passion, Resurrection and Last Judgement, in a creative adaptation of an established Eucharistic symbol, distinct from the more pointed application of snake decoration, in whose invention the *Kells* artists are likely to have participated (cf Mac Lean 1993), leaving the indications of their delight in the discovery in the snakes found in all five major initial pages. Both snakes and vines were new motifs, but vines were comparatively more alien, however well the *Kells* artists mastered their depiction. Henry (1974, 209) described the *Kells* vine as 'a product of the imagination of the painter who had probably never seen the real plant', but something must have stimulated the artists' imagination.

FORMAL ORIGINS

Since 'no one has yet found a convincing Carolingian model for the plant forms in *Kells*', Schapiro (1980, 215, 217) derived them 'from one stream of Northumbrian art, which issued from or passed through Wearmouth and Jarrow' a suggestion made in his study of the *St Petersburg Bede* (*Pub Lib, MS Q.I.18*), a Wearmouth-Jarrow product of c 746 (Alexander 1978, no 19). The two loops of the initial B of *Brittania* at the beginning of Book 1 (fol 3v) contain differentiated plant forms. Of these, the upper is closer to the *Book of Kells*, with its trefoil arrangements of leaves, buds or berries and others with a central, elongated pointed leaf (Schapiro 1980, 215, Fig 4). Comparable groupings, with and without pointed central leaves, appear early in Northumbrian sculpture, on the c 700 Jarrow no 20 'Hunter' relief (Cramp 1984, 115, Pl. 98 525), although the *St Petersburg* vine is uninhabited.

The lower plant form in the *St Petersburg* B has no cognates in *Kells*, but offers other connections. The closest parallels Schapiro (1980, 205, 222 n 31) found to its 'distinctive central flower, set like a trefoil in the palmette', occur on the gilt bronze repoussé plaques on the tie-rods in the Dome of the Rock in Jerusalem, completed in 691. Creswell (1969, I, 1, 86–7, 121–2, pls 27c, e, 29c) established the plaques' early Umayyad date and their Syrian stylistic origins (cf Åberg 1945, 51–3), but 'whether the motif got to England directly from the East or by way of Continental art', Schapiro (1980, 205) did 'not venture to guess'.

Kitzinger (1936, 67–8, pl V) found undulating Northumbrian sculptural vine-scrolls with alternately oriented grape clusters comparable to mosaics in the Dome of the Rock. Cramp (1974, 134) detected similarities between the gilt bronze plaques on both the tie-beams and entrance lintels in the same building and similarly uninhabited vine-scrolls of the Hexham school of Northumbrian sculpture. Rounded leaves predominate in the *Book of Kells* in two of the canon tables (fols 3r, 4r), the incipits of Matthew's and Luke's *capitula* (fols 8r, 19r), the Christ portrait (fol 32v) and the end of the Lucan Genealogy (fol 202r). Similar leaf formations decorate the lintel plaques (Fig 15.7) over the doorways of the Dome of the Rock (Creswell 1969, I, 1, 82, pls 3a–c). The *Kells* artists, it seems, had access to the same sources that informed Hexham, whether independently or through a Northumbrian intermediary. Like Schapiro, Cramp (1974, 134–5) doubts 'direct contact between Hexham and the Middle East', preferring 'either

Fig 15.7. Dome of the Rock, Jerusalem: gilt bronze plaque, north entrance lintel. (The Ashmolean Museum, University of Oxford)

the importation of an artist, or of a notable model from that area on which several different types of vine-scroll co-existed'. The gilt bronze plaques in Jerusalem offer the likely medium of such an import, enabling Cramp to envision 'a particularly remarkable golden cross' brought to Northumbria from afar.

The visit of Iona's abbot Sléibíne to Ripon in the mid-8th century (Ó Cróinín 1983, 84–5) suggests one avenue by which the artists of the *Book of Kells* could have learned of such an imported model. But a single exemplar seems unlikely to explain all the vine-scrolls in the manuscript, which embraces both inhabited and uninhabited variants. One cross carved by the Iona sculptors demonstrates familiarity with inhabited vine-scrolls: two birds peck at a bunch of grapes on the east face of the constriction of the upper cross arm on the Kildalton cross (RCAHMS 1984, 211). The Iona sculptor's experimentation with cross structure

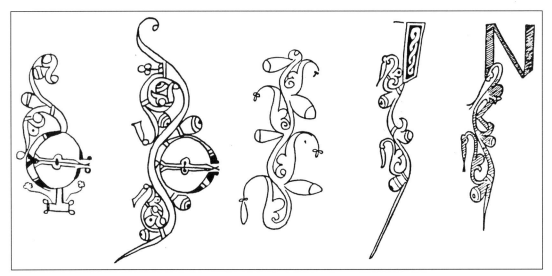

Fig 15.8.   Examples of floriated Coptic *coronis*. (After Meyvaert 1989, figs 6–10)

reflects an awareness of technical developments in Northumbria (Mac Lean 1995), exemplified in their early stages by the Ruthwell and Bewcastle crosses. The use of both inhabited and uninhabited vines in the *Book of Kells* best evokes Bewcastle, which incorporates both types in its ornamental repertoire (Bailey & Cramp 1988, 20, 63–8, ills 91–3, 99–100, 102, 107, 112–5). But Bewcastle is already an amalgamation of competing tendencies in Northumbrian sculpture, reflecting multiple sources. We should imagine a similar set of choices available to the *Kells* artists.

Meyvaert (1989, 15–17) suggests one such possibility. The tips of pointed and rounded leaves in the *Book of Kells* are frequently decorated with double lines, a detail Meyvaert derives from the *coronis*, one of the three types of paragraph marks in Coptic manuscripts. Single lines decorate Meyvaert's earliest example (Fig 15.8, centre), datable to the 8th or early 9th century, while only rounded buds have double lines in the others, dated between 861 and 889, wherein pointed leaves are reduced in importance (Jansma 1973, 41, 45, 93, 129–30, 228–30; Petersen 1954, 314, 316). Lacking clear evidence for the 'earlier stages' of the floriated *coronis*, Meyvaert attributes the *Kells* motif to Arculf's sojourn in Alexandria, prior to calling at Iona in the early 680s, but Arculf must have arrived heavy laden indeed, if he were truly responsible for all the artistic baggage that has been attributed to him (*pace* Werner 1994, 455–6, 465–6, 477–9, 486 n 121). Meyvaert deserves praise, however, for identifying the criteria also characteristic of three-dimensional, if non-Coptic, antecedents of the *Kells* motif.

Åberg (1945, 82–4, figs 78–9) isolated a 7th-century Lombardic type of foliate metalwork ornament, with Visigothic counterparts, bearing pointed and rounded leaves with segmented tips, in response to Byzantine stimuli, with compositional

Fig 15.9. Foliate designs in Lombardic metalwork. (After Åberg 1945, fig 78)

equivalents on the bronze plaques in the Dome of the Rock. A pertinent reliquary in Utrecht (Fig 15.9, centre) parallels another in Beromünster, Switzerland, inscribed with the name of Warnebertus, an obscure bishop of Soissons (d 676), although both reliquaries or their makers came from further south (Hubert et al. 1969, 311; Roth 1979, 280, pl 230b). Cramp (1986, 132) notes the Lombardic hospitality accorded Wilfrid in 679 by King Perctarit, whose successor Cunicpert married the Anglo-Saxon Hermelinda (Plummer 1896, II, 279, 325). Distinctly western developments, begun as effects of a Byzantine cause, may therefore culminate in the later 8th century in the double lines decorating the foliate buds of the Northumbrian silver-gilt Ormside Bowl (Webster & Backhouse 1991, no 134).

Schapiro (1980, 215, 224 n 79) reminds us that over eighty years ago, Zimmermann (1916, 22, 29) cited 'with some reservation, the gold cross of the Emperor Justin II [565–578] in . . . Rome as an example of the parent style' of the foliate ornament in the *Book of Kells* (Fig 15.10). Its pointed leaves between paired rounded buds, some with double lines, parallel others on the Ormside Bowl and in *Kells* (cf Bruce-Mitford in Kendrick et al. 1960, 254), while its veined leaves and stem prefigure the vine-scrolls at the end of the manuscript's Lucan Genealogy (Fig 15.6). The Lamb of God superimposed over the centre of the same face of the cross foreshadows the Eucharistic theme repeated by the vine-scroll imagery throughout the *Book of Kells*. The vines of the cross of Justin II lack true inhabitants, as do those in the Dome of the Rock, but the concentric circles of the round bud between pointed leaves, at the lower left corner of the right-hand inhabited vine-scroll panel on the Jedburgh shrine (Fig 15.3), a form akin to the lower one in the *St Petersburg* B, may bring us closer to Kitzinger's

Fig 15.10. Cross of Justin II, Vatican, Rome. (Di proprietà del Capitolo di San Pietro in Vaticano)

(1936, 69) 'western late antique source [still] unknown to us', an inhabited cousin of the Byzantine cross of Justin II.

The inclusion of inhabitants in *Kells* vine-scroll compositions pays tribute to contemporary developments in Northumbria, some of whose sources made their way to the artists of the *Book of Kells*. But one may have done so independently. 11th-century prefaces to *Altus Prosator* report that Columba wrote the hymn in gratitude for the 'Great Gem', a cross sent by Gregory the Great (Bernard & Atkinson 1898, I, 63; II, 23), identified, however wishfully, with one on Tory Island in 1532 (Kelleher 1915, 234–5). Did one version of Kitzinger's western late antique source bypass Northumbria for Iona?

ACKNOWLEDGEMENTS

I thank the Samuel H. Kress Foundation for its travel grant, Jane Hawkes for her hospitality and Michelle Brown, Oleg Grabar, Lawrence Nees and Éamonn Ó Carragáin for bibliographical and photographic rescue.

CHAPTER 16

THE NECESSARY DISTANCE: *IMITATIO ROMAE* AND THE RUTHWELL CROSS

Éamonn Ó Carragáin

This chapter examines a paradox. It is difficult to find, in the pre-Carolingian Europe of the 7th and 8th centuries, any parallel to the intellectual sophistication of the Ruthwell cross. Yet this monument was situated, not in a great centre of Northumbrian monastic culture, but in a border land. It is reasonable to suppose that it should be seen in some relationship to the Northumbrian expansion which in the 730s saw Pehthelm, a friend and correspondent of Bede, installed as the first Anglo-Saxon bishop of the ancient British monastery of *Candida Casa* or Whithorn (Cramp 1960, 12; 1995c; Mac Lean 1992, 70; Howlett 1992, 92). But why should a monument erected at the periphery of Northumbrian culture be the least provincial, the most urbane, of early English monuments? I shall argue that the quality of the monument may be bound up precisely with its apparent peripherality. Being at a distance from controversies and from great libraries, and preserving a salutary distance, appropriate to a religious community, from local Northumbrian politics, may have contributed to the contemplative quality, and hence the sophistication, of the Ruthwell cross.

It is remarkable that the Ruthwell cross can be read as a para-liturgical document. Its iconography and inscriptions are alike closely related to liturgical practices. The liturgy of the 8th century was changing fast, and this may provide some additional evidence for dating the cross. In the course of a short chapter, I shall restrict myself to listing four of the principal ways in which the 8th-century Roman liturgy is relevant to the Ruthwell cross:

(a) Both the Ruthwell and the neighbouring Bewcastle crosses have prominent *Agnus Dei* panels. At Bewcastle, a standing John the Baptist points with his right hand at the *Agnus Dei*, which he cradles in his left arm; the existence of his pointing finger was confirmed in July 1996, on an excursion during the conference on the Golden Age of Northumbria, by Jane Hawkes, Catherine Karkov and Jim Higgins. The weathering of the Bewcastle cross renders it impossible to rely on photographic evidence about such details, but these three scholars confirmed John's pointing finger by close visual examination and by touch: by carefully exploring that part of the panel with their own fingers. At Ruthwell, John the Baptist again points across his body at the *Agnus Dei*, which he cradles in his left arm. The existence of the pointing finger (now broken off at the upper knuckle) was confirmed in a close examination of the panel by Jane Hawkes, Ross Trench-Jellicoe, and the present author in July 1997 (our conclusions will be fully presented in a forthcoming joint article). At Ruthwell, there is a clear continuity between the folds of John's broad pallium visible just above and just below the pointing hand. Therefore it was clear that John was cradling no other object above his pointing hand. In neither the Bewcastle nor the Ruthwell panel could any of these scholars discern any trace of a book (as proposed by Meyvaert 1982; reiterated in Meyvaert 1992, 112–25). At Ruthwell, the *Agnus Dei* scene is placed firmly in a Eucharistic context: just above the recognition of Christ in the desert by the beasts, and the scene in which Saints Paul and Anthony 'broke bread in the desert'. To give an *Agnus Dei* image such prominence, and such a Eucharistic context, suggests that it was particularly important to whatever small clerical or monastic communities lived at Ruthwell and Bewcastle. The most likely context for such familiarity is that these communities sang the chant, '*Agnus Dei, qui tollis peccata mundi, miserere nobis*' at the Mass. As this chant was only introduced into the Roman liturgy at the very end of the 7th century, the recurrence of prominent *Agnus Dei* images on both monuments suggests that these monuments were erected in the 8th century (see Ó Carragáin 1978).

(b) At Ruthwell, a central image in the Eucharistic sequence is the adoration of Christ by the beasts (Figs 16.1 and 16.2). At Ruthwell as at Bewcastle this panel was placed directly below the *Agnus Dei* scene. In the Old Roman liturgy, two responsory chants, each familiar from separate daily or weekly use, were sung together at one crucial moment: the ceremony of readings which at the ninth hour on Good Friday commemorated the death of Christ. The first of these chants was the Old Latin Canticle of Habbakuk. The canticle would have been familiar to any conscientious cleric, who should have sung it every week on Friday at Lauds. On Good Friday, as well as being sung in the morning at Lauds, the opening verses were sung, to a much more complex musical setting, at the ninth hour, as a responsory after the first Old Testament reading. These opening verses included the words 'You will be known in the midst of two animals'. The second of these chants was Psalm 90 (Vulgate numbering), '*Qui habitat*'. Our hypothetical conscientious cleric would have been even more familiar with this psalm, as he should have sung it every night just before going to bed; in the Roman liturgy it was always sung at compline. At the Good Friday Adoration of

Fig 16.1. Detail of panel depicting Christ Adored by the Beasts. Ruthwell cross. (Photograph: Ross Trench-Jellicoe)

Fig 16.2. Detail of inscription accompanying panel depicting Christ Adored by the Beasts. Ruthwell cross. (Photograph: Ross Trench-Jellicoe)

193

the Cross in the Old Roman liturgy, Psalm 90 was sung as a responsory after the second Old Testament reading. It included the words, 'You will walk on the asp and the basilisk, and tread down the lion and the dragon' (Psalm 90.13). At both Ruthwell and Bewcastle, the sculptors have referred to the iconography which traditionally represented this verse. But they avoided representing lions or dragons and they converted their anonymous beasts from evil to good. By transforming the traditional iconography, the sculptors were able to refer also to the Canticle of Habbakuk. At Ruthwell Christ is presented as recognized by, and between, the two animals. They cross their inner paws between their bodies in a clear visual reference to the *Chi* symbol, the first Greek letter of his Messianic title, Christ (Fig 16.1). The details of the crossed paws were carefully presented by the sculptors. The paw of the animal on the left crosses over the paw of the animal on the right. Each paw is equipped with three pads: they are animal paws, not human fingers. These paws can be closely observed (and felt) by the onlooker. As the cross now stands, they come some 5 ft above ground level: perhaps, eye-level for a medieval audience. The Ruthwell community encouraged literate onlookers to recognize in the animals' crossed paws a visual pun.

The extensive inscription to the panel consists not of one sentence but two. These two sentences are spatially distinguished from each other in an epigraphic equivalent of the manuscript practice of layout *per cola et commata*: distinguishing between sentences by laying out each new sentence on a new line (Parkes 1993, 14–15; Fig 16.2). The first sentence runs across the top margin of the panel, and continues down the right side. The second begins at the top of the left side of the panel, runs down that side, and is completed on the right side, after the end of the first sentence. The first sentence consists of two two-stress phrases, linked together by alliteration. This sentence links the *nomen sacrum* to a Latin formula composed from the vocabulary of the psalms (cf Vulgate Ps 9.9; 66.5; 95.13 etc), in order to form a single acclamation, the metrical equivalent of a line of Old English verse:

IHS XPS IVDEX AEQVITATIS

The Ruthwell community may well have found this metrical *sententia* suitable for chanting, communally or in solo, as an acclamation. As its *incipit* (the *nomen sacrum*) has pride of place on the top margin of the panel, the sacred name functions as a *titulus*, directing our attention to the crossed paws below where the *Chi* of the *nomen sacrum* is wittily imitated by dumb beasts in the desert. In this way the prophecy is fulfilled: Christ's Messianic title is acknowledged, precisely, between their bodies: '*in medio duorum animalium*'. It is likely that a similar visual pun existed at Bewcastle. Although thirteen centuries of rain have practically washed away the crossed paws, there was space for them, and traces of them remain. At Bewcastle this visual reminiscence of the *nomen sacrum* was encouraged by the runic name '+ *gessus kristtus*' inscribed above the panel (Ó Carragáin 1987b, 16–17).

Psalm 90 was sung at the ninth hour on Good Friday only in the Old Roman liturgy. In Romano-Frankish use it was gradually replaced, from the late 8th century, by Psalm 139, 'Eripe me' (Hesbert 1935, no 78a, lix n 4). Thus it is clear that the extremely original panels at Ruthwell and Bewcastle would have made most sense in the context of the Old Roman liturgy. Here, the liturgy may suggest a *terminus ad quem*, however tentative, for both the Ruthwell and Bewcastle monuments: perhaps before the end of the 8th century, and certainly before Carolingian liturgical chant reached Northumbria.

(c) The relation of the Anglo-Saxon poem at Ruthwell to the iconography of that monument also suggests a date in the 8th century. In the third column of runes (across the top and down the right hand side of the vine-scroll) the followers of Christ gather at the Cross on Calvary ('eager ones came thither from afar, the noble ones [came] together'). It is reasonable to suggest that this may be a reference to the way in which, at Rome for the ninth hour on Good Friday, the papal liturgy involved a solemn procession to the Basilica of Holy Cross in Jerusalem to adore a relic of the True Cross. This symbolic papal pilgrimage to the Roman equivalent of Calvary was imitated throughout Europe in the 8th century. One of the most original features of the Ruthwell poem is the way it describes the Cross as bowing, presumably to present the body of Christ to his followers (if we accept the close parallel between this line of the Ruthwell poem and line 59 of *The Dream of the Rood* in the Vercelli Book, 'I bowed [to the hands of the men]'). The likelihood that this detail once existed in the Ruthwell poem is confirmed by the final column of runes (on the left hand side of the vine-scroll). This fourth column describes those followers as contemplating Christ's body ('Wounded with arrows, they laid him down, limb-weary. . . . There they looked on [the Lord of Heaven]'). The poem (apart from a brief *incipit* at the top of the lower stone above the vine-scroll on each of the narrow sides) is inscribed in four great columns of runic script. The order in which these unique columns must be read directs the reader around the cross, clockwise or sunwise (see Ó Carragáin 1988b, 11–12, 50–2). It is natural, then, to expect a relationship between the final sentence of the poem (the fourth column of runes), and the second half of the iconography, on the broad side just to the left of that fourth column. This broad side contains the series of images we have already discussed, connected with the recognition of Christ in the Eucharist (Paul and Anthony, Christ acclaimed by the beasts, the *Agnus Dei*). As we have seen, one of these Eucharistic images, Christ acclaimed by the beasts, in addition refers to the two chants which were sung, in the Old Roman liturgy of the early 8th century, at the Adoration of the Cross on Good Friday.

The Good Friday ceremony of readings was subject to much experiment during the 8th century. Should the readings and chants accompany the Adoration of the Cross, as in the papal liturgy at Rome (Andrieu 1931, 3, 271–3, *Ordo XXIII*, pars 12–22), or should the readings come first and the adoration follow (op. cit. 3, 291–4, *Ordo XXIV*, pars 22–37)? Should the ceremony take place in the chief church of a town, or in a special church at which the people should gather, in imitation of the papal synaxis at Santa Croce in Gerusalemme in Rome (op. cit. 3, 291–2, *Ordo XXIV*, par 22)? Above all, it is clear that, in the 8th century, clerics working within the Roman tradition tried to combine the Adoration of the Cross as closely as possible with the reception of the Eucharist. To receive Communion directly after the Adoration of the Cross was a recent innovation of the late 7th century, inspired by Eastern devotion. At Rome it was a feature of the presbyteral basilicas (such as St Peter's or Sta Maria Maggiore), not of the conservative papal liturgy in the Lateran; it thus appears in the earliest Gelasian sacramentaries (Mohlberg 1960, 64–7). The fact that on the Ruthwell cross a vernacular poem describes the Cross handing the body of Christ to his followers may provide us with a precious piece of evidence about the Good Friday liturgy at Ruthwell. This totally original narrative detail would make sense if we assume that Christians at Ruthwell in some way 'received' the body of Christ at the end of their Good Friday ceremony of the Adoration of the Cross, perhaps as prescribed in the early Gelasian sacramentaries. The design of the lower stone made it natural for the viewer to move from the fourth column of the poem to the adjoining Eucharistic iconography; and poem and iconography, seen in relation to each other, suggest that for the Ruthwell community the Good Friday Adoration of the Cross was related to and completed by the reception of the Eucharist. This liturgy suggests a date. In the 8th century, the unique design of the Ruthwell monument would have made perfect sense, as a particular expression of the general clerical interest, throughout western Europe, in how the Adoration of the Cross on Good Friday should be closely combined with reception of the Eucharist.

(d) We have considerable evidence on the Ruthwell cross that the Ruthwell community celebrated the new Marian feasts which gradually came into the Roman liturgy from the East in the latter half of the 7th century. One of these was the Annunciation, which was celebrated on 25 March, the spring equinox in the Julian calendar. At Ruthwell, the Annunciation panel is inscribed precisely with the verse from Luke's gospel which was most used, in various forms, as the basis for antiphons for the new feast of the Annunciation (Luke 1.28; cf Hesbert 1935, no 33, 42–5; Ó Carragáin 1995, 631, n 3). Another of these new feasts was the Nativity of the Virgin, on 8 September. Only in the Roman liturgy, and only in the late 7th and early 8th centuries, was the Visitation story read at Mass on the Nativity of the Virgin. In the course of the 8th century, the Visitation lection was gradually replaced by a more appropriate Mass lection, the genealogy of Christ from Matthew's gospel. The greatest of the new Marian feasts was the Dormition or Assumption of the Virgin on 15 August. The lection for this great feast was the story of Martha and Mary from Luke's gospel. Thus, if indeed the name Martha does appear on the Ruthwell Visitation panel, it by no means indicates, as Howlett (1974) and Meyvaert (1992, 138) have argued, that that panel does not represent the Visitation. Instead a reference to Martha of Bethany on a Visitation panel would insert that panel more firmly than ever within the early 8th-century way of celebrating the new Marian feasts (see Ó Carragáin 1994a, 34–6). A 'Martha' reference on the Visitation panel would, for 8th-century clerics, make that panel more Marian, not less. The panel would then refer to two new Marian feasts which fell less than three weeks apart each autumn. With a reference to 'Martha', the panel would also have become an epitome of Mary's historical importance, uniting the gospel lection read on her Nativity and which included her great canticle the Magnificat (which she sang at the Visitation; Luke 1.39–47) with the gospel read on the celebration of her Dormition (Luke 10.38–42). The four Marian feasts (Candlemass, 2 February; Annunciation of the Lord, 25 March; Dormition of the Virgin, 15 August; and Nativity of the Virgin, 8 September) were made into a special set or cycle by Pope Sergius I, at the very end of the 7th century, with solemn processions from the Forum to Sta Maria Maggiore. Sergius's action was known to Bede in the first decades of the 8th century. On the first side of the Ruthwell iconography, we seem to have references to three of the new Marian feasts: the Annunciation, the Nativity of the Virgin (through the Visitation scene) and her Dormition (through the possible Martha reference). Again, the liturgy directs our attention to the first half or middle of the 8th century, when these feasts were recent innovations, and when just these three lections were used at Rome for three of the new Marian feasts (for the early history of the feasts in England, see Clayton 1990, 30–40).

All four pieces of evidence adduced in this brief and partial survey suggest that the monument was erected after the beginning of the 8th century and probably before the end of that century. But it is advisable to be tentative about dating the cross by the liturgy; I put forward these four examples as suggestive, not as conclusive, evidence for dating. Liturgical evidence may occasionally provide a reasonably firm terminus a quo (as in the case of the Agnus Dei panels, discussed above). However, we can be much less sure about any terminus ad quem: in an isolated monasteriolum there was little to prevent the community from hanging on to the chants it had always sung, long after these chants had been superseded at great monastic centres. I do not wish to propose the liturgy as a solution to the problem of dating the Ruthwell cross. It does no more than provide confirmatory evidence to back up indications from other disciplines.

The hypothesis of a liturgical context for the Ruthwell cross is more important than any help it may offer in the question of dating. It encourages us to think in a more realistic manner than previously possible about the likely commissioners and early audiences of the Ruthwell cross and the associated Bewcastle cross. The liturgy was a series of actions, performed communally, at set times (daily, weekly or yearly), and to set music. To perform these actions correctly, a clerical community above all had to cultivate the art of memory. The library of necessary books would have been very small, certainly fewer than a dozen. These books must have been used primarily as aids to memory, as works of occasional reference out of which the song and actions of a living liturgy had to be recreated by the community itself. As there was in this period no way of writing music down, the chants accompanying the liturgical actions all had to be preserved in the memory. In such a situation, the relations between word and music would have been far more intimate than anything we are used to. The easiest way to recall a liturgical chant must have been to remember the relevant *incipit* (opening phrase: '*Kyrie*'; '*Gloria*'; '*Credo*'; '*Agnus Dei*') or other phrases from the text. Conversely, a convenient way to recall the words of a liturgical text must often have been to recall the music to which the text was chanted (see Ó Carragáin 1994a, 24–5).

Liturgical performance provides a context within which we can imagine deep and rich learning without our having to imagine a large and rich library. Depth and richness would have come above all from the way in which the liturgy must have shaped each day, each week, and each year for any group of conscientious clerics, monks or nuns. We must try to imagine ourselves within a world of experience in which a phrase like '*in medio duorum animalium innotesceris*' recalled, not a page reference in a Bible (the Old Latin text of Habbakuk 3.3), but a particular time each week (Friday, at sunrise), and a particular piece of music (the tone to which the canticle was chanted). In the same world of experience that phrase would (at any time of the year) carry, latent within it, a memory of the special day (Good Friday, at the ninth hour) when it was sung to particularly elaborate music, and when it was associated with the other great text, sung every single night but also, on Good Friday, solemnly sung just after '*in medio duorum animalium*': '*Super aspidem et basiliscum ambulabis; et conculcabis leonem et draconem*' (Ps 90.13).

The liturgy was of necessity a do-it-yourself art. Ceremonies had to be adapted to the needs of the local community, however remote or small that community was. You learned about how to do the liturgy by listening, if possible, to someone who had been there (either Rome, or some great centre such as York or Wearmouth-Jarrow or Hexham). Even when such oral traditions were written down and have survived, they have come down to us in informal, makeshift documents (the classic analysis is Andrieu 1931, 2, xvii–xlix). Any group who wished to enact the liturgy had to make their own decisions about how to adapt details to the local situation. Thus a basic principle about early medieval liturgical action is that in it, imitation of the model also involved its profound adaptation and, therefore, a considerable amount of independence from it. Local communities must often have had to imagine what their models were like, even though they had never seen the models themselves. We may possibly have an example of this in the Bewcastle cross. It is clear that one of its central functions is to commemorate aristocratic patrons. The runic text which fills one of the large panels of its west side seems to have begun with some such words as 'this victory sign was set up by . . .' and to have ended with some formula like 'pray for their souls' (Page 1973, 148). I have suggested elsewhere that this panel of runes may have been put to liturgical use. The text on the panel was clearly not designed to be read out at Mass: the inscription was in English, after all, not in Latin, and in runes (with their associations of secrecy and mystery), not in Roman letters. But precisely in the Roman liturgy, the names of the living and dead to be commemorated were not read out aloud. Instead of this, the priest usually commemorated them implicitly, by pausing at the appropriate points of the Mass for a moment of mental prayer while gazing at a diptych or at a *liber vitae*. If Mass were ever celebrated within sight of the west side of the Bewcastle cross, the priest and congregation could make an implicit commemoration of all their benefactors (not just those actually listed on the cross) by simply glancing at the cross for a moment of silent prayer at the appropriate moments of the Mass. The very inaccessibility of runic script could have contributed to its symbolic value. The runic panel may have been valued not simply because it preserved the names of certain powerful patrons, but also because it suggested the deeper mystery of the *liber vitae*, a mystery also suggested by the closed scroll in Christ's left hand in the panel just above. There, Christ significantly blesses the scroll (and perhaps also the audience) with his raised right hand (Ó Carragáin 1987b, 38).

In the early medieval Mass, the liturgical commemorations of the living and the dead were often actually known as 'the diptychs'. This was because, ideally, the names of those to be commemorated were recorded on two leaves of material, which folded to form an elementary book. On occasion, ancient ivory diptychs, originally distributed by imperial consuls to their friends and clients at the beginning of their term of office, were reused as liturgical diptychs (for a list of surviving examples, see Vezin 1971, 34–5). Because these ivory diptychs were of great value, some of them have been preserved and have come down to us, often with early medieval lists of those to be commemorated inscribed on the inner, undecorated leaves (for a good illustration of one such reused diptych, that of Boethius at Brescia, see Hubert et al. 1969, 134–5).

Let us assume for a moment that the Bewcastle community, of whatever kind it was, had never seen an ivory diptych. Even so, it is very likely that they would have known the liturgical term 'the diptychs', and heard about the objects which this phrase signified (for references to diptychs on the Rothbury cross, see Hawkes 1997, 34–9). They may even have heard that on diptychs secular as well as sacred iconography was to be found. Those possibilities provide us with a context in which it would have been natural to associate a list of those to be remembered with a series of iconographic panels. There is a close connection between the two 'inner panels' of the sequence of four on the west face at Bewcastle: Christ's blessing hand, and the scroll he holds in his left hand, form a perfect visual complement to the runic request for prayers for the souls of local aristocrats, which fills the panel immediately below (Ó Carragáin 1987b, 38–9). The identification of the two 'outer' panels, above and below, has been much disputed. The recent examination of the panel, on the occasion of the Golden Age of Northumbria conference in 1996, has made it once more seem likely that it is John the Baptist who holds the *Agnus Dei* (in the panel above). But who bears the eagle or falcon in the lowest panel: John the Evangelist or a local aristocratic donor? The tradition of diptychs can provide parallels for either possibility, for both religious and secular portraits. Indeed, the whole tradition of diptychs involved the adaptation of secular iconography for religious purposes (which could have happened at Bewcastle if secular iconography were adapted to represent John the Evangelist). Whatever the interpretation of this panel, if the Bewcastle community provided for its secular patrons a sort of diptych in stone, it exercised just that freedom and creativity which the early medieval liturgy normally demanded: to learn (perhaps at second- or third-hand) what was done at a great centre, and then to make your own version of what you had heard about, from local materials and in terms that made sense to your own community.

It is exciting to study the ways in which in the 7th and 8th centuries the Roman liturgy was changing fast, and how these changes were originally linked to theological and political developments at Rome and Byzantium. But the Ruthwell community was remote from such great events. This remoteness gave them a great opportunity. In their isolation, they could use images, which had their origins in controversy, in new ways for contemplative purposes. If at Ruthwell they heard at all about the threat posed by iconoclasm to the western church in the late 720s and in the 730s, the threat must to them have seemed remote. In Jarrow Bede knew of the threat before 730, and in his *De Templo* penned a page against iconoclasm (Meyvaert 1979, 38–9). But clerics at Ruthwell may simply have known that images were, since iconoclasm, increasingly valued as a way of expressing, in fidelity to ancient Christian tradition, the physical reality of the incarnation of the invisible God in human flesh and in human history. They used images to make close and deep connections between the historical facts of Good Friday (described in original and dramatic terms in their vernacular Crucifixion poem), and their own liturgical participation in these historical events (reflected in various ways in the iconography and inscriptions of their cross).

There are, as we have seen, remarkable similarities between the Ruthwell and Bewcastle crosses: but they are very different monuments. The Bewcastle cross acts as a memorial for a set of English people, whose names we can no longer know with certainty, but who are likely to have been lay aristocratic patrons. It is striking that the Ruthwell monument completely avoids any such commemoration of the surrounding secular society. Instead, it provides a remarkably coherent paradigm of the central themes of Christianity. This paradigm is organized around the classic sequence of the Christian rites of initiation. In the first half of the iconography images of conversion and repentance (the blind man and the woman who was a sinner) are fittingly placed between images of Christ's growth to birth in Mary's womb (Annunciation and Visitation). We have seen that the second half of the iconography is centred on images of the Eucharist, the climax towards which Christian initiation was directed.

The complex unity of the Ruthwell cross would have gradually come to make sense to any clerics who, in the course of a lifetime spent in its vicinity, performed the major liturgical ceremonies at the proper times during each liturgical year. They would not have needed any book-reading to supplement the knowledge which would have come to them naturally from their public communal actions. I do not believe, however, that the full unity of the cross could have meant much to the illiterate laity of the surrounding area. It was not merely that there are two languages on the cross, Latin and English, and two scripts. It is more that, without actually participating in the liturgy, appreciation of the way in which the monument reacts with that symbolic system would have remained abstract and unreal. I am therefore quite sceptical about efforts to explain the whole cross in terms of preaching or instruction of the laity. Individual panels, or groups of panels, might on occasion have been useful for preaching. The vernacular poem may have been widely sung, in various versions (such as the version that crops up centuries later in the Vercelli Book as *The Dream of the Rood*. That version is equipped with a dream-vision frame, of which there is no trace at Ruthwell). But such partial or occasional use is rather different from a deep appreciation of the unity of the monument. That could only come from long acquaintance. I suspect that the Ruthwell cross was, like the liturgy itself, designed to be lived or lived with, rather than to be talked about.

I am even less convinced that we should see the monument primarily in political terms, as though it was intended to blazon the recent Anglo-Saxon control of the area. Instead, it seems to me likely that the monument is symbolically so rich and confident because of another necessary distance: the distance which, Benedict Biscop believed, should be kept between the life of a monastic community and that of the local aristocratic lay society, so that a monastery could be sufficiently detached from local traditions of aristocratic heredity (Wormald 1976). Only in this way would the community be free, when appointing its abbot and priors, to follow its own independent judgement about an individual's holiness and talent, without reference to the accident of aristocratic birth. Monks in the Wearmouth-Jarrow tradition saw that aristocracy was bound up with values of a world that was transient and evanescent; they saw the monastery, on the other hand, as providing a foretaste of the better society of the kingdom of God (Mayr-Harting 1976). How vital this principle was to the Wearmouth-Jarrow tradition, and how much it was under threat from aristocratic interference by the end of Bede's life, we can learn from Bede's letter to Ecgberht of York (Plummer 1896, 1, 403–23). The close links which Rosemary Cramp (1965, 10–12) established between Ruthwell and Wearmouth-Jarrow may extend, not simply to a style of sculpture, but also to a style of monastic life and liturgy. Ruthwell, with its synthesis of Roman and Celtic ideals, is the embodiment in stone of the Gregorian ideal of diversity within unity, an ideal which we know of through Bede and which, Bede records, was vitally important to Benedict Biscop and his community (Ó Carragáin 1994a, 26–7). Ruthwell is also an eschatological monument, and stands as a silent but eloquent criticism of all man-made power-structures, racial divisions and especially (with such scenes as the man blind from birth and the woman who was a sinner) of the importance of aristocratic birth. The Ruthwell and Bewcastle animals who acclaim Christ with their crossed paws have been converted from evil to good, but also to anonymity. In order to acclaim Christ in the desert, they have given up long iconographic lineages, not to say promising iconographic careers, as asps, basilisks, lions or dragons. Their crossed paws, which form the Messianic title (Christ, the anointed one), provide a witty warning: with the advent of '*Iesus Christus, iudex aequitatis*' the dynastic dreams of lesser kings would wither away.

Central to the vision of the Ruthwell cross is an element of what Henry Mayr-Harting has called 'monastic classlessness'. The nobility which the cross explores and celebrates is entirely dependent on a spiritual and sacramental relationship to Christ. In the Ruthwell cross there is no room for any other kind of aristocracy. It is reasonable to see in the Ruthwell cross, with all its sacramental references, the classic sculptural expression in pre-Carolingian Europe of that 'clericalism' which Mayr-Harting (1976, 15–18) has carefully defined as central to Gregory the Great and Bede.

I do not wish to deny that politics may have been an important external factor in the commissioning of the Ruthwell cross. It is likely to be because of politics that Anglo-Saxon clerics or monks were there in the first place, and that they had money to commission such a fine piece of sculpture. But if politics is reflected in that iconography, it is a highly subversive kind of politics, which ignores and circumvents racial, dynastic and ecclesiastical dividing lines. It is highly significant that a number of scholars, following Meyer Schapiro (1944), have convincingly shown that the Ruthwell cross, far from celebrating an Anglo-Saxon triumph or simple propaganda for the Roman *ordo*, includes important Irish, non-Roman elements (Neuman de Vegvar 1987, 203–27; Mac Lean 1992, 68–70). The Ruthwell cross at many points reflects the Old Roman liturgy; but it cannot be accused of making simplistic pro-Roman liturgical statements. The monument is remarkably eirenic, and forms the classic example of friendly contact between Roman and Irish liturgical traditions (Ó Carragáin 1978, 137; 1988b, 51–4; Cramp 1995c sees Ruthwell as being possibly 'a monument to the reconciliation of the British and Irish churches with the Anglo-Saxon'). The most outstanding aspect of the monument's originality, an aspect that unites poem and iconography, is the intimate relationship it establishes between Christ's incarnation and his Passion. Both Irish and Roman monastic scholars, even when they disagreed about how to calculate the next Good Friday, always agreed that the first Good Friday fell on 25 March, the anniversary of Christ's incarnation. Here, as in the Paul and Anthony panel, Ruthwell emphasizes the great symbolic riches that united the Roman and Celtic clerical traditions, not the scholarly computistics that caused tension between them. Preaching and polemic lead to simplification, and simplification is not something one can easily associate with the Ruthwell cross.

Preserving a necessary distance enabled the Ruthwell *monasteriolum*, whatever sort of clerical community it may have been, to avoid provincialism, and get its sculptors to create a monument that is European and universal in its scope. In such range and scope, the monument faithfully reflects the developing art of communal liturgical worship, the great achievement of Christian culture in the early Middle Ages. Worship in that period was intensely local, in that every community had in the end to work out its way of doing things. But at its best the liturgy combined intense local creativity with profound universality: central to it was an objective sense of the communion of the church in East and West, on earth and in heaven. This communion naturally embraced the Irish churches to the west and north. The Ruthwell community emphasized the ideals it, as a clerical community, held in common with the Irish monks: the importance of withdrawing *in deserto* the better to recognize Christ in the breaking of bread, like Paul and Anthony, the Egyptian prototypes of this vocation.

No cultural discourse could subvert the distinction between cultural centre and cultural periphery more surely than the liturgy, precisely because the liturgy offered all its participants, equally, membership in the communion of saints. Any small clerical community at Ruthwell would have known that it could participate sacramentally, with all Christians living and dead, in the fruits of the incarnation, death and resurrection of Christ – participate as fully as the Pope himself. Their monument suggests that ecclesiastical controversy at Rome and secular power-politics in Northumbria were of little account to them, compared to the patterns of their communal sacramental worship, of which they provided such a memorable synthesis. By preserving a necessary distance from the strident simplifications of preaching and politics, by concentrating on their monastic and liturgical vocations, the members of the Ruthwell *monasteriolum* created for themselves a great contemplative monument, of European and universal significance.

CHAPTER 17

ANGLO-SAXON SCULPTURE: QUESTIONS OF CONTEXT

Jane Hawkes

Over 100 years ago the Revd Browne (1887, 156) was sufficiently perplexed by the context of the carved figural decoration of some of the Anglo-Saxon crosses he encountered to ask, quoting the Old Testament prophet, Joshua (4.6), 'What mean these stones?'. It is a question few scholars have attempted to answer, let alone ask of the stone carvings of Anglo-Saxon England.

In part this is due to the fact that early systematic study of the monuments this century was concerned largely with establishing a chronology for the material (eg Collingwood 1915; 1927; 1932; Clapham 1930, 60–76; Brown 1937; Kendrick 1938, 126–42, 164–78, 194–204; 1949, 42–86), while more recently they have been examined in the light of local groups, or schools, of carving (eg Cramp 1965; 1977; Bailey 1978b; Lang 1978a). Methodologies such as these demand, almost of necessity, that the material be analysed in terms of the motifs which occur frequently in its decoration. Thus the chronological approach, based on notions of stylistic development, concentrated on analysing motifs such as the vine-scroll and animal ornament (cf Brøndsted 1924; Kitzinger 1936). The more recent interest in identifying regional centres of production also focused on these motifs, but for different reasons: through them it sought to identify local similarities and variations.

The result for the overall study of Anglo-Saxon sculpture has meant that while a broad general chronology has been agreed on, and while some regional groups of sculpture have been identified, analysis of the figural sculpture (particularly its iconography, as opposed to its style) has been comparatively neglected. Figural carving simply does not occur as frequently as the more decorative motifs. Of the 113 pieces of Anglian (pre-Scandinavian) sculpture surviving in Northumberland, for instance, only 9 have figures carved on them, and 3 of these were part of the

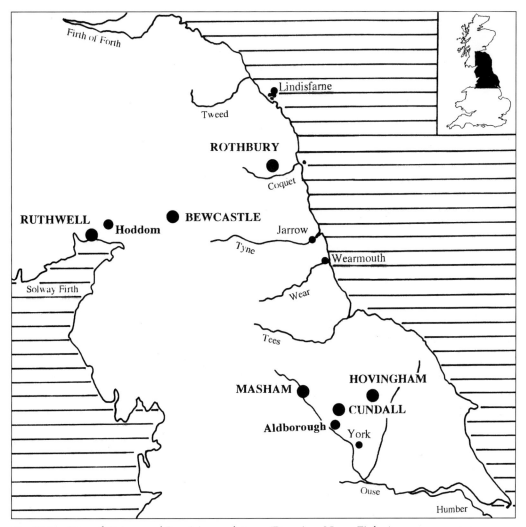

Fig 17.1. Sites of Deiran and Bernician sculpture. (Drawing: Nyree Finlay)

same monument: the Rothbury cross (Cramp 1984, 217–21). This has meant that, with some notable exceptions – namely the monuments at Ruthwell, Dumfriesshire, and Bewcastle, Cumbria (Ó Carragáin 1978; 1986; 1987a; 1987b; 1988b; 1992), and more recently those from Hovingham in Yorkshire, Wirksworth, Derbyshire and Rothbury, Northumberland (Hawkes 1993, 1995; 1996b; cf Bailey 1996b) – consideration of the cultural context of the sculpture has been largely overlooked. Yet, one of the topics iconographic studies can address is the context of the stones: what the carvings signify, as opposed to the question of the models lying behind the images. Implicit in such studies is consideration of their significance both for those who commissioned the monuments, and for the audiences anticipated by those patrons.

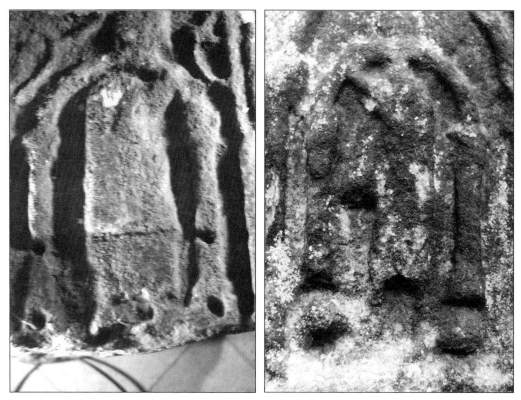

Fig 17.2. Left, Samson with the gates of Gaza, Cundall shaft. Right, Samson with the gates of Gaza, Masham column. (Photograph: Jane Hawkes)

Study of the iconographic significance of the figural programmes carved on the Anglo-Saxon monuments should therefore be of value in attempts to assess their cultural context, particularly those which seem to have emerged from common 'centres' of production within the same general time-frame. The carvings at Hovingham and Masham and that now divided between Cundall and Aldborough, all in Yorkshire, are three such monuments, as are those from Rothbury, Bewcastle, Ruthwell and Hoddom, Dumfriesshire (Fig 17.1).

THE DEIRAN GROUP

The first of these groups of figural carvings, produced in Deira in the early part of the 9th century (at Masham, Hovingham and Cundall-Aldborough), are linked by a number of common details: a distinctive trefoil foliate motif set in some of the arcade spandrils at Hovingham and Masham (Collingwood 1927, figs 54–5); the delicate 'miniaturist' presentation of the figural decoration within the arcades on these two monuments (Cramp 1970a, 60; 1977, 224); and a figural scene repeated at both Cundall and Masham which portrays Samson Bearing the Gates

Fig 17.3. Hovingham slab. (Photograph: Ross Trench-Jellicoe)

of Gaza (Fig 17.2). These two scenes are, in fact, mirror images of each other: Samson walks to the right at Cundall, and to the left at Masham. It is a phenomenon best explained in 'template' terms, and is strongly indicative of a common centre of production (Bailey 1978b; Lang 1978a).

Yet, despite this shared background, the monuments have little in common in terms of their figural iconography. As I have suggested elsewhere (Hawkes 1993), the Hovingham stone (Fig 17.3) seems to present a message of the promised Resurrection using images taken from the life and death of Christ: the Annunciation; the Visitation; and the Resurrection, illustrated by the Women at the Sepulchre (although cf Cassidy 1996, 153). Recalling specific doctrinal tracts on the Incarnation, Resurrection and Salvation of Humanity, these scenes collectively present the beginning of Christ's life as a man and his Resurrection in the flesh – the inception and fulfilment of the promise of salvation.

At Masham (Fig 17.4) it is no longer possible to identify many of the figural scenes due to the extremely weathered condition of the column. Nevertheless, in the uppermost arcade a composite scheme of Christ flanked by his twelve apostles can still be discerned, while in the register below there is a Eucharistic scheme of two peacocks confronting a vine emerging from a chalice (Fig 17.5), as well as the Samson scene, and images of David slaying the lion, and composing the psalms (Henderson 1986, pls 5.8a, b). No sign of the scenes found at Hovingham can be discerned, although in itself this is not a particularly revealing observation given the damaged state of the monument. The figural scenes which have survived, however, do suggest the existence of a rather different iconographic programme – one which referred to the central Christian doctrines of Redemption, Resurrection and Salvation as preserved and confirmed by Christ's church on earth.

Within this programme the Samson scene functioned as a Type of Christ's redemptive death. The actions of the Old Testament hero at Gaza (Judges 16.1–3) were not commonly discussed in early medieval exegesis, but in sermons on Easter Sunday, the day of the Resurrection of Christ, Samson was invoked as a particularly apt example. Gregory the Great, for instance, followed by later Anglo-Saxon writers, interpreted the story as foreshadowing Christ's death, descent into hell, resurrection and ascension:

The deeds of Samson, related in the Book of Judges, foreshadowed this day. . . . What Samson did we know. At midnight he took the gates of the city and carried them to the top of a hill outside. Whom does Samson symbolize . . . in this, if not our Redeemer? What does Gaza symbolize, if not the gates of hell? And what the Philistines, if not the perfidy of the Jews, who seeing the Lord dead, and His Body in the sepulchre, placed guards before it, rejoicing that they had Him in their power, and that He Whom the Author of life had glorified was now enclosed by the gates of hell: as they had rejoiced when they thought they had captured Samson in Gaza. But in the middle of the night Samson, not only went forth from the city, but also bore off its gates, as our Redeemer, rising before day, not only went forth free from hell, but also destroyed the very gates of hell. He took away the gates, and mounted with them to the top of a hill; for by His Resurrection He bore off the gates of hell, and by His Ascension He mounted to the kingdom of heaven (Toal 1958, 244–5, *Hom 21.7*; cf Ælfric, Crawford 1922, 414, *Pref*; Thorpe 1844, 226–8, *Sermon on Easter Sunday*).[1]

Here a clear analogy is made between the Old Testament story and those actions of Christ which provided the basis of the Christian doctrines of Redemption and Resurrection. Elsewhere the link between the actions of the Old and New Testament redeemers was made, by inference, in the apocalyptic account of the harrowing of hell described in the Gospel of Nicodemus, a text known in Anglo-Saxon England by the 8th century (James 1924, 183; Der Nersessian 1954, 210; Osborne 1984, 170–97). In this account Christ is described approaching hell declaring, in 'the voice of a great thundering, "Lift up, O princes, your gates and be ye lift up, ye everlasting doors, and the King of Glory shall come in"'. Hearing this, David admonishes Satan to 'Open thy gates, that the King of Glory may come in' (James 1924, 132). The words are taken from Psalm 23–4, one of those attributed to David. Thus, the scene at Masham can be understood to depict, not just the Old Testament story, but Samson as a type of Christ the Redeemer. His actions at Gaza foreshadow those of Christ in

Fig 17.4. Masham column. (Photograph: Jane Hawkes)

Fig 17.5. Masham peacocks. (Photograph: Jane Hawkes)

hell, an event foretold by David in the psalms, and understood to refer to the Resurrection.

The carved image of David composing and dictating his psalms is (fortuitously) preserved next to that of Samson at Masham (Henderson 1986, pl 5.8a). Such images carry a matrix of ideas surrounding the salvation of the future Messiah. Because Christ as the Son of Man was David's descendant, events from David's life were interpreted as paradigms of faith and salvation (Milburn 1954, 111–2; Bailey 1978a, 20). More specifically, Nathan's description of the House of David as an institution given by God (2 Samuel 7), meant that prophetic messages concerning the future salvation of humanity were inextricably linked with David. Thus, scenes of him dictating the psalms illustrated not only the spontaneous and divine inspiration of the psalms, but also the King of Israel who was the forefather, prophet and embodiment of the future King of Israel, the Son of God. This association of ideas was widespread in the writings of the early Christian church, and through these were familiar to Anglo-Saxon writers, such as Bede and Alcuin (eg Augustine, *CCSL* 48, 598–611, *De Civ Dei*, XVIII.8–20; *PL* 36, 183–7; 646–61; 673–92; 37, 1729–36, *Comm Ps* 24; 55; 57; 132; Jerome, *PL* 22,

545–9, *Ep 53*, 8; Hilary of Poitiers, *PL* 9, 337–46, *Tr in Ps* 53; Bede, *PL* 93, 764–71; 778–82, *Comm Ps* 55; 57; Alcuin, Godman 1982, 50–1, *On the Bishops, Kings and Saints of the Church of York*, lines 601–5; cf Ælfric, Crawford 1922, 35–6, *Pref*; Skeat 1885, 340–2, *Hom XVI*; Thorpe 1844, 64, *Sermon for the Second Sunday after Epiphany*).

Against this background the image of David slaying the lion at Masham (Henderson 1986, pl 5.8b) signifies the deliverance of Christians from the power of evil through Christ's death. In commentaries on the psalms, such as that by Augustine, it is made clear that just as David saved the sheep from the lion, so Christ in his death, descent and resurrection, saved humanity from death and the devil (*PL* 36, 98, *Comm Ps* 7.2; cf 36, 127–8; 684, *Comm Ps* 9.9; 57.7). To paraphrase Ælfric, as David 'took the sheep from the lion', so Christ in his death, descent and resurrection, took 'all the faithful into his fellowship' having 'easily vanquished the cruel devil' (Crawford 1922, 35–6, *Pref*).

At Masham, the effect of these redemptive actions on the lives of individual Christians is then expanded in the iconography of the other surviving schemes. The institution of the church and its sacraments, founded on Christ, his teachings, and his redemption, are represented by the composite image of Christ and his disciples at the top of the column (Burke 1930, 165–70; Morey 1942, 58–65), while the Eucharistic scheme of the peacocks refers to the immortality open to those participating in the sacraments of that church. It is a theme common in the writings of the early church, and was not unknown in Anglo-Saxon England (eg Augustine, *CCSL* 48, 762, *De Civ Dei* XXI.4; Aldhelm, *MGH: Auct Antiq* 15, 103–4; 237, *Riddle XIV*; *De Virg* IX).

This interpretation of the images suggests a potentially coherent iconographic programme: the redemptive death and resurrection of Christ are illustrated through Samson and referred to by David dictating the psalms; the implied connection is made more explicit with the depiction of David killing the lion; the result for mankind is entry into immortality as expressed by the peacocks; it is achieved through faith in Christ and his salvation on which the church is founded. Overall, the iconographic concern of the Masham column centres on the institution of the church on earth, its foundation (and legitimization) in Christ and his apostles, and its role (through the sacraments) in the salvation of each Christian soul. Although incomplete, it does seem that the monument preserves not only a different selection of scenes to that found at Hovingham, it also presents a very different iconographic programme.

Furthermore, although the Samson scene is repeated at both Masham and on the Cundall-Aldborough pieces, it is associated with a very different set of images on the cross shaft (Collingwood 1927, fig 32). At Cundall it is isolated in the middle of panels devoted to animal, foliate and geometric motifs (which may or may not have been intended as signifiers). Busts of angels figure at the top of the shaft, and a now unidentifiable scene was set at the base (Fig 17.6). It is not possible to recreate the overall iconographic programme of this monument, given

Fig 17.6. Aldborough fragment. (Photograph: Jane Hawkes)

the condition of this last scene, but if a redemption message was intended (as would be suggested by the Samson scene), that message was certainly being conveyed in a very different manner to the methods adopted at Masham.

Although all three monuments emerged from a common background, those responsible for their production apparently intended very different iconographic functions. In this particular case, this is not too surprising; the different monument-types represented by these stones must have played some part in determining their varied iconographies. The Cundall-Aldborough stone was clearly a monumental cross; the Hovingham slab was once part of a shrine; and the large column at Masham recalls, possibly deliberately, the triumphal columns of imperial Rome. We can assume that such different monuments served different purposes, and could, therefore, be expected to have had different iconographies.

THE BERNICIAN GROUP

The 8th- and early 9th-century products of the Bernician centre (from Rothbury, Bewcastle, Ruthwell and Hoddom; see Fig 17.1) are, however, all monuments of the same type: the free-standing stone cross. Here again they have many details in common: the vine-scroll derived from a single-stemmed 'root' with V-shaped bindings at the offshoots; the distinctive portrayal of the beasts, viewed from above; the deep-dished triple cruciform halo used for Christ; the distinctive moustaches displayed by some of the figures; and the repetition of figural scenes at Bewcastle and Ruthwell which illustrate Christ standing over the beasts, and a figure supporting a lamb (Cramp 1984, pls 212.1210, 213.1214–5, 1218–9, 214.1220, 215.1224; Bailey & Cramp 1988, ills 94–5, 102; Cassidy 1992, pls 21,

23, 26, 28). Furthermore, the cross heads from Rothbury and Hoddom had central medallions filled with a portrait of Christ (Radford 1953, pl III). Together these suggest a common centre of production.

Yet, despite these shared features, the figural decoration of these monuments differs greatly. In the surviving pieces from Rothbury, for instance, there is no sign of a figure supporting the lamb which features at Ruthwell and Bewcastle – in itself not a telling detail given how much of the monument has been lost. There is a portrait of the *Majestas* at Rothbury, but this is a half-length figure holding a book, not the full-length figure standing over the beasts found at Ruthwell and Bewcastle. Conversely, on the more complete crosses at Ruthwell and Bewcastle, there is no sign of the scenes which *have* survived at Rothbury (Cramp 1984, 218, fig 20). There is no Ascension, no image of hell, no scene involving a crowd of figures. And, although the centre of both the Hoddom and Rothbury cross heads portrayed Christ, different figures holding different attributes are set in the cross arms (Radford 1953, pls IV–V).

The implication is, that although these monuments emerged from the same sculptural centre, those responsible for their production were not in the business of mass-producing the same monument. This supposition is born out by even the most cursory glance at the iconographic programmes of the Bewcastle and Ruthwell crosses. Although these two monuments display two very similar images, they function in quite different ways.

The Bewcastle cross features only three figural scenes: the two repeated at Ruthwell and the man with the bird of prey which Karkov has recently (and convincingly) argued should be identified as a secular portrait (Karkov 1997; cf Kitzinger 1993, 10–12). The presence of this figure, along with the inscription above, implies that the monument probably had a strongly commemorative function in addition to any Eucharistic and liturgical significances which Ó Carragáin (1978; 1986; 1987b) has demonstrated are conveyed by the other two scenes.

By contrast, the Ruthwell cross is decorated with about a dozen figural schemes, and despite the ongoing debate surrounding the details of its iconographic significance, it does seem to have had a strong, probably primary, liturgical function (Ó Carragáin 1978; 1986; 1987b; 1988b; 1992; 1994a; but cf Howlett 1974; 1992; Meyvaert 1982; 1992; Henderson 1985). The images and inscriptions work together as a complex commentary on the liturgical rituals of Easter Week and the Eucharist in the 8th-century churches of Rome and Northumbria. In this Ruthwell undoubtedly has some points of contact with Bewcastle, but expectations surrounding the actual (or primary) iconographic roles of the two monuments were probably different – the one being primarily Eucharistic and potentially extremely erudite, the other being perhaps more commemorative in its frame of reference.

What remains of the figural iconography of the Rothbury cross reinforces this impression of intended iconographic (and therefore, surely, of functional)

1. Bede's World: *Gyrwe* Building 1. The completed timber hall from the south. The building is used by museum staff and living history groups as a focus for demonstrations of life in Bede's time. (Photograph: Susan Mills)

2. Bede's World: *Gyrwe* Building 2. The *grubenhaus* and the timber hall from the south-east. In the background is the modern industrial landscape which forms the backdrop to the project. (Photograph: Susan Mills)

3. *Sæ Wylfing* at 7 knots on the River Deben. (Photograph: B.C. Hoppitt)

4. Aerial view of the Flixborough site taken immediately before the excavation. The sand dune is in the centre; just beyond it is the sandpit where the eleven graves were found. On the nearest edge of the dune is the trial excavation carried out by Scunthorpe Museum. To the left of the dune is the site of All Saints' church, demolished in the late 18th century. The boundary of its circular churchyard can be seen as a relict hedge line. The main area of the site lay under, and to the north, of the dune. (Photograph: Kevin Leahy)

5. A succession of buildings under excavation at Flixborough. The post-holes of one hall are partly overlain by its successor. Two of the pad-stones on which the posts rested can be seen in the foreground of the left-hand wall trench. This intercutting of structures provides important evidence for the phasing of the site. (Photograph: Kevin Leahy)

6. 8th-century metalwork from Flixborough. (Photograph: Kevin Leahy)

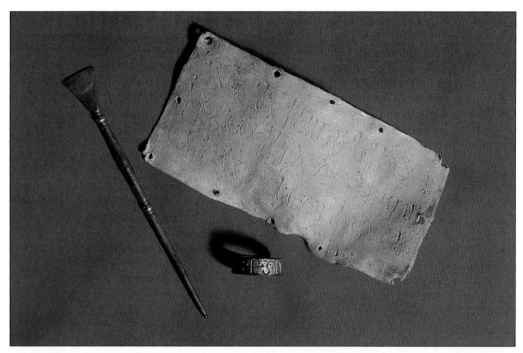

7. Evidence of literacy. The excavation produced twenty-seven styli made from iron, copper alloy and, in one case, silver. The silver gilt ring bears half the alphabet (A–L) around its edge. The lead plaque is incised with a list of seven Old English names: ALDUINI: ALDHERI: HAEODHAED: EODUINI: EDELGYD: EONBERECH(T): EDE --- N. Two of the names are feminine and three may be of people referred to by Bede as Lindsey clerics. (Photograph: Kevin Leahy)

8. Ripon Jewel, front × 2.

9. Ripon Jewel, rear × 2.

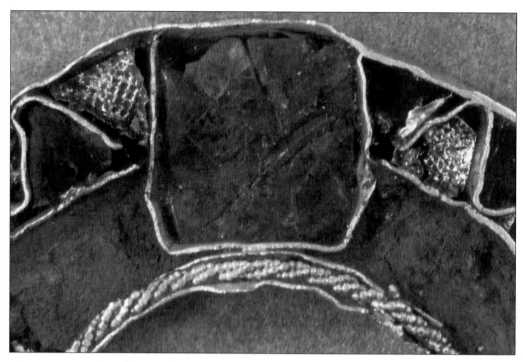

10. Ripon Jewel, Amber 1 and the adjacent areas: the amber is 6 mm square.

11. Ripon Jewel, beaded cable three-strand filigree: the cable diameter is 0.6–0.7 mm.

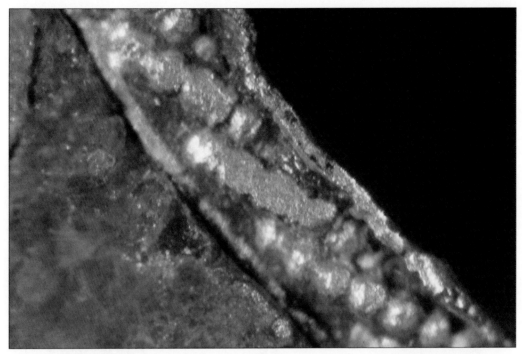

12. Ripon Jewel, beaded cable three-strand filigree, showing flattening.

13. Ripon Jewel, foil 4g.

14. Hunterston Brooch: front view. Scale 1:1. (Photograph: National Museums of Scotland)

diversity. As I have argued elsewhere (Hawkes 1996b), the surviving scenes of this monument appear to present a fairly systematic message concerning the life-saving power and authority of Christianity. Over and over the iconography emphasizes the power and glory of Christ, and the importance of faith in that power (and in the written Word) in the individual getting of salvation. Although this monument emerged from the same centre of production as the Ruthwell and Bewcastle crosses, and although it too must have played some part in liturgical celebrations, given the fact that it probably stood inside the church and may have held lighted candles or wicks in its cross arms (Cramp 1984, pl 212.1211), it presented a very different iconographic programme.

CONCLUSIONS

It would seem, therefore, that the monument form did not always determine the iconography of the figural carvings, as might be deduced from considering only the products of the Deiran school: the stones at Masham, Hovingham and Cundall-Aldborough. In fact, those responsible for the production of sculpture in Anglo-Saxon Northumbria employed a variety of figural scenes to create very different iconographic programmes. Furthermore, this variation was not simply the result of making the iconography fit the type of monument; rather, different iconographic functions were intended, even when the monuments were of the same type. In other words, the carvings were made for different purposes, and the concerns of both the patrons and the perceived audiences were taken into account at each production.

At Hovingham the programme is potentially very learned, albeit canonically orthodox. It is, moreover, a programme ideally suited to the original function of the stone as part of a shrine. It has relevance both for the body presumably contained within, and for those worshipping at it. Its repeated use of the Virgin Mary in the scenes may also imply that the body may have been that of a woman and (or), that those worshipping at the shrine included a strong female presence.

The concerns of those responsible for the Masham column are expressed not simply in the iconography of the monument but also in its setting. Although the stone is no longer set exactly in its original position (Rodwell 1981, 161–2), it still stands on the same site, a strategic promontory commanding a bend in the River Ure. The centre responsible for this site was probably of some importance given its location, extent, and the subsequent impressive (Norman) rebuilding of the Saxon foundation (— 1988; Lang forthcoming). Furthermore, the column, like many stone monuments in Anglo-Saxon England, could well have been originally brightly coloured and inset with glass and metal (Bailey 1996a, 5–11). Certainly metal bands once separated the registers of carved images – an addition which could have served to identify the scenes. It would thus have been a highly visible, very public monument deliberately designed to impress an audience wider than any immediate ecclesiastical community. Such a context means it would not have been necessary to understand the carved iconographic niceties of the column to appreciate its significance, although its programme, celebrating as it does the institution of Christ's church on earth and all that it stands for, would clearly have reinforced the appearance and setting of the monument.

Similarly multivalent audience responses are also perceptible in the Bernician monuments. Here, liturgical considerations certainly played a part, although this may not have always been the primary or sole function; commemoration, and more general statements about Christianity and the church were also communicated. In some cases an extremely learned and highly trained audience was being anticipated, whether that audience was conceived as being individuals or communal, but this was not the only type of audience expected; the responses of more general, uninitiated audiences are also apparently catered for in the iconography. The programme of the Rothbury cross, for instance, is informed, but orthodox, canonical and relatively easy to comprehend (compared with the extreme erudition of the Ruthwell cross). While it suggests the presence of a literate, theologically aware, audience, on another reading it operates on a very immediate level. Images such as that of the Damned in Hell do not require a learned response (Fig 17.7). Viewed in a darkened church, painted and set with

Fig 17.7. The Damned in Hell, base of cross shaft, Rothbury, Northumberland. (Photograph: Jane Hawkes)

paste glass, illuminated by glittering candlelight, and set at eye level at the base of the cross, the deformed figures struggling eternally in the symmetrical coils of the beasts, their genitals threatened by the jaws of the creatures, elicit responses at a very basic level.

Considered from the point of view of the figural iconography, in conjunction with the type of monument and its setting, the cultural context of Anglo-Saxon sculpture clearly varied. Each monument was probably intended to function in a way specific to itself; the roles could, and evidently did, vary, and iconographically there was the possibility of a number of different levels of audience response being anticipated. There is probably no easy, or indeed, no single, answer to Browne's question as to what these stones 'mean'.

NOTE

1. *'Quod bene in libro Judicum Samson illius facta significant. . . . Sed quid Samson fecit agnovimus. Media nocte portas civitatis abstulit, et montis verticem ascendit. Quem . . . hoc in facto, quem nisi Redemptorem nostrum Samson ille significat? Quid Gaza civitas nisi infernum designat? Quid per Philisthaeos nisi Judaeorum perfidia demonstratur? Qui cum mortuum Dominum viderent, eiusque corpus in sepulcro iam positum, custodes illico deputaverunt, et eum qui auctor vitae claruerat, in inferni claustris retentum quasi Samsonem in Gaza se deprehendisse laetati sunt. Samson vero media nocte non solum exiit, set etiam portas tulit, quia videlicet Redemptor noster ante lucem resurgens, non solum liber de inferno exiit, set et ipsa etiam inferni claustra destruxit. Portas tulit, et montis verticem subiit, quia resurgendo claustra inferni abstulit, et ascendendo coelorum regna penetravit'* (PL 76, 1173, Hom 21.7).

CHAPTER 18

NORTHUMBRIAN SCULPTURE (THE RUTHWELL AND BEWCASTLE MONUMENTS): QUESTIONS OF DIFFERENCE

Fred Orton

Difference is of two kinds as oppos'd either to identity or resemblance.

Hume

Every individual has something that differences it from another.

Locke

There is a feeling in the air that study of the Ruthwell cross and what the *British Academy Corpus of Anglo-Saxon Stone Sculpture* refers to as Bewcastle 1 has reached an impasse. The various research programmes that once seemed on the verge of delivering new accounts of these monuments have run into the sand. Interesting work is being done, such as that on the representation of women on the Ruthwell cross, but the most productive studies ask questions not usually asked of the Ruthwell cross and Bewcastle 1, and ask them of other objects. These questions – for example, about relationships between monuments in a specific local area, cutting and carving techniques, and ways of arranging decorative schemes – seem to be questions scholarship should find most worth asking of the Ruthwell cross and Bewcastle 1, even though both the scholarship and objects contain all kinds of resistance to asking and answering them. In part, at least, this chapter is about some of those resistances and how we might overcome them.

One way out of the impasse might lie in proposing another set of descriptions that could embrace the objects. How would it alter things if we chose to look at the monuments in another way? How different would they look from the way we usually regard them, and from each other? The idea of 'difference' is important, especially for the Ruthwell cross and Bewcastle 1 which scholarship sees and understands as similar.

Previously (Orton 1995), I have been concerned to grasp the Ruthwell cross from its false familiarity of belonging to a particular chronology and setting, a certain type of monument and point of view, in order to find a way of making it an object again, to retrieve its material and visual specificity for art history by attending to its inconsistencies and incongruities – what the Revd Henry Duncan (1883), who put it together between 1802 and 1823, referred to as its 'peculiarities' and 'anomalies'. These features, which make the Ruthwell cross what it is, are all matters of difference. The fragments that Duncan brought together are of two different kinds of sandstone; the inscriptions on the upper and lower stones are laid out and cut differently; there are differences in the way the figures are arranged, represented and carved on the two stones. My point was that all the material and ideological anomalies between the upper and lower stones should encourage us to see them as distinct, and to keep them apart, even as their very togetherness as the object that Duncan created, forces us to see them as a unity. Rereading his 'An Account of the Remarkable Monument in the shape of a Cross' I was struck by how scrupulous Duncan was in always referring to the lower stone as 'the column' or 'the pillar' and to the upper stone as 'the cross'. When he refers to both stones together, to the object he constructed, he calls it 'the monument' and on one occasion, 'the Ruthwell monument' (1883, 314). I think we should follow his example.

In the 17th century there were several monuments in Ruthwell church that the General Assembly considered idolatrous. Though they were not all Anglo-Saxon survivals, at least one certainly was. Almost 200 years after their destruction Duncan (op. cit. 315) thought he had reconstructed a column or pillar which 'at a later period' had been remodelled with the addition of a cross. Whether this column, pillar or pyramid (remembering what Lancfrith and William of Malmesbury recorded concerning, respectively, the monuments at Winchester and Glastonbury),[1] and the cross that make the Ruthwell monument what it is, first came together in medieval Northumbria or 19th-century Dumfriesshire is a moot point for scholarship, and one it is ill-equipped to deal with. We have to find ways of explaining the Ruthwell monument as an object that is both a column *and* a cross, each part, separate and together, with its own historical and cultural specificity.

For the present the Ruthwell cross remains a medieval monument made of a column and cross. But it does so against evidence suggesting that what was destroyed in 1642 was not a cross but a column or obelisk. The Ruthwell monument became a 'fact' between 1599 and 1601 when Reginald Bainbrigg remarked on it in a note apparently sent to Camden as material worth considering for inclusion in any future edition of his 1586 *Britannia* (Page 1959, 287). It reads:

> . . . unexpectedly I encountered a cross of wonderful height which is in the church at Ruthwell. It has on it beautiful images telling the story of Christ. It is wonderfully decorated with vines and animals, and on two sides, ascending from the base to the top, and then opposite descending from the top to the base, it is incised with strange and unknown letters. The inscription runs thus . . . (Meyvaert 1982, 3).

And he gives a sample of the inscription, laying it along the top of his note and down its right margin. What Bainbrigg saw as worthy of note, and what the sample gives, are the runes in the border at the 'top' of the east side of the lower stone and the first fourteen lines (minus line 5) in its right border. We can be certain Bainbrigg knew top from bottom; he attached some importance to the terms, insisting on them twice. But when it came to representing what was worthy of note he did not include the runic inscription on the east side of the upper stone. The 'top' of what Bainbrigg considered notable did not include the upper stone or cross. Why? It is unlikely that he chose not to see something that was there because he considered it unworthy of note – he had, after all, decided that 'strange and unknown letters' were worth noting. It is more likely that the upper stone or cross was not there to be seen and noted. In his 'Account of the Curiosities at Dumfreis [*sic*]', probably penned in the 1690s, George Archibald, a native of Dumfriesshire who was born within living memory of the monument's destruction, seems to confirm that this was the case. In the course of providing what was a 'statistical account', he observed that:

> Here is also in this County, St Ruths Church, called Ruthwall, where lyes a Monument broken in two pieces, which was a Pillar quadrangle of stone, reaching from the bottom of the Church unto the Roof (Mitchell & Clark 1908, 187–8).

Bainbrigg saw a column, but he referred to it as a cross.

As Wittgenstein and N.R. Hanson have shown, seeing is a 'theory laden' experience determined by prior knowledge, ideas and beliefs, interests and competencies, and by the language or notation used to express what we see (Harrison & Orton 1984, 57–68, 69–83). The scholar of Anglo-Saxon stone sculpture seeing an upright or recumbent oblong object attempts to make her observation cohere against a background of established knowledge and a set of appropriate descriptions with which to represent it. There has always been a tendency among those persons who are interested in such things to refer to columns and pillars situated in or near churches as crosses. Two examples will suffice to develop this point beyond Bainbrigg's note and return us to a discussion of scholarship and difference. The first is taken from the letters of William Nicolson who, in 1697, referred to 'a famous cross' in the church at Ruthwell, 'a square stone cross' (Nicolson 1809, nos 23, 24).[2] As we know, what Nicolson saw in 1697 was not a cross: he *saw* two blocks of stone, one of lying them in Murray's Quire, which he referred to *as* a cross.[3] Seeing the fragments in the church, Nicolson, canon and later bishop of Carlisle, was predisposed to see and tell a cross.

The second example is taken from the *Corpus of Anglo-Saxon Stone Sculpture* (Bailey & Cramp 1988, 61–72), where Bewcastle 1 is described and classified as a 'cross-shaft and base', largely because that is what it has come to be seen as, but also because those who compile *Corpus* entries are restricted to allocating their objects of study to a typology comprising 'free-standing crosses' (cross shafts and cross heads), 'tombs and grave-markers', and 'architectural sculpture and church furnishings'; they have no way of classifying this particular object other than as a 'cross-shaft'. Thus, the entry for Bewcastle 1 continually refers to it as 'the Bewcastle cross' although, as the entry under Bewcastle 2, the cross head, makes clear, there is no evidence for doing so (Bailey & Cramp 1988, 61–71, 72). It is unclear why the representation of a broken cross head in the drawing of Bewcastle 1 now in the collection of the Society of Antiquaries of London (op. cit. ills 117–18) is thought to pre-date the plate in Cox's *Magna Britannia* of 1720 (see Farrell 1977, 140). Both are surely associated with each other rather than with a lost cross head intimately related to Bewcastle 1. And both are spurious. The latter is a composite that was made by appropriating the single line of 'Cyneburh' runes and the chequer-pattern from the north side of the column and adding them to an imagined cross.[4] The former is more or less completely wild, and the *Corpus* is wrong to see in it an 'accurate recording' of the chequers panel and to take that representation as lending 'some plausibility' to its 'rendering of the head'. The drawn chequers panel is thirty-nine squares deficient of accuracy, and the shape of the head, though it 'would be perfectly appropriate in a Cumbrian setting in the Anglian period', is almost implausible (Bailey & Cramp 1988, 72). Moreover, although a now-lost rune-inscribed fragment of stone may have been found in 1615, we should not assume, as was done in the 17th century, that it formed 'the head of a cross', or that it was once part of a presumed Bewcastle 2 or an actual Bewcastle 1 (Page 1959, 54–7; Page in Bailey & Cramp 1988, 172–3).[5]

Bewcastle 1 is probably best seen and understood as another column or obelisk, a type of monument that cannot be accommodated within the *Corpus* without doing violence to its order of things. And, since Bewcastle 1 and the Ruthwell monument are usually discussed together as similar monuments, seeing and understanding the former as a column means that we need to rethink its relation of similarity with the latter.[6] What are generally accepted as the two key Anglo-Saxon stone sculptures, high crosses, now have to be seen as unrelated or as only related in a very contingent way, not as similar but as different. Bewcastle 1 is a column. The Ruthwell monument is a cross. Or rather, it became a cross. At some moment in its history the Ruthwell monument was a column, and at that moment the two monuments would have been similar. But even then, as we will see, the Bewcastle and Ruthwell columns would have to be seen and understood as different kinds of column.

The study of Anglo-Saxon stone sculpture progresses within a kind of Kuhnian paradigm or disciplinary matrix composed of symbolic generalizations, shared beliefs, values and exemplars that tell a community of practitioners how their object of study is to be approached and characterized, and how that characterization relates to some view of the world (Harrison & Orton 1984, 229–42). The paradigm governs how objects are seen, understood and explained; it provides model problems and solutions, tools, standard illustrations; and it and its institutions are dominated by a particular classic work. It both enables and facilitates, and controls and inhibits the production of knowledge. As far as the study of Anglo-Saxon stone sculpture is concerned, the classic work is, of course, Collingwood's 1927 *Northumbrian Crosses of the Pre-Norman Age*. Out of date now, it provides the base or core of the *Corpus of Anglo-Saxon Stone Sculpture*. A paradigmatic key commitment and belief, first stated by Collingwood, is that there can be little progress in the study of Anglo-Saxon stone sculpture without a comprehensive descriptive and visual catalogue of every extant example (Collingwood 1927, Preface, unpaginated; Zarnecki's preface in Cramp 1984; esp Lang 1983, 187). Hence the *Corpus*, whose scholarship believes that any individual sculpture cannot be studied and understood in isolation; the monuments have to be studied together, conceived in series and connection (Collingwood 1927, 184). As one corpus scholar put it: 'it is almost impossible to consider the Bewcastle Cross without reference to the Ruthwell monument and indeed the whole corpus of carved stones which is left to us' (Farrell 1977, 113). It seems that the effect of theorizing the Ruthwell monument and Bewcastle 1 in terms of difference may be considerable.

Within the limits of this chapter a critical discussion of corpus scholarship, its commitment to the criterion of exhaustiveness and the search for origins, the way it organizes its materials around the theme of development and progress, and the privilege it accords to gradual transformation and continuity, will have to be confined to a criticism of one aspect or effect of its concerns: style. To investigate style is to look for constants that are explained by an organizing principle regarded as determining the character of the parts and the patterning of the whole. More specifically, corpus scholarship is concerned with organizing its objects into series where each member is characterized by the degree of its similarity to the other members – it is based on seeing and explaining the development of similarities of form, decorative elements, and occasionally quality and expression, ways of cutting and carving. My point is not that we should do away with style but that we should not permit our scholarship to be structured by it, or to be so cavalier with asserting 'similarity' either directly or indirectly via a catalogue of connected approximates, such as 'practically identical to', 'obviously derived from', 'most closely associated with', 'very reminiscent of', 'corresponding to', 'analogous to', 'resembles' and 'parallels'. Corpus scholarship needs 'similarity', based as it is in the project of establishing a system of homogeneous relations between all the stone sculptures in its defined spatio-temporal area. A problem arises, however, when it turns its attention to any individual monument because the universal cannot explain the specific. Though mobilized to do so, 'similarity', corpus scholarship's main concern and tool, will not do the job.[7]

With Nelson Goodman's work on 'similarity' in mind (Harrison & Orton 1984, 85–92) we could say that although statements of similarity might be useful in the street, they are not to be trusted in the study of Anglo-Saxon stone sculpture. 'Similarity', for example, 'cannot be equated with, or measured in terms of, possession of common characteristics' (op. cit. 90–1). To assert that two things are 'similar' in having a specific property in common, as when one corpus scholar writes that 'Like the animated vine-scroll on the east face [of Bewcastle 1] the plant details are [also] most closely associated with Ruthwell' (Cramp 1965, 8), is to say nothing more than that the Bewcastle and Ruthwell monuments have those properties in common. How is one to decide what is an unrelated or accidental similarity and what is a related or non-accidental similarity? Surely not on the basis that she 'feels that the likeness is so striking' it must be significant (Bailey & Cramp 1988, 66). Not surprisingly, perhaps, it is quite usual for similarity to be stated and then taken as insubstantial, as in this example where one scholar:

> . . . discusses the Bewcastle interlace at some length. She notes . . . that the six-cord double-stranded pattern occurs in the Lindisfarne Gospels, but [then] states: 'the essential concept does not come from the Lindisfarne Gospels although the well gridded double-stranded patterns have a superficial similarity' (*ibid*).

The value of 'similarity' is diminished at the moment it is asserted, or, in this example, at the moment it is *reasserted* in the knowledge that its value is superficial.

While we usually take 'similarity' as offering empirical evidence on which to form metaphors or principles of classification and discrimination, judgements of similarity may actually follow from metaphorical modes or principles of classification and discrimination already established. Such judgements may merely affirm those types of relationship that the paradigm has already established as a means to organize our observations and deliberations as, for example, in the *Corpus*. We might, now, suspect that finding or 'feeling' stylistic similarities is often a sign that some principle of classification has already been applied or that some interest is already at work. Similarity 'tends . . . to require for its explanation just what it purports to explain' (Harrison & Orton 1984, 92).

Not surprisingly, there will be times when we find corpus scholars classifying objects together which defeat our strenuous efforts to find them similar. The Ruthwell monument (column *and* cross) and Bewcastle 1 are two such objects. Thinking only of the Ruthwell monument as it was when a column, I wonder what kind of knowledge we would gain of it and Bewcastle 1 if we insisted on their dissimilarity, listed (even briefly) their differences, and took these as signs of their circumstances of production.

Resourced, as they surely were, by a knowledge of the obelisks or triumphal columns of Rome, the Bewcastle and Ruthwell columns would have been intended to be seen as monuments of imperial power. Northumbria appropriated the form of an important type of Roman monument to its own imperial project; it imitated, and perhaps even saw itself as identical with, Rome. However, the two columns are not structured or carved in the same way, and so affect us, as they presumably affected their medieval beholders, differently. Bewcastle 1 rises from a square base while the Ruthwell column rises from an oblong. Each side of Bewcastle 1 is edged with a broad outer roll moulding echoed by a fine inner roll moulding; the ornamental panels on the north and south sides are separated by flat band mouldings. Each side of the Ruthwell column is edged with a flat band moulding, as are the figure panels on the north and south sides. Though both columns are deeply cut in high relief, the carving of the Ruthwell column can be characterized as more 'Mediterranean' with details that in several places may have been free of the supporting block. The slender, tapering form of Bewcastle 1, neatly supplemented by the dimensions and compositions of its ornamental and figure panels, effects a dynamic upward movement. The Ruthwell column seems to be less slender and less free of the ground, its visual and textual programmes less upwardly mobile compared with Bewcastle 1. Each column supports its sculptural and ideological weight differently and to different effect.

Although both columns share a representation of Christ on the Beasts (I shall leave aside that they also share inhabited vine-scroll, although the differences there should also be attended to), they differ in important details and contexts. Over and above differences of gesture, dress and other properties, we have to keep each panel's context of use in mind. The Bewcastle Christ on the Beasts effects its meanings in relation to ways of seeing and understanding different patterns of interlaced or plaited ornament that are missing from the Ruthwell column. The Ruthwell Christ on the Beasts on the other hand, effects its meanings within an integrated iconographical and textual programme that may relate *Ecclesia* to *Vita Monastica* that is not present on Bewcastle 1 (Meyvaert 1992; Wood 1995).

It is possible that the Ruthwell Christ on the Beasts may have served as a resource for the Bewcastle panel, or vice versa. Or possibly both were adapted from a resource(s) elsewhere. These possibilities are commonplaces of corpus scholarship. But more importantly, these and the other panels, figurative and abstract, are not mere tokens or types, but *representations* and, as such, they have to be theorized as actively manufactured renderings of their referents made from available cultural resources (see Barry Barnes in Harrison & Orton 1984, 101–11, esp 106–7) – seen and understood for what they are and how they have been made to reflect the functions they were required to perform when the procedures were carried out, competencies executed, or techniques applied. These functions will be generally intelligible in terms of the objectives of some social group. We can be sure that these columns were put up to function in the performance of some institutionalized activity, designed to further particular aims or ends. The difference between, for example, the details and contextualization of Christ on the Beasts on Bewcastle 1 and the Ruthwell column, together with other differences (including those of cutting and carving), should be taken to signify different social groups, viz the different communities, institutional activities and aims that produced the two columns.

Both columns exhibit a wealth of inscriptions. Bewcastle's surviving texts are all runic; Ruthwell's are runic and Roman. On Bewcastle's north side, the Old English personal name, 'Cyneburh', has been read, and on the west (and probably the north) side there is a Latin form of 'Jesus Christ'. These seem to function as labels, although it is difficult to make out what they label. The longest inscription on the Bewcastle column is located on the west side between Christ on the Beasts and the figure with a bird. (It is mainly the Bewcastle column's forced relation of similarity to the Ruthwell monument that turns the latter figure into John the Evangelist.) This inscription seems to tell us that the column was erected as a 'token of victory' to the memory of someone; it is commemorative and invokes us to prayer (Page 1959, 61, 63, 65; cf Page in Bailey & Cramp 1988, 65). Ruthwell's runic texts are laid out around the vine-scroll on its narrow east and west sides, and provide verses representing the Crucifixion. The Roman texts are inscribed around the figure panels. On the south side they are fragments of scripture, and on the north they are denotative or descriptive statements that render the panels effective illustrations of Bible stories. Here, contrary to the way it is inscribed at Bewcastle, we read 'Jesus Christ' in the six-letter Greek form taken into Roman with the *Eta* given as a minuscule 'h'. Another difference concerns the relation of Latin to vernacular at Ruthwell compared with the predominance of vernacular on Bewcastle 1, where the commemorative text is in the vernacular. The texts on the main sides of the Ruthwell column are in Latin; the verses on its narrow sides are in the vernacular. Latin and vernacular, each treated as proper to its function and place. There is a difference here. Latin, the language of clerics, was becoming the universal instrument of church and state bureaucracies. It knew no bounds other than those of the Christian faith obedient to Rome. Latin is the language of the main sides of the Ruthwell column. In contrast to Latin, and related to the particularism of medieval polity, its political, social and economic diversity, there was the linguistic diversity of the vernacular. This native language does its signifying on the narrow sides of the Ruthwell column, literally and perhaps metaphorically marginalized by the Latin on the main sides. Vernacular is predominant on the Bewcastle column, telling us what we are looking at and how we should behave. I take this to be a major difference. What determined the scope and compass of the dominant textual language of each column almost certainly determined its ideological form and content as well.

Another difference worth listing is the way the columns represent women. This is a quantitative and qualitative difference. On the Ruthwell column there are several representations, textual and sculptural: Mary at the Annunciation and post-partem going into or leaving Egypt, and Mary Magdalene attending to Christ's feet. These and other 'worthy women' on the Ruthwell monument have been discussed elsewhere (Farr 1997b). On the Bewcastle column there is, as far as can be discerned, only one representation, and that is textual: 'Cyneburh'. It is clear that whenever the columns were erected what it was to be a woman, a noble woman, was being redefined and redescribed as a lived reality. We have to understand the different ways that women are represented on the two monuments as different aspects of, and effects in, that process. In 8th-century Anglo-Saxon England, secular and religious power shifted increasingly to men.[8] After Æthelburh (Edwin's queen), Eanflæd (Oswiu's queen), Cyneburh (the wife of Oswiu's son Alchfrith), Æbbe (Oswiu's sister and abbess of Coldingham), Æthelthryth and Iurminburh (Ecgfrith's queens), Hild (princess of Deira and abbess of Whitby), Ælfflæd (Oswiu's daughter and Hild's successor), Verca (abbess of a convent of virgins at the mouth of the Tyne), Kenswith (Cuthbert's foster mother), and Cynethrith (the abbess given care of Wilfrid's robe), women vanish from the historical record of Northumbria, their names displaced on to funerary monuments. Whatever and whoever was commemorated in the Bewcastle column's main inscription, 'Cyneburh' is the most legible name to have survived. Assuming she was kin to the persons recorded in the main inscription (and there seems little point in her being there if she was not), 'Cyneburh' keeps kin relations between men and women in place at the moment when they were being dislocated by the progress of the Roman church. For this reason, despite the variety of types of women represented on the Ruthwell column which gives them a special value, perhaps we should value 'Cyneburh' more, whether the reference is to Alchfrith's wife or not. If Anglo-Saxon kin relations are represented on the Ruthwell column, then they are represented differently.

Hwæt, no time for the sun-dial on Bewcastle 1 and its absence from the Ruthwell column! No. That is my incomplete listing of the differences between the two monuments with some hints as to how they might be made meaningful: the Ruthwell column with its predominantly religious significance that, especially for those persons who knew its verses on the Crucifixion, probably effected the identity of a cross; and Bewcastle 1 with its predominantly secular programme that effected the identity of a commemorative obelisk, albeit one with some religious significance. The differences should now be studied together for what they might tell us about an individual monument's complex relation to its actual determining moment in the 'Golden Age of Northumbria'. And then, if that monument is the Ruthwell monument, we will have to add the cross to the column. That is work to be done. But not here. All I wanted to do was raise a few questions of difference.

NOTES

1. Dodwell (1982, 113–18) discusses what Anglo-Saxon documents refer to as 'pyramids', concluding that they were tall, slender, probably flat-topped columns or obelisks erected as memorials. He points out that 'this aberrant use of the word seems to be peculiar to England and can be explained, perhaps, by the penchant of the Anglo-Saxons for visiting Rome' where they would have been able to see not only columns and obelisks but also 'two famous classical tombs which actually were pyramids'.

2. Nicolson, who was first informed about the Ruthwell monument in 1690, had come across Bewcastle 1 some years before. In his diary entry for 20 October 1684 he refers to the 'Pedestal at Bewcastle', but what he then saw as a 'pedestal', he later saw as a 'pyramid' or 'cross' (Farrell 1977, 133–7).

3. The lower fragment of the column that lay in Murray's Quire was noted by Nicolson at the time of his second visit to Ruthwell, in 1704 (Nicolson 1809, 195–7).

4. Farrell (1977, 139–40) points this out and comments that the inscription at the foot seems to have been recut from the transcription in Nicolson's note of 30 July 1703.

5. In the 18th century George Smith recorded a socket at the top of Bewcastle 1 (Farrell 1977, 142–3). He referred to the monument as an obelisk and described it as 'a Square Pyramid . . . wherein a Cross was fixed' (op. cit. 158). In the 19th century the Lysons recorded a socket in the top of the shaft measuring '8½ by 7½ inches'. Hewison (1914, 40–1), who surveyed 'Bewcastle 1' in 1913, recorded: 'There was a cavity on the apex, measuring 8½ inches square and 7½ inches deep, which is now filled with cement'. It is unclear, in these circumstances, how he was able to determine its depth. It is also unclear why he claimed the Lysons' measurement of the cavity to be '7½ inches by 5½ inches'. Though the *Corpus* cites the Lysons, it does not confirm the presence of the cemented cavity. Evidently it still exists, off-centre and more towards the west face than the east, but there is little reason to assume it was put there to take a cross rather than a capital (for example). Note also, for what it is worth, that like Smith, Hewison (1914, 40–1) tended towards seeing Bewcastle 1 as an obelisk that may have had 'a finial such as a cross, or a Mithraic cone, like those to be seen in the museums at Chesters (Northumberland) and Carlisle'.

6. It is worth noting that Brown and Webster went out of their way *not* to do this in their 1920 'Report on the Ruthwell Cross with some Reference to that at Bewcastle in Cumberland'.

7. There is a danger that I will be misunderstood to be talking about actual persons here, especially those who have completed work on or are presently compiling volumes of the *Corpus*. Rather, I have in mind a community, apparatus or institution that I have come to know from reading published texts, and I am trying to denote, much as one might try to denote, for example, Russian 'formalism' or American 'New Criticism', a kind of work, a set of basic commitments, an attitude – both enabling and disenabling – with regard to an object of study which has reached a point where further extensions of it may well produce diminishing

returns. Even when corpus scholars have undertaken research and writing beyond the *Corpus* brief, no matter how useful and productive of new knowledge, what they have produced has been, to my mind, constrained by the parameters of corpus scholarship. That said, I take it that this chapter, not produced from within corpus scholarship, is itself symptomatic of a paradigm shift already under way there.

8. Amending Farr (1997b), who thinks that the programme on Ruthwell, including Mary and Martha paired with Paul and Anthony on the cross, acknowledged the presence of monastic females only to recategorize and subordinate them, I would contend that the representation of women on the Ruthwell *column* might best be understood as an attempt to hang onto and assert the power and presence of women in monasticism and at court at the moment when that power was being contested and successfully diminished – the Ruthwell column might have been a site of resistance to the recategorization and subordination of noble women in Anglo-Saxon society. In which case, the addition at a later date, of Mary and Martha, paired with Paul and Anthony, should be theorized in terms of how it commented on – worked with and against – the representation of women on the column below to secure an altered female identity.

CHAPTER 19

THE ICONOGRAPHIC PROGRAMME OF THE FRANKS CASKET

Leslie Webster

Ever since its debut on the stage of world scholarship (Franks 1859) the Franks or Auzon Casket has been acknowledged as a unique and fascinating enigma, at once legible as an assemblage of separate texts and images, but at the same time obscure in detail, and opaque in meaning and intent (Fig 19.1). At least two of the scenes lack any direct iconographic or written parallel, which have made its forthright juxtaposition of pagan Germanic and Judaeo-Christian elements particularly difficult to understand, let alone reconcile in a convincing universal interpretation.[1] Equally, because any reading of the iconography presents so many difficulties, it has hardly been possible to arrive at a clear idea of the casket's purpose or context. This chapter suggests a fresh approach, which attempts to circumvent the gaps in our knowledge of its sources by examining broader visual and thematic relationships between the individual panels, and the key part which the presentation of the accompanying texts plays in this. Through such strategies, a thematic structure can be perceived, even if it is not legible in every detail, and key elements identified.

Central to such a reading is the fact that, in common with other early medieval societies, the Anglo-Saxons had a long, preliterate tradition of non-verbal messages, often structured in a complex and riddling manner (Archibald, Brown & Webster 1997, 211–12, 236). The fondness for visual riddles goes back into pagan Germanic culture, and was reinforced and extended after the conversion by the introduction of the learned traditions and expositive techniques of classical and Christian visual narrative. In particular, the conventions of early Christian condensed narrative were quickly absorbed by Anglo-Saxon painters and sculptors. These abbreviated representations of biblical episodes held symbolic meaning which transcended the original text, often referring to the function of the object they adorn, or to the commissioning patron's life (Dinkler 1979); this convention was certainly known to the maker of the casket.

Fig 19.1.   The Franks Casket. (Photograph: Trustees of the British Museum, by permission)

A literary equivalent to this tradition exists in the considerable body of Anglo-Saxon wisdom poetry – the *Maxims I* and *II*, and *Deor*, for example – gnomic statements from which the audience may learn to evaluate past and present, transposing and mentally extending a general truth into an understanding of their own experience (Tuttle Hansen 1988; Webster 1996). But there is also an important parallel sense in which these skilful and deceptively simple texts are also a kind of riddle, exploiting syntactic and semantic ambiguity to provoke the reader into a deeper reading of the message, in very much the same way that the visual images work. Indeed, a fascination with learned verbal games – word play, encryption, the complexities of orthography and of parallel scripts – is an integral part of Anglo-Saxon Christian learning. Within this, the riddle functioned as an instrument for developing mental agility, as well as an exercise in reading texts in different ways and at different levels. Anglo-Saxon scholars, as Patrizia Lendinara has reminded us (Lendinara 1991, 266) had to be *larum leoþfæst*, limber in learning, and *enigmata*, riddles, were one of the standard classical ways of stretching the cerebral muscle. But the Anglo-Saxon versions were often much more inventive, even when they used classical models. Roberta Dewa, for example, has recently argued how artfully the runic riddles in the Exeter Book manipulate the possibilities of texts within texts; in various ways, they all employ the power of an alternative script to achieve a creative linguistic and intellectual dislocation (Dewa 1995). On the Franks Casket, a similar learned mindset ingeniously combines verbal and visual riddles to deliver a serious message in an appropriately memorable, engaging, and intellectually exercising way. This riddling interplay of text and image is one of the keys to the casket; the other is the creation of a discourse of contrapuntal images to develop the encrypted message which is at the heart of the casket's meaning and function.

The Franks Casket, assigned on runological, philological and art-historical grounds to northern England in the first half of the 8th century, belongs unequivocally in the highly learned milieu implied by all of the above (Webster 1991). The messages it contains are structured in a complex, cross-referential manner, indicating that more than one level of reading is involved; and though its juxtaposition of widely differing themes has sometimes too readily been identified as nothing more than a scholastic *welthistorisch* compilation from some cosmographical source, it is now possible to see how it might repay that deeper inspection for which it was surely intended.

The casket's history is unknown before the early 19th century, when it was discovered in private hands in the village of Auzon, Haut-Loire (Napier 1901). The supposition is that it was former church property, secularized at the Revolution, but attempts to track it down in the likely inventories have so far been fruitless. Most probably, however, it reached France during the Anglo-Saxon period; its survival into modern times suggests that it came as a prestigious gift to a church, where, barring accidents, its chances of survival would have been much better than in a royal treasury.

Since the casket's original context is unknown, any attempt to understand it must rely on the internal evidence of the object itself. Central to any understanding of the casket and its iconographic programme, is the nature of its model. There can be no doubt that it is based – admittedly at some remove – on an early Christian reliquary of the type represented by the 4th-century Brescia Lipsanothek (Kollwitz 1933; Volbach 1976, cat 107). As we know, ecclesiastical objects of all kinds were bulk-imported into 7th-century Anglo-Saxon England, to serve the worship and teaching needs of the newly established Christian church; ivory reliquaries were surely among them. Indeed, the formal parallels between the Brescia reliquary and the Franks Casket are striking: constructionally they are very similar, down to such details as the nature of the corner-posts and their fixings and the integration of the lock; and in both narrative organization and visual layout, they are even more closely matched. On each, the panels have a central theme or themes, framed by a border which gives a commentary on the main subjects. On the Brescia reliquary, all the themes and border commentaries are presented through images, using no text. The main themes derive from the New Testament, and the subsidiary themes from the Old. Thus for example, the front panel has as its main subjects the miracle of the issue of blood; Christ teaching in the Temple; and Christ the shepherd. The supporting scenes extend the discourse with abbreviated representations from the Jonah story, foreshadowing Christ's resurrection and, via the Susannah/Daniel cycle, the topic of the saved soul. These icons of salvation are contrapuntally echoed in the iconographic organization of the other panels, which (with the exception of the lid) again enclose narrative from the New Testament within a frame of themes from the Old. The reliquary panels also divide into three thematic groups: front and back, centring on Christ's ministry and discipleship; the two ends, which focus on miracles; while the two panels of the lid have related scenes from the Passion.

On the Franks Casket, the central pictorial themes are accompanied, not by supporting images, but by short textual commentaries written almost entirely in Old English and runes, and of an equally careful construction. These texts have usually been discussed in terms of their verbal content; but their visual presentation and organization is very carefully manipulated to emphasize the message of each panel. Even so apparently simple a matter as the relief cutting of the runes, for example, reveals that although the techniques of the two media are so different, the craftsman/designer was fully familiar with the traditions of penmanship associated with manuscript writing; the runic letters, just as much as the roman lettering on the back of the casket, show a clear sense of *ductus*; indeed, now and again – as in the 'm' and 'd' runes – this verges upon an ornamental propensity to knotwork. Not only does this confirm the learned impression given by the casket's varied array of pictorial themes, it also confirms very graphically the relationship of these inscriptions to the display scripts of the great gospel manuscripts, themselves sometimes incorporating rune-like letters. Such scripts are powerful visual icons as much as any figural representation or verbal discourse; this is the Insular world where texts can be images, and images texts. It is a topic we shall return to in detailed discussion of the individual panels.

The idiosyncratic presentation and subtle integration of the Franks Casket's framing textual commentary is central to any interpretation. But equally dependent on a late antique model is the idea of a contrapuntal overall programme, such as we see in the Brescia Lipsanothek; as with the framing commentary, this approach has been adapted in the casket's case to suit an Anglo-Saxon audience. The key to the purpose and context of this enigmatic object is indeed the carefully ordered juxtaposition of exemplars from Judaeo-Christian and Germanic iconography in one coherent programme. In this, as I will argue, the casket may be read as three pairs of opposed scenes in each of which a Christian topos offers a commentary on a pagan Germanic one. The panels are discussed below, one by one, and in the order in which I think the paired themes were intended to relate to one another.

THE FRONT (FIG 19.2)

Here uniquely, two scenes are set alongside one another, on either side of the missing central lock which gives access to the casket's contents; this arrangement occupies the prominent position on the casket, and thereby gives a prompt to the

Fig 19.2. The front panel of the Franks Casket. (Photograph: Trustees of the British Museum, by permission)

audience from the outset that the scenes on the casket are to be read in pairs. On the right is a representation of the Adoration of the Magi, identified by an incised runic label, '*mægi*' (the only text not carved in relief on the casket); the three kings present their homage to the Christ-child enthroned with his mother, an image of Christ as *rex regum*. Opposite, is a highly compressed representation of the Germanic tale of Weland the smith, who, exiled, imprisoned and cruelly lamed by King Nithhad, was compelled to work for him alone. Weland took a terrible revenge, murdering the king's sons and impregnating his daughter, before escaping on artfully constructed wings; out of this tale of vengeance in the end, a hero, Widia, was born (see Dronke 1997, 255–84). Around the panel runs a riddling verse in Old English and runes, which refers to the physical origin of the casket, and may be translated (I use the versions of Page 1973 throughout) as follows:

> The fish beat up the seas onto the mountainous cliff; the king of ?terror became sad when he swam aground onto the shingle. Whale's bone.

The passage which refers to the king of terror runs retrograde along the base of the panel.

What can this tell us? First of all, the obvious Christian message of redemption: Christ came into this world to take on the sins of mankind. His birth signifies this. Opposite, the evil deeds of Nithhad and Weland's revenge seem to provide a shadowy parallel outcome in the consequent birth of the hero Widia. The Anglo-Saxon wisdom poem *Deor* reflects upon this theme:

> To Beadohild, her brothers' death was not so sore upon her spirit as her own situation, in that she had clearly realized that she was pregnant. Never could she confidently consider what must needs become of that. That passed away; so may this (Bradley 1982, 364).

Dronke (1997, 280–1) has very reasonably objected that, as there is no obvious moral reference in the refrain lines of *Deor*, Widia's birth is not seen there as a triumph of good over evil. Nevertheless, even a minimalist reading of *Deor* suggests that, as in the Nativity story, consolation may be found in bitterest adversity. Dronke's alternative interpretation, based on Weland's airborne rescue of the princess said to be depicted on certain later sculptures, that the escape may represent an image of the soul's deliverance, is attractive, but rests on unsure identification (Dronke 1997, 271–2, 281–5). As it is, both interpretations suggest a reading of the casket's version of the Weland story which gives a redemptive analogue to the Christian scene.

But there are also subtexts. The theme of exile is latent in both scenes; it is of course the warning delivered by the Magi that precipitates the flight into Egypt, while Weland, a *figura* of Christ in Dronke's argument, is also an exile as well as an image of deliverance. Perhaps the unexpected presence of a label identifying the Magi may be intended to stress a significance they carry both in relationship to the idea of exile, and to the theme of kingship which is also prominent here. Christ the child-king, enthroned before the Magi, accepts the homage of the three kings in an icon of Christian rule. Humility, magnanimity, and deference to the king of heaven are among the virtues to be expected of earthly kings. At the same time, the spectator is invited by implication to compare this topos with that of the wicked ruler exemplified opposite by the tale of Nithhad's cruelty – here also a parable of how evil rulers are punished. These themes, of exile, and of good and bad rule, recur in other guises on the casket.

The main text seems at first sight to be a simple riddle on the casket's origins, with the answer, 'whale's bone' delivered at its end. Like all the other texts, it is carefully laid out so that the words fit properly in the spaces available. However, almost every panel organizes the text in a different way, as if to demonstrate everything that can be done with an inscription and still keep it intelligible. Upside-down, retrograde, cryptic and roman texts – all possibilities are paraded in an apparent display of scholarly ingenuity. But there is more to it than that; this particular text is a riddle, and in a very prominent position on the casket. It can be surely be no coincidence that the passage that refers to the 'king of terror' is the *only* text on the casket which is retrograde. This is unlikely to be merely decorative. It seems to signal that at this point it describes the death of something unnatural and evil, as indeed the text explicitly presents the creature. Whales were of course a physical reality to Anglo-Saxons, as the still tangible fate of this particular individual certainly demonstrates; but Anglo-Saxon scholars also knew their *Physiologus*. In this late antique text, widely read in the early medieval world, and translated into Old English, the whale was a dangerous monster, 'dangerous and cruel . . . skilled in trickery' (Squires 1988, 41–2); for Bede, the huge fish which tried to consume Tobias, was the 'ancient devourer of the human race' (Connolly 1997, 46, 12.6.1–2), the king of the underworld who seduced and destroyed the unwary. This riddle is the casket's primary text, both by reason of its placing, and because its content alone does not describe the scenes it surrounds. Its riddling nature also requires the reader to be aware that the message of the front panel, and indeed, because that is the entry point, that of the casket as a whole, is a text to be read carefully. This is then at one level, a tale of a whale; but at another, it signals the fate that awaits wicked kings (the 'king of terror' gets his just deserts); and at yet another, it is a primary key to the understanding of this remarkable object.

Quite literally, indeed, the front panel is the key to the casket; to gain access to its precious contents, you have to turn the key in the lock and, in doing so, you are also invited to unlock its meaning. A literary analogy exists in *Exeter Book* riddle 24, which uses the same trope of unlocking an answer which, in the riddle, is encrypted in runes; 'who has unlocked, with the craft of a key, the fetters of the treasure door that held the riddle fast in the mind against men skilled in runes, its

Fig 19.3.   The lid of the Franks Casket. (Photograph: Trustees of the British Museum, by permission)

234

heart wrapped up in cunning?' It is that heart, the content, that matters; specifically, in the case of our three-dimensional riddle, there is a precious three-dimensional content, which is accessed physically, by means of the lock, and intellectually, through the unlocking of its riddling iconography.

THE LID (FIG 19.3)

If the front of the casket occupies the user's first attention, because of access to the lock, the lid which opens to reveal the contents comes next in the interactive hierarchy. The user has already learnt from examining the front that its twin scenes are to be read together, introducing the idea that the four other panels are also organized in contrapuntal pairs. In this argument, the lid and the back panel should be read in tandem, while the two side panels form another conjugation. This analysis gains support from the fact that the iconographical programme of the Brescia Casket is, as noted, organized along similar lines, suggesting that a similar structure was also present in the Franks Casket's model.

The lid also exemplifies one of the crucial difficulties with certain scenes on the casket: we do not know the tale behind the image represented. In the case of the lid, this problem is compounded by the fact that at least two of its major constructional components are missing. It is likely that the surviving panel, which has a fixing for a handle, stood at the centre of the lid, and was thus flanked by subsidiary panels. As it seems to comprise a discrete scene, it is probable that the accompanying panels carried texts, rather than additional scenes; but we cannot be sure of that. One text only is present now, the name '*Ægili*' above the head of the archer. This is usually taken to refer to the brother of Weland, the famous archer Egil, and there can be no reason to doubt that this probably represents some lost episode from an Egil story (Dronke 1997, 270, 290–1).

Accepting that we may never know the plot, what can this panel tell us? We see here a fortified precinct, within which fiercely armed warriors besiege an elaborate structure, defended by the lone archer. Behind him, an apparently female figure proffers another arrow, beneath an architectural setting framed by imaginary creatures of unknown significance. Prominent among the attackers is a helmeted warrior, who appears to be the victim of a treacherous sword stab.

The scene evidently depicts an heroic defence, the outcome of which is unknown to us. The prominent attacker who receives the secret blow, like the figure of the Emperor Titus on the back panel (see below), wears the Roman-style crested helmet of exalted rank. Could this be, like Nithhad, a *rex iniquus*, depicted in the process of receiving his just deserts? What is certainly evident is that, in both its organization and principal elements, the lid offers too many parallels with the central elements of the back panel for this similarity to be a coincidence. In addition to the visual likeness between Titus on the back panel and the prominent helmeted warrior on the lid, both scenes feature a siege which focuses on the defence of an elaborate architectural structure, in each of which symbolic creatures seem to protect an inner sanctum. Those on the back panel are associated with the Holy of Holies; the significance of those on the lid is obscure, but their closest parallels suggest a religious or magical context (Webster 1982, 24–5). Is this indeed some other sacred place? Finally, the emphatic and distinctive architectural settings of both scenes place their events in the civilized, man-made world – a significant point, as will be seen when the end panels are discussed.

To proceed much beyond this would be foolhardy, but if the many visual parallels between the two panels are accepted (see Lang below), that at least suggests they were, like the two frontal scenes, meant to be read in tandem. A final review follows examination of the back panel.

THE BACK PANEL (FIG 19.4)

This complex scene is divided into two registers, comprising four acts which relate to the story of the Fall of Jerusalem in AD 70. At the top left Titus, wearing a crested helmet, leads his troops in the attack upon Herod's Temple, represented by the arched structure which dominates the centre of the panel. At its heart is the Ark of the Covenant in the Holy of Holies, around which are four interlacing eagles, and below, two winged bovine creatures. It is usually suggested that these represent the two cherubim above the Ark, and the twelve oxen below the great brazen sea, though this deserves re-examination (see below). In the upper right-hand panel, the Jews flee. Below left, an enthroned male figure dispenses justice, labelled by the single word *dom*, 'judgement'. Opposite, on the right, a muffled figure is apparently escorted away; the equivalent label reads *gisl*, 'hostage'. Both lower scenes contain unclear elements. The main inscription refers to the upper register only, and reads 'Here Titus and a Jew fight; here its inhabitants flee Jerusalem'. It is notable that, uniquely on the casket, the text above the scene of flight shifts briefly out of Old English and runes into Latin and the roman alphabet – only to remain in Latin but move back into runes, as it rounds the corner. As with the other texts, such a marked deviation from normal convention is unlikely to be an accident.

Jerusalem, its Temple and the Tabernacle, are prominent topics in patristic exegesis; in Bede, for instance, Jerusalem appears as an image of the origins of the universal church (McClure 1983, 81). Bede also wrote detailed commentaries on both Solomon's Temple and the Tabernacle, and allusions to both regularly occur elsewhere in his works (Connolly 1995; Holder 1994). Another example of Anglo-Saxon interest in the theme is provided by the *Codex Amiatinus*, copied from the Cassiodoran *Codex Grandior* at Wearmouth-Jarrow during Ceolfrith's abbacy (688–716), which contains a diagram combining elements of both the Temple and Tabernacle. This seems to embody, as O'Reilly (1995, lii–lv) has suggested, a simultaneous reference to the Old and New Covenants, and to the idea of the Temple as the body of Christ. The Temple certainly trails a complex

Fig 19.4. The back panel of the Franks Casket. (Photograph: Trustees of the British Museum, by permission)

exegetical freight, which leads far beyond the remit of the present chapter (see O'Reilly 1995, for a masterly examination of this topic). As well as prefiguring the divine temple which is encapsulated in the incarnate body of Christ, and the community of the church on earth, the Temple featured in exegesis in many other ways; for Bede, for example, its destruction was also seen as a turning point in the history of the church and its forms of worship (Plummer 1896, II, 190).

The casket's central image, then, is a complex symbol – at one level, it represents the continuity of the universal church, and its earthly community; at another, the destruction of the Temple at the hands of the Roman, Titus, seems to contain within it a prefiguration of the new order in which the church is established in Rome. Bede, in his homily for the anniversary of the dedication of Jarrow (O'Reilly 1995, xix, xxix, xlviii), certainly discusses the successive destructions of the Temple as things ordained 'as an example for us' (citing I Cor, 10–11). Thus the very destruction may serve as an image of the continuity of the universal church which is continually renewed in the body of its members. That this theme has specific resonance on the casket is emphasized by the fact that this image of the Fall of Jerusalem is counterbalanced by that of the Foundation of Rome, depicted on the left-hand end (see below). In such a reading, Titus' Roman victory may then be interpreted as the replacement of the Old Covenant by the New (Epistle to the Hebrews, 8–10), and given particular emphasis here by the Ark of the Covenant, emptied of its Mosaic testimony, which lies at the centre of this panel.

If the eagle figures above the Ark are indeed intended to represent the cherubim, another Bedan reading is of interest here; in his commentary on Solomon's Temple, *De Templo* (Connolly 1995, 1, 13.7, 8) and in *De Tabernaclo* (Holder 1994, 1, 25.22), following Jerome, he explains that the cherubim represent the Old and the New Testaments, the former as a prefiguration of the latter (Holder 1994; O'Reilly 1995). This would be an apt reading in the context as interpreted. However, their unusual form suggests another reading which might relate them and the oxen beneath the Ark to the four living creatures of Ezekiel's vision (Ezekiel 1, 5–10) which were adopted as the evangelist symbols. Bede, again in *De Tabernaclo* (Holder 1994, 1, 25.12), divides these symbols in two pairs, the man and the calf signifying Christ's passion, and the lion and eagle standing for Christ's victory over death. The clearly delineated animal features of the casket creatures, and the fact that the oxen are, like the evangelist symbol, winged (unlike the descriptions of the oxen beneath the brazen sea) suggests that Christ's Passion and Ascension, and hence Redemption, could also be implicit in this complex image.

Indeed, as the choice of the Fall of Jerusalem seems to imply, a related subtext of the entire panel seems to be that out of suffering comes transformation, renewal and salvation. Perhaps the casket's sudden gear-shift into Latin at precisely this juncture – 'here its inhabitants flee Jerusalem' – is another of the symbolic ways in which the text comments visually on the panel subjects. The casket's unique use of Latin and the roman alphabet at this point in the text emphasizes the pictorial message of a new world order.

But there is another level at which this panel may be read. Titus, the future emperor, is also a model of the victorious and virtuous pagan ruler. He was portrayed admiringly by Josephus as a reluctant destroyer and (by the standards of the day) magnanimous victor; Suetonius and others praised his goodness to his people, his justice and liberality.[2] He is thus fittingly depicted dispensing justice in the lower register. The hostage scene – with all its implications of exile – though obscure, must also be in some way connected with the role of victorious kingship. Such an icon of kingship, and the wider virtues it represents, would have plenty of contemporary resonance in 8th-century Anglo-Saxon England; the *prudentia*, *fortitudo*, *iustitia* and *temperantia* which Bede saw as the ideal attributes of the good king are surely exemplified here in the person of the Emperor Titus (Wallace-Hadrill 1971, 76).

Turning finally in this section to the question of the relationship of this panel to the surviving scene on the lid, there is, as outlined above, a clear set of visual prompts between the two which are exclusive to these scenes. In the absence of confident identification of the lid scene, one can only sketch a possible structure. If the outcome of the siege of Jerusalem bears, among other meanings, the idea that renewal and redemption come through adversity and suffering, it may be that the siege of Egil's fortress offers a Germanic counterpart; out of that, perhaps also came good. The prominence of warrior leaders in both – the good pagan, Titus, on the back panel, and the presumably evil opponent of the hero Egil – reinforce this parallelism, and add confirmation to the possibility that the casket is in part a series of texts on rulership as well as on salvation.

THE LEFT-HAND END (FIG 19.5)

A thematic link between the back panel and this end has been noted, but there is a more immediately striking visual parallel between the two ends. Whereas the elaborate buildings of the lid and back panel suggest the civilized world, both end scenes are set in dangerous wilderness, symbolized by the wood; and appropriately, therefore, animals dominate the centre of both scenes. Here, we see Romulus and Remus fed by the wolf, whose mate accompanies her (but see Neuman de Vegvar below, 263); the naked boys are discovered by shepherds in a dense forest, and the scene is neatly divided into three elements. The inscription reads:

Romulus and Remus, two brothers, a she-wolf nourished them in Rome city, far from their native land.

This scene constitutes a paramount symbol of Rome itself, and also of the Christian church. The she-wolf has saved Romulus and his brother, and nurtures them, Romulus subsequently becoming the founder of Rome; at the same time the

Fig 19.5. The left-hand end panel of the Franks Casket. (Photograph: Trustees of the British Museum, by permission)

image of the wolf and twins represents the Roman mother church, which both offers salvation and nourishes the faithful. These secular and religious aspects of Rome had particular meaning for the recently converted; Bede, in *Homily* 1.6, speaks about how God ordained the rise of the Roman Empire:

> since it bestows on the preachers of his word the capacity of travelling over the world and spreading abroad the grace of the Gospel wherever they wished, and this would have occurred to a much less extent if the whole world had not been under the rule of one empire (Scully 1997, 32).

But again, there may be another strand to the message. In tradition, as recounted by Livy, Romulus was a great and powerful king, founder and protector of the kingdom. Perhaps significantly, the accompanying text goes out of its way to emphasize the fact that the two brothers are exiles, 'far from their native land'. The arrangement of the inscription also gives a steer to this message. On the casket, this most structured of textual artefacts, the careful positioning of the words 'brothers' and 'far from their native land' in opposing frames on the short sides of this panel seems to give intentional visual support to the exile topic. The image of exile is further compounded by the setting in the wood, always for Anglo-Saxons a place of dangers, outcasts and lawlessness. Anglo-Saxon kings, even the most powerful among them, often endured exile, as numerous references in the *Historia Ecclesiastica* and elsewhere testify. As has been noted, the theme is also latent in the scenes on the front and back panels. Are we then to read in this some contemporary political reference, beyond the idea of salvation implicit in the image of the rescuing she-wolf as the church? Have we in fact entered once more the world of princes, whose own temporal authority depends upon the church? Certainly, the image of the wolf and twins was well known in Anglo-Saxon England from earliest times (see Neuman de Vegvar below; cf Archibald, Brown & Webster 1997, 235–7; Webster & Backhouse 1991, no 139). It was also a familiar motif in early medieval cosmographies, one of which is known to have been brought back from Rome by Benedict Biscop, and was acquired by that most learned of Northumbrian kings, Aldfrith, in exchange for eight hides of land (Plummer 1896, 380, *Hist Abb* 15). In other words, it is a topos of demonstrably flexible resonance in Anglo-Saxon contexts, to be considered carefully.

THE RIGHT-HAND END (FIG 19.6)

We are back in the impenetrable world of an unknown Germanic story, despite the presence of a text commentary. Like the left-hand end, the scene is set in a wilderness of forest and marsh, with animal protagonists, and it, too, is divided into three elements. The central part depicts a horse apparently mourning over a barrow in which a skeleton can be made out. An enigmatic female figure with a

Fig 19.6. The right-hand end panel of the Franks Casket. (Photograph: Trustees of the British Museum, by permission)

rod and goblet stands before him, and a bird flies below. Three labels, 'wood', 'rushes' and 'biter' define the scene. To the left of this, a composite winged creature, half-human, half-beast, sits on a mound, its muzzle bound by a serpent. A helmeted warrior confronts or guards this creature. To the right, two cloaked figures appear to seize a third.

The main inscription is in alliterative verse, and is encrypted, by substituting unique forms for all the vowels. It reads:

> Here Hos sits on the sorrow mound; she suffers distress as Ertae had imposed it upon her, a wretched den (?wood) of sorrows and torments of mind.

This presumably refers to the scene at the left, and possibly to that on the right; the barrow might also be described as a sorrow mound, and it is likely that all three scenes are elements of the same story. But what are we to make of it?

First, the setting explicitly places the story in a wilderness of wood and marsh, as the labels *wudu* and *risci* make clear; in contrast to the civilized world of buildings depicted on the lid and back, this scene, like that on the other end, takes place in the natural world of dangers and terrors. We may think not only of the perils of fugitives and robbers, revealed by the laws of Ine (688/694), which prescribe severe penalties for those who go through the wood off a track (Whitelock 1979, 366, Ine 20), but also of Felix's account of Guthlac's fenland hermitage (Colgrave 1956). Like the mysterious Hos figure on her hillock, the saint is isolated on the island of Crowland, beset with *incognita monstra . . . diversarum formarum terrores;* his retreat is in *vastissimi heremi inculta loca.* This includes woods – he dwells *inter umbrosa solitudinis nemora* – as well as rushy marshes, *inter densas harundinum compagines* (Colgrave 1956, 86–9, 116–19, XXIV, XXV, XXXVII). This is a world of spiritual dangers, of demons and evil spirits, at least as much as physical ones. So too with the casket; its carefully labelled wasteland of wood and rushes, and the reference in the main inscription to suffering and mental torment make it abundantly clear that this wild setting also is a place of more than mere physical peril.

A deeper comparison with the Romulus scene on the left-hand end then presents itself. Though both scenes share a reference to exiled or imprisoned beings at risk from the dangers of the wild wood, it is immediately apparent that, whereas the Christian interpretation of the wolf and twins signifies Life, the church's life-giving nourishment and the deliverance of mankind, this panel's theme is Death, capture, punishment and imprisonment. Whatever the nature of Erta's oppression of Hos, the context clearly shows it as an evil constraint; the burial mound with its accompanying figures also takes us into the world of death, while the scene of capture at the right of the panel reinforces the ominous message. This is an image of the harsh and terrible world of the old paganism, in which man is cast out from God's mercy. Is this perhaps also why the main text had to be encoded, to suggest through its abnormal appearance the unnatural, inverted nature of this theme? To try any closer reading of these enigmatic and highly condensed representations can only be speculation; but the presence yet again of an armed and helmeted figure, perhaps portrayed in the act of imposing the punishment on the Hos figure, may represent yet another type of *rex iniquus*, balancing the good ruler symbolized by Romulus in the matching end panel. And even though we cannot infer more than a general sense of the programme which connects these two panels, the fact that they oppose scenes of suffering and exile, one an image of Christian salvation, the other of damnation and torments again emphasizes how the casket's Christian and Germanic themes are intimately connected.[3]

At the end of all this, where have we arrived? and what does this tell us about the casket's function and context? It is clear that the casket's themes are organized contrapuntally, providing three pairs of scenes, in each of which a Christian topos offers a commentary on a pagan Germanic one. In the three Judaeo-Christian scenes, aspects of the redemptive nature of Christianity are implicit; despite the difficulties of interpretation involved in two of the Germanic scenes, each seems to represent a situation in which pagan tribulation or suffering of various kinds either end in deliverance, or offer a stark contrast to divine salvation. Exile is also a common strand in every scene except the lid (so far as we know). But it is also particularly striking that each scene appears to contain some reference to the concept of good and bad rule, again shown through contrasted examples from Judaeo-Christian and Germanic tradition. In 8th-century England, where all these issues were of central importance to church and laity, the casket's role both as a Christian text on salvation, and as a mirror for princes, surely suggests a context for its making.

The ideology of kingship was a central theme for all early medieval societies, whether encountered in the pages of Bede or *Beowulf* (see especially Wallace-Hadrill 1971, 72–97; McClure 1983, 76–98). An iconic presentation of rule among the Anglo-Saxons, as with other Germanic peoples, goes back far into their past; we may think only of the transformation of the Roman emperor's image on Scandinavian bracteates, of Childeric's accoutrements of Roman officialdom, or nearer to home and the date of the casket, the carefully constructed expression of *Romanitas* that is the burial assemblage from Mound I at Sutton Hoo (Webster 1992; Archibald, Brown & Webster 1997, 222–4). The concept of successful kingship, and particularly of the Christian ruler in his various aspects – victorious warrior, saintly martyr (and of course sometimes both) – whose exemplary deeds would bring prosperity and good fortune for his people was a crucial matter in the competitive climate of 8th-century England, and its ecclesiastical and secular institutions (Wallace-Hadrill 1971, 76). The exercise of secular power was sustained by the divine authority of the heavenly king, and abused at peril. For Bede, 'each king had a special place in the divine plan, and . . . moral judgments could and must be passed on all his actions'

(McClure, 1983, 90). This theme recurs in Insular culture in many ways; just as the Old Testament kings of Israel were cited by Bede and others as role models for contemporary kings, David iconography is prominent in the late 8th-century Pictish royal sculptural monuments at Dupplin and St Andrews (Henderson 1986; 1994a; 1994b; above; Archibald, Brown & Webster 1997, 225–30). A similar process is seen in the Christian framing of Germanic heroic tradition apparent in *Beowulf*, *Deor*, and *Widsith* (Bradley 1982, *passim*). As the Pictish sculptural parallels show, kings themselves were keen to illustrate their relationship with authoritative role-models; this could obviously extend to the favourable comparison of good with bad kings. A splendid example of this is described in Ermoldus Nigellus's poem on the Carolingian palace at Ingelheim, addressed to Charlemagne's son, Louis the Pious (Duemmler 1884). The poet describes how the palace was adorned with sumptuous wall paintings which opposed the deeds of good rulers, 'much closer to the faith', with those of pagan rulers, great, but flawed by evil. The roll-call of the former included Roman emperors such as Constantine and Theodosius, and culminated unsurprisingly with Charles Martel, Pepin, and Charlemagne himself. The pagan conquerors included Cyrus, Phalaris, Romulus (here in a less than approving light), Hannibal and Alexander. The Franks Casket suggests that Northumbrians too knew how to make such comparisons.

It is therefore not at all surprising that so many Middle Saxon texts which touch on the topic of kingship were – naturally enough – presented to or associated with kings. Bede dedicated the *Historia Ecclesiastica* to King Ceolwulf of Northumbria (abdicated 737), and had already given him the first draft; later, Offa and Alfred owned copies; Felix addressed his *Life* of the former princely warrior and saint, Guthlac, to King Ælfwald of East Anglia (d c 749); and the *Life* itself gives certain emphasis to the pious deeds of that powerful king, Æthelbald of Mercia (d 757). Aldfrith of Northumbria (d 705), *rex in scripturis doctissimus* to Bede, and *rex simul atque magister* to Aldhelm (who compared him punningly to Solomon) sought, as noted above, a cosmography; and in this context of kings and texts with messages for kings, one should not disdain the internal evidence which suggests that *Beowulf* itself may have been set down in substantially its present form for the spiritual benefit and temporal honour of Offa (Whitelock 1958, 59–64; Wallace-Hadrill 1971, 120–1).

Weighed against the freight of such a background, this learned and complex artefact, with its carefully composed set of messages about Christian authority and salvation, which at the same time, like *Beowulf*, acknowledges a Germanic ancestry, has to have been made in a monastic context, and for a royal patron. The theme of exile may also be significant in a royal connection, but since this was usually at some stage the lot of almost any 8th-century king of standing, it cannot point to an identification. We must content ourselves with the conclusion that there are several plausible contenders among the early to mid-8th-century kings of Northumbria, let alone Mercia, not forgetting that it could equally have been made for a nameless young heir who never came to power. We can at least say that whoever it was intended for was expected to have the mental agility and learned disposition required to unlock the lesson contained in this three-dimensional riddle.

Finally, if it is a gift fit for a king or prince, what, precisely, is its function? Commentators have often been reluctant to identify it as an ecclesiastical product, because of the unambiguously pagan content, of the right-hand end in particular, and of the Germanic scenes in general – the 'What has Ingeld to do with Christ?' argument (eg Blair 1970, 282–3). But this assimilation of a Germanic past to a Christian message is by no means unusual in Anglo-Saxon and indeed, other early medieval contexts; for example, in the form in which it has come down to us, *Beowulf* presents a pagan Germanic hero as a model of wise and generous kingship for royal Christian successors – a pagan hero who nevertheless operates in a world ordained by God. In such an expositive context, the casket's equally robust and highly learned cultural counterpoint suggests that not only was it made in a religious context, but served an instructional purpose – as a container for a gospel book, perhaps, or other suitable exemplary text. The fact that it is so clearly modelled on a late antique reliquary supports this suggestion of a religious intent, as does the probability that it was a gift to a Frankish church. In the end, however, this casket is *sui generis*; this extraordinary object will never cease to excite speculation and debate.[4]

NOTES

1. It is, however, true to say that many scholars now suspect the casket is designed to a coherent plan (eg Neuman de Vegvar 1987, 259–73). Here I owe a particular debt to Jim Lang, who gave a memorable paper at the Franks Casket symposium organized by Sid Bradley at York in 1986; his approach opened up for me a whole set of new ways in which one could profitably start looking at this ingenious artefact. For a recent bold try at an overall scheme, Peeters 1996 offers a complicated reading which, though failing to convince in its detailed identification of Babylonian, Gregorian and Visigothic themes, is surely on the right lines in suggesting that an overall programme exists, and that it is centred on aspects of Christian salvation.

2. Williamson 1959, *passim*; Graves 1957, 287–93. Both authors were known in 8th-century England; see Levison 1946, 144 for comment on the transmission of Suetonius manuscripts.

3. Ian Wood has suggested to me that this tableau may encapsulate an inverted parallel to Golgotha – while this may be a step too far on present understanding of the scene, I suspect that were we to know more of the story behind it, such a parallel reading would seem very plausible.

4. Over the untold years in which I have failed to write about the iconography of the Franks Casket, I have benefited immensely from discussions with many friends and colleagues, some of whom would be surprised to know that those discussions had any bearing on the casket. Among them, I am especially grateful to the late Rupert Bruce-Mitford who encouraged me to work on it in the first place, and to Ray Page for continuing to point out that speculation needs to be judiciously tempered with fact. Thanks are also due to the late Jim Lang, and to Richard Bailey, Michelle Brown, Marjorie Caygill, Bob Farrell, the late Chris Fell, Marco Mostert, Carol Neuman de Vegvar, Else Roesdahl, David Wilson, Ian Wood, David Wright and Sue Youngs.

CHAPTER 20

THE IMAGERY OF THE FRANKS CASKET: ANOTHER APPROACH

James Lang

In the 4th century Basil belaboured 'certain writers of the church who, under the shadow of high and sublime conceptions, have launched into metaphor':

> I know the laws of allegory. . . . There are those who do not admit the common sense of the scriptures, who see in a plant, in a fish whatever their fancy wishes, who change the nature of reptiles and of wild beasts to suit their allegories. . . . For me, grass is grass; plant, fish, wild beast, domestic animal, I take all in the literal sense (Klingender 1971, 151–2).

This tirade is not only a warning to today's scholars but an affirmation of figurative habits of thought made respectable, if subtle by early commentators such as Gregory, Augustine, Cassiodorus and Bede. It is, perhaps, their voices that might echo through the imagery of the Franks Casket (see above Fig 19.1) to give us some clue towards the unlocking of its programme. To call it a programme implies that the scenes are not discrete, self-contained or random, even though their narrative sources are diverse. The links between them are not so much in the narrative as in the motifs; the scenes are images rather than illustrations and relate to each other metaphorically rather than as episodes in sequential prose. Augustine, in *The City of God*, confirms this habit of mind:

> Now, this class of prophecy in which there is a compounding and commingling, as it were, of both references, is of the greatest importance in the ancient canonical books *which contain historical narratives* and it still exercises the wits of those who examine sacred scripture (Bettenson 1972, 714).

Type and antitype, juxtaposed as they were at Jarrow, are a clear pairing but the casket presents nine or ten scenes which, if they comprise a single programme, need a more complicated syntax. There are, I believe, four recognizable devices used on the box to signpost the direction of a thematic progression.

Firstly, there is juxtaposition, in the Old Testament versus New Testament manner, of episodes with a common or developing theme. Davidson (1969, 219) demonstrated this on the front plate of the casket where Weland's revenge in the smithy is placed alongside the Epiphany (see above Fig 19.2): common themes of treasure, gifts and miraculous birth tie the scenes together.

Secondly, there is a series of small, almost incidental images which serve as *leitmotifs*. The most cheerful of these is the bird: on the front plate Egil quietly strangles birds in preparation for Weland's flying-machine escape. One seems to have escaped into the next panel and stands safely between the kneeling Magus and the Virgin and Child. Its flight does not end there, however, for it continues round the corner on to the right side where it skims beneath the disconsolate horse (see above Fig 19.6). Its function may well be to lead the eye onwards and, visually, to imply a connection between adjacent scenes. Another example of such a *leitmotif* could well be the branch held by a hand, and certainly the image of the cup. Few of these *leitmotifs* are common in the artistic repertoire of Northumbria at that period; their 'free-style', naturalistic treatment belongs not to decorative ornament but to narrative and symbolic conventions. It is the art style for communication.

A third device in what might be termed the 'grammar' of the programme is the provoking of visual associations by a kind of theme-and-variations approach to some motifs. The dominant example is the pillared and arched structure that represents the canopy over the Virgin and Child, the frame around the lady in Egil's house on the lid, and the Temple with its empty Ark of the Covenant on the back plate. A route is established from front to back over the lid of the casket, implying that the front and back work together, even though they are not adjacent (see above Figs 19.2–4).[1] All three arches share triple-stepped bases and capitals, and both Mary's canopy and the Temple in Jerusalem have medial examples added to the pillars. The structure on the lid associated with Egil's battle is a close architectural cousin.[2] Furthermore, it lies to the right, as indeed does Mary's canopy. The arched structure similarly encloses a woman, a reminder of Mary below, despite a radical difference in their activities. The Egil arch sits within an embattled rectangle which, as Bruce-Mitford (1969, 16) showed, strongly resembles the plan of the Tabernacle in the *Codex Amiatinus*.

This prepares the informed viewer for the back plate and its image of the Temple with the Ark. It is a visual bridge between front and back, as indeed is the left-hand sequence of Weland's smithy with Egil, Egil's battle on the lid, and Titus's battle on the back. There, there is also a thematic link. If Weland and Titus are joined by this bridge, then there must be a common factor. At first the destruction of Jerusalem seems to have little in common with a hamstrung smith decapitating Germanic princes, but both stories are about revenge and its wider consequences after a major injustice. This would not have been an unlikely interest for a Christian Anglo-Saxon who, if he were a monk, would have read the psalms on a daily basis, psalms which are often full of cries for vengeance upon the ungodly, often in terrible language. Divine retribution and heroic come-uppance are not far apart. The correspondence between Weland and Titus is a perfect example of Augustine's 'compounding and commingling . . . historical narratives'.

The trick of repeating a variation of a visual image is used to reinforce the relationship of the two battles on the lid and back: the large circular disc which held the handle of the lid and the arch of the Temple on the back are each incorporated into the battle scene in a similar way. The attack advances from the left, the armour of both armies corresponds, and figures either topple or clamber from the curving slopes of the central elements. On the back this is more than a design feature, for the two upper panels depict the storming of Jerusalem by Titus in AD 70 followed by a group of refugees in flight. The two frames are united by figures who slide down the roof of the Temple. It is an important detail, culled from Josephus's account of the assault; it justified Titus's action in destroying the sanctuary. Josephus makes it clear that the Jews had used the top of the Temple as a military vantage point and had therefore, themselves, desecrated their holy building which Titus had been scrupulous in sparing (Williamson 1959, 322). Thus Josephus exonerates Titus, since it was a Hebrew, not a Roman act of sacrilege.

The back plate (see above Fig 19.4) is designed as four panels set round the Temple and its empty Ark, with captions in various scripts and languages. The left-hand border has a runic inscription which begins at a point midway up the side of the lower panel, ascends, and continues along the top where it is punctuated by a figure climbing on the arch. It reads at the side: *her fegtaþ*, and can refer only to the top left panel. At the top, *Titus end giuþeasu*, stands close to both parties named in the caption. The top left panel is the only one appropriate to the inscription (Page 1973, 178–80).

The upper right-hand panel showing refugees is surmounted by *HIC FUGIANT HIERUSALIM*, not in runes, and down the right-hand edge in runes, *afitatores*, perhaps a corruption of '*habitatores*'. The change in both script and language, as well as the varying content of the inscriptions, reinforces the impression that this caption refers only to the upper right panel. The inscriptions of both the left- and right-hand borders do extend below the upper frames but do not refer to the lower ones at all, even on the right where the scenes are so similar.

The captions for the lower panels sit in the bottom corners of the plate and run horizontally to distinguish them from the inscriptions above. They are the two monosyllables *dom* (judgement) and *gisl* (hostage). Their brevity may result from the crowded composition of the panels but another possibility, hinted at by their horizontal placing at the extreme corners, might be that the words relate not only to the lower frames of the back plate, but also to the progression of scenes which work outwards from them around the box. It is important to interpret the box three-dimensionally.

For the moment, however, let us stay with the *dom* panel on the back. There is no indication of the identity of either the dispenser of *dom* or its recipient. The scene has a three-fold composition: on the left a man seizes another by the hair; on the right is a pair, one with a spear and the other with a debatable object. Dominating the centre is an enthroned figure whose right hand emerges from folds of drapery to hold a cup, gripped distinctively between upright fingers and thumb. The lower parts of the seated figure are obscured by a small person seated in profile upon the floor. His foot is stretched out awkwardly before him, and his left hand grasps what might well be a staff. His other hand, disproportionately large, extends beyond the side of the throne to hold a second cup, in exactly the manner of that held above him on the throne.

Hitherto, it has been assumed that the whole back plate is devoted to Titus and Jerusalem, and that the *dom* panel shows Fronto, the appointed judge of defeated Jerusalem, dispensing justice from his throne (Williamson 1959, 37; Wadstein 1900, 30). Among the many scholars who have strayed into the Franks Casket, only Becker has paid any real attention to the figure seated on the floor. He saw him as a servant to the judge, crammed into the limited space available in the panel, and suggested that some exchange of cups and scrolls was being undertaken (Becker 1973, 65–9). At this point we should reflect on the manner in which the front plate of the box operates: the juxtaposition of thematically related images from two distinct historical or literary sources. On the front (see above Fig 19.2), the left-hand panel shows Weland proffering the drugged cup to Beaduhild in exactly the same posture adopted by both figures in the *dom* scene on the back: between upright fingers and thumb. The repetition of this *leitmotif* not only relates the front and back plates, but allows us to interpret the *dom* scene.

King Nithhad sits enthroned on the front plate, holding one of the skull goblets made by Weland from the heads of his princes, one of whom lies decapitated beneath the anvil, his head in the smith's tongs. Weland, hamstrung as he is, not only needs a staff, but is obliged to sit at the king's feet to witness his revenge. He offers the second goblet in exactly the manner he adopted when he presented Beaduhild with the spiked drink, a *leitmotif* which relates scenes on front and back and reinforces the theme of revenge-cum-judgement. In later centuries, the Old Norse *Volundarkviða* (35) confirmed these particular iconographic elements:

> But the bowls, that were beneath their bobbed hair, I enclosed in silver, I gave them to [Nithhad] (Dronke 1997, 252).

Revenge is, in effect, the wreaking of personal judgement by the victim upon the offender. If the word *dom* allows, Weland here exerts judgement upon Nithhad;

as a consequence of his crime against Weland, a crime that included theft, mutilation and enforced exile, Nithhad received terrible judgement.

This is exactly the theme expressed in the panel above: Titus's destruction of Jerusalem, prophesied by Christ upon the city that had used him ill. It comes very close to divine revenge, a constant theme in the psalms, and the gospel passage interestingly refers to the empty Temple and the dispersal of the Jews, as depicted on the back of the casket.

> O Jerusalem, Jerusalem, thou that killest prophets and stonest them that are sent to thee, how often would I have gathered thy children together, even as a hen gathereth her chickens under her wings, and ye would not. Behold, your house is left unto you desolate (Matthew 23.37–24.2).

So, just as left and right are juxtaposed on the front, and front and back plates are also juxtaposed, so too on the back plate itself, top and bottom are set against each other. The theme of *dom* is common to both registers, though source and context differ, the one myth, the other biblical history. Augustine would have relished such compounding and commingling.

It is not as tidy as one would hope, however. If top and bottom left are related, one might expect top and bottom right to have a similar relationship. Are they from two separate sources? Literary sources tell us nothing of hostages in the Weland myth, but in the Old English poem *Deor* the famous smith is loosely associated with the idea of exile (Bradley 1982, 362–5). If we follow the direction of the hostages and fleeing inhabitants of Jerusalem, we should turn the corner onto the adjacent side panel which depicts Romulus and Remus suckled by the wolf (see above Fig 19.5). The runic inscription reads:

> Romulus and Remus, two brothers, a she-wolf nourished them in Rome, far from their native land (Page 1973, 177–8).

We have only just left images of two other, less fortunate brother princes (the sons of Nithhad), and, as Rome takes over the Hebrew power-centre, hostages and refugees fleeing *their* native land. If the journey continues anticlockwise from Romulus and Remus, we arrive back in Weland's smithy where he is confined like any hostage on his island. Indeed, all these exiled people (Weland, Romulus and Remus, the refugee Jews), are confined to the left half of the casket, the half which on the back carries the caption: *gisl*.

It is more difficult to unite the panels on the right, principally because of the enigmatic nature of the right side-plate whose imagery and inscriptions are exceptionally oblique.

The creator of the programme was literary, well-read and familiar with the subtleties of 'compounding and commingling' his sources. In c 700 his formidable library can only have been in a Northumbrian monastery where he would have recited the psalms regularly, informed by commentaries upon them by Augustine and Cassiodorus. One psalm in particular appears to generate caption after caption appropriate to the scenes on the casket: it is Psalm 68 (67), *Exsurgat Deus*, Let God Arise.[3]

The battles and refugees of the box spring to mind in verses such as: 'Let his enemies be scattered; let those who hate him flee before him' (verse 1), and 'the kings of the armies, they flee, they flee' (verse 12), and again, 'scatter the peoples who delight in war' (verse 30). Often this theme is closely associated in the psalm with images of ascent: 'Thou didst ascend . . . leading captives in thy train, and receiving gifts among men, even among the rebellious' (verse 18). At least three of the casket's images are encapsulated there. 'Lift up a song to him who rides upon the clouds' (verse 4); 'to him who rides in the heavens, the ancient heavens' (verse 33); 'his power is in the skies' (verse 34). These verses celebrate divine revenge from the skies, while Weland's heroic vengeance hovered 'against the clouds on high', as *Volundarkviða* (37) put it centuries later (Dronke 1997, 253). In Psalm 68.13 the means of flight is as full of artifice as Weland's contrivance and it is expressed in terms of fine metalworking: 'wings of a dove silvered, and between the shoulders thereof in the freshness of gold', a line earning two whole sections of Augustine's commentary on this psalm. It is probable that Weland's ham-strung exile, and his escape from it, is the lot of those described by Augustine who must wait for redemption:

He who leadeth forth men fettered, in strength – For he looseth the heavy bonds of sins wherewith they are fettered, so that they could not walk in the way of the commandments; but he leadeth them forth in strength which before His grace they had not (Schaff 1956, 287).

It is this psalm which provides an extraordinary gloss on the enigmatic right side of the casket. Verse 30 reads: *Increpa feras arundis* (rebuke the beasts that dwell among the reeds). Immediately above the horse's head is the word *bita* (biter) in runes, a reasonable name for a fierce beast, though both Sweet and Toller in their Anglo-Saxon dictionaries gave the meaning as 'wild beast' (Sweet 1896, 25; Toller 1898, 105). Over its back is the word *risci* (reeds). The line in the psalms is as obscure as the carving, yet the correspondence is startlingly close. A third runic word buried within the scene is *wudu* (wood). The word *arundis* (reeds) is used in one text of the psalm, that used by Augustine in his commentary where he even plays with a synonym for reeds (*calami*) so that he can make a pun on the act of writing with a pen (*CCSL* 39, 895–6; Schaff 1956, 297). In Cassiodorus's commentary, however, this verse reads: *Increpa feras siluarum* (the beasts abide in the wood), 'wood' being the third runic word below the animal's feet and undergrowth of its setting (*CCSL* 97, 600). The difference lies in the fact that Cassiodorus was using the 'Roman' version, the oldest of Jerome's three revisions. This Psalter evidently dominated in England throughout most of the

Anglo-Saxon period and it is very likely to have been familiar in early 8th-century Northumbria. The Gallican Psalter, which has *harundinis* in place of the Roman *siluarum*, was in both Ireland and Gaul 200 years before the casket was made, and a Northumbrian monastery at that time, with its Janus head turned to both the Celtic west and the continent, might easily have enjoyed access to both texts. The casket, then, gives a glimpse of the library: either two versions of the Psalter text, and (or) the commentaries of both Augustine and Cassiodorus.[4]

Now that we are accustomed to comparing front and back, top and bottom of the casket, perhaps we should be juxtaposing left and right. The brothers Romulus and Remus are suckled by a wild beast, the she-wolf, in a wood. The connection may be further strengthened by Page's possible alternative reading of the runic caption for the cryptic (right) panel, where *sarden sorga* can be translated as either 'wretched den of sorrows' or 'wretched wood of sorrows' (Page 1973, 182).

The debris of scholarly attempts to disentangle the imagery of the right side is enough to deter one from identifying a particular narrative source, but in terms of motifs within imagery it is striking that the free-floating objects and some of the figures are found as conventions in later Old English poetry. *The Wanderer*, for example, contains an *ubi sunt* passage that cries:

> Where has gone the steed? Where has gone the man? Where has gone the giver of treasure? Alas, the gleaming chalice; alas the armoured warrior (Bradley 1982, 324).

Naturally, this is not to say that the right side illustrates *The Wanderer* whose extant text is much later, but the conventions of the *anhaga* (wanderer) may well have been current in the period of the casket's manufacture. In this context it is worth contemplating the date of the two texts of *The Dream of the Rood*. Certainly there are other echoes in *The Wanderer* of the casket's imagery: 'So I . . . separated from my home'; 'Him the paths of exile preoccupy'; 'Some war snatched away and carried off along the onward road' (Bradley 1982, 322–4). It is equally possible that the imagery of the psalms continued to feed literary conventions.

Psalm 68 is, however, a more hopeful text. In verse 5 the phrase 'the father of orphans' goes some way to explaining the miraculous suckling and survival of Romulus and Remus, and the psalm continues: 'God gives the desolate a home to dwell in; he leads out the prisoners to prosperity, but the rebellious dwell in the tomb'. Immediately following the 'father of orphans' comes, appropriately for the casket, the crucial line: *Deus in loco sancto suo* (God in his holy place); but on the back of the casket God is manifestly not in his holy place. The Ark is empty. The juxtaposition of back and front, coupled with verse 29 of the psalm, appears to clinch the connection between the two: 'Because of Thy temple at Jerusalem, kings bear gifts to Thee.'

This pairing of the Temple and Mary at the Epiphany is illuminated by the commentaries of both Augustine and Cassiodorus on this verse. Both refer to Jerusalem as a mother. Cassiodorus has *Jerusalem mater omnium* (*CCSL* 97, 600) and Augustine, significantly for the casket, relates the verse to Galatians 4.26:

> Jerusalem, which is our free mother, because the same also is thy holy Temple; from that Temple then, to thee kings shall offer presents (Schaff 1956, 297).

This brings us to the front plate where the Magi come to Christ and the Virgin under that visual echo of the Temple in Jerusalem. The Christ Child is depicted in an unusual way; his head is contained in a *vesica* within Mary's body. Grabar identified this iconography as a representation of the Incarnation, though his earliest example was from the 9th century (Grabar 1968, 128, pl 304). It is clear, however, that it existed before the date of the Franks Casket, since it appears in a fresco in Santa Maria Antiqua in Rome, as well as on a late 6th-century stone stele from Khandesi in Georgia (Grabar 1966, 170, fig 180; Tschubinaschivili 1972, pl 2; Mepisashvili & Tsintsadze 1979, 235).

It is interesting that the Incarnation image is adopted for the Epiphany – surely because it was meant to stand against the empty Ark in Jerusalem. In Bethlehem, God is indeed in his holy place. In the future that holy place would be in the members of his church, as Bede insists (Connolly 1995, xxix, 5), hence the Ark must remain empty and the new church, geographically, follows in the footsteps of Romulus and Remus to Rome. It is in Rome that early churches such as SS Cosmas and Damian in the 6th century filled the triumphal arch of the apse with Christ victorious on a ladder of clouds (Mancinelli 1981, 59) and in Rome that we find in St Clement's both Bethlehem and Jerusalem juxtaposed on either side of such an arch, reworked from an earlier mosaic in the 12th century (Boyle 1989, 26, pl). It was also to Rome that Titus returned with the booty wrenched from Jerusalem's Temple. His arch, raised to commemorate his conquest, so vividly depicted on the casket, stands in the Forum, and in the highest point of its coffered soffit is a carving of Titus borne into the heavens at his apotheosis by an eagle. The principal reminders of Jerusalem in Rome are surmounted by one 'who rides upon the clouds' of Psalm 68, 'whose enemies are scattered'. He also has more than a passing resemblance to a flying Germanic smith who would have had more than a professional interest in the metalwork of the Temple.

Psalm 68 was considered by early commentators to be about escape from death. Cassiodorus lists its themes as future judgement, vengeance falling upon the faithless and the enemies of the Lord, and recompense for the faithful who delight in their reward, all themes of the casket's iconography (*CCSL* 97, 585). Both psalm and casket, as well as their respective commentaries, remain obscure, but that was the intention of that riddling mind which created the programme.

Caskets can be locked as well as opened. It was a relief in preparing this risky chapter to find Augustine, still commenting on this psalm, praying:

> May then the Lord open unto us that knock, and may the secret things of his mysteries be disclosed (Schaff 1956, 288).

ACKNOWLEDGEMENTS

I am grateful to Jane Hawkes and John McKinnell for their help in providing literary sources, and to Hilda Ellis Davidson who, years ago, recognized the possibilities of this topic.

The editors would like to thank Diana Whaley for her help with the Old Norse literary sources.

NOTES

1. Another trick may lie in the runes and the directions in which they are read, but there the routes are perilous, so I shall confine myself to the arched features and what they contain.
2. The carving of the lid panel is probably by a different hand from that which cut the front and back plates. The style of the kirtles and leggings of the warriors, for example, is more sophisticated on the lid, and the interior of their shields (a detail not shown elsewhere) is dished, the only instance of such cutting on the box which is generally carved in flat planes. The border mouldings of the lid are also distinctive.
3. The numbering of the psalm follows that of the Vulgate edition of Sixtus V and Clement VIII, and of the Authorised Version. Verse numbers are those of the Vulgate.
4. I am most grateful to Richard Marsden for this textual information (pers comm).

CHAPTER 21

THE TRAVELLING TWINS: ROMULUS AND REMUS IN ANGLO-SAXON ENGLAND

Carol Neuman de Vegvar

In considering the programme of the Franks Casket, the well-known whalebone box in the British Museum, no one has satisfactorily explained the iconographic peculiarities of the Romulus and Remus panel that serves as the casket's left side (Fig 21.1). The scene shows the discovery of Romulus and Remus rather than the more common motif of the suckling of the twins. The discovery has its own traditions in classical art; however, the scene on the Franks Casket includes several iconographic anomalies in which it deviates from all classical exemplar. To the best of the ability of an artist unfamiliar with foreshortening, the twins are shown as young adults, possibly bearded, sprawling on the ground beside a recumbent wolf, rather than as infants seated underneath the belly of a standing wolf, as is the classical norm. There are four shepherds, whereas normally in classical depictions there are at most three; also, the shepherds carry spears rather than crooks, and they kneel in homage rather than gesturing their surprise or standing by. Last and most anomalous is the second wolf at the top of the panel. The *titulus* should most probably be read as 'Romulus and Remus, two brothers, a she-wolf nourished them in Rome, far from their native land' (Page 1987, 41).

The story of the exposure, nourishment, and discovery of Romulus and Remus survives in multiple classical sources, including Livy, Florus, Plutarch, Justinus, and Eusebius (Souers 1935, 200). The king of Alba orders the twins to be cast into the Tiber. The servants entrusted with the task place the infants in a cradle or trough at the edge of the flooded river that in receding leaves the twins safe, according to some at the foot of a sacred fig tree. A she-wolf, bereft of her litter, finds and suckles them. They are discovered by Faustulus, the king's shepherd, and adopted by him and his wife, Acca Larentia. A variation of the story, given

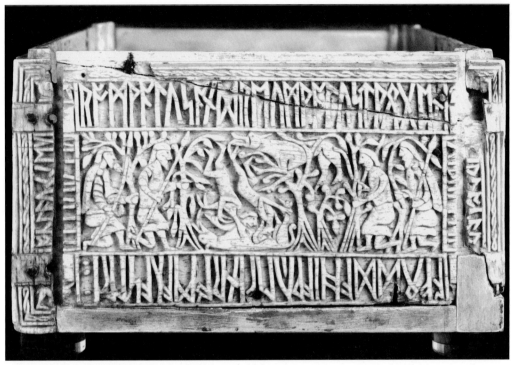

Fig 21.1. Franks Casket, left side: *Discovery of Romulus and Remus*: British Museum, London. (Photograph: Trustees of the British Museum, by permission)

by Dionysius of Hallicarnassus, who claims to be quoting Quinctus Fabius (op. cit. 201–2), describes an unnamed shepherd discovering the wolf and twins and calling other shepherds to view the unnatural phenomenon. They approach the scene and drive the wolf away with their shouting; she hides in a cave in a nearby grove dedicated to Pan. The shepherds take the children and on their way meet Faustulus, who takes the children home (*ibid*).

Current scholarly consensus asserts an origin for the Franks Casket in Anglo-Saxon England, in either Northumbria or Mercia, in the first half of the 8th century (Webster & Backhouse 1991, no 70). The Franks Casket is not alone in 8th-century Anglo-Saxon art in depicting the story of Romulus and Remus, but the other extant examples show the suckling rather than the discovery of the twins. A fragment of a whalebone plaque, now housed in the Castle Museum in Norwich (Fig 21.2), was found in 1970 at Larling, Norfolk (Green 1971). It was most likely part of a book cover or writing tablet and is usually dated to the late 8th century because of the resemblance of its decorative motifs to those on the Gandersheim casket and the Rothbury cross (Webster & Backhouse 1991, no 138 and fig 13). On the Larling fragment, the wolf and twins fill the re-entrant angle of a cross. The plaque was found near a church dedicated to Æthelberht, the sainted king of East Anglia executed in 794 by his overlord, Offa of Mercia.

Fig 21.2. Whalebone plaque fragment from Larling, Norfolk; Norwich, Castle Museum.
(Photograph: Norfolk Museums Service: Norwich Castle Museum)

Historians suspect the execution was the result of a failed rebellion by
Æthelberht against Offa, for which the physical evidence is an East Anglian *sceat*
(penny) issued by Æthelberht; shortly afterwards Offa also issued an East
Anglian penny in what has been interpreted as a reassertion of hegemony (Yorke
1990, 64). Æthelberht's *sceattas* show the wolf and twins, along with the word
REX on the reverse, and a head along with the king's name in Latin letters and the
moneyer's name in runes on the obverse (Fig 21.3). The bust portrait obverse is
common among Anglo-Saxon 8th-century mintings. Its gesture toward the
validating authority of *romanitas* is strengthened here by giving the king's name
in Latin letters while the moneyer's name, Lul, is given in vernacular runic script.
Æthelberht's coins are also not unique among early Anglo-Saxon coins in
showing the wolf and twins: several secondary series V *sceattas* produced in
southern England in the first quarter of the 8th century feature the group, derived
from Roman coins by a process of geometricizing abstraction (Rigold 1977,
25–6; 1–30; Stewart 1984, 7, 16, 18; Rigold & Metcalf 1984, 245–68; Webster
& Backhouse 1991, no 74b; Fig 21.4). But the clarity with which the theme is
depicted on Æthelberht's penny, compared to the typically abstracted versions on
the southern *sceattas*, suggests political intent.

A gesture toward the founders of Rome would have been appropriate for a
leader of the Wuffingas, a dynasty whose genealogy also claimed Caesar as an
ancestor.[1] The East Anglian moneyer, Lul, who also produced pennies for
Eadwald of East Anglia and Offa and Coenwulf of Mercia, does not repeat the
wolf and twins motif for them (Webster & Backhouse 1991, no 222a–d). So the
wolf and twins on Æthelberht's coins may well represent the dynastic and
genealogical claims he asserted to back his ill-fated struggle to break free of
Mercian hegemony. However, as Leslie Webster has pointed out, the find site of

Fig 21.3. Penny of Æthelberht of East Anglia (d 794); British Museum, London. (Photograph: Trustees of the British Museum, by permission)

Fig 21.4. *Sceat*, secondary series V, wolf and twins/bird-in-vine type, c 725; British Museum, London. (Photograph: Trustees of the British Museum, by permission)

the Larling plaque, near a church dedicated to the sainted East Anglian rebel king, may be purely fortuitous, and have no bearing on the meaning of the scene on the plaque itself. Her explanation that the wolf and twins 'were commonly used to symbolise the Church nourishing the faithful' (op. cit. 179) would mesh well with the cross and vine-scroll in an ecclesiastical, possibly eucharistic context.

An earlier example of the wolf and twins motif from Anglo-Saxon art is the c 475 gold type-A bracteate found at Undley in Suffolk (British Museum, London), which bears both a helmeted head and the wolf and twins (Fig 21.5). Hills (1991) has convincingly demonstrated a strong possibility that this bracteate was made in East Anglia, rather than Scandinavia as was contended by Hines and Odenstedt (1987). Both motifs on this bracteate seem to be derived from a coin or medallion of the URBS ROMA type (Fig 21.6). The closest parallel, a coin minted at Trier in 330–5, circulated widely in the 4th century; two occur in Kentish graves.

Clearly, when the Anglo-Saxons got to England, Romulus and Remus were already there, having hitched a ride with the Romans. Beside the widespread distribution of the motif on coins, evidence for its availability in Roman England includes a mosaic pavement at Aldborough, Yorkshire (Elgee & Elgee 1933, 163–4, pl vii), a circular ornament in stamped copper from Moorfields (Museum of London; Smith 1854, 11–12, pl iii:2), and a pediment from the *cardo* of Corstopitum on Hadrian's Wall (Corbridge Museum; Dulière 1979, no 114, fig 292). However, there is no evidence for continuity in the use of the motif into the Anglo-Saxon period; instead the theme seems to be periodically reintroduced, and in the case of the Franks Casket, reinvented.

The Undley bracteate, Larling plaque, and Anglo-Saxon pennies show the suckling scene rather than the discovery seen on the Franks Casket. Indeed the suckling scene is the primary visualization of the Romulus and Remus story in broad circulation in the Middle Ages. It occurs at the foot of the cross on the late Carolingian Rambona diptych (Museo Cristiano, Vatican; Goldschmidt 1914, 86, pl 84) and on a Tuscan stone base of 12th- to early 13th-century date (Museum of Fine Arts, Boston; Herman & Bliss 1987, 74–5; Cahn & Seidel 1979, 111–13). This is not surprising considering that the suckling scene is more common than the discovery in Roman art. It appears on many altars and tombstones, and particularly and critically in portable media such as coins and gems.[2] The discovery scene is less common in Roman art, but does appear in both stationary and portable contexts. However, these do not provide a complete set of sources for the Franks Casket scene. The earliest examples show the suckling wolf observed by a single shepherd, as on two Republican sards in the British Museum (Walters 1926, 115, no 984, 988, pl XIV, XV).[3] On a denarius minted by Sextus Pompeius Fostulus in 129 BC (Souers 1935, 202; Carson 1962, 113, pl 201), the name of the minter serves also to identify the shepherd as Faustulus. The availability of such models in northern Europe in the early Middle Ages is demonstrated by the use of a late Republican carved gem, showing the wolf and twins discovered by a single shepherd, as the bezel of an early 7th-century Merovingian ring now in the British Museum (Walters 1926, 380–1, no 4051).

The single-shepherd type fades from use in the 1st century BC and is progressively replaced with a motif showing wolf and twins discovered by two (or occasionally more) shepherds (Dulière 1979, I, 88–9), coinciding with Dionysius of Halicarnassus' version of the story. Scenes of discovery by multiple shepherds usually show them springing back in astonishment, or simply standing adjacent to the wolf and twins. A Hadrianic relief on the side of an altar from Ostia, dated to 124 (Museo delle Terme, Rome), shows the wolf and twins with the personified Tiber in the lower register; the upper contains the imperial eagle and three shepherds holding short crooks, two of whom spring back in surprise while the third sits on a rock at the left (Strong 1907, 241–3, pl LXXIV). On a relief showing the facade of the Hadrianic temple of Venus and Rome (Museo delle Terme, Rome), the pediment shows two shepherds who flee from the wolf and twins (op. cit. 238–41, pl LXXII). Astonishment is gestured more quietly by two shepherds on the ceiling of the eastern arch of the Porta Martis in Reims (Dulière 1979, II, 46 no 118, fig 317). Most typically on the gems, two shepherds flank the wolf and twins in an arch representing the cave.[4] On a small chrysoprase in Berlin (Furtwängler 1898, 117, no 2487) two shepherds holding crooks start back in fright to the left, as on the Hadrianic pediment. Four Italic scarab-style brown and blue pastes in Berlin show three shepherds, two facing left and one facing right, above a crude image of the wolf and twins (op. cit. 40, no 435–8). The shepherd facing right is also distinguished from the others by a beard and cloak, possibly reflecting a conflation of the multiple shepherds and Faustulus types. Antique multiple-shepherd models may be influential in the Franks Casket scene. Additionally, a bronze coin minted at Ostia between 309 and 312 showing the wolf and twins flanked by the Dioscuri, who hold spears and the reins of horses (Fig 21.7), may have been a model for the Franks Casket's flanking shepherds with spears (Dulière 1979, II, M124, 98–9). However, no extant

Fig 21.5. Bracteate from Undley, Suffolk;
British Museum, London. (Photograph:
Trustees of the British Museum, by
permission)

classical image could have provided a model for the reclining she-wolf, the
four shepherds holding spears and revering the wolf and twins, the second wolf,
or the size and age of the twins.[5]

Some aspects of the scene may be linked to classical texts available in 8th-century
England. One of these is Virgil's *Aeneid*, known to Bede and his contemporaries
either in its entirety or in excerpts. In Book VIII, Virgil describes the imagery on the
shield given by Venus to Aeneas. Here, the wolf was portrayed 'couched after the
birth in the green cave of Mars' (MacKail 1934, 166). An artist unfamiliar with
Roman prototypes and presented with this phrasing might well depict a recumbent
wolf; the cave is missing in the image but the foliage arches suggestively above the
wolf and twins. Similarly, the reverence that the Franks Casket shepherds show for
the wolf and twins may also have a textual source. The shepherds recognize the
authority of the twins only in the writings of the chronicler Cassius Hemina of the
2nd century BC. The passage survives as quoted by the 4th-century AD grammarian
Diomedes, whose *Three Books on the Grammatical Arts* were used by Boniface and
others in the 7th- and 8th-century Insular world (Law 1982, 20):

> Of the shepherds, the multitude, agreeing without strife, appointed equally
> as masters Remus and Romulus, in such a way that they would provide in
> matters of authority between themselves (Keil 1857, 384).

Whether there was an independent oral Romulus and Remus cycle in early
Anglo-Saxon England (Hunter 1974, 40), and whether these sources were
influential in its formation, is unknown.

Fig 21.6.   URBS ROMA coin of
Constantine I, minted at Trier
(330–5); British Museum, London.
(Photograph: Trustees of the British
Museum, by permission)

Fig 21.7.   Bronze coin, minted at Ostia (309–12):
wolf and twins with Dioscuri; American Numismatic
Society, New York. (Photograph: courtesy of the
American Numismatic Society, New York)

However, neither classical visual models nor antique texts can explain the second wolf, the large number of reverent spear-carrying shepherds, or the adult twins on the Franks Casket. Souers (1935, 206–7) declared that the extra wolf and the shepherds to the right were added as decorative fill to a model with two shepherds to the left, by an artist who was unfamiliar with the story and who wished to adapt the model to a wider rectangular format. Today's medievalists are more cautious about pleading the ignorance or decorative invention of artists to explain away whatever does not fit a tidy set of prototypes. Ignorance may explain deletions of forms already unclear in available models, as Souers suggested of the cave which had much earlier become a simple arch on the carved gemstones. But it is difficult to imagine how curled crooks could be misread as spears, how infants have been misconstrued as adults, or how a second wolf has been mistakenly allowed to creep into the woods.

The spears may, at least in part, reflect the realities of keeping flocks in 8th-century England. Wolves were the primary large predators of the English wilderness, and the spear is the weapon most commonly found in Anglo-Saxon graves (Härke 1992, 156–7), suggesting that if Anglo-Saxon shepherds were armed against wolves, they would have been armed with spears.

As for the second wolf, two proposals by early scholars may be set aside as neither is completely satisfactory. Holthausen (1900, 210) speculated that this large and clearly ferocious canine might be the shepherd's dog; however, no visual connection is made to the shepherds. Goldschmidt (1918, 57) suggested that the second canine might be the mate of the she-wolf, but this has no basis in any source, and the sex of the second wolf is not explicit. It might equally be read as the she-wolf fleeing from the shepherds, conflating Dionysius's narrative sequence, although no classical visual prototypes exist.

The selection of scenes on the Franks Casket indicates a strong preference for non-biblical subject matter – only half the front panel is given over to the Adoration of the Magi; the rest of the panels deal with either classical mythology, Roman secular history, or Anglo-Saxon heroic legend. Given this choice of subject matter, the Franks Casket was most probably made for a secular patron, albeit by an artist with access to both the resources and literate advice of a monastic community. By the 8th century the Anglo-Saxon aristocracy was thoroughly converted to Christianity, and concepts of rulership were beginning to be reformulated to fit with the new faith.[6] But the *titulus* of the Romulus and Remus scene hints at neither a Eucharistic reading, with the wolf as a type for the church nourishing the faithful, nor a reading of the adult Romulus as a fratricide comparable to Cain, as in Augustine's *City of God* 15.6. However, Augustine's reading of the suckling of the twins as evidence of divine intervention may be more applicable:

> And yet, if to convict the man who was king, who had cruelly ordered them to be flung into the water, God wished to aid those infants through whom a great city was destined to be founded after their divine escape from the water, by letting a wild animal suckle them, what is surprising in that? (Sanford & Green 1988, 437, XVIII: xxi).

The role of destiny in claims to rulership was a matter of major concern to Anglo-Saxon kings and magnates. The selection of Romulus and Remus as a theme for a casket made at a monastery but destined for a secular aristocrat would send a message of the role of God in assuring the destiny of successful claimants. The unusual aspects of the scene may have been intended to make the meaning of the scene more vivid for its anticipated audience by drawing on indigenous tradition.

The duplication of the wolves suggests that they are to be considered together with the twins. The Old English poetic record, as in the *Exeter Book Maxims I(C)* (Muir 1994, 257, lines 9–11, 146–8), refers to wolves as the characteristic companions and assailants of outcasts in the wilderness. Romulus and Remus are themselves identified by the *titulus* as outcasts, exiles 'far from their native land', and the story details the exposure of the infants in the wild, the space associated in the Anglo-Saxon mind with outsiders and wolves. Recent demolition by Stanley (1992) of the old equation 'wolves = outlaws' permits a reading of the wolves as a danger to the twins. In the minds of Christian Anglo-Saxons this perception may well have made the story of their rescue by a wolf all the more miraculous evidence of God's intervention on behalf of the future founders of Rome.

Exposed infants who are rescued or nurtured by wild animals and later become founders of states or successors to thrones is a widespread Indo-European folkloric topos (Dunn 1960; Binder 1964; de Vries 1956, 212–14). It can be traced in the Germanic world in the six Middle High German versions of the story of Wolfdietrich, the earliest of which dates to the early 13th century, where Dietrich is delivered from exposure by a wolf (Dunn 1960, 102–3). Insular parallels are also found in Ireland where a wolf is rescuer and nurturer in the story of Cormac mac Airt, recorded in the *Book of Ballymote* around 1400, and in the legends of Saints Albeus and Amargenus, both recorded in the 12th century or later. (Dunn 1960, 104–5; Carney 1955, 291 n 6). Besides the poem *Beowulf*, the Anglo-Saxon oral epic tradition has survived primarily in the form of scattered references in the poetic record and the derogatory remarks of churchmen. The Anglo-Saxon artisan and audience of the Franks Casket could have understood the Romulus and Remus scene in the light of a now-lost indigenous epic which included the exposure topos; the type is so common that its complete absence from stories current in Anglo-Saxon England seems improbable.

The Anglo-Saxon poetic record does refer to wolves in the context of warfare, as the scavengers of the battlefield, but they are also associated with victory in battle, as in *Elene*, where the wolf is *holtes geletha*, 'woodland companion', to the victorious Constantine (Gradon 1958, 30, line 113; Toller 1898, 401).[7] Victory in battle was one of the continuing conditions of the maintenance of authority in the early Anglo-Saxon period; hegemonies were held together as often by combat as by diplomacy. Wolves were a frequent totem of warrior societies in Indo-European cultures, including the early Germanic world. Norse sources mention not only *berserkr* or bear-warriors but also *ulfhethinn* or wolf-skin warriors (Höfler 1934, 170–2). Both of these belong to the widespread Indo-European tradition of shape-changing warriors, who were believed to become the animals of which they wore the pelts (Eliade 1970, 1–20; Przyluski 1940; Dumèzil 1970, 139–47). Visual evidence of such beliefs may have been found both on the now-lost 5th-century Danish Gallehus horns, one of which showed a wolfheaded figure probably bearing a weapon (Oxenstierna 1956, abb 3c) and on a 7th-century metalwork plaque from Torslunda in Öland where a dancing warrior is accompanied by a figure part man and part wolf or bear (Bruce-Mitford 1978, 209, fig 156a). Although Anglo-Saxon art lacks explicit visual references to this tradition, the role of wolves in the poetic record suggests that wolves and warriors were also linked in England. Such animal warriors were rarely part of the mainstream cultures in which they lived, but rather sometimes successful outsiders, a parallel for Romulus and Remus.[8] Several Franks Casket anomalies may be explained by this association: the twins may have been shown as adults to suggest their role as outcast warriors, and the two wolves may have signified not only the twins' temporary exile but also their destiny for rulership via victorious military campaigns. The kneeling armed shepherds may also take on a new meaning in this context, as victory in battle in early Anglo-Saxon England was premised on the loyalty of one's warband.

Furthermore, the duality of the protagonists may have been a familiar mythic element in the Anglo-Saxon setting. Many Germanic origin legends include stories of migration from an ancient homeland to a new place of settlement, often led by a pair of brothers. Paul the Deacon names the Lombards' leaders as Ybor and Agio and those of the Vandals as Ambri and Assi; Dio Cassius gives Raos and Raptos as the leaders of the Vandalic Astingar into Dacia in 170 (Ward 1968, 50–3). These myths may well reflect early Germanic dioscurism, the worship of twin or brother gods who protect travellers and warriors, which was in turn widespread among Indo-European cultures (Turville-Petre 1957, Wagner 1960, Ward 1968). The earliest documentary source is Tacitus's *Germania* 43, where the Naharvali are said to worship the Alcis, whom Tacitus identifies as equivalent to Castor and Pollux (Mattingly 1970, 137). Possible visual evidence can be traced back to the Bronze Age in Denmark, where ritual razors and incised stones show pairs of gigantic figures either in or hovering over ships (Naumann 1950).[9] One surviving Anglo-Saxon origin legend has similar elements. According to Bede (Colgrave & Mynors 1969, 50–1, 1.15), the earliest Anglo-Saxon settlers were led by a pair of brothers, Hengest and Horsa.[10] The legend of these brothers also appears in the *Anglo-Saxon Chronicle*, where they figure additionally in the genealogy of the Kentish royal house (Swanton 1996, 12–14). Bede was probably using a Kentish source, a dynastic propaganda piece stressing the seniority of the Kentish dynasty, possibly premised on actual joint kingship in Kent (Miller 1975; Yorke 1983).[11] Hengest and Horsa's names, respectively 'stallion' and 'horse', appear to have a dioscuric cultic component; the names Hengst and Hors were applied in Schleswig-Holstein up to the 19th century to paired horsehead roof finials thought to have protective powers (Ward 1968, 54).

In England, place-names associated with Hengest occur mostly in the south east, extending northwards only as far as Cambridgeshire, suggesting the primarily local origins of the legend (Yorke 1993). However, paired dancing warriors on one of the ornamental panel types on the Sutton Hoo helmet (Bruce-Mitford 1978, 186, fig 140) suggest that if Hengest and Horsa were not known as far north as East Anglia in the 7th century, they may have had regional analogues. In the 8th century, Bede's *Ecclesiastical History* made the Hengest and Horsa legend more widely known and accepted. The late 9th-century Old English translator of Bede renders the Hengest and Horsa text with unusual fidelity, suggesting that the passage had acquired canonical status (Howe 1989, 70). An oral tradition concerning Hengest may also have been in circulation in Anglo-Saxon England, perhaps contributing to the appearance of the character of the same name in *Beowulf*. So the legend of a pair of outcast or traveller brothers who led a people and contributed to the formation of a kingdom was probably not unfamiliar in the 8th-century Anglo-Saxon milieu of the Franks Casket and could stand as a reference to destined rulership.

The scene of the nurturing of Romulus and Remus on the Franks Casket thus found sympathetic echoes in indigenous culture, and its meaning was likely enhanced by comparisons that such similarities invited. The scene was designed to bring attention to the duality of the twins, their identification as young warriors with the wolves, and the reverence with which they are regarded by the shepherds; to focus the viewer's mind on their role as successful leaders, saved from certain death and exalted by a destiny reflecting the will of God.

ACKNOWLEDGEMENTS

My profound gratitude is owed to the following: Dr John Hines (University of Wales, Cardiff) and Mrs Leslie Webster (British Museum) for their kind assistance concerning the Undley bracteate; and Professor John Osborne (University of Victoria) for allowing me to present a preliminary version of this chapter at the 14th Canadian Conference of Medieval Art Historians in 1994, the critique of which encouraged the evolution of the project to its present form. All errors remaining are the responsibility of the author.

NOTES

1. Hauck (1986, 261) suggested a dynastic connection for the Undley bracteate to the Wuffingas; neither Hills (1991, 148) nor I find this association convincing in that early context, but by the date of the Æthelberht coins the dynastic reference may be plausible.
2. Examples include: a carved sard of the Republican period, British Museum 983 (Walters 1926, 115, pl XIV); a didrachm of 269 BC (Carson 1962, 108, pl 191); and three examples in Berlin: a convex Hellenistic stone (1128); a brown paste of 1st-century BC to 1st-century AD date (4375); a flat Hellenistic/Roman carnelian (6896; Furtwängler 1898, 73, 181, 256). Dulière (1979) gives a wide variety of examples, including many altars and funerary stelae; however, none is of English origin. The formula showing the wolf turning her head toward the twins is followed in the Rambona diptych but not in the Boston relief, indicating that a variety of sources for the scene were available to the later Middle Ages.
3. Other examples include a flat dark brown paste, Berlin 4381 (Furtwängler 1898, 181) which is virtually identical in composition to British Museum 984.
4. Examples include a stone from the Roman Republic, British Museum 987 (Walters 1926, 15, pl XV); the Ara Casali (Brunn & Bulle 1898, 44–5, pl 16); a lateral face of the Mattei sarcophagus (Dulière 1979, II, 48–9 no 125, fig 318); a violet convex late Roman paste, Berlin 3120 (Furtwängler 1898, 139; cf 181).
5. An engraved mirror back, now in the Antiquarium Communale in Rome and allegedly originally from Bolsena, shows two shepherds flanking a standing wolf with twins that are shown as young children rather than as infants (Dulière 1979, I, 73; II, 100, fig 321). The shepherd at left holds a club and wears the wolfskin of a celebrant of the Lupercalia; the one at right holds a spear. Below the wolf and twins reclines a second wolf. However, although originally claimed as Etruscan work the mirror is now believed to be a sophisticated 19th-century forgery (ibid; Klügmann & Körte 1887, 172; Souers 1935, 204–5).
6. Becker's (1973, 106–10) reading of the casket as casting a spell of protection on the owner is problematic; the Christianized elite of the 8th century would have found the use of magic

repugnant or at least inappropriate. Becker's reading of the Romulus and Remus scene as referring to the protection of travellers, with reference to the cult of the Dioscuri, is difficult to accept in an 8th-century context (cf Frank 1979, 120–2).

7. See also, in the 12th century, Laȝamon's *Brut*, where Arthur identifies himself with the wolf (Deskis & Hill 1995).

8. The association of werewolfism with warrior societies is found also in Ireland, where McCone (1984, 12–16; 1986; 1987; 1991, 213–15) has traced the association of lycanthropy with the age-grade warrior outcast group, the *fían*, that served to keep the peace in disputes over bride price and between neighbouring kingdoms.

9. See also the object with two helmeted warriors wielding axes found in Seeland in the 18th century and primarily known from early drawings (Derolez 1963, abb 6) and a pair of similarly helmeted warriors on the Gallehus horns (Oxenstierna 1956, abb 4a).

10. Although Wallace-Hadrill (1988, 23–4) did not question Hengest's historicity, Turville-Petre (1957), Brooks (1989, 58, 251 n 20) and Yorke (1993) have seen Hengest and Horsa as mythic, possibly recruited to support a tradition of dual kingship in Kent. Yorke (1993) suggests that the ecclesiastical powers of Canterbury may have assisted in the promotion of this legend of Kentish regnal primacy in order to sustain the primacy in religion of the see of Canterbury (cf Dumville 1977a, 72–104).

11. Joint kingship was also practised in Sussex, Wessex, Essex, and possibly Northumbria (Yorke 1985, 25–7; 1990, 170). Wood (1977, 19–20) has examined the continental parallels. Alföldi (1931) links double kingship to the exposure myths among several Turkic peoples of the Eurasian steppe.

CHAPTER 22

THE RIPON JEWEL

*R.A. Hall & E. Paterson (York Archaeological Trust)
& C. Mortimer (Ancient Monuments Laboratory), with
a contribution by Niamh Whitfield* [1]

INTRODUCTION

The Ripon Jewel (Plates 8, 9) is a 29 mm diameter gold cloisonné roundel, constructed on an annular gold base and inlaid with garnets, amber and other material. Filigree wire enhances the setting's inner edge, and stamped gold- and silver-coloured metal foils lie behind most of the garnet and amber inlays.

The Jewel was discovered during excavation in 1977 in the grounds immediately east of the former Deanery, presently The Old Deanery, some 50 m northeast of Ripon Cathedral.[2] It was found near the base of the stratigraphic sequence in an aceramic layer of brown soil containing mortar, plaster and stone fragments. This layer, and a small number of associated strata sharing similar characteristics, form a distinctive grouping spatially and stratigraphically, and may represent the erection, use and rebuilding of a structure. There is neither evidence for earlier occupation or activity, nor dating evidence for this series of layers apart from the presence of the jewel itself; layers sealing this horizon contain 13th- and 14th-century pottery (Hall & Whyman 1996).

DESCRIPTION

The Gold Base

The base is made from a circular disc of gold sheet, 0.1 mm thick, with a circular hole cut in the centre (Plate 9). The diameter of the whole is 29 mm maximum and the inner circle is 13–14 mm in diameter, leaving a 7–8 mm wide section on to which the decoration is applied. The surface is damaged by dents, scratches, tears and small holes. Impressions of some of the cloisonné cell walls are visible on the reverse as raised lines, suggesting the layout of the design was first scored into the base before the cell walls were mounted; there is evidence for this practice on the 7th-century pendant from Cranmer House, Canterbury (Webster 1987, 283) and on broadly contemporary composite disc brooches (Pinder 1995, 7).

There is no evidence in the form of wear, scars or rivet holes to indicate the former presence of a pin, catchplate or suspension loop to allow use as a brooch or pendant; indeed there is nothing to show how the Jewel articulated with its surrounds. It must be assumed that it was one component in a composite arrangement. A separately mounted stud presumably filled the centre, fixed by a direct attachment to the background upon which the whole device was mounted. This background might have been a circular (or other) mounting with a border collar securing the Jewel; alternatively, a suitable mounting may have been fabricated as just one decorative element in some larger piece of metalwork.

Outer and Inner Collars

The outer and inner collars are constructed from 2–2.5 mm wide strips of gold which, like the base, are 0.1 mm thick. They are joined to the base, possibly using copper salts, any excess metal being carefully pared off with a knife or chisel (Ogden 1992, 266). No solder is visible, but microscopy reveals fine diagonal scratches made at the inner edge by the cutting tool. Here, the base overlaps the collar all the way round, suggesting the base plate was trimmed after the inner collar was attached. At the outer edge, the base slightly overlaps the collar in some places, while in others the relationship is reversed.

Close beside the inner collar a second strip of the same size is attached to the base. The two strips are separated by a ring of gold filigree wire set almost flush with their upper edges and, presumably, soldered in place.

The Gold Cloisons

Cells containing the inlays are constructed in the space between the outer and inner collars, using the same thickness of gold sheet cut into strips 2–2.5 mm wide. It is unclear how these were attached to the base since no solder is visible. It is likely, however, that they were spot soldered, as Pinder (1995, 7) has demonstrated, and were further secured by the cement used to hold the inlay, described by Arrhenius (1985, 89) as the 'fused paste technique'.

Four approximately square cloisons were constructed to hold the amber inlays. They were contrived by folding a gold strip at approximately right angles in two places to create three sides of a square, the Jewel's outer rim serving as the fourth side (Plate 10). These cells are positioned equidistantly and fill the whole width of the jewel.

Slightly curved gold strips divide the arcs between the square cloisons, creating narrow, subrectangular areas, 3–3.5 mm wide, with longer strips bent zigzag fashion and placed in each outer arc to produce rows of cells, each of roughly

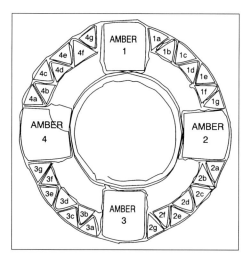

Fig 22.1. The Ripon Jewel: identification key.

equilateral triangular shape and sides about 3 mm long. Cell areas 1, 2 and 4 (Fig 22.1) have seven triangular cells. In cell area 3, the gold strip appears to have been slightly too long to create seven similarly sized triangles. Instead of trimming it, one end was bent upwards to create another half triangle; there is no evidence that this half-sized cloison was inlaid. This suggests that the Jewel is not the work of experienced craftsmen of the highest technical sophistication.

The upper edges of some of the gold strips, especially in cell area 2, have been flattened slightly. This thickening helped to secure the inlays, but is probably the result of polishing the surface of the object after construction rather than being evidence for intentionally tooled edges (Arrhenius 1985, 79). Indeed, there are extensive signs of wear, with the outer and inner collars and many of the internal cell walls distorted by dents and small tears.

Analysis of the gold at the Ancient Monuments Laboratory, London, using X-ray analysis (Mortimer 1996, 3) suggests that at least three different compositions were used to construct the Jewel. A low purity gold (24.5% Ag, 2% Cu) was used for the back plate, but a comparatively pure gold for the beaded wire (11.5% Ag, 2.5% Cu) which is more easily fabricated from gold of a higher caratage. The gold content of the cell walls is also relatively high but variable, with silver compositions of 9.5–19.5% and copper of 1–2%.

The Filigree Work

The decorative wire consists of a 0.6–0.7 mm diameter cable composed of three strands of fine beaded wire, each 0.2 mm in diameter, which have been S-twisted together. One section of the cable and adjacent inner collar has been torn apart, showing clearly the three strands of wire (Plate 11). The upper surface of the wire has been damaged in several places, creating smooth flat surfaces where the tops of beads have been flattened (Plate 12). It is unclear whether this damage occurred during antiquity, burial or after excavation.

Dr Niamh Whitfield writes:

The probability is that the gold wire was block-twisted, since this is the only method observed on fine gold wire from Anglo-Saxon England prior to the late 8th or early 9th century (Whitfield 1990, 16–18; cf fig 16).

However, as the Ripon wire is fully and regularly beaded, there are no blank spans which might retain tell-tale manufacturing marks and, therefore, we cannot be certain how it was made. Beaded wire manufactured with the aid of a grooved swage held at right angles is the norm for Anglo-Saxon jewellery and in this respect the Ripon Jewel conforms.

Three-strand beaded cables almost certainly occur on the Taplow gold buckle, an object also decorated with the more common two-strand beaded type (Campbell 1982, pl 39). Although there is no other definite Anglo-Saxon example, this can be attributed to the fact that it is not always possible to assess the exact number of wires in a strand, particularly if more than two are involved, without finding an unravelled strand tip. Three-strand beaded cables are not confined to early medieval Anglo-Saxon gold. They occur in Merovingian contexts (eg on a very ornate late 6th- to 7th-century brooch from Meckenheim, Rhineland, BM, MLA 99, 7–17.1), and also on the 'Tara' brooch from Ireland, c 700 (Whitfield 1993, figs 14.7g, 14.13). The use of ornamental wire at the base of a circular stud setting is normal on late 6th- to 7th-century Anglo-Saxon gold and garnet jewellery and also later Anglo-Saxon work, such as the 8th-century Ormside bowl (Webster & Backhouse 1991, no 134) and the 9th-century Gravesend silver cross pendant (Wilson 1964, no 20). It is also well known on Hiberno-Saxon work, where the tradition continued from at least c 700 to the 12th century.

The Inlay – Amber

The four approximately square pieces of inlay were identified as amber by visual examination and X-ray fluorescence by Ian Panter at York Archaeological Trust. They vary considerably in condition, dimensions and colour, which now ranges from mid-orange to dark orange/brown. Polyvinyl acetate in acetone was applied to the amber as a consolidant during the 1978 conservation process, and therefore the original colour may have been altered.

The dimensions of these inlays vary from a minimum of 6 mm^2. Amber 1 is 6 mm^2, with four straight sides (Plate 10). Ambers 2 and 4 are keystone-shaped; each has sides 6 mm long, but with outer and inner edges of 6.5 mm and 6 mm, and 7 mm and 6.5 mm, respectively. Ambers 2, 3 and 4 have slightly curved outer edges; amber 4 also has a slightly curved inner edge. At a missing corner of amber 4 it is possible to measure its thickness as 1 mm, and see that a gold foil lies behind it.

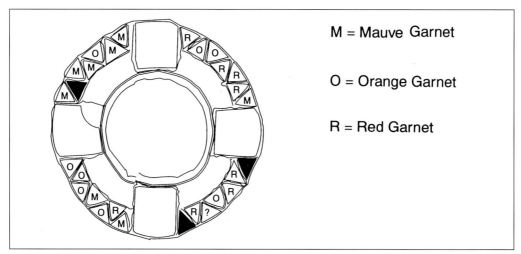

Fig 22.2.   The Ripon Jewel: the position of garnets of various colours.

Together, the amber inlays form a prominent cruciform pattern which, at least in the present incomplete state of the Jewel, is the dominant motif.

The Inlay – Garnet

Twenty-five of the twenty-eight triangular cells still contain garnet inlays. These have been designated a–g in a clockwise direction within each quadrant (Fig 22.1). Garnets 2a, 2g and 4b are missing. Examination and analysis of twelve of the garnets at the English Heritage Ancient Monuments Laboratory and Gem Testing Laboratories, London, identified three types of garnet which vary in chemical composition and hence colour and appearance. They are orange (orange pyrope), mauve (pyrope/almandine) and red (red pyrope). The garnets which were not removed have been examined *in situ* under a binocular microscope and their colour compared to the analysed garnets. Most of the mauve stones appear to be grouped together in the fourth quadrant, while the orange and red stones are concentrated in the first and second quadrants (Fig 22.2).

The garnets were cut from plates 1 mm thick, flat on both sides and presumably originally split by cleaving. They are roughly triangular in shape with sides 2–2.5 mm long; the edges are bevelled and uniformly set so that the side with the smaller surface area is at the bottom. Only the upper surfaces were polished. Half the gems examined have one very uniform and possibly wheel-cut edge, with two more uneven edges similar in appearance to window glass which has been grozed (ie nipped with pincers). The other six garnets examined have three grozed edges. This may suggest that all these gems were recycled from larger pieces and trimmed to fit the triangular cells.

Garnets 1d and 3d have parallel scored lines or scratches on their surface which are possibly polishing scars. Some of the gems lie flush with the top of the cells but many have settled to the bottom or lie at an angle within it. The space between each garnet foil and the bottom of its cell was presumably packed originally with an adhesive paste/filler which secured the gem, but this has since decayed, leaving no visual evidence in the empty cells. The most likely material for such a paste/filler is a beeswax and calcite mixture which shrinks as it sets, pulling the cell walls inwards and thus securing the garnets (Arrhenius 1985, 88). This normally survives as a yellow/white cement-like deposit (Shearman 1993, 30).

Other Inlay

The inner cloisonné arcs in each quadrant now contain what appears to be a consolidated dark brown silty soil incorporating quartz grains. During conservation this was recorded as 'bluey-grey, soft and powdery . . . with a lot of dirt' (YAT 1978). Analysis of it, carried out by Dr A. Cox at the University of York using X-ray diffraction, demonstrated the presence of a range of elements (potassium, sodium, iron, magnesium, aluminium, silica, calcium, manganese and various metals including gold, silver, copper, zinc and lead). All of these, apart from the metals, are to be expected in glass. Further investigation using X-ray analysis and X-ray diffraction analysis at the Ancient Monuments Laboratory did not confirm the presence of potassium and sodium but did detect a non-crystalline silicate which could be glass.

The nature of this inlay remains unclear although some possibilities, including white inlays such as shell or magnesite (La Niece 1988, 236), have been ruled out through the analyses. Arrhenius (1985, 36) notes that glass is one of the other inlays sometimes found on garnet cloisonné artefacts, but the results achieved here indicate only that glass may have been used. The lack of lead in the X-ray analysis may be significant if it reflects the original composition; enamels would normally contain substantial amounts of lead, whereas glass inlays could have been made from a soda-lime-silica glass, probably fabricated from small flat pieces chipped into shape. However, it is unclear why a soda-lime-silica glass would have decayed so thoroughly, as it is usually well preserved in most types of burial context.

One further possibility is that what remains in these arcs is not a residue of their original inlay, but soil introduced after loss, a residue of some paste or filler, or a mixture of both. In this case, the alternative types of inlay noted above are possible; it is also conceivable that gold filigree foils occupied these areas, although such a juxtaposition with a central stud would be unique in contemporary jewellery.

The Foils

Thin metal foils, both gold- and silver-coloured, back most of the garnets as well as the only amber inlay where the presence of a foil could be tested. In the case of the garnets, foils are visible through and at the edges of the gems; a row of four

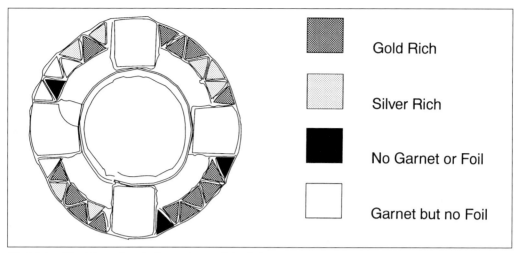

Fig 22.3. The Ripon Jewel: the position of the foils.

cells in the top left quarter has no foils. The foils are made from thin metal sheet cut into roughly triangular shapes and folded up around the edges of the gems, thus helping to secure them and hide any opaque crystalline paste. In two cases only small scraps of metal were used, not fully covering the back of the gems. The positioning of the two differently coloured foils does not appear to follow any pattern (Table 22.1; Fig 22.3).

1a gold	2a empty	3a gold	4a no foil
1b gold	2b gold	3b silver	4b empty
1c gold	2c gold	3c gold	4c no foil
1d silver	2d gold	3d gold	4d no foil
1e silver	2e gold	3e silver	4e silver
1f silver	2f gold	3f gold	4f gold
1g gold	2g empty	3g no foil	4g silver

Table 22.1. The colour of the foil in each cloison.

It was possible to examine eleven foils in greater detail. Some had been stamped to produce a patterned surface, thus increasing the lustre of the garnets (Plates 10, 13). The pattern appears as small square indentations comparable to the pointillé pattern found on similar foils in cloisonné jewellery from the early 7th-century Sutton Hoo, Suffolk, ship burial (Bruce-Mitford 1983, 631). The pattern is quite fine, measuring 3.5–4 squares per mm, and was made with stamps cut from bone or wood rather than using textiles as suggested by Arrhenius (1985, 39). In at least two cases, the pattern appears to have been reversed, presumably because the foils were placed upside down in the cells (Table 22.2).

1a	only lightly stamped with a possible pointillé in one corner
1b	pointillé
1f	pointillé
1g	no stamp
3a	no stamp
3b	reversed pointillé
3c	no stamp
3f	no stamp, small scrap of metal
4e	reversed pointillé
4f	no stamp, small scrap of metal
4g	pointillé

Table 22.2. Descriptions of eleven recorded foil patterns.

The gold foil below amber 4 has deeply scored lines creating a cross-hatched pattern of squares measuring approximately 1 mm across. In this instance the pattern has been made using a cutting tool. One corner is bent up showing the foil to be very thin sheet of similar thickness to that used for the garnet foils. The other amber fragments are not translucent enough to confirm the existence of foils.

X-ray analysis in the scanning electron microscope confirmed the gold-coloured foils, including amber 4 foil, to be gold rich, and the silver-coloured foils to be rich in silver. One silver-coloured foil, 4e, seemed to have an equal proportion of gold and silver. Small mercury peaks were detected for the foils under amber 4 and garnet 4e, suggesting the silver foils may have originally been mercury gilded (Mortimer 1996, 4).

DISCUSSION

The combination of garnet and amber cloisonné inlays on the Ripon Jewel is highly unusual, if not unique. Stevenson (1974, 27) speculated that garnets or red glass filled some small, now empty panels on the Hunterston brooch of c 700, although all the surviving inlays are amber. Arrhenius (1985, 36–8) does not mention amber as an inlay material used alongside garnet in Merovingian and other cloisonné workshops and, if a continental origin is ruled out, the combination of cloisonné goldwork with garnets identifies the Jewel as a piece of Anglo-Saxon workmanship rather than an importation from elsewhere in Britain. The principal Anglo-Saxon comparanda (see below) are dated to the 7th century on the basis, ultimately, of numismatic evidence (Webster & Backhouse 1991, 25–8; 47–54). There are no firmly dated later examples of Anglo-Saxon garnet cloisonné jewellery; Wilson (1964, 17–19) suggests the Kirkoswald trefoil, dated to the 8th century, is the latest piece to incorporate garnet inlay.

Analysis of the gold alloy composition provides one means of assessing the date of the piece. It is widely thought that gold artefacts of the 6th and 7th centuries were made by melting down coinage, particularly Merovingian, but also

Byzantine. As some coins are datable to the reigns of particular kings, the relationship between the date of the coins and the fineness of their gold can be examined (Kent 1972). Three different series of Merovingian coins were investigated, showing that there were three different standards of purity, the highest being the 'high Provençal' and the lowest being those from outside Provence. There was a general downward trend in the purity of each standard, from consistently above 85% gold at the end of the 6th century to well below 50% gold in the second half of the 7th century. On the basis of coins found at Sutton Hoo, Suffolk, and Crondall, Hampshire, it has been suggested that many more coins, other than the Provençal types, were available in England; thus the 'extra-Provençal' standard is considered the most appropriate in assessing the likely date of artefacts of this period. Earlier coins, Provençal coins, or earlier gold objects could, however, have been included in the melt; a misleadingly early date for manufacture might thus be estimated on the basis of gold purity (Brown & Schweizer 1973, 182–4). Dating of Anglo-Saxon gold artefacts by their composition, therefore, can only be an estimate, one which quite often gives what seems to be too early a date. Furthermore, scanning electron microscope X-ray analyses and the results of X-ray fluorescence analysis commonly carried out on gold artefacts (Hawkes et al. 1966; Brown & Schweizer 1973), should be compared with caution. Since X-ray fluorescence analysis penetrates deeper, information from the gold-enhanced zones of the metal surface is more important in scanning electron microscope X-ray results than in X-ray fluorescence results.

With this in mind, the values for the Ripon Jewel can be considered. Most of the parts analysed had gold contents of 80–90%. Even allowing for slight surface enrichment and any inaccuracy due to surface preparation, this implies a date before 625 and, if the extra-Provençal standard is used, a date before 610. The back of the artefact, however, has a lower gold content (72%), perhaps the result of deliberate selection. This might suggest the Jewel was not made until coinage of this lower purity was in circulation, that is after 610 by the extra-Provençal standard, or after 640 by the other standards. However, uncertainties about the gold source(s), and about how often and to what extent its alloy composition may have changed with possible reuse, mean these dates must be treated with considerable caution.

There are relatively few gold artefacts from this period outside the south, especially the south east, of England. It is therefore difficult to make any statement about regional patterning in compositions. More detailed analyses, including trace element data, might show this, but it would require sampling of a large number of gold objects, which traditionally have tended to be analysed less frequently than some others.

In general form, size, layout of the decorative elements, and use of gold and garnets, the Ripon Jewel most closely resembles the front plate of a plated disc brooch. Avent (1975, 62–5) catalogued twenty-four examples of these, all found in Kent except for two from Suffolk, which he dated to c 600–20. In a number of respects, however, the Jewel differs from the Kentish material: the absence of filigree at its outer edge; the position of the zone of garnet cloisonné decoration at the outside of the Jewel; the simplicity of the cloisonné cell pattern; the square shape of the four cardinal cloisonné fields; and the presence of amber as their inlay. Nonetheless, its generic similarities may indeed indicate that the Jewel was part of such a brooch, as Cramp (1995b, 27) has suggested, albeit a unique regional copy or variant of the type.

Alternatively, it was part of a composite pendant. There is a well-known series of circular garnet-inlaid pendants, variously dated to the 7th century, including those with garnet cloisonné surrounding a coin (from Bacton, Norfolk, and Forsbrook, Staffs; Smith 1923, 61–2, pl 4; Jessup 1950, 119–20, pl 28), or those where cloisonné garnets or a cabochon garnet embellish a design largely consisting of filigree (Webster & Backhouse 1991, nos 9, 33, 36). However, the only parallel for a composite pendant broadly comparable to the Ripon Jewel is that from Canterbury (Webster 1987; Webster & Backhouse 1991, no 10). There is no evidence on the Jewel for a suspension loop as on the Canterbury pendant, though another style of loop might not have impinged upon the cloisonné work. Such an ostentatious item of display jewellery would fit the secular milieu of any hypothetical pre-monastic royal estate-centre at Ripon; equally, it could reflect a secular visitor or gift to Wilfrid's monastery.

Nonetheless, the Jewel's findspot, near the heart of the monastic precinct, and its cruciform principal motif, inevitably raise the possibility that it was made, perhaps at Ripon, for a specifically ecclesiastical purpose. It could, for example, have been part of the decoration of a reliquary, cross, or elaborate book cover. Such possibilities are raised by Wilfrid's biographer, Stephen of Ripon. Within about a decade of his patron's death in 709/10 he wrote that Wilfrid marvellously decorated his new Ripon church with gold, silver and varied purples (*auro et argento purpuraque varia mirifice decoravit*) and that the treasury at Ripon contained gold, silver and precious stones (*aurum et argentum cum lapidibus pretiosis*; Colgrave 1927, 34, 136, xvii, lxiii). Furthermore, in the context of Wilfrid's dedication of his church at Ripon, Stephen mentions an altar vested in purple woven with gold (*purpuraque auro texta induentes*), and an illuminated copy of the four gospels written in letters of purest gold on purpled parchment; it was contained in a case made of the purest gold and set with most precious stones which Wilfrid had ordered his jewellers to construct (*quattuor evangelia de auro purissimo in membranis depurpuratis, coloratis . . . et bibliothecam librorum eorum, omnem de auro purissimo et gemmis pretiosissimis fabrefactam, compaginare inclusores gemmarum praecipit . . .*; op. cit. 36, xvii).

Given the near total archaeological ignorance about the range and appearance of 7th- to 8th-century Northumbrian and, indeed, Anglo-Saxon ecclesiastical metalwork, it is possible, using generally later comparanda, only to give some indications of how the Ripon Jewel might have been employed.

Applied decorative roundels occur on some of the earliest surviving Insular reliquary shrines of the 8th and early 9th century. Examples include the shrine at Abbadia San Salvatore, Siena, Italy. This, unusually, has a small amount of garnet inlay with gold foil backing on its ridge piece, as well as an imitation cloisonné pattern on its front and lid. The Monymusk shrine is another example of the type (Youngs 1989, no 129), and records of further examples are coming to light, such as the 'Shrine of Winifrid' from Gwytherin, Denbighshire (Butler & Graham-Campbell 1990; Edwards & Hulse 1992). Another possible position is suggested by the so-called Rupertus Cross, Anglo-Saxon workmanship of the mid- to late 8th century from Bischofshofen, Pongau, Salzburg, Austria, which had circular glass insets decorating its gilt-bronze sheets (Webster & Backhouse 1991, no 133).

The number of stylistic variations from the norms for plated disc brooches suggests that the Jewel is not a product of the Kentish workshops which presumably made most of the specimens represented in Avent's corpus, nor of the East Anglian workshop which he also suggests produced the two examples from Suffolk (Avent 1975, 65). Indeed, a case for the Jewel being a product of a local Northumbrian school can be constructed on archaeological grounds, to complement the documentary insights mentioned above. There is certainly evidence that the Northumbrians wore garnet-decorated accoutrements. Simple *en cabochon* garnets are found on a copper alloy buckle-plate from East Boldon, Tyne and Wear (Cramp & Miket 1982, 9–10); a more spectacular piece, now missing, was the gold and garnet ring from Driffield, Yorkshire East Riding (Sheppard 1923). In Deira, garnets form elements in decorated gold pendants, such as those from burials at Acklam Wold or Garton Slack in the Wolds area of eastern Yorkshire (Mortimer 1905, 94, 248). Within Northumbria, garnet decorated swords also occur, representative examples being the horn hilt from Cumbria with garnet and gold filigree decoration (Smith 1923, 92–3, pl VII), and the gold and garnet 'pyramidal' mount from Dalmeny, West Lothian (Bruce-Mitford 1974a, 268; Alcock 1981, 173).

Ecclesiastical objects of garnet-inlaid gold cloisonné are also known from Northumbria. A 10 mm long fragment from the arm of a pectoral cross was found in excavations at Dunbar, East Lothian, a site and area in Northumbrian hands from the mid-7th century (Holdsworth 1991; 1993, 40–2). The best known and most precisely dated gold object from Northumbria which incorporates garnets is the 6 cm tall equal-armed pectoral cross recovered from Cuthbert's tomb in Durham Cathedral in 1827 (Raine 1828). Cuthbert died in 687; his remains were enshrined in 698. Although there were several later documented openings of the tomb-shrine, it is unanimously accepted that the pectoral cross had been with his remains since the 7th century. The cross had been broken and repaired on two occasions before being consigned to the grave; Bruce-Mitford (1956, 325) suggested it was made c 640–70, and Webster places it in the second half of the 7th century (Webster & Backhouse 1991, no 98; cf Bruce-Mitford 1974b; Evison 1987, 44–5 for further discussion).

Cuthbert's cross stands apart from other, broadly contemporary Anglo-Saxon garnet-inlaid crosses and jewellery by reason of its shape, 'architectural' or 'three-dimensional' construction, the small size of the garnets (a trait shared with the Dunbar cross and the Ripon Jewel), and the absence of foil backings behind the garnets. Both Bruce-Mitford and Webster have concluded that it is probably of Northumbrian workmanship; Bruce-Mitford (1956, 322–3) further suggested it was the sole surviving product of a workshop under the patronage of the Northumbrian royal court. For Coatsworth (1989, 295), however, shared characteristics between architectural fragments, sculpture, manuscript painting and metalwork indicate the small, closely-knit Northumbrian monastic milieu which, she believes, produced them all.

Some confirmatory evidence exists for garnet-working in the region. Two tiny mineral fragments, thought to be garnet, and possibly used as settings in jewellery, were recovered in excavations by York Archaeological Trust at 46–54 Fishergate, York (Rogers 1993, 1376–8). Both have the chemical composition of the pyrope class of garnets. The context from which they were recovered dates to late 7th to mid-9th century (cf Kemp 1996), and although they could represent redeposited evidence for Roman garnet-working, brought to the site from elsewhere in York (for there was only Roman agricultural activity at Fishergate), it is more probable that they represent Anglian garnet-working.

The zigzag or chevron arrangement of the Ripon Jewel's garnet cloisonné zone is also noteworthy in the context of possible regional manufacture, for a carved stone cross head from Ripon has a similar motif defining the border of the head (Collingwood 1915, 234), and it has been suggested that this stone is part of a Ripon school of carving (Collingwood 1927, 94–5). Though difficult to date, it may belong to the late 8th or early 9th century (Tweddle pers comm). As Bailey has pointed out (1996a, 38–41), the same type of zigzag border also occurs on stone crosses at Hexham, Northallerton, Jarrow, Heysham, Hornby and Lancaster. (Of these, Hexham, Hornby and Lancaster, as well as Wycliffe, Hackness and Whitby, also share with Ripon the form in which script was laid out on cross shafts; Higgitt 1995, 230). The occurrence at Ripon of this simple geometric motif on both relatively immovable stone sculpture and easily portable metalwork may be no more than coincidence; alternatively it suggests a favoured local style of decoration, part of a regional ecclesiastical artistic tradition.

As noted above, garnet inlay, in either cabochon or cloisonné form, is attested in Northumbria. Amber beads are found in Northumbrian pagan Anglo-Saxon graves, but amber is not employed as an inlay in metalwork there nor, it seems, elsewhere in Anglo-Saxon England. Amber inlays, however, generally in the form of studs, appear on Celtic metalwork from the mid-7th century onwards (Youngs 1989, 52), including ecclesiastical pieces such as the mid-8th-century Ardagh Chalice (op. cit. 128, colour plate on 160).

Within later 7th- or early 8th-century Northumbria, the Ripon Jewel would reflect an innovative and experimental employment of amber as an inlay, prompted by its other uses in Anglo-Saxon contexts, or by the importation of amber-inlaid Celtic artefacts. Later 7th-century Northumbria was, of course, particularly open to the contacts which would have brought such workmanship into view, and there were a number of mechanisms for the transmission of craftsmen's skills (Campbell & Lane 1993, 61). A reciprocal of such artistic cross-fertilization is represented at Dunadd, in Dalriada, where top quality imported Germanic gold and garnet work has been found, as well as moulds for brooches of Celtic form but with Germanic decoration (Youngs 1989, 52–3, no 181; Campbell & Lane 1993, 53–6).

Finally, it may be noted that the materials and colours of the surviving components of the Ripon Jewel – gold, the golden orange/yellow of the amber, and the orange, red and mauve of the garnets – correspond closely to the colours favoured for Wilfrid's altar vestment and gospel book. It would have formed an appropriately rich and colour coordinated accessory to these documented items. The Ripon Jewel could thus be considered a small but significant relic of the milieu which Wilfrid fostered in his monastery at Ripon.

ACKNOWLEDGEMENTS

Richard Hall would like to thank the Dean and Chapter of Ripon Cathedral and Robert Lambie, Chapter Steward, for facilitating study of the Jewel. Mark Whyman provided the details of the Jewel's findspot. Richard Bailey, Leslie Webster and Niamh Whitfield have offered helpful comments and criticism, but neither they nor Angela Evans, Dominic Tweddle, Tania Wilson, Ian Panter, Jim Spriggs, Andrew Foxon and Christopher Loveluck, who supplied a variety of information, can be held responsible for the conclusions presented here. The photographs of the front and rear of the Jewel are by Simon I. Hill, and those of details by Erica Paterson; the drawings are by Kate Biggs, and Heather Dawson has merged and tailored the various text components. I am grateful to them, and to other colleagues at York Archaeological Trust, for their support and interest.

NOTES

1. Erica Paterson was responsible for conserving the Jewel and has contributed the descriptive elements of the text; Catherine Mortimer undertook the scientific analyses and wrote the associated sections of the text; Richard Hall is responsible for the discussion and has produced the integrated report in consultation with the other authors.
2. The excavations were directed by D. Greenhaugh on behalf of the Ancient Monuments Inspectorate of the Department of the Environment.

CHAPTER 23

A NORTHUMBRIAN PLAQUE FROM ASBY WINDERWATH, CUMBRIA

Susan Youngs

An unusual decorative bronze mount was discovered by metal detectorists in Cumbria in 1993 on an upland site at Asby Winderwath Common (NY 664 107; Fig 23.1). This is open karst limestone country with a road line, continuing as a bridleway, running across it towards Orton; there are some enclosed fields and much rough pasture. The local landscape is dominated by the scarp slope of the Pennines to the west. The plaque came from an area where the remains of three rectangular stone buildings can be seen, but without excavation their date and functions remain unknown. Intensive aerial survey had already revealed a number of such enclosures and buildings in the Orton Scar area pre-dating modern land units (Higham 1979, 34–7).

The context is important because this was not a solitary piece. It was found in loose association with significant amounts of other metalwork, over 100 items so far. These are mainly iron implements (ranging from knives and sickle blades to hasps and four bells) and fastenings but they also include bronze Anglo-Saxon strap ends and a pin of 9th-century type; at least one later medieval pin is included and a clog iron so it is by no means a closed assemblage. There were no coins reported, but among the ironwork are two slide keys which are of a type common from the 5th to 9th century but rare thereafter (Ottaway 1992, 674–5). Thus, while the main range of medieval iron tools and fittings cannot be closely dated there remains a group of metalwork associated with the bronze plaque datable to 800–900. These are not excavated finds and certainly some weeding has gone on, but there remains a core group of datable items which suggests activity at Asby Winderwath during the 9th century at least.[1]

The plaque (Reg. MLA 1995, 9–1,1) is of bronze with a cast openwork design and a plain back (Fig 23.2). It measures 84.2 x 63 mm and is about 3 mm thick. In antiquity it was slightly cut about at the upper end, presumably modified for

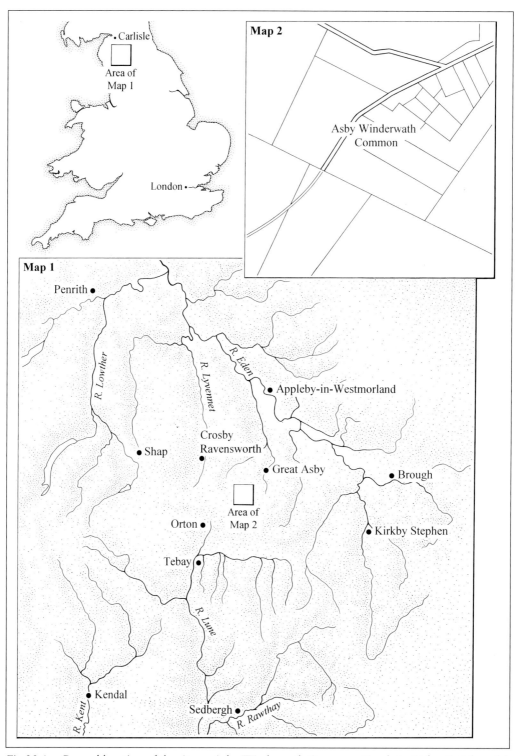

Fig 23.1.   General location of the site on Asby Winderwath Common, Cumbria. (After B. Edwards)

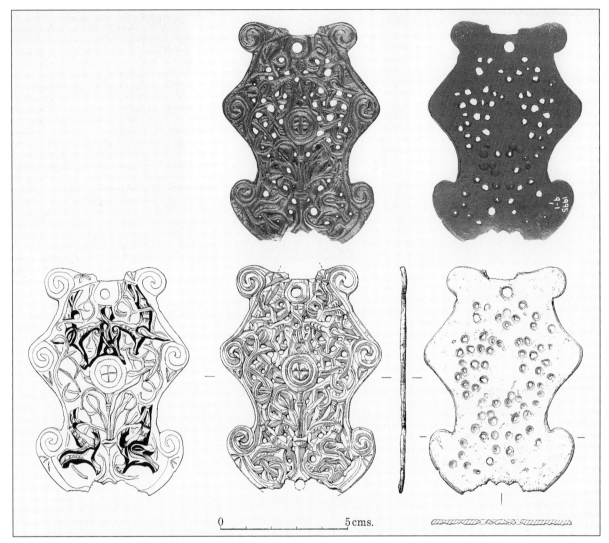

Fig 23.2.   Photographs and drawings of a bronze plaque from Asby Winderwath Common, Cumbria. (Copyright the Trustees of the British Museum. Scale 1:1)

reuse. The front is gilded, despite its present coppery pink appearance, and it is suggested that this coppery look to the gilding could be the result of copper alloyed in the gold, interdiffusion between the gilding and body metal during heating, or a result of post-excavation treatment.[2] The first two explanations are more likely as the phenomenon has been noted and observed elsewhere. The bronze alloy is 91.58% Cu, 7.2% tin with lead and iron and a trace of zinc (qualitative XRF results, Department of Scientific Research, British Museum).

The distinctive outline of the piece is created by the three spirals on each long side, widely spaced but ornamentally linked, with panels of trumpet pattern behind them at top and bottom. This heavy frame of abstract ornament dictates a fluid shape to the complex but more representational decoration of the main field. This, although clumsily executed, is filled by a coherent pattern of a plant with a vertical trunk which divides into thick curling branches, some with heavy pinnate leaves at the end. On and among the branches are two pairs of creatures. An equal-armed cross in a double circular frame dominates the centre of the panel. The details of jaws and leaves are difficult to read as the whole design is not only in openwork but also in low relief, faceted in 'chip-carved' style.

Before becoming entangled in this ornament the form of the piece deserves further consideration. Here, the sinuous outline and crude Celtic trumpet and spiral pattern of the border panels most resemble a group of Irish metal mounts where running spirals and trumpet patterns give a plastic outline. Parallels are found among a number of single finds (Wamers 1985, 24–6, Taf 19–22, 24–7), as well as the well-known series of Irish mounts recovered from Viking-period graves, the best known being those from Navan, Co Meath, and Soma and Gausel in Norway (Fig 23.3). These pieces are sometimes associated in the ground with horse bridles and are considered therefore to be harness mounts, strap unions principally. There are, however, problems about the original function of the interlocking pieces in these sets; when linked together some form rigid units, incompatible with use on flexible straps (Spearman 1993). Their primary function, therefore, remains unclear but they formed large sets of complementary but unidentical pieces. The Irish mounts are broadly dated to the 8th century on stylistic grounds.

There appear to be no openwork Irish examples and the Asby Winderwath Common plaque also differs from them in two important respects. Firstly, the back is plain; there is no integral attachment lug. Such lugs are typical of Irish decorative components. Even within the narrow casing of the Moylough, County Sligo belt mount or on the house-shaped shrines, the plaques are attached by lug and pin. While there are exceptions which have external lugs, such as an enamelled plate from the Shanmullagh, Blackwater hoard (Bourke 1993, 34), and the frames of the Donore handles (Ryan 1987b), on the Asby Winderwath plaque holes for rivets were incorporated within the design of the main field. The second difference lies in the semi-representational ornament of the main field, the plant, animals and birds. The relatives of the Asby Winderwath creatures are found in Anglo-Saxon ornament, as is the whole central design.

There are media other than metal in which Celtic spirals form decorative frames. Discrete panels with sinuous outlines of trumpet and spiral ornament also feature in Insular manuscript decoration, in particular as panels appended to the main body of decorated initials. One such panel, similar in outline to the metal plaque, occurs on the opening *Chi* of Matthew in the *Barberini Gospels* (Fig 23.4), but here as elsewhere in the manuscripts the interior is also filled with abstract curvilinear decoration and the ornament is asymmetric (Alexander 1978, cat 36). Simple parallels to both frame and content are found on some of the column bases of the canon tables in the *St Petersburg Gospels* (Bakka 1963,

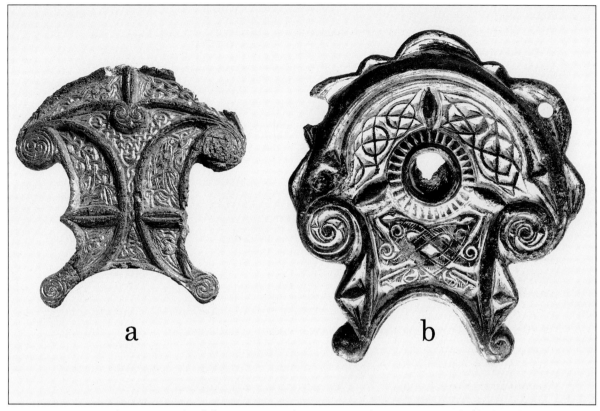

Fig 23.3. 8th-century Irish gilt bronze mounts from: (a) Gausel, Stavanger, Rogaland; (b) Belle, Aurland, Sogn og Fjordane, Norway. (Copyright Bergen Museum, Universitetet I Bergen)

fig 37; Alexander 1978, ill 188–9, frontispiece) where spiral-tipped curving borders frame vines and animals, a small but interesting combination of details (Fig 23.5). In sculpture, the arms of the Pictish cross at Dupplin, near Forteviot (see Henderson above) have a plastic outline with heavy scrolls; the east face of the cross head is filled by two vines, while the central image on the west face is a prominent boss with an equal-armed cross in fretwork inside a roundel. This is particularly interesting because the first name on the weathered inscription has been identified as Custantin mac Forcussa, Constantine King of the Picts and Dál Riata Scots who died in 820 (Forsyth 1995, 242–3), although this does not end the debate on its dating, as the cross in both form and decoration is acknowledged to show strong Anglo-Saxon influence, and because by its size and material it is firmly provenanced to Perthshire, unlike easily portable books and fittings. We also know from Bede's record that the Pictish church deliberately fostered relations with Northumbrian craftsmanship from the early 8th century (Colgrave & Mynors 1969, 532–5, V.21).

The main field of the Asby Winderwath plaque, with its balanced pattern of semi-naturalistic plant and beasts, comprises an inhabited double vine-scroll. The structural details of the plant show it is rooted in depictions of the grape-bearing vine of the classical world. The diagnostic features distinguishing it from a tree are the divisions of the trunk where the dividing tendrils grow from clearly marked joints, or nodes, as though an extended folding telescope. While the cup shape at the base could be read as an etiolated vessel, as seen on the Croft-on-Tees cross, for example (Cramp & Lang 1977, no 3), the pattern repeats further up the stem below the cross roundel. These botanically incorrect interlocking joints are a marked characteristic of most Insular vine-scrolls. Botanical exactitude departs early in the sculptural tradition. Some of the apparently naturalistic and least stylized vines bearing recognizable bunches of grapes also bear large flowers, possibly derived from other plants in classical art such as the lotus, acanthus or pomegranate. This other plant is probably the source of the marked junctions. Thus the tendency to refer to unberried vegetal patterns of this sort as 'plant-scroll', while strictly correct, disguises the viniferous and hence symbolic nature of the plant (Wilson 1984, 64–79). Discussing Anglo-Saxon vine-scroll ornament in sculpture Kitzinger (1936, 66) observed:

> In the English examples the scroll itself and its undulating movement plays a much more important part; it is emphasized by an almost entire omission of leaves and other details, which are allowed very often to conceal the main stem in the oriental example. The uninterrupted growth of the stem is made still more evident by the fatness of its form and it is then complicated by the winding and interlacing of the stem with itself and with the animals and birds.

This description suits the plaque well. A double scroll here turns the vine into a tree, but the segmental structure reveals its iconographic ancestry. In his important study of the vine in Insular metalwork Bakka (1963, 23) identified a much-used bifurcating form as a 'bush-vine', but the present subject does not divide just above the base, nor is it crowned by a central bud or frond. Obscure within the panel are a few pinnate leaves with three divisions, one at the bottom and two in profile at the top being eaten.

Four creatures feed within the tendrils of the vine. At the bottom right is a bird with its wing demarcated and its head thrown back, right leg raised against the trunk; facing it is a less clearly identifiable creature in a similar pose. Their bodies are divided internally by narrow lines with attached nicks. Above the central cross is a pair of quadrupeds carefully delineated to show all four legs and intertwined tails. The bodies are textured with chevrons and hip joints are marked by spirals. I have so far failed to identify any animals paired in this distinctive rump-to-rump pose, which is an alternative version of that exemplified by two quadrupeds in the central panel of one of the canon table frames in the *St Petersburg Gospels* (Fig 23.5). The general disposition and decorative style on the Asby Winderwath panel is, however, familiar on a larger scale in stone.

Fig 23.4. Detail from the *Barberini Gospels*, fol 18r (*Rome, Vatican, MS Barb. lat.570*). (Copyright La Biblioteca Apostolica Vaticana)

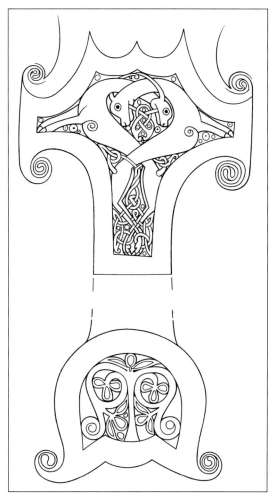

Fig 23.5. Drawing of two details from the canon table frames, fol 12v, in the *St Petersburg Gospels*. (*St Petersburg, Public Library, Cod. F.V.1.8*)

A prescient observation was made by Henderson (1983, 252) about the panel of inhabited vine-scroll on the Croft-on-Tees shaft in North Yorkshire (Fig 23.6): 'Croft is carved with an angular precision and delicacy which evokes even more strongly the miniature arts of ivory and metal'. The ornament of the Asby Winderwath plaque is indeed close to this panel in many respects, despite the disparity of scale. It shares the basic framework of a double, unberried scroll of jointed type, all the beastly inhabitants are in profile and have their far forelegs raised (Fig 23.7). The birds which sit at the base have exaggerated raised feet and confront each other; the right-hand animal on the next layer resembles the pair on the plaque. The style of the latter is similar to the delicate carving of the former. The differences are also interesting: there is no central framed cross; the backward turn of the feeding heads is absent, as is the distinctive entwined tails and rump-to-rump pose of the quadrupeds; the animal bodies are untextured although the birds are feathered; the leaves are of a different type – one common in 9th-century manuscripts and metalwork associated with Mercia. Croft itself lay within the ancient kingdom of Northumbria on the border between Bernicia and Deira; the cross shaft has been dated to the late 8th century (Cramp & Lang 1977, no 3).

Surviving metalwork provides some help with the ornamental scheme of the plaque: an unprovenanced belt chape, independently attributed to Northumbria, has some related features in addition to the shared Christian theme of two birds, here peacocks, confronting a double plant-scroll (Webster & Backhouse 1991, no 101). It too is in openwork and the birds share the distinctive chevron markings on wings and tail seen on the Asby Winderwath animals but otherwise unknown to me, although a central line on the peacocks' tails turns them into feathers. A gilt bronze disc from Hillesøy, Lenvik, Norway has a double axis, repeating motif where winged beasts and bush-vines are intermixed (Bakka 1963, 7–9, figs 1, 4). Here the animal bodies are divided with distinctive cross-lines and nicks in the same way as the Asby Winderwath birds. The disc is not in openwork and the foliage has 9th-century features, but it is of some importance because it comes from a grave datable by a pair of oval brooches to the mid-9th century and shares the texturing trait with the openwork plaque.

The best-known metalwork example of inhabited vine-scroll was found nearby in Cumbria, in the Viking burial at Ormside (Webster & Backhouse 1991, no 134). It is interesting that it is so unlike the small plaque, both in its repoussé technique and its style, despite sharing a common theme. The Ormside bowl has been dated stylistically to the second half of the 8th century; it shows Carolingian influence and has been compared with the Rupertus cross (op. cit. no 133) which also bears segments of double vine-scroll with feeding animals. On the bowl one pair of birds sits back to back, heads over shoulders and with claws raised to grasp grapes, a more self-explanatory version of the pose seen on the Asby Winderwath plaque. The vine here divides from the base. All these examples show that there were several ornamental traditions relating to the iconography of

Fig 23.6.   Panel of inhabited vine on a cross shaft from Croft-on-Tees, North Yorkshire. (Copyright the Department of Archaeology, University of Durham. Photograph: T. Middlemass)

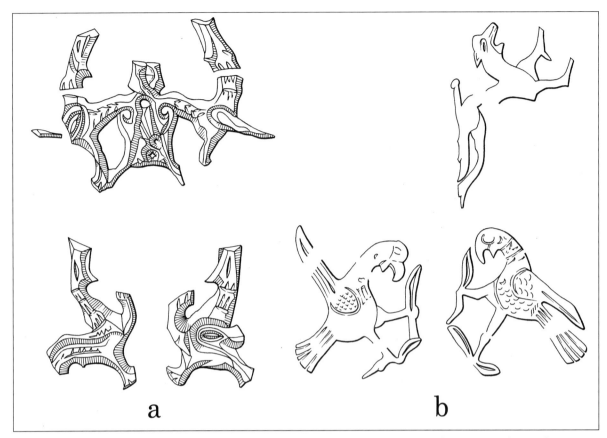

Fig 23.7. Comparative drawing of the creatures on: (a) the Asby Winderwath Common plaque; (b) the Croft-on-Tees cross shaft reduced to the same scale.

the inhabited vine present in 8th-century and later Anglo-Saxon metalwork, a case first made by Bakka (1963).

Within this tradition the Asby Winderwath Common mount has a unique element: the whole plant with its feeding menagerie frames and supports the central equal-armed cross set in a heavy frame. This motif is not otherwise known in the Anglo-Saxon vine-scroll tradition. There is good evidence from the *Book of Kells* that small discs with the simple, straight-armed cross, represent the Eucharistic bread (Lewis 1980, 146; Meehan 1994a, 44–6; cf Galavaris 1970), and there are several examples of circular loaves depicted in Irish sculpture and manuscripts, as well as some Anglo-Saxon and Pictish representations (Ó Carragáin 1988a). The 8th-century Anglo-Saxon chrismal from Mortain depicts the archangels Gabriel and Michael holding discs identified as the host (Webster & Backhouse 1991, no 137).[3] On the plaque from Asby Winderwath, the motifs present a unified theme of Divine sustenance, with Creation feeding upon the True Vine (John 15.1), combined with elements representing both the bread and the wine. This association is found again in the art of the *Book of Kells* (fol 32v), where peacocks marked with Eucharistic ringed crosses stand upon pots of vines framing the head of Christ (Fig 23.8). Although an apparently simple, even rudimentary sign of the Passion, this particular cross form is not widespread in *Kells* where a number of more complex small types are used, frequently the Maltese cross; the deliberate exception is the opening to John's Gospel, the great 'I' of *In principio* with its portrait of Christ, where numerous crosses of this type again play on the Word becoming flesh and the importance of transubstantiation. There is therefore a late 8th-century Ionan iconographic convention in which the simple cruciferous disc has a Eucharistic meaning. Similarly the decorative programme of the Dupplin cross is interpreted as centred on the Eucharist as well as on David (see Henderson above). In Anglo-Saxon art the characteristic cross form has expanding arms and was constructed from a pattern of arcs. The use of the straight-armed Greek cross on the plaque is an unexpected further link with Irish Christian iconography of the 8th century. But perhaps this suggested iconography is not so surprising in a Northumbrian context where early 8th-century hagiography places considerable emphasis on the divine provision of bread, as in some of the first miracles described in the anonymous *Life of Cuthbert* as validating signs of his holy nature (Colgrave 1940, 71, 79, *V Anon* I.6, II.2).

There are a number of bronze shrine mounts of typically Irish domed form, all broadly dated to the 8th century, which incorporate panels of vine-scroll, most of which were discussed and illustrated by Bakka (1963; 1965), with addenda in Wamers' 1985 corpus. Bakka argued that most were Northumbrian, a view strongly influenced by contemporary opinions on the origins and influence of the *Book of Durrow* and the *Lindisfarne Gospels*. The pieces are all Norwegian finds; among them are a domed shrine mount from Komnes (buried in the second half of the 9th century) and another from Lilleby which also has snake bosses (deposited in the first half of the 10th century), while from Kaupang comes a rather crude boss of distinctive form and decoration (Wamers 1985). All these shrine mounts carry panels of simple, uninhabited vine-tree ornament but all have a variety of other motifs in various styles. There now seems no compelling reason to argue for manufacture in Northumbria, both in the light of the workshop evidence from Dunadd in former Scottish Dál Riata (Campbell & Lane 1993) and with improved understanding of the complex relationships hidden by post-medieval use of the labels 'Celtic' and 'Roman'. The workshop moulds show it was possible for 7th-century craftsmen to work in a variety of styles. A rectangular pyramidal mount buried before 800 at Fure, Sogn og Fjordane, is particularly tantalizing – it has Insular animals on three panels and an inhabited vine-scroll panel on the fourth (Bakka 1963, fig 54; Wamers 1985, Kat 54). There is another stylistic hybrid, a domed boss found at Ribchester, now lost (Laing 1993, no 258). Why should decorative metalwork be any less culturally ambiguous than the *Lindisfarne Gospels* or the *Book of Durrow*? What did the shrines and fittings of Lindisfarne or at Coldingham look like in 750? Without

Fig 23.8. A pair of peacocks standing on vines framing the head of the portrait of Christ in the *Book of Kells*. A bright red cross stands out on their wings. (*Dublin, Trinity College Library, MS 58*, fol 32v. (Copyright the Board of Trinity College Dublin)

integral texts or scripts we have far less information on which to form judgements on provenance. We know from the *Book of Kells* and the shrine bosses that the vine was used in religious imagery in Ireland and the wider world of the Columban federation towards the end of the 8th century. Edwards (1986, 31–3) listed seven later examples in sculpture on the Irish high crosses and concluded 'vine-scroll is little used on Irish sculpture' positing a single model, with the possible exceptions of two crosses. The Irish metalwork tradition, if it is agreed to incorporate Bakka's 'Northumbrian' pieces, is surprisingly strong but limited to simple panels in the style seen on the north cross at Duleek. What we do see, however, on many of these bosses is a dominant central cross with panels of animals, interlace and vines within the arms of the cross. The imagery of the *Book of Kells* as a product of the Ionan scriptorium can itself be understood as reflecting a wider range of influences from the Pictish kingdom and Northumbria.

The style of the main field, however, leaves no doubt that the Asby Winderwath Common plaque was not made in an Irish workshop, whether in Ireland or north Britain but was produced in an Anglo-Saxon cultural milieu, albeit with strong Irish influence. There are Anglo-Saxon gospel books with Insular decoration in which spiral and trumpet patterns and inhabited vine-scroll are juxtaposed. On the great *Chi* of the *Barberini Gospels* the latter hangs from the former (Fig 23.4); here the style of the inhabited vine-scroll has been compared with that of the Ormside bowl. The origins and affinities of this codex have been much debated but, whether it reflects Mercian influence or Northumbrian, there seems to be consensus on a late 8th-century date. The *St Petersburg Gospels* (Fig 23.5), which also have elements reflecting the composition of the plaque, are also dated to the second half of the 8th century; although the cultural roots of this manuscript are controversial it too is considered to be Northumbrian (Alexander 1978, nos 36, 39).

On the Asby Winderwath Common plaque the means of attachment as well as the artistic affiliations of the principal ornament confirm its Anglo-Saxon provenance. The spiral hip joints of the two quadrupeds compare with those on the York helmet (Tweddle 1984) and are typical of Hiberno-Saxon art of the 8th century. The same observation must hold good for the trumpet and spiral borders, although the date of the Dupplin cross carries this to the end of the 8th century and beyond. On the basis of the Cumbrian plaque's iconographic and stylistic links I therefore suggest it was made in Northumbria, in the late 8th century.

The composition plays upon pairs, double images, for not only are the beasts in mirrored pairs and of two kinds, but the central cross and the plant itself give a second doublet, the living tree behind the wood of the cross. All is contained within two borders of three interlinked spirals. I know of no precise parallel to this combination of cross superimposed on the tree but it is a powerful juxtaposition, despite its small scale and the crudity of its execution, with a wealth of associative significance for what Lewis (1980, 141) has called 'the initiated eye'. Technically and artistically the plaque is a modest production, not an innovatory masterpiece. It does not carry a new message but a rather indistinct version of what must have been an established iconography.

We should also remember that such images, whether of holy places or holy symbols, were not necessarily keepsakes but were representative of the Divine, not evocative but invocative. This raises the question of the function of this plaque – for what and for whom it was made. Here speculation should allow for the concentrated Eucharistic significance of the design, its demonstrable artistic connections with Irish decorative traditions, in form as well as decoration, and for the simple fact that this piece has a top and bottom if the decoration is to make sense. That is not a feature of the related Irish metal mounts. Like the related sculptural panels this was designed to be read and perhaps set with the long axis vertical. It has been suggested that the piece is itself a cross arm but there would be serious difficulties in devising an appropriate motif for the central crossing of the cross such as a bust or *Agnus Dei* in the space available.

Bearing these considerations in mind, it seems unlikely that the plaque was made to be worn, whether by a man or a horse, and that it was probably used within an ecclesiastical context. It would, for example, be particularly appropriate on the chest, satchel or cupboard where the materials for the

Eucharist were stored or for the reserved sacrament, and the Mortain casket supports such an association of iconography and function (Warren 1987, 138–9; Webster & Backhouse 1991, no 137). The openwork panels filled with intertwined plants and animals which surround the central cross on the back cover of the *Lindau Book* (Haseloff 1990, 86–8, pl 66) also remind us that such a plaque could have been made for a book cover. The original binding of the *Stonyhurst Gospel* bears a vine. There is here complex Christian significance in the imagery with explicit Eucharistic association, albeit employed on a small-scale piece of metalwork. This is not a public monument or object of communal devotion like a stone cross. It could have been made for personal use with some prophylactic function or been part of a larger decorative programme.

Finally there is the question of its presence at Asby Winderwath Common. Before four iron bells and a clapper make a monastery, it should be noted that the bells are not of Celtic type with riveted side seams (Bourke 1980, 52–4) but have braised joints and are of a kind relatively widespread in Anglo-Saxon areas, not closely dated although one has been found at the complex Saxon settlement site of Flixborough, Lincolnshire (Leahy 1995; Loveluck 1998). The plaque had been modified for reuse suggesting it may have been recycled in the 9th or 10th centuries, the time when many Irish and Anglo-Saxon mounts reached Norway. Asby Winderwath Common can be seen in the context of Viking activity in the area – it is about 8 km from the burial at Ormside, which itself confirms a Viking presence in the second half of the 9th century, and a silver bossed penannular brooch and armlet were found in Orton Scar, although the expansion of the kingdom of Strathclyde to the Eamont in this period points to the 10th century as the period of major Viking settlement (Birley 1964; Higham 1985).

By itself this small plaque epitomizes the Insular style, taking that to be a hybrid of Irish and Anglo-Saxon traits feeding on the post-classical Christian iconographic tradition and growing into something new, distinctive and influential; it is a modest but interesting addition to the art of the Golden Age of Northumbria.

ACKNOWLEDGEMENTS

I am grateful for help and observations from Professor Richard Bailey, David Buckton, Professor Rosemary Cramp, Ben Edwards, Dr Isabel Henderson, Dr Nicholas Higham, Kevin Leahy, Dr Nancy Netzer, Professor Éamonn Ó Carragáin, Leslie Webster and Christopher Verey and also for the patience and forbearance of the Editors. The artwork was produced by Lisa Reardon, Jim Farrant and Jim Thorn.

NOTES

1. The whole find, the site and its regional context will be published by Ben Edwards and I am much indebted to him for permission to pull the plum from the pie in advance of his study and for comments on the find-place. This has deliberately not been precisely located on Fig 23.1. I

should also acknowledge the assistance of Brian Wilson and associates who found the material and, most particularly, the role of Kevin Leahy who first recognized the importance of the plaque and sent details to the British Museum. The group has been acquired by the Department of Medieval and Later Antiquities, British Museum.

2. Report and observations by Susan La Niece, Department of Scientific Research, British Museum.

3. My thanks to Leslie Webster for pointing out the iconography of this important parallel.

CHAPTER 24

DESIGN AND UNITS OF MEASURE ON THE HUNTERSTON BROOCH

Niamh Whitfield

This investigation of the design of the Hunterston brooch was prompted by three separate but interrelated lines of study.

The first was the increasing amount of research on the geometry underlying many Insular artefacts, in particular the work of Bruce-Mitford (1960) and Stevick (1994) on the use of the compass and straight edge in Insular manuscripts.

The second was the identification of various units of linear measure in the Old Irish laws by Professor Fergus Kelly, who kindly made available his results in advance of publication. These sources suggest that craftsmen in the early Middle Ages used defined measurements. For example, an 8th-century account in the *Additamenta* of the *Book of Armagh* states that various items of precious metal were of regular ancient dimensions (*senairotib*) (Kelly 1997, 583).

The third impetus was the independent identification by the late Robert Stevenson (1989, 242) of an apparent unit of measure of 9 mm on the Westness brooch, and by the late Jim Lang (1988, 99) of the same unit on some 10th-century bossed penannular brooches from Ireland. Indeed, it was at the latter's suggestion that I began to look for such units myself, so I am very pleased to be able to publish some of my results in this volume dedicated to his memory.

THE GENERAL DESIGN OF THE HUNTERSTON BROOCH

The brooch (Plate 14; Fig 24.1) was found in Ayrshire, and can be dated (partly on the basis of features it has in common with the *Lindisfarne Gospels*)

Fig 24.1. Hunterston Brooch: back view. Scale 1:1. (Photograph: National Museums of Scotland)

to the later 7th or early 8th century (Stevenson 1974; Whitfield 1993). It is one of the earliest, largest and most elaborate examples of the pseudo-penannular series, a type of brooch which clearly descends from the zoomorphic penannular type (cf Youngs 1989, nos 17, 69). Common features, identified on Fig 24.2, include expanded terminals, a movable pin with a decorative pin-head which swivels around the hoop, and buffers at the end of the hoop which prevent the pin from slipping on to the terminals. In the earlier penannular type the pin slips through the gap between the terminals, but on the Hunterston brooch and other pseudo-penannular examples, the terminals are joined. Nevertheless, the concept of a gap between the terminals is acknowledged in the design.

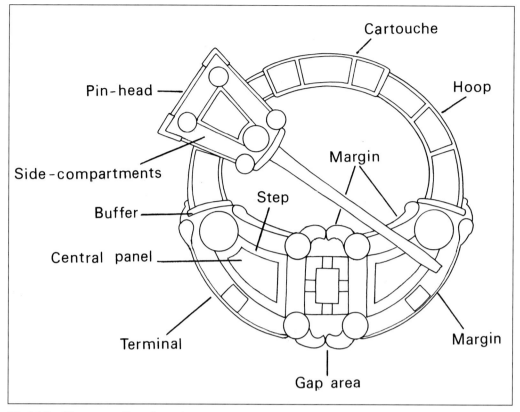

Fig 24.2. Hunterston Brooch: main components.

On the Hunterston brooch, the decorative surface is much enlarged to maximize the scope for ornament while acknowledging the traditional form. Sunken compartments surrounded by gilt walls on the front hold gold filigree and amber insets, while those on the back hold chip-carved plates. A numbering system for the insets is given in Fig 24.3. Matching features share the same number, the suffix 'L' being used for those on the left, and the suffix 'R' for those on the right.

Despite the profusion of decoration, the design is simple and orderly. Ornament on each decorative zone displays a bold and separate character. Furthermore, the centre of each zone is clearly distinguished from the surrounding area. In the middle of the hoop is a 'cartouche' enclosing a filigree panel bounded by amber studs. The matching terminals and pin-head each have a wedge-shaped, stepped central filigree panel surrounded by filigree side compartments, in turn edged by gilt chip-carved margins - birds' heads on the outer edge of the terminals, scrolls elsewhere. The 'gap' area likewise has a clear centre bordered by filigree panels, those on the left and right also being an integral part of each terminal. Like the latter, the 'gap' area is edged by a margin, in this case composed of relatively large eagles' heads of amber and filigree.

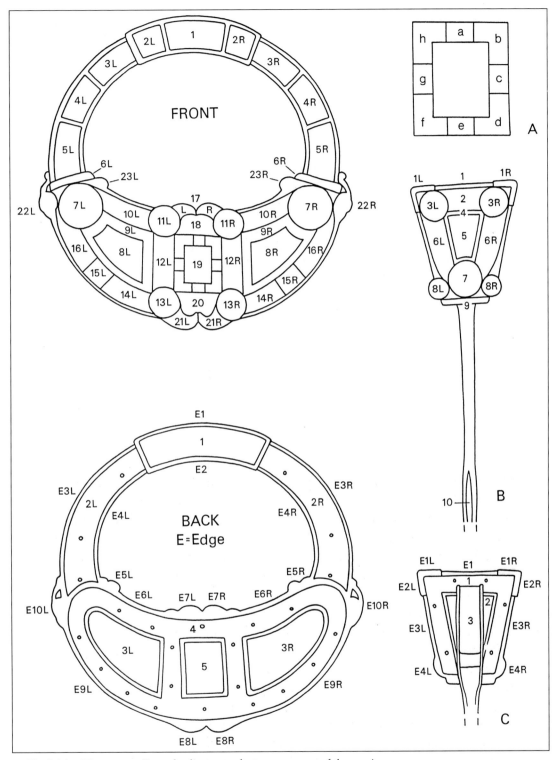

Fig 24.3.   Hunterston Brooch: diagram of compartments of decoration.

METHODS OF INVESTIGATION

To discover the underlying geometry and measurements of the Hunterston brooch two steps were taken. First, ideas were suggested by experiments with a compass and ruler on tracing paper superimposed on photographs of the brooch. Second, the hypotheses were verified by measurements of the brooch itself, using plastic vernier callipers.

Unless otherwise stated, measurements of filigree compartments were made at their surface rather than on their sunken floors. This gave a more accurate view of the overall plan of the brooch because many compartments have inward sloping walls and therefore a relatively small floor area. The edges of the brooch itself also taper, the back being slightly broader than the front; overall dimensions represent the maximum, ie those at the back. Many elements on the brooch have curved sides. It was not possible to measure these curves in full; instead chords (the shortest distance between the two extreme ends) were recorded.

Some very short lengths were involved and it is important to consider just how accurate the measurements were. In theory it should have been possible to be accurate to 0.1 mm, but in practice this was not always possible and it will be seen that the appended tables, recording various dimensions, positively bristle with 'c's, standing for 'circa'. These were included for the following reasons:

(i) The Hunterston brooch is not flat: for safety reasons the calliper points could not be allowed to probe into it. As a result, the height of steps and studs, as well as the diameter of stud cells at their base, were estimated to the nearest millimetre or half millimetre (Table 24.3).

(ii) It was sometimes difficult to pinpoint the precise edge in question, particularly in the case of studs and stud cells (Tables 24.1 and 24.3).

(iii) More clearly defined edges, such as the sharp angles in compartment corners or at the edge of steps, sometimes gave readings which appeared to be within 0.1–0.2 of a full millimetre. Again the digit was rounded up (Tables 24.1–4).

It is to be borne in mind that the intended proportions of the Hunterston brooch could have altered slightly during its manufacture. First the design must have been sketched on a trial-piece or wax tablet. Then a model was carved, possibly in wax. Next this model was cast in silver, and the body of the brooch polished and gilded. Finally, the decorative elements (filigree, chip-carved plates and amber) were fixed in place. Casting, if not skilfully done, may lead to some shrinkage, while polishing may also result in some slight changes in proportion.

Yet, it was striking that when spans which are significant in terms of the overall geometry were measured, readings were often obtained in whole millimetres which were fractions or multiples of 9 mm. A lower common factor was 3 mm which was the working figure used in the course of this study. Such results are consistent with Stevenson and Lang's findings, as well as measurements of other pieces of Celtic metalwork to which I will refer below. They also suggest a very high standard of craftsmanship on the part of the manufacturer.

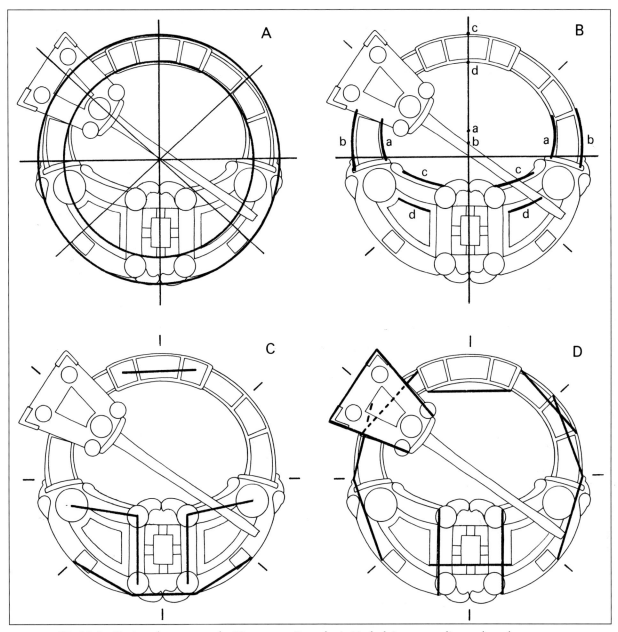

Fig 24.4.   Design elements on the Hunterston Brooch: A. Underlying cross, diagonals and concentric circles. B. Compass points and arcs which define expansion of hoop and inner areas on each terminal. C. Lengths of 33 mm. D. Lengths of 42 mm.

THE GEOMETRY OF THE HUNTERSTON BROOCH (FIG 24.4)

A relatively simple geometry determines the form of the Hunterston brooch, but it is subtly disguised and does not immediately meet the eye. Deductions from compass work and measurements suggest a series of interrelated steps, now to be described, each illustrated by a different diagram drawn by Nick Griffiths.

Figure 24.4A

Robert Stevick has pointed out the importance in manuscript design of the figure of a cross with equal arms within a circle (1994, Figs 1–2). This figure is also the basis of the design of the Hunterston brooch.

The perimeter of the brooch is based on a circle with a radius of c 60 mm, masked by the projecting outer edge of the cartouche and parts of the margin; the eye is also misled by the way in which the hoop splays inwards at filigree panels 5L and 5R.

The vertical arms of the notional cross within the circle are easier to identify: they bisect both the cartouche in the centre of the hoop and the 'gap' area between the terminals. Better disguised is the continuous line formed by the two horizontal arms. However, it likewise accurately bisects the brooch, as tests with a ruler both above the brooch itself and on photographs showed. On the inner edge it exactly cuts the left and right junction of the hoop and terminals. On the outer edge it passes above both junctions and touches instead the inconspicuous tips of the ear-lappets of the left and right marginal bird – a very neat piece of camouflage, since the eye is drawn away from this underpinning line by the continuation below it of the outer part of the hoop and by the large circular amber studs 7L and 7R.

The centre of the circle can also be identified not only in the centre of the cross, but also at the intersection of the diagonal lines which link the upper edges of the four-sided stud cells on the hoop and terminals. It might be thought that these diagonal lines bisect the right angles in the centre of the cross, but measurements with a protractor showed that this is not the case. A different principle operated as will be explained below.

A second circle, concentric with the first, defines the inner edge of the hoop. On the terminals, this same circle follows the curvature of the top of the outer wall bounding the central panels (though it seems to deviate a little by panel 8R). This inner circle, which appears to have a radius of 48 mm, is quite clear on the diagram, but is not immediately obvious on the brooch itself, because the eye is misled by the inward curve of the hoop by the junction.

Figure 24.4B

Now to explain this veering from the circumference of the hoop at panels 5L and 5R which is one of the most subtle aspects of the design.

The curves which define the inner edge of panels 5L and 5R are centred on a point on the vertical arm of the underlying cross which is 15 mm (a quarter of the radius) above the centre of the circle (Fig 24.4B, a–a). However, those which define the outer edges of panels 5L and 5R have a centre midway between that point and the centre of the circle (Fig 24.4B, b–b). The radii of the arcs are respectively c 48 mm (the radius of the inner circle on Fig 24.4A) and c 54 mm (a dimension which also recurs elsewhere, for example, on the chord linking the outer corners of the cartouche on the back of the hoop).

Next to be considered is the way the inner edge of the terminals and also of the central panels within each terminal were delineated. Again two different, but related compass points are involved. An arc springing from the top of the brooch outlines the trumpet pattern on the margins of side compartments 10L and 10R (Fig 24.4B, c–c). A second arc, springing from a point immediately below the first one, at the centre of the inner edge of the cartouche, outlines the wall on the inner edge of panels 8L and 8R, the central panel on the terminals (Fig 24.4B, d–d). Despite their different centres, each of these arcs has a radius of 75 mm.

On the back of the brooch (Fig 24.1) the outlines of the terminals within the margin and their central panels (3L and 3R) are laid out in the same way, except that there the radii are c 76 mm and 72 mm respectively.

A further concordance is that the vertical distance from the intersection of the beaks of the inner pair of eagles to the inner arc of the cartouche is c 60 mm, which is also the radius of the brooch.

Figures 24.4C and 24.4D

Recurrent dimensions also determine the layout of the panels around the outer edge of the brooch. Chords of 33 mm (Fig 24.4C) and 42 mm (Fig 24.4D) are repeated around the circumference, dimensions which are divisible by 3 mm, and therefore related to the 9 mm unit of measure observed by Stevenson and Lang.

Three chords of 33 mm appear at the base of the brooch. This is the distance between the outer corners of panels 14L and 14R measured horizontally across the 'gap' area; it is also the distance between these points and the upper edges of studs 15L and 15R.

Above this the unit of measure changes to 42 mm. This is the length of the chords linking the lower corner of panels 16L and 16R to the tips of the ear-lappets of the marginal birds at the half-way point of the circle (22L and 22R). Chords of 42 mm also link the ear-lappets of the marginal birds to the outer corner of studs 4L and 4R on the hoop, while further overlapping chords link the lower corners of the same studs to the outer corners of the cartouche.

What is more, the inner edge of the cartouche itself measures 42 mm, and this is also the precise distance across the 'gap' between the outer corners of the wall surrounding the central panels on each terminal (8L and 8R). These notional lines match in more ways than one because they form chords of the inner circle outlining the brooch, so their tips are equidistant from the centre of the circle.

This does not complete the list of recurrences of 42 mm in the design of the Hunterston brooch. It is the length of each of the three sides of the pin-head, and also of each terminal at its junction with the 'gap' area (measured along the edges of steps 9L and 9R from the corners of panels 10 and 14 on either side of the brooch). This is a significant correlation because, as already pointed out, the correspondence between the pin-head and the terminals is an important part of the design.

Finally, 33 mm seems to be the distance between the centres of studs 2L and 2R on the cartouche, the centres of studs both 7L and 11L, and 11R and 7R on the terminals, and the centres of studs 11L and 13L, and 11R and 13R flanking the 'gap'.

THE 'GAP' AREA (FIGS 24.5, 24.6B)

Subtle planning is also evident in the layout of the 'gap' area on the front of the brooch. At first sight this looks like a regular oblong (Plate 14, Fig 24.5), and indeed, the long sides on the left and right side *do* match: the notional outer edges each measure 42 mm (ie 9 mm + 24 mm + 9 mm), while the inner and outer long sides of the central oblong filigree and amber frame are likewise identical in length: 13.5 mm and 22.5 mm respectively (Table 24.1). However, as Fig 24.6B shows, the 'gap' area is, in fact, considerably narrower on its inner edge than on its outer one. This tapering effect is masked by the apparently similar distances between the studs forming the eyes of the inner and outer pairs of eagles' heads.

On the back of the brooch (Fig 24.1; Table 24.4) the oblong panel in the 'gap' area also tapers towards the centre.

ASYMMETRY OF THE TERMINALS (FIG 24.6A)

One other small asymmetry is to be noted. As Fig 24.6A, c–f, and Table 24.1 show, the central panel 8L on the left terminal is approximately 1 mm shorter on its outer edge than the matching panel 8R on the right terminal. Moreover, the adjoining gapside side-compartments 12L and 12R show corresponding small differences in width. This may simply be due to an error in layout. However, given the high standard of accuracy observed elsewhere on the brooch, it is tempting to see it as a deliberate variation, analogous to the numerous small differences observed under the microscope on the Hunterston filigree panels (Whitfield 1993, 121–2). The *Lindisfarne Gospels* also has some defects which seem to be deliberate: it has been suggested that there the scribe was practising humility by avoiding absolute perfection (Backhouse 1981, 55).

Fig 24.5. Hunterston Brooch: 'gap' area. Not to scale. (Photograph: National Museums of Scotland)

Below: Fig 24.6. Dimensions on the Hunterston Brooch. All measurements in millimetres. A. Chords of 18 mm on hoop and asymmetry on the terminals. B. Horizontal spans between corresponding pairs of panels across inner and outer edge of 'gap' area. a = from 10L–10R; b = from 14L–14R; c = maximum span of eagles' beaks 17L–17R; d = maximum span of eagles' beaks 21L–21R; e = minimum span of eagles' beaks 17L–17R; f = minimum span of eagles' beaks 21L–21R; g = from inner corners of steps 9L–9R; h = from outer corners of steps 9L–9R; i = inner wall of oblong frame in 'gap'; j = outer wall of oblong frame in 'gap'.

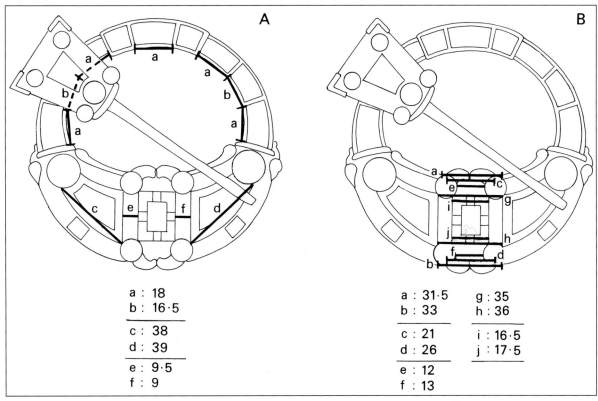

A

a : 18
b : 16·5

c : 38
d : 39

e : 9·5
f : 9

B

a : 31·5   g : 35
b : 33   h : 36

c : 21   i : 16·5
d : 26   j : 17·5

e : 12
f : 13

DESIGN TECHNIQUES ON THE *LINDISFARNE GOSPELS*, AND DUNADD AND NENDRUM TRIAL-PIECES

No marks on the Hunterston brooch demonstrate that the guidelines were used. These would have appeared on now lost, preparatory sketches rather than on the object itself. However, there is confirmation on other Insular artefacts for some of the design techniques described above.

For example, Bruce-Mitford's reconstruction (based on the study of pinpricks and rulings) of the geometry underlying the Ultimate La Tène patterns on fol 138v of the *Lindisfarne Gospels*, conveniently illustrated by Alexander (1978, fig 3) and Wilson (1984, fig 28), shows familiarity with the following procedures:

(i) the layout of a design on an underlying cross in a circle (albeit laid out at an oblique angle) which is further subdivided by oblique intersecting lines (cf Fig 24.4A).

(ii) The subdivision of the underlying radial lines to pinpoint the location of compass points from which spring curves which are integral to the design (cf Fig 24.4B). This particular design technique is typical of La Tène art and was used, for instance, on the Iron Age Bann disc (Raftery 1987, fig 2:3). It is interesting to discover it on the later Hunterston brooch.

Just as relevant are two trial-pieces which show the outlines of two small pseudo-penannular brooches, one on a piece of slate from Dunadd, Argyll (Fig 24.7A), the other on a piece of greywacké stone from Nendrum, Co Antrim, which also bears a sketch of a brooch pin (Fig 24.7B). Each clearly represent the planning stage of the brooches shown. Although neither pseudo-penannular brooch belongs to the same typological sub-group as Hunterston, each provides confirmation for some of the design processes inferred from its shape. As on Hunterston, compass work is crucial: the small holes dug by the point of the compass are discernible on both trial-pieces. Though some features are roughly sketched in freehand, in each case there is also evidence for the use of a straight edge.

The following similarities with the design stages proposed above can be identified:

(i) The outline of both sketched brooches is formed by a circle, each with a visible centre ('A' on Fig 24.7A).

(ii) On both trial-pieces the inner edge of the hoop is defined by a semicircle concentric with the outer circle.

(iii) A ruled diagonal runs through the centre of the Dunadd brooch (C–C on Fig 24.7A) (although, as it runs diagonally across the stone, it was probably only to centre the circle upon it).

(iv) On the Dunadd brooch the roughly sketched arc which acts as the inner edge of the terminals springs from an extremely noticeable point at the top of the brooch (cf B on Fig 24.7A and Fig 24.4B, c–c).

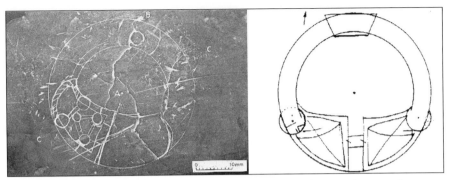

Fig 24.7.   Brooches on trial-pieces: A. Dunadd, Argyll. Scale 1:1. (Photograph: N Whitfield.) B. Nendrum, Co Antrim. Scale 1:1. (After O'Meadhra 1979)

(v) On the Nendrum brooch circular compass-drawn studs mark the junction of the hoop and terminals (cf studs 7L and 7R on Fig 24.3).

(vi) On the hoop of the Nendrum brooch, as on Hunterston, is a straight-ended cartouche.

(vii) On both trial-pieces the outer radius is in units of measure related to 3 mm. In the case of the Dunadd brooch the radius is 18 mm, while the Nendrum pseudo-penannular brooch has a radius of 21 mm. This is also the radius of the brooch pin on the Nendrum trial-piece, a feature which again recalls the Hunterston brooch since, as already observed, repetition of the same length is a noteworthy characteristic of the latter.

All this is suggestive of a unit of measure related to 3 mm (or 9 mm) in early medieval times. It is therefore necessary to return to the Hunterston brooch and look more closely at further evidence for such a unit there.

UNITS OF LINEAR MEASURE ON THE HUNTERSTON BROOCH

The appended Tables 24.1–4 record the size of individual compartments, measured internally or externally (ie from within the compartment wall or from the outer edges of that wall).

The plan of the brooch determined the size of individual compartments. Therefore, not all will exactly display dimensions which neatly correspond to the proposed unit of measure, even assuming flawless workmanship. That said, the recurrence of 3 mm and its multiples is remarkable.

Not all dimensions conform to a discernible pattern. The circular studs on the front of the brooch and pin-head, for instance, do not seem to have been measured exactly in the way proposed (Table 24.3). Yet, they are exceptional and some other 'non-conforming' dimensions can be shown, on closer inspection, to be a function of the use of a unit of measure related to 3 mm (or 9 mm).

One example is the panelling on the left and right side of the hoop (Table 24.1). On compartments 3L and 3R, 4L and 4R, and 5L and 5R the presence of lengths such as c 17.25 mm or c 20.5 mm are clearly not multiples of 3 mm. However, as demonstrated on Fig 24.4D, the layout of these panels was determined by striking overlapping chords of 42 mm. The apparently anomalous units of measure are therefore dictated by the underlying logic.

Moreover, elsewhere on the hoop appear chords based on the suggested units. Filigree compartments 1, 5L and 5R are each 18 mm long on their inner edges (Fig 24.6A, a). Now, the hoop flares towards the junctions with the terminals, and the edges of the two last-named compartments were struck from points on the cross in a circle underlying the brooch (Fig 24.4B). Thus a reading of 18 mm on panels 5L and 5R as well as on panel 1 is an unexpectedly orderly result. This is also the length of the inner edges of filigree compartments 3L and 3R when measured from their topmost corners to the end of the dividing wall between each and its neighbour. Such results suggest a clear mathematical understanding of the geometry of the Hunterston brooch on the part of the designer.

Most panels on the Hunterston brooch also generally conform to the system proposed here. Examples will be found on the tables and just a few will be highlighted, as follows:

(i) A number of elements measure 9 mm, eg: (a) the sides of the angle-pieces on the pin-head (1L and 1R); (b) the narrow ends of most of the side compartments on the terminals; (c) the sub-triangular trumpet patterns on the marginal birds' heads on the terminals (22L and 22R); (d) the trumpet spirals on the inner margins of the terminals (23L and 23R). One third of this length, 3 mm, is the width of the filigree panels in the oblong frame in the 'gap' (Fig 24.3A: b, d, f, h).

(ii) The beaded steps surrounding the central panels on the terminals on the front (9L and 9R) each measure c 21 mm on the inner edge; c 12 mm on the top-side edge; and c 24 mm on the gapside edge (Table 24.1).

(iii) The beaded step on the pin-head (4) measures 12 mm across the top; 18 mm along the left and right side; and 12 mm across the (plain) bottom edge adjoining stud 7 at the apex (Table 24.2).

(iv) A dimension on the pin-head not shown on Table 24.2 is the distance between the outer tips of filigree side compartments 6L and 6R, which measure 15 mm across stud 7. This is also the length of the top end of compartment 5 in the centre of the pin-head, which indicates that an underlying oblong was used in the planning of the pin-head.

(v) The filigree-decorated side compartments 10L and 10R on the terminals each measure c 21 x 9 mm internally (Table 24.1).

(vi) The rectangular frame surrounding the central panel on the 'gap' area (Fig 24.3A) is 18 x 24 mm from mid-point to mid-point when measured at the base of the compartment walls (though not on their upper surface, as Table 24.1 shows). The equivalent panel on the reverse of the brooch, no 5, has similar dimensions (Table 24.4).

The tables also give some readings which fall approximately half-way between figures divisible by 3 mm. Examples on Table 24.1 include c 10.5 mm (compartment 1); c 13.5 mm (compartment 19); and c 22.5 mm (compartment 1). Of course, the smaller the unit, the greater the possibility of error, so it would be unwise to postulate a further sub-unit of 1.5 mm. Nevertheless, these readings may be significant. Bruce-Mitford's (1960, 221–31) detailed analysis of the grids underlying the patterns on the *Lindisfarne Gospels* revealed some minute modules, some 1.5 mm long, others as little as 1 mm × 1mm.

In summary, the dominant use in the layout of the brooch of 15 mm, 33 mm, 42 mm, c 48 mm, 54 mm, 60 mm and 75 mm (*v sup*), and the frequent appearance on the tables of units of 6 mm, 9 mm, 12 mm, 15 mm, 18 mm, 21 mm, 24 mm, 30 mm, or of dimensions of approximately these lengths, must go beyond coincidence. The evidence of the Hunterston brooch is thus consistent with the hypotheses of Stevenson and Lang. It is also consistent with many (though not all) of Bruce-Mitford's measurements of the *Lindisfarne Gospels*, and with measurements I have made of other pieces of Insular metalwork. There is no space to discuss these here. It is worth noting, however, that they included the Iron Age Bann disc (Raftery 1987, fig 2:3) and the zoomorphic penannular brooch from Caledon, Co Tyrone (Kilbride-Jones 1980, fig 37.76), as well as late 7th- to 9th-century objects, such as the Steeple Bumpstead boss (Youngs 1989, no 140; Youngs 1993), the Londesborough and Breadalbane brooches (Youngs 1989, nos 71, 72).

WHAT BASIC UNITS OF LINEAR MEASURE UNDERLIE THE DIMENSIONS OF THE HUNTERSTON BROOCH?

The final question to consider is the basic unit. Was it 9 mm (as Stevenson and Lang suggested); 3 mm (the working measures used in the course of this study); or some larger unit of which 3 mm and 9 mm represent recognized subdivisions?

The subject of ancient systems of measure is a difficult one. Nevertheless, common sense suggests that, although near perfect, small-scaled work is typical of the best Insular art, diminutive lengths like 3 mm and 9 mm probably represent fractions of much larger measures. This supposition is supported by the evidence of the Old Irish laws.

Kelly has recently surveyed the units of measures attested there and found that shorter units of length are generally based on the human hand and foot of an average adult male (Kelly 1997, 560). Not only is this method highly reminiscent of Roman metrology, so too is the nomenclature and the relationships between the various units.

In ancient Rome, a standard measure was the *pes* (foot). This was subdivided into four *palmi* (palms), twelve *unciae* (inches) and sixteen *digiti* (digits).

The Irish foot (*traig*) was likewise subdivided into palms though these represented a third (rather than a quarter) of a foot, the following terms being used for the same apparent length: *bas* (the palm of the hand or handbreath), *crob* (hand, claw, paw), and *ferglac* (a man's hand). Moreover, the *traig* was also divided into inches, the word for an 'inch' being *ordlach* (a derivative of *ordu*, thumb), used as a measure of circumference as well as length. A similar (though not necessarily identical) unit was the *mér* (finger or digit), used to describe the dimensions of tools, vessels and salted meat (Kelly 1997, 561–5).

An even smaller unit recorded in the Old Irish laws is the *gráinne* (cereal grain) which equalled a third of an inch (*ordlach*) (op. cit. 560–1). Unlike the lengths itemized above, it had no Roman counterpart. However, the cereal grain as a unit of linear measure is known elsewhere in the early medieval period, and represents a move towards greater precision.[1] It was attested in a Carolingian source, the *Pauca de mensuris* in the *Codex Gudianus*, where five grains make up a digit (Kidson 1990, 82). Moreover, Welsh medieval law tracts (Fernie 1985, 247; Jenkins 1986, 120), record the barleycorn which equalled a third of an inch, as do medieval English sources. For instance, in 1324 a statute of Edward II defines an inch as three barleycorns round, dry and in a row (Hallock & Wade 1906, 36). A Middle Irish text of approximately 11th-century date, on the other hand, specifies a grain of oats, barley and wheat should be used (Kelly 1997, 561).

Lang (1988, 100) has already drawn attention to the possible relevance of the barleycorn inch to Insular art. He observed that 9 mm is approximately a third of a modern inch which measures 25.4 mm. Since 3 x 9 = 27, there is a shortfall of just 1.6 mm. This is certainly a striking correlation.

However, we do not need to assume that the early medieval Celtic metalworking inch was precisely the same as the modern (imperial) one.[2] As Fernie (1991, 1–2) has noted, a sharp distinction needs to be drawn between systems of length on the one hand and absolute lengths on the other. The mention of inches in documents from different places does not permit one to assume that the units referred to are of the same length, only that they are likely to bear a similar relationship to other named units, such as the foot, in both places. Indeed, the length of a natural measure like the foot varied from culture to culture, or even (over time) within a single culture. The Romans used the classical Roman foot (*pes monetalis*) of 29.6 cm (Kidson 1990, 75); the Drusian foot (*pes drusianus* of c 33.3 cm (Grierson 1972, 35; cf Fernie 1985, 251); and the *Philetairos* ('royal') foot, probably 35.52 cm long and related to the classical Roman foot by a ratio of 6:5 (Kidson 1990, 83). As for the early medieval period, there is considerable controversy about the precise length of the various feet attested there. Thus the Anglo-Saxon foot, for instance, has been estimated with varying degrees of reliability as 25 cm, 31.44 cm, 33.3 cm or 30.48 cm (the length of the modern English foot) (Fernie 1985, 250–3); 28 cm (Bettess 1991);

31 cm and 33.5 cm (Huggins 1991, 26). To return to the Hunterston brooch and the units related to 9 mm upon it, if we follow Lang in assuming that this may have represented a third of an inch, then (on the basis of the Old Irish laws) we should also assume an inch of 27 mm (incidentally, the radius of the Westness brooch) and a foot of 32.4 cm.

None of the feet listed above exactly match this, but there is one historical foot which is precisely this length. This is the French *pied du roi*, attested at 32.4 cm in 1742, but in use an indeterminate number of centuries earlier, which is a candidate for the (hotly debated) Carolingian foot (Fernie 1978, 386–7). Is this a simple coincidence or a significant correlation? The case for a Celtic foot of 32.4 cm, subdivided into inches of 27 mm, in turn subdivided into barleycorns of 9 mm, further subdivided into thirds of 3 mm and perhaps even smaller fractions, is not proven, but there is sufficient evidence to encourage further measurement and discussion.

CONCLUSION

The Hunterston brooch was planned in a geometrical way and includes subtle drawing techniques derived from La Tène art. Some of the same techniques can also be identified on trial-pieces showing sketches of pseudo-penannular brooches. Detailed measurements of the brooch produced evidence for a unit of measure also found on other pieces of Insular metalwork, which is related to 9 mm. The evidence of the Old Irish laws suggests familiarity with the Roman system of measurement, and 9 mm may represent a third of an inch of 27 mm, which is, in turn, a twelfth of a foot of 32.4 cm. Further research is needed to confirm this.

ACKNOWLEDGEMENTS

I am grateful to Alison Sheridan, Mike Spearman, Jim Wilson, Fraser Hunter, and especially Ian Scott, for facilitating repeated examination of the Hunterston brooch, and to Adrian Whitfield for much help with its geometry. I have also benefited from the advice of Fred Bettess, Fergus Kelly, Nick Griffiths (who, in addition, drew all the diagrams), John Lee, Peter Northover, Robert Stevick and Richard Warner. Finally, I acknowledge grants from the British Academy and Royal Irish Academy towards drawings for a catalogue of penannular brooches, some of which are illustrated here.

NOTES

1. The cereal grain also appears as a unit of weight of precious metals in the Old Irish *Uraicecht Becc* (Kelly 1997, 584), and in the early 7th-century laws of Æthelberht of Kent (Grierson 1972, 3).
2. Measurements of early medieval Irish sculpture by Edwards (1983), Lang (1988) and Gelly (1995) have, however, produced results more consistent with the modern inch. On the other hand, Kelly (1996, 138–9) suggested that the significant dimension on Columban high crosses was the Roman foot, while Stalley (1998) proposed that this unit was also used in the design of Irish round towers.

Compartments	Location	Measurement	Inner Edge	Outer Edge	Topside Edge	Gapside Edge
1	Centre of hoop	Internal	18 mm	c 22.5 mm	left: c 10.5 mm	Right: c 10.5 mm
2L & 2R	Stud cells in 'cartouche' on hoop	External	c 12.5 mm	15 mm	c 12.5 mm	12 mm
Ditto	Ditto	Stud cell: external dimensions	c 9 mm	c 10.5 mm	c 9 mm	c 9 mm
3L & 3R	Hoop	Internal	c 17.25 mm	c 20.5 mm	c 9.5 mm	c 9.5 mm
4L & 4R	Hoop	Compartment as a whole: internal dimensions	c 15.5 mm	c 20 mm	c 9.5 mm	c 10 mm
Ditto	Ditto	Stud cells: external dimensions	4L: c 13 mm 4R: c 12.5 mm	c 14 mm	c 4 mm	c 4.5 mm
5L & 5R	Hoop	Internal	18 mm	22.5 mm	c 10 mm	c 13.5 mm
6L & 7R	Buffers at junctions of hoop and terminals	External				c 20 mm (=maximum width of buffers)
8L & 8R	Centre of terminals	Internal	15 mm	8L: c 25 mm 8R: c 26 mm	c 8.5 mm	c 16 mm
Ditto	Ditto	External	c 16 mm	8L: c 29 mm 8R: c 30 mm	c 9 mm	c 18 mm
9L & 9R	Beaded step surrounding central panel on terminals	External	21 mm	9L: c 38 mm 9R: c 39 mm	12 mm	24 mm
10L & 10R	Side compartments on terminals	Internal	21 mm	c 21 mm	c 9 mm	c 9 mm
12L & 12R	Side compartments on terminals	Internal	12L: c 9.5 mm 12R: c 9 mm	12L: c 9.5 mm 12R: c 9 mm	24 mm	c 22.5 mm
14L & 14R	Side compartments on terminals	Internal	14L: c 16.5 mm 14R: c 16 mm	14L: c 21.5 mm 14R: 21 mm	14L: c 8 mm 14R: c 7.5 mm	9 mm
15L & 15R	Stud cell on outer side compartments on terminals	External, measured at base of cell wall	c 9 mm	c 10 mm	15L: c 8 mm 15R: c 7.5 mm	15L: c 7.5 mm 15R: c 7 mm
16L & 16R	Side compartments on terminals	Internal	15 mm	c 26 mm	16L: 9 mm 16R: c 9 mm	16L: c 8 mm 16R: c 7.5 mm
17L & 17R	Marginal eagles' beaks on inner edge of 'gap' area	External		Shorter chord of beak: c 5.75 mm	base of beak: 6 mm	
18	B-shaped compartment on inner edge of 'gap' area	Internal		Length of straight edge at base of compartment: 16.5 mm	vertical dimensions: 7 mm	
a–h	Oblong frame of central panel on 'gap' area	External	c 16.5 mm	c 17.25 mm	c 22.5 mm	c 22.5 mm
Ditto	Ditto	Measured between mid-points of base of oblong: 18 × 24 mm				
19	Rectangular panel in centre of 'gap' area	Internal	c 9 mm	c 9.5 mm	Left: c 13.5 mm	Right: c 13.5 mm
20	B-shaped compartment on outer edge of 'gap' area	Internal	Length of straight edge at base of compartment: c 17.25 mm		vertical dimension: c 7.5 mm	
21L & 21R	Marginal eagles' beaks on outer edge of 'gap' area	External	Shorter chord of beak: c 6 mm		Base of beak: c 7.75 mm	

Table 24.1: Dimensions of compartments on front of Hunterston Brooch.

Note: (a) 'Inner edges' are those closest to the notional centre of the brooch; (b) 'Outer edges' are those opposite the inner edges; (c) On truly central panels the remaining edges are marked in the relevant box as 'left' and 'right', as seen by the viewer (not wearer); (d) On panels which are not central, 'topside' and 'gapside' denote those edges which, following the circumference of the brooch, respectively face towards either the central panel on the hoop or towards the 'gap' area between the terminals.

Compartment	Location	Measurement	Upper Edge	Lower Edge	Left Edge	Right Edge
1	Undecorated part of margin on upper edge	Maximum length	24 mm			
1L	Angle-piece at left corner of upper edge	Length of each side	9 mm		9 mm	
1R	Angle-piece at right corner of upper edge	Length of each side	9 mm			9 mm
2	Top side compartment	Internal	24 mm	12 mm	c 8 mm	c 8 mm
4	Beaded surround of central panel	External	12 mm	12 mm	18 mm	18 mm
5	Centre of pin-head	Internal	15 mm	7.5 mm	18 mm	18 mm
6L	Side compartment on left side	Internal	c 7 mm	c 4.5 mm	c 26.5 mm	c 18 mm
6R	Side compartment on right side	Internal	c 7 mm	c 4.5 mm	c 18 mm	c 25.5 mm
9	Buffer at apex	Maximum width	c 20 mm			

Table 24.2: Dimensions of compartments on front of pin-head of Hunterston Brooch.

Stud	Location	Measurement	Diameter	Height
Brooch: 7L & 7R	Junctions of hoop and terminals	Diameter of studs	c 12.5 mm	
Ditto	Ditto	Diameter of base of settings	c 17 mm	
Ditto	Ditto	Height of settings		c 4.5 mm
Brooch: 11L, 11R, 13L & 13R	Eyes of four eagles' heads at corners of 'gap' area	Diameter of stud (only 11R *in situ*)	c 10.25 mm	
Ditto	Ditto	Diameter of base settings	c 13 mm	
Ditto	Ditto	Height of settings		c 5 mm
Pin-head: 3L & 3R	Empty stud settings at corners at top of pin-head	Internal diameter of settings	c 7.5 mm	
Ditto	Ditto	Diameter of base of settings	c 10 mm	
Ditto	Ditto	Height of empty setting		c 6 mm
Pin-head: 7	Apex of pin-head	Diameter of stud	c 9.5 mm	
Ditto	Ditto	Diameter at base of setting	c 14 mm	
Ditto	Ditto	Height of setting		c 6 mm

Table 24.3: Dimensions of circular studs on Hunterston Brooch and pin-head.

Note: to protect the brooch only approximate measurements were made of the base of stud settings and the depth of setting.

Compartment	Location	Measurement	Inner Edge	Outer Edge	Topside Edge	Gapside Edge
1 on brooch	Centre of hoop	External	c 43.5 mm	c 54 mm	Left: 14 mm	Right: 14 mm
Ditto	Ditto	Internal	c 41 mm	c 48.25 mm	c 10 mm	c 10 mm
3L & 3R on brooch	Sub-triangular panels in centre of terminals	External	Max length: 3L: c 32.5 mm 3R: c 33 mm			24 mm
Ditto	Ditto	Internal	Max length: 3L: c 29.5 mm 3R: c 30 mm			c 20 mm
5 on brooch	Oblong panel in centre of 'gap' area	External	c 17 mm	c 18 mm	24 mm	24 mm
Ditto	Ditto	Internal	c 12 mm	c 13 mm	c 18.25 mm	c 18.25 mm
3 on pin-head	Decorative panel on loop	Internal			Width: 6 mm	

Table 24.4: Dimensions of compartments on back of Hunterston Brooch and pin-head (for terminology see Table 1).

MANUSCRIPTS

CHAPTER 25

THE *BOOK OF DURROW*: THE NORTHUMBRIAN CONNECTION

Nancy Netzer

Such is the known provenance of the *Book of Durrow* (*Dublin, Trinity College Library MS 57*; Alexander 1978, no 6): a partially erased and rewritten colophon (fol 247v), originally in the same hand as the text of the manuscript, solicits prayers for a scribe called Columba; an inscription, including a dedication to St Columba (d 597), was copied in 1677 from the now-lost 10th-century *cumdach* of the *Book of Durrow*; a document concerning the Columban monastery of Durrow, entered on the last leaf (fol 248v), suggests the manuscript resided at that monastery sometime between the late 11th and 12th centuries, but gives no clue to its length of residence. Henry Jones, bishop of Meath and scoutmaster of Cromwell's army, acquired the manuscript from Durrow and gave it to Trinity College in 1661. The question is, how the tale of origin has been spun around this evidence over the last 400 years and, for present purposes, what role has Northumbria, or more precisely, the Anglo-Celtic missionary foundations of northern England, come to play in it? The tale became tightly entangled in the political and cultural aspirations of the antiquarians and scholars who published the *Book of Durrow* and other Insular manuscripts. As a result, especially for much of the 19th century and until recently, many publications reveal more about the national biases of the authors than about the origin of the manuscript itself. Constrained by space, I shall present but a streamlined analysis of these developments.[1]

The saga begins in 1639 when James Ussher, archbishop of Armagh, collated the texts of both the *Book of Durrow* and the *Book of Kells (Dublin, Trinity College Library, MS 58*; Alexander 1978, no 52) with that of the Vulgate, stating that both manuscripts were by the hand of Columba (Ussher 1639, 691).[2] Moreover, as early as the 17th century, scholars of both English and Irish origin, like the Anglo-Irish historian and collector of manuscripts Sir James Ware, were familiar with Bede's assertion that the Irish had taught most of the English how to write. Bede's account, however, was of little consequence for the great ancestor of English palaeographers, Humfrey Wanley, who in his catalogue of Anglo-Saxon manuscripts (1705, sig cv–c2r, 81–2), claimed that all manuscripts written in Insular majuscule, including *Durrow*, were Anglo-Saxon.

English antiquarians throughout the 18th century perpetuated Wanley's bias. Indeed, John Obadiah Westwood (1845, *Kells* 2), a somewhat more even-handed English antiquarian of the mid-19th century, says that 'Wanley, Casley and others appear never to' have suspected 'the existence of an ancient school of art in Ireland'. Such oversights should not surprise us. In 1171, Henry II used the image of crude Irish heathens masquerading as Christians as a pretext for invading Ireland. Indeed, Giraldus Cambrensis, archdeacon of St David's, who accompanied Prince John to Ireland in 1185, at once described an early illuminated gospel book (previously thought to be *Kells*) as one of the 'miracles of Kildare' (Fox 1990, 265), and labelled the Irish barbarous beasts, cannibals and a 'filthy race, a race sunk in vice, a race more ignorant than all other nations of the first principles of the faith' (Wright 1863, 134–5). Often quoted, Cambrensis's description generated similar historical assertions for the next seven centuries (Lebow 1973, 6–35).

Late 16th- and 17th-century English histories and accounts of Ireland, like *A View of the State of Ireland* (Edmund Spenser 1596, first published 1633), *The Irish Rebellion* (Sir John Temple 1646) and *Hibernia Anglicana* (Richard Cox 1689), also frequently indulge in the stereotypical image of the Irish as primitive, licentious, poverty-stricken, barbarous, violent, bloodthirsty and backward. Their authors rationalized, therefore, that the Irish were fortunate to have fallen under the 'more civil and regular' government of England (Cox 1689, 'An Apparatus'). Clearly, political union did little to erode cultural separation. Rather, in the 19th century, it nurtured the even more invidious backdrop of ethnic prejudice upon which antiquarian publications of the *Book of Durrow* must be viewed and in which the manuscript seems to have become ensnared as a national symbol of Ireland.

Many 19th-century English historians, recounting the theories of Cambrensis and the Elizabethans as dogma, constructed an image of English nationality in almost exclusively Anglo-Saxon terms. As they told it, 5th-century Saxon incursions effaced, rather than augmented Celtic-British culture. Above all, Victorians viewed themselves as Anglo-Saxons, not as inheritors of mixed Celtic and Saxon traditions. They saw their descent from the savage Celtic peoples, recorded by Caesar and Tacitus, as an inauspicious beginning to British history and, some notable exceptions notwithstanding, took the Saxon foundation of England as their dominant historiographic model. The volatile history of Ireland, marked by forced occupation, civil disturbance and insurrection from the 16th through 18th centuries, was their proof of the Celts' inability to accept the finer tenets of civilization – a convenient explanation of poverty in Ireland during the 19th century. In this light, the troubled past appeared not as the result of an imperfect political and economic union with Ireland, but rather as the natural tendency of the Celtic race (Smiles 1994, 113–17). The source of the negative stereotypes of the Irish is epitomized in a paragraph from the *History of England* by David Hume, the most influential historian and philosopher of the 18th century.

> The Irish from the beginning of time had been buried in the most profound barbarism and ignorance; and as they were never conquered or even invaded by the Romans, from whom all the western world derived its civility, they continued still in the most rude state of society, and were distinguished by those vices alone to which human nature, not tamed by education, or restrained by laws, is forever subject (Hume 1802, 424).

To counter such wickedly racist views in constructing a revisionist theory to the British model of Irish history, Irish antiquarians sought to develop a better informed archaeology and anthropology.[3] In the latter half of the 18th century some, like Thomas Comerford (in his *History of Ireland from the Earliest Accounts of Time to the Invasion of the English under King Henry II*, 1751), began to reconsider Anglo-Irish relations, often, albeit absurdly, exaggerating Irish claims to antiquity and culture. Between 1775 and 1850, however, several serious historians examined aspects of Irish history relying on new primary sources, including manuscripts and objects that various Irish scientific societies had collected and published (Lebow 1973, 30–5). Beginning in the early 19th century, official institutions, like the Royal Irish Academy and the Public Record Office of Ireland, sponsored a series of publications (some excessively lavish) of Celtic objects and manuscripts. In 1814, the Irish historian, Charles O'Conor (in his *Rerum Hibernicarum scriptores veteres*), assigned a group of manuscripts to early medieval Ireland in his attempts to dispel the myth that the Celts were uneducated and uncivilized. O'Conor (1814, cxxix–ccxxxvii) published a list of twelve manuscripts using the *Rushworth Gospels* (*Oxford, Bodleian Library MS Auct D 2 19*; Alexander 1978, no 54) as a linchpin, pointing out that it is signed by a scribe with the Irish name, MacRegol. Establishing that MacRegol was the abbot of Birr (d 822), O'Conor used this manuscript to reverse Wanley's argument and reclaimed the lot of Insular manuscripts for Ireland. In this game, turnabout was fair play. If the *Rushworth Gospels* were Irish, so too were other manuscripts written in what he calls the ancient 'unadulterated Irish [meaning not

Roman] hand': Insular majuscule. This included the *Book of Durrow* which he thought was *Kells* (1814, ccxxxvii–ccxli) and, like Ussher nearly 200 years earlier, assigned to Columba himself and consequently to a date before the saint's death in 597.[4] By thus assigning *Durrow* to Columba, O'Conor delivered a group of splendid early manuscripts to Ireland, thereby promoting the nationalist agenda to show the Celts as civilized and educated in the early Middle Ages. In so doing, he also stoked the nationalistic controversy over distinguishing Irish from Anglo-Saxon manuscripts in this early period.

Sir William Betham, in his *Irish Antiquarian Researches* (1826–7), takes O'Conor's work one step further. Applying O'Conor's formula of using scripts to establish origin, Betham set out to date each manuscript more strategically in rebuttal of the English ethnic assault. From the outset he reveals his purpose:

> The state of Ireland, at the periods preceding the existence of written testimony, is only to be ascertained from the remains of art which exist upon or may be discovered below its surface. . . . A people capable of the production of works which exist only in a state of civilization cannot justly be declared barbarous by the verdict of posterity (Betham 1826, 11).

Betham then controverts Hume's argument of some twenty years earlier, saying that the Irish experienced a 'high degree of civilization above their neighbours . . . shortly after the province was overrun by Saxons, who were invited over about the year 449' (op. cit. 13). He contends that the Irish, who had been 'instructed and civilized by the introduction of Christianity from Britain' were, over the next two or three centuries, 'free from the effects of the inroads of barbarians, and would be infinitely superior in refinement after that province fell under the debasing and uncivilizing power of the Saxons' (op. cit. 13–14). Betham viewed early Irish manuscripts, for whose dates he drew on the local lore about the books in question, as:

> national muniments, of which all Irishmen may be justly proud . . . evidences of the civilization and literary acquirements of their country . . . when other nations of Europe, if not in utter ignorance and barbarism, were in their primers, their very horn-books (1827, 243).

Just after Betham's publication the most sumptuous of the Insular manuscripts, primarily the great gospel books, came to be recognized as achievements of international importance and worthy of prominence in a general history of medieval art. In 1837, in a series of books on artworks and artists in England and Paris, Gustaf Wilhelm Waagen, director of the Art Museum in Berlin, describes several Insular manuscripts at length, including the *Lindisfarne Gospels* (*London, British Library Cotton MS Nero D IV*; Alexander 1978, no 9) and *Echternach Gospels* (*Paris, Bibliothèque Nationale MS lat 9389*; Alexander 1978, no 11).

Some years later (1843–5), English entomologist-turned-palaeographer, Westwood, published specimens of several Insular manuscripts in colour lithography in his *Paleographia sacra pictoria*. He saw manuscripts like the *Macdurnan Gospels* (*London, Lambeth Palace MS 1370*; Alexander 1978, no 70), the *Lichfield Gospels* (*Lichfield, Cathedral Library*; Alexander 1978, no 21), and the *Book of Kells* as proof that, from the 5th through the 8th century, Ireland developed a style of art distinct from those of other parts of the civilized world. Convinced that this style came to Lindisfarne via Iona, Westwood, unlike many of his countrymen who insisted it was the other way around, argued that all Irish manuscripts, including *Durrow* and *Kells*, must have pre-dated the *Lindisfarne Gospels*.

Without the nationalistic pressures that fell upon his Irish colleagues, Westwood tried to study the manuscripts systematically and to categorize the distinguishing elements of their style, much as he had classified butterflies and other insects. His limitations, however, become obvious as, for example, he describes what he calls the lion of Mark, which (even though it precedes John in *Durrow*), he says, would be a 'respectable beast were it not for the harlequin's dress in which it is represented' (1868, 21).

Encouraged by such new-found support, Irish antiquarians continued to find ingenious ways to use manuscripts to bolster the Irish cause. Perhaps the most ambitious and lavish statement of the significance of the Irish manuscripts appears in the folio-size publications, revealingly entitled, *Facsimiles of National Manuscripts of Ireland*. The first volume deemed worthy of this pretentious title was published in 1874 by Gilbert, secretary of the Public Record Office of Ireland. This publication, containing descriptions and photozincographs of eight Insular manuscripts, followed a similar English and Scottish series that focused on later historical manuscripts. The Irish chose to distinguish their series, notably the last, by selecting older and splendidly decorated 'national' manuscripts. Indeed, in his introduction Gilbert explains the importance of the publication:

> The want of a comprehensive Irish Palaeographic series has been long felt – more especially as Ireland, though noted for letters in early times, is one of the few European countries for which a publication of this nature has not already been executed (Gilbert & James 1874, v).

Here, the manuscripts become virtual metaphors for Irish civility and culture in the early medieval period.

Gilbert marshals a number of creative arguments to prove that *Durrow* was written by Columba in the 6th century: the manuscript's provenance at the monastery of Durrow, founded by Columba in 553; the colophon mentioning the scribe Columba; the fact that Cuiminé, the 7th-century abbot of Iona, 'bore testimony to Columba's diligence as a scribe'; and (my favourite) the inclusion among the manuscript's capital letters of some from the Greek, a language that Columba knew, according to his contemporary, the poet Dallán (op. cit. viii–ix).

In the 19th century *Durrow* clearly remained, for the most part, the province of Irish scholars who mined it to bolster the nationalist cause, without attempting careful study. Not until the early 20th century did scholars study specific aspects of the manuscript and the English reaction intensify. By 1904 the Swedish archaeologist, Salin, had recognized the Anglo-Saxon origin of the animals on the last carpet page in *Durrow* (Fig 25.1); a German scholar, Zimmermann (1916, 22), while still assigning *Durrow* to Ireland in about 700, said that although the manuscript was without imitators there, it influenced later English illumination (a reference taken up by later scholars touting the Northumbrian cause, eg Lowe in *CLA* II, xiv). The two-century-old Ireland–Northumbria question, however, remained in the wings until 1934 when the Englishman Sir Alfred Clapham called it to centre stage. Clapham refuted the artistic priority of Ireland and, reacting partly to the non-Irish style of manuscripts produced at the Columban monasteries of Luxeuil and Bobbio, concluded that Irish Christian art was unknown in Ireland before the close of the 7th century. Clapham (1934, 52–5) suggested instead, in an excessively convoluted and improbable treatise, that the Insular style indeed evolved through the hands of Irishmen, but in Northumbria – citing the *Lindisfarne Gospels* as the best example. He then speculated that Irish missionaries from Northumbria returned to Iona and Ireland, bringing with them 'the developed art of manuscripts', and produced the *Book of Durrow* probably at Iona (op. cit. 56–7).

A year later, the English biblical scholar Burkitt (1935, 36) reinforced Clapham's theories. After, at best, a perfunctory examination, he declared that the gospel text of *Durrow* represented a curious state half-way between the Italo-Northumbrian texts of the *Codex Amiatinus* and *Lindisfarne Gospels* and the Irish text of the *Book of Kells*, which he assigned to Iona. He then reasoned that *Durrow* must be Northumbrian. He augmented his conclusions with an analysis of the *Durrow* and *Kells* scripts so creative and worthy of 19th-century ethnic prejudice that it bears repeating: the thick downstrokes of the letters, he said, indicated that the scribes held their right elbows close to their sides, and, thus they had been taught to write in the classical way, the way that both Celts and Teutons have always in their hearts so disliked (op. cit. 37).

The same year, the renowned palaeographer, Lowe, argued from a similar poorly veiled, essentially racially biased perspective, that Irish scribes were 'less bound by rules and regulations and often guided by whim and fancy', whereas the work of English scribes was in comparison, 'balanced and disciplined'. This argument remains, surprisingly unaltered, in Lowe's second edition of 1972 (*CLA* II, xvi). Such arbitrary criteria left Lowe free to assign to Northumbria the finer manuscripts like *Durrow* (op. cit. no 273) and the *Echternach Gospels* (*CLA* V, no 578).

I confess that the *Book of Durrow* has always seemed to me a book apart among the group of early Irish manuscripts now in Dublin, and gradually the suspicion woke in me that perhaps English workmanship accounted for the orderliness of its script and the balance and sobriety of its ornamentation (*CLA* II, xiv–xv).

In 1947, the Anglocentric arguments asserting the priority of Northumbria came to a climax. Masai, a Belgian librarian, asserted in his book, provocatively entitled *Essai sur les origines de la miniature dite irlandaise*, that the Anglo-Saxons invented Insular majuscule script and that the style of manuscript illumination, formerly called Irish, originated in the scriptorium at Lindisfarne (1947, 52, 103). Indeed, armed with a series of simplistic historical, textual and art-historical arguments, Masai (1947, 126) advanced a view nearly as radical as Wanley's nearly 150-year-old theory that *Durrow, Kells, Lindisfarne, Echternach* and the *Durham Gospels (Durham, Cathedral Library MS A II 17*; Alexander 1978, no 10) were all written in the scriptorium at Lindisfarne.

In the same year, Nordenfalk's (1947, 162–74) introduction of the *Durham Gospel Fragment (Durham Cathedral Library MS A II 10*; Alexander 1978, no 5), preserved in a Northumbrian library and shown to mark one stage earlier in both script and decoration (lacking the Celtic trumpet and Germanic animal ornaments) than *Durrow*, provided more ammunition for the Northumbrian cause. Despite its provenance, the Durham manuscript might well have been brought to Northumbria from Iona; as Verey has shown (1969, 137–242; 1973, 575–9; 1989, 145–6), a section of its text is close to that of the Irish gospel book, *Usserianus Primus (Dublin, Trinity College Library MS 55*; Alexander 1978, no 1).

The publication of a facsimile of *Durrow* in 1960 provided an opportunity in the commentary volume for more systematic study of the manuscript. Here, Bieler suggests that the majuscule script of *Durrow* fits best in Northumbria half-way between those of the *Durham Fragment* and *Echternach*, where he sees it as having achieved perfection. In his eyes, comparable volumes in Ireland lacked their high standard of penmanship (Luce et al. 1960, 94). This vision, however informed it might have been at the time, pales in the light of subsequently discovered fragments (previously known only as the lower script in a palimpsest) of a gospel book that came from the Irish Columban foundation at Bobbio and are now in Turin (*Biblioteca Nazionale MSS O IV 20, F IV 14, F IV 16, F VI 2, G V 2; CLA* IV, no 446; *CLA* suppl, 52; Ferrari 1973, 9–12). This fragmentary gospel book is thought to be, at least, in a hand from the same scriptorium, if not from the identical hand that produced the *Book of Durrow* (O'Sullivan 1985, 353–4; Brown 1993, 205–6).

Bieler also argues that frames of red dots around display script are found nowhere else in illumination of Irish origin (Luce et al. 1960, 94). Once again, recent research shows that this feature occurs in the *Augsburg Gospels (Augsburg, Universitätsbibliothek Cod I.2.4°.2*; Alexander 1978, no 24), a gospel book based on an Irish model, probably written by Irish-trained scribes, and produced in the Echternach scriptorium early in the 8th century (Ó Cróinín 1988, 28–30; Netzer 1994, 112–19).

The discovery of the ship burial at Sutton Hoo in 1938, and Bruce-Mitford's (1978, esp 432–611) close examination of the find, however, provide the strongest evidence that *Durrow* originated in Northumbria. More recently, George Henderson assembled a series of compelling comparisons between the metalwork from Sutton Hoo (found with coins datable between 625 and 635) and motifs found on various folios of the *Book of Durrow*. He summarizes the most relevant arguments (Henderson, G 1987, 29–55). For example, he points to the relationship between various mounts of gold and garnets from Sutton Hoo (op. cit. pl 27) and the rectangular panels surrounded by interlace on a *Durrow* carpet page (Fig 25.2); between the millefiori glass settings in the pyramidal mounts (op. cit. pl 27) and the square blocks of the eight-centred cross on the *Durrow* carpet page (Fig 25.6); between scabbard bosses (op. cit. pl 30) and the three black and white circular ornaments in the centre of the John carpet page (Fig 25.1); and between the two varieties of beasts on the Sutton Hoo purse (op. cit. pl 28) and the symmetrically placed short and long ribbon beasts forming the borders of the same carpet page. Later still, regarding the latter comparison, Bailey (1992, 37–9) shows a similar beast on a small gold foil fragment from Bamburgh to prove that the style was known in 7th-century Northumbria (see title page).

It is a welcome relief finally to encounter the work of these recent scholars who are well aware of the several possible conclusions that could be drawn from the metalwork, but have not exploited the evidence to argue for origin on one side of the Irish sea or the other. Indeed, Bailey (1992, 39) points the way to a more productive future line of enquiry, declaring: 'What sources were available in Northumbria were equally accessible to Ireland and vice versa.'

As the excavation of metalwork in Ireland continues, and its yield, like the hoard from the River Blackwater at Shanmullaghound, now in the Ulster Museum, Belfast (Bourke 1993, 24–39), is better published, tangible evidence for Bailey's statement is likely to multiply. Already, Sue Youngs (1995, 38–45) has made compelling comparisons between enamels with interlace recently excavated in Ireland and interlace in *Durrow*, and I have seen several fine comparisons to *Durrow* ornamental motifs among the drawers of unpublished excavated metalwork in the National Museum of Ireland.

When seeking parallels for the rectangular inserts of the *Durrow* carpet page with interlace and panels of pattern (Fig 25.2) among recently excavated material, one must take into account the sides of the Derrynaflan paten (Youngs 1989, no 125a, plate on 162; Ryan 1983, pl 35) with its application of rectangular monochrome glass studs, some of which are inlaid with silver grills in stepped patterns and placed against mounts with chip-carved interlace above and below (Fig 25.3). Inlaid glass studs on the Irish Moylough belt shrine (Youngs 1989, no 47; Fig 25.4) are probably closer to the black and white discs with stepped cross designs in the central medallion of the *Durrow* animal carpet page (Fig 25.1), than they are to the Sutton Hoo scabbard bosses (Henderson, G 1987, pl 30). Similarly, the design of the openwork silver medallions on the same belt

Fig 25.1. Carpet page, *Book of Durrow*
(*Dublin, Trinity College Library MS 57*),
fol 192v. (Copyright the Board of Trinity
College, Dublin)

Fig 25.2. Carpet page, *Book of Durrow*,
fol 125v. (Copyright the Board of Trinity
College, Dublin)

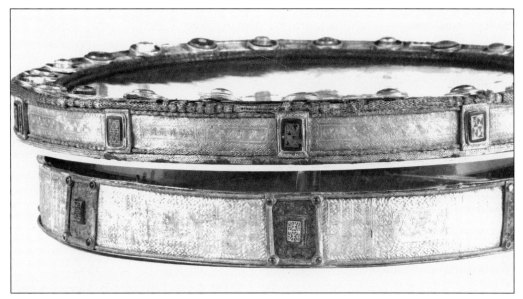

Fig 25.3. Glass stud, Derrynaflan paten, detail. (National Museum of Ireland)

Fig 25.4.   Belt shrine, Moylough, Co Sligo, detail. (National Museum of Ireland)

Fig 25.5.   Carpet page, *Book of Durrow*,
fol 3v. (Copyright the Board of Trinity College,
Dublin)

Fig 25.6.   Carpet page, *Book of Durrow*,
fol 1v. (Copyright the Board of Trinity College,
Dublin)

shrine is very close to that of the four lateral medallions in the central medallions of the *Durrow* carpet page with trumpet spirals (Fig 25.5). Moreover, black and white checked millefiori patterns, approximating those on the *Durrow* cross-carpet page (Fig 25.6), appear already on Irish penannular brooches, like the one from Ballinderry crannog, thought to date from the early 7th century (Youngs 1989, no 19). On the *Durrow* page, the representation of what must have been inspired by a metal frame around the millefiori squares suggests that the painter was looking at class 3 millefiori, such as that found, for example, on the Ashmolean terminal (op. cit. no 55), practised in Ireland in the 8th and 9th centuries (Youngs 1995, 39; Carroll 1995, 55). Clearly, we must analyse the precise relationship between the two media if we are to determine its usefulness as a potential source of evidence for the manuscript's origin.

Along these lines, any reasoned analyst of the origin of the *Book of Durrow* must also reckon with the evidence revealed in the recent commentary volume to the facsimile of the *Book of Kells*. Here, McGurk demonstrates the close relationship between the unique arrangement of the various preliminary texts and those texts themselves in *Durrow* and *Kells*. In both manuscripts even the *incipits* and *explicits* are identical, such that both omit the same colophons. This correspondence thus reveals that both manuscripts probably derive from a common exemplar. McGurk further shows that the text of the elaborate arched canon tables in *Kells* owes a debt to that found in simple rectangular frames in *Durrow*. Moreover, he has correctly analysed the retention in *Kells* of particular errors in *Durrow* to conclude that *Durrow* was a direct ancestor of *Kells*, via one or two intermediaries (Fox 1990, 37–58). Such a relationship surely has implications for the single origin of both manuscripts – perhaps at Iona – and must be considered in any even-handed discussion of the question.

To those who now view me as a spoiler, I say only that I wish to dampen the nationalist flame, rather than rekindle it. We all may hope that the scholarly direction of the last few years will continue and expand and that arguments more rooted in nationalism than in scholarship will lie low. The commercialization of the *Book of Durrow* – it has become a national symbol of Ireland, showing up on merchandise ranging from travel posters to dish towels in Shannon airport – will impede such progress, however. So far, we see that historical circumstances are favourable to *Durrow*'s origin in Ireland, Iona or Northumbria, but that is only the setting for the gem. For all the publications that mention the *Book of Durrow*, we still know astoundingly little about the book itself. Analysis must now focus on the evidence found in connections among *Durrow*, sculpture and metalwork on the one hand, and other scripts and texts on the other. To use the *Book of Durrow* at this time as a scaffolding on which to attach other works, manuscripts in particular, to the Golden Age of Northumbria would only result in a constructed framework too feeble to support an argument that might otherwise have much to recommend it.

NOTES

1. This article is part of the first chapter of a monograph on the *Book of Durrow* the author is writing.

2. '*In regio Comitatu ea est, Durrogh vulgo appellata: quae monasterium habuit S. Columbae nomine insigne; inter cujus* ΧαΜΗλΙα *Euangeliorum codex vetestissimus asservabatur, quem ipsius Columbae fuisse monachi dictitabant. ex quo, & non minoris antiquitatis altero, eidem Columbae assignato (quem in urbe Kelles sive Kenlis dicta Midenses sacrem habent) diligenti cum editione vulgata Latina collatione facta, in nostros usus variantium lectionum binos libellos concinnavimus.*'

3. The 'revisionist thesis' of Irish history actually begins in the 17th century with several historical tracts written by Irish clerics in defence of their religion and country. For discussion see Lebow 1973, 25–35.

4. Apparently, neither *Durrow* nor *Kells* was available when O'Conor made his initial list. *Durrow*, however, was discovered in time to be described in an appendix under the mistaken belief that it was *Kells*.

CHAPTER 26

LINDISFARNE OR RATH MAELSIGI? THE EVIDENCE OF THE TEXTS

Christopher D. Verey

A conference on the 'Golden Age' of Northumbria could not pass without reference to those spectacular creations of the Northumbrian scriptoria of the late 7th and early 8th centuries. Indeed it was fitting that the exhibition 'Treasures from the Lost Kingdom of Northumbria' in the Laing Art Gallery, Newcastle (Hawkes 1996a), which coincided with the conference on the Golden Age of Northumbria, was able to bring together two of the masterpieces of the Lindisfarne scriptorium, the *Lindisfarne Gospels* and the *Durham Gospels*. That we regard these two as contemporary Lindisfarne books is due primarily to the work of Brown and Bruce-Mitford in the facsimile edition of the *Lindisfarne Gospels* (Kendrick et al. 1960). Their work envisaged at Lindisfarne at the turn of the 7th and 8th centuries one of the great creative centres of early medieval Europe. But, with so much lost (eg Gameson 1994), and given the particularly portable nature of books, to be able to be confident about the origin of one book from this early period is to be fortunate; but to be confident about the common origin of three of the most celebrated early Insular gospel books, the *Lindisfarne Gospels* together with the *Durham* and *Echternach Gospels*, the latter two allegedly written by the same scribe, might be regarded by some as fanciful, by others as reckless.

In the nearly forty years since the publication of the commentary on the facsimile of the *Lindisfarne Gospels*, and in the fifteen or so since the publication of the *Durham Gospels* (Verey et al. 1980), the central place given to Lindisfarne has been challenged – though not as much as one might have expected. The ideas of Ó Cróinín (1982; 1984; 1989) about the possible influence of Rath Maelsigi in Ireland, rather than Lindisfarne, on the development of the scriptorium at Echternach and on the evolution of Insular hands, have been described by O'Sullivan (1994, 94) as 'cracks in the facade' of Brown's Lindisfarne edifice. Other commentators have been less emotive: I tend to sympathize with George Henderson's judgement (1987, 6) that Ó Cróinín's work has given the subject a 'useful jolt'. 'Jolted' by Ó Cróinín's different perspective, this chapter considers the extent to which the evidence of the texts of the gospel books might further undermine or underpin the Lindisfarne edifice.

One of the less 'golden' gospel books of the period is that preserved in *MS A.II.16* in the Dean and Chapter Library in Durham. The present *A.II.16* contains all four gospels. The gospel of John may well come from a different source. This chapter is concerned with the gospel book from which Matthew, Mark and Luke survive. *A.II.16* contains one or two fine initials (Alexander 1978, no 16), but it does not fall into that category of luxury books epitomized by the *Lindisfarne Gospels*. The descriptions of the hands which trip most readily off the pens of palaeographers include the not very flattering 'somewhat artificial', 'not very expert' (*CLA* II, 148a), and 'not very graceful' (*CLA* II, 148b). This is a second-class book; it does not excite competing claims across the Irish Sea!

The main text of *A.II.16* is written in two closely similar uncial hands and one Insular majuscule. The two uncial hands wrote nine quires, the majuscule three. The evidence suggests that the majuscule quires were not a later production to complete a damaged uncial book, but part of the original production. For example, the uncial portions have rubrics in the hand of the majuscule portion, and it is a common Insular hand that provides the marginal apparatus (Eusebian sections) throughout.

The evidence would tend to point to *A.II.16* coming from a centre competent, but not very expert, in both uncial and Insular majuscule. But where? The uncial is not of the typical Wearmouth-Jarrow type; the majuscule shares little of the expertise associated with the Lindisfarne products. We can almost certainly discount an Irish import into Northumbria: 'one cannot speak of Irish uncial' (*CLA* II [rev 1972], xx). Though the book cannot be firmly associated with Durham before the 12th century, in the absence of evidence to the contrary, the survival of an early, 8th-century book in the monastic library at Durham is fairly persuasive evidence for early Northumbrian provenance. Moreover, there is no serious reason to question the Northumbrian production of *A.II.16*.

The text of *A.II.16* contains a distinct feature which associates it with products of the two celebrated Northumbrian scriptoria. The chapter divisions in the book belong to a distinct family whose origins in the Insular world are intrinsically associated with the introduction of the Italo-Northumbrian text of the gospels. This is the gospel text type found in the *Lindisfarne Gospels* and in the gospels copied at Wearmouth-Jarrow. It is a version likely to have been imported into Wearmouth-Jarrow directly from Italy; and if the liturgical elements in these particular chapter lists are taken as an integral element of the imported gospel archetype, then this may well have come from the Naples region. Only one chapter list now survives in *A.II.16*, that prefacing Mark. But the margins of both Matthew and Mark contain an incomplete, but fairly comprehensive set of numbers indicating the openings of chapters according to this particular family.

In contrast, the text of neither Matthew nor Mark in *A.II.16* belongs to the Italo-Northumbrian family. The juxtaposition of a fairly complete set of marginal chapter numbers with a type of gospel text to which they would not have belonged, would suggest not a chance survival, but a conscious decision to introduce a particular usage at some stage in the transmission behind the text of *A.II.16*. That usage was distinctly associated with Lindisfarne and Wearmouth-Jarrow.

The texts of the gospels in *A.II.16* display a variety of types. Luke is a mixture of Vulgate and Old Latin and the type of free textual handling often characterized as 'Irish' (Verey et al. 1980, 70–1). While Luke may be said to have affinities with this type of text, the association with other examples of the so-called 'Irish' text is a loose one, and, to date, I can discern no other texts with which Luke in *A.II.16* may be said to have a significant affinity.

In Matthew there is a change of text type at about the point at which the majuscule hand takes over from the uncial, folio 24. Up to this point, for some twenty-two chapters (that is the modern standardized biblical chapter divisions) *A.II.16* shares its text type with the *Echternach Gospels*. Looking at the conspectus of all pre-9th-century evidence (Fischer 1988), for these chapters of Matthew the *Echternach Gospels* and *A.II.16* share a textual affinity far closer than either shares with any other surviving book. It is certainly much closer than that suggested by the scatter of readings shared between the *Echternach Gospels* and the much later *MacDurnan Gospels* to which McNamara (1990, 102–11) has drawn attention.

There are 363 places in these twenty-two chapters where the *Echternach Gospels* and *A.II.16* individually or jointly contain readings at variance with the text in the critical edition of Wordsworth and White (1898). In other words, except for these 363 readings, the two gospel books agree both with each other and with the text judged by Wordsworth and White to be closest to the original state of the Vulgate revision. It is in these 363 readings that both the disagreements between the two gospel books, and, more significantly, their distinct common ground are to be found. Some 60 of the 363 variants represent obvious simple scribal errors in one gospel book or the other – often promptly corrected. Of the balance, *A.II.16* and *Echternach* agree in over 50% of readings.

The disagreements between the two contain a fair measure of examples of that freedom of textual handling which seems to characterize much of the Insular tradition, and whose pronounced presence is a feature of the so-called 'Irish' text type (Wordsworth & White 1898, 714; Verey et al. 1980, 70–1) – features such as the inversion of word order, the addition or omission of pronouns or adjectives to aid comprehension. This 'textual overlay' reflects a largely random editorial process. Differences in such readings may have little significance for understanding the tradition of the particular text, and agreements in such features between two books may indicate two scribes thinking alike rather than a shared text type. If such features are discounted, in the first twenty-two chapters of

Matthew there are only about fifty significant disagreements between the *Echternach Gospels* and *A.II.16*. This would suggest a measure of agreement between the two gospel books of anything up to three-quarters of the significant variants against the text of Wordsworth and White. By the standards of the surviving material this would suggest a close relationship.

In *A.II.16* Matthew there is a clear and very close Northumbrian association with the text type found in the *Echternach Gospels*; moreover, it is found in association with chapter divisions belonging to the text type found at Lindisfarne and Wearmouth-Jarrow. The degree of agreement in the gospel text does not seem to be paralleled in surviving Irish or continental material. The early gospel books associated with Willibrord's foundation at Echternach do not show close textual affinity with the *Echternach Gospels* (Netzer 1994, 13–16).

The close association with the *Echternach Gospels* does not appear to end precisely at the point at which the majuscule hand takes over in *A.II.16* Matthew. It seems to survive for about a further (modern) chapter. Thereafter the last five (modern) chapters of Matthew in *A.II.16* display a different text type, one found also in another surviving gospel book, almost certainly of Northumbrian origin, the *Cambridge-London Gospels*. This book contains the leaves of most of Matthew and Mark in the Cotton collection in the British Library, albeit much damaged in the 1731 fire, and an incomplete Luke and John donated by Archbishop Parker to Corpus Christi College, Cambridge.

Because of the fire damage, comparison between the last five chapters of Matthew in *A.II.16* and in the Cotton leaves is much limited. But where the texts of the two can be compared there are in the Cotton leaves some thirty-two variants against the text of Wordsworth and White (excluding scribal errors and common orthographic variants). In all but eight of these readings, that is in three-quarters, the same reading occurs in *A.II.16*. This is significant affinity.

The text of Mark in *A.II.16*, which is back with the uncial hand, is of the same type as that at the end of Matthew and displays markedly close parallels with the text of the Cotton leaves. The text type in Mark in *A.II.16* and the *Cambridge-London Gospels* is, moreover, found in the *Durham Gospels*. The same text type is found also in two Italian uncial gospel books known to have been in England at an early date, the 6th-century *St Augustine's Gospels* in Corpus Christi College, Cambridge, and the slightly later Oxford Bodleian *MS Auct D.2.14*.

The text in the *Durham Gospels* is close to that in *Auct D.2.14* (Verey et al. 1980, 72). The relationship between the Bodleian book and the *Durham Gospels* extends also to the other two Insular books. My study of the *Durham Gospels* identified forty-two places in Mark where *Durham* shared distinct variants with Bodleian *MS Auct D.2.14*. *A.II.16* is extant for forty-one of these, and in all but one of these forty-one places shares a common reading with the *Durham Gospels* and the Bodleian book. Because of their fragmentary state, the Cotton leaves of the *Cambridge-London Gospels* preserve only twenty-four of the forty-one, but in all twenty-four they share the reading with the *Durham Gospels*, *A.II.16* and *Auct D.2.14*.

Though all three of these Insular gospel books closely share a text type for Mark, the relationships between the three differ. The texts of the *Durham Gospels* and the *Cambridge-London Gospels* are more closely related than either is with *A.II.16*. Where the *Durham* and *Cambridge-London Gospels* can be compared (because of the damage to the latter) there are 240 places where one or the other or both differ from the text in Wordsworth and White (excluding common orthographic variants). In 60% of these places the two agree against Wordsworth and White. The remaining 40% include simple scribal errors, often promptly corrected, and the textual overlay attributable to the random editorial processes of Insular scribes, referred to above. When such features are discounted there is no more than a handful of differences between the texts of the two books. These suggest that neither text is the product of emendation against another distinct text type.

The relationship between *A.II.16* and these other two books shows that the *Durham* and *Cambridge-London Gospels* are descended in parallel from a common archetype for Mark, and not one from the other. Where all three gospel books are extant there is a total of 280 variants where one or two or all three individually or jointly differ from Wordsworth and White. In 66% of these *A.II.16* agrees with either one or both of the *Durham* and the *Cambridge-London Gospels*. But in only 36% of the 280 does *A.II.16* agree with both of the other books. The agreement between *A.II.16* and one or other of the other two books is evenly balanced. *A.II.16* agrees with the *Durham Gospels* against the *Cambridge-London Gospels* in forty-four readings, and with the *Cambridge-London Gospels* against the *Durham Gospels* in forty readings. This pattern of agreement, whereby readings shared with *A.II.16* survive in one or other of the other two gospel books, but not both, would suggest that the *Durham* and *Cambridge-London Gospels* derive from a common archetype and are not descended one from the other.

Returning to the total of 280 readings where one, two or three of these books differ from Wordsworth and White, there are a total of 101 places where all three agree. If these are added to the agreements between *A.II.16* and either of the other two, the level of agreement is 145 (or 52%) between *A.II.16* and the *Durham Gospels*, and 141 (or 50%) between *A.II.16* and the *Cambridge-London Gospels*. Remembering that these are percentages of agreement on differences from the presumed Vulgate standard, and that in all other respects the books agree, this indicates a close textual relationship between *A.II.16* and the other two. But the agreement between the *Durham* and *Cambridge-London Gospels* is significantly closer.

In some places where *A.II.16* differs from the other two gospel books it reflects a reading found in the earlier Italian uncial gospel books referred to above. This could suggest that it preserved readings in the imported Italian source (not necessarily either of the two surviving Italian books, but with the same text type), readings which were then lost in the tradition of the *Durham* and *Cambridge-*

London Gospels. These two were produced almost certainly earlier than *A.II.16*, possibly by half a century or more. That would not prevent the survival of earlier readings into *A.II.16*. The evidence is not overwhelming or conclusive (readings can be re-imported into a tradition).

To summarize the relationships between the three texts of Mark, the degree of close relationship between the *Durham* and *Cambridge-London Gospels*, coupled with the lack of evidence of alternative influence, would suggest that these two could be regarded as little more distant than 'cousins'. In other words the two appear to share a common ancestor possibly as little as one removed. *A.II.16* could be seen as relating as closely as a second or third cousin to the other two.

There is a further conclusion. Because of the relationship between the three, the text type of Mark cannot have been imported into Northumbria by the agency of one of the three surviving Insular books. The idea that the *Durham Gospels* were imported into Northumbria (O'Sullivan 1994, 89), though not susceptible to conclusive disproof by textual evidence, nonetheless is distinctly implausible. The evidence above suggests that a very closely related version of the text of Mark found in the *Durham Gospels* pre-existed in Northumbria. While that same text could, in theory, have been exported and then reimported by Insular agency, when one considers not only the close relationship between the texts in the three books, but that the text type finds no close parallel in any known likely Irish or Echternach book, it is difficult to understand why a highly involved hypothesis should take precedence over the more obvious conclusion.

But the evidence of the text of Mark is not all that there is to go on. I have argued elsewhere (Verey et al. 1980, 106–7) the close relationship between the *Durham Gospels* and the *Lindisfarne Gospels*. The *Durham Gospels* are corrected and punctuated *per cola et commata* by reference to an exemplar very close to *Lindisfarne*. This work was done in a hand which, if not identical, is of identical training with a correcting hand in the *Lindisfarne Gospels*. The idea that the revision to the *Durham Gospels* follows the book's supposed importation into Lindisfarne or Northumbria does not accord with the evidence: the same correcting hand was responsible for some of the apparatus which, as in the case of the family of chapter numbers, came from the original exemplar of the *Durham Gospels*, and could not have come from the tradition of the *Lindisfarne Gospels*. On the balance of probabilities the textual evidence reinforces the conclusion that the *Durham Gospels* originated at Lindisfarne at around the same time as the production of the *Lindisfarne Gospels*.

The *Cambridge-London Gospels* and the *Durham Gospels* are closely related not only in the text of Mark, but also in Luke and in some of their gospel prefaces. But the close similarities between these two gospel books does not stop with the texts. There are close parallels not only in the structure of the decoration of the two books, but also in scribal tricks (Verey 1998). The former feature would suggest closely shared models, the latter a common scribal tradition. The relationship can be seen readily by reference to the plates in Chapter 3 of *From Durrow to Kells* (Henderson, G 1987). It is reasonable to conclude an origin for the *Cambridge-London Gospels* in the sphere of influence of Lindisfarne around the turn of the 7th and 8th centuries.

Turning to the *Echternach Gospels*, even a superficial glance at the same chapter in Henderson's book (1987) will show close parallels between the decoration of the *Echternach* and *Cambridge-London Gospels*, for example in the shared models for, and similar (but by no means identical) treatment of the evangelist symbols, and in the structure of the initial opening to Mark. Moreover, the closest parallels for the prefatory matter in the *Echternach Gospels* is found in the *Cambridge-London Gospels* (Verey 1998). The closest parallel so far identified for the original gospel text (that is not the systematic marginal revision) in the *Echternach Gospels* is that with Durham *A.II.16* for Matthew. (There is much more work needed on the text of the other three gospels in the *Echternach Gospels*). In contrast, the architecture and textual substance of the *Echternach Gospels* are not closely related to the early products of the Echternach scriptorium (Netzer 1994).

To draw the various textual threads together, Durham *MS A.II.16* contains a chapter family that points to a distinct Lindisfarne and Wearmouth-Jarrow usage. The gospel text of most of Matthew in *A.II.16* provides the closest parallels so far identified with the original text of the *Echternach Gospels*. The last five chapters of Matthew in *A.II.16* are closely related to the text in the *Cambridge-London Gospels*. The text of Mark is also closely related to that of the *Cambridge-London Gospels*, and the same text type is shared with the *Durham Gospels*. The text type is identifiable to central Italy in the 6th and 7th centuries. The nature of the relationship between the texts of Mark in these three Insular gospel books would suggest that the *Cambridge-London* and *Durham Gospels* could be as closely related as textual 'cousins', and that *A.II.16* is a slightly more distant relative reflecting a version of the text behind the common ancestor of the other two. (The same text type is shared for Luke in the *Durham* and *Cambridge-London Gospels*, but not in *A.II.16*.) The gospel prefatory matter in the *Echternach Gospels* is closely related in layout and text to that found in the *Cambridge-London Gospels*. The *Durham Gospels* mix the prefatory matter of the Italian tradition behind its gospel text (the chapter family and the prologues) with the tradition found in the *Echternach* and *Cambridge-London Gospels* (layout and the inclusion of Hebrew names; Verey et al. 1980, 18–25).

The nature of the textual relationships suggests that the scriptoria that produced these four Insular books, Durham *A.II.16*, the *Cambridge-London*, the *Durham* and the *Echternach Gospels* had access to closely related exemplars. This alone cannot prove that all four originated from the same cultural province. But such strong textual evidence does add considerable weight to the other evidence concerning these books.

Durham *A.II.16* is almost certainly of Northumbrian origin. Several aspects of the production of the *Durham Gospels* point to close association with Lindisfarne. The nature of the relationship between the texts of Mark in *A.II.16* and the form found in the *Durham* and *Cambridge-London Gospels* reinforces the Northumbrian identity of the *Durham Gospels*. Given the close parallels between the *Cambridge-London Gospels* and the *Durham Gospels* in script and ornament, as well as the textual affinities between the two, the most obvious conclusion is that the *Cambridge-London Gospels* are also Northumbrian in origin, reflecting a closely similar background to that of the *Durham Gospels*. The *Echternach Gospels* show similar close relationships in script and ornament with the *Durham Gospels*, and with the *Cambridge-London Gospels*. This, coupled with the close textual relationship with *A.II.16*, would also, reasonably, point to Northumbria as the likely origin of the *Echternach Gospels*.

There is always a need for caution with the fragmentary nature of the surviving evidence, the more so with the very portable nature of manuscript and textual evidence. But these four books, Durham *A.II.16*, the *Cambridge-London, Durham* and *Echternach Gospels*, are interrelated in such a way as to suggest that all four belong to Northumbria in its 'Golden Age', and in their various relationships each to a lesser or greater degree connects with Lindisfarne. Northumbria would seem the least convoluted explanation of their various relationships.

ACKNOWLEDGEMENTS

I acknowledge with pleasure the support in many very practical ways, and the continuing friendship of Patrick McGurk, Michelle Brown and Nancy Netzer. I should like to thank also Roger Norris for a most magnificent afternoon at Durham at the close of the conference on the Golden Age of Northumbria, when Nancy Netzer, Dáibhí Ó Cróinín and I were able to examine *A.II.16* along with other early manuscripts in the Dean and Chapter Library (Fig 26.1). The comments here on the *Cambridge-London Gospels* are based on my work in contribution to a study by several scholars including Michelle Brown, Nancy Netzer and Mildred Budny, which it is hoped to publish as a monograph.

Fig 26.1 Dáibhi Ó Cróinín, Christopher Verey and Nancy Netzer examine *A.II.16* in the Dean and Chapter Library, Durham, July 1996. (Photograph: Mark Stansbury)

APPENDIX: MANUSCRIPTS CITED IN THE TEXT OF THE CHAPTER

Cambridge, Corpus Christi College, MS 286 (Gospels of St Augustine). CLA II, 126; McGurk (1961) no 3. *Sigla*: Fischer (1988–91) Jx; Wordsworth & White (1898) X.

The Cambridge-London Gospels: Cambridge, Corpus Christi College, MS 197(b) + London, British Library, MS Cotton Otho C.V. CLA II, 125; McGurk (1961) no 2; Alexander (1978) no 12. *Siglum*: Fischer (1988–91) Eg.

Durham, Dean and Chapter Library, MS A.II.16, folios 1–102 + Cambridge, Magdalene College, Pepysian MS 2981 (18). CLA II, 148a and 148b; McGurk (1961) nos 10 and 11; Alexander (1978) no 16. *Sigla*: Fischer (1988–91) Nd and Ne.

The Durham Gospels: Durham, Dean and Chapter Library, MS A.II.17, folios 2–102 + Cambridge, Magdalene College, Pepysian MS 2981 (19). Facsimile: Verey et al. (1980). CLA II, *149*; McGurk (1961) no 13; Alexander (1978) no 10. *Siglum*: Fischer (1988–91) Ef.

The Echternach Gospels: Paris, Bibliothèque Nationale, MS lat. 9389. CLA V, no 578; McGurk (1961) no 59; Alexander (1978) no 11. *Siglum*: Fischer (1988–91) Ge; Wordsworth & White (1898) Ep.

The Lindisfarne Gospels: London, British Library, MS Cotton Nero D.IV. Facsimile: Kendrick et al. (1960). CLA II, 187; McGurk (1961) no 22; Alexander (1978) no 9. *Sigla*: Fischer (1988–91) Ny; Wordsworth & White (1898) Y.

Oxford, Bodleian Library, MS Auct. D.II.14. CLA II, 230; McGurk (1961) no 32. *Sigla*: Fischer (1988–91) Jo; Wordsworth & White (1898) O.

CHAPTER 27

THE SHAPE OF LEARNING AT WEARMOUTH-JARROW: THE DIAGRAM PAGES IN THE *CODEX AMIATINUS*

Carol A. Farr

Three diagram pages in the *Codex Amiatinus (Florence, Biblioteca Medicea-Laurenziana, Amiatinus 1)* arrange the books of the Bible according to Hilary, Jerome, and Augustine (fols 6, 7, 8; Figs 27.1–3). Rarely the subject of art-historical comment, they are nearly always taken at face value as having relevance to studies of Bible texts, not to visual art. Decoration and figural images in them are minimal, and they are virtually unique as decorated pages, offering no obvious comparisons with other examples of Insular manuscript art. The most interesting comment on them has been Schapiro's (1958, 207) comparison of the diagram according to Hilary with the complex frames of certain decorated pages of the *Book of Kells (Trinity College, Dublin MS 58)*, such as folio 114r, the so-called 'Arrest of Christ' (Fig 27.4). Schapiro was speaking as a formalist: the ornamented structure of medallions, arch, and crosses are echoed in the composition of the frames of the picture on folio 114r and others, including the Enthroned Christ (fol 32v) and Portrait of John (fol 291r). Diagram and full-page illumination thus speak of a stylistic interplay in Northumbria between the restrained art of late 7th- and early 8th-century Wearmouth-Jarrow and sumptuous Insular gospel book ornament. Today's scholars would object to his stylistic use of the *Book of Kells*'s decoration to support the *St Petersburg Bede*'s Northumbrian origin, but the likeness between the two images is thought-provoking. The comparison of the pages could be made in another way, to see them as visual tools of early medieval learning and interpreting.

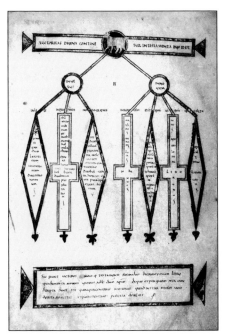

Fig 27.1. *Codex Amiatinus (Florence, Biblioteca Medicea-Laurenziana Amiatinus 1)*, fol 6. Books of the Bible according to Jerome. (By permission of the Ministero per i Beni Culturali e Ambientali)

Fig 27.2. *Codex Amiatinus*, fol 7. Books of the Bible according to Hilary. (By permission of the Ministero per i Beni Culturali e Ambientali)

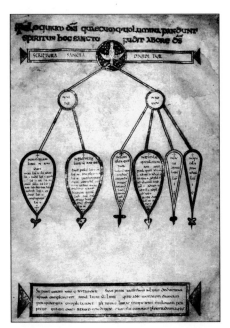

Fig 27.3. *Codex Amiatinus*, fol 8. Books of the Bible according to Augustine. (By permission of the Ministero per i Beni Culturali e Ambientali)

Fig 27.4. *Book of Kells (Dublin, Trinity College Library, MS 58)*, fol 114r. Arrest or Passion of Christ. (By permission of The Board of Trinity College Dublin)

Alexander (1978, 34) has pointed out that the *Amiatinus* diagrams are rare and important early examples of teaching schemata. In modern scholarship, however, they are usually discussed in terms of their believed source in Cassiodorus's *Codex Grandior*, the one-volume (pandect) *Vetus Latina* (or pre-Vulgate) copy of the Bible kept at his monastery in South Italy, the Vivarium. The three diagrams in the *Codex Amiatinus* are thought to have been copied from, or at least based upon, the lists or diagrams of the divisions which Cassiodorus mentions, in his *Institutiones*, as having been inserted into the pandect (Mynors 1937, 36–40, I.12–14). To what degree the diagrams in the *Codex Amiatinus* represent copies or creative emulations of those in Cassiodorus's Bible is a question beyond the scope of this chapter (see Marsden 1995a, 115–23; Corsano 1987, 5, 22–34; Michelli below). That the monks of Wearmouth-Jarrow chose to present the lists as they did is indicative of their particular monastic environment. Parkes (1982, 16–22) has pointed out its uniqueness, evident in its manuscripts' recognizability and consistency, a feature atypical of what little is known of Insular centres in general. Their distinct scribal and artistic qualities, he explains, were produced within a scrupulously maintained educational and religious discipline which went hand in hand with a consciously specialized monastic culture.

The diagrams were rooted in a diligent cultivation of Italianate monasticism. Its meticulous discipline and organization generated distinctive visual forms linking the monastery to the authority of Rome (Parkes 1982, 16–22). The diagrams' precision and rigorous order, as well as their textual subject, resemble stylistic qualities and references to books and texts seen in other manuscript art associated with Wearmouth-Jarrow. The diagrammatic layout of the frontispiece to the uncial gospel fragments bound into the *Utrecht Psalter* (*Utrecht, Universeteitsbibl MS 32*, fol 101v; Fig 27.5; Bruce-Mitford 1967, 16) provides a good example. It resembles the *Amiatinus* diagrams in its abstract, geometric shapes, minimal decoration, and solemn clarity and presents further likeness in that it, too, bears a symbolically meaningful, diagrammatic layout to list books of scripture. The names of the gospels are placed within a circle of arcs, indicating the wholeness, perfection, and harmony of their divine truth, a truth incited by the first words of the inscription: 'incipit in nomine d[omi]ni n[ostr]i ih[es]u xp[ist]i evangelia numero IIII'. A Greek letter resides in each small arc of the circumference decoration, together spelling out a prayer for the Virgin's intercession in aid of the scribe (Lowe 1952, 237). The perfection and truth expressed by the circular diagrammatic list of gospels becomes almost amuletic, its powers drawn upon in an erudite verbal and visual sidelight by its learned creator. It becomes much more than a list of titles. The *Codex Amiatinus* diagrams gain elevated significance in similar ways. But to return to the original point, the important thing here is not the issue of copy or free interpretation but that, either way, the diagrams and frontispiece, with their rigor and precise textual erudition, are cooperative with the romanizing monastic discipline cultivated at Wearmouth-Jarrow. They functioned within a consciously specialized environment of learning.

In cip
IN NOMINE ÐNI
NI IĦU XPI EUANGE
LIA NUMERO IIII
SEC MATTHEUM
SEC MARCUM
SEC LUCAN
SEC IOHANNEM

Fig 27.5. *Utrecht, Universeteitsbibl MS 32* (gospels bound with the *Utrecht Psalter*), fol 101v. Frontispiece. (By permission of Universiteit Utrecht, Universiteitsbibliothek)

Diagrams aid understanding and learning, and on one level that must have been the purpose of those in the *Codex Amiatinus*. Cassiodorus explained in the *Institutiones* that, despite their differing arrangements, the three divisions of the Bible according to Jerome, Hilary, and Augustine actually complement rather than contradict each other. Study of the divisions, he said, will reveal how they make each other mutually intelligible (Mynors 1937, 36–40, I.12–14; Corsano 1987, 23; Henderson, G 1993, 84). Implicit in this statement, however, is the assertion of universal scriptural truth and of the genuine spiritual wisdom of the fathers in explaining it. There is no contradiction, the diagrams tell their audience: truth is revealed through different means. This idea is expressed in the depictions of the three persons of the Trinity, one in each of the discs at the top of each diagram. Each portrait subsumes the diagram below within a statement of the derivation of all scripture and orthodox understanding from divine authority. Lists and categories are put in play on a higher field of significance.

An additional diagram in the *Codex Amiatinus*, listing the books of the Pentateuch (fol 7v), refers to the idea of the diverse revelation of truth. The page shows a large circle, painted purple on an orange ground, within which five smaller circles are arranged in a cross, each bearing an encapsulation of passages from Jerome's letter to Paulinus on the absolute essence of spiritual truth in scripture (Quentin 1926, 21–2, *Ep* 53, I.25). The community at Wearmouth-Jarrow knew of the letter and may have known Cassiodorus's praise of its expression of the unity of Old and New Testament in his *Institutiones* (Mynors 1937, 59–60, 21.2). The page may have been copied from one in the *Codex Grandior*, or the monks of Wearmouth-Jarrow, immersed in high-powered biblical studies, may have compiled it from patristic texts on scriptural divisions and harmony. Its purpose, however, was a statement of the spiritual unity underlying the verbal diversity of scripture as the basis and objective of Christian learning, a lesson furthermore couched in the discourse on sacred texts handed down from Jerome, possibly via the Roman Cassiodorus.

How can the diagrams with their strict order and narrow textual basis be compared with the visually splendid, seemingly shifting and ambiguous images in the *Book of Kells*? Even though made for a time and place quite distinct from that of the *Codex Amiatinus*, pictures such as the Temptation of Christ (fol 202v, see Fox 1990, fol 202v; Henry 1974, 68) and the 'Arrest' (fol 114r; Fig 27.4) may be seen to present interpretative figures or, said in another way, diagrammatic shapes that are meant to reveal true understanding of scripture. In the illustrations, the 'diagrams' are large, clearly defined shapes, such as the X-shape of the body of Christ on folio 114r and the rectilinear shape of the Temple in Jerusalem joined to Christ's head and shoulders in the Temptation, both of which possess a semiosis of references to divine perfection and Christian salvation, as will be seen. Within these bold visual shapes, the artist(s) organized rich detail of small-scale shapes and patterns. In this way, the Temptation illustration and the picture on folio 114r resemble both antique mnemonic schemes used in medieval learning, such as Quintilian's house of rooms (Carruthers 1990, 107–8, 114–21; Farr 1997a, 74), and historiated letters, which install visual imagery within text, harmonizing and merging the functions of both – a recognized feature of Insular manuscript art (Alexander 1978, 10–13; Parkes 1991, 8–9; 1993, 24–5). Furthermore, both are internal within the gospel text, a feature distinguishing them from the other full-page images in the *Book of Kells* or any surviving early Latin gospel manuscript (Farr 1997a, 50 n 31; Alexander 1978, 73–4; Henry, 1974, 163; McGurk 1955, 106). Their intended integration with the text may be seen in the conjoining of text and illustration by the inscription of Matthew 26.30 (*et ymno dicto exierunt in montem oliveti*) in the arch over the scene on folio 114r, so that the picture is placed like a letter or punctuation in the text. Both pictures are placed at points of chapter divisions known from Old Latin and early Vulgate copies of the gospels and which are emphasized in Insular gospel manuscripts by extensive punctuation and enlarged, sometimes decorated, initial letters (de Bruyne 1914, 506, 513; McGurk 1955, 106–7; Farr 1997a, 50, 80–5, 117–31). The images act like enlarged decorated letters to articulate the division of following text from preceding, but also, by means of the richly multivalent significance of the figures of the X-shaped body of Christ and the square shape of the Temple joined with the head and shoulders of Christ, the two pictures refer to the text preceding and following them, functioning like punctuation marks to indicate relationships between sense units (Farr 1997a, 80–8, 119–33, 166–70; O'Reilly 1994, 351–97; Lewis 1980, 155–8). The pictures seem to merge into a complementary relationship of the didactic functions of interpretative figures or diagrammatic shapes with the textual articulation achieved by the graphic shapes of punctuation and decorated letters.

According to patristic and early medieval exegesis and grammatical studies, the shape of a letter represents the first level of its identity, and this shape (its *figura*) can be as meaningful as a Christian sign. For example, the *Tau* or *T* and *Chi* or X may be figures of Christ, his body, or the cross (Holtz 1981, 603, Donatus, *Ars Maior* II.2; Hertz 1855, 6–8, Priscian, *De littera* I.3, 7–8; Polara 1979, 8, 9, Virgilius Maro Grammaticus, *Epitomae* II. 121–7; Parkes 1991, 3, 16; Irvine 1994, 97–104; Law 1995, 68–9, 72). Letters can become signs of the cross, evoking its extensive and complex meaning, narrative and symbolic (Farr 1997a, 116–18, 132). A letter is a meaningful shape, a *figura*, comparable with the conceptual *figura* of exegesis. Bede uses the word to discuss the shape, form, and meaning of the Tabernacle and the Temple:

> In addition, the figure of each sanctuary can be generally distinguished thus: the structure of the Tabernacle is the time of the Synagogue, that is of the ancient people of God; but the structure of the Temple is the Church, that is the multitude of the elect which has come to faith after the Lord's incarnation (cf Holder 1994, 46).[1]

The two buildings merge as a single *figura* of the church revealing through the reader's deep contemplation their allegory of the church's temporal stages:

> But if we look more carefully into each one, the building of one as well as the other house describes mystically the status of the whole church of the present which, from the beginning of the creation of the world until the last elect who is to be born at the end of the world, does not ever cease to be built and, by means of the truth of figures, also marvellously depicts the glory of the future life which it now enjoys in part but after the end of this world it is going to be enjoyed in all of its members into eternity (cf Holder 1994, 46).[2]

In the *Book of Kells*, one sees the Temple transformed into an interpretative shape or figure, and the picture associates the building with the Tabernacle by depiction of the embroidered scarlet, blue, and purple curtains with loops at the top which God instructed Moses to make (Ex 2.61–6; Farr 1997a, 53–66). Moreover, depiction of the multivalent Temple as the body of Christ posits in the gospel text the figure of the Head and Body, a figure which the Donatist Tyconius, in his *Liber Regularum* (I), developed from biblical examples into a tool for Christological interpretation (Burkitt 1895, 1–8). Augustine cited Tyconius's rule of the Head and Body as a tool, when placed in the right hands, for orthodox interpretation of scripture (Robertson 1958, 104–17, III.30–7; *CCSL* 39, 1266, *Enarr in Ps* II.1; Farr 1997a, 68–75). Bede's interpretations of the Temple and Tabernacle bring to mind the diagram of the Tabernacle in the *Codex Amiatinus* (fols 2v–3), which is based on the descriptions in Exodus 26 and Numbers 2–3, as well as patristic exegeses which may associate it with the Temple, although like the diagram pages, it clearly differs conceptually from the depiction in the *Book of Kells* (Revel-Neher 1982; Kühnel 1987, 157–9).

The *Book of Kells*'s interpretative figures, however, present some commonalties with the *Codex Amiatinus*'s diagrams. In both, visual shapes participate in early medieval traditions of learning, known under the heading *grammatica*, which refers to all levels of literacy from reading and grammar through interpretation and communication of divine truth (Irvine 1994). Where the *Book of Kells* uses historiated figures as punctuation, the *Amiatinus* diagrams associate themselves with *grammatica* through use of graphic forms as decoration, such as the leaf-shaped *hederae* sprouting from panels containing the lists. *Hederae* are distinctively antique punctuation marks seen in the luxurious Mediterranean uncial books imitated at Wearmouth-Jarrow (Parkes 1982, 12, 16–17; 1993, 180–1). In both manuscripts, one sees the use of shapes as meaningful signs, *figurae*, which carry within themselves complex, multivalent significance for the viewer to contemplate and learn from. The *Codex Amiatinus* diagrams use cross shapes as well as circles and four-sided shapes with their significance of cosmic perfection and universality. In the diagram of lists according to Hilary (Fig 27.2), *hederae* grow from cross-shaped panels, associating them with the Eucharist and salvation, references made also by folio 114r, the *Book of Kells* (Farr 1997a, 104–31, 157)

Nevertheless, shapes and multivalent images in the two manuscripts present contrasts in their function and relationship to text. The images in the *Book of Kells* function within textual structure, in narrative texts, although they are not primarily narrative (Farr 1997a). The *Codex Amiatinus* frontispieces associate themselves with high-status Mediterranean literacy by incorporating graphic signs and shapes such as *hederae* and *tabulae ansatae*, the rectangular panels with triangular 'handles' used in official Roman presentations of public inscriptions. The script, also, is the revered uncial which Wearmouth-Jarrow scribes skilfully imitated (Parkes 1982, 5, 20–2). The *Codex Amiatinus* diagrams reproduce

Roman forms to affirm the particular Christian learnedness of the Wearmouth-Jarrow community and the attendant grace and authority of that learning.

That they probably were not seen mainly as functioning diagrams to guide the reader in Bible study may be supported by evidence of Bede's attitude toward diagrams. He seems to have considered them distracting or misleading. Although Bede wrote several didactic texts, no evidence exists that he provided any diagrams to aid the learner. The lack of diagrams in Bede's *De Natura Rerum* is especially conspicuous compared with contemporaneous uses of them. Isidore of Seville seems to have considered diagrams (*rotae* or *figurae*) essential to his *De Natura Rerum*. Evidence of other manuscripts associated with Insular production suggests that Anglo-Saxon and Irish scholars created figures and diagrams in the tradition of Isidore, despite Bede's disapproval of the pictures. When later, post-Conquest scribes copied Bede's text, they inserted diagrams in the manuscripts, often copying them from Isidore, because the pictures were accepted as aids for understanding a difficult text. Bede worked, however, within a specialized intellectual context (*CCSL* 123A, 186). Although he was a student of Irish teachers, one of his reasons for writing didactic texts was his dissatisfaction with theirs, besides his own commitment to Gregorian traditions (*CCSL* 123A, viii). Works like the *computus* texts of anonymous Irish authors were usually compilations of textual excerpts, tables, diagrams, calendars, and formulae assembled to respond to the particular needs of an individual monastic teacher. Very often they contained errors (*CCSL* 123A, xii–xiv, 174). An error in a text may be detectable, but something misplaced in a diagram or left out usually would not be obvious to the student user. Skill or knowledge, Bede believed, should reside within the scholar, and this belief is evident in his interpretation of natural phenomena in a way that depends on highly abstract numeric and computational knowledge (see also Stevens 1985).

The multivalency of the *Book of Kells figurae* may overlap with the diagrams' references to multivalent visual forms and the revelation the figures provide, such as the Tabernacle diagram's associations with the Temple and the cross-shaped panels, but the narrative textual references are missing from the *Amiatinus* pages. They do not refer to events and are not inserted into the text of the manuscript. The *Amiatinus* diagrams produce meaning by association rather than direct multivalent, interpretative depiction of events. In contrast, the illustrations in the *Book of Kells* are like maps with stories in them, like the later medieval maps with images of the Fall and Passion. Moreover, the images in the two manuscripts stand in different relationships to reading. The *Kells figurae* are set within a specific reading context. The *Codex Amiatinus* diagrams function with a much higher degree of autonomy. They are static in the sense that they are about texts and attitudes to texts rather than about interpretation of texts. More absolute and pure, they expand meaning by association with Roman learning and the spiritual authority of that learning. Such authority with its prestige, resources, and claim to access to divine wisdom could in turn make the community autonomous from its context in both spiritual and material ways, thus enhancing its own control and status (Parkes 1982, 21–2). Where the *Book of Kells* illustrations represent interpretative images for specific contexts and recognize more fully the multivalency of interpretation – with the attendant need to control interpretation – the *Codex Amiatinus* diagrams represent overriding statements of authority through learning and exclusive access to truth. Thus, they create an expression of the Wearmouth-Jarrow community's central place in the Christianity of Northumbria.

ACKNOWLEDGEMENTS

I wish to thank the following institutions for providing photographs and for granting permission to publish them: The Board of Trinity College Dublin (Fig 27.4); Biblioteca Medicea-Laurenziana, Florence, by permission of the Ministero per i Beni Culturali e Ambientali (Figs 27.1, 2, 3); Universiteitsbibl Utrecht (Fig 27.5). I also thank Dr Brian Martine for an English translation of the Greek inscription, Dr Faith Wallis for her discussion of graphic glosses, and Dr A.J. Hawkes for her assistance.

NOTES

1. '*Item figura utriusque sanctuarii potest ita generaliter distingui. Opus tabernaculi tempus sinagogae, hoc est antiquae Dei plebis, opus vero templi ecclesiam, id est illam electorum multitudinem quae post incarnationem dominicam ad fidem.*' (*CCSL* 119A, 42–3, *De Tabernaculo* II.i)
2. '*Verum si diligentius singula inspiciamus, utriusque domus aedificatio totius ecclesiae praesentis statum mystice describit quae ab initio mundanae conditionis usque ad ultimum qui in fine saeculi nasciturus est electum semper aedificari non desinit et futurae quoque gloriam vitae qua nunc ex parte fruitur sed post huius terminum saeculi in omnibus suis membris in aeternum fruitura est mirabili figurarum veritate depingit.*' (*CCSL* 119A, 43, *De Tabernaculo* II.i)

CHAPTER 28

WHAT'S IN THE CUPBOARD? EZRA AND MATTHEW RECONSIDERED

Perette Michelli

The relationship between the *Lindisfarne Gospels* and the *Codex Amiatinus* has been presented with such detail and authority that challenge now seems unlikely. It has been argued convincingly that the *Codex Amiatinus* reproduces the concept of a 6th-century Bible pandect (the *Codex Grandior*) in Cassiodorus's library at Vivarium, and that its text is largely derived from a nine-volume 'Vulgate' (the *Novem Codices*) also from Vivarium. Less convincingly, it has been argued that the gospel volume was rejected at Wearmouth-Jarrow in favour of a 6th-century Neapolitan gospel book, which was also used for the *Lindisfarne Gospels* (Brown in Kendrick et al. 1960, 50). The situation is complicated by the suggestion that the *Amiatinus* Ezra is a direct copy of a Vivarium miniature that may have been a portrait of Cassiodorus himself (Bruce-Mitford 1960, 148; Courcelle, letter reported by Bruce-Mitford, op. cit., 148; Bruce-Mitford 1969, 14). This leads inevitably to the further inference that the *Lindisfarne* Matthew is an adaptation of the *Amiatinus* or Vivarium image, and that the remaining *Lindisfarne* Evangelists are culled from another source, different from the text (Bruce-Mitford 1960, 154–5, 156). So established are these views that doubts concerning them had to remain until recent work on Insular attitudes to art and authorship (Michelli 1996) brought new considerations to bear on the issue.

In the light of these studies it is now possible to suggest that the *Amiatinus* Ezra (Fig 28.1) is an Insular adaptation of a pure Ezra portrait invented by Cassiodorus, who derived it from a Greek Evangelist type, and that it makes a specific claim that all the *Novem Codices* were held at Wearmouth-Jarrow. It also seems likely that all the *Lindisfarne* Evangelists are derived from a single source, almost certainly the same as the text of the book itself, and that this was not a Neapolitan book but the gospel volume of the *Novem Codices*, a work fully illustrated with Evangelist portraits and canon tables. Thus the *Amiatinus* Ezra and the *Lindisfarne* Matthew derived from independent models, both of which were Cassiodoran. Finally, it becomes apparent that the *Novem Codices* did not contain the Vulgate text, but a hybrid conflated by Cassiodorus and that this version has accidentally usurped the Vulgate identification in the minds of modern scholars.[1]

The development of scholarly debate on this topic is complex. It has been set out with admirable clarity by Neuman de Vegvar (1987, 143–9), and it would be superfluous to reiterate it here. Suffice it to say that it has two main origins: an iconographical idea by Courcelle and Bruce-Mitford which results in discrediting the *Novem Codices* gospel illustrations, and a textual idea by Julian Brown which results in discrediting the *Novem Codices* gospel text.

Courcelle was the first to suggest that the *Amiatinus* Ezra accurately reflects the frontispiece to the first volume of the *Novem Codices*, and he saw that original image as a conflation of Cassiodorus and Ezra (Courcelle 1949; 1969, 379). Bruce-Mitford preferred to see the original image as an actual portrait of Cassiodorus, and believed that it had acquired its Ezra veneer in Northumbria (in Kendrick et al. 1960, 146–8). In consequence, he had to see the Vivarium version as an original, creative work, and therefore the *Lindisfarne* Matthew, which looks so similar, was necessarily derived from it and could not reflect a pre-existing Evangelist tradition. He was thus forced to argue that while the other three *Lindisfarne* Evangelists were, in fact, based on the *Novem Codices* gospel volume, the Matthew image was not. As he put it, 'we know . . . that this Matthew figure . . . was certainly derived from a source different from the rest of the portrait set, and not even an Evangelist' (op. cit. 142).

To challenge this, we must examine the early Insular definition of art and its purpose. The Insular concept of art embraced all kinds of creation, whether visual, literary, mathematical, or scholarly. It is set out fully in the 11th-century preface to the *Martyrology of Oengus*, which states that 'four things are required by every work of art, to wit a Place, and a Time, an Author and a Cause of invention' (Stokes 1905, 3). The writer then explains that these establish the value, origin and date of the work – in other words, its credentials. The concept seems to be very old. It is found in an Irish letter, written by Cuimíne c 632 concerning the Easter calculation at Iona (Walsh & Ó Cróinín 1988). To support his preferred calculation, Cuimíne cited ten alternatives, together with their authors (op. cit. 84–6, lines 208–20). He did not mention where and when they were produced because this information was either included in their prefaces or could be deduced from the identities of their authors (op. cit. 29–47). Most only had a single author but the ninth, dictated to Pacomius by an angel, had two; and the tenth, 'the cycle of the 318 bishops', had 318 (op. cit. 44–6)! This huge number was the authority Cuimíne claimed against the computation used at Iona, which he denigrated as 'one whose author, place and time we are uncertain of' (op. cit. 86–7, line 221).

This approach to authorship and credentials seems to have been international. There are clear indications of it in Carolingian circles but the present discussion can be illustrated with Cassiodorus. His *Institutiones* sets out a study programme, and every work he cites is qualified with information about the identity, reliability and skill of its author and translator. When he recommends a worthy anonymous commentary on Job, he raises its potential credibility by suggesting, on stylistic grounds, that its author might be Hilary of Poitiers (Mynors 1937, 26, 6.3). He also says that ideally his monks should consult the Greek Fathers because they are well established, although he acknowledges that most will be limited to Latin translations and the Roman authorities which were newer and less satisfying (op. cit. 6, *Pref 5*).

In Insular circles, this attitude seems to have applied to Cassiodorus himself. Courcelle (1969, 82) notes that although the *Codex Amiatinus* reproduces almost everything we know of the *Codex Grandior* and the *Novem Codices*, Cassiodorus's own material (some chapter summaries he wrote to fill gaps in his exemplar) was 'consistently omitted'. Laistner (1966, 95–7, 102) also notes that apart from his commentary on the Psalms, Cassiodorus's own works were never popular, but his compilations, like *Institutiones* volume II, and his editions of important works were well known and often copied. Thus it seems that Cassiodorus's main credibility lay in the editing and transmission of authenticated texts, rather than in his new scholarship. This inference, that authorship, origins and credentials were all-important, must be of crucial relevance to the claims made by the *Codex Amiatinus* and the *Lindisfarne Gospels*.

These findings undermine current theories about the Ezra portrait (Fig 28.1). Bruce-Mitford wanted to see the original image as a portrait of Cassiodorus himself (in Kendrick et al. 1960, 146–8). His evidence was the nine-volume Bible in the cupboard which seems to correspond with our understanding of the *Novem Codices*. Thus, the image appears to be a portrait of the author of the *Novem Codices*. But there is a significant problem with this. Neither Ezra nor Cassiodorus was the author of the *Novem Codices* in any terms which would have been accepted at Vivarium.

In *Institutiones* Cassiodorus states that he was the author of several works (for example, his commentary on the Psalms, and the diagrams, commentary material, and tabernacle image in the *Codex Grandior*). But although he claims directly to have written out the *Novem Codices* and the *Codex minutiore manu conscribendum* himself, and implies that he also transcribed the *Codex Grandior* (Mynors 1937, 5, 7–9, 22–3, 37, *Pref* 4, 8, 9, *Inst* 5.22, 12.3), he never suggests that he was their author. In fact, he maintains that the scribe's prime duty is to transmit texts honestly and accurately, and not to interfere with them in any way (Hodgkin 1886, 512–13, XII, *Letter 21*; cf Mynors 1937, 41–51, 75–8, *Inst* 15, 30). So

Fig 28.1. The 'Ezra Portrait', *Codex Amiatinus*
(*Florence, Biblioteca Medicea-Laurenziana
Amiatinus 1*), fol Vr. (By permission of the
Ministero per i Beni Culturali e Ambientali)

Cassiodorus could hardly have set himself up as the 'author' of a Bible, and thus it is unlikely that the image was ever a pure portrait of him.

Nevertheless, Cassiodorus could be connected with the image in another way. His classical education, his desire to create a specifically Christian version of that education, his concern for establishing the authenticity and quality of his texts, and his knowledge of, interest in and practice of art, might well stimulate or endorse an interest in the classical author portrait, as known, for example, in the *Vienna Dioscurides* (dated 512–18). We know that he took a lively interest in the visual arts. Of his 468 letters, eleven concern public figures' responsibilities towards art. His consistent theme is that art must be maintained and restored as a valuable and enjoyable visual amenity for the public good, and that the production and maintenance of art is both a mark of respect and a labour of love. His letters include detailed descriptions of public statues, marble *spolia*, and *opus sectile* work, and in one case he shows a respectable knowledge of the history of art too (Hodgkin 1886, 423, X. 8). We also know that he was a resourceful and enterprising person, who loved to clarify his work with diagrams and illustrations. His *Institutiones*, for example, were evidently informatively illustrated (Milkau 1928, 38–44), and he states that he invented and executed (*aptavi*) diagrams of the organization of the Bible, and an image of Solomon's tabernacle in the desert (Mynors 1937, 22–3, 5.2). If he invented all these, it is quite possible that he could have invented the Ezra portrait too. Indeed, he may actually suggest this himself: when he gives the credentials of his tabernacle image (the person who explained its appearance to him), Cassiodorus adds that he learned about priestly garb from the same man (ibid.). If this is not a direct acknowledgement of the authorship and credentials of the Ezra image, it is something akin.

It would not be difficult for Cassiodorus to invent this image. It is clearly derived from the same Greek Evangelist type which was used for the *Lindisfarne* Matthew, and this may suggest that there was no established archetype for Ezra. Profiled Evangelists are known to have existed by Cassiodorus's time. The profiled Matthew in the choir of S Vitale, Ravenna, is one example, although at c 540–7 it was produced a little after Cassiodorus left that city. On the other hand, the profiled Mark of the 6th-century *Rossano Gospels* is surely comparable with what Cassiodorus could have seen during his stay in Constantinople before he founded Vivarium and produced his great Bibles. Thus Cassiodorus's invention of this portrait is well within the bounds of possibility. All he had to do was borrow the type and superimpose his knowledge of priestly garb.

He would have needed the portrait either for the Octateuch volume of his *Novem Codices* or for the Old Testament of his *Codex Grandior*. Each contained the work of several authors as well as anonymous texts, so any portrait set would necessarily have been oversupplied yet incomplete. Thus the choice of Ezra was enterprising. The story appears in 4 Ezra, which is not part of the Vulgate and is not included in the *Codex Amiatinus* or in the Old Testament as we have it today. But it was part of the Septuagint and was translated by Jerome for his Hexaplaric version, and Marsden (1995b, 117) has shown that this was the text used for the *Codex Grandior*.

4 Ezra tells that many books had been destroyed but is ambiguous about what those books were: 14.21 refers to them as the books of the Law (Moses's Pentateuch), while 4.23 refers to the books of the Torah (the whole of Scripture). At Ezra's own request, the Lord enabled him to dictate the entire series to five scribes in the wilderness, by giving him a fiery drink which inspired him (Stone 1990, 440–2, 14.37–49). This is somewhat different from the more famous version of the story, that Ezra wrote out the books from memory. However, that version seems to have originated with later commentators such as Isidore of Seville (Marsden 1995b, 120 n 57). Ezra gave twenty-four books back to the people, which implies that he replaced the whole of scripture: a Talmudic gloss of c 500 lists twenty-four canonical books of the Torah (Harley, 1979, 46; cf Mynors 1937, 37, 12.2). Cassiodorus informs us that by counting the books in groups, Jerome is able to produce twenty-two canonical books of the Old Testament, which matches the number of letters in the Hebrew alphabet. So Ezra works quite well as an honorary author for the whole Old Testament, but he cannot be made to fit an Octateuch. It is likely, then, that the portrait originally

appeared at the beginning of the Hexaplaric *Codex Grandior* which would also
have contained the story to which it referred.

This has further implications, however: if the picture introduced the text of the
Codex Grandior, it must also be argued that the cupboard did not originally
contain the *Novem Codices*. To be true to the story, it should have contained
twenty-four books, which seems rather full. However, the cupboard may not have
appeared in the original picture at all. 4 Ezra is explicit that the dictation to five
scribes took place in the wilderness and we could expect the original picture to
have shown at least the scribes, if not also the wilderness. The circular
arrangement of the Seven Physicians' pages that introduce the *Vienna Dioscurides*
suggest that such an iconography might have made a satisfactory complement to
the Majesty page, which occasionally introduces the New Testament of later
Bibles (including the *Codex Amiatinus*).

Such speculation aside, the Ezra image today shows him in a study with,
apparently, Cassiodorus's *Novem Codices* in a cupboard behind him. The picture
is set at the front of a Bible which does not contain the necessary story and this
may be the reason for the explanatory caption above the picture. Not only would
such a caption have been unnecessary in Cassiodorus's original text, but there are
later indications which associate it with Northumbria rather than Vivarium. It is
echoed by Bede in his commentary on Ezra, and it also appears in a poem
attributed to Alcuin (Marsden 1995a, 3 and n 2). The caption reads: *Codibus
sacris hostili clade perustis, Esdra dõ fervens hoc reparavit opus* (the sacred
books having been destroyed by the enemies' flames, Ezra on fire with the Lord
repaired this need). This not only identifies the portrait, but defines the terms
of the story by its generalized reference to 'sacred books' rather than the
more limited 'books of the Law', by which the couplet has been inaccurately
rendered (Bruce-Mitford 1969, 11). Thus the caption also justifies the use of the
portrait as a frontispiece to the Old Testament. However, the famous idea that the
couplet makes an analogy between Ezra and Cassiodorus cannot be supported
(op. cit., 14). *Institutiones* reveals an educator who talked about collecting the
best versions of the most important texts, and making his monks read them so
that they would be able to apply the classical exegetical technique to the
scriptures and thus gain a proper understanding of them (Mynors 1937, 4, 6,
Pref 2, 6). As we have seen, he never suggests that he is the 'author' of any of
these texts, nor that they were in any danger of being lost. There is no connection
between him and Ezra.

So why has the picture been so thoroughly adapted? To address this question,
we must first consider what we know of the *Novem Codices*. All our information
about this Bible comes from Cassiodorus's *Institutiones*. This account is
problematic because Cassiodorus's main purpose is to catalogue and comment on
his library holdings at Vivarium with a view to directing his 'simple' monks'
reading after his death. As he writes, thoughts apparently occur to him about his
own editorial work and these are incorporated abruptly into the text without

introduction or explanation, and sometimes without an obvious end-point. The first nine chapters of *Institutiones* concern sections of the Bible and recommended commentaries. Since Cassiodorus refers to these as '*codices*', it is not always clear whether he is speaking metaphorically about biblical sections, or descriptively about a nine-volume Bible. However, he does seem to be speaking about the physical Bible when he says 'with the Lord's help we have assembled sacred letters in nine *codices* . . .' (Mynors 1937, 36, 11.3). He seems to refer to the same nine codices when he says:

> . . . insofar as my age has allowed, I have gone over all nine *codices* of divine authority, reading [emending] them carefully, after a comparison of ancient *codices* and previous reading on the part of friends (op. cit. 7–8, *Pref* 8).

Immediately afterwards, he comments that:

> We too, impressed by the authority of this very great man [Jerome], have decided that this system [layout *per cola et commata*] ought to be followed (op. cit. 8, *Pref* 9).

His final comment is rather ambiguous:

> In the second book of his work *On Christian Learning* the blessed Augustine, in accordance with the afore-mentioned nine *codices*, which the Holy Church approves, describes the Scriptures as being contained in seventy-one books (op. cit. 39, 13.2).

This last has been taken to indicate that Cassiodorus arranged the *Novem Codices* according to the Augustinian order (Marsden 1995b, 133), but seems more likely to refer to the number of canonical books he actually included in the *Novem Codices*. Thus Cassiodorus seems to be saying that he produced a Bible in nine volumes, checked and emended it in the approved manner, laid it out according to Jerome's system of breaking the lines to indicate natural pauses in the readings, and included the seventy-one books authorized by Augustine.

From this evidence, most scholars have inferred that the layout conclusively indicates that Cassiodorus used the Vulgate for the *Novem Codices* (Marsden 1995b, 136, n 125). Marsden argues persuasively, however, that Cassiodorus seems rather to be explaining why he used Jerome's layout for a text with which it is not normally associated – that the text of the *Novem Codices* was not the Vulgate. Thus, we do not know what text was used in the *Novem Codices*, because Cassiodorus's information is extraordinarily ambiguous. Cassiodorus arranged his whole reading programme and the text of *Institutiones* around the *Novem Codices*, and yet his references to them are consistently obscure. Every other text he mentions is clearly defined by reference to its authorship, translation, strengths and weaknesses. Thus, the mystery surrounding the *Novem Codices* seems to have been created deliberately. Understanding of why Cassiodorus found it necessary to do this throws light on his clues about the identity of the text.

Cassiodorus states his position with regard to textual authority and scholarship very clearly. It has already been shown that he directly claimed authorship of a commentary on the Psalms, and the diagrams, commentary material and tabernacle image in the *Codex Grandior*, but only claimed to have transcribed the rest of the *Codex Grandior* and the *Codex minutiore manu conscribendum*, which contained Jerome's Hexaplaric and Hebraic versions respectively (Marsden 1995b, 116–17, 132). Thus, Cassiodorus discriminated carefully between authorship and scribal transmission. With regard to authority, he is equally clear. In *Institutiones* he repeatedly recommends his monks to consult the most well-established and orthodox sources first, and only to turn to more recent sources if the older ones were insufficient (Mynors 1937, 5–6, 34–5, *Pref* 4, *Inst* 10.1–5). He particularly deplores the kind of scholarship which delights in disproving established canons: 'There are, indeed, some who think it a fine thing to know some fact which is at variance with the ancients and to find something new that they may thereby seem clever'. (op. cit. 11.1).

This commitment to orthodoxy over evidence leads Cassiodorus to necessary compromises. For example, where his three authorities on the organization of the Bible conflict, he decides that they are not contradictory but complementary (op. cit. 40, 14.2), and he reproduces them all in the *Institutiones* and in the *Codex Grandior* (Fig 28.2). This takes a more interesting twist with respect to the text of *Institutiones* itself. It is well known that the first nine chapters concern divisions of the Bible text. The titles fall more or less into the order Cassiodorus describes for Jerome, but the text follows another order because in Chapters 3–5 the text and titles do not coincide. Thus, Chapter 3 is titled 'Prophetarum', but the text concerns the Psalter; Chapter 4 is 'Psalteri', but the text concerns the books of Solomon; and Chapter 5 is 'Salomonis', where the text is about the Prophets. The text therefore follows Hilary's order in contrast to the titles and Cassiodorus has successfully represented two possible orders without having to choose between them. With regard to the titles of the *Novem Codices* themselves, it can be seen that unless they had volume numbers clearly displayed on their covers, they could be permuted to reflect either Augustine's order or Hilary's order and, again, no choice has to be made.

But organization is not the only problem with Biblical texts. The various authoritative translations also conflict periodically. Cassiodorus's response to this is an unusually long chapter (15) with detailed instructions for dealing with the problem. His main thrust is to avoid interference wherever possible and, where not, to consult and compare Jerome's Hexaplaric and Vulgate texts, and especially the Greek text which was the most authoritative of all (op. cit. 47–8, 15.11). In fact, Cassiodorus made these texts easily accessible,

COMPARISON OF TITLES AND ORGANIZATION							
Institutiones Chapter Titles	St Jerome	Institutiones Text Order	Codex Amiatinus	Septuagint, Hilary	St Augustine	Books in Cupboard	Institutiones Abbreviations
Octateuchus	Octateuch	Octateuch	Octateuch	Octateuch	('Historia') Octateuch	OCT LIB LEG	OCT
Regum	Kings	Kings Chronicles (Paralipomenon)	Kings Chronicles	Kings Chronicles	Kings Chronicles	REG PAR L VI	REG
Prophetarum	Prophets Job (from Wri)	Psalms	Psalms	Psalms	Writings	HIST LIB VIII	PSL
Psalterii	Psalms	Solomon	Solomon	Solomon	('Prophetarum') Psalms	PSAL LIB I	SAL
Salomonis	Solomon	Prophets	Prophets	Prophets	Solomon	SAL LIB V	PROP
Agiographorum	Chronicles Writings	Writings	Writings	Writings	Prophets	PROPH L XVI	AGI
Evangelia	Gospels	Gospels	Gospels	Gospels	Gospels	EVANG L IIII	EV
Epistuli Apostolorum	Epistles	Epistles	Acts Epistles	Acts Epistles	Epistles	EPIST AP XXI	AP
Acta Apostolorum et Apocalypsi	Acts and Apocalypse	Acts and Apocalypse	Apocalypse	Apocalypse	Acts and Apocalypse	ACT AP APOC IS	AAA

Fig 28.2. Textual organizations as presented by Cassiodorus and the *Codex Amiatinus*.

each in a distinctive pandect: the Greek pandect in the eighth bookcase, the Hexaplaric *Codex Grandior*, and the Vulgate *Codex minutiore manu conscribendum* (op. cit. 22–3, 37, 40–1, 47–8, 5.2, 12.3, 14.2, 14.4, 15.11). As Marsden (1995b, 137) has indicated, Cassiodorus showed a high regard for all these translations, but, as is well known, their texts do not match. It may be suggested, therefore, that the fourth great Bible at Vivarium was a new Latin edition in which Cassiodorus sought to reconcile all these versions, using the methods outlined in his Chapter 15. He may be referring to this project when he says:

> And so it appears that the Divine Scriptures of the Old and the New Testament from the very beginning to the end have been expounded in the Greek language . . . But with the Lord's aid we follow rather after Latin writers, that, since we are writing for Italians, we may most fitly seem to have pointed out Roman interpreters as well. For more gladly is that narration undertaken by every man which is told in the language of his fathers (Mynors 1937, 5–6, *Pref* 4)

and again:

> I have spent the greatest and most zealous toil upon the Psalter and the
> Prophets and the Epistles of the Apostles . . . I have worked hard not to lack
> melodious eloquence and not to mutilate the holy books with rash
> presumption (op. cit., 7–8, *Pref* 8).

Thus, it may be that *Institutiones* was conceived in concert with the *Novem
Codices*, as a means of propagating an all-embracing grasp of the Scriptures in
the clearest possible manner consonant with orthodoxy. Cassiodorus's admiration
for long-established orthodoxy, and his horror of religious or scholarly heresy,
could have made it difficult or undesirable for him to outline this project
explicitly. Instead, by demonstrating all the ways his new edition harmonized
with existing translations and commentaries, he could present it as an 'authorized
version' backed by the highest authorities.

The result is that, despite the apparent clarity of Cassiodorus's account in
Institutiones, there is no specific description of the *Novem Codices* from which
the artist of the *Codex Amiatinus* could have reconstructed them. Indeed, if he
was 'reconstructing' them, he made some surprising decisions. For example,
rather than duplicating the chapter titles in *Institutiones*, the artist substituted
Augustine's umbrella title '*Historia*' for the otherwise universal group title
'*Agiographorum*' (Fig 28.2). Likewise, the abbreviations for these titles do not
match those recommended by Cassiodorus (Corsano 1987, 15–16; Henderson, G
1993, 82; cf Mynors 1937, 67, 26.1–2). So this image of the *Novem Codices* does
not seem to be based on Cassiodorus's clues. The conclusion is hard to avoid: that
the books in the cupboard are likely to have been done 'from life', and the
Novem Codices would therefore appear to have been at Wearmouth-Jarrow
(cf Marsden 1995a, 12).

It is worth noting in this respect that the *Amiatinus* text could be seen as an
'authorised version' rather than a Vulgate. Marsden (1995b, 183) has discussed
its content and sources in detail and concludes that since it is the earliest
surviving exemplar of the 'Vulgate', it has become the best one by default.
Presumably it follows that, if its text is not a pure Vulgate after all, it would be
difficult to establish this. But there are indications that this may actually be the
case. Scholars have noted the conflict between the prologue of the *Codex
Amiatinus*, which states that it contains seventy canonical books (as did the
Codex Grandior), and the list of contents which states accurately that it contains
seventy-one: the same number as the *Novem Codices*. Moreover, Marsden
(op. cit. 140–83) notes that the *Amiatinus* text tends to be 'contaminated' with
Roman and Hexaplaric sources, and where older Vulgate texts survive, they are
generally considered more accurate than the *Codex Amiatinus*. Given
Cassiodorus's approach to emendation, ideas of accuracy and contamination are
probably misleading. The evidence seems rather to indicate that the text of the

Codex Amiatinus is not a 'contaminated Vulgate' but the carefully emended, 'authorized version' of Cassiodorus as preserved in the *Novem Codices*. This provides a possible motive for their incorporation into the Ezra miniature. If they were available for copying and were the source of the text in the *Codex Amiatinus*, there would be good reason to document this in some way, and it has been shown that it was one of the functions of art to preserve this kind of information. Thus, the *Amiatinus* Ezra portrait seems to be a historical document as explicit as any written source. Its location at the front of a pandect containing Cassiodoran diagrams, illustrations and prefatory material acknowledges the source of the concept and opening material, and the incorporation of the *Novem Codices* acknowledges the source of the text.

These findings have implications for the *Lindisfarne Gospels*, whose text and canon tables so closely match the *Codex Amiatinus* that it has long been accepted that it derives from the same exemplar. This exemplar is generally identified as having been either the *Novem Codices* (assumed to have been Vulgate) or the *Codex minutiore manu conscribendum*, which Cassiodorus clearly identified as a Vulgate, although it is not known whether this pandect ever reached Northumbria. Brown (in Kendrick et al., 1960, 56) has further argued that the gospel text was replaced in Northumbria by a superior Neapolitan exemplar, and this must now be examined.

The Neapolitan exemplar was suggested by the liturgical apparatus of the *Lindisfarne Gospels*. Brown (op. cit., 24–7, 34–6, 50) suggested that the *Novem Codices* would have no need for liturgical apparatus because they were a study Bible, so this Neapolitan text could not have belonged to them. Against this, it might be suggested that liturgical apparatus would not interfere with the use of a study Bible. Furthermore, there are indications that this liturgy could have referred directly to Vivarium. The identification of the liturgy rests on two references to one Neapolitan saint, Januarius, and the dedication of a basilica of St Stephen. Is this enough? St Stephen cannot be a unique name for a church, and one Neapolitan saint may not indicate a Neapolitan liturgy. In fact, Januarius is not limited to Naples: it seems that there was a church of St Januarius at Vivarium. The earliest surviving copy of *Institutiones* is in an 8th-century manuscript associated with Montecassino now in Bamberg (*Staatsbibliothek, Cod Patr 61*, fols 1–67v). It includes a colophon at the end of the text (on folio 67v) which seems to have been copied from the exemplar. This states: *codex archetypus ad cuius exemplaria sunt reliqui corrigendi* (the original book, in accordance with whose examples others are to be corrected). Like many later versions, this text is lavishly illustrated, and since the illustrations are consistent in all the versions, they are believed to derive from Cassiodorus's original. O'Donnell (1979, 22ii–xxiii) has drawn attention to the view of Vivarium on folio 29v (Fig 28.3). With its four-square approach, its colonnade placed sideways, and its generally informative nature, it is reminiscent of Cassiodorus's tabernacle image, so it could indeed be a copy of one of his illustrations. This

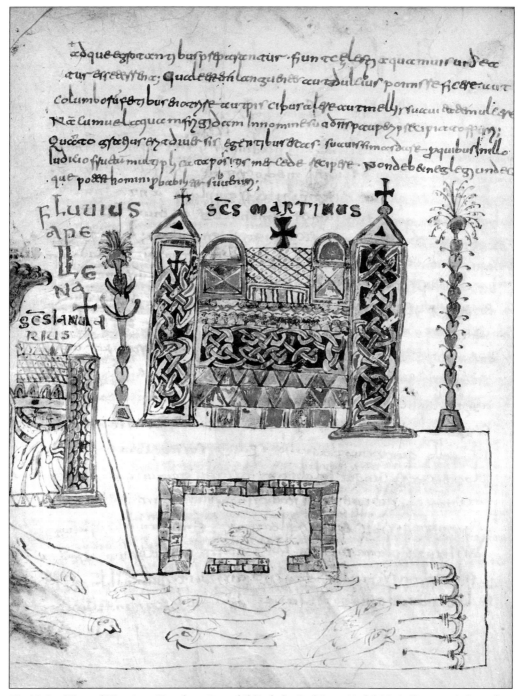

Fig 28.3.   View of Vivarium (*Bamberg Staatsbibliothek, Cod Patr 61*, fol 29v). (By permission of Staatsbibliothek, Bamberg)

makes the name of the church on the left particularly valuable since it is not recorded in the text. It is labelled 'St Januarius'. If Cassiodorus had such a church at Vivarium, it seems quite possible that that saint could be commemorated in one of his own gospel books. So the 'Neapolitan' exemplar may have had a Vivarian origin after all.

But was it the gospel volume of the *Novem Codices*? The evidence suggests that it was. Numerous indications have been cited to show that text of the *Codex Amiatinus* was taken from the *Novem Codices*, and it has been shown that the Ezra picture was considerably modified in order to document the same source. It is not tenable to suggest that only some volumes were used (*pace* Brown in Kendrick et al., 1960, 56). The gospel text in the *Codex Amiatinus* is claimed to be that of the *Novem Codices*, and since this text matches that of the *Lindisfarne Gospels*, we must say the same for that book too. The reference to Januarius is quite compatible with this, and may even have been included to record the same claim. The 'Neapolitan' liturgical material could indeed have been in the *Novem Codices* gospel, as Chapman originally suggested (op. cit. 52–3).

Giving an ambiguous 'clue' to the origin of a work in this way is a demonstrably Insular approach to authentication. While the Italian Cassiodorus gave the credentials of every work in writing, Insular artists and scribes tended to treat this kind of information as esoteric knowledge, scattering clues throughout the work rather than providing explicit information. The *Book of Durrow* contains a colophon copied on to the end of the text which clearly implies that the exemplar was by Columcille. But a reader would only find it if he knew what he was looking for; and only someone who knew the story of the illicitly copied text would understand it (cf Lawlor 1916). The *Echternach Gospels* seem to be based on the same exemplar as the *Lindisfarne Gospels* and the *Codex Amiatinus* and, like *Durrow*, they contain a colophon copied on to the end of the text. Known as the *promendavi* note, its geographical, linguistic and textual implications would all suit Cassiodorus emending his *Novem Codices*. But, again, a reader would find it only if he knew what he was looking for, and he would only understand it if he knew who would be in a position to emend what and where (cf Brown in Kendrick et al., 1960, 50; cf Mynors 1937, 23.1). So there is no need to discredit the gospel text of the *Novem Codices*. All his material could have been included in it, and with it a complete set of Evangelist portraits and canon tables. Like the text itself, these decorative elements occur in remarkably similar form in the *Lindisfarne Gospels* and in the *Codex Amiatinus* where an Evangelist portrait is transformed into Ezra, and short canon tables are transformed into tall ones.

Thus, true to the Insular ideal, the books declare their own credentials. Both are derived from the *Novem Codices*, which evidently contained Cassiodorus's new 'authorised version', and were fully illustrated. And the *Lindisfarne Gospels* has been underestimated: it is a complete 6th-century Italian Gospel book in disguise.

NOTE

1. In the original version of this paper, I glossed over the issue of which translation was contained in the *Novem Codices* because I could find no evidence for the Vulgate and thus found myself in conflict with all published accounts. I am therefore grateful to Richard Marsden for tactfully embarrassing me after the presentation of this paper at the conference on the Golden Age of Northumbria, by pointing out that he had already established that the *Novem Codices* were not a Vulgate but an Old Latin (Marsden 1995b, 137). As a result of this, I reconsidered the matter and have entered into dialogue with him in this version of the paper.

BEDE

CHAPTER 29

THE CHURCH AS NON-SYMBOL IN THE AGE OF BEDE

George Hardin Brown

In the middle of the 9th century, Amalarius of Metz in his *Liber officialis* summarily explains the various words for church:

> The Church is the people assembled by its ministers by 'Him who makes those of one spirit to dwell in the house' (Ps 67.6). The house itself is called church, because it contains the church. It is called church, because it is dominical; for *kurios (κύριος)* in Greek is Latin *dominus*, and therefore, *kyrica* mean dominical. It is called *basilica*, that is royal, from *basileo*. *Basileus (βασιλεύς)* means king, the basis of the people; *laos (λαός)* means people; *basilaus*,[1] the basis of the people. Hence Isidore: 'The dwellings of the kings were formerly called *basilicas*, whence they possess the name. Now, however, divine temples are designated *basilicas*, because cult and sacrifices are offered there to God the King.' (Hanssens 1948, 261; cf Lindsay 1911, II, XV.iv.11)[2]

In the 13th century William Durandus in his *Rationale* (I.1–2) adds to this explication: 'For as the material church is constructed from the joining together of various stones, so is the spiritual church by that of various people' (Webb 1906, 10; *CCCM* 140, 11–12). Such definitions serve as a convenient demonstration that for the medieval Christian the word 'church' possessed the same double valence as it does for us, signifying the people and the edifice in which the people worship. During the Northumbrian Golden Age a wide range of texts contain the ubiquitous term *ecclesia*, to which the vernacular, *cyrice*, source of modern English 'church', corresponds. *Basilica* appears, but less frequently, sometimes indicating a grander church and sometimes serving as a pretentious alternate for *ecclesia*. For instance, the author of the anonymous *Life of St Cuthbert* uses *basilica* for the church of Lindisfarne, whereas Bede uses *ecclesia* for that same church (Colgrave 1940, 132, 286, *V Anon* IV.13, *V Pros* 40). According to context *ecclesia* and *cyrice* can refer either to the faithful or to their sacred edifice, whereas *basilica* historically always refers to the building.[3]

In the light of the bivalent meaning of the word 'church' from late antiquity onwards as both assembly of the faithful and sacral building, I wish first to register the striking metaphoric reversal that occurs in the Pauline epistles, where the members of the church themselves are compared to a temple or consecrated building: 'Do you not know that you are God's temple and God's spirit dwells in you?' (I Cor 3.16; cf 3.17, 6.19), or:

> You are built upon the foundation of the apostles and prophets with Christ Jesus himself as the chief cornerstone, in whom the structure is closely fitted together into a dwelling place for God in the Spirit (Eph 2.20–2).

Bede asserts:

> We must not suppose that only the building in which we come together to pray and celebrate the mysteries is the Lord's temple, and that we ourselves, who come together in the Lord's name, are not more fully his temple and are not so named, since the Apostle clearly says, 'You are the temple of the living God'; as God says, 'I will live in them and walk among them' [2 Cor 6.16] (Martin & Hurst 1991, II, 242, *Hom* II.24).

So, in the New Testament the church in its one meaning as an assembly of faith is collectively and individually compared to, among other things, a temple in which the Spirit of God dwells, a living *domus Dei*.

Our question now is, do Northumbrian texts also symbolize the church building in which the people congregate? Are the church building, its structure, layout, proportions, furniture and decoration allegorized? Is the location of the church with respect to other churches and shrines understood in spatial allegorical terms, such as the way of the cross or the pilgrimage to Jerusalem, as it was later on the continent? I suppose that most, especially those who are familiar with later medieval ecclesiastical symbolism would answer, 'Yes, very likely.' For, in the later Carolingian period, Amalarius of Metz, with whom we started, extensively allegorized not only the parts of the Mass but also the various elements of the edifice in which the liturgy takes place: the altar and the furnishings, such as the candles, the censer, and the vessels. After the paragraph quoted at the beginning of this chapter, Amalarius compares the Christian basilica to Solomon's royal palace adjacent to the Temple (Hanssens 1948, 261, II.2). In the later Middle Ages even Amalarius is outdone in symbolic comparison by Durandus and his epigoni, whose allegorical interpretations of the liturgy and of the church building strike the modern reader as ingeniously contrived and arbitrary (Thibodeau 1988).

For instance, the cruciform shape of the church is compared to the shape of the human body of Christ, with the rounded apse the head (with lights for its eyes and turrets for its ears), the transept the arms, and the nave the trunk. If, as in some churches, the apse is out of alignment with the nave, that indicates Christ's head tilted to the axis of the cross. Or if the body of the church is the Virgin Mary's, then the vaults are her rib cage, under which Jesus rests. Or, in another interpretation, the pillars are the apostles, the crypt the hermits, the cock on the steeple the preachers, and so on. Or the procession and Mass indicate in every liturgical detail the *via crucis* from Jerusalem to Calvary.

However, the fact is, in the early western exegetical tradition before the Carolingian period, such an allegorical treatment of either the Mass or the church building and its parts is not found. In the ecclesiastical histories and commentaries of the Northumbrian Golden Age, replete as they are with descriptions of all sorts of ecclesiastical structures, the church building and its furnishings are not treated symbolically. Likewise the configurations of monastic and ecclesiastical buildings within a related geographic area are not treated as symbolic of the biblical sites in Palestine. Some recent attempts have been made to argue the contrary, but unconvincingly, because textual and other hard evidence in support of such a thesis is lacking. Granted, students of periods post-dating our 8th century have found plenty of evidence for such allegorical treatments in continental authors symbolically explaining cathedrals such as Liège or Chartres. However, when they turn to English cathedrals such as Durham, their efforts have been disappointed.

The fact is puzzling for a number of reasons. Northumbrian texts, such as the *Lives of Cuthbert*, the *Life of Wilfrid*, the *Histories of the Abbots of Wearmouth and Jarrow*, and of course, Bede's *Ecclesiastical History* and the *Letter to Bishop Ecgberht*, all supply opportunities for allegorical treatment. They feature a variety of local wooden and stone churches of different sizes, patterns, and shapes, oratories, monastic chapels, and martyria (Higham 1986, 280, 282–4, 296–302). Authors such as Eddius and Bede write about ecclesiastical builders like Wilfrid and Benedict Biscop and Ceolfrith, who had all travelled widely in Gaul and Italy and knew great churches and Roman basilicas; these writers describe the noble qualities of various Northumbrian churches, especially those built in the continental (Gallic and Roman) style. Bede had access to European manuscripts, illustrations, and accounts of Roman stational churches. He knew and excerpted in Book Five of the *Ecclesiastical History* parts of Adomnán's *De locis sanctis*, which contains a description of the churches and shrines of the Holy Land, accompanied by illustrations and ground plans of the major sacred sites. Bede knew Eusebius's florid descriptions of eastern basilicas, but he did not adopt Eusebius's comparison of the basilica to the heavenly Temple. Despite numerous opportunities, the Northumbrian authors, as well as Bede's older contemporary in Wessex, Aldhelm, never aggrandize the sacred buildings by allegorical symbolism or comparisons with the biblical Temple, New Testament sites, or the glories of the heavenly Jerusalem. Nor do they apply to the church building the Augustinian and Boethian number and ratio symbolism, so exuberantly developed in the later Middle Ages.

Because Bede in his biblical commentaries makes use of the various meanings of the church as a community of Christians and makes use of the biblical and patristic symbols for the church, we might well expect him to exploit the symbolic potential of the plan of the Christian church. Bede's penchant for allegory and typology and also what Jones (1970, 169) aptly calls 'Bede's rather exceptionally architectural approach to Revelation' intensify our expectation. As Holder (1994, xv) comments:

> Indeed, there seems to have been something about the balance, harmony, and regularity of architectural design that appealed to Bede's imagination and stimulated him to formulate a comprehensive theological and pastoral vision in relation to the various sacred structures described in the Bible.

Note, however, that Holder stipulates 'sacred structures described in the Bible', not extra-biblical sacred structures, such as contemporary churches. The ensemble of works that Bede dedicates to the allegorical interpretation of the biblical sacred structures is impressive, highly detailed and figurative, but also remarkably unified thematically. The commentaries on the Tabernacle, on the Temple, on Ezra and Nehemiah (which deals with the restoration of the Temple after the Exile), the Thirty Questions on the Books of Kings, and the three special homilies on the topic (Martin & Hurst 1991, II, 1–12, 241–69, *Hom* II.1, 24, 25), are uniquely Bedan. Of all the Fathers only he has programmatically presented a sustained allegorical commentary on the Tabernacle and Temple (*CCSL* 122, xviii). We might well expect that Bede and his contemporaries would use the same symbolic approach for allegorical treatment of the church. We may think from Bede's love of allegory and constant dealing with it that it extended to all areas of his world and culture.

This is not true. In all his detailed allegorical interpretation of the Tabernacle and Temple, even in his two homilies on the dedication of a church, the physical church is scarcely mentioned. Manifestly, the only arena open for allegorical interpretation was infrabiblical. Bede's precedent for that was Christ himself, the head of the church, and from Peter and Paul, the apostles of the church, and from the Fathers. A key text, central to Bede's hermeneutics and often quoted by him, is I Corinthians 10.11, as, for instance, in the prologue to *De Tabernaculo*:

'For all these things', as the Apostle says, 'happened to them in figure but were written down for us'. 'All these things' includes not only the deeds or words that are contained in the Sacred Writings, but also the description of the locations and hours and times and the things themselves, as well as the circumstances under which they were done or said (Holder 1994, 1).

In all the Northumbrian writings of the 8th century, in all the thousands of references to church as an assembly of Christians or the building in which they worshipped, there is no symbolic treatment of the church building whatever. This, despite the fact that Bede, who with his scientific mind just as enthusiastically applied the hermeneutic tools of numerology as did Augustine and Gregory, would find the proportions and arrangement of the church building as susceptible to numerological interpretation as the mathematical relationships in the measurements of the Tabernacle and Temple. The church is not the subject of allegorical symbolism but the object of it. That is to say, Bede and his contemporaries understood that a biblical person (such as the Bride of the Song of Songs), place (such as Jerusalem or Zion), or thing (such as the Tabernacle or Temple) prefigured the church. But the church building was the real, non-symbolic liturgical site.

If in England, guided by Bede, the church building is for historical and theological reasons not treated symbolically, what is the likely source of such treatment beginning during the Carolingian era on the continent? The East. Neoplatonic views of the material world as symbolic of the higher reality enter the western liturgy through the *De Ecclesiastica Hierarchia* of pseudo-Dionysius whose allegorical interpretations to some degree had already filtered into the West through Isidore of Seville but were, like other of Isidore's trends, resisted by Bede. Other Greek patristic texts influenced Carolingian exegesis at the same time as Byzantine architectural concepts came to markedly influence Frankish iconography, art and architecture. Even though a reaction against the liturgical symbolism of Amalarius was led by Agobard (d 840) and Florus (d 860), the way was set for the symbolic extravagances culminating in the works of Durandus in the 13th century. What is ironic (and historically confusing) in that development is the fact that allegoricists like Amalarius mine Bede's commentaries on the Tabernacle and Temple and their furnishings and apply them to the Christian church edifice and its furniture. Durandus titles his legalistic and allegorical treatise the *Rationale*, the name of the Jewish high priest's vestment; and Durandus elaborately treats the bishop's vestments after his allegorical description of the church. Bede, although he explicates every detail of the *Rationale* in the *De Tabernaculo* (3.5) as he does the Temple, applies that interpretation neither to Christian vestments nor Christian church (Holder 1994, 118–25). Bede and his Northumbrian colleagues, despite their fondness for allegory, would have none of that.

NOTES

1. Amalarius seems to have invented a Greek work, *basilaus*, based on a combination of βασι– and λαός.

2. '*Ecclesia est convocatus populus per ministros ecclesiae ab eo qui facit unianimes habitare in domo. Ipsa domus vocatur ecclesia, quia ecclesiam continet. Ipsa vocatur kyrica, quia est dominicalis; kyrius grece, latine dominus, ac ideo kyrica, dominicalis. Ipsa vocatur basilica, id est regalis, a basileo. Basileus rex dicitur, quasi basis populi; laos populus dicitur, basilaus basis populi. Unde Isidorus: "Basilicae prius vocabantur regum habitacula, unde et nomen habent. Nam Basileus rex, et basilicae regiae habitationes. Nunc autem ideo divina templa basilicae nominantur, quia ibi regi Deo cultus et sacrifician offeruntur."*'

3. The extended meaning of the collective noun, the church, in an institutional sense of the term, as in the phrase, 'the church teaches', was familiar from credal and synodal formulas, even though the papal hierarchical understanding of the term had not yet evolved as it would in the 13th century. For an example of Bede's use of church in this sense, see his *Homily II.24* (CCSL 122, 23–30, 250–69; Martin & Hurst 1991, 242, 250). Bede in his commentary on Acts speaks of the church of Christ spreading throughout the whole world, and in the *Ecclesiastical History* he traces its spread to this corner of the world, England. Following the precedents of Paul, who writes letters to the churches of Rome and Corinth, and John in the Book of Revelations, who addresses the seven churches that are in Asia, and Pope Gregory, with his vast correspondence with bishops and missionaries, Bede speaks to the Christian English community. However, writing from the standpoint of Northumbria, his primary concern in the *Ecclesiastical History*, in the homilies, and especially in the pastoral letter to Bishop Ecgberht of York is with the Anglo-Saxon north.

CHAPTER 30

BEDE: SCHOLAR AND SPIRITUAL TEACHER[1]

Gerald Bonner

When Charles Plummer, in his great edition of Bede's historical writings, came to describe his hero's death, he wrote: 'And so he passed away, the very model of the saintly scholar-priest' (Plummer 1896, I, lxxviii–ix). Plummer's choice of words deserves attention, since he might equally justly have described Bede as the model of the learned monk, of a type long familiar from the history of the Benedictine Order. Bede had, after all, lived as a religious from the age of seven, when his kinsmen entrusted him to the care of Benedict Biscop and Ceolfrith to be educated at Wearmouth, and subsequently spent his life as a monk of Jarrow. He had taken holy orders, the diaconate at nineteen and the priesthood at thirty, at the direction of Abbot Ceolfrith (Colgrave & Mynors 1969, 566, V.24), so that we cannot be certain that it was by his own will – it may have been in virtue of monastic obedience. Nevertheless, it is unlikely that Plummer would have chosen his words carelessly. If he called Bede a scholar-priest, it was because he regarded those words as being the best description of his life and work. Half a century after Plummer, Sr Mary Carroll (1946, 257–8) came to the same conclusion: 'Lofty as was Bede's appreciation of [the monastic] state of life, he valued still more his life as a priest, and his writings turn frequently to the duties of the clergy.' Bede's spirituality seems, therefore, to be more pastoral than claustral; he is not simply concerned with his monastic brethren but rather with all the members of Christ's church, clerical and lay, monastic and secular. I would suggest that it is Bede's conception of pastoral responsibility which conditions the character of his works and the topics upon which he chooses to write.

It should first be observed that Bede sees the priestly office as a ministry, not only of the sacraments, which he takes for granted, but also of pastoral teaching: the Christian priest is a minister who presides over and instructs a Christian congregation, and it was with instruction that Bede was particularly concerned, for few theologians have been more conscious of the missionary and catechetical apostolate of the church. So he declares, in his *De Tabernaculo* III (*CCSL* 119A,

110–11), that a priest's perfection is grounded in good works and in teaching the truth, according to what the evangelist Luke says about himself: that he had 'made a treatise of all that Jesus began to do and to teach' (Acts 1.1). But Bede goes further. He does not confine the notion of Christian priesthood to the ordained ministry but, drawing upon the text in I Peter 2.9, that Christians are 'an elect race, a royal priesthood, a holy nation, a people of god's own possession', he extends the priestly office to all the faithful, since they are members of the one high priest, Jesus Christ (*PL* 93, 192C, *Expl Apoc* 20; *CCSL* 119A, 194, *De Templo* II); and this in turn leads him to a high evaluation of anyone concerned, however humbly, with teaching the faithful the rudiments of the faith. In his letter to Bishop Ecgberht of York, Bede urged his disciple to ordain priests and to establish teachers 'who, by preaching the word of God in individual villages and consecrating the holy mysteries, and most of all by performing the office of holy baptism where opportunity offered', would promote the evangelization of Northumbria, adding that he himself often provided English translations of the Lord's Prayer and the Creed for unlettered priests, unable to make their own (Plummer 1896, I, 408–9).

I have said, following Plummer and Carroll, that Bede is to be seen primarily as a priest and only secondarily as a monk. Such exact distinctions, however, do not apply in northern Britain in the 7th and 8th centuries; the parochial system, as we understand it, did not yet exist (Addleshaw 1963, 1–2). There were some local churches, erected on their estates by pious landowners like the *thegns* Puch and Addi mentioned in the *Ecclesiastical History* (Colgrave & Mynors 1969, 462, 464, V.4, 5), or in a village, like the unidentified *Medilwong*, where Cuthbert comforted the bereaved mother of a sick child and assured her that no more of her family would die of the plague (Colgrave 1940, 118–20, 258–61, *V Anon* IV.6; *V Pros* 33);[2] but such places of worship did not suffice for the population as a whole. Where a monastery existed, lay people could join in its worship; but there were many settlements, as Bede pointed out in his letter to Bishop Ecgberht, in remote and inaccessible places, which never saw their bishop for years on end (Plummer 1896, I, 410). This meant that many people either never heard the gospel message or, having accepted it, were left without any regular pastor. In such circumstances it was natural that the monasteries should be expected to exercise an external pastoral ministry. Bede speaks of the peripatetic ministry of his hero, Cuthbert, at Melrose and Lindisfarne (Colgrave 1940, 184–6, 208, *V Pros* 9, 16). Again, the great Northumbrian crosses, situated at convenient meeting places in the countryside, may well have served as assembly places for people to meet a visiting minister (Addleshaw 1963, 10–11).[3] Back in his monastery the itinerant priest followed the rule of his house; on his mission tours he was the parson for those who had no parish.

I suggest that Bede is to be classed in this category. Of his devotion to the monastic rule there is no question, and we have the delightful story, recorded by Alcuin, of how Bede would never absent himself from the divine office because, he explained: 'I know that the angels visit the canonical hours and the assemblies of the brethren. Will they not say: "Where is Bede? Why does he not come to the devotions of the brethren?"' (Hadden & Stubbs 1871, 471). And there is his own reference at the conclusion of the *Ecclesiastical History* to 'the observance of the discipline of the Rule and the daily task of singing in church' (Colgrave & Mynors 1969, 566, V.24). His priestly concern is to be seen in his writings. Whether he imitated Aidan and Cuthbert by travelling around the territory of his monastery, we do not know; though it may be that his teaching duties and his writing would have left him little time for such physical activity. In any case, Bede's pastoral ministry was essentially literary and this needs to be remembered if we seek to understand the meaning of Plummer's phrase: 'scholar-priest'. In speaking of Bede's scholarship we need to avoid any conception of the originality which is commonly implied when we speak today of scholarship. In the early western Middle Ages the vital need was not originality of thought but the preservation and transmission of the learning of the past at a time when so much was being lost through the break-up of the Roman order and the incursion of the barbarian peoples who were founding the kingdoms which would succeed the Roman rule. This task did not exclude the possibility of both originality and learning on the part of the custodians of Christian doctrine and classical culture; but these were not essential. What was essential was transmission, and that was what Bede understood himself to be providing.

Bede, then, did not seek to make new discoveries but to hand on the legacy of the past to his own day because of its practical value to Christian civilization. Accordingly, Bede's writings fall approximately into three categories: textbooks, works of edification, and biblical commentaries. The textbooks, works like *De Arte Metrica* and *De Orthographia*, are designed to help the student to learn the Latin language, the language of the western church, with a view to applying the knowledge gained to the service of Christianity. Bede's grammars are not humanist writings, in the Renaissance sense of the word, intended to encourage classical studies; rather, they enable the student to read the Bible and the Fathers, and to understand the language of public worship.

The writings which I have described as works of edification cover a wide range of topics, including hagiographical compositions, like the two lives of St Cuthbert; geography, in the *De Locis Sanctis*; science – *De Natura Rerum*, *De Temporibus* and *De Temporum Ratione* – and history, of which the *Historia Ecclesiastica* is the supreme example. All these varied compositions have as their end the winning of souls for Christ. The writings on time are no exception to this intention. Their aim is to enable the reader to determine with accuracy the date when Easter will fall in any particular year according to the Roman usage, and this is not out of a simple desire for uniformity. The early Middle Ages in which Bede lived were a period in which men were increasingly concerned that the rites which they used in their worship should be exact, because errors of form might lead to invalidity, and invalidity would imperil the soul of the worshipper. The

Patristic Age had accepted the fact that different local churches used different liturgical forms, all of which were equally valid, so long as certain basic conditions were satisfied. We can see this conception expressed in the letter to Pope Gregory I to Augustine, permitting him to compile a liturgy for the English church from other sources than the Roman, if these seemed more suitable (Colgrave & Mynors 1969, 80–2, I.27), and Gregory's liturgical liberalism may be contrasted with the requirement of his successor, Gregory II, in his letter of 15 May 719 to Boniface, the apostle of Germany:

> . . . we command you that in admitting within the church those who have some kind of belief in God, you will insist upon using the sacramental discipline prescribed in the official ritual formulary of the Holy Apostolic See (Talbot 1954, 68).

In 1977, Angenendt argued that this requirement should not be understood simply as an ecclesiastico-political piece of self-aggrandizement by the Roman see, but in the wider context of a development in religious sentiment: one's salvation might depend on a correct formula, and the formula of the greatest see in Christendom could hardly be in error. Hence, at the Synod of Whitby, King Oswiu and his ministers, 'having abandoned the less perfect practice, hastened to transfer themselves to the things which they had recognized to be better' (Colgrave & Mynors 1969, 306–9, III.25), while Bede himself, despite his love and veneration for Aidan, nevertheless took care to dissociate himself from Aidan's paschal observance while applauding his personal holiness (Colgrave & Mynors 1969, 264, III.17; cf 218, III.3). Thus Bede's writings on time are works of edification, since they instruct priests how to do the things which are necessary for the salvation of themselves and their flock.

In his commentaries on the Bible, that corpus of writings which constitutes the foundation of Christian belief and devotion, Bede follows the tradition of the Fathers, particularly Augustine of Hippo's teaching in *De Doctrina Christiana*. The meaning of difficult passages must be explained for the uneducated; the doctrinal import must be made clear to save the faithful from falling into heresy, and thence to damnation; but there is a further consideration, and perhaps a particularly monastic one: *meditatio* – the prayerful reading and reflection upon a passage of Scripture which may, under grace, raise the devout mind to *contemplatio*, that anticipation while still in the flesh of the vision of God, which will only be truly experienced in the life to come. It is in meditation that the allegorical interpretation of Scripture acquires the power to raise the mind to contemplation, as is particularly apparent in the treatises *De Tabernaculo*, *De Templo* and *In Ezram et Neemiam*, all of which are interpreted by Bede as describing the Christian church and the Christian life in allegorical form. Moses, going up the mountain to receive the ten command-ments, represents the need to lay aside earthly considerations if one wishes to understand divine matters (*CCSL* 119A, 5, *De Templo* I); the temple of Solomon was made in the figure of Holy Church universal, from the first of the elect to the last man who will be born in the world (op. cit. 147); the repose of the Sabbath (Neem 10.31), spiritually understood, is to refrain from all servile work, that is from sin, always keeping holiday and resting and understanding that the Lord himself is God, so that after such a Sabbath, freed from sin in our conscience, we may come to the Sabbath of future glory in heaven (*CCSL* 119A, 373, lines 1358–62, *In Ez et Neem* III). Such exegesis anticipates later writings on spirituality, making the literal biblical text a theme for contemplation.

Bede's biblical commentaries are, by their very nature, addressed to the educated, those persons, clerk and lay, who could read Latin. Did he offer material to the less well-instructed? His *Homilies on the Gospels* are written in Latin, but it is an open question whether they were actually preached in the form in which we have them. It is at least possible that the *Homilies* are based upon conferences delivered in English in the course of divine worship at Jarrow, in order to edify those humbler members of the community whose Latinity was confined to the Latin office. Ward has found them 'full of passion and poetry' (Martin & Hurst 1991, I, ix); yet the theology underlying them assumes a thorough grounding in Christian doctrine, of a sort not very common in church congregations today. Let us take a passage from *Homily* 1.8, a sermon for Christmas Day:

> Christ was born God from God, but He did not wish to remain only the Son of God: He deigned to become also Son of Man, not losing what he had been, but taking up what He had not been, so that by this He might transform human beings into children of God, and might make them co-heirs of His glory so that they might by grace begin to possess what He Himself had always possessed by nature (Martin & Hurst 1991, 80, *Hom* I.8, slightly modified by author).

This is the doctrine of deification – 'He became man that we might become gods' – often said to be peculiar to the Greek East, but known and on occasion taught by Augustine of Hippo (Bonner 1986), from whom Bede presumably received it. If Bede's *Homilies on the Gospels* are indeed based upon discourses actually delivered (Martin & Hurst 1991, xi–xv; cf v–vii), they may point to a higher degree of theological instruction among his hearers than we are sometimes accustomed to assume. Wearmouth-Jarrow was, however, an exceptionally well-instructed institution in Northumbria, and Bede never forgot the simpler souls who needed the milk of the gospel, as his *Letter to Ecgberht* makes clear. This, his last work, reveals his lifelong pastoral concern for Christ's little ones, which continued to the day of his death. Plummer was wholly justified in his description of Bede as a saintly scholar-priest.

NOTES

1. This communication includes material, in an abridged version with some additions from an article, 'Bede – Priest and Scholar', read to the Friends of Bede's World at Jarrow Hall, Tyne and Wear, on 12 June 1996, printed in *Milltown Studies* (Dublin) 39 (1997), 66–77. I am grateful to the editor, Gervase Corcoran, OSA, for permission to reproduce it here.

2. The common assumption that the child's sickness was bubonic plague (*Pasteurella pestis*) is untenable. It may have been smallpox; alternatively measles or influenza (Shrewsbury 1971, 20–1; McNeill 1977, 114 and note).

3. It should not, however, be too readily assumed that the primary purpose of the erection of a cross was as an assembly point for worship conducted by a visiting priest. It may well have served a liturgical function in a wooden church which has not survived or an apotropaic role as a defence against demons haunting the locality.

CHAPTER 31

BEDE AND THE GOLDEN AGE OF LATIN PROSE IN NORTHUMBRIA

Christopher Grocock

The aim of this short chapter is to present a rhetorical and linguistic analysis of five passages taken from Bede's extensive prose writings: *Historia Ecclesiastica*, preface, II.13 and IV.24, and *Sermones* I.13 and I.20. Most studies on Bede focus (quite correctly) on the importance of *what* he wrote; *how* he wrote it tends to be neglected, though his corpus survives in a better condition than most of the stone sculpture, paintings, or other artefacts from the period.

THE LATIN LANGUAGE AND BEDE

The background to the linguistic situation in c 700 in the Anglo-Saxon kingdoms, particularly Northumbria, and on the continent is a complex one, though we may safely assume that Bede worked and wrote in a multilingual context, with Old English, Celtic/British, and at least one kind of Latin in use. This situation is not unfamiliar nowadays: at the newsagent where the present author regularly bought his Saturday newspaper in Jarrow, he was served by two ladies behind the counter in English (with a Geordie accent) but this was frequently a parenthesis in a conversation conducted in a language from the Indian sub-continent.

Similar situations would certainly have arisen in Bede's experience. Old English was obviously in use, not only outside the monasteries but inside them, too: writing c 734 to Bishop Ecgberht, Bede suggests he makes use of translations of the Lord's Prayer and the Apostles' Creed which he himself has made for the benefit of those brothers who do not know Latin, those whom Bede terms *idiotae . . . qui propriae tantum linguae notitiam habent*: 'simpletons, who know only their own tongue' (Plummer 1896, I, 409). We may posit a bilingual religious community on the banks of the Tyne and the Wear.

There is no evidence in Bedan writings that the author can recall of Celtic languages being in common use in Northumbria in Bede's day; Aidan, for example, had to make use of Oswald's fluency in his native Irish (Colgrave & Mynors 1969, 220–1, III.3).

Latin was 'the language of Western Christianity' (Mohrmann 1961, I, 51), as well as the legacy of the Western Empire. By the 5th century, under the direction of the church Fathers, a kind of 'Christian humanism' supplanted the classical and pagan rhetoric. Augustine in his *De Doctrina Christiana* provided the main dynamic which produced a major development, drawing from both classical sources following the 'Ciceronian' style and also a hitherto unseen beauty in the Bible, which became a guide for 'Christian orators' – that is, preachers (op. cit. 356).

Bede himself furthered this tradition with his summary of rhetorical devices based on scripture, the *De Schematibus et Tropis*:

> [Augustine] left us in his sermons an example of sacred eloquence which continues on the one hand the tradition of the first Christian centuries . . . and which on the other introduces a new and essential element: the imitation of biblical style. . . . Instead of acquiring a system of rhetorical rules, Augustine proposes the possibility of developing a natural talent by the reading of good models. These models however are no longer the Classical authors, but the Bible and the Fathers of the Church (op. cit. 71, 360).

In this way a 'Christian Humanist' style emerged by the 5th century (op. cit. 68) and we can see why reading proved such a delight for Bede, who seems to have been ideally suited to this curriculum.

For Christian writers, clear communication was crucial. Jerome noted of Hilarius that his 'Gallic oratorical style, its Greek rhetorical flowers, and especially its long sentences, "*a lectione simplicium fratrum procul est*"' (Herman 1991, 32). Augustine stressed that the purpose to which eloquence is put is paramount, and classical rhetoric not necessary. His conclusions in the *De Doctrina Christiana* were to be the foundation for the education of Bede and his contemporaries (Mohrmann 1961, I, 359–62).

However, from the latter years of the empire to the Merovingian period the situation became increasingly problematic. In Romance areas:

> . . . for Christian writers and especially the most eminent ones, the conditions under which a written text could or could not be understood, was or was not suitable, when read or recited, to persuade and attract a heterogeneous public, represented an ever-present and central issue (Herman 1991, 31).

Much of the Christian public had difficulty understanding complex texts. A 'utilitarian' prose style was becoming a necessity by the Merovingian period, as Gregory of Tours had noted (Auerbach 1965, 87–8).

For Bede and his contemporaries in the Anglo-Saxon kingdoms, bilingual from the outset, a different situation applied, not unlike that noted in Germany where 'Church Latin was a foreign tongue, unrelated to the language of the people' (Auerbach 1965, 120). This experience may well have had a bearing on the attitude of Alcuin and a later generation when faced with a similar situation in Charlemagne's realms in Francia.

For Bede, Latin was a learned language, a *Vatersprache*, but he would also have come into contact with 'native speakers' – one of them taught him to sing, after all. We might wonder what sort of spoken Latin he could have heard. Was there already proto-Romance in Francia? What about Italy, represented by John the Chanter? What about Theodore and Hadrian, slightly earlier but from further afield? One might ask, slightly tongue-in-cheek, whether Geordie Latin was spoken in Wearmouth-Jarrow! Did Benedict Biscop return from his continental tours with more than books and pictures – a hint of continental pronunciation? The development of proto-Romance on the continent is now regarded as quite late:

> . . . even in the 8th century, *rusticitas* and *grammatica* were not yet identified as separate languages . . . but they were beginning to crystallize into two separate categories within the same language (Wright 1993, 82).

The need for clear enunciation was noted, two generations after Bede and in a continental context, by Alcuin in his *Dialogus de Rhetorica*, and by 813 Latin appears to have been unintelligible to the general audience, as the famous *Canon 17* of the Council of Tours illustrates. Might proto-French already have been well into its development by c 700? (Wright 1993, 87; Mohrmann 1961, II, 151; Banniard 1991, 173).

The very basis of classical Latin language, quantity and accent, was being lost from c 500–700 in those ex-provinces of Rome where Latin was still spoken, in the same way that inflections were giving way to prepositional phrases and an abandonment of declined forms. The change in word order from Subject-Object-Verb (SOV) to Subject-Verb-Object (SVO) is a vexed question, and Bede's treatment of main verbs is examined below. The change from SOV to SVO has implications not only for style but also on the mental constructs associated with communicating in a language.

In non-Romance Christianized areas, the means of learning Latin was via the Bible, and above all the Psalms. George Hardin Brown reminds us in a recent article that *Psalteratus* means 'learned', 'literate', and that the Psalms were learned by heart, and almost certainly without explanation in the native tongue in the Anglo-Saxon culture of Bede's day (Brown 1995, 77). They were learned as a *Vatersprache*, but with some contact with 'native speakers'.

Anglo-Saxon monastic culture stood four-square in the tradition of Christian Latin, which stressed the importance above all of *sacra scriptura* and hence Latin as the *lingua sacra*. Auerbach (1965, 87) pointed out the fundamentally Christian context of all church writing: the church's teaching 'was a product of the old Mediterranean cultures and, based as it was on a book and the interpretation of a book, markedly literary even by Mediterranean criteria'.

Above all, it was Augustine who left as his legacy a corpus which became the model for those who came after. It is worth noting that the transmission of the collection of Augustine's sermons seems to come from the Anglo-Saxon kingdoms (*CCSL* 41, 19), and a recent evaluation of Bede concludes that he is a model scholar according to the pattern laid down by Augustine, noted above, in the *De Doctrina Christiana* (Davidse 1996, 8–11). George Hardin Brown has recently remarked (1996, 1) that 'Bede . . . was impressive, but not flashy or spectacular. He left that to Aldhelm' and that the hallmark of Bedan style is 'moderation and measure in style and content'. This does not mean that Bede is a dull writer – indeed I hope to show the remarkable compass of his skill as a prose stylist, and the dexterity he employs as storyteller and preacher (which two go hand in hand!). Hisperic mannerisms such as occur in Aldhelm or Columbanus are entirely absent in Bede, as indeed are (with a few very minor but significant exceptions) what might be termed 'Vulgarisms'. One such will be noted later. Apart from the study of his writing, Bede's competence as a Latinist is evident from his twin handbooks *De Arte Metrica/De Schematibus et Tropis*. This shows his mastery of theory and is illustrative as much for what he does not remark on as for what he does.

GRAMMATICAL CONSTRUCTION OF SENTENCES

The complexity of sentences is perhaps the most useful indicator of the capabilities of understanding of both author and audience: the need for simplicity to achieve clear communication has been noted above. There are various ways of examining this, and Tables 31.1 and 31.2 show a comparative statistical analysis of sentence and clause length, and of clauses per sentence in Bede *vis-à-vis* other patristic and late Latin specimen sermons of Augustine, Jerome, and Columbanus, and passages from Cassiodorus, Gildas, and Ætheria's *Peregrinatio*.

	HE Pref.	*HE* II.13	*HE* IV.24	*Serm* II.13	*Serm* I.20
No of words	716	568	893	1,739	1,884
No of clauses	149	126	167	288	319
No of sentences	18	26	32	45	63
Averages:					
Words per clause	4.80	4.85	5.35	6.04	5.94
Clauses per sentence	8.28	5.04	5.21	6.40	5.06
Words per sentence	39.77	21.85	27.91	38.64	29.90

Table 31.1: Words and clauses per sentence in Bede.

	Augustine Serm I	Augustine Serm II	Augustine Serm VI	Augustine De Civ Dei I Pref, I.1, V.11, XIX.17	Augustine De Cat Rud 1–5
No of words	1,069	2,148	1,181	1,240	2,485
No of clauses	190	458	292	210	434
No of sentences	51	171	99	21	69
Averages:					
Words per clause	5.63	4.69	4.04	5.90	5.73
Clauses per sentence	3.73	2.68	2.95	10.00	6.29
Words per sentence	20.97	12.56	11.93	59.05	36.01
	Jerome Tr Ps VII XVIII.7–9	Jerome Hom Matt XVI.19–31	Jerome Hom in Luc	Cassiodorus Institut Pref	
No of words	2,116	1,088	2,912	1,323	
No of clauses	450	256	692	216	
No of sentences	157	78	250	37	
Averages:					
Words per clause	4.70	4.25	4.21	6.13	
Clauses per sentence	2.86	3.28	2.76	5.83	
Words per sentence	13.48	13.95	11.65	35.76	
	Columbanus Instruct I	Columbanus Instruct VI	Columbanus Instruct XI	Gildas De Excid Brit 1–10	Ætheria Peregrinatio
No of words	1,183	696	780	1,932	2,510
No of clauses	272	198	185	370	463
No of sentences	53	40	47	42	75
Averages:					
Words per clause	4.35	3.52	4.22	5.22	5.42
Clauses per sentence	5.13	4.95	3.94	8.81	6.17
Words per sentence	22.32	17.40	16.60	46.00	33.47

Table 31.2: Words and clauses per sentence in other sources.

The basic clause length and sentence length differ more in the sermons and other didactic/historical works in the 5th-century writers than in either of the later ones. Gildas in particular writes with great complexity and, for a document intended to be read out loud (as his first sentence makes explicit), with convoluted constructions. Bede's own aim was certainly clarity and communication, as much as his predecessors', but these figures indicate that the complexity of how, by his time, the message was being communicated was perhaps closer to the written than the spoken idiom. The punchy, direct style of the sermons of Augustine and Jerome in particular is replaced by a more fluid, gentle use of Latin, with fewer rhetorical questions and direct *apostrophe* to the congregation. Gildas's Hisperic style, evinced in part in Columbanus (whose style can also be fiery on occasion) was continued by Aldhelm, but except for some writers of Celtic background, was a 'dead end' so far as the development of what we might call 'mainstream Latinity' was concerned in the period after Bede. Northumbria, not Wessex, was the dominant school in Carolingian Europe.

SUBORDINATE CLAUSES

Numeric analysis of the length of sentence or use of a number of clauses is not sufficient in itself to demonstrate the complexity of a given author's Latinity. For example, Ætheria's sentence length and the number of clauses she employs compare with the other authors; where she falls short is in her use of Latin in all its richness and rhythm. A second and very necessary measure of an author's ability to use the Latin language is therefore an examination of the type and variety of dependent clauses used. Table 31.3 gives an indication of the breadth of Bede's resources in writing Latin: the present participle clauses are not classical but follow the style of the Bible, adopted by the Fathers, as a part of the 'Christian humanist' manner of Latin prose.

Type of Clause	*HE* Pref	*HE* II.13	*HE* IV.24	*Serm* II.13	*Serm* I.20	Total
Ablative absolute	4	15	3	5	5	32
Ablative attend circ			2	4	3	9
Relative	24	21	18	43	40	146
Present part.	3	9	12	13	10	47
Past part.	2	2	2	4		10
Future part.			1			1
Conditional	3	1	1	2	1	8
Final	3	3	4	5	3	18
Causal		3	5	14	17	39
Indirect (acc + inf)		2	7	4	7	20
Concessive			2	5	4	11
Temporal	2		6			8
Gerundive			3	3		6
Totals	41	56	66	102	90	355

Table 31.3: Subordinate clauses in selected Bedan passages.

WORD ORDER

Style may also be evaluated by word order within the sentence. Table 31.4 shows the number of main verbs (ie verbs governing main clause) found in the 'final' or SOV position in the Bede passages:

Passage	HE Pref	HE II.13	HE IV.24	Serm II.13	Serm I.20
No of main verbs in final position	18	18	15	15	18
Sentences	18	26	32	34	37
% of main verbs in final position	100	69	47	44	48

Table 31.4: Main Verbs in Final Position in Bede.

It is an (erroneous) commonplace that in classical Latin 'the main verb goes at the end'. Word order in classical, early and late medieval Latin is complex; in particular there can no longer be any thought of a simple development from SOV to SVO. Cicero especially can be very free with word order to alter emphasis (Pinkster 1991, 71–3, 77–80). Bede is equally skilful in varying his word order to good effect, though the *HE* preface is very 'correct', often with a main verb deliberately left to the end after a parenthetical dependent clause. Is it possible that the Anglo-Saxons might have been attuned to this in having an inflected language of their own, whereas Romance had evolved from the abandonment of such means of differentiation and as a result depends on rectilinear word order to a much greater degree? This question is outside the scope of this chapter but might be worth some comparative study.

CLAUSULAE

Clausulae are the quantitative metrical patterns used in clause and sentence endings commonly employed in classical antiquity which are based on the metrical values given to syllables (long [_], and short [uu]). They are most notable in Cicero but are common in other classical authors. The most common patterns, which have long been recognized, are shown in Table 31.5 (Clark 1905, x–xi; Norden 1958, II, 930, 938–9).

1a. Cretic + trochee	_ u _ / _ x
1b. Variant (common in Cicero as *esse uideatur*)	_ u uu / _ x
1c. Second variant	_ u _ / uu u
1d. Third (rarer) variant	uu u _ / _ u
2. Two cretics	_ u _ / _ u x
3. Cretic and two trochees or one molossus	_ u _ / _ u _ x
4. Two trochees	_ u / _ x
5. Spondee and trochee	_ _ / _ u

Table 31.5: *Clausulae*.

The use of the *clausula* survived into the 4th and 5th centuries but it appears to have had a mixed value for the Christian Fathers. Norden's comments on Jerome and Augustine are illuminating: 'Jerome's practice is again quite instructive; when he deals with simple questions he gives no consideration to rhythm, but as soon as his writing reaches to a higher plane, he attunes himself to it' (Norden 1958, II, 947) – as though it is something he tries not to use, but which 'comes out' when he gets worked up about a topic. Tension between classical Latin and biblical simplicity is never quite resolved in Jerome; he admits it himself, most notably in his own account in *Ep XXII*.30 of the dream in which he was accused of being a Ciceronian.

On Augustine, Norden comments:

> Unless I am mistaken, Augustine is the first to make allowance not only for the quantities of the syllables, but also for the accents of the *clausula*. Understandably enough, he himself says of the Africans that they do not know how to distinguish the quantities of syllables with their ears, on account of which he had based his celebrated *Hymn against the Donatists* only on syllable-accent (Norden 1958, II, 948).

Now Bede has a 'near-perfect understanding of quantity' which is shown by the 'metrical excellence of his verse' (Lapidge 1993, 15) as much as by his treatment of matters metrical – and accentual, for that matter – in the *De Arte Metrica*. However, neither in that work nor in its second part, the *De Schematibus et Tropis*, does he refer to the *clausula*. Nevertheless, as the examples show, he does make use of it. I suspect that his extensive reading and extraordinary ability to absorb and make use of the Latin language expressed by Augustine especially, but also by the other writers available to him, has simply meant that he has an 'ear' for the rhythmic patterns in 'good' Latin prose, and writes it unconsciously. The same of course may well have been true of classical authors, including Cicero himself (Simpson & Vellacott 1970, 33).

Table 31.6 (below) shows instances in the Bede passages of the *clausula*: only three types are used, with a variant of Type 2, _ u _ / _ _ _ also occurring. In addition a hexameter ending, _ u u / _ x, is also found; this is generally avoided by prose writers, though Tacitus and Livy do use it. This data should also be compared with that below, on the *cursus*.

Clausula Type	*HE* Pref	*HE* II.13	*HE* IV.24	*Serm* II.13	*Serm* I.20
1a	10	10	5	16	7
1b	1	3	3		
2	14	9	2	3	
(2)	4	2	6	6	3
3					1
Hex	2	2	3		
Totals	31	26	19	25	11

Table 6 contd.

Clausula Type	HE Pref	HE II.13	HE IV.24	Serm II.13	Serm I.20
No of clauses	149	126	167	288	319
No of sentences	18	26	32	45	63
Clausulae per x clauses	4.80	4.84	8.79	11.52	29
Average per sentence	3.87	1.00	0.59	0.55	0.17

Table 31.6: *Clausulae* in Bedan passages.

THE *CURSUS*

Norden's comment on Augustine gives a possible clue to the origin of the other hallmark of prose style, the *cursus*. This was an important feature of Latin prose style in the Middle Ages, and is based on rhythmical rather than quantitative endings for clauses and sentences. It reached its heyday under Leo the Great at the end of the 11th century – hence its common name the 'leonine *cursus*' – and finally became fixed (one might say ossified) in the 13th century. Curtius notes that the *cursus* begins to degenerate even as early as the 8th century, though he does not specify where.

The four basic types of *cursus* are shown in Table 31.7. The symbols u and _ refer to stressed, not quantitative syllables.

Cursus planus (cf *clausula* type 1)	⁄ ⁄ uniuersi fideles	⁄ ⁄ uu _ u / u _ u
Cursus uelox (cf *clausula* type 1 var b)	⁄ ⁄ firmiter iniungentes	⁄ ⁄ _ u u / u u _ u
Cursus tardus/ecclesiasticus (cf *clausula* type 2)	⁄ ⁄ mater ecclesia	⁄ ⁄ _ u / u _ u u
Cursus medius (cf *clausula* type 2)	⁄ ⁄ uoluit domino	⁄ ⁄ _ u u / _ u u

Table 31.7: Types of *Cursus*.

Table 31.8 shows Bede's use of the *cursus* identified in the five passages considered.

Cursus Type	HE Pref	HE II.13	HE IV.24	Serm II.13	Serm I.20
Planus	7	10	19	15	20
Velox	10	3	14	11	6
Tardus	9	1	1	6	8
Medius	9	8	5	2	2
Totals	35	22	39	34	36
No of clauses	149	126	167	288	319
No of sentences	18	26	32	45	63
Cursus per x clauses	4.45	5.73	5.76	8.47	8.86
Average per sentence	1.83	0.85	0.91	0.76	0.57

Table 31.8: *Cursus* in Bedan passages.

LINK WORDS

Another way of judging complexity of prose style is to examine relationships between sentences, and the way in which connections, link words, assist the development of argument and narrative. A specific instance of this will be noted later but first it is useful to consider the link words and devices used to build a coherent narrative or argument in the five passages under scrutiny, as shown in Table 31.9.

Word	HE Pref	HE II.13	HE IV.24	Serm II.13	Serm I.20
Et		1	1	4	5
Vnde		3	2	4	4
Qui, etc	4	6	6	5	6
Siue	1				
Nec, neque				2	1
Vt autem	1				
Si					2
Exinde	1				
Denique	1				
Sed, sed et	1				3
Qualiter	1				
Porro	1				
Ideo					2
Inter quae	1				
Praeterea	1				
Ita, itaque		1			1
Autem (2nd word)		1			1
Nunc		1			1
Cum, cumque		1	1		1
Siquidem		1			
Rursum, rursus		1			1
Quin					1
-que (enclitic)		2			1
Item		1			
Nam, namque		1			5
Ergo (2nd word)			1	1	1
Sic, sicque			1	1	2
Vbi				1	
Alioquin				1	
Quia				2	
Atque				1	
Quoque (2nd word)					1
Totals	13	20	12	22	39
Total sentences	18	26	32	45	63
% of sentences beginning with 'link'	78	58	69	51	60

Table 31.9: Link words in Bedan passages studied.

OTHER STYLISTIC FEATURES

In addition to the features examined above, some other stylistic features in the passages may briefly be noted. Words and clauses are frequently used in a parallel 'biblical' style often using a chiastic structure, though as with the other features noted there is variety within the passages: the *HE* preface is written in a 'high' style, redolent of pomp and ceremony, with developed and lengthy sentence structure, carefully balanced, and using much parallelism; Bede is after all addressing the king as well as writing the introduction to his most famous work. In *HE* II. 13 the narrative is dynamic and flows freely; we may note some lively vulgarisms from Cædmon in *HE* IV.24 with a very vivid use of direct speech (note that the angel does not use the 'vulgar' idiom). In *Homily I*.13 there is extremely grammatically complex rhetoric, which is a show of sheer power particularly in the central section extolling Benedict Biscop's work for the monastery (*CCSL* 122, 93, lines 172–85 are the key section). *Homily I*.20 illustrates how Bede masterfully handles a complex argument while maintaining a lively pace.

In conclusion we can see in these extracts from Bede's huge extant corpus that his Latin is firmly rooted in that of the church Fathers, but it is not mannered or boring, and stands as a high point from which, according to Auerbach, the 'Carolingian revival' produced but a pale imitation: 'Einhard is correct . . . and relatively elegant, but lifeless. There is much more life in Gregory of Tours and sometimes even in Bede' (Auerbach 1965, 119). This author cannot agree about the robust if limited Gregory of Tours; Bede shows more subtlety than may have been recognized. Grounded in the finest of the Christian writers from the 4th and 5th centuries there is almost a 'time-warp' in his style, as indeed we might expect. In particular there is a variety of registers in which he is able to write, showing a light touch where necessary but also equipped with all the weaponry available to the rhetorician and preacher to stir the hearts of his audience without ever becoming maudlin or melodramatic. For Bede, as for his master Augustine, preaching was the pinnacle of the Christian teacher's role, for it led not to eloquence but to salvation itself. As for Augustine, writing in his sermon on Ezekiel 33.2–11, for Bede it was the *magnum onus, magnum pondus, magnus labor.*

We should be grateful that he had such models to follow. The linguistic situation of c 410 is set out neatly by Herman, and details much of the argument above:

Written texts, when read or listened to, were considered to be normally and usually understood by large popular publics, even unschooled and illiterate, on condition that authors and orators conformed to some seemingly obvious limitations: the texts had to be 'simple', without long and complicated periods, without neologisms or new foreign words, and when said or read aloud, this had to be done without undue speed, with clear and distinct pronunciation (Herman 1991, 37–8).

How far from the Hisperic ideal this is! Bede, as George Hardin Brown (1996, 1) has said, left verbal pyrotechnics to Aldhelm, and it is because Bede is not part of the Hisperic tradition, among other reasons, that this study has deliberately not attempted the type of analysis undertaken by Howlett in his recent studies (1994; 1995), based on numeric analysis and Hebraic biblical style.

No evidence was produced by this study for innovation in Bede's work – it would frankly have been surprising to find any – but as an emulator he stands at the very highest rank. The clarity of his expression is remarkable. There is no ambiguity, and his aim as a writer was clearly to communicate, to express himself so that his audience understands well (Cross 1996, 28), though the demands on his audience are not slight, and indicate a highly developed level of Latinity expected if not actualized among those monks who did speak Latin at Wearmouth-Jarrow and beyond (and indeed his secular audience too), bearing in mind, as we must, that *lectio* means 'reading out loud' (Chaytor 1945, 10, 12, 53). Bede may even have profited from his relative geographic isolation: Auerbach sees better Latin occurring in early medieval Insular contexts because 'Latin had been introduced only as a literary language and for this reason continued to be employed far more correctly'. The author expected to find variety, evidence of creativity, polish and skill – choosing a title before getting the results from the passages analysed seemed a safe bet – but this admittedly limited analysis is a clear insight into the breathtaking mastery and skill which Bede employs in his Latin works. Bede is like an early medieval star belatedly added to the galaxy whose brightest beacons were Augustine and Jerome. He was certainly regarded in precisely this way by successive generations in the monastic world, including Notker Balbulus at St Gallen, who regarded him (using a slightly different metaphor) as a 'new sun to illuminate the whole earth' (Allen 1996, 65). With Bede at its heart the early 8th century was indeed a Golden Age for Latin prose.

CHAPTER 32

SOURCE-MARKS IN BEDE'S BIBLICAL COMMENTARIES

Mark Stansbury

Bede's commentary on Luke, commissioned by Acca, bishop of Hexham, for those who needed a simple commentary on that gospel, is interesting not only for what Bede said about the gospel text, but also for the way he said it. Two aspects of the way Bede structured his commentary are significant: firstly, his extensive use of quotations from other writers; and secondly, the graphic conventions he employed to indicate those quotations. Composing biblical commentaries by making extensive use of other writers' works became common among Carolingian exegetes, but in Bede's time, the practice required explanation and justification, both of which were provided in letters between Acca and Bede prefaced to the Luke commentary. For this commentary Bede also developed a graphic system to indicate in the margins of the manuscript both the source and extent of the excerpts he used, a system he continued in the commentary on Mark, but not mentioned in any of his other exegetical works. Bede may have become especially sensitive to attributing quotations after criticism he received for his earlier commentary on Acts and may also have developed his system of marginal source-marks to ease his scribal labours.

Bede's commentary on Luke is among his earlier exegetical works. It was composed after the commentary on Acts (also commissioned by Acca), and both were composed before 716. Two letters comprise the preface of the Luke commentary: one from Acca to Bede requesting the commentary and answering several of Bede's objections to writing it, and a second letter from Bede replying to Acca's letter. Acca's letter begins by reminding Bede of his long-standing commitment to write a commentary on Luke and then answers Bede's objections, which are that the commentary was too difficult to write, that Ambrose had already done it better than Bede could, that Bede would be called a plagiarist (*compilator*), that Bede feared he would 'be thought to compose new things to replace the study of old writers', and that there were those who would ask why it was necessary to write a commentary on a book for which commentaries already existed when there were many books without commentaries that still needed them. Acca replies to these objections that nothing is said that has not been said before, that both Gregory in his homilies and Augustine and other Fathers have used the works of other writers in making their own works, that Ambrose's commentary is accessible only to the learned, not to the sort of reader so common today, and finally that Augustine used this very technique in his letter to Paulina *On seeing God*, where he took a portion of an Ambrose commentary, inserted it in his letter, and then explained it. Acca adds that his letter should be prefaced to Bede's commentary so that it will be clear that the commentary was written because of the esteem Bede had for him and to fulfil the need of the unlearned for a commentary *simpliciori stilo*. Finally, Acca adds that Bede should answer the objections raised against his, Bede's, interpretation of the evangelist symbols in his commentary on the Apocalypse, in which he had written that Matthew was the lion and Mark the man.

Bede's letter begins by marvelling that Acca could write the preface for the commentary before Bede had agreed to write it. Bede then goes on to say that he has done the work of the *dictator*, *notarius*, and scribe himself, and that after looking through the works of Ambrose, Augustine, Gregory, Jerome and other fathers to see what they said about Luke, he copied into the work exactly what they said or, in some cases, paraphrased their words. Because, Bede writes, it was a great deal of work to insert the name of the writer each time he used a passage; he gave each of the four writers a two-letter abbreviation and used the first letter in the margin of the manuscript to show where the quotation began and the second letter to show where it ended. Bede also implores subsequent scribes to include these source-marks so that he will not be accused of stealing the work of the *maiores*. After adding that he has also included some of his own thoughts on certain passages of Luke, Bede justifies the evangelist symbols he used in his Apocalypse commentary with three lengthy quotations from Augustine.

These two letters are, in a way, odd because they justify the practice of excerpting from other writers' works, which Bede had previously done in his earlier commentaries on the Apocalypse and Acts. From Acca's letter we can infer that this practice was not without its critics, to whom Acca replied that Bede's commentaries would still be useful because they explained the text (as well as the older commentaries) in ways that readers of his day could understand. Evidence of further criticism of Bede's exegesis can be found in his commentary on Acts (written shortly before the Luke commentary) and the *Retractatio* (written ten to fifteen years later). Bede used citations from other writers' works in composing his commentary on Acts, and indeed his explanation of Acts 2.6 in the story of Pentecost ('Because each heard them speaking in his own language') is composed entirely of an unattributed quotation from Rufinus's translation of Gregory Nazianzen. In the passage cited by Bede, Gregory Nazianzen wonders whether this verse means that the apostles went to each group of people and spoke different languages or whether the apostles spoke only once and their words were miraculously understood by each person in his or her own language. Apparently this explanation caused problems, for in the *Retractatio* (2.6), Bede writes:

> I know that I have been criticized by some because I said that this phrase could be understood in two ways, or rather because I wondered how it should be understood. I briefly answer them that I offered absolutely everything I wrote about this phrase in my previous book not from my own understanding, but took it from the words of a holy and totally irreproachable teacher, namely Gregory Nazianzen (*CCSL* 121, 110).[1]

After explaining the alternatives again in the *Retractatio*, Bede concludes that 'I think he has not erred who believes either of these could have happened' (*CCSL* 121, 111).[2] In other words, those who criticized Bede had not recognized that his 'commentary' on this verse was in fact a quotation from an 'irreproachable teacher', and Bede's response is to point this out. Because the Luke commentary was written after the commentary on Acts and before the *Retractatio*, this criticism could have arisen while Bede was composing the Luke commentary and could account for Bede's desire to be clear about when he is quoting others' work. In addition, if Bede did in fact do all the scribal work for the Luke commentary himself, then using marginal signs would have had the double advantage of not only lightening his work but would also have ensured that the quotations were clearly marked. The criticism of Bede's exegesis in the Acts commentary also shows that Acca was correct in saying that there were those who needed a commentary in simpler style – those who needed to have all the quotations marked for them, who could not be expected to recognize Bede's elegant borrowings.

How, then, did Bede hit upon this system for indicating quotations? Although no writer before Bede mentions using a system like it, there is evidence in manuscripts that marking citations with marginal signs was not unusual, and that such signs were added in Anglo-Saxon England. In 1928, E.A. Lowe published a continuation of an earlier study of the oldest Latin manuscripts. He recorded the graphic means used to indicate citations, and of the ninety-eight manuscripts in his second study, twenty-nine employ some device to indicate citations, usually indenting the quoted text or marking it in the margin with small S- or hook-shaped signs (Lowe 1928). Only one of the manuscripts in Lowe's list, a 4th-century fragment of Cyprian's letters in which the citations are in red ink and indented, is said to have been in England before 1100 (Gneuss 1981).[3] But the number of manuscripts and the range of authors represented in Lowe's list makes it possible that some sort of graphic device for marking citations was used widely enough that Bede could have seen such devices in the manuscripts he read. In addition, one manuscript, *Boulogne-Sur-Mer, Bibliothèque Municipale MS 32* (*CLA* VI, no 734), shows that such signs were added in England. *Boulogne 32* is a 6th- or 7th-century uncial manuscript of Ambrose. In *Codices Latini Antiquiores*, Lowe assigns the origin of the manuscript to Italy, but marginalia on folios 61 and 62 show that the manuscript was in England in the 8th century. During the manuscript's stay in England an Anglo-Saxon reader also added marginal signs to mark biblical citations in the first ten folios of the manuscript, which contain Ambrose's *Apologia pro David Propheta*.

Bede also used Primasius, the 6th-century bishop of Hadrumetum as one of his sources in his commentary on the Apocalypse. In the preface to his commentary Primasius wrote that he had included whatever he could find from the works of Augustine on the Apocalypse, but that primarily he excerpted 'the known Donatist Ticonius', always being careful to select only Tyconius's orthodox sentiments.[4] *Oxford, Bodleian MS Douce 140 (CLA II, no 33)*, from the 7th or 8th century, is the oldest manuscript of Primasius on the Apocalypse and has marginal annotations in 8th-century Anglo-Saxon minuscule; in addition, the biblical and patristic citations in this manuscript are marked with marginal signs reminiscent of those Lowe found in older manuscripts (Clark 1918, 104–23) and those in *Boulogne 32*. Could Bede have known Primasius's commentary in this manuscript or its exemplar? If he had, might this have furnished him with an example not only of method (a commentary using extensive citations from other authors) but also inspiration for marginal indications of these citations? Several problems make answering these questions difficult. Firstly, when Bede quotes Tyconius it is difficult to know whether Bede quoted from a Tyconius manuscript now lost or quoted him through Primasius. The 'catholicized' text of Tyconius survives in only one manuscript of the 11th century from Bobbio (Matter 1992, 41) and its text could thus have been 'corrected' from other works quoting Tyconius on the Apocalypse, making any argument about the text essentially circular. Secondly, Bede often mentions Tyconius in his Apocalypse commentary but Primasius only once.

Bede may also have been acquainted with marginal signs through the *Expositio Psalmorum* of Cassiodorus. The thirteen signs he used functioned in this work as marks of reference to show the reader where, for example, syllogisms or etymologies were being discussed in the Psalms. For Cassiodorus, the signs form an index that refers firstly to passages within the commentary and secondly, by extension, to the Psalms. Using these signs as an index, a student can, for example, scan the margins of the codex to find every marked discussion of the thirteen topics. Thus, by looking at the layout of Cassiodorus's commentary we can infer not simply what Cassiodorus thought about the Psalms, but what a student was supposed to take from their study. It is tempting to speculate that, in fact, Bede took the idea for his own signs from Cassiodorus, whose work he knew in its full form (Bailey 1983). Because the textual history of Cassiodorus's Psalm commentary has yet to be unravelled, it is impossible to know whether Bede's text contained these marginal signs.

Bede, then, may have drawn on graphic devices he saw in other manuscripts, and now we should turn to his sources for composing a biblical commentary by excerpting the works of previous writers. As we have seen, Acca cited a passage from Augustine in which Augustine does the same thing, but there are other possible sources as well. From antiquity, private reading had been accompanied by excerpting, presumably to create commonplace books. In a picturesque passage, Pliny the Younger described his uncle's habit:

> Often during the summer after a meal (which he ate lightly and easily as old men are wont) if there was leisure, he lay in the sun, a book was read, he annotated, and excerpted it. For he never read anything from which he did not take excerpts. He also used to say that there was no book so bad that some part of it was not useful (Mynors 1963, 73, 18–22, *Plin Sec Ep* 3.5.10).[5]

Such series of excerpts, often with specifically didactic ends, were popular in the late Roman world, and can be found in the *Noctes Atticae* of Aulus Gellius, the *Saturnalia* of Macrobius, and Cassiodorus's *De Orthographia*. In all of these works, excerpts from many works are joined into one book.

Yet another kind of excerpt can be seen in the ones made of a single author, such as those from Augustine made by Eugippius and from Gregory made by his notary, Paterius. In this kind of excerpt, the rationale is often that the writer wrote so much that few could have access to all these books, and even possessing them, few would be able to search through all of them. This is significant because later these same reasons were used by Bede and by Carolingian biblical commentators. At least five writers prior to Bede composed collections from the works of Augustine (Dekkers 1990); and three writers composed collections from the works of Gregory the Great (Wasselynck 1962).

It is also clear that Bede knew these sorts of excerpts and, in fact, created them himself. Among the catalogue of his works at the end of the *Historia Ecclesiastica*, Bede lists a work composed 'from whatever commentary I found on the Apostle in the works of St Augustine transcribed in the order of the Bible' (Colgrave & Mynors 1969, 569, V.24).[6] Wilmart (1926) identified Bede's collection as part of the one attributed in Migne to Florus of Lyon, and later, Fransen (1987), in the course of editing the work for the *Corpus Christianorum*, found persuasive evidence that Bede had, at times, used Eugippius's Augustine excerpts in composing his own.

Bede created a similar selection of excerpts from Gregory to serve as the sixth book of his commentary on the Song of Songs. Bede wrote that he drew from all Gregory's works except the sermons to form the sixth book of his commentary, and adds that anyone who wants should feel free to excerpt the sermons and add a seventh book. He concludes that:

> I have heard (*audiui*) that Paterius, a student of this same blessed Pope Gregory, collected whatever Gregory commented on in all of holy scripture

and put it into one volume, and if I had this work in my hands, I could have fulfilled the study I desired better and much more easily; but because I have not been worthy to see this book, I have undertaken, insofar as I could with the help of the Lord, to imitate it (*CCSL* 119B, 359, *In Cantica Canticorum* 6.17–23).[7]

These two examples show that Bede knew about the collections of Eugippius and Paterius, that he found them useful, and that such collections are linked to biblical commentary of the sort that Bede did.

As obscure as the origins of Bede's system may be, its fate in the Carolingian world of the 9th century is clear, and we can also shed light on these techniques by seeing how Carolingian scholars used his work. Perhaps the most significant fact is that by the 9th century Bede had become a *pater*, an exegete whose work was cited along with that of Augustine, Ambrose, Gregory, and Jerome. This authority seems to have applied not only to the words Bede wrote, but the way he wrote them as well, for at least four Carolingian scholars – Smaragdus, Claudius of Turin, Hrabanus Maurus, and Paschasius Radbertus – used Bede's technique of marginal source-marks and attribute this technique to Bede. None did so more often and more systematically than Hrabanus, the abbot of Fulda and student of Alcuin. In the preface to his commentary on Matthew, for example, Hrabanus said that his commentary was written not so much because a new commentary was necessary, but as it was convenient: because, he said, he had distilled many sayings and opinions into one volume, the reader who does not have many books or cannot understand the opinions of the Fathers can find something appropriate for him.[8] Then Hrabanus described how he used the initials of his sources to mark their citations in the margins of his commentary. Ironically, this passage about quoting authors is, in fact, a long quotation from Bede's letter to Acca at the beginning of Bede's commentary on Luke. Hrabanus then explained another feature he added to his commentary. He has, he wrote, included two sets of titles in the commentary: one written in black, the other written in red. The black titles are the same as the ones found in his copy of Matthew, so that if a monk reading this copy of Matthew finds a passage whose meaning (*allegoria*) he does not understand, he can note the chapter heading and then look for the identical chapter heading in Hrabanus's commentary to find an explanation of the text. The set of red titles, on the other hand, were composed by Hrabanus not for the gospel itself, but for the commentary and refer to the list of titles at the beginning of the commentary; thus they form an internal index to the commentary itself.

Bede stands at a pivotal point in biblical exegesis. He is among the first to write biblical commentaries by including long quotations from previous exegetes. His use of this technique has parallels in previous biblical commentary, but the way Bede uses these excerpts sets his commentaries apart. Bede also developed a new graphic technique to represent his way of doing exegesis by including marginal source-marks to indicate his borrowings. This technique may have come from two concerns: first, to ensure that his readers who were less erudite than he would know when Bede was quoting previous writers, and second as a labour-saving device for Bede the busy scribe. Finally, both these aspects of Bede's exegesis were widely used by Carolingian exegetes in the 9th century, for whom Bede had become one of the *patres*. For these Carolingian writers, too, simple commentaries that took the place of many books proved useful.

NOTES

1. '*Scio me esse reprehensum a quibusdam, quod hanc sententiam duobus modis posse intellegi dixerim, uel potius qualiter sit intellegenda quasierim. Quibus breuiter respondeo quod omne quicquid de eadem sententia in praecedente meo uolumine scripsi non hoc ex proprio sensu protuli, sed ex uerbis sancti et irreprehensibilis per omnia magistri, hoc est, Gregorii Nazianzeni assumpsi.*'

2. '*Non autem errasse reor illum, si quis utrumque fieri posse credat . . .*'.

3. No 297 in Gneuss (1981). He gives the shelf-mark as Add 40165 A 1 and the date and provenance as iv *ex* (Africa).

4. CCSL 92, 1, prol 4–10: '*ut non meis tantum solis fuerim contentus inuentis, sed quamquam numero pauca, si qua tamen a sancto quoque Augustino testimonia exinde exposita forte repperi, indubitanter adiunxi. Sed etiam a Ticonio quandam donatista certa, quae sano congruunt sensui, defloraui et ex eis quae eligenda fuerant, exundantia reprimens inportuna resecans et inpolita conponens catholico moderamine temperaui.*'

5. '*Post cibum saepe (quem interdiu leuem et facilem ueterum more, sumebat) aestate, si quid otii iacebat in sole, liber legebatur, adnotabat, excerptebatque. Nihil enim legit, quod non excerperet. Dicere etiam solebat, nullum esse librum tam malum ut non aliqua parte prodesset.*'

6. '*In Apostolum quaecumque in opusculis sancti Augustini exposita inueni, cuncta per ordinem transcribere curaui.*'

7. '*Audiui autem quia Paterius eiusdem beati papae Gregorii discipulus de tota sancta scriptura quaeque ille per partes in suis operibus explanauit collecta ex ordine in unum uolumen coegerit, quod opus si haberem ad manus facilius multo ac perfectius studium meae uoluntatis implerem; uerum quia necdum illud uidere merui ipse per me hoc prout potui imitari domino adiuuante curaui.*' I have not been able to discover how Bede knew of Paterius's collection.

8. PL 107.727 C-D: '*non quasi pernecessarium, cum multi scriptores me in illo vestigio praecesserint, sed quasi magis commodum, cum plurimorum sensus ac sententias in unum contraxerim, ut lector pauperculus, qui librorum copiam non habet, aut cui in pluribus scrutari profundos sensus Patrum non licet, saltem in isto sufficientiam suae indigentiae inveniat.*'

CHAPTER 33

(UN)DATING BEDE'S *DE ARTE METRICA*

Arthur Holder

At the end of his grammatical treatise *De Arte Metrica*, Bede addressed the recipient of the work as his 'most beloved son and *conlevita* [fellow Levite] Cuthbert' (Kendall 1991, 141, I.25). Since early Christian authors often identified the Old Testament Levites with the ecclesiastical order of deacons, Plummer concluded a century ago that Bede's use of the term *conlevita* in this context implied that *De Arte Metrica*, as well as the companion piece *De Schematibus et Tropis*, must have been composed some time after Bede's own ordination to the diaconate in 691 or 692, at the age of nineteen, but before his ordination as priest in 702 or 703, at the age of thirty (Plummer 1896, I, cxlv). This approximate dating of the work was further refined by Laistner, who argued that the paternal tone of Bede's address to Cuthbert would have been uncharacteristically patronizing unless there had been a difference of some years between the ages of the two men. Even if Cuthbert, like Bede, had been ordained a deacon before attaining the canonical age of twenty-five, Bede must have been nearly a decade older to have thought of his younger pupil as a 'son'; on this basis Laistner concluded that *De Arte Metrica* should be dated to the very last years of Bede's diaconate, in 701 or 702 (Laistner & King 1943, 131–2).

At least partly as a result of the early dating provided by scholars as influential as these, Bede's grammatical treatises have sometimes been disparaged or even dismissed as immature, derivative, and relatively insignificant 'school books' not worthy of comparison with the great works of history, hagiography, and biblical exegesis which were the principal products of his more mature years. In fact, his other grammatical treatise, *De Orthographia*, has until recently likewise been assigned an early date and treated as a slight composition, simply on the assumption that as a work on grammar it too must have belonged to an immature and unsophisticated period of Bede's literary career. However, Dionisotti (1982) has shown that a point of Greek translation about which Bede was in error in his commentary on Acts is correctly interpreted in *De Orthographia*, which means that the date of the latter must be after 709 –

perhaps much later – and that Bede's treatise on orthography is quite a sophisticated piece of work. Similar questions have been raised about the dating of *De Arte Metrica*, and, although some progress has been made, I do not think the matter can yet be considered fully resolved. My hope here is to bring us a few steps closer to a satisfactory conclusion.

The first person to question the dating of *De Arte Metrica* to the time of Bede's diaconate was Jones, in his preface to the critical editions of Bede's didactic works published in 1975 (*CCSL* 123A, x–xi). He was followed by Irvine (1986, 43) in a concluding note to an important article on Bede's grammatical studies. The redating of *De Arte Metrica* to a later period in Bede's life seems well on its way to becoming the new scholarly consensus, having been accepted by Brown in his book *Bede the Venerable* (1987, 35–6) and Kendall, who in the introduction to his recent edition and translation of *De Arte Metrica* and *De Schematibus et Tropis* from *St Gall MS 876* has suggested that they may have been published later, but based on some of Bede's old lecture notes (1991, 28–9).

We may sum up the force of the combined arguments of Jones and Irvine as follows: (1) Bede may have been using *conlevita* as a general term meaning 'fellow minister' or 'fellow cleric' rather than as a technical term for 'fellow deacon' (both Jones and Irvine say this); or (2) he may have been referring only to some conventual office within the monastery (so Jones); or (3) he may have been thinking of himself as still a deacon in a sense, since he had previously been ordained to the diaconal office and still exercised a diaconal function upon occasion (so Irvine). In any case, say both these scholars, if anyone was a deacon at the time of writing it was Cuthbert, not Bede, and on other grounds entirely *De Arte Metrica* is more probably dated much later in Bede's literary career. Not to prolong the suspense unduly, my own view is that they were right in their conclusion but mistaken in their grounds. I believe that I can offer a better, more convincing explanation of Bede's usage of the term *conlevita*, but first I must briefly address myself to the three distinct (and incompatible) explanations put forth by Jones and Irvine.

Firstly, could *levita* in the 8th century have simply meant 'fellow ordained minister'? I seriously doubt it. My investigations have convinced me that when Christian authors of the patristic and early medieval periods applied the term not to Old Testament Levites but to Christian ecclesiastics, they were consistently referring to ordained deacons. This was in accord with the widespread tendency in both East and West to assimilate the ecclesiastical ministries of bishop, presbyter, and deacon to the threefold Old Testament hierarchy of high priest, priest, and Levite (Dassmann 1970, 198–214). I cite only a few representative Latin examples from among many: Jerome used the word *levita* to refer to the deacon who sang the *Exsultet* at the Easter Vigil (Morin 1913, 55); the ordination prayers for deacons in both the Roman and Gallican sacramentaries explicitly speak of the diaconate as a Levitical office (Porter 1967, 30, 32, 54); Isidore of Seville in his *De ecclesiasticis officiis* explained that 'the order of deacons took its beginning from the tribe of Levi' (*CCSL* 113, 66, II.8.1); in the 9th century, Paschasius Radbertus, deacon and abbot of Corbie, composed an acrostic on his own name in which the first letters of each line spell out RADBERTUS LEVITA (*PL* 120, 1387–8); and the early 11th-century *Liber vitae* from New Minster in Winchester customarily uses the term *levita* to identify the deacons in its lists (Gerchow 1988, 320–6). But most pertinent here is a passage in Bede's own commentary on Ezra and Nehemiah. Commenting on Ezra 2.70, where some Levites are said to have returned to Jerusalem from exile in Babylon, Bede says that this is fulfilled in a spiritual sense 'when, with the Lord's assistance, any deacon of Holy Church resumes possession of the virtue of perfection which he had squandered when he was led astray by the devil' (*CCSL* 119A, 262). In short, the term *levita* applied to a Christian cleric throughout the patristic and early medieval periods is consistently used as a technical term for 'deacon'.

As for Jones's second suggestion, that *levita* might refer to some functionary within the monastic community, we can only surmise what sort of functionary he might have had in mind. It is true that the Greek word *diakonos* originally meant simply 'servant' or 'steward', and that on occasion it continued to be used in those senses by Christian authors writing in Greek, but this secular usage does not seem to have carried over into Latin. Perhaps Jones was thinking of the traditional parallel between the New Testament deacon and the monastic cellarer, such as is implied in Chapter 31 of the Benedictine *Rule* when it applies to the cellarer a line which in 1 Tim 3.13 refers to deacons: 'Those who carry out their duties well will earn a high standing' (Vogüé 1988, 2:273–83). But this is only an analogy of function, not an identification of office. I have found no patristic or early medieval evidence that either the Latin *diaconus* or its Hebrew antitype *levita* was ever used outright to designate a monk who was not an ordained deacon.

Now we come to the third suggestion, put forth by Irvine (1986, 43), that Bede may have considered himself Cuthbert's *conlevita* since 'they shared the duties as well as the office of deacon'. It is true that, from the 4th century on, the various orders of clergy had come to be understood as a *cursus honorum*, analogous to secular dignities and arranged hierarchically as steps on a ladder, rather than organically in pre-Nicene fashion, as interdependent and equally respectable roles (Dix 1946, 284; Faivre 1977; Gibaut 1995, 367–91). Accordingly, Eddius Stephanus reports in his *Vita Wilfridi* that Chad was advanced 'through all the ecclesiastical degrees' when Theodore reconsecrated him in the Roman succession to be bishop of Mercia (Colgrave 1927, 32). By Bede's time, direct *per saltum* ordination to the presbyterate was no longer the norm, and it was customary for priests to have had prior service as deacons – though Popes were often chosen directly from the diaconal ranks of the Roman church and frequently seem to have been made bishop without going through the presbyteral stage (Barnett 1981, 110–11; Gibaut 1995, 377–8). Moreover, the 8th-century Roman *Ordo*

XXXIV called for one who was about to be consecrated bishop to be vested with a dalmatic, implying that the diaconal function was subsumed within the episcopal (though not necessarily the presbyteral) office (Bradshaw 1990, 220). And when Photius was consecrated patriarch of Constantinople in the 9th century he was ordained to several orders on successive days – but note that there is no evidence to support the often-repeated claim that the catechumen Ambrose similarly passed through the various orders after being elected bishop of Milan in the 4th century (Barnett 1981, 109–11; Weil 1996, 205–8). Undoubtedly, the cumulative theology of ordination to which Irvine refers was developing rapidly throughout the church.

And yet, it is anachronistic, I believe, to imagine that an 8th-century Anglo-Saxon priest such as Bede might have filled in as liturgical deacon at solemn High Mass, or might have continued to exercise other specifically diaconal functions. This was a later development that would only have been necessary after the demise of the diaconate as a permanent (or at least long-term) vocation; but there was apparently no shortage of deacons to serve at monastic altars in Bede's time. As I have already noted, Bede himself remained a deacon for eleven years (op. cit. 566, V.24). The Cuthbert who wrote the well-known account of Bede's death was in deacon's orders, whether or not he was the same Cuthbert to whom *De Arte Metrica* was addressed (op. cit. 580). The venerable cleric Pehthelm, who later became the first bishop of Whithorn, was said by Bede to have been both deacon and monk *multo tempore* (op. cit. 1969, 512, V.18). Even in the Carolingian period, both Alcuin and Radbertus had distinguished careers as theologians and abbots while remaining deacons until the ends of their lives. A theology of holy orders as cumulative and sequential (a theology of the sort that would be necessary to support the notion 'once a deacon, always a deacon'), was certainly beginning to emerge by the time of Bede, but it was not yet fully in place.

In any event, there is a simpler, and happily less speculative, approach to interpreting Bede's use of the term *conlevita*, which is to see it within the context of an ancient, widespread, and well-documented convention of Christian Latin epistolary style (O'Brien 1930; Jerg 1970). For while Bede is the earliest known author to have used the term *conlevita*, patristic Latin contains hundreds of attested citations of analogous forms consisting of the prefix *con* plus the name of an order of ordained ministry. A search via CD-ROM of the CETEDOC patristic corpus yields 453 occurrences of *conepiscopus*, 156 occurrences of *consacerdos*, 43 occurrences of *conpresbyter*, and 14 occurrences of *condiaconus*. Most of these occurrences appear in letters, either in the opening address or with reference to a third party, but some are in canons of church councils or other literary genres. Behind this usage lie many examples of comparable patristic Greek forms beginning with *sum*, as well as the *consenior* ('fellow elder') of Latin versions of 1 Peter 5.1, and classical forms such as *conservus* ('fellow servant') and *commilito* ('fellow soldier').

A remarkable feature of this body of data is that 27% of the total number of Latin patristic occurrences of all these forms appears in the writings of Augustine (Holder 1996, 100–4). When we look at the two forms *conpresbyter* and *condiaconus*, in which the reference is to a member of the lower clergy, the results are even more striking: Augustine provides 31 out of 43 (or 72%) of the examples of 'fellow presbyter' and 12 out of 14 (or 86%) of the examples of 'fellow deacon'; this accords well with Augustine's emphasis on the communal character of diocesan clergy which led him to require all the clergy of Hippo to live together in the bishop's own household under a monastic rule (Van der Meer 1987, 200–6; Lawless 1987). An examination of Augustine's usage quickly persuades us that the term *condiaconus* need not indicate that both parties are in deacon's orders, for the bishop of Hippo often addressed not only his own deacons but deacons in other dioceses in this way. Furthermore, we can confidently rule out any notion that Augustine's use of the term *condiaconus* was somehow dependent on his own prior ordination as a deacon, because we know from his biographer Possidius that Augustine was never a deacon at all, having been ordained directly to the priesthood, as was standard procedure in the 4th century (*PL* 32, 36–7).

As an example of Augustine's usage we may consider *Letter 149* which is addressed to his 'most blessed, venerably esteemed and estimably venerable, holy and religiously cherished brother and fellow bishop, Paulinus', and then in the first paragraph makes reference to 'our brother and fellow presbyter, Quintus', as well as 'our son and fellow deacon, Rufinus' (*CSEL* 44, 348). Notice the combination of familial language such as 'brother' and 'son' with words indicating that the cleric (of whatever rank) has a share along with the writer in the common ministry of Christ, each according to his own office. The *Letter* which contains these forms is of particular interest to us, inasmuch as Bede quoted from it extensively in his *Collectaneum* on the Pauline epistles (Ogilvy 1967, 87; Fransen 1961, 64). Could we not describe Bede's usage 'son and fellow Levite' in *De Arte Metrica* as a not-very-distant echo of Augustine's 'son and fellow deacon'? In both cases, the paternal tone is appropriate for a bishop or presbyter in relation to a deacon occupying a subordinate position, who is probably a younger man as well.

This letter is the only one of Augustine's writings certainly known to Bede that contains any of the forms in question. However, in *De Temporum Ratione* Bede quoted a passage containing the word *conepiscopus* from a letter of Leo the Great (*CCSL* 123B, 419), and in the prologue to his prose *Vita Cuthberti* Bede refers to himself as Bishop Eadfrith's *conservus* (Colgrave 1940, 142). In addition, there is further evidence for knowledge of this epistolary style among Bede's circle of friends. Bishop Acca's letter which stands as the prologue to Bede's commentary on Luke hails Bede himself as 'most reverend brother in Christ and *consacerdos*' (*CCSL* 120, 5) and Cuthbert's account of the death of Bede is addressed to one Cuthwin, his *conlector*, which might mean 'fellow teacher' but could just as easily be translated as 'fellow lector', with apparent reference to the minor order of clergy by that name (Colgrave & Mynors 1969, 580).

When we consider Bede's term *conlevita* in the context of this well-attested patristic (and characteristically Augustinian) style of epistolary address, it no longer appears as a puzzling anomaly, but rather as a variation on a common Christian literary theme. A *conlevita* is a 'fellow Levite', which is equivalent to 'fellow deacon', but is perhaps more readily understood if we paraphrase it as something like 'deacon who is my colleague in the ministry of Christ'. This, I suggest, is how it would have been intended by Bede and understood by Cuthbert his addressee. In subsequent centuries, the term *conlevita* crops up in only two other texts known to me. At the end of the 9th century, Abbo of St Germain des Prés used this word in referring to himself as 'the last of God's creatures, a humble fellow Levite', and the Winchester Troper (which is found in 10th- and 11th-century manuscripts) employed the plural form in reference to the fellow deacons of St Stephen who sing with joy on the day of his feast (Waquet 1964, 2; Frere 1894, 7). It is hardly surprising that a term used so infrequently should present commentators with difficulties in interpretation, and in the 9th century its true meaning was already lost to Remigius of Auxerre, who in his gloss on Bede's *De Arte Metrica* explained with reference to the word *conlevita*: 'that is, a Levite at the same time, because blessed Bede was then a deacon also' (CCSL 123A, 141). Modern scholars who have misunderstood the term for so many years can take solace in the realization that in this state of confusion we have not been alone.

In conclusion, lest anyone should wonder if a single word is really deserving of so much attention, let me recall once more the issue at stake. If Bede's use of *conlevita* in *De Arte Metrica* does not indicate that he was a deacon at the time of writing (as I believe I have demonstrated upon grounds more convincing than those previously put forth), then both this treatise and *De Schematibus et Tropis* could have been written (or at least revised) in Bede's maturity. Whatever the date of their composition may finally be determined to be, the grammatical texts should no longer be considered as mere warm-up exercises for his allegedly more 'serious' work in the fields of history and exegesis. On the contrary, as King has said (1979, 1:146), with Bede 'grammar had become the handmaid of monastic spirituality'. In this regard, perhaps we ought to note that a handmaid is a servant, to be sure, but also a constant companion. The grammatical treatises, no less than Bede's other works, should always be viewed as an integral part of his programme of theological education and ecclesiastical reform. Then we shall be better able to appreciate this more well-rounded Bede whose vocation as a Christian teacher included his work in grammar as well as his more celebrated efforts in history and theology.

CHAPTER 34

AUGUSTINE AND GREGORY THE GREAT IN BEDE'S COMMENTARY ON THE APOCALYPSE

Thomas W. Mackay

In his masterful 1966 Jarrow Lecture, Gerald Bonner reported his cataloguing of Bede's sources in the Apocalypse commentary and the role of Tyconius in western exegesis of the Apocalypse. He evinces an astute and tender appreciation of Bede's spirituality and mind. This article expands upon Bonner's lecture particularly for Augustine and Gregory the Great.

Much of the evidence relevant to source and stylistic analysis results from the intense and minute examination of words, phrases and the critical apparatus. This article will detail some pieces of evidence, though it will not bring forth the full array. For the sake of comparison we will observe Bede's use of both Augustine and Gregory the Great in his Apocalypse commentary, the *Expositio Apocalypseos* as he termed it in his commentary on Acts.[1] Here Bede names Gregory as a source three times, but at current tabulation there are at least a dozen other passages where he has interwoven phrases or sentences from Gregory who did not write explicitly on the Apocalypse and had not previously been drawn into the western tradition of exegesis on that book. All Bede's quotations are direct and without intermediary – an interesting counterpoint to his use of passages from Augustine.

For Apocalypse 20 Bede is dependent primarily on Augustine through Primasius with some indications of direct borrowing or confirming reading.[2] Likewise he is greatly dependent on Augustine for shaping his thoughts, doctrinal perspective, and verbal expression. But some of the doctrine, exegesis and expression comes ostensibly from Augustine while he has in turn drawn from others; for the Apocalypse that often means from Tyconius (Fredrickson 1992; Matter 1992). Certainly this is true for the basic non-literalist approach to exegesis, for the symbolic interpretation of words, numbers and ideas in the Apocalypse, and for the application of Tyconius's seven rules for interpreting Scripture, the *Liber Regularum*. Augustine has expanded on his source, refined and developed the ideas, and integrated them into his masterpiece, the *City of God*.[3] A comparative study of Apocalypse commentaries demonstrates that some expressions in Augustine have verbal parallels in Tyconian derivatives because they were all from a common source.

Bede's *Expositio Apocalypseos* has several quotations or adaptations of Gregory the Great's *Moralia in Iob*, though the source itself is not named. Nevertheless early manuscripts of his commentaries on Mark and Luke, contemporary with the *Expositio* and adopting a practice perhaps prompted by fashioning it, often exhibit 'source-marks' or letters in the margins to signal the beginning and end of a patristic quotation. These are an early type of footnote where Bede, who implores the scribes to copy the source notations as well as the text, at least attempts to alert his readers to the major Latin Father he is quoting: 'HR' means Hieronymus; 'AM', Ambrosius; 'AV', 'Au', or 'AG' indicates Augustinus; and 'GR', Gregorius (Sutcliffe 1926; Laistner 1933; Jones 1937; see Stansbury above).[4] There is no marginal notation of sources in manuscripts of Bede's Apocalypse commentary, but occasionally he names sources in the commentary proper.

Definitions in Jerome's *Liber Interpretationis Hebraicorum nominum* (CCSL 72, 59–161) that Bede uses on Apc 7.5–8 (150C–152C) without mention of Jerome were already in Primasius. Bede does name Jerome when he takes two extracts from his commentary on Daniel: for Apc 8.1 (154C) he uses *in Dan* 4 on 12.12, and for Apc 14.18 (176C) he draws from Jerome's *in Dan* 2 on 7.10, not his *in Isaiam* as Bonner suggested (CCSL 75A, 943.670–944.677, 679; 846.655–8); Primasius did not use Jerome on Daniel. By contrast Gregory sometimes is named, more often not, though all of Bede's quotations appear to be at first hand.

In the preface Gregory is named as a historical figure (*non dudum, id est temporibus beati papae Gregorii*), and Bede had copies of his correspondence with Augustine and others in England (Colgrave & Mynors 1969, 78–103, 1.27). For Apc 4.2 (143A) Bede's comment draws upon Gregory, *Moralia in Iob* 2.38 on Job 1.6, fashioning one shorter sentence from a single sentence in Gregory – two phrases of three words each, one of two words, and three single words, of which two are adapted (CCSL 143, 83.75–7).[5] In his comment for Apc 5.10–13 (146C) Bede uses the same work on 5.11 (CCSL 143, 65.53–4, *Mor* 2.10 on Job 1.8); it is one sentence of eleven words from Gregory, unchanged. Finally, for Apc 14.18 (176D) Bede makes one sentence of twenty-one words from a single sentence in Gregory's *Homilia in Euangelia* 2.35.2 (PL 76, 1260D.47–50). Bede uses it as his final comment, before dropping the last two words (transition), writing *quamlibet* for *quamuis*, *mundi finis* inverted from *finis mundi*, and *quia* for *qui* (perhaps an Insular confusion).

Bede also quotes from Gregory's *Homilia* in his commentaries on Mark and Luke and his own *Homilies on the Gospels*. The earliest extant manuscript of Gregory's *Homilia* is from 7th-century Anglo-Saxon England, *Cambridge Corpus Christi College MS 69* (Gneuss 1981, no 42; Budny 1997, I.89–94), so we have a manuscript containing the text (or rather, half of the homilies) essentially as Bede knew it.

Bede's exegesis of Apc 5.8 (146A) states that *fialis ureo corda latitudine caritatis patula designatur*, a paraphrase of Gregory (*PL* 76, 1098BC, *Hom I.6.6*). Moreover, Bede's exegesis of Apc 19.9 (188D) includes a direct quotation of two sentences from Gregory, dropping the first two transition words, *id circo enim*, and slightly compressing the end, *non ad prandium . . . ueniunt*, which he follows by *profecto ad coenam Agni uocantur*, paraphrasing Gregory's *non ad Agni prandium sed ad coenam uocantur* (*PL* 76, 1187D–1188A, *Hom II.24.6*; cf 1267AB, 2.36.2).

In the lengthy discussion of the stones in Apc 21.19–20 (201CD), Bede also alludes to a passage from Gregory's *Homilies* where he comments on the nine stones of Ez 27.13 (*PL* 76, 1249–50B, *Hom II.34.7*).

For the conclusion of his comment on Apc 14.3 (173CD), Bede quotes two sentences – forty-two words in Bede, after eliminating *quippe* transition as the second word in the first of the two sentences – from Gregory's *Regula Pastoralis* 3.28 (*PL* 77, 106B, *Admonitio* 28), a text known to Bede (cf Laistner 1935; Gneuss 1981, esp nos 771, 894).

Another eight passages come unacknowledged from the *Moralia in Iob*. On Apc 3.21 (142C) Bede quotes verbatim four lines on Job 36.7 (*CCSL* 143B, 1307.32–7, *Mor* 26.53). The first twelve words are the *lemma*, followed immediately by a sentence of which Bede quotes the first twenty-five words, adapting *sedisse se asserit* into *sedit*.

For Apc 6.11 (148B) Bede quotes Is 61.7, the same passage Gregory quotes in the *Moralia* in connection with Apc 6.11 (*CCSL* 143B, 1789.29–36, *Mor* 35.25 on Job 42.10; cf *CCSL* 143, 66.64–71, *Mor* 2.11 on Job 1.8).[6] Also, Bede's statement regarding the resurrected state is a mosaic paraphrase of Gregory's context.

The source of Bede's scriptural parallel in his comment on Apc 10.6 (161C) is Gregory's *Moralia* 4.5 on Job 3.3 (*CCSL* 143, 116, with lines 116–17 for Apc *lemma* in connection with Ps 80.16). There Gregory cites Ps 80.16 as *erit tempus eorum in aeternum*, a quotation taken from Jerome's *Psalterium Romanum*, the earliest of his three versions of the Psalms. His later revisions, the *Gallicanum* and the *Hebraicum*, both read *erit tempus eorum in saeculo*.[7] When Bede paraphrases Ps 80.16, he writes *erit utique tempus impiorum in aeternum* – with *in aeternum* echoing Gregory's quotation of the *Romanum*. The remainder of Bede's words in this comment are modelled after or suggested by the passage in Gregory, and the quotation that Bede appends from 1 Cor. 15.52 also uses the words *in aeternum*.

In the fontes notes to Romero-Pose's edition of Beatus (1985, 2, 140.2–3),[8] there is reference to a verbal source for Bede on Apc 13.11 in Gregory's *Moralia*:

quia per hypocrisin sanctitatis eam quam in se ueraciter dominus habuit singularem sibi inesse et sapientiam mentitur et uitam (*CCSL* 143B, 1724.17–19; *PL* 76, 711.19–33, *Mor* 33 xxv.59).

This is affixed to the first eight words of his sentence that come from Tyconius but for which there is no echo in Gregory except *agni cornua*, from the *lemma*. Bede has fashioned one part from Tyconius and completed it with nineteen consecutive words from Gregory.

For the explanation of Apc 14.14 (176B) Bede has relied on Gregory's *Moralia* 33.21 on Job 40.21 (*CCSL* 143B, 1691. 23–6, and 18–20 for Bede's *lemmata*, all one verse reference in Gregory).[9] From this Bede has drawn the first three sentences after the *lemma* in Gregory to use a phrase of nine words to which he then appends Gregory's previous sentence – five words, drop two, take two more – thus inverting Gregory's sentence order. The last word, the verb *cadet* in Bede, corresponds to the reading of manuscripts C and M of Gregory (*Monte Cassino 77 DD, sx, Benevento* and *Manchester, Rylands MS 83*, from Spain, AD 914) versus the printed edition *cedit*.

For Apc 16.8 (180A) Bede gives an extensive explanation including a verbatim quotation from Gregory's *Moralia* 34.25 on Job 41.21 (*CCSL* 143B, 1750.29–1751.35, verbatim lines 33–5), but he also paraphrases the interpretation of the entire passage. He freely reverses the order of the paraphrased portions.

Bede's explanation of Apc 20.12 (193D) is drawn from Gregory's *Moralia* 24.16 on Job 33.27 (*CCSL* 143B, 1199.64–5 for *lemma*; 58, 63, 66–8 for comment).[10] In this discussion Bede curiously interweaves a passage from Tyconius with words from *Moralia in Iob* 24.16 (a ten-word phrase plus another ten words used in a mosaic-like construction). The Tyconius background is attested by words in Caesarius and Beatus (Caesarius, Morin 1942, 270.24–30; Beatus, Romero-Pose 1985, 2, 373.1–3, 16–374.1; Sanders 1930, 615).

Finally, Bede cites Job 38.32 in connection with the *sublemma* for Apc 22.16 (206B), *stella splendida et matutina*. Commenting on Job Gregory cites the same Apocalypse *sublemma*, including the *et* that is not in Primasius (*CCSL* 143B, 1487.1–14, esp 1–2, 7, 9, 11–14, *Mor* 29.75). Moreover, several words in the comment between the two Scriptures in Bede are fashioned in a mosaic from Gregory's exegesis.

Bede knew these texts of Gregory directly, the quotations are deliberate, and so this provides a pattern of use and verbal adaptation characteristic of Bede. We will now detail some of Bede's extensive use of Augustine.

Bede knew and read Augustine both directly and indirectly. For his account of Tyconius's seven rules in the preface, Bede compressed Augustine's summary at the end of *De Doctrina Christiana* 3, as variants and the critical apparatus to Augustine indicate (*CCSL* 32, 102–16, *De Doc Chr* 3.30, 42–3.37, 56; cf Mackay 1979). To read Bede, it would appear that he was reading Tyconius directly, perhaps from the preface to his own commentary, but Augustine is mentioned twice in that context and is in fact the source. Furthermore, he is named for another quotation, this time the last sentence of *Contra Adversarium Legis et Prophetarum*, Book 1 (*CCSL* 49, 86.1543–4), a line also quoted by Bede as the last sentence of *In Lucam I*, 31.73–4:

> *Nescio quo enim modo, ut beatus [om in Luc] Augustinus ait, ita libri termino reficitur lectoris intentio secut labor viatoris hospitio.*

This work is also used five times as a source for *In Genesim*.

In the commentary proper, Bede cites Augustine by name four times (144AB, 173D, 175C, 191D; cf Mackay 1995). Augustine's words are also woven into the fabric of Bede's comments on several passages. When at Apc 4.7 (144A) Bede refers to the four animals and the evangelists, he apparently relies on Primasius (*CCSL* 92, 53.167–55.199) for a passage from Augustine's *Tractatus in Iohannis* (*CCSL* 36, 327.10–35; cf Caesarius, Morin 1942, 220.7–13).[11]

Primasius refers to Augustine's *De Virginitate* at Apc 14.4 and quotes extensively, but Bede (173D–174A) skips two pages in Primasius to pick out another passage from the same work of Augustine.[12] Even then he trims it, quoting the first complete sentence of seven lines, compressing the next sentence by omitting seventeen, then nine words, and then dropping twelve lines except for one group of two words, another of six, to which is adjoined four lines minus five words. The last lines include 1 Peter 2.21 that Bede quotes with his distinctive Vulgate twists following the *Codex Amiatinus* text for *uobis* instead of *nobis*, but accepting from Augustine an omission of *et* and an inversion *pro uobis passus est*. Based on Tyconius's *Liber Regularum* Reg 1 (Burkitt 1895, 5.25–6), Augustine apparently has interpreted the Virgin as being the church (*CSEL* 41, 244.16–17, *De Virg* 11–13; cf Bede on Apc 14.5, 174B). Beatus has the same Scripture references as Bede and also the same interpretation of the Virgin.[13] This interpretation goes back to a very early Christian approach and may have been in the Apocalypse explanations by Victorinus and Hegesippus and the identification in Hermas (Mackay 1990).

Again at Apc 14.11 (175C), Bede names Augustine, for he has interwoven words and phrases from *City of God* but not through Primasius (cf *dCD* 20.9 in Primasius as part of a comment on Apc 20.4). Augustine underlies much of Primasius's exegesis on Apc 14 though he is not named or overtly quoted there as source.

Primasius used Augustine's *City of God* 20.7–15 – effectively a commentary on Apc 20 – frequently without acknowledgement of author or source. For that chapter, Bede summarized Augustine as it was written and adapted by Primasius. Given his mind, memory, and methods, together with independent citation of *City of God*, Bede was probably sometimes aware of the ultimate source, perhaps sometimes not. Verbal clues indicate occasional direct quotation from Augustine, but most commonly it was through Primasius.

At Apc 20.3 (191D), near the beginning of the section in Primasius on Apc 20 drawn directly from Augustine, *City of God* 20.7–15, Bede interjects *ut sanctus Augustinus ait* for the first extended passage from Augustine, though Primasius has not named him (nor did the recent *CCSL* editor, Adams, detect the borrowing at any time in Apc 20). In his 1966 Jarrow Lecture, Bonner correctly notes a wider extent of Bede's indirect dependence on Augustine through Primasius for Apc 20.3–21.1. In fact, Augustine in *City of God* 20.7–17 underlies even more from Apc 20.1–21.2 than Bonner observed.

When quoting Augustine for Apc 20.6, Bede includes the words *qui proprie uocantur in ecclesia sacerdotes* that Primasius omitted.[14] Clearly he has directly quoted the words.

Conversely, at Apc 22.4, Primasius has named Augustine for another passage from *Epist* 147 that Bede does not use and introduces yet another thus: *Item in libro uicesimo secundo de Ciuitate Dei idem sic dicit* (dCD 22.29). But when Bede uses this quotation from Augustine in his commentary (204CD), he does not identify the origin by author or work. By retaining *dei* in Primasius, Bede further demonstrates that he has not taken the quote directly from Augustine himself.[15]

In his commentary on the last of Apc 20.4 (192A), Bede quotes from Augustine through Primasius for two and half lines, skips sixteen lines, then quotes an additional three and a half lines. All of this is in a section of some fifty lines directly and continuously quoted by Primasius. But Bede has already used words from the sixteen lines to fashion a mosaic-like sentence at the end of Apc 14.11 (175C) where he identifies *sanctus Augustinus . . . dicit* as source. Clearly, Bede was in control of his sources directly, yet he chose to follow Primasius's reading of Augustine, *City of God* for convenience, except the language for comments on Apc 14.11, 20.1, 3B, 6 (175C, 191AB, 191C, 192C). Yet, for 20.3 (191D) where Bede acknowledges the ultimate literary source, and elsewhere, variants of the Fulda manuscript (*Kassel Theol MS*, fol 24) show the passage comes from Primasius.

Bede's independence from his sources also includes splitting the *lemmata* and commenting on many more phrases than his sources, Tyconius, Augustine, Primasius and others. He is also very conscientious about using the Vulgate for his *lemmata*, while his sources typically had an Old Latin text. But when he quotes them, he normally does not change their words that make internal reference to the Old Latin *lemmata*.

Even a cursory examination of Bede's other works (exegetical, historical and didactic) reaffirms that he often did not identify the source of quote or paraphrase. Still, as noted above, the presence of 'source-marks' in some early manuscripts attests to his integrity as a writer and scholar. Unfortunately, there is no consistent pattern of naming literary sources in the actual text of his commentaries. There is, however, one curious feature of composition, a feature quite noticeable as Bede borrows from his sources. He will frequently abbreviate a passage by quoting the first few lines and, less often, also the last sentence or so. For example, in his comment on Apc 20.4 (192AB), the Northumbrian monk has used the initial and final statements of Augustine (718.92–4 and 111–14, *dCD* 20.9). By contrast, Primasius quotes most of eighty lines, except for some short gaps totalling less than a dozen lines.[16]

As to why Bede does not use a longer or different selection, the explanation is merely one of length and bulk, not doctrinal disagreement. In general, the *Expositio Apocalypseos* has rather brief comments for any scriptural *lemma*. There are exceptions, namely the prefatory summary of the seven rules of Tyconius, the names of the Twelve Tribes of Israel, and the twelve stones on the temple at the New Jerusalem. But Bede, with his concern for what actually works in instruction, generally restricts his own composition to a more modest scale than that of his predecessors (Palmer 1959).

To understand why we find indirect quotations in Bede, we must merely look at his method of composition. Apparently he would make notes, including textual variants, for some time as he gathered information. But his own writing, where possible, would rest primarily on one or two sources, with the other evidence inserted appropriately (this is clear from an examination of Plummer 1896; cf Mackay 1976). Occasionally he would also revise in the light of new information though his exegetical works do not appear to have been transmitted in different recensions (Meyvaert 1964).[17] The fundamental composition, developed from one or two main sources, was the only text copied for dissemination. Such is the case with the *Expositio*; Bede relied on Tyconius and Primasius, interweaving other sources as appropriate. Yet he does not hesitate to name an author whom his source cites as, for example, when he names Tyconius in the preface though Bede was using Augustine's *De Doctrina Christiana* for his summary. Hence, if Bede elsewhere used quotations from Augustine via Primasius, it may be that to do so was far more convenient, given his normal *modus operandi* or it may possibly have been that he did not recognize the passage in its borrowed form as having originally been stated by another author.

Those commentaries dependent on Tyconius enable us to control, in a certain measure, Augustine's interpretation and phraseology for his discussion of Apc 20. Thus, in comparing Bede and Augustine, those expressions which we consistently find elsewhere in the traditional exegesis of the Apocalypse we may well suspect to have been borrowed from Tyconius's commentary.

The beginning of Bede's *Expositio* is replete with allegorical interpretations. These interpretations follow the guidelines of the *Liber Regularum* that Bede summarizes in the preface. For instance, the names of the seven cities are given allegorical interpretations, and at Apc 2.10 (138B) the ten days are taken to be the ten persecutions from Nero to Domitian. At Apc 4.4 (143BC) the two testaments are taken to be the Twenty-four Elders, just as at Apc 1.13 (136A) the two breasts are the two testaments. Numerous other examples could be adduced, but these few will suffice.

SUMMARY AND CONCLUSIONS

When Bede infuses words from Gregory he does so directly. When he has quoted Augustine for the Apocalypse it is as well first to check Primasius to ascertain whether the passage came to Bede directly or indirectly. However, the *CCSL* edition of Primasius is not strong on literary sources and parallels, so the reader must compare Augustine to Primasius independently.

Often Bede will take the first three sentences after a *lemma* and apply them to his text, although he is always free to modify grammatical structure, to abbreviate, to refashion in a literary mosaic. Generally he will preserve entire phrases with little or no disruption. But indirect usage can often be determined by the adaptations or manuscript variants of the intermediate source: Augustine for Tyconius's seven rules and Primasius for Augustine's *City of God*, for instance. Bede is quite aware of his own sources, both direct and indirect, and he is rather conscientious about informing his readers.

It is indisputable that Bede has relied heavily on Tyconius and Primasius in composing the *Expositio*. Nevertheless there are a number of other passages where Augustine is quoted or where references are made to ideas found in the *City of God*. This notion of the last days is reinforced by Bede's comments in *De Temporibus* and *De Temporum Ratione*, especially the chronicles (Jones 1943, 303, *De Temp* 16.17–18; *CCSL* 123B, 463–4, *De Temp Rat* 66–71). We further see this attitude in his letter to Plegwin on the ages of the world (Jones 1943, 308–15, esp 308, para 4, lines 23–4). In all these works the fundamental viewpoint is that the church began to reign on earth commencing with Christ's Incarnation and that the millennium is an endless age which will occur after the Resurrection and Judgement; these two notions fuse in Augustine and his intellectual heirs. The fact that this attitude towards the seven ages of the world is found in such widely disparate writings that Bede composed throughout his productive years indicates that this has been a basic tenet of his understanding. Apparently this idea has come from *City of God*, though early Christian exegesis was literal and espoused positions Augustine later abhorred. Yet, as we examine more closely Bede's *Expositio*, one of his earliest writings, we discern that several of the fundamental elements that dovetail completely with this world view in fact come to Bede from earlier commentators on the Apocalypse and in particular from Tyconius. All of this leads to the conclusion that either Bede has, under the influence of *City of God*, culled those parts of his earlier commentators which corresponded with his view or else Augustine's *City of God* incorporates and develops the world view of Tyconius (Monceaux 5.216; Markus 1970, 115–18; Lauras & Rondet 1953). And it is from this world view that Bede has drawn his perspective.

Consequently, we may state that, based on the evidence seen in the various commentators on the Apocalypse, Augustine has adopted some of the interpretations of Tyconius as his own. Tyconius's works later went out of wide circulation except for the portion that Augustine himself had quoted or summarized or that had become the foundation of western exegesis of the Apocalypse. This phenomenon is, of course, paralleled in other situations in late antiquity when the epitome and digest took the place of the original full-length work; Augustine's summary of Tyconius's *Liber Regularum* is part of that trend. This does not diminish the achievement of Augustine, but it does illuminate his methods and the importance of his considered judgement for our cultural tradition.

This study also shows Bede working within the patristic tradition, paying attention to minute nuances of word, text, grammar, presentation, and precise orthodoxy while being eclectic in gathering and evaluating sources. His mind was magnificent, his research methodical, and his writings illuminating and balanced.

NOTES

1. References to Bede's *Expositio Apocalypseos* are by column to *PL 93*; I am preparing the edition for *CCSL*.
2. Adam's edition of Primasius used here, *CCSL 92*, takes into account *Oxford Bodleian Douce MS 140* which was known in Bede's England and annotated by Boniface (Clark 1918; *CLA* II, 33, no 237, and 53).
3. References to Augustine's *City of God* (dCD) will be by page and line to *CCSL 48*.
4. In the next century Rhabanus Maurus adopted and expanded this practice.
5. See Gneuss 1981, no 858, for the 8th-century Northumbrian manuscript of the *Moralia*, as well as seven others from Anglo-Saxon England. There is also an 8th-century manuscript of Paterius *De expositione Veteris et Novi Tesamenti* (Gneuss 1981, no 772; *PL 79*, 683C–1136D, with passages on the Apocalypse at 1107C–1122A). Bonner 1966, n 62, also suggests Gregory, *Hom in Ezech* I.vii.19 (*PL 76*, 862D), but that passage has only *angelicae potestates/uirtutes*, while Bede's words are directly from the *Moralia*.
6. Gregory gives the full verse (*CCSL 143*, 66.69–71), differing from Bede's language by quoting the Old Latin *impleatur numerus conseruorum eorum et fratrum eorum* for Bede's *impleantur conserui eorum et fratres eorum*.
7. The *Gallicanum* normally appears as the Vulgate Psalms; it was the revision by Jerome, based upon the Septuagint or Greek Old Testament, often in the manuscripts as *iuxta* or *secundum LXX*. The *Hebraicum* was another revision, this time considering the Hebrew text.
8. Here Romero-Pose cites *CCSL 143B*, 1724.12–13, Gregory's comment following his quotation of Apc 13.11 (*duo cornua agni similia quia . . . et uitam*; cf Primasius (*CCSL 92*, 197.116, 118–19).
9. The earliest manuscripts of Bede's commentary read *inciditur*, the same as in Gregory. The *PL* text, taken from Giles's edition, erroneously has *includitur*, a common late manuscript error in the tradition but one already appearing in manuscript D (*Paris BN lat MS 12284*, dated to the early 9th century).
10. For the *lemma*, Bede has *scripta sunt*; Gregory and Vulgate, including the *Codex Amiatinus*, have *scripta erant*; Augustine and Primasius read *ex ipsis scripturis librorum secundum facta sua*.
11. The verbal parallels are rather weak, and I suspect Bede has another source or parallel, but it is not in Beatus, and Bede is closer to Augustine than to Primasius.
12. Augustine, *De Virg 27* (*CSEL 41*, 263.7–264.19, selectively) through Primasius 4.14 (*CCSL 92*, 212.75–81, 83–5, 86–8, 98–103 [with elipsis]), with variants closest to Augustine

manuscript G (*St Gall MS 178, s.ix*). Primasius quotes Augustine's *De Virg* 12, 14.26–9 (*CCSL* 92, 211.69–214.136).

13. Both 2 Cor 11.2 and 1 Cor 6.11 are cited in this context by Bede 174C and Beatus 6.8.11–12 and 6.8.8 (Romero-Pose 1985, 2, 185–86; Sanders 1930, 511), while Augustine cites them only at the first of the segment Primasius quotes chs 11–14 (*CSEL* 41, 244–6).

14. Augustine, *dCD* 20.10 (719.21–720.29, with the phrase in question at 720.25–6); Primasius 5.20 (*CCSL* 92, 278.159–65). They both quote 1 Pet 2.9, but Augustine has *plebs*, as does Bede; Primasius has *gens*, as does the Vulgate. Bede's quote from Augustine begins at 719.23. The scripture is not in Beatus.

15. Augustine *dCD* 22.29 (857.41) *praemium fidei nobis uisio ista seruatur*; Primasius 5.22 (*CCSL* 92, 303.77) *praemium fidei nobis uisio dei seruatur*, as Bede. Primasius 303.77–85 quotes Augustine 857.41–5 followed by 861.202–862.206. Bede uses only the first line.

16. Primasius 5.20 (*CCSL* 92, 275.92– 277.159 from Augustine 717.56–719.137). There are two short gaps from 74–9 and 82–4, and lines 62–4 have been changed into *quae a suo rege probabili meruit audire sanctione*, an expression which is used by Bede at 191D.

17. Twice in his *Homilies*, I.9 and II.21(*CCSL* 122, 63.125–34; 341.206–19), Bede discussed at length Apc 1.9 *fui in insula . . . textimonium Iesu*. Neither draws on his own commentary though all three passages have some similar language due to *HE*; cf Jerome *De Vir Inl* 13.25–7.

BIBLIOGRAPHY

(———) 1838 Sepulchral Stones at Hartlepool, *Gentleman's Magazine*, (NS), 10, 536.

(———) 1843 In Antiquarian Researches, *Gentleman's Magazine*, (NS), 20, 637.

(———) 1844 Sepulchral Stones found at Hartlepool, *Gentleman's Magazine*, (NS), 21, 187–8.

(———) 1928 The missing Hartlepool gravestone, *Antiqs J*, 8, 524.

(———) 1988 Interim Report on Excavations at Dixon Keld, Masham (unpublished. Harrogate Museums and Art Gallery Service).

ÅBERG, N 1926 *The Anglo-Saxons in England*. Uppsala.

—— 1945 *The Occident and the Orient in the art of the 7th century. II. Lombard Italy*. Stockholm.

ADAMS, M 1996 Excavation of a pre-Conquest cemetery at Addingham, West Yorkshire, *Medieval Archaeol*, 40, 151–91.

ADDLESHAW, G W O 1963 The pastoral organization of the modern dioceses of Durham and Newcastle in the time of Bede. Jarrow Lecture (repr in *Bede and his World. 1. The Jarrow Lectures 1958–1978*, Aldershot, 1994).

AIRLIE, S 1994 The view from Maastricht. In Crawford, 32–46.

AKERLUND, H 1963 *Nydam skeppet*. Göteborg.

AKERMAN, J Y 1855 *Remains of Pagan Saxondom*. London.

ALCOCK, L 1963 *Dinas Powys. An Iron Age, Dark Age, and Early Medieval Settlement in Glamorgan*. Cardiff.

—— 1981 Quantity or Quality: the Anglian graves of Bernicia. In Evison, V I (ed) *Angles, Saxons and Jutes: Essays presented to J N L Myres*, 168–86. Oxford.

—— 1983 Gwyr y Gogledd: an Archaeological Appraisal, *Archaeologia Cambrensis*, 132, 1–18.

—— 1987 *Economy, Society and Warfare among the Britons and Saxons*. Cardiff.

—— 1988 *Bede, Eddius, and the forts of the North Britons*. Newcastle.

—— 1996 Ur-Symbols and the Pictograph-system of the Picts, *Pictish Arts Society Journal*, 9, 2–5.

ALCOCK, L & ALCOCK, E A 1990 Reconnaissance excavations on Early Historic fortifications and other royal sites in Scotland, 1974–84: 4, Excavations at Alt Clut, Clyde Rock, Strathclyde, 1974–5, *Proc Soc Antiq Scotl*, 120, 95–149.

—— 1992 Reconnaissance excavations on Early Historic fortifications and other royal sites in Scotland, 1974–84, *Proc Soc Antiq Scotl*, 122, 215–87.

ALEXANDER, J J G 1978 *Insular manuscripts 6th to the 9th century. A Survey of Manuscripts Illuminated in the British Isles*. I. London.

—— 1990 The illumination. In Fox, 305–14.

ALFÖLDI, A 1931 Über die theiromorphe Weltbetrachtung in der hochasiatischen Kulturen, *Archäologischer Anzeiger*, 43, 393–418.

ALLEN, J R 1892 Report on the sculptured stones older than AD 1100, with symbols and Celtic ornament, in the district of Scotland south of the River Dee, *Proc Soc Antiq Scotl*, 26 (1891–2), 251–9.

ALLEN, J R & ANDERSON, J 1903 *The Early Christian Monuments of Scotland*, 3 parts. Edinburgh (repr with an introduction by Isabel Henderson, 2 vols, Balgavies, 1993).

ALLEN, M I 1996 Bede and Frechulf at medieval St Gallen. In Houwen & MacDonald, 61–80.

AMORY, P 1993 The Meaning and Purpose of Ethnic Terminology in the Burgundian Laws, *Early Medieval Europe*, 2.1, 1–28.

ANDERSON, M O 1980 *Kings and Kingship in Early Scotland* (rev edn). Edinburgh.

—— 1982 Dalriada and the creation of the kingdom of the Scots. In Whitelock, D, McKitterick, R & Dumville, D (eds) *Ireland in Early Mediaeval Europe*, 106–32. Cambridge.

—— 1991 *Adomnán's Life of Columba* (rev edn). Oxford.

ANDRIEU, M 1931–61 *Les Ordines Romani du haut Moyen Âge*, 5 vols (= Spicilegium Sacrum Lovaniense, 11, 23, 24, 28, 29). Louvain.

ANGENENDT, A 1977 Bonifatius und das Sacramentum initionis, *Romische Quartalschrift fur christliche Altertumskunde und Kirchengeschichte*, 72, 133–83.

—— 1986 The Conversion of the Anglo-Saxons considered against the background of the early medieval mission, *Settimane di Studi sull' Alto Medioevo*, 32.2, 747–92.

ARCHIBALD, M with BROWN, M & WEBSTER, L 1997 Heirs of Rome: the shaping of Britain AD 400–900. In Webster & Brown, 208–48.

ARNOLD, T 1885 (ed) *Symeonis Monachi Opera Omnia*, II (= Rolls Series, 75). London.

ARRHENIUS, B 1985 *Merovingian garnet jewellery. Emergence and social implications.* Stockholm.

AUERBACH, E 1965 *Literary Language and its Public in Late Latin Antiquity and in the Middle Ages.* London.

AUSTIN, D 1987 The medieval landscape and settlement of Castle Eden, Peterlee, Co Durham: Excavations 1974, *Durham Archaeol J*, 3, 57–78.

—— 1990 The 'proper study' of medieval archaeology. In Austin, D & Alcock, L (eds) *From the Baltic to the Black Sea: Studies in Medieval Archaeology*, 9–42. London.

AVENT, R 1975 *Anglo-Saxon Garnet Inlaid Disc and Composite Brooches.* Oxford. (= BAR Brit Ser, 11).

BACKHOUSE, J 1981 *The Lindisfarne Gospels.* London.

BAILEY, R N 1978a The Durham Cassiodorus (Jarrow Lecture).

—— 1978b The Chronology of Viking-Age Sculpture in Northumbria. In Lang, 173–203.

—— 1983 Bede's Text of Cassiodorus' Commentary on the Psalms, *The Journal of Theological Studies*, (NS), 34.1, 189–93.

—— 1992 Sutton Hoo and Seventh-Century Art. In Farrell & Neuman de Vegvar, 31–41.

—— 1996a *England's Earliest Sculptors.* Toronto.

—— 1996b 'What Mean These Stones?' Some Aspects of Pre-Norman Sculpture in Cheshire & Lancashire, *Bulletin of the John Rylands Library*, 78.1, 21–46.

BAILEY, R N & CRAMP, R 1988 *Cumberland, Westmorland and Lancashire-north-of-the-sands.* Oxford (= Corpus of Anglo-Saxon Stone Sculpture, II).

BAKKA, E 1963 *Some English Decorated Metal Objects found in Norwegian Viking Graves.* Oslo (= Årbok for Universitetet I Bergen Humanistisk serie, I).

—— 1965 Some decorated Anglo-Saxon and Irish metalwork found in Norwegian graves. In Small, A (ed) *The Fourth Viking Congress*, 32–40. Edinburgh.

BANNIARD, M 1991 Rhabanus Maurus and the Vernacular Languages. In Wright, 164–76.

BARNETT, J M 1981 *The Diaconate: A Full and Equal Order.* New York.

BARRETT, J 1990 The Monumentality of Death: the character of early Bronze Age mortuary mounds in Southern Britain, *World Archaeology*, 22.2, 179–89.

BARTY, E 1967 *Anglo-Saxon Non-runic Inscriptions.* Unpublished Ph.D. thesis. Cambridge. (= Okasha).

BASSETT, S 1989 (ed) *The Origins of Anglo-Saxon Kingdoms.* Leicester.

BATEMAN, T 1861 *Ten Years' Digging in Celtic and Saxon Grave Hills in the Counties of Derby, Stafford and York, from 1848 to 1858.* London.

BECKER, A 1973 *Franks Casket: Zu den Bildern und Inschriften des Runenkästchens von Auzon.* Regensburg.

BERESFORD, M & HURST, J G 1990 *Wharram Percy: Deserted Medieval Village*. London.

BERNARD, J H & ATKINSON, J 1898 *The Irish Liber Hymnorum*, 2 vols. London (= Henry Bradshaw Society, 13–14).

BETHAM, W 1826 *Irish Antiquarian Researches*, I. Dublin.

—— 1827 *Irish Antiquarian Researches*, II. Dublin.

BETTENSON, H 1972 (ed) *Augustine: City of God*. Harmondsworth.

BETTESS, F 1991 The Anglo-Saxon Foot: A Computerized Assessment, *Medieval Archaeol*, 36, 44–50.

BIDDLE, M & KJØLBYE-BIDDLE, B 1985 The Repton Stone, *Anglo-Saxon England*, 14, 233–92.

BIÈVRE, E DE 1996 (1997) *Utrecht. Britain and the Continent: Archaeology, Art and Architecture*. London (= British Archaeological Association Conference Transactions, 18).

BINDER, G 1964 *Die Aussetzung des Königskindes Kyros und Romulus*. Meisenheim am Glan.

BIRLEY, E 1964 The Orton Scar find and Thomas Reveley of Kendal, *Cumberland Westmorland Antiq Archaeol Soc*, (NS), 64, 81–9.

BLACKBURN, M 1993 Coin finds and coin circulation in Lindsey, c 600–900. In Vince, 90–6.

BLAIR, J & SHARPE, R 1992 (eds) *Pastoral Care before the Parish*. Leicester.

BLAIR, P H 1970 *The World of Bede*. London.

—— 1976 *Northumbria in the days of Bede*. London.

—— 1985 Whitby as a centre of learning in the seventh century. In Lapidge, M & Gneuss, H (eds) *Learning and Literature in Anglo-Saxon England*, 3–32. Cambridge.

BONNER, G 1966 Saint Bede in the Tradition of Western Apocalyptic Commentary (Jarrow Lecture).

—— 1986 Augustine's conception of deification, *Journal of Theological Studies*, (NS), 37, 369–86.

BONNER, G, ROLLASON, D & STANCLIFFE, C 1989 (eds) *St Cuthbert, His Cult and His Community to AD 1200*. Woodbridge.

BOURKE, C 1980 Early Irish Hand-Bells, *J Roy Soc Antiqs Ireland*, 110, 52–66.

—— 1993 *Patrick: The Archaeology of a Saint*. Belfast.

—— 1995 (ed) *From the Isles of the North. Early Medieval Art in Ireland and Britain*. Belfast.

BOWMAN, W 1855 (ed) *Reliquiae Antiquae Eboracenses*. Leeds.

BOYLE, L 1989 *St Clement's, Rome*. Rome.

BRADLEY, S A J 1982 *Anglo-Saxon Poetry*. London.

BRADSHAW, P F 1990 *Ordination Rites of the Ancient Churches of the East and West*. New York.

BRENAN, J 1991 *Hanging Bowls and their Contexts*. Oxford (= BAR Brit Ser, 220).

BREWIS, P 1936 A cruciform brooch from Benwell, Newcastle upon Tyne, *Archaeol Aeliana*, 4 ser, 13, 117–21.

BREWSTER, T C M 1969 Cowlam, Kemp Howe, *Medieval Archaeol*, 13, 241.

BRISCOE, T 1968 The Anglo-Saxon S-shape brooch in England with special reference to one from Lakenheath, Suffolk, *Proc Cambridge Antiq Soc*, 61, 45–53.

BROER, C J C & BRUIJN, M W J DE 1994 De Heilig-Kruiskapel in Utrecht: Sint-Maarten of Sint-Salvator?, *Bulletin van de Koninklijke Nederlandse Oudheidkundige Bond*, 93, 162–8, English summary at 194.

—— 1995 *De eerste Kerken in Utrecht: Sint-Thomas, Sint-Salvator, Sint-Maarten*. Utrecht.

BROMWICH, R 1961 *Trioedd Ynys Prydein*. Cardiff.

BRØNDSTED, J 1924 *Early English Ornament*. London and Copenhagen.

BROOKS, N 1989 The creation and early structure of the kingdom of Kent. In Bassett, 55–75.

BROWN, D 1977 Firesteels and pursemounts again, *Bonner Jahrbucher*, 177, 451–77.

BROWN, G B 1915 *The Arts in Early England – Saxon Art and Industry in the Pagan Period*, III–V. London.

—— 1919 The Hartlepool Tombstones, and the relations between Celtic and Teutonic art in the early Christian period, *Proc Soc Antiq Scotl*, 5 ser, 5 (1918–19), 195–228.

—— 1937 *The Arts in Early England. VI.2. Anglo-Saxon Sculpture*. London.

BROWN, G B & WEBSTER, A B 1920 Report on the Ruthwell Cross with some reference to that at Bewcastle in Cumberland, *The Royal Commission on the Ancient and Historical Monuments and Constructions of Scotland, Seventh Report with Inventory of the Monuments and Constructions in the County of Dumfries*, 219–86. Edinburgh.

BROWN, G H 1987 *Bede the Venerable*. Boston.

—— 1995 The Dynamics of Literacy in Anglo-Saxon England, *Bulletin of the John Rylands University Library of Manchester*, 77.1, 109–42.

—— 1996 Bede the Educator (Jarrow Lecture).

BROWN, P 1996 *The Rise of Western Christendom*. Cambridge, Mass.

BROWN, P D C & SCHWEIZER, F 1973 X-ray Fluorescent Analysis of Anglo-Saxon Jewellery, *Archaeometry*, 15.2, 175–92.

BROWN, T J 1972 Northumbria and the *Book of Kells*, *Anglo-Saxon England*, 1, 219–46.

—— 1993 The Irish Element in the Insular System of Scripts to circa AD 850. In Bately, J, Brown, M & Roberts, J (eds) *A Palaeographer's View: The Selected Writings of Julian Brown*, 201–20. London.

BROWNE, G F 1887 Brief précis of the early sculptured stones of Cheshire, *Archaeol J*, 44, 146–56.

BRUCE-MITFORD, R L S 1956 The Pectoral Cross. In Battiscombe C F (ed) *The Relics of St Cuthbert*, 308–25. Oxford.

—— 1960 Decoration and Miniatures. In Kendrick et al., II, 109–258.

—— 1967 The Art of the *Codex Amiatinus* (Jarrow Lecture).

—— 1969 The Art of the *Codex Amiatinus*, *J Brit Archaeol Assoc*, 3 ser, 32, 1–25.

—— 1974a Six interesting pieces of cloisonné jewellery. In Bruce-Mitford, 262–80.

—— 1974b The Pectoral Cross of St Cuthbert. In Bruce-Mitford, 281–302.

—— 1974c (ed) *Aspects of Anglo-Saxon Archaeology*. London.

—— 1975 *The Sutton Hoo Ship-Burial. I. Excavations, background, the ship, dating and inventory*. London.

—— 1978 *The Sutton Hoo Ship Burial. II. Arms, Armour and Regalia*. London.

—— 1983 *The Sutton Hoo Ship Burial. III.2. Late Roman and Byzantine Silver, Hanging Bowls, Drinking Vessels, Cauldrons and other Containers, Textiles, the Lyre, Pottery Bottle and other Items*. London.

BRUNN, H & BULLE, H 1898 (eds) *Heinrich Brunn's kleine Schriften*. Leipzig.

BRUYNE, D DE 1914 *Sommaires, divisions et rubriques de la bible latine*. Namur.

BUDNY, M 1997 *Insular, Anglo-Saxon and Early Anglo-Norman Manuscript Art at Corpus Christi College, Cambridge. An Illustrated Catalogue*. Kalamazoo and Cambridge.

BULLOUGH, D 1975 'Imagines Regum' and their significance in the early medieval west. In Robertson, G & Henderson, G (eds) *Studies in Memory of David Talbot Rice*, 223–76. Edinburgh.

BURKE, W L M 1930 A Bronze situla in the Museo Cristiano of the Vatican Library, *Art Bulletin*, 12, 163–78.

BURKITT, E C 1935 Kells, Durrow, and Lindisfarne, *Antiquity*, 9, 33–7.

BURKITT, F C 1895 (ed) Tyconius, *Liber Regularum*. Cambridge (= *Texts and Studies, Contributions to Biblical and Patristic Literature* 3.1, 1–85).

BUTLER, L & GRAHAM-CAMPBELL, J 1990 A lost reliquary casket from Gwytherin, North Wales, *Antiqs J*, 70, 40–8.

CAHN, W & SEIDEL, L 1979 *New England Museums*. New York (= *Romanesque Sculpture in American Collections*, 1).

CAMPBELL, E 1989 A Blue Glass Squat Jar from Dinas Powys, South Wales, *Bulletin of the Board of Celtic Studies*, 36, 239–45.

—— forthcoming Glass vessels or Cullet: a taphonomic study of the Early Medieval glass from Dinas Powys.

CAMPBELL, E & LANE, A 1993 Celtic and Germanic interaction in Dalriada: the 7th-century metalworking site at Dunadd. In Spearman & Higgitt, 52–63.

CAMPBELL, J 1982 (ed) *The Anglo-Saxons*. Oxford.

—— 1986 *Essays in Anglo-Saxon History*. London.

—— 1989 Elements in the background to the Life of St Cuthbert and his early cult. In Bonner et al., 3–19.

CARDWELL, P 1988 Catterick Triangle excavations – interim report, *Yorkshire Archaeol Soc*, 11–14 (= *Roman Antiquities Section Bulletin*, 5, Winter 1987–8).

CARNEY, J 1955 *Studies in Irish Literature and History*. Dublin.

CARROLL, J 1995 Millefiori in the Development of Early Irish Enamelling. In Bourke, 49–57.

CARROLL, M T A 1946 *The Venerable Bede. His Spiritual Teachings*. Washington DC (= Catholic University of America, Studies in Medieval History, (NS), 9).

CARRUTHERS, M 1990 *The Book of Memory: A Study of Memory in Medieval Culture*. Cambridge (= Cambridge Studies in Medieval Literature 10).

CARSON, R A G 1962 *Coins, Ancient, Medieval and Modern*. London.

CARVER, M 1989 Kingship and material culture in Early Anglo-Saxon East Yorkshire. In Bassett, 141–58.

—— 1992 (ed) *The Age of Sutton Hoo: the Seventh Century in North-western Europe*. Woodbridge.

CASEY, J 1994 The end of fort garrisons on Hadrians Wall: a hypothetical model. In Vallet, F & Kazanski, M (eds) *L'Armée Romaine et les Barbares du III au VIIe Siécle*, 259–67. Paris.

CASSIDY, B 1992 (ed) *The Ruthwell Cross: chapters from the colloquium sponsored by the Index of Christian Art, Princeton University, 1989*. Princeton, NJ.

—— 1996 The Dream of St Joseph on the Anglo-Saxon cross from Rothbury, *Gesta*, 35.2, 149–55.

CCCM = *Corpus Christianorum Continuatio Mediaevelis*, 1968–. Turnhout.

CCSL = *Corpus Christianorum Series Latina*, 1953–. Turnhout.

CESSFORD, C 1993 The Borthwick Mains Salmon, *Hawick Archaeol Soc*, 1993, 26–9.

—— 1994a The death of Aethelfrith of Lloegr, *Northern History*, 30, 179–83.

—— 1994b Early Historic Chains of Power, *Pictish Arts Society Journal*, 6, 19–26.

—— 1994c Pictish Raiders at Trusty's Hill?, *Transactions of the Dumfriesshire and Galloway Natural History and Antiquarian Society*, 69 (1996), 81–8.

—— 1995 Where are the Anglo-Saxons in the Gododdin Poem?, *Anglo-Saxon Studies in Archaeology and History*, 8 (1996), 95–8.

—— forthcoming a Exogamous marriages between Anglo-Saxons and Britons in seventh-century Northern Britain, *Anglo-Saxon Studies in Archaeology and History*.

—— forthcoming b The Pictish Mirror Symbol and archaeological evidence for mirrors in Scotland, *Oxford Journal of Archaeology*.

—— forthcoming c Ur-Symbols or formal and utilitarian scripts?, *Pictish Arts Society Journal*.

CHADWICK, H M 1901 Early Inscriptions in the North of England, *Transactions of the Yorkshire Dialect Society*, 1.3, 79–85.

CHAYTOR, H J 1945 *From Script to Print*. Cambridge.

CLA = Lowe, E A 1934–72 *Codices Latini Antiquiores*, 11 vols & supplement. Oxford.

CLANCY, T 1996 Iona, Scotland and the Céli Dé. In Crawford, 111–30.

CLAPHAM, A W 1930 *English Romanesque Architecture before the Conquest*. Oxford.

—— 1934 Notes on the Origin of Hiberno-Saxon Art, *Antiquity*, 8, 43–57.

CLARK, A C 1905 *Ciceronis Orationes*, I. Oxford.

—— 1918 *The Descent of Manuscripts*. Oxford (repr. 1969).

CLARK, M K 1935 *A Gazetteer of Roman Remains in East Yorkshire*. Malton. (= *Roman Malton and District Reports*, 5).

—— 1943 Bracelet and Toilet Set from Burton Fields Gravel Pit, *Proceedings of the Leeds Philosophical and Literary Society (Literary and Historical Section)*, 5 (1938–43), 339–43.

CLAYTON, M 1990 *The Cult of the Virgin Mary in Anglo-Saxon England*. Cambridge.

CLEARY, S E 1989 *The Ending of Roman Britain*. London.

CLEMENCE, H 1993 *The Timber-Framed Structures at West Heslerton Anglo-Saxon Settlement: Analysis and Comparison*. Unpublished undergraduate dissertation. Nottingham.

CLOSE-BROOKS, J 1984 Pictish and other burials. In Friell, J G P & Watson, W G (eds) *Pictish Studies: Settlement, Burial and Art in Dark Age Northern Britain*, 87–114. Oxford.

—— 1986 Excavations at Clatchard Craig, Fife, *Proc Soc Antiq Scotl*, 116, 117–84.

COATSWORTH, E 1989 The pectoral cross and portable altar from the tomb of St Cuthbert. In Bonner et al., 287–301.

COGGINS, D 1979 Durham: Binchester (NZ 210313), *Medieval Archaeol*, 23, 236, fig 1.

COGGINS, D, FAIRLESS, K J, & BATEY, C E 1983 Simy Folds: An early medieval settlement in Upper Teesdale, Co Durham, *Medieval Archaeol*, 27, 1–26.

COLGRAVE, B 1927 (ed) *The Life of Bishop Wilfrid by Eddius Stephanus*. Cambridge.

—— 1940 (ed) *Two Lives of Saint Cuthbert*. Cambridge.

—— 1956 (ed) *Felix's Life of Saint Guthlac*. Cambridge.

—— 1968 (ed) *The Earliest Life of Gregory the Great by an Anonymous Monk of Whitby*. Lawrence, Kansas.

COLGRAVE, B & MYNORS, R A B 1969 (eds) *Bede's Ecclesiastical History of the English People*. Oxford (repr 1991).

COLLINGWOOD, W G 1915 Anglian and Anglo-Danish sculpture in the West Riding, with addenda to the North and East Ridings and York, and a general review of the Early Christian monuments of Yorkshire, *Yorkshire Archaeol J*, 23, 129–299.

—— 1927 *Northumbrian Crosses of the Pre-Norman Age*. London.

—— 1932 A Pedigree of Anglian Crosses, *Antiquity*, 6, 35–54.

COLLINGWOOD-BRUCE, J 1880 (ed) *A Descriptive Catalogue of Antiquities, chiefly British, at Alnwick Castle*. Newcastle.

CONNOLLY, S 1995 (ed) *Bede. On the Temple*. Liverpool.

—— 1997 (ed) *Bede on Tobit and on the Canticle of Habakkuk*. Dublin.

CORSANO, K 1987 The first quire of the *Codex Amiatinus*, *Scriptorium*, 41.1, 3–34.

COURCELLE, P P 1949 *Les lettres grecques en Occident, de Macrobe a Cassiodore*. Paris.

—— 1969 *Late Latin Writers and their Greek Sources*. Cambridge, Mass.

COWEN, J D 1931 The Capheaton Bowl, *Archaeol Aeliana*, 4 ser, 8, 328–39.

COX, R 1689 *Hibernia Anglicana*. London.

CRAIG, D 1991 The sculptured stones from Hoddom, 1991. In Lowe, C E *Transactions of the Dumfriesshire and Galloway Natural History and Antiquarian Society*, 3 ser, 66, 11–35, Appendix I, 27–34.

CRAMP, R 1960 The Anglian Sculptured Crosses of Dumfriesshire, *Transactions of the Dumfriesshire and Galloway Natural History and Antiquarian Society*, 3 ser, 38 (1959–60), 9–20.

—— 1965 *Early Northumbrian Sculpture* (Jarrow Lecture).

—— 1967 *The Monastic Arts of Northumbria II*. London.

—— 1969 Excavations at the Saxon Monastic Sites of Monkwearmouth and Jarrow, Co Durham: an Interim Report, *Medieval Archaeol*, 8, 21–65.

—— 1970a The position of the Otley crosses in English sculpture of the eighth and ninth centuries, *Kolloquium über Spätantike und Frühmittelalterliche Skulptur*, 55–63. Mainz.

—— 1970b The Anglo-Saxon Period. In Dewdney, J C (ed) *Durham County with Teesside*, 199–206. Durham.

—— 1974 Early Northumbrian sculpture at Hexham. In Kirby, D P (ed) *Saint Wilfrid at Hexham*, 115–40. Newcastle.

—— 1976a Monastic Sites. In Wilson, 201–52.

—— 1976b Analysis of the Finds Register and Location Plan of Whitby Abbey. In Wilson, 453–7.

—— 1977 Schools of Mercian Sculpture. In Dornier, A (ed) *Mercian Studies*, 191–233. Leicester.

—— 1978 The Anglian Tradition in the ninth century. In Lang, 1–14.

—— 1983 Anglo-Saxon Settlement. In Chapman, J C & Mytum, H C (eds) *Settlement in North Britain 1000 BC–AD 1000*, 263–97. Oxford (= *BAR Brit Ser*, 118).

—— 1984 *County Durham and Northumberland*, 2 parts. Oxford (= *Corpus of Anglo-Saxon Stone Sculpture*, I).

—— 1986 Anglo-Saxon and Italian sculpture, *Angli e Sassoni al di qua e al di là del mare*, 125–40. Spoleto (= *Settimane di Studio del Centro Italiano di Studi sull'Alto Medioevo*, 32).

—— 1988 Northumbria: the archaeological evidence. In Driscoll & Nieke, 69–78.

—— 1992 *Studies in Anglo-Saxon Sculpture*. London.

—— 1993 A reconsideration of the monastic site of Whitby. In Spearman & Higgitt, 64–73.

—— 1994 Monkwearmouth and Jarrow in their Continental Context. In Painter, K (ed) *'Churches Built in Ancient Times': Recent Studies in Early Christian Archaeology*. London (= Society of Antiquaries of London, Occasional Paper 16), 279–94.

—— 1995a Nature redeemed. In Brown, D & Loades, A (eds) *The Sense of the Sacramental*, 122–36. London.

—— 1995b The Making of Oswald's Northumbria. In Stancliffe & Cambridge, 17–32.

—— 1995c Whithorn and the Northumbrian Expansion Westwards. (Whithorn Lecture, 3).

—— 1997 The Insular Tradition: An Overview. In Karkov, Ryan & Farrell, 283–99.

CRAMP, R & DANIELS, R 1987 New finds from the Anglo-Saxon monastery at Hartlepool, Cleveland, *Antiquity*, 61, 424–32.

CRAMP, R & LANG, J T 1977 *A Century of Anglo-Saxon Sculpture*. Newcastle.

CRAMP, R & MIKET, R 1982 *Catalogue of Anglo-Saxon and Viking Antiquities in the Museum of Antiquities, Newcastle upon Tyne*. Newcastle.

CRAWFORD, B E 1994 (ed) *Scotland in Dark Age Europe*. St Andrews.

—— 1996 (ed) *Scotland in Dark Age Britain*. St Andrews.

CRAWFORD, S J 1922 (ed) *The Old English version of the Heptateuch, Ælfric's Treatise on the Old and New Testaments and his Preface to Genesis*. London (= Early English Text Society, (OS), 160).

CRESWELL, K A C 1969 *Early Muslim architecture*, 2 vols (2nd edn). Oxford.

CRONE, B A 1991 Buiston, *Curr Archaeol*, 127, 295–7.

CROSS, J E 1979 A lost Life of Hild of Whitby: the evidence of the *Old English Martyrology*, *The Early Middle Ages*, Acta, V, 21–43.

—— 1996 Bede's influence at home and abroad: an introduction. In Houwen & MacDonald, 17–29.

CSEL = *Corpus Scriptorum Ecclesiasticorum Latinorum*, 1866–. Turnhout.

CUBITT, C 1995 *Anglo-Saxon Church councils c 650–850*. Leicester.

CURLE, A O 1914 Report on the excavation, in September 1913, of a Vitrified Fort at Rockliffe, Dalbeattie, known as the Mote of Mark, *Proc Soc Antiq Scotl*, 48 (1913–4), 125–68.

—— 1923 *The Treasure of Traprain*. Glasgow.

CURLE, C L & HENRY, F 1943 Early Christian art in Scotland, *Gazette des Beaux-Arts*, 6 ser, 24, 257–72.

DALTON, O M 1926 (ed) *The History of the Franks by Gregory of Tours*, 2 vols. London.

DANIELS, R 1987 Hartlepool, *Curr Archaeol*, 104, 273–7.

—— 1988 The Anglo-Saxon Monastery at Church Close, Hartlepool, Cleveland, *Archaeol J*, 145, 158–210.

—— 1990 The development of medieval Hartlepool: excavations at Church Close, 1984–5, *Archaeol J*, 147, 337–410.

—— 1992 The Anglo-Saxon monastery at Hartlepool, England, (no editor cited) *Medieval Europe 1992 Pre-Printed Papers. 6. Religion and belief*, 171–6. York.

DARK, K R & DARK, S P 1996 New archaeological and palynological evidence for a sub-Roman reoccupation of Hadrian's Wall, *Archaeol Aeliana*, 5 ser, 24, 57–72.

DASSMANN, E 1970 Die Bedeutung des Alten Testaments für das Verständnis des kirchlichen Amtes in der frühpatristischen theologie, *Bibel und Leben*, 11, 198–214.

DAVIDSE, J 1996 On Bede as Christian Historian. In Houwen & Macdonald, 1–15.

DAVIDSON, H R E 1969 The Smith and the Goddess, *Frühmittelalterliche Studien*, 3, 216–26.

DAVIS, J B & THURNAM, J 1865 *Crania Britannica*, II. London.

DEKKERS, E 1990 Quelques notes sur des florilèges augustiniens anciens et médiévaux, *Augustiniana*, 40, 27–38.

DENT, J 1984 The Yorkshire Dykes, *Archaeol J*, 141, 32–3.

DEPARTMENT OF THE ENVIRONMENT 1968 *Department of the Environment – Archaeological Excavations*. London.

DEROLEZ, R L M 1963 *Götter und Mythen der Germanen*. Einsiedeln, Zürich and Köln.

DESKIS, S & HILL, T D 1995 The Wolf Doesn't Care: The Proverbial and Traditional Context of Laȝamon's *Brut* lines 10624–36, *The Review of English Studies* (NS), 46, 41–8.

DEWA, R 1995 The Runic Riddles of the Exeter Book: Language Games and Anglo-Saxon Scholarship, *Nottingham Medieval Studies*, 39, 26–36.

DICKINSON, T M 1982 Fowler's Type G Penannular Brooches Reconsidered, *Medieval Archaeol*, 26, 41–68.

—— 1990 Annular brooch. In Wrathmell, S & Nicholson, A (eds) *Dalton Parlours: Iron Age settlement and Roman villa*, 286–7. Wakefield (= *Yorkshire Archaeology*, 3).

DIERKENS, A 1996 Willibrord und Bonifatius: die angelsächsischen Mission und das fränkische Königreich in der ersten Hälfte des 8. Jahrhunderts. In Wieczorek et al., 459–65.

DINKLER, E 1979 Abbreviated Representation. In Weitzmann, K (ed) *The Age of Spirituality: Late Antique and Early Christian Art, Third to Seventh Century*, 396–402. New York.

DIONISOTTI, A C 1982 On Bede, Grammars, and Greek, *Revue Bénédictine*, 92, 111–41.

DIX, G 1946 The Ministry in the Early Church c AD 90–410. In Kirk, K E (ed) *The Apostolic Ministry: Essays on the History and the Doctrine of Episcopacy*, 183–303. London.

DIXON, P 1982. How Saxon is the Saxon House? In Drury, P J (ed) *Structural Reconstruction*, 275–87. Oxford.

DODDS, M E 1897 (ed) *A History of Northumberland*, IV. London.

DODWELL, C R 1982 *Anglo-Saxon Art: A New Perspective*. London.

DOUGLAS, LORD, & ALEXANDER, J 1881 Notice of the Discovery of a Massive Silver Chain of Plain Double Rings or Links at Hardwell, Berwickshire, with Notes on Similar Chains Found in Scotland, *Proc Soc Antiq Scotl*, 15 (1880–1), 64–70.

DRISCOLL, S & NIEKE, M 1988 (eds) *Power and Politics in Early Medieval Britain and Ireland*. Edinburgh.

DRONKE, U 1997 (ed) *The Poetic Edda. II. Mythological Poems*. Oxford.

DRURY, P J, & WICKENDEN, N P 1982 An Early Saxon Settlement within the Romano-British Small Town at Heybridge, Essex, *Medieval Archaeol*, 26, 1–40.

DUDLEY, H 1949 *Early Days in North-West Lincolnshire*. Scunthorpe.

DUEMMLER, E 1884 (ed) *Ermoldus Nigellus. In Honorem Hludowici Imperatoris*, IV, 181–283. Berlin (= *MGH: Poetae Latini Ævi Carolini*, II, 63–6).

DULIÈRE, C 1979 *Lupa Romana: recherches d'iconographie et essai d'interprétation*, 2 vols. Brussels and Rome (= *Études de philologie, d'archéologie, et d'histoire anciennes*, 18, Institut Historique Belge de Rome).

DUMÉZIL, G 1970 *The Destiny of the Warrior*. Chicago and London.

DUMVILLE, D N 1977a Kingship, Genealogies and Regnal Lists. In Sawyer & Wood, 72–104.

—— 1977b Sub-Roman Britain: History and Legend, *History*, 62, 173–92.

DUNCAN, H 1883 An Account of a Remarkable Monument in the shape of a Cross, inscribed with Roman and Runic Letters, preserved in the Garden of the Ruthwell Manse, Dumfriesshire, *Archaeologica Scotica: or, Transactions of the Society of Antiquaries of Scotland*, 4.2, 313–26.

DUNN, C W 1960 *The Foundling and the Werwolf; A Literary Historical Study of Guillaume de Palerne*. Toronto.

EAGLES, B N 1979 *The Anglo-Saxon Settlement of Humberside*. Oxford (= *BAR Brit Ser*, 68).

EAGLES, B N, & EVISON, V I 1970 Excavations at Harrold, Bedfordshire, 1951–3, *Bedfordshire Archaeol J*, 5, 17–56.

EDWARDS, A J H 1939 A Massive Double-Linked Silver Chain, *Proc Soc Antiq Scotl*, 73 (1938–9), 326–37.

EDWARDS, N 1983 Some Observations on the Layout and Construction of Abstract Ornament in Early Christian Irish Sculpture. In Thompson, 3–17.

—— 1986 The South Cross, Clonmacnois (with an appendix on the incidence of vine-scroll on Irish sculpture). In Higgitt, 23–36. Oxford.

EDWARDS, N & HULSE, T G 1992 A fragment of reliquary casket from Gwytherin, North Wales, *Antiqs J*, 72, 91–101.

ELGEE, F 1930 *Early Man in North-East Yorkshire*. Gloucester.

ELGEE, F & ELGEE, H W 1933, *The Archaeology of Yorkshire*. London (repr 1971).

ELIADE, M 1970 *Zalmoxis the Vanishing God: Comparative Studies in the Religions and Folklore of Dacia and Eastern Europe*. Chicago and London.

EMMERSON, R K & MCGINN, B 1992 (eds) *The Apocalypse in the Middle Ages*. Ithaca and London.

EVERITT, A 1986 *Continuity and Colonisation: The Evolution of Kentish Settlement*. Leicester.

EVISON, V I 1975 Pagan Saxon Whetstones, *Antiqs J*, 55, 70–85.

—— 1982 Anglo-Saxon glass claw-beakers, *Archaeologia*, 107, 43–76.

—— 1987 *Dover: The Buckland Anglo-Saxon Cemetery*. London (= Historic Buildings & Monuments Commission for England Archaeological Report, 3).

FAIRWEATHER, A D, & RALSTON, I B M 1993 The Neolithic timber hall at Balbridie, Grampian region, Scotland: the building, the date, the plant macrofossils, *Antiquity*, 67, 313–23.

FAIVRE, A 1977 *Naissance d'une hiérarchie: les premières étapes du cursus clérical*. Paris.

FARR, C 1991 Liturgical influences on the decoration of the *Book of Kells*. In Karkov, C & Farrell, R (eds) *Studies in insular art and archaeology*, 127–41. Oxford, Ohio (= *American early medieval studies*, I).

—— 1994 Textual structure, decoration and interpretive images in the *Book of Kells*. In O'Mahony, 437–49.

—— 1997a *The Book of Kells: Its Function and Audience*. London (= The British Library Studies in Medieval Culture, 4).

—— 1997b Worthy Women on the Ruthwell Cross: Woman as a Sign in Early Anglo-Saxon Monasticism. In Karkov et al., 45–61.

FARRELL, R T 1977 (ed) *The Anglo-Saxon Cross*. Hamden, Conn. (= reprint of Cook, A S 1914 'Some Accounts of the Bewcastle Cross between the Years 1607 and 1861', and Stevens, W O 1904, 'The Cross in the Life and Literature of the Anglo-Saxons').

FARRELL, R T & NEUMAN DE VEGVAR, C 1992 (eds) *Sutton Hoo: Fifty Years After*. Oxford, Ohio (= *American Early Medieval Studies*, 2).

FARRELL, R T with KARKOV, C 1992 The Construction, Deconstruction, and Reconstruction of the Ruthwell Cross: Some Caveats. In Cassidy, 35–47.

FAULL, M L 1977 British survival in Anglo-Saxon Northumbria. In Laing, L (ed) *Studies in Celtic Survival*, 1–55. Oxford (= *BAR Brit Ser*, 37).

—— 1979 *British Survival in Anglo-Saxon Yorkshire*. Unpublished Ph.D. thesis. Leeds.

—— 1981 The Early Anglo-Saxon Period. In Faull, M L & Moorhouse, S A (eds) *West Yorkshire: An Archaeological Survey to AD 1500*, 179–86. Wakefield.

FELL, C E 1981 Hild, Abbess of Strenaeshalch. In Bekker-Nielsen, H, Foote, P, Jørgensen, J H, Nyberg, T (eds) *Hagiography and Medieval Literature: A Symposium*, 76–99. Odense.

FENWICK, V 1978 *The Graveney Boat*. Oxford (= *BAR Brit Ser*, 53).

FERNIE, E 1978 Historical Metrology and Architectural History, *Art History* 1.4, 383–99.

—— 1985 Anglo-Saxon Lengths: the 'Northern' System, the Perch and the Foot, *Archaeol J*, 142, 246–54.

—— 1991 Anglo-Saxon Lengths and the Evidence of the Buildings, *Medieval Archaeol*, 35, 1–5.

FERRARI, M 1973 Spigolature Bobbiesi, *Italia Medioevale e Humanistica*, 16, 1–41.

FISCHER, B 1988–91 *Die lateinischen Evangelien bis zum 10. Jahrhundert*. Freiburg im Breisgau (= *Aus der Geschichte der lateinischen Bibel*, 13, 15, 17, 18, Matthew 1988, Mark 1989, Luke 1990, John 1991).

FORDYCE, W 1857 *The History and Antiquities of the County Palatine of Durham*. Newcastle.

FORSYTH, K 1995 The inscriptions on the Dupplin Cross. In Bourke, 237–44.

FOWLER, P J 1997 Farming in Early Medieval England: some Fields for Thought. In Hines, 245–68.

FOWLER, P J & MILLS, S A forthcoming An Early Medieval Landscape at Bede's World, Jarrow. In Jameson, J (ed) *Archaeology and Reconstructions*.

FOX, C 1959 *The Personality of Britain*, (4th edn). Cardiff.

FOX, P 1990 (ed) *The Book of Kells MS 58 Trinity College Library Dublin*. Luzern (= facsimile and commentary).

FRANK, R 1979 Review of 'Becker, *A Franks Casket*', *Speculum*, 52, 120–22.

FRANKS, A W 1859 On an ancient casket, *Archaeol Jnl*, 16, 391

FRANSEN, I 1961 Description de la Collection de Bède le Vénérable sur l'Apôtre, *Revue Bénédictine*, 71, 22–70.

FRANSEN, P–I 1987 D'Eugippius à Bède le Vénérable: à propos de leurs florilèges augustiniens, *Revue Bénédictine*, 97, 187–94.

FREDRICKSEN, P 1992 Tyconius and Augustine on the Apoalypse. In Emmerson & McGinn 20–37.

FRERE, W H 1894 *The Winchester Troper from MSS of the 10th and 11th Centuries*. London.

FURTWÄNGLER, A 1898 *Königliche Museen zu Berlin: Beschreibung der Geschnittenen Steine im Antiquarium*. Berlin.

GAGE, J 1836 Sepulchral Stones found at Hartlepool in 1833, *Archaeologia*, 26, 479–82.

GALAVARIS, G 1970 *Bread and the Liturgy*. Milwaukee and London.

GALLAGHER, D B 1987 The Anglo-Saxon Cemetery of Hob Hill, Saltburn, *Yorkshire Archaeol J*, 59, 9–27.

GAMESON, R 1994 The Royal 1.B.vii Gospels and English book production in the seventh and eighth centuries. In Gameson, R (ed) *The Early Medieval Bible*, 24–52. Cambridge (= *Cambridge Studies in Palaeography and Codicology*, 2).

GATES, T & O'BRIEN C 1988 Crop-marks at Milfield and New Bewick and the Recognition of *Grubenhäuser* in Northumberland, *Archaeol Aeliana*, 5 ser, 16, 1–9.

GEAKE, H 1992 Burial Practice in Seventh and Eighth Century England. In Carver, 83–94.

—— 1997 *The Use of Grave-Goods in Conversion-Period England, c 600–c 850*. Oxford (= *BAR Brit Ser*, 261).

GEARY, P 1983 Ethnic Identity as a Situational Construct in the Early Middle Ages, *Mitteilungen der Anthropologischen Gesellschaft in Wien*, 113, 15–26.

—— 1994 *Phantoms of Remembrance: Memory and Oblivion at the end of the first Millenium*. Princeton, NJ.

GELLY, M A 1995 The Irish High Cross: Methods of Design. In Bourke, 157–66.

GERCHOW, J 1988 *Die Gedenküberlieferung der Angelsachsen*. Berlin and NY.

GIBAUT, J ST H 1995 Sequential Ordination in Historical Perspective: A Response to J Robert Wright, *Anglican Theological Review*, 77, 367–91.

GIFFEN, A E VAN, VOLLGRAFF, C W & HOORN, G VAN 1934–8 *Opgravingen op het Domplein te Utrecht: Wetenschappelijke verslagen*. Haarlem.

GIFFORD, E & GIFFORD, J 1995 The sailing characteristics of the Saxon ships as derived from half-scale working models with special reference to the Sutton Hoo ship, *International Journal of Nautical Archaeology*, 24.2, 121–4.

—— 1996 The sailing performance of Anglo-Saxon ships as derived from the building and trials of half-scale models of the Sutton Hoo and Graveney ship finds, *Journal of the Society of Nautical Research*, 82.2, 131–53.

GILBERT, J T & JAMES, H 1874 *Facsimiles of National Manuscripts of Ireland*. Dublin.

GILCHRIST, R 1994 *Gender and Material Culture: the archaeology of religious women*. London.

GNEUSS, H 1981 A preliminary list of manuscripts written or owned in England up to 1100, *Anglo-Saxon England*, 9, 1–59.

GODDEN, M & LAPIDGE, M 1991 (eds), *The Cambridge Companion to Old English Literature*. Cambridge.

GODMAN, P 1982 (ed) *Alcuin: The Bishops, Kings and Saints of York*. Oxford.

GOLDSCHMIDT, A 1914 *Die Elfenbeinskulpturen aus der Zeit der Karolingischen und Sachsichen Kaiser VIII. – XI. Jahrhundert*, I. Berlin (repr 1969, Berlin and Oxford).

—— 1918 *Die Elfenbeinskulpturen aus der Zeit der Karolingischen und Sachsichen Kaiser VIII. – XI. Jahrhundert*, II. Berlin (repr 1970, Berlin).

GOMME, G L 1886 *Gentleman's Magazine Library: Archaeology*. London.

GOODBURN, D 1986 Do we have evidence of a continuing Saxon boat-building tradition? *International Journal of Nautical Archaeology*, 15.1, 39–47.

—— 1993 A side-rudder from the London waterfront, *A spirit of enquiry*, 56–60. Exeter (= WARP Occasional Paper 7).

—— 1994 Anglo-Saxon boat finds from London, are they English? *Crossroads in ancient ship building*, 97–104. Oxford (= Oxbow Monograph, 40).

GRABAR, A 1966 *Byzantium from the Death of Theodosius to the Rise of Islam*. London.

—— 1968 *Christian Iconography: a study of its origins*. Princeton, NJ.

GRADON, P O E 1958 (ed) *Cynewulf's 'Elene'*. London.

GRAHAM-CAMPBELL, J 1991 Dinas Powys and the Dating of Enamelled Zoomorphic Penannular Brooches, *Bulletin of the Board of Celtic Studies*, 38, 220–32.

GRAVES, R 1957 (trans) *Suetonius: the Twelve Caesars*, XI, 287–93. Harmondsworth.

GREEN, B 1971 An Anglo-Saxon Plaque from Larling, Norfolk, *Antiqs J*, 51, 321–3.

GREENWELL, W & ROLLESTON, G 1877 *British Barrows*. Oxford.

GRIERSON, P 1972 *English Linear Measures: An Essay in Origins*. The Stenton Lecture (1971). Reading.

GRIERSON, P & BLACKBURN, M 1986 *Medieval European Coinage. 1. The early Middle Ages*. London.

GROOT, H L DE 1994 De Heilige Kruiskapel te Utrecht, *Bulletin van de Koninklijke Nederlandse Oudheidkundige Bond*, 93, 135–49, English summary at 193–4.

HADDEN, A W & STUBBS, W 1871 *Councils and Ecclesiastical Documents relating to Great Britain and Ireland*, 3. Oxford.

HAIGH, D H 1846 Notes on Monumental Stones discovered at Hartlepool, *Journal of the British Archaeological Association*, 1, 185–96.

—— 1858 *Notes on the History of S Begu & S Hild; and on some Relics of Antiquity discovered in the sites of the Religious Establishments founded by them*. Hartlepool.

—— 1875 On the Monasteries of S Heiu and S Hild, *Yorkshire Archaeol J*, 3, 349–91.

HALDENBY, D 1990 An Anglian site on the Yorkshire Wolds, *Yorkshire Archaeol J*, 62, 51–63.

—— 1992 An Anglian site on the Yorkshire Wolds – continued, *Yorkshire Archaeol J*, 64, 25–39.

—— 1994 Further Saxon finds from the Yorkshire Wolds, *Yorkshire Archaeol J*, 66, 51–6.

HALL, R 1994 *Viking Age York*. London.

HALL, R A & WHYMAN, M 1996 Settlement and monasticism at Ripon, North Yorkshire, from the 7th to 11th centuries AD, *Medieval Archaeol*, 40, 62–150.

HALLOCK, W & WADE, H T 1906 *The Evolution of Weights and Measures and the Metric System*. New York.

HAMEROW, H 1993 *Excavations at Mucking 2: The Anglo-Saxon Settlement*. London (= English Heritage Research Report, 21).

—— forthcoming *From the Migrations to Charlemagne: Early Medieval Settlements in Northwest Europe*.

HAMEROW, H & PICKIN, J 1995 An Early Anglo-Saxon Cemetery at Andrew's Hill, Easington, Co Durham, *Durham Archaeol J*, 11, 35–66.

HANSSENS, J M 1948 (ed) *Amalarii Episcopi Opera Liturgica Omnia*, tomus II, Liber officialis III.2.1, *De situ ecclesiae*. Vatican.

HARBISON, P 1986 A Group of Early Christian Carved Monuments in Co Donegal. In Higgitt, 49–85.

—— 1992 *The High Crosses of Ireland, An Iconographical and Photographic Survey*, 3 vols. Bonn (= RGZM Forschungsinstitut für Vor-und Frühgeschichte, Monographien, Band 17).

HARDEN, D B 1956 (ed) *Dark Age Britain – Studies Presented to E T Leeds*. London.

HARDING, A 1978 Northumberland: Milfield South (NY939335), *Medieval Archaeol*, 22, 149.

HARGROVE, E 1789 *The History of the Castle, Town and Forest of Knaresborough with Harrogate, and its Medicinal Waters*. York.

HÄRKE, H 1992 Changing Symbols in a Changing Society: the Anglo-Saxon weapon burial rite in the seventh century. In Carver, 149–65.

HARRISON, C & ORTON, F 1984 (eds) *Modernism, Criticism, Realism*. London and New York.

HASELOFF G 1990 *Email im Frühen Mittelalter Frühchristliche Kunst von der Spätantike bis zu den Karolingern*. Marburg.

HAUCK, K 1986 Kontinentale und Insulare Götterbildamulette, *Settimane di Studio*, 32, 249–52.

HAWKES, J 1993 Mary and the cycle of resurrection: the iconography of the Hovingham panel. In Spearman & Higgitt, 254–60.

—— 1995 The Wirksworth slab: an iconography of Humilitas, *Peritia*, 8, 1–32.

—— 1996a *The Golden Age of Northumbria*. Morpeth.

—— 1996b The Rothbury Cross: an iconographic bricolage, *Gesta*, 35, 77–94.

—— 1997 Symbols of Passion or Power? The Iconography of the Rothbury Cross Head. In Karkov et al., 27–44.

HAWKES, S C, MESSICK, J M & METCALF, D M 1966 X-ray fluorescent analysis of some Dark Age coins and jewellery, *Archaeometry*, 9, 98–138.

HAYFIELD, C 1988 The origins of the Roman landscape around Wharram Percy, East Yorkshire. In Price J & Wilson P R (eds) *Recent Research in Roman Yorkshire: Studies in honour of Mary Kitson Clark*, 99–122. Oxford (= BAR Brit Ser, 193).

HAY FLEMING, D 1931 *St Andrews Cathedral Museum*. Edinburgh.

HAYWOOD, J 1991 *Dark Age naval power*. London.

HEDEAGER, L 1993 The Creation of Germanic Identity – A European Origin Myth. In Brun, P, Leeuw, S van der & Whittaker, C R (eds) *Frontières d'Empire – Nature et signification des frontières romaines*, 121–31. Nemours (= *Actes de la Table Ronde Internationale de Nemours 1992 – Mémoires du Musée de Préhistoire d'Île-de-France*, 5).

HENDERSON, G 1985 The John the Baptist panel on the Ruthwell cross, *Gesta*, 25, 3–12.

—— 1987 *From Durrow to Kells: the insular gospel-books 650–800*. London.

—— 1993 Cassiodorus and Eadfrith once again. In Spearman & Higgitt, 82–91.

HENDERSON, I 1978 Sculpture north of the Forth after the takeover by the Scots. In Lang, 47–73.

—— 1979 The Silver Chain from Whitecleugh Shieldholm, Crawfordjohn, Lanarkshire, *Transactions of the Dumfriesshire and Galloway Natural History and Antiquarian Society*, 54, 20–28.

—— 1983 Pictish Vine-Scroll Ornament. In O'Connor, A & Clarke, D V (eds) *From the Stone Age to the 'Forty Five. Studies presented to R B K Stevenson*, 243–68. Edinburgh.

—— 1986 The 'David Cycle' in Pictish Art. In Higgitt, 87–123.

—— 1987 *The Book of Kells* and the snake-boss motif on Pictish cross slabs and the Iona crosses. In Ryan 1987a, 56–65.

—— 1993 The Shape and Decoration of the Cross on Pictish Cross-Slabs Carved in Relief. In Spearman & Higgitt, 209–18.

—— 1994a The Insular and continental context of the St Andrews Sarcophagus. In Crawford, 71–102.

—— 1994b The Picts written records and pictorial images. In Burt, J R F, Bowman, E D & Robertson, N M R (eds) *Stones, Symbols and Stories. Aspects of Pictish Studies. Proceedings from the Conferences of the Pictish Arts Society, 1992*, 44–66. Edinburgh.

—— 1997 *Pictish Monsters: Symbol Text and Image*. Cambridge (= H M Chadwick Memorial Lectures, 7).

HENIG, M 1975 *Vindolanda Jewellery*. Newcastle.

HENRY, F 1965 *Irish Art in the early Christian period, to 800 AD*. London.

—— 1967 *Irish Art During the Viking Invasions 800–1020 AD*. London.

—— 1974 *The Book of Kells*. London.

HERBERT, M 1988 *Iona, Kells and Derry. The History and Hagiography of the Monastic Familia of Columba*. Oxford.

HERMAN, J 1991 Spoken and written Latin in the last centuries of the Roman Empire: a contribution to the linguistic history of the western provinces. In Wright, 29–43.

HERMAN, K B & BLISS, G 1987 24 Capital with ornamental relief: foliage with figures of Romulus and Remus, bearded masks, and griffins. In Bonde, S (ed) *Survival of the Gods: Classical Mythology in Medieval Art*. 74–5. Providence, RI.

HERTZ, M 1855 (ed) Priscian *Institutiones grammaticae*. Leipzig (= *Grammatici Latini*, 2).

HESBERT, R 1935 *Antiphonale Missarum Sextuplex*. Brussels.

HEWISON, J K 1914 *The Runic Roods of Ruthwell and Bewcastle with a Short History of the Cross and Crucifix in Scotland*. Glasgow.

HIGGITT, J 1982 The Pictish Latin inscription at Tarbat in Ross-shire, *Proc Soc Antiq Scotl*, 112, 300–21.

—— 1986 (ed) *Early Medieval Sculpture in Britain and Ireland*. Oxford (= *BAR Brit Ser*, 152)

—— 1995 Monasteries and Inscriptions in Early Northumbria – The Evidence of Whitby. In Bourke, 229–36.

HIGHAM, N J 1979 An aerial survey of the Upper Lune Valley. In Higham, N J (ed) *The Changing Past. Some recent work in the archaeology of Northern England*, 31–8. Manchester.

—— 1985 The Scandinavians in North Cumbria: Raids and Settlement in the later Ninth to mid-Tenth Centuries. In Baldwin, J R & Whyte, I D (eds) *The Scandinavians in Cumbria*, 27–63. Edinburgh.

—— 1986 *The Northern Counties to AD 1000*. London.

—— 1992 *Rome, Britain and the Anglo-Saxons*. London.

—— 1993 *The Kingdom of Northumbria AD 350–1100*. Stroud.

—— 1995 *An English Empire: Bede and the early Anglo-Saxon Kings*. Manchester.

—— 1997 *The Convert Kings: Power and Religious Affiliation in early Anglo-Saxon England*. Manchester.

HILDYARD, E J W 1953 A Roman and Saxon site at Catterick, *Yorkshire Archaeol J*, 38, 241–5.

—— 1957 Cataractonium, fort and town, *Yorkshire Archaeol J*, 39, 224–65.

HILL, D & METCALF, D M 1984 (eds) *The Seventh Oxford Symposium on Coinage and Monetary History*. Oxford (= *BAR Brit Ser*, 128).

HILL, P 1988 Whithorn, *Curr Archaeol*, 110, 85–91.

—— 1997 *Whithorn and St Ninian. The Excavations of a Monastic Town 1984–91*. Stroud.

HILLS, C 1991 The gold bracteate from Undley, Suffolk: some further thoughts, *Studien zur Sachsenforschung*, 7, 145–51.

HINDERWELL, T 1811 *History of Scarborough*. York.

HINES, J 1997 (ed) *The Anglo-Saxons from the Migration Period to the Eighth Century. An Ethnographic Perspective*. Woodbridge.

HINES, J & ODENSTEDT, B 1987 The Undley Bracteate and its Runic Inscription, *Studien zur Sachsenforschung*, 6, 73–94.

HIRST, S M 1985 *An Anglo-Saxon inhumation cemetery at Sewerby, East Yorkshire*. York (= *York University Archaeological Publications*, 4).

HODDER, I 1982 *Symbols in Action: ethnoarchaeological studies of material culture*. Cambridge.

HODGES, C C 1894 The Pre-Conquest Churches of Northumbria, *Reliquary* (NS), 8, 1–12.

—— 1905 Anglo-Saxon Remains. In Page, W (ed) *The Victoria History of the Counties of England: Yorkshire*, II, 211–40. London.

HODGKIN, T 1886 *The letters of Cassiodorus, being a condensed translation of the Variae Epistolae of Magnus Aurelius Cassiodorus Senator, with an introduction by Thomas Hodgkin*. London.

HODGSON, J 1827 *History of Northumberland*, II.1. Newcastle.

HÖFLER, O 1934 *Kultische Geheimbünde der Germanen*, I. Frankfurt-am-Main.

HOLDER, A G 1994 (trans) *Bede: On the Tabernacle*. Liverpool. (= Translated Texts for Historians, 18).

—— 1996 Styles of Clerical Address in the Letters of Augustine, *Studia Patristica*, 33, 100–4.

HOLDSWORTH, P 1991 Dunbar, *Curr Archaeology*, 127, 315–7.

—— 1993 Excavations at Castle Park, Dunbar: an interim report on the Anglian evidence, *Transactions of the East Lothian Antiquarian and Field Naturalists Society*, 22, 31–52.

HOLLIS, S 1992 *Anglo–Saxon Women and the Church: Sharing a Common Fate*. Woodbridge.

HOLTHAUSEN, F 1900 Review of 'Wadstein, E *The Clermont Runic Casket*', *Literaturblatt für germanische und romanische Philologie*, 21.6, 208–12.

HOLTZ, L 1981 (ed) *Donat et la tradition de l'enseigement grammatical*. Paris.

HOPE-TAYLOR, B 1977 *Yeavering: an Anglo-British centre of early Northumbria*. London (= *Department of the Environment Archaeological Report*, 7).

—— 1980 Balbridie . . . and Doon Hill, *Curr Archaeol*, 72, 18–19.

HORNSBY, W 1912 An Anglian Cemetery at Hob Hill, near Saltburn, *Yorkshire Archaeol J*, 22, 131–7.

HOUWEN, L A J R & MACDONALD, A A 1996 (eds) *Beda Venerabilis. Historian, Monk & Northumbrian*. Groningen.

HOWE, N 1989 *Migration and Mythmaking in Anglo-Saxon England*. New Haven and London.

HOWLETT, D 1974 Two panels on the Ruthwell cross, *Journal of the Courtauld and Warburg Institutes*, 37, 333–6.

—— 1992 Inscriptions and Design of the Ruthwell cross. In Cassidy, 71–94.

—— 1994 *The Book of Letters of Saint Patrick the Bishop*. Dublin.

—— 1995 *The Celtic Latin Tradition of Biblical Style*. Dublin.

HOWLEY, G C D 1997 (ed) *The Pickering Bible Commentary for Today*. London and Glasgow.

HUBERT, J, PORCHER, J & VOLBACH, W F 1969 *Europe in the Dark Ages*. London.

HUGGINS, P J 1991 Anglo-Saxon Timber Building Measurements: Recent Results, *Medieval Archaeol*, 35, 6–28.

HUME, D 1802 *The History of England*, I (rev edn). London.

HUNTER, M 1974 The sense of the past in Anglo-Saxon England, *Anglo-Saxon England*, 3, 29–50.

HURST, J G 1984 The Wharram Research Project: Results to 1983, *Medieval Archaeol*, 28, 77–111.

IRELAND, C 1991 Aldfrith of Northumbria and the Irish Genealogies, *Celtica*, 22, 64–78.

IRVINE, M 1986 Bede the Grammarian and the Scope of Grammatical Studies in Eighth-century Northumbria, *Anglo-Saxon England*, 15, 15–44.

—— 1994 *The Making of Textual Culture: 'Grammatica' and Literary Theory 350–1100*. Cambridge (= Cambridge Studies in Medieval Literature, 19).

JACKSON, K H 1959 Edinburgh and the Anglian Occupation of Lothian. In Clemoes, P (ed) *The Anglo-Saxons. Studies Presented to Bruce Dickens*, 35–42. Cambridge.

—— 1969 *The Gododdin. Scotland's Oldest Poem*. Edinburgh.

JACKSON, S 1988 Copper Alloy Objects. In Daniels, R The Anglo-Saxon Monastery at Church Close, Hartlepool, Cleveland, *Archaeol J*, 145, 182–3.

JAMES, E 1989 The origins of barbarian kingdoms: The continental evidence. In Bassett, 40–52.

JAMES, M R 1924 *The Apocryphal New Testament*. Oxford.

JAMES, S, MARSHALL, A & MILLETT, M 1984 An Early Medieval Building Tradition, *Archaeol J*, 141, 182–215.

JANSMA, N S H 1973 *Ornements des manuscrits coptes du Monastère Blanc*. Groningen.

JARMAN, A O H 1988 (ed) *Aneirin: Y Gododdin, Britain's oldest heroic poem*. Llandysul.

JENKINS, D 1986 *Law Texts from Medieval Wales*. Llandysul.

JERG, E 1970 *Vir Venerabilis: Untersuchungen zur Titulatur der Bischöfe in den ausserkirchlichen Texten der Spätantike als Beitrag zur Deutung ihrer öffentlichen Stellung*. Vienna.

JESSUP, R 1950 *Anglo-Saxon Jewellery*. London.

JOBEY, G & MAXWELL, D 1957 A square-headed brooch from Benwell, *Archaeol Aeliana*, 4 ser, 35, 282–4.

JONES, B 1922 Discoveries at Hartlepool, *Antiquaries Journal*, 2, 141–3.

JONES, C W 1937 Manuscripts of Bede's *De Natura Rerum*, *Isis*, 27, 438.

—— 1943 (ed) *Bedae Opera de Temporibus*. Cambridge, Mass.

—— 1970 Some Introductory Remarks on Bede's Commentary on Genesis, *Sacris Erudiri*, 19 (1969–70), 115–98.

KARKOV, C E 1997 The Bewcastle cross: some iconographic problems. In Karkov et al., 9–26.

KARKOV, C, RYAN, M & FARRELL, R T 1997 (eds) *The Insular Tradition*. Albany, NY.

KEENEY, G S 1935 *The Occupation of the Counties Northumberland, Durham, Cumberland and Westmorland from the Fourth to the Eighth Centuries*. Unpublished Ph.D. thesis. Oxford.

—— 1936 Anglo-Saxon Burials at Galewood, within Ewart, near Milfield, *Proc Soc Antiq Newcastle*, 4.7 (1935–6), 14–17.

—— 1939 A Pagan Anglian Cemetery at Howick, Northumberland, *Archaeol Aeliana*, 4 ser, 16, 120–8.

KEIL, H 1857 (ed) *Flavii Sosipatri Charisii Artis Grammaticae Libri V; Diomedis Artis Grammaticae Libri III; ex Charisii Arte Grammatica excerpta*, Leipzig (= *Grammatici Latini*, 1).

KELLEHER, A 1915 Betha Coluimb Chille (continuation), *Zeitschrift für Celtische Philologie*, 10, 228–65.

KELLY, D 1992 The high crosses of Ireland: a review article, *J Roy Soc Antiq Ir*, 122, 67–78.

—— 1993 The relationships of the crosses of Argyll: the evidence of form. In Spearman & Higgitt, 219–29.

—— 1996 A Sense of Proportion: The Metrical and Design Characteristics of some Columban High Crosses, *Proc Royal Soc Antiq Ir*, 126, 108–46.

KELLY, E P 1993 The Lough Kinale book-shrine. In Spearman & Higgitt, 168–74.

KELLY, F 1997 *Early Irish Farming*. Dublin.

KEMP, R 1996 *Anglian Settlement at 45–54 Fishergate, York*. London (= Addyman, P V (ed) *The Archaeology of York*, 7/1).

KENDALL, C B 1991 *Bede: Libri II De Arte Metrica et De Schematibus et Tropis: The Art of Poetry and Rhetoric*. Saarbrücken.

KENDRICK, T D 1938 *Anglo-Saxon Art to* AD *900*. London.

—— 1949 *Late Saxon and Viking Art*. London.

KENDRICK, T D, BROWN, T J, BRUCE-MITFORD, R L S, ROOSENRUNGE, H, ROSS, A S C, STANLEY, E G & WENER, A E 1960 *Evangeliorum Quattuor Codex Lindisfarnensis*, 2 vols. Olten and Lausanne.

KENT, J P C 1972 Gold standards of the merovingian coinage AD 580–700. In Hall, E T & Metcalf, M (eds) *Methods of Chemical and Metallurgical Investigation of Ancient Coinage*, 69–74. London.

KIDSON, P 1990 A Metrological Investigation, *J Warburg Courtauld Inst*, 53, 71–97.

KILBRIDE-JONES, H E 1980 *Zoomorphic Penannular Brooches*. London.

KING, M H 1979 *Grammatica mystica*: A Study of Bede's Grammatical Curriculum. In King & Stevens, 145–59.

KING, M H & STEVENS, W M 1979 (eds) *Saints, Scholars, and Heroes: Studies in Medieval Culture in Honour of Charles W. Jones*, 2 vols. Collegeville, MN.

KIRBY, D P 1974 The Kingdom of Northumbria and the destruction of the Votadini, *Transactions of the East Lothian Archaeological and Natural History Society*, 14, 1–13.

—— 1991 *The Earliest English Kings*. London.

KITZINGER, E 1936 Anglo-Saxon vine-scroll ornament, *Antiquity*, 10, 61–71.

—— 1993 Interlace and Icons: form and function in early Insular art. In Spearman & Higgitt, 3–15.

KLINGENDER, F 1971 *Animals in Thought and Art*. London.

KLÜGMANN, A & KÖRTE, G 1887 *Etruskische Spiegel*, vol 5 (1884–7), Berlin. (repr 1974, Berlin and New York).

KNÖGEL-ANRICH, E 1992 *Schriftquellen zur Kunstgeschichte der Merowingerzeit*, 2nd ed. Hildesheim, Zürich and New York (originally published under the name Knögel as *Bonner Jahrbücher*, 140–1, 1936).

KOLLWITZ, R 1933 Die Lipsanothek von Brescia. Berlin (= *Studien zur Spätantike Kunstgeschichte*, 7).

KRIER, J 1996 Echternach und das Kloster des hl. Willibrord. In Wieczorek et al., 466–78.

KÜHNEL, B 1987 *From the Earthly to the Heavenly Jerusalem: Representations of the Holy City in Christian Art of the First Millennium*. Rome (= Römische Quartalschrift für christliche Altertumskunde und Kirchengeschichte. Supplementheft 42).

LAING, L 1973a The Angles in Scotland and the Mote of Mark, *Transactions of the Dumfriesshire and Galloway Natural History and Antiquarian Society*, 50, 38–52.

—— 1973b The Mote of Mark, *Curr Archaeol*, 39, 121–5.

—— 1975 The Mote of Mark and the origins of Celtic Interlace, *Antiquity*, 49, 98–108.

—— 1993 *A Catalogue of Celtic Ornamental Metalwork in the British Isles c* AD *400–1200*, Oxford (= Nottingham Monographs in Archaeology No 5, *BAR Brit Ser*, 229).

LAING, L, & LAING, J 1993 *The Picts and the Scots*. Stroud.

LAISTNER, M L W 1933 Source Marks in Bede Manuscripts, *Journal of Theological Studies*, 24, 350–4.

—— 1935 The Library of the Venerable Bede. In Thompson, A H (ed) *Bede: his Life, Times, and Writings. Essays in Commemoration of the Twelfth Centenary of his Death*, 237–66. London.

—— 1966 *Thought and Letters in Western Europe*, AD *500 to 900*. Ithaca, New York.

LAISTNER, M L W & KING, H H 1943 *A Hand-List of Bede Manuscripts*. Ithaca, NY.

LANG, J 1978a Continuity and Innovation in Anglo-Scandinavian Sculpture. In Lang, 145–72.

—— 1978b (ed) *Anglo-Saxon and Viking Age Sculpture and its context*. Oxford (= *BAR Brit Ser*, 49).

—— 1983 Recent Studies in the Pre-Conquest Sculpture of Northumbria. In Thompson, *Studies in Medieval Sculpture*, 177–89.

—— 1988 Some Units of Linear Measure in Insular Art. In Mac Niocaill & Wallace, 95–101.

—— 1991 *York and Eastern Yorkshire*, Oxford (= *Corpus of Anglo-Saxon Stone Sculpture*, III).

—— forthcoming *Northern Yorkshire*, Oxford (= *Corpus of Anglo-Saxon Stone Sculpture*, VI).

LANG, J & MORRIS, C 1978 Recent finds of pre-Norman sculpture from Gilling West, N. Yorkshire, *Medieval Archaeol*, 22, 127–30.

LAPIDGE, M 1993 *Bede the Poet* (Jarrow Lecture).

LAURAS, A & RONDET, H 1953 Le Thème des deux cités dans l'oeuvre de saint Augustin, *Etudes Augustiniennes*, 28, 99–160.

LAW, V 1982 *The Insular Latin Grammarians*. Woodbridge.

—— 1995 *Wisdom, Authority and Grammar in the Seventh Century: Decoding Virgilius Maro Grammaticus*. Cambridge.

LAWLESS, G 1987 *Augustine of Hippo and His Monastic Rule*. Oxford.

LAWLOR, H J 1916 The Cathach of St Columba, *Proc Roy Ir Acad*, 33C, 241–443.

LEAHY, K A 1995 The Flixborough hoard, *Curr Archaeology*, 141 (1994–5), 352.

—— forthcoming a Middle Saxon metalwork and the productive site phenomenon in Yorkshire. In Geake, H (ed) *Anglo-Saxon Yorkshire*: Conference Proceedings 1995.

—— forthcoming b The Anglo-Saxon Metalwork. In Manby, T G *Excavations on a Bronze Age and Anglo-Saxon site at Paddock Hill, Octon, Yorks*.

LEBOW, N 1973 British Historians and Irish History, *Eire-Ireland*, 4, 3–38.

LEEDS, E T 1949 *A Corpus of Early Anglo-Saxon Great Square-Headed Brooches*. Oxford.

LEEDS, E T & POCOCK, M 1971 A Survey of the Anglo Saxon Cruciform Brooches of the Florid Type, *Medieval Archaeol*, 15, 13–36.

LEES, C & OVERING, G 1994 Birthing bishops and fathering poets: Bede, Hild and the relations of cultural production, *Exemplaria*, 6.1, 35–65.

LENDINARA, P 1991 The World of Anglo-Saxon Learning. In Godden & Lapidge, 264–81.

LEVISON, W 1946 *England and Continent in the Eighth Century*. Oxford.

LEWIS, S 1980 Sacred Calligraphy: the Chi Rho Page in the *Book of Kells, Traditio*, 36, 139–59.

LINDSAY, W M 1911 (ed) *Isidori Hispalensis Episcopi Etymologiarum sive Originum Libri XX*, 2 vols. Oxford.

LONGLEY, D 1982 The Date of the Mote of Mark, *Antiquity*, 56, 132–4.

LOUGHLIN, N & MILLER, K R 1979 *A Survey of Archaeological Sites in Humberside*. Hull.

LOVELUCK, C P 1998 A high-status Anglo-Saxon settlement at Flixborough, Lincolnshire, *Antiquity*, 72, 146–61.

LOWE, E A 1928 More Facts about our Oldest Latin Manuscripts, *The Classical Quarterly*, 22, 43–62 (repr Bieler, L 1972 (ed) *Palaeographical Chapters*, I, 251–74, Oxford).

—— 1952 The Uncial Gospel Leaves Attached to the Utrecht Psalter, *Art Bulletin*, 34, 237–8, figs 1–4.

LUCE, A A, SIMMS, G O, MEYER, P & BIELER, L 1960 *Evangeliorum quattuor codex Durmachensis*, 2 vols. Olten and Lausanne.

LUCY, S J 1998 *The Early Anglo-Saxon Cemeteries of Eastern Yorkshire: An Analysis and Reinterpretation*. Oxford (= *BAR Brit Ser*, 272).

—— forthcoming Early Medieval Burials in East Yorkshire: Reconsidering the Evidence. In Geake, H (ed) *Anglo-Saxon Yorkshire: Conference Proceedings 1995*.

MAC AIRT, S & MAC NIOCAILL, G 1983 (ed) *The Annals of Ulster (to AD 1131)*. Dublin.

MACKAIL, J W 1934 (trans) *Virgil's Works; The Aeneid, Eclogues, Georgics*. New York.

MACKAY, T W 1976 Bede's Hagiographical Method His Knowledge and Use of Paulinus of Nola. In Bonner, G (ed) *Famulus Christi. Essays in Commemoration of the thirteenth Centenary of the Birth of the Venerable Bede*, 77–92. London.

—— 1979 Bede's Biblical Criticism. The Venerable Bede's Summary of Tyconius's *Liber Regularum*. In King & Stevens, 1, 209–31.

—— 1990 Early Christian Millenarianist Interpretation of the Two Witnesses in John's Apocalypse 11:3–13. In Ricks, S D & Lundquist, J (eds) *By Study and also by Faith: Studies in Honor of*

Hugh Nibley on the Occasion of his Eightieth Birthday, 27 March 1990. 2 vols. 1, 222–331. Salt Lake City.

—— 1995 Sources and Style in Bede's Commentary on the Apocalypse, *Studia Patristica*, 30 (1997), 54–60.

MACKENZIE, E & ROSS, M 1834 *An Historical, Topographical and Descriptive View of the County Palatine of Durham.* Newcastle.

MACLAUCHLAN, H 1867 *Notes not included in the Memoirs Already Published on Roman Roads in Northumberland.* London.

MAC LEAN, D 1992 The Date of the Ruthwell Cross. In Cassidy, 49–70.

—— 1993 Snake-bosses and redemption at Iona and in Pictland. In Spearman & Higgit, 245–53.

—— 1995 Technique and contact: carpentry-constructed Insular stone crosses. In Bourke, 167–75.

MAC NIOCAILL, G & WALLACE, P 1988 (eds) *Keimelia. Studies in Medieval Archaeology and History in Memory of Tom Delaney.* Galway.

MACQUARRIE, A 1992 Early Christian religious houses in Scotland: foundation and function. In Blair & Sharpe, 110–33.

MANBY, T G 1986 *Thwing, Excavation and Field Archaeology in East Yorkshire 1986, The Anglo-Saxon Cemetery.* Leeds.

—— 1988 Excavation and Field Archaeology in East Yorkshire, The Thwing Project 1973–87, *Council for British Archaeology Forum*, 16–18. London.

—— forthcoming *Thwing, Paddock Hill, A Bronze Age and Anglo-Saxon site in East Yorkshire.*

MANCINELLI, F 1981 *The catacombs of Rome and the origins of Christianity.* Florence.

MARKUS, R A 1970 *Saeculum: History and Society in the theology of St Augustine.* Cambridge.

MARSDEN, R 1995a *The Text of the Old Testament in Anglo-Saxon England.* Cambridge (= Cambridge Studies in Anglo-Saxon England, 15).

—— 1995b Job in his place: the Ezra miniature in the *Codex Amiatinus, Scriptorium*, 49, 3–15.

MARSHALL, A & MARSHALL, C 1994 Differentiation, Change and Continuity in Anglo-Saxon Buildings, *Archaeol Jnl*, 150, 366–402.

MARTIN, L T & HURST, D 1991 (trans) *Bede the Venerable. Homilies on the Gospels*, 1. Kalamazoo, Mich.

MASAI, F 1947 *Essai sur les origines de la miniature dite irlandaise.* Brussels.

MATTER, E A 1992 The Apocalypse in Early Medieval Exegesis. In Emmerson & McGinn, 38–50.

MATTINGLY H 1970 (trans and ed) *Tacitus: The Agricola and the Germania.* Harmondsworth.

MAYR-HARTING, H 1976 The Venerable Bede, the Rule of St Benedict, and Social Class (Jarrow Lecture).

—— 1991 *The Coming of Christianity to Anglo-Saxon England.* London.

MCCLURE, J 1983 Bede's Old Testament Kings. In Bullough, D, Collins, R & Wormald, P (eds) *Ideal and Reality in Frankish and Anglo-Saxon Society: Studies Presented to J M Wallace Hadrill*, 76–98. Oxford.

MCCONE, K 1984 *Aided Cheltchair maic Uthechair*: Hounds, Heroes, and Hospitallers in Early Irish Myth and Story, *Ériu*, 35, 1–30.

—— 1986 Werewolves, Cyclopes, *Díberga*, and *Fíanna*: Juvenile Delinquency in Early Ireland, *Cambridge Medieval Celtic Stud*, 12, 1–22.

—— 1987 Hund Wolf und Krieger bei den Indogermanen. In Meid, W (ed) *Studien zum indogermanischen Wortschatz*, 101–54. Innsbruck.

—— 1991 *Pagan Past and Christian Present in Early Irish Literature.* Maynooth.

MCGURK, P 1955 Two Notes on the *Book of Kells* and Its Relation to Other Insular Gospel Books, *Scriptorium* 9, 105–7.

—— 1961 *Latin gospel books from AD 400 to AD 800.* Paris-Brusselles, Anvers-Amsterdam. (= *Les Publications de Scriptorium*, V).

—— 1990 Appendix of Gospel readings. In Fox, 71–152.

MCNAB, S 1988 Styles used in twelfth-century Irish figure sculpture, *Peritia*, 6–7, (1987–8), 265–97.

MCNAMARA, M 1990 *Studies on Texts of Early Irish Latin Gospels (A.D. 600–1200)*. Steenbrugge-Dordrecht.

MCNEILL, W 1977 *Plagues and Peoples*. New York.

MEANEY, A L 1964 *A gazetteer of early Anglo-Saxon burial sites*. London.

MEEHAN, B 1994a *The Book of Kells*. London.

—— 1994b The division of hands in the *Book of Kells*. In O'Mahony, 183–95 (= rev of Meehan, B The division of hands. In Fox 1990, 249–56).

MEEHAN, D 1958 (ed & trans) *Adamnan's De Locis Sanctis*. Dublin. (= *Scriptores Latini Hiberniae*, III).

MEER, F VAN DER 1961 *Augustine the Bishop: The Life and Work of a Father of the Church*. London and New York.

MEPISASHVILI, R & TSINTSADZE, V 1979 *The arts of ancient Georgia*. London.

MEYVAERT, P 1964 *Bede and Gregory the Great* (Jarrow Lecture).

—— 1979 Bede and the Church Paintings at Wearmouth-Jarrow, *Anglo-Saxon England*, 8, 63–77.

—— 1982 An Apocalypse panel on the Ruthwell cross. In Tirro, F (ed) *Medieval and Renaissance Studies*, 3–32. Durham, NC (= Proceedings of the Southeastern Institute of Medieval and Renaissance Studies, Summer 1978, Medieval and Renaissance Series, 9).

—— 1989 The *Book of Kells* and Iona, *Art Bulletin*, 71.1, 6–19.

—— 1992 A New Perspective on the Ruthwell Cross: Ecclesia and Vita Monastica. In Cassidy, 95–166.

—— 1996 Bede, Cassiodorus, and the *Codex Amiatinus*, *Speculum* 71, 827–83.

MGH: Auct Antiq = Monumenta Germaniae Historica: Auctorum Antiquissimorum.

MICHELLI, P E 1996 The inscriptions on pre-Norman Irish reliquaries, *Proc Roy Ir Acad*, 96C, 1–48.

MIKET, R 1975 Thirlings, *Medieval Archaeol* 18, 182–3.

—— 1978 Two early Anglo-Saxon brooches from Chesters and Chesterholm, *Archaeol Aeliana*, 5 ser, 6, 177–80.

—— 1980 A restatement of evidence from Bernician Anglo-Saxon burials. In Rahtz, P A, Dickinson, T M, Watts, L (eds) *Anglo-Saxon Cemeteries 1979*, 289–305. Oxford (= *BAR Brit Ser*, 82).

—— 1982 An Anglo-Saxon small-long brooch from Hylton, *Archaeol Aeliana*, 5 ser, 10, 209–11.

—— 1984 An Anglo-Saxon small-long brooch from Cleadon, Tyne and Wear, *Archaeol Aeliana*, 5 ser, 12, 245.

—— 1985 Two Anglo-Saxon brooches provenanced to near Corbridge, Northumberland, *Archaeol Aeliana*, 5 ser, 13, 214–16.

MIKET, R & POCOCK, M 1976 An Anglo-Saxon Cemetery at Greenbank, Darlington, *Medieval Archaeol*, 20, 62–74.

MILBURN, R L P 1954 *Early Christian Interpretations of History*. London.

MILES, G T & RICHARDSON, W 1911 *A History of Withernsea: with notices of other parishes in South Holderness*. Hull.

MILKAU, F 1928 Zu Cassiodor, *Von Büchern und Bibliotheken: Festchrift Kuhnert*, 38–44. Berlin.

MILLER, M, 1975 Bede's use of Gildas, *English Historical Review*, 355, 241–61.

MILLETT, M 1983 Excavations at Cowdery's Down, Basingstoke, Hants, 1978–1981, *Archaeol J* 140, 151–78.

—— 1990 *The Romanization of Britain: an essay in archaeological interpretation*. Cambridge.

MILNE, G & RICHARDS J D 1992 *Wharram: A Study of Settlement on the Yorkshire Wolds, VII. Two Anglo-Saxon Buildings and Associated Finds*. York (= York University Archaeology Publications, 9).

MITCHELL, A & CLARK, J 1908 (eds) *Geographical Collections Relating to Scotland Made by Walter Macfarlane*, III (1906–8). Edinburgh.

MOHLBERG, L C 1960 (ed) *Liber Sacramentorum Romanae Aeclesiae Ordinis Anni Circuli.* Rome (= Rerum Ecclesiasticarum Documenta, Series Maior, Fontes, IV).

MOHRMANN, C 1961 *Etudes sur le Latin des Chrétiens,* 2 vols. Rome.

MOLONEY, C 1996 Catterick Racecourse, *Curr Archaeol,* 148, 128–32.

MONCEAUX, P 1901–23 *Histoire littéraire de l'Afrique chrétienne,* 7 vols. Paris. (repr Brussels 1963).

MOREY, C R 1942 *Early Christian Art.* Oxford.

MORIN, G 1913 Pour l'authenticité de la lettre de S. Jérôme á Présidius, *Bulletin d'ancienne littérature et d'archéologie chrétiennes,* 3, 52–60.

—— 1942 (ed) *Expositio de Apocalypsi Sancti Iohannis.* In *Sancti Caesarii Episcopi Arelatensis Opera Omnia nunc primum in unum collecta. Volumen II. Opera Varia,* 210–77. Maredsous.

MORRIS, I 1987 *Burial and Ancient Society – The rise of the Greek city-state.* Cambridge.

MORRIS, J 1980 (ed) *Nennius. British History and Welsh Annals.* London.

MORRIS, M C F 1907 *Nunburnholme, its History and Antiquities.* London and York.

MORRIS, R K 1983 *The Church in British Archaeology.* London (= CBA Research Report, 47).

MORRIS, R W B, & HOEK, M A M VAN 1987 Rock Carvings in the Garlieston area, Wigtown District, *Transactions of the Dumfriesshire and Galloway Natural History and Antiquarian Society,* 62, 32–9.

MORTIMER, C 1996 Technical Analysis of the Ripon Jewel, *Ancient Monuments Laboratory Report,* 3 (96). London.

MORTIMER, J R 1905 *Forty Years' Researches in British and Saxon Burial Mounds of East Yorkshire.* London.

MUIR, B J 1994 (ed) *The Exeter Anthology of Old English Poetry; An Edition of Exeter Dean and Chapter MS 3501. 1. Texts.* Exeter.

MUNRO, R 1882 *Ancient Scottish Lake-Dwellings or Crannogs.* Edinburgh.

MYNORS, R A B 1937 (ed) *Cassiodori Senatoris Institutiones.* Oxford.

—— 1963 (ed) *C. Plini Caecili Secundi Epistularum Libri Decem.* Oxford.

MYRES, J N L 1969 *Anglo-Saxon Pottery and the Settlement of England.* Oxford.

—— 1977 *A Corpus of Pagan Anglo-Saxon Pottery.* Oxford.

NAPIER, A S 1901 The Franks Casket. In *An English Miscellany Presented to Dr Furnival,* 362–81. Oxford.

NAUMANN, H 1950 Neue Beiträge zum altgermanischen Dioskurenglauben, *Bonner Jahrbücher,* 150, 91–101.

NENK, B S, MARGESON, S & HURLEY, M 1994 Medieval Britain and Ireland in 1993, *Medieval Archaeol,* 38, 228–9.

NERSESSIAN, S DER 1954 An Armenian version of the Homilies on the Harrowing of Hell, *Dumbarton Oaks Papers,* 8, 201–24.

NETZER, N 1994 *Cultural Interplay in the Eighth Century: The Trier Gospels and the Making of a Scriptorium at Echternach.* Cambridge.

NEUMAN DE VEGVAR, C L 1987 *The Northumbrian Renaissance: a study in the transmission of style.* London and Toronto.

NEWMAN, J forthcoming Barham, Suffolk – Middle Saxon market or meeting place? In Metcalf, D M & Blackburn, M (eds) *Productive Sites of the Middle Saxon Period,* Proceedings of the 12th Oxford Coin Symposium.

NICOLSON, J 1809 (ed) *Letters on Various Subjects, Literary, Political, and Ecclesiastical, to and from W Nicolson,* I. London.

NIECE, S LA 1988 White Inlays in Anglo-Saxon Jewellery. In Slater, E S & Tate, J O (eds) *Science and Archaeology. Proceedings of a conference on the application of scientific techniques to archaeology, Glasgow, 1987,* 235–46. Oxford (= BAR Brit Ser, 196.1).

NIEKE, M R 1993 Penannular and related brooches: secular ornament or symbol in action? In Spearman & Higgitt, 128–34.

NIEKE, M R & DUNCAN, H B 1988 Dalriada: the establishment and maintenance of an early historic kingdom in northern Britain. In Driscoll & Nieke, 6–21.

NORDEN, E 1958 *Die antike Kunstprosa*, 2 vols. Darmstadt.

NORDENFALK, C 1947 Before the *Book of Durrow*, *Acta Archaeologica*, 18, 141–74.

—— 1977 Another look at the *Book of Kells*. In Piel, F & Traeger, J (eds) *Festschrift Wolfgang Braunfels*, 275–9. Tübingen.

O'BRIEN, M B 1930 *Titles of Address in Christian Latin Epistolography to 543 AD*. Washington.

O'BRIEN, C & MIKET, R 1991 The Early Medieval Settlement of Thirlings, Northumberland, *Durham Archaeol J*, 7, 57–91.

Ó CARRAGÁIN, É 1978 Liturgical innovations associated with Pope Sergius and the iconography of the Ruthwell and Bewcastle croses. In Farrell, R T (ed) *Bede and Anglo-Saxon England*, 131–47. Oxford (= *BAR Brit Ser*, 46).

—— 1986 Christ over the beasts and the Agnus Dei: two multivalent panels on the Ruthwell and Bewcastle crosses. In Szarmach, P E & Oggins, V D (eds) *Sources of Anglo-Saxon culture*, 377–403. Kalamazoo, Michigan (= *Studies in Medieval Culture*, 20).

—— 1987a The Ruthwell cross and Irish High Crosses: some points of comparison and contrast. In Ryan 1987a, 111–28.

—— 1987b A liturgical interpretation of the Bewcastle Cross. In Stokes, M & Burton, T L (eds) *Medieval Literature and Antiquities: studies in honour of Basil Cottle*, 15–42. Cambridge.

—— 1988a The Meeting of St Paul and Saint Anthony: visual and literary uses of a Eucharistic motif. In Mac Niocaill & Wallace, 1–58.

—— 1988b The Ruthwell Crucifixion poem and its iconographic and liturgical contexts, *Peritia*, 6–7 (1987–8), 1–71.

—— 1992 Seeing, Reading, Singing the Ruthwell cross: vernacular poem, Old English liturgy and implied audience. In *Art and Symbolism*, 91–6. York (= pre-printed papers 7. Medieval Europe: Conference on medieval archaeology in Europe, York, 1992).

—— 1994a The City of Rome and the World of Bede (Jarrow Lecture).

—— 1994b 'Traditio evangeliorum' and 'sustentatio': the relevance of liturgical ceremonies to the *Book of Kells*. In O'Mahony, 398–436.

—— 1995 Rome pilgrimage, Roman liturgy and the Ruthwell Cross, *Akten des XII. internationalen Kongresses für christliche Archäologie, Bonn, 22. bis 28. September 1991*, 2, 630–9 (= *Jahrbuch für Antike und Christentum*, Ergäanzungsband, 20, 2 parts. Münster).

O'CONNOR, T P 1991 *Bones from 46–54 Fishergate*. York (= Archaeol York, 15 (4)).

—— 1994 8th–11th century economy and environment in York. In Rackham J (ed) *Environment and Economy in Anglo-Saxon England*, 136–47. London (= *CBA Research Report*, 89).

O'CONOR, C 1814 *Rerum Hibernicarum scriptores veteres*. Buckingham.

Ó CRÓINÍN, D 1982 Pride and Prejudice, *Peritia*, 1, 352–62.

—— 1983 Early Irish annals from Easter tables: a case restated, *Peritia*, 2, 74–86.

—— 1984 Rath Maelsigi, Willibrord, and the earliest Echternach manuscripts, *Peritia*, 3, 17–49.

—— 1988 *Codices illuminati medii aevi 9: Evangeliarium Epternacense*. Munich.

—— 1989 Is the Augsberg Gospel Codex a Northumbrian Manuscript?. In Bonner et al., 189–202.

—— 1995 *Early Medieval Ireland 400–1200*. Harlow.

O'DONNELL, J J 1979 *Cassiodorus*. Los Angeles and London.

OGDEN, J 1992 Gold in Antiquity, *Interdisciplinery Science Reviews (The Institute of Materials, London)*, 17, 261–70.

OGILVY, J D A 1967 *Books Known to the English, 597–1066*. Cambridge, Mass.

OKASHA, E, 1971 *Hand-list of Anglo-Saxon Non-Runic Inscriptions*. Cambridge.

—— 1992 A second supplement to *Hand-List of Anglo-Saxon Non-Runic Inscriptions*, *Anglo-Saxon England*, 21, 37–85.

—— 1995 Literacy in Anglo-Saxon England: the Evidence from inscriptions, *Anglo-Saxon Studies in Archaeology and History*, 8 (1996), 69–74.

O'MAHONY, F 1994 (ed) *The* Book of Kells: *proceedings of a conference at Trinity College Dublin, 6–9 September 1992*. Aldershot.

O'MEADHRA, U 1979 *Early Christian, Viking and Romanesque Art: Motif-Pieces from Ireland. An Illustrated and Descriptive Catalogue*. Stockholm. (= Theses and Papers in North-European Archaeology, 7).

O'REILLY, J 1993 The *Book of Kells*, folio 114r: a mystery revealed yet concealed. In Spearman & Higgitt, 106–114.

—— 1994 Exegesis and the *Book of Kells*: the Lucan Genealogy. In O'Mahony, 344–97.

—— 1995 Introduction. In Connolly, xvii–lv.

Ó RIAIN-RAEDEL, D 1995 Edith, Judith, Matilda: the role of royal ladies in the propagation of the continental cult. In Stancliffe & Cambridge, 210–29.

ORTON, F 1995 The Ruthwell Cross: Fragments and Critique. Unpublished paper. International Medieval Congress. Leeds.

OSBORNE, J 1984 *The early medieval wall-paintings in the lower church of San Clemente*. New York and London.

O'SULLIVAN, W 1985 Insular Caligraphy: Current State and Problems, *Peritia*, 4, 346–59.

—— 1994 The Lindisfarne Scriptorium: For and Against, *Peritia*, 8, 80–94.

OTTAWAY, P 1992 *Anglo-Scandinavian Ironwork from 16–22 Coppergate*. London. (= *The Archaeology of York. 17. The Small Finds*, fasc 6).

OWEN, D 1971 *Church and Society in Medieval Lincolnshire*. Lincoln (= *The history of Linconshire*, 5).

—— 1975 Medieval chapels in Lincolnshire, *Lincolnshire History Archaeol*, 10, 18.

OXENSTIERNA, E 1956 *Die Goldhörner von Gallehus*. Lidingö.

PACITTO, A 1971 The excavation of two Bronze Age burial mounds at Ferry Fryston in the West Riding of Yorkshire, *Yorkshire Archaeol J*, 42, 295–305.

PÄFFGEN, B & RISTOW, S 1996 Christentum, Kirchenbau und Sakralkunst im östlichen Frankenreich (Austrasien). In Wieczorek et al., 407–15

PAGE, R I P 1959 An Early Drawing of the Ruthwell Cross, *Medieval Archaeol*, 3, 285–8.

—— 1973 *An introduction to English runes*. London.

—— 1987 *Runes*. Berkeley and Los Angeles.

PALMER, R B 1959 Bede as a Textbook Writer: A Study of his *De Arte Metrica*, *Speculum*, 24, 573–84.

PAOR, M DE & PAOR, L DE 1958 *Early Christian Ireland*. London.

PARKES, M 1982 The Scriptorium of Wearmouth-Jarrow (Jarrow Lecture).

—— 1991 The Contribution of Insular Scribes of the Seventh and Eighth Centuries to the 'Grammar of Legibility'. In Parkes, M (ed) *Scribes, Scripts and Readers. Studies in the Communication, Preservation and Dissemination of Medieval Texts*, 1–18. London (= reprint of Maierú, A 1987 (ed) *Grafia e interpunzione del latino nel medioevo*, 15–29, Rome).

—— 1993 *Pause and Effect: An Introduction to the History of Punctuation in the West*. Berkeley and Los Angeles.

PARSONS, D 1996 England and the Low Countries at the time of St Willibrord. In De Bièvre, 30–48

PEARCE, S M 1982 Estates and church sites in Dorset and Gloucestershire: the emergence of a Christian society. In Pearce, S M (ed) *The Early Church in Western Britain and Ireland: studies presented to C A Ralegh Radford*, 117–38. Oxford (= *BAR Brit Ser*, 102).

PEERS, C R & RADFORD, C A R 1943 The Saxon monastery at Whitby, *Archaeologia*, 89, 27–88.

PEETERS, L 1996 The Franks Casket: a Judeo-Christian Interpretation, *Amsterdamer Beiträge zur Älteren Germanistik* 46, 17–52.

PETERSEN, T 1954 The paragraph mark in Coptic illuminated ornament. In Miner, D (ed) *Studies in art and literature for Belle da Costa Greene*, 295–330. Princeton, NJ.

PHILLIPS, J 1853 *The Rivers, Mountains and Sea-Coast of Yorkshire, with essays on the climate, scenery and ancient inhabitants of the county.* London.

PICKIN, J 1991 An Anglo-Saxon Cemetery at Easington, County Durham, *Archaeology North*, 2, 16.

—— 1993 An Anglo-Saxon Cemetery at Easington, County Durham, *Archaeology North*, 3, 6–8.

PINDER, M 1995 Anglo-Saxon Garnet Cloissonné Composite Disc Brooches Some Aspects of their Construction, *J Brit Archaeol Assoc*, 148, 6–28.

PINKSTER, H 1991 Evidence for SVO in Latin. In Wright, 69–82.

PL = Migne, J-P (ed) 1844–64 *Patrologiae Cursus Completus, Series Latina*, 221 vols. Paris.

PLUMMER, C 1896 (ed) *Venerabilis Baedae Opera Historica*, 2 vols in 1. Oxford.

POCOCK, M 1970 A note on two early Anglo-Saxon brooches, *Yorkshire Archaeol J*, 42, 407–9, pl 1.

POLARA, G 1979 (ed) *Virgilio Marone Grammactico, Epitomi ed Epistole*. Naples.

PORTER, H B 1967 *The Ordination Prayers of the Ancient Western Churches*. London.

POULSON, G 1841 *The History and Antiquities of the Seigniory of Holderness, in the East Riding of the County of York*, II. Hull.

POWLESLAND, D 1989 *West Heslerton 1989, The Anglian Settlement, an interim report*. Unpublished.

—— 1997 Early Anglo-Saxon Settlements, Structures, Form and Layout. In Hines, 101–24.

—— in press *West Heslerton: The Anglian Cemetery*.

POWLESLAND, D & HOUGHTON, C A forthcoming *West Heslerton – The Anglian Cemetery* (= English Heritage Monograph).

POWLESLAND, D, HOUGHTON, C A & HANSON, J H 1986 Excavations at Heslerton, North Yorkshire 1978–82, *Archaeol J*, 143, 53–173.

PRZYLUSKI, J 1940 Les confréries de loups-garous dans les sociétés indo-européennes, *Revue de l'Histoire des Religions*, 121, 128–45

PURDY, J D 1974 Ganton. In Allison, K J (ed) *A History of the County of York: East Riding*, III, 208–16. London.

QUENTIN, H 1926 (ed) *Librum Genesis ex interpretatione Sancti Hieronymi*. Rome (= *Biblia Sacra iuxta latinam vulgatam versionem ad codicum fidem*, 1).

RADFORD, C A R 1953 Hoddom, *Transactions of the Dumfriesshire & Galloway Natural History & Antiquarian Society*, 31 (1952–3), 174–97.

RAFTERY, B 1987 *A Catalogue of Irish Iron Age Antiquities*. Marburg.

RAHTZ, P 1976a Buildings and rural settlement. In Wilson, 49–98.

—— 1976b The building plan of the Anglo-Saxon monastery of Whitby Abbey. In Wilson, 459–62.

RAINE, J 1828 *St Cuthbert: with an account of the state in which his remains were found upon the opening of his tomb in Durham Cathedral in the year MDCCCXXVII*. Durham.

RALSTON, I B M, & INGLIS, J 1984 *Foul Hordes: The Picts in the North-east and their background*. Aberdeen.

RAU, R 1988 *Briefe des Bonifatius, Willibalds Leben des Bonifatius, nebst einigen zeitgenössischen Dokumenten*. Ausgewählte Quellen zur deutschen Geschichte des Mittelalters, Freiherr von Stein-Gedächtnisausgabe, IVb. Darmstadt.

RCAHMS 1982 = Royal Commission on the Ancient and Historical Monuments of Scotland, *Argyll, An Inventory of the Monuments*. 4. Iona. Edinburgh.

—— 1984 = Royal Commission on the Ancient and Historical Monuments of Scotland, *Argyll: an inventory of the monuments*. 5. Islay, Jura, Colonsay & Oronsay. Edinburgh.

—— 1994 = Royal Commission on the Ancient and Historical Monuments of Scotland, *South-East Perth, an Archaeological Landscape*. Edinburgh.

REVEL-NEHER, E 1982 La double page du *Codex Amiatinus* et ses rapports avec les plans du tabernacle dans art juif et dans l'art byzantin, *Journal of Jewish Art*, 9, 6–17.

RICHARDS, J D 1991 *Viking Age England*. London.

—— 1994 Cottam Evaluation, *Yorkshire Archaeol J*, 66, 57–8.

—— in prep Cottam: Anglian and Anglo-Scandinavian Settlement on the Yorkshire Wolds.

RICHTER, M 1994 *The Formation of the Medieval West: studies in the oral culture of the barbarians*. Dublin.

RIDYARD, S 1988 *The Royal Saints of Anglo-Saxon England*. Cambridge.

RIECK, F 1993 The Man from Nydam Ross, *Marine Archaeology Newsletter*, 1, 3–4.

RIGOLD, S E 1977 The principal series of English *sceattas*, *British Numismatic Journal*, 47, 21–30.

RIGOLD, S E & METCALF, D M 1984 A revised checklist of English finds of *sceattas*. In Hill & Metcalf, 245–68.

RIJNTJES, R 1994 De *ecclesiola* in het Utrechtse castellum: bouwhistorische interpretatie van de resten van de Heilig-Kruiskapel, *Bulletin van de Koninklijke Nederlandse Oudheidkundige Bond*, 93, 150–61. English summary at 194.

—— 1996 Porticus or pastophorion? Eighth-century St Martin, Utrecht, between Anglo-Saxon and Frankish traditions. In De Bièvre, 49–57.

RILEY, D N, *Fieldwork diary, 1933–37*, North Lincolnshire Museums. Unpublished.

RITCHIE, A 1989 *Picts*. Edinburgh.

RITCHIE, G, & RITCHIE, A 1991 *Scotland. Archaeology and Early History*. Edinburgh.

RIVET, A L F & SMITH, C 1979 *The Place-names of Roman Britain*. London.

ROBERTSON, D 1958 (trans) *Saint Augustine: On Christian Doctrine*. New York and London.

RODWELL, W 1981 *The Archaeology of the English Church: the study of historic churches and churchyards*. London (repr 1989 *Church Archaeology*. Manchester).

ROGERS, N S H 1993 *Anglian and Other Finds from 46–54 Fishergate*. London (= Addyman, P V (ed) *The Archaeology of York*, 17/9).

ROMERO-POSE, E 1985 (ed) *Sancti Beati a Liebana Commentarius in Apocalypsin*, 2 vols. Rome.

ROTH, H 1979 (ed) *Kunst der Völkerwanderungszeit*. Frankfurt am Main (= *Propyläen Kunstgeschichte*. Supplementband IV).

RYAN, M 1983 (ed) *The Derrynaflan Hoard I: A Preliminary Account*. Dublin.

—— 1987a (ed) *Ireland and Insular art AD 500–1200*. Dublin.

—— 1987b The Donore Hoard: early medieval metalwork from Moynalty, near Kells, Ireland, *Antiquity*, 61, 57–63.

—— 1992 The Sutton Hoo Ship Burial and Ireland: Some Celtic Perspectives. In Farrell & Neuman de Vegvar, 83–116.

SALIN, B 1904 *Die altgermanische Thierornamentik*. Stockholm.

SAMSON, R 1992 The Reinterpretation of the Pictish Symbols, *J Brit Archaeol Assoc*, 145, 29–65.

SANDERS, H A 1930 (ed) *Beati in Apocalypsin Libri Duodecim*. Rome (= Papers and Monographs of the American Academy in Rome, 7).

SANFORD, E M & GREEN, W M 1988 *Saint Augustine: The City of God Against the Pagans (books XVI–XVIII:xxxv)*. Cambridge, Mass and London.

SAWYER, P H & WOOD, I N 1977 (eds) *Early Medieval Kingship*. Leeds (repr 1979).

SCHAFF, P 1956 (ed) *The Nicene and Post-Nicene Fathers*, 1 ser, 8. Michigan.

SCHAPIRO, M 1944 The Religious Meaning of the Ruthwell Cross, *Art Bulletin* 26, 232–45.

—— 1958 Decoration of the Leningrad Manuscript of Bede, *Scriptorium*, 12, 191–207.

—— 1980 Decoration of the Leningrad Manuscript of Bede. In Schapiro, M *Late Antique, Early Christian and Medieval Art, Selected Papers*, 3, 199–224. London. Repr from *Scriptorium*, 12, 1958, 191–207.

SCHLOSSER, J VON 1892 *Schriftquellen zur Geschichte des karolingischen Kunst*. Vienna (repr Hildesheim, Zürich and New York, 1988).

SCOTT, F S 1956 The Hildithryth stone and the other Hartlepool name-stones, *Archaeol Aeliana*, 4 ser, 34, 196–212.

SCULL, C 1991 Post-Roman Phase 1 at Yeavering: A re-consideration, *Medieval Archaeol*, 35, 51–63.

—— 1995 Approaches to material culture and social dynamics of the Migration period of eastern England. In Bintliff, J & Hamerow, H (eds) *Europe Between Late Antiquity and the Middle Ages*, 71–83. Oxford (= *BAR Inter Ser*, 617).

SCULL, C & HARDING, A 1990 Two early medieval cemeteries at Milfield, Northumberland, *Durham Archaeol J*, 6, 1–29.

SCULLY, D 1997 Introduction. In Connolly, 17–37

SELKIRK, A 1989 Piercebridge, *Curr Archaeol*, 113, 204–5.

SHARPE, R 1995 (trans) *Adomnán of Iona, Life of St Columba*. London.

SHEAHAN, J J & WHELLAN, T 1856 *History and Topography of the City of York; the Ainsty Wapentake; and the East Riding of Yorkshire*, II. Beverley.

SHEARMAN, F 1993 Excavation, Examination and Conservation of Anglo-Saxon Jewellery from Bosshall, Ipswich, *The Conservator*, 17, 26–33.

SHEPPARD, J 1979 *Anglo-Saxon Barrows of the Later Sixth and Seventh Centuries AD*. Unpublished Ph.D. thesis. Cambridge.

SHEPPARD, T 1902 Quarterly Record of Additions. I, *Hull Museum Publications*, 9, 9–10.

—— 1918 An Anglo-Saxon Cemetery at Hornsea, *Transactions of the Hull Scientific and Field Naturalist Club*, 4, 258–72.

—— 1923 Saxon Gold Ring Found at Driffield, East Yorks, *Hull Museums Publication No. 134 (Hull)/Trans E. Riding Antiquarian Society*, 24, 43–50.

—— 1938 *Anglo-Saxon Cemeteries in East Yorkshire* (= *Hull Museum Publications*, 195).

—— 1940 Saxon Remains at Elloughton, East Yorkshire, *Hull Museum Publications*, 208, 161–4.

SHERLOCK, S J 1988 An Anglo-Saxon spearhead from Thornaby, Cleveland, *Archaeol Aeliana*, 5 ser, 16, 251.

SHERLOCK, S J & WELCH, M G 1992a *An Anglo-Saxon Cemetery at Norton, Cleveland*. London (= *CBA Research Report*, 82).

—— 1992b Anglo-Saxon Objects from Maltby, Cleveland, *Durham Archaeol J*, 8, 71–6.

SHREWSBURY, J F D 1971 *A History of Bubonic Plague in the British Isles*. Cambridge.

SIMPSON, D P & VELLACOTT, P H 1970 (eds) *Writing in Latin: Style and Idiom for Advanced Latin Prose*. London.

SKEAT, W W 1885 (ed) *Ælfric's Lives of Saints*. London (= Early English Text Society (OS), 76, 82, 1881–5).

SMILES, S 1994 *The Image of Antiquity: Ancient Britain and the Romantic Imagination*. New Haven, Conn.

SMITH, A H 1933 *Three Northumbrian Poems: Caedmon's Hymn, Bede's Death Song and The Leiden Riddle*. London.

SMITH, A N et al. 1995 The excavation of Neolithic, Bronze Age and early historic features near Ratho, Edinburgh, *Proc Soc Antiq Scot*, 125 (1995), 69–138.

SMITH, C R 1854 *Catalogue of the Museum of London Antiquities*. London.

SMITH, I M 1991 Sprouston, Roxburghshire: an early Anglian centre of the eastern Tweed Basin, *Proc Soc Antiq Scotl*, 121, 261–94.

SMITH, J 1919 Excavation at the forts of Castlehill, Aitnock and Coalhill, Ayrshire, *Proc Soc Antiq Scotl*, 53 (1918–9), 123–36.

SMITH, J A 1874 Notice of a Silver Chain or Girdle, the property of Thomas Simpson of Blansie, Esq, Berwickshire; Another in the Possession of the University of Aberdeen, and Other Ancient Scottish Silver Chains, *Proc Soc Antiq Scotl*, 10 (1872–4), 321–47.

SMITH, R A 1912a The excavation by Canon Greenwell FSA, in 1908, of an Anglo-Saxon cemetery at Uncleby, East Riding of Yorkshire, *Proc Soc Antiq*, 24, 146–58.

—— 1912b Anglo-Saxon Remains. In Page, W (ed) *The Victoria History of the Counties of England: Yorkshire*, II, 73–108. London.

—— 1923 *British Museum. A Guide to the Anglo-Saxon and Foreign Teutonic Antiquities*. London.

SMITH, W 1881–91 (ed) *Old Yorkshire*. London.

SMYTH, A P, 1984 *Warlords and Holy Men: Scotland AD 80–1000*. London.

SNAPE, M E 1992 Sub-Roman brooches from Roman sites on the Northern Frontier, *Archaeol Aeliana*, 5 ser, 20, 158–60.

SOUERS, P W 1935 The Franks Casket: Left Side, *Harvard Studies and Notes in Philology and Literature*, 18, 199–209.

SPEARMAN, R M 1993 The mounts from Crieff, Perthshire, and their wider context. In Spearman & Higgitt, 135–142.

SPEARMAN, R M & HIGGITT, J 1993 (eds) *The Age of Migrating Ideas: early medieval art in northern Britain and Ireland*. Edinburgh and Stroud.

SQUIRES, A 1988 (ed) *The Old EnglishPhysiologus*. Durham.

STALLEY, R 1998 Some New Thoughts on Irish Round Towers, unpublished paper to the 33rd International Congress on Medieval Studies, Kalamazoo, Michigan, 7–10 May 1998.

STAMPER, P A & CROFT, R A forthcoming *Wharram: A Study of Settlement on the Yorkshire Wolds, VIII. The South Manor Area Excavations*. York (= York Univ Archaeol Publ, 10).

STANCLIFFE, C 1989 Cuthbert and the polarity between pastor and solitary. In Bonner et al., 21–44.

STANCLIFFE, C & CAMBRIDGE, E 1995 (eds) *Oswald: Northumbrian King to European Saint*. Stamford.

STANLEY, E G 1992 Wolf, My Wolf. In Hill, J H, Doane, N & Ringler, D (eds) *Old English and New. Studies in Language and Linguistics in Honor of Frederic G. Cassidy*, 42–62. New York and London.

STEAD, I M 1991 Garton Station. In Stead, I M (ed) *Iron Age Cemeteries in East Yorkshire: excavations at Burton Fleming, Rudston, Garton-on-the-Wolds and Kirkburn*. 17–24. London (= *English Heritage Archaeological Report*, 22).

STENTON, F M 1971 *Anglo-Saxon England*. Oxford.

STEVENS, W 1985 *Bede's Scientific Achievement* (Jarrow Lecture).

STEVENSON, R B K 1949 The Nuclear fort of Dalmahoy, Midlothian, and other Dark Age Capitals, *Proc Soc Antiq Scotl*, 83 (1948–9), 186–98.

—— 1955 Pictish art. In Wainwright, F T (ed) *The Problem of the Picts*, 97–128. Edinburgh.

—— 1956 Pictish chains, Roman silver and bauxite beads, *Proc Soc Antiq Scotl*, 88 (1954–6), 228–30.

—— 1974 The Hunterston Brooch and its Significance, *Medieval Archaeol*, 18, 16–42.

—— 1989 The Celtic Brooch from Westness, Orkney, and Hinged Pins, *Proc Soc Antiq Scotl*, 119, 239–69.

STEVICK, R D 1994 *The Earliest Irish and English Bookarts. Visual and Poetic Forms before AD 1000*. Philadelphia.

STEWART, I 1984 The early English denarial coinage, c 680–c 750. In Hill & Metcalf, 5–26.

ST JOSEPH, J K 1982 Sprouston, Roxburghshire: an Anglo-Saxon Settlement Discovered by Air Reconnaissance, *Anglo-Saxon England*, 10, 191–9.

STOCKER, D 1993 The early church in Lincolnshire: a study of the sites and their significance. In Vince, 101–22.

STOKES, W 1905 *The Martyrology of Oengus the Culdee*. London.

STONE, M E 1990 *Fourth Ezra*. Minneapolis.

STÖVER, J 1994 De afmetingen van de Salvator-of Oudmunsterkerk in de afbeeldingen van de Monumenta van Van Buchel en in de collectie Booth: Toetsing en interpretatie aan de hand van opgravingsresultaten, *Bulletin van de Koninklijke Nederlandse Oudheidkundige Bond*, 93, 169–85. English summary at 195.

—— 1996 Willibrord's cathedral? An investigation of the first phases of the construction of the Salvatorkerk in Utrecht. In De Bièvre, 69–81.

STRONG, E 1907 *Roman Sculpture from Augustus to Constantine*. London and New York.

SURTEES, R 1823 *The History and Antiquities of the County Palatine of Durham*. London.

SUTCLIFFE, E F 1926 Quotations in the Ven. Bede's Commentary on S Mark, *Biblica*, 7, 428–39.

SWANTON, M 1996 (ed) *The Anglo-Saxon Chronicle*. London.

SWANTON, M J 1964 An Anglian Cemetery at Londesborough in East Yorkshire, *Yorkshire Archaeol J*, 41, 262–86.

—— 1974 *A Corpus of Pagan Anglo-Saxon Spear Types*. Oxford (= *BAR Brit Ser*, 7).

SWANTON, M J & MYRES, J N L 1967 An early Alamannic brooch from Yorkshire, *Antiquaries Journal*, 47, 43–50.

SWEET, H 1896 *The student's dictionary of Anglo-Saxon*. Oxford (repr 1958).

SWINDELLS, N, & LAING, L 1980 Metalworking at the Mote of Mark Kirkcudbright in the 6th and 7th centuries AD. In Oddy, W A (ed) *Aspects of Early Metallurgy*, 121–8. London.

TALBOT, C H 1954 *The Anglo-Saxon Missionaries in Germany*. London and New York.

TEMPLE, J 1646 *The Irish Rebellion*. London.

THACKER, A 1989 Lindisfarne and the origins of the cult of St Cuthbert. In Bonner et al., 103–22.

—— 1992 Monks, preaching and pastoral care in early Anglo-Saxon England. In Blair & Sharpe, 137–70.

—— 1995 *Membra disjecta*: the division of the body and the diffusion of the cult. In Stancliffe & Cambridge, 97–127.

THIBODEAU, T 1988 A Study of William Durand's (ca 1230–1296) Commentary on the Divine Office in Book 5 of the *Rationale Diviniorum Officiorum*, Ph.D. thesis. University of Notre Dame (pub Ann Arbor).

THOMAS, C 1992 The Early Christian Inscriptions of Southern Scotland, *Glasgow Archaeol J*, 17, 1–10.

THOMAS, J 1991 *Rethinking the Neolithic*. Cambridge.

THOMPSON, F H 1983 (ed) *Studies in Medieval Sculpture*, London (= Society of Antiquaries of London, Occasional Paper (NS), 3).

THORPE, B 1844 (ed) *The Homilies of the Anglo-Saxon Church*, I. London.

TINNISWOOD, A & HARDING, A 1991 Anglo-Saxon occupation and industrial features in the henge monument at Yeavering, Northumberland, *Durham Archaeol J*, 7, 53–108.

TOAL, M F 1958 (ed) *The Sunday Sermons of the Great Fathers*, 2. London.

TOLLER, T N 1898 *An Anglo-Saxon Dictionary based on the manuscript collections of Joseph Bosworth*. Oxford (repr 1980).

TSCHUBINASCHIVILI, K 1972 *Kandisi*. Tbilissi.

TURVILLE-PETRE, J E 1957 Hengist and Horsa, *Saga Book of the Viking Society*, 14, (1953–7), 273–90.

TUTTLE HANSEN, E 1988 *The Solomon Complex: Reading Wisdom in Old English Poetry*. Toronto.

TWEDDLE, D 1984 *The Coppergate Helmet*. York (= *York Archaeological Trust*.)

USSHER, J 1639 *Britannicarum ecclesiarum antiquitates*. Dublin.

VEREY, C 1969 A Collation of the Gospel texts contained in Durham Cathedral MSS A II 10, A II 16 and A II 17. Unpublished MA thesis, Durham.

—— 1973 Some Observations on the Texts of Durham Cathedral MSS A II 10 and A II 17, *Studia Evangelica*, 6, 575–9.

—— The Gospel Texts at Lindisfarne at the Time of St Cuthbert. In Bonner et al., 143–50.

—— 1998 A Northumbrian Text Family in Sharpe, J L & Kampen, K Van (eds) *The Bible as Book, The Manuscript Tradition*, 105–22. London and New Castle.

VEREY, C D et al. 1980 (eds) *The Durham Gospels*. Copenhagen (= *Early English Manuscripts in Facsimile*, 20).

VEZIN, J 1971 Une nouvelle lecture de la liste de noms copiÿeae au dos de l'ivoire Barberini, *Bull archÿeaol du comitÿea des travaux hist et scientif* (NS), 7, 19–53.

VINCE, A 1993 (ed) Pre-Viking Lindsey. Lincoln.

VOGÜÉ, A DE 1988 *Community and Abbot in the Rule of St Benedict*, 2 vols. Kalamazoo, Michigan.

VOLBACH, W F 1976 *Elfenbeinarbeiten der Spätantike und des Frühen Mittelalters*. Munich.

VRIES, J DE 1956 *Altgermanische Religionsgeschichte*, 1. Berlin.

WAAGEN, G F 1837 *Kunstwerke und Künstler in England und Paris*, I–III. Berlin.

WADE, K 1984 Barham (excavation summary). In Martin E, Plouviez J & Ross, H (eds) Archaeology in Suffolk, *Proc Suffolk Inst Archaeol*, 35, 326.

WADSTEIN, E 1900 *The Clermont runic casket*. London.

WAGNER, N 1960 Dioskuren, Jungmannschaften, und Doppelkönigtum, *Zeitschrift für Deutsche Philologie* 79, 1–17, 225–47.

WALLACE-HADRILL, J M 1971 *Early Germanic Kingship in England and the Continent*. Oxford.

—— 1988 *Bede's Ecclesiastical History of the English People: a historical commentary*. Oxford.

WALSH, M & Ó CRÓINÍN, D 1988 *Cummian's Letter De Controversia Pascali and the De Ratione Conputandi*. Ontario.

WALTERS, H B 1926 *Catalogue of the Engraved Gems and Cameos Greek Etruscan and Roman in the British Museum*. London.

WAMERS, E 1985 *Insularer Metallschmuck in wikingerzeitlichen Gräbern Nordeuropas*. Neumünster (= Offa–Bücher, 65).

WANLEY, H 1705 *Antiquae Literaturae Septentrionais liber alter*. Oxford (= George Hickes *Linguarum Vett. Septentrionalium Thesaurus*, II).

WAQUET, H 1964 *Abbon: Le siège de Paris par les Normands*. Paris.

WARD, D 1968 *The Divine Twins: an Indo-European myth in Germanic tradition*. Berkeley and Los Angeles.

WARE, H 1902 (ed) Bishop Nicolson's Diaries, Part II, *Transactions of the Cumberland and Westmorland Antiquarian and Archaeological Society* (NS), 2, 155–230.

WARNER, G F 1915 *The Stowe Missal*, II. London (= Henry Bradshaw Society, 32, repr Woodbridge, 1989).

WARREN, F E 1987 *The Liturgy and Ritual of the Celtic Church* (2nd edn). Ipswich.

WASSELYNCK, R 1962 Les compilations des 'Moralia in Job' du VIIe au XIIe siècle, *Recherches de théologie ancienne et médiévale*, 29, 5–15.

WEBB, B 1906 (trans) *The Symbolism of Churches and Church Ornaments: A Translation of the Rationale Divinorum Officiorum written by William Durandus* (3rd edn). London.

WEBSTER, H 1996 *Old English Gnomic Poetry*. Unpublished.

WEBSTER, L 1982 Stylistic Aspects of the Franks Casket. In Farrell, R T (ed) *The Vikings*, 20–32. Chichester.

—— 1987 The Gold Pendant. In Frere, S S & Bennett, P (eds) Canterbury Excavations: Intra- and Extra-Mural Sites, 1949–55 and 1980–84, *The Archaeology of Canterbury*, VIII, 282–4. Maidstone.

—— 1991 The Franks Casket. In Webster & Backhouse, 101–3.

—— 1992 Death's Diplomacy: Sutton Hoo in the light of other male princely burials. In Farrell & Neuman de Vegvar, 75–82.

WEBSTER, L & BACKHOUSE, J 1991 (eds) *The Making of England: Anglo-Saxon art and culture AD 600–900*. London and Toronto (= exhibition catalogue).

WEBSTER, L & BROWN, M 1997 (eds) *The Transformation of the Roman World AD 400–900*. London (= exhibition catalogue).

WEBSTER, L E & CHERRY, J 1973 Yorkshire, North Riding: Catterick (SE225988), *Medieval Archaeol*, 17, 150.

WEIL, L 1996 Aspects of the Issue of *Per Saltum* Ordination: An Anglican Perspective. In Mitchell, N & Baldovin, J (eds) *Rule of Prayer, Rule of Faith: Essays in Honor of Aidan Kavanagh, OSB*, 200–17. Collegeville, MN.

WELIE, E VAN 1996 St Salvator's, St Martin's and Pepin the Younger. In De Bièvre, 58–68.

WERNER, M 1994 Crucifixi, sepulti, suscitati: remarks on the decoration of the *Book of Kells*. In O'Mahony, 450–88.

WESTWOOD, J O 1845 *Paleographia Sacra Pictoria* (1843–5). London.

—— 1868 *Facsimiles of miniatures and Ornaments in Anglo-Saxon and Irish Manuscripts*. London.

WHELLAN, T 1859 *History and Topography of the City of York and the North Riding of Yorkshire*, II. Beverley.

WHITE, R H 1988 *Roman and Celtic Objects from Anglo-Saxon Graves*. Oxford.

WHITELOCK, D 1958 *The Audience of Beowulf*. Oxford.

—— 1979 (ed) *English Historical Documents. I. c 500–1042*, 2nd ed. London.

WHITFIELD, N 1990 Round Wire in the Early Middle Ages, *Jewellery Studies*, 4, 13–28.

—— 1993 The filigree of the Hunterston and 'Tara' Brooches. In Spearman & Higgitt, 118–27.

WHITWELL, J B 1991 Flixborough, *Curr Archaeol*, 126, 244–7.

WIECZOREK, A, PÉRIN, P, WELCK, K VON & MENGHIN, W 1996 *Die Franken: Wegbereiter Europas*, 2 vols. Mannheim and Mainz.

WILLETT, F 1957 The Ruthwell and Bewcastle Crosses – A Review, *Memoirs of the Manchester Library and Philosophical Society*, 98 (1956–7), 94–136.

WILLIAMS, J 1971 Tynron Doon, Dumfriesshire: a history of the site with notes on the finds, 1924–67, *Transactions of the Dumfriesshire and Galloway Natural History and Antiquarian Society*, 47, 106–20.

WILLIAMS, J E C 1968 *The Poems of Taliesin. Edited and annotated by Sir Ifor Williams*. Dublin.

WILLIAMSON, C A 1959 *Josephus: the Jewish war*. Harmondsworth.

WILMART, A 1926 La collection de Bède le Vénérable sur l'apôtre, *Revue Bénédictine*, 38, 16–52.

WILSON, D M 1964 *Anglo-Saxon Ornamental Metalwork 700–1100*. London (= *Catalogue of Antiquities of the Later Saxon Period*, I).

—— 1976 (ed) *The Archaeology of Anglo-Saxon England*. London.

—— 1984 *Anglo-Saxon Art from the Seventh Century to the Norman Conquest*. London.

WILSON, P R 1982 Yorkshire, North: Catterick, Bainesse Farm (SE241973), *Medieval Archaeol*, 26, 212.

WILSON, P R et al. 1996 Early Anglian Catterick and *Catraeth*, *Medieval Archaeol*, 40, 1–61.

WOOD, I N 1977 Kings, Kingdoms and Consent. In Sawyer & Wood, 6–29.

—— 1995 Ruthwell: In Search of a Historical Context. Unpublished paper, International Medieval Congress. Leeds.

WOOLER, E 1913 *Historic Darlington*. London.

WORDSWORTH, J & WHITE, H J 1898 *Novum Testamentum Domini Nostri Iesu Christi secundum editionem Sancti Hieronymi: pars prior, Quattuor Evangelia* (1889–98). Oxford.

WORMALD, P 1976 Bede and Benedict Biscop. In Bonner, G (ed) *Famulus Christi*, 141–69. London.

—— 1996 The emergence of the *Regnum Scottorum*: A Carolingian hegemony? In Crawford, 131–53.

WRIGHT, R 1991 (ed) *Latin and the Romance Languages in the Early Middle Ages*. London.

—— 1993 Review article 'On Michel Banniard's *Viva Voce*', *Journal of Medieval Latin*, 3, 78–94.

WRIGHT, T 1863 (ed) *The Historical Works of Giraldus Cambrensis*. London.

X. Y. 1833 Runic Gravestones found at Hartlepool, *Gentleman's Magazine*, 103.2, 218–20.

YAT 1978 *York Archaeological Trust Ripon Jewel Conservation Report*. Unpublished.

YORKE, B A E 1983 Joint Kingship in Kent c 560 to 785, *Archaeologia Cantiana*, 99, 1–19.

—— 1985 The kingdom of the East Saxons, *Anglo-Saxon England* 14, 1–36.

—— 1990 *Kings and Kingdoms of Early Anglo-Saxon England*. London.

—— 1993 Fact or Fiction? The written evidence for the fifth and sixth centuries AD, *Anglo-Saxon Studies in Archaeology and History*, 6, 45–50.

YOUNGS, S 1989 (ed) *The Work of Angels: masterpieces of Celtic metalwork, 6th–9th centuries AD*. London (= exhibition catalogue).

—— 1993 The Steeple Bumpstead Boss. In Spearman & Higgitt, 143–50.

—— 1995 Medium and Motif: Polychrome Enamelling and Early Manuscript Decoration in Insular Art. In Bourke, 37–47.

ZIMMERMANN, E H 1916 *Vorkarolingische Miniaturen*, I–IV and text. Berlin.

INDEX OF SITES

Note: *Italic* page numbers indicate illustrations

INDEX OF SUBJECTS

Note: **Bold** page numbers indicate plates; *italic* page numbers indicate illustrations